BLACK ATHENA

Black Athena

The Afroasiatic Roots
of Classical Civilization

VOLUME I
The Fabrication of Ancient Greece 1785–1985

Martin Bernal

Rutgers University Press
New Brunswick, New Jersey

First published in the United States by
Rutgers University Press, 1987
Second paperback printing, 1988

First published in Great Britain by
Free Association Books, 1987

Library of Congress Cataloging-in-Publication Data

Bernal, Martin
  Black Athena.
  (The fabrication of ancient Greece, 1785–1985; v. 1)
  Bibliography: p.
  Includes index.
  1. Greece—Civilization—Egyptian influences.
  2. Greece—Civilization—Phoenician influences.
  3. Greece—Civilization—To 146 B.C.   I. Title.
  II. Title: Afroasiatic roots of classical civilization.
  III. Series: Bernal, Martin. Fabrication of ancient
  Greece, 1785–1985; v. 1.
  DF78.B398   1987   949.5   87–16408
  ISBN 0-8135-1276-X
  ISBN 0-8135-1277-8 (pbk.)

The publication of *Black Athena* was aided by
the Hull Memorial Publication Fund
of Cornell University.

To the memory of my father,
John Desmond Bernal,
who taught me that things
fit together, interestingly

Contents

Preface and Acknowledgements

THE STORY BEHIND *Black Athena* is long, complicated and, I believe, sufficiently interesting as a study in the sociology of knowledge to deserve extended treatment; thus I can give only a brief outline of it here. I was trained in Chinese studies; for almost twenty years I taught about China and carried out research on both intellectual relations between China and the West at the turn of the 20th century and contemporary Chinese politics. After 1962, I became increasingly concerned with the war in Indo-China, and in the virtual absence of any serious scholarship on Vietnamese culture in Britain, I felt obliged to study it. This was both to contribute to the movement against the American repression there, and for its own sake as a fascinating and extremely attractive civilization that was at the same time both thoroughly mixed and entirely distinctive. Thus in many ways Vietnam and Japan – whose history I had also studied – have served as my models for Greece.

In 1975 I came to a mid-life crisis. The personal reasons for this are not particularly interesting. Politically, however, it was related to the end of the American intervention in Indo-China and the awareness that the Maoist era in China was coming to an end. It now seemed to me that the central focus of danger and interest in the world was no longer East

Asia but the Eastern Mediterranean. This shift led me to a concern for Jewish history. The scattered Jewish components of my ancestry would have given nightmares to assessors trying to apply the Nuremburg Laws, and although pleased to have these fractions, I had not previously given much thought to them or to Jewish culture. It was at this stage that I became intrigued – in a Romantic way – by this part of my 'roots'. I started looking into ancient Jewish history, and – being on the periphery myself – into the relationships between the Israelites and the surrounding peoples, particularly the Canaanites and Phoenicians. I had always known that the latter spoke Semitic languages, but it came as quite a shock to discover that Hebrew and Phoenician were mutually intelligible and that serious linguists treated both as *dialects* of a single Canaanite language.

During this time, I was beginning to study Hebrew and I found what seemed to me a large number of striking similarities between it and Greek. Two factors disinclined me to accept these as random coincidences. First, having studied Chinese, Japanese and Vietnamese as well as a little Chichewa – a Bantu language spoken in Zambia and Malawi – I realized that this number of parallels is not normal for languages without contacts with each other. Secondly, I now realized that Hebrew/Canaanite was not merely the language of a small tribe, isolated inland in the mountains of Palestine, but that it had been spoken all over the Mediterranean – wherever the Phoenicians sailed and settled. Thus there seemed to me no reason why the large number of important words with similar sounds and similar meanings in Greek and Hebrew – or at least the vast majority of those which had no Indo-European roots – should not be loans from Canaanite/Phoenician into Greek.

At this stage, led by my friend David Owen, I became heavily influenced by the works of Cyrus Gordon and Michael Astour on general contacts between Semitic and Greek civilizations. Furthermore, I was convinced by Astour that the legends concerning the foundation of Thebes by the Phoenician Kadmos contained a kernel of truth. Like him, however, I dismissed the legends of Egyptian settlement either as complete fantasy or as cases of mistaken identity, believing that – whatever the Greeks had written – the colonists had really been Semitic speakers.

I worked along these lines for four years, and became convinced that anything up to a quarter of the Greek vocabulary could be traced to Semitic origins. This, together with 40–50 per cent that seem to be Indo-European, still left a quarter to a third of the Greek vocabulary unexplained. I hesitated between seeing this irreducible fraction conventionally as 'Pre-Hellenic' or of postulating a third outside language, either from Anatolian or – as I preferred – Hurrian. When I looked into these languages, however, they provided virtually no promising material. It was only in 1979, when I was glancing through a copy of Černy's *Coptic Etymological Dictionary*, that I was able to get some sense of Late Ancient Egyptian. Almost immediately, I realized that *this* was the third outside language. Within a few months I became convinced that one could find plausible etymologies for a further 20–25 per cent of the Greek vocabulary from Egyptian, as well as the names for most Greek gods and many place names. Putting the Indo-European, Semitic and Egyptian roots together, I now believed that – with further research – one could provide plausible explanations for 80–90 per cent of the Greek vocabulary, which is as high a proportion as one can hope for in any language. Thus there was now no need for the 'Pre-Hellenic' element at all.

At the beginning of my research I had had to face this question: Why, if everything is as simple and obvious as you maintain, has nobody seen it before? This was answered when I read Gordon and Astour. They had seen the East Mediterranean as a cultural whole, and Astour had demonstrated that anti-Semitism provided an explanation for the denial of the role of the Phoenicians in the formation of Greece. After hitting upon the Egyptian component, I soon became even more acutely involved in the problem of 'why hadn't I thought of Egypt before?' It was so obvious! Egypt had by far the greatest civilization in the East Mediterranean during the millennia in which Greece was formed. Greek writers had written at length about their debts to Egyptian religion, and other aspects of culture. Furthermore, I found my failure still more puzzling because my grandfather was an Egyptologist, and as a child I had been extremely interested in Ancient Egypt. Clearly there were very profound cultural inhibitions against associating Egypt with Greece.

At this point I began to investigate the historiography of the origins of Greece, to make sure that the Greeks had really believed they had been colonized by Egyptians and Phoenicians and had taken most of their culture from these colonies, as well as from later study in the Levant.

Once again, I had a big surprise. I was staggered to discover that what I began to call the 'Ancient Model' had not been overthrown until the early 19th century, and that the version of Greek history which I had been taught – far from being as old as the Greeks themselves – had been developed only in the 1840s and 50s. Astour had taught me that attitudes towards the Phoenicians in historiography were profoundly affected by anti-Semitism; it was therefore easy for me to make a connection between the dismissal of the Egyptians and the explosion of Northern European racism in the 19th century. The connections with Romanticism and the tensions between Egyptian religion and Christianity took rather longer to unravel.

Thus, one way and another, the scheme set out in *Black Athena* has taken me more than ten years to develop. During this time I have been a public nuisance in both Cambridge and Cornell. Like the Ancient Mariner, I have waylaid innocent passers-by to pour my latest half-baked ideas over them. I owe these 'wedding guests' a tremendous debt, if only for their patient listening. I am even more grateful for the extremely valuable suggestions they made, which – although I have been able to acknowledge only a few of them – have been of incalculable help to my work. Most important of all, I want to thank them for their excitement about the subject and for the confidence they gave me that it was not madness to challenge the authority of so many academic disciplines. They appeared to believe in what I was saying and they convinced me that although some of my ideas were probably wrong in particular, I was on the right track.

I owe the experts a different kind of gratitude. They were not simply in my way. I pursued them into their lairs and pestered them with requests for rudimentary information and explanations of the reasons behind their ideas or conventional wisdom. Despite the fact that I took up much of their valuable time and sometimes upset their most cherished beliefs, they were uniformly courteous and helpful, often going to considerable efforts on my behalf. The help of the 'wedding guests' and the experts has been central and essential to the project. In many ways I see the whole thing as a collective rather than an individual effort. One person could not possibly have covered all the many fields involved. Even with this massive outside help, however, I have inevitably fallen short of the thoroughness one would rightly expect of a monographic study. Furthermore, I am fully aware that I have not understood or properly assimilated much of the best advice given to me. Thus none of the people mentioned below is in any way responsible for many errors of fact and interpretation the reader will find. Nevertheless, the credit for this work belongs to them.

First, I should like to thank the men and women without any one of whom I could never have completed this work: Frederic Ahl, Gregory Blue, the late and very much lamented Robert Bolgar, Edward Fox, Edmund Leach, Saul Levin, Joseph Naveh, Joseph Needham, David Owen, and Barbara Reeves. In different proportions, they gave me the information, advice, constructive criticism, backing and encouragement that have been crucial for these volumes. All of them are exceptionally busy people and working on extremely important and fascinating projects of their own. I am more moved than I can say at the great amounts of time they spent on my work, which was often presented to them when it was at a very primitive level.

I also want to thank the following men and women – and record my gratitude to those who are now dead – for the time and trouble they took to help me: Anouar Abdel-Malek, Lyn Abel, Yoël Arbeitman, Michael Astour, Shlomo Avineri, Wilfred Barner, Alvin Bernstein, Ruth Blair, Alan Bomhard, Jim Boon, Malcolm Bowie, Susan Buck Morse, Alan Clugston, John Coleman, Mary Collins, Jerrold Cooper, Dorothy Crawford, Tom Cristina, Jonathan Culler, Anna Davies, Frederick de Graf, Ruth Edwards, Yehuda Elkana, Moses Finley, Meyer Fortes, Henry Gates, Sander Gilman, Joe Gladstone, Jocelyn Godwin, Jack Goody, Cyrus Gordon, Jonas Greenfield, Margot Heinemann, Robert Hoberman, Carleton Hodge, Paul Hoch, Leonard Hochberg, Clive Holmes, Nicholas Jardine, Jay Jasanoff, Alex Joffe, Peter Kahn, Richard Kahn, Joel Kupperman, Woody Kelley, Peter Khoroche, Richard Klein, Diane Koester, Isaac Kramnick, Peter Kuniholm, Annemarie Kunzl, Kenneth Larsen, Leroi Ladurie, Philip Lomas,

Geoffrey Lloyd, Bruce Long, Lili McCormack, John McCoy, Lauris Mckee, Laurie Milroie, Livia Morgan, John Pairman Brown, Giovanni Pettinato, Joe Pia, Max Prausnitz, Jamil Ragep, Andrew Ramage, John Ray, David Resnick, Joan Robinson, Edward Said, Susan Sandman, Jack Sasson, Elinor Shaffer, Michael Shub, Quentin Skinner, Tom Smith, Anthony Snodgrass, Rachel Steinberg, Barry Strauss, Marilyn Strathern, Haim Tadmor, Romila Thapar, James Turner, Steven Turner, Robert Tannenbaum, Ivan van Sertima, Cornelius Vermeule, Emily Vermeule, Gail Warhaft, Gail Weinstein, James Weinstein, and Heinz Wismann. I should particularly like to thank the few among them who objected strongly to what I was trying to do but still knowingly and willingly provided very useful aid.

I should like to express my deep gratitude to everybody at the Department of Government at Cornell who not only tolerated but encouraged my involvement in a project so far from the usual concerns of a government department. Equally, I should like to thank all at Telluride House for many years of hospitality and for the intellectual stimulus that led me to turn to my new field. I am also very grateful to everybody at the Society for the Humanities at Cornell, where I spent a very productive and happy year in 1977/8.

I owe a deep debt to my publisher, Robert Young, for his confidence in the project and the constant help and encouragement he has given me. At the same time, I want to thank my editor, Ann Scott, for the huge amount of work she has put into this volume, her patience, and the sympathetic way in which she has vastly improved the quality of the text without bruising my *amour propre*. I am deeply indebted to the two scholarly readers, Neil Flanagan and Dr Holford-Strevens, and the copy-editor, Gillian Beaumont. I can assure the readers that the many errors, inconsistencies and infelicities still lurking in this book are nothing to those abounding in the text before it came under their expert scrutiny. Despite the frustrations of their Augean task, they have been extraordinarily patient and charming in all their dealings with me. I should like, too, to thank Kate Grillet for her first draft of the maps and charts and her extraordinary skill in interpreting my rushed and imprecise directions. I am also very grateful to my daughter, Sophie Bernal, for help with the bibliography and for her cheerful and patient gofering.

I owe an incalculable debt to my mother, Margaret Gardiner, who gave me my basic education and self-confidence. More specifically, she has provided the means for me to complete this volume and has given valuable editorial help with the introduction. I should like to thank my wife, Leslie Miller-Bernal, for her useful judgement and criticism, but above all for providing the warm emotional base upon which so large an intellectual undertaking is utterly dependent. Finally, I should like to thank Sophie, William, Paul, Adam and Patrick for their love and for keeping me so firmly rooted in the things that really matter.

Transcription
and Phonetics

THE ORTHOGRAPHY USED in Egyptian words is the standard one accepted by modern Egyptologists, the only exception being the ꜣ used to represent the 'vulture or double 'aleph', which is often printed as two commas on top of each other.

Whatever the exact sound of the ꜣ in Old Egyptian it was transcribed into Semitic scripts as r, l, or even n. This consonantal value was retained at least until the 2nd Intermediate Period in the 17th century BC. In Late Egyptian it appears to have become an 'aleph and later, like the Southern English r, it merely modified adjacent vowels. The ꜣ is the first sign of the alphabetical order used by Egyptologists, and I shall continue with other letters with obscure or difficult sound values.

The Egyptian i̥ corresponds to both the Semitic 'aleph and yōd. 'Aleph is found in many languages, and nearly all Afroasiatic ones. It is a glottal stop before vowels, as in the Cockney 'bo'le' or 'bu'e' ('bottle' and 'butter').

The Egyptian 'ayin, which also occurs in most Semitic languages, is a voiced or spoken 'aleph. The Egyptian form seems to have been associated with the 'back' vowels o and u.

In early Egyptian the sign w, written as a quail chick, may have had purely consonantal value. In Late Egyptian, the form of the language which had the most impact on Greek, it seems to have been frequently pronounced as a vowel, either o or u.

The Egyptian sign written as r was more usually transcribed as l in Semitic and Greek. In later Egyptian it seems, as with the ꜣ, to have weakened into becoming merely a modifier of vowels.

The Egyptian and Semitic letters Romanized as ḥ appear to have been pronounced as an emphatic h.

The Egyptian and Semitic ḫ represents a sound similar to the ch in 'loch'. In later times it became thoroughly confused with the letter š.

The Egyptian letter ẖ appears to have represented the sound ḫy. It too became confused with š.

The letter written here as s was transcribed as either s or z.

š was pronounced as sh or skh. In later times it became very confused with ḫ and ẖ.

ḳ represents an emphatic k. Inconsistently, I have followed the common practice of Semitists and have employed q to represent the same sound in Semitic.

The letter t was probably originally pronounced as tʸ. However, even in Middle Egyptian it was being confused with t.

Similarly, the ḏ was frequently alternated with d.

EGYPTIAN NAMES

Egyptian divine names are vocalized according to the commonest Greek transcription – for example, Amon for ʾlmn.

Royal names generally follow Gardiner's (1961) version of the Greek names for well-known pharaohs, for instance, Ramessēs.

COPTIC

Most of the letters in the Coptic alphabet come from Greek and the same transcriptions are used. Six extra letters derived from Demotic are transcribed as follows:

ⲷ š	ⲵ ḫ	ⲝ ḏ
ⳓ f	ⳉ h	ⳓ ǧ

Semitic

The Semitic consonants are transcribed relatively conventionally. Several of the complications have been mentioned above in connection with Egyptian. Apart from these, one encounters the following:

> In Canaanite the sound ḫ merged with ḥ. Transcriptions here sometimes reflect the etymological ḫ rather than the later ḥ. ṭ is an emphatic t.
>
> The Arabic sound usually transcribed as th is written here as tʸ. The same is true of the dh/dʸ.
>
> The letter found in Ugaritic which corresponds to the Arabic *Ghain* is transcribed ġ.
>
> The Semitic emphatic k is written q, rather than ḳ as in Egyptian.
>
> The Semitic letter *Tsade*, almost certainly pronounced ts, is written ṣ.
>
> In Hebrew from the 1st millennium BC the letter *Shin* is written as š. Elsewhere, however, it is transcribed simply as s, not as š, because I question the antiquity and the range of the latter pronunciation (Bernal, forthcoming, 1988). This, however, causes confusion with Samekh, which is also transcribed as s. Sin is transcribed as ś.

Neither *dagesh* nor *begadkepat* is indicated in the transcription. This is for reasons of simplicity as well as doubts about their range and occurrence in Antiquity.

Vocalization

The Masoretic vocalization of the Bible, completed in the 9th and 10th centuries AD but reflecting much older pronunciation, is transcribed as follows:

Name of sign	Plain	with י y	with ו w	with ה h
Pataḥ	בַ ba	–	–	– –
Qåmeṣ	בָ bå	בָּי bâ	–	בָּה båh
Ḥireq	בִ bi	בִּי bî	–	– –
Ṣērê	בֵ bē	בֵּי bê	–	בֵּה bēh
Sᵉgōl	בֶ be	בֶּי bệ	–	בֶּה beh
Ḥōlem	בֹ bō	– –	בּוֹ bô	בֹּה bōh
Qibûṣ	בֻ bu	– –	בּוּ bû	– –

The reduced vowels are rendered:

ְ bᵉ   ֲ ḥă   ֱ ḥĕ   ֳ ḥŏ.

Accentuation and cantillation are not normally marked.

GREEK

The transcription of the consonants is orthodox.

υ is transcribed as y.

The long vowels η and ω are written as ē and ō, and where it is significant the long α is rendered ā.

Accentuation is not normally marked.

GREEK NAMES

It is impossible to be consistent in transliterating these, because certain names are so well known that they have to be given in their Latin forms – Thucydides or Plato – as opposed to the Greek Thoukydidēs or Platōn. On the other hand, it would be absurd to make Latin forms for little-known people or places. Thus the commoner names are given in their Latin forms and the rest simply transliterated from Greek. I have tried wherever possible to follow Peter Levi's translation of Pausanias, where the balance is to my taste well struck. This, however, means that many long vowels are not marked in the transcription of names.

Maps and Charts

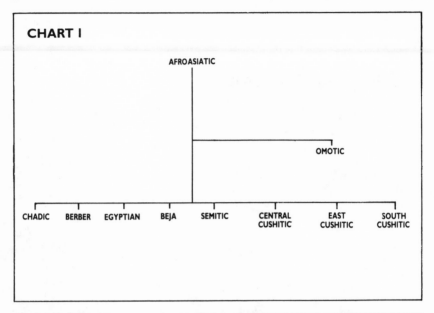

CHART I

AFROASIATIC

OMOTIC

CHADIC   BERBER   EGYPTIAN   BEJA   SEMITIC   CENTRAL   EAST   SOUTH
                                              CUSHITIC   CUSHITIC   CUSHITIC

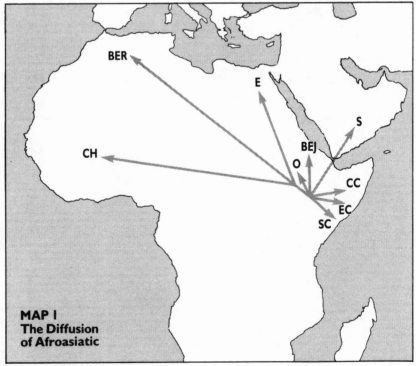

MAP I
The Diffusion
of Afroasiatic

CHART 2   XXV

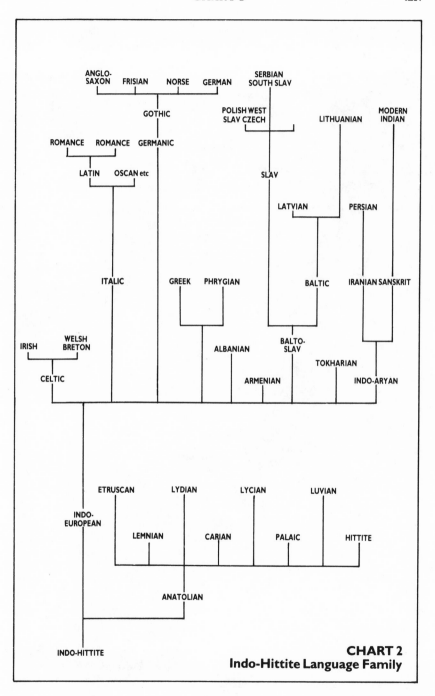

CHART 2
Indo-Hittite Language Family

BLACK ATHENA

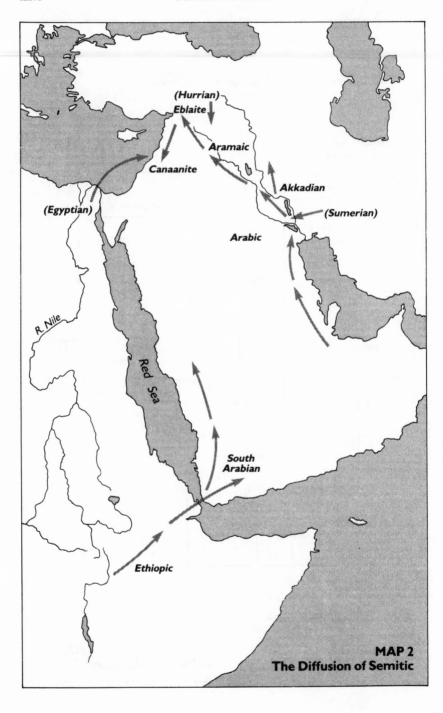

MAP 2
The Diffusion of Semitic

MAP 3   xxvii

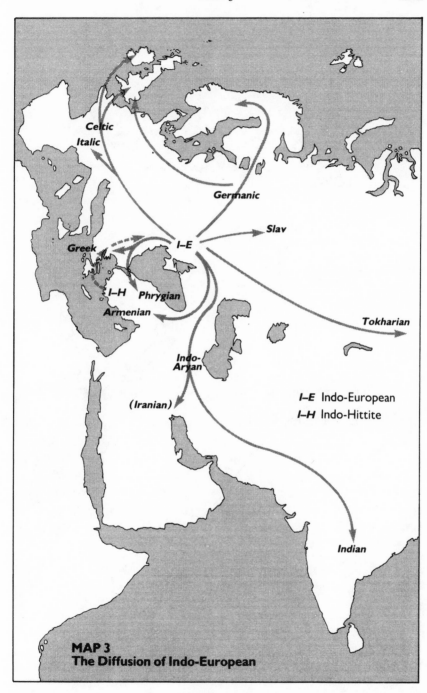

MAP 3
The Diffusion of Indo-European

Celtic
Italic
Germanic
Slav
Greek
I–E
I–H
Phrygian
Armenian
Tokharian
Indo-Aryan
(Iranian)
Indian

I–E Indo-European
I–H Indo-Hittite

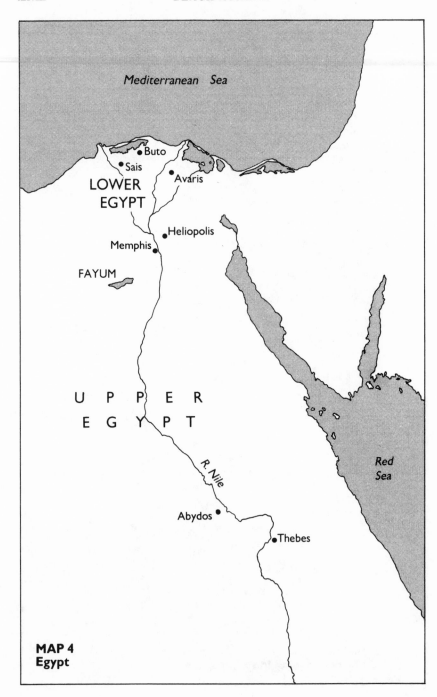

MAP 4
Egypt

MAP 5 xxix

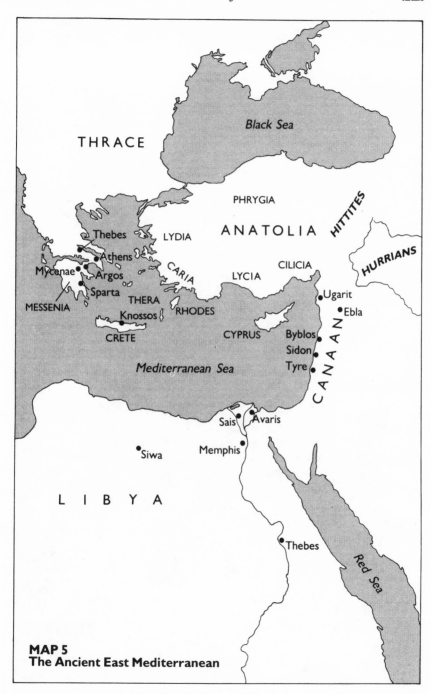

MAP 5
The Ancient East Mediterranean

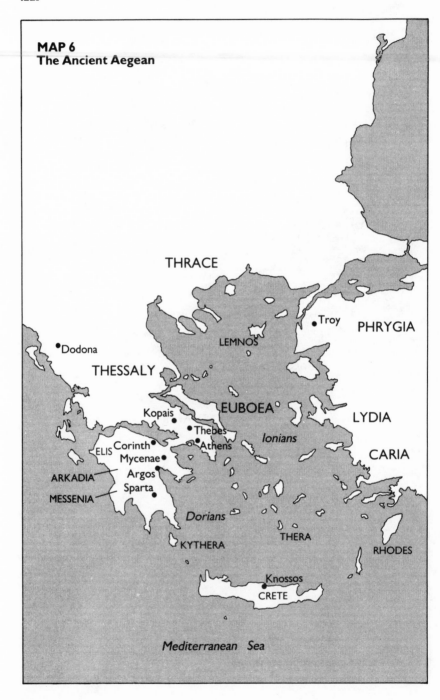

MAP 6
The Ancient Aegean

THRACE

PHRYGIA

Troy

LEMNOS

Dodona

THESSALY

EUBOEA

LYDIA

Kopais

Thebes

Ionians

Corinth
Athens

ELIS

Mycenae

CARIA

ARKADIA

Argos

MESSENIA

Sparta

Dorians

KYTHERA

THERA

RHODES

Knossos

CRETE

Mediterranean   Sea

CHRONOLOGICAL TABLE

Aryan Model, Crete	Aryan Model, Greece	Revised Ancient Model	BC
			3300
			3200
			3100
Early Minoan I		Early Minoan I	3000
	Early Helladic I	Early Helladic I	
			2900
			2800
			2700
			2600
EM II	EH II	EM II, EH II	2500
			2400
			2300
EM III	EH III Coming of the Greeks ??	EM III, EH III	2200
			2100
MM I First palaces	MM I	Menthotpe/ Rhadamanthys suzerain in Crete and Boiotia ??	2000
	MH I Coming of the Greeks?	Senwosre/Hpr Kɜ Rˁ Kekrops suzerain of Attica ??	1900
			1800
Destruction of palaces		MM III Hyksos invasions	
MM III		Danaos and Kadmos 1st Shaft Graves	1700
	MH III 1st Shaft Graves	LM IA Alphabet introd. Thera eruption	

LM IA			1600
	LH IA or Mycenaean IA		
		LM IB	
LM IB	Thera eruption ?		1500
LM II Mycenaean conquest	Thera eruption ?	LM II Mycenaean conquest of Crete, Egyptian suzerainty	1400
	LH/Myc. II		
Final destruction of Cretan palaces	LH/Myc. III Mycenaean palaces	LH/Myc. III Pelops' invasion?	
LH/Myc. IIIB	LH/Myc. IIIB Thebes destroyed	LH/Myc. IIIB Thebes destroyed	1300
Trojan War	Trojan War	Trojan War	1200
	Dorian invasion	Return of the Heraklids	
	Mycenae destroyed	Mycenae destroyed	
LH/Myc. IIIC	LH/Myc. IIIC	LH/Myc. IIIC Philistines	1100
	Ionian migrations	Ionian migrations	1000
		Hesiod	900
	Corinth ruled by Bakchiadai	Corinth ruled by Bakchiadai Homer	
	Alphabet introduced ? Homer	Lykourgos reforms Sparta	800
	First Olympic Games	First Olympic Games Colonies established in Italy and Sicily	
	Colonies established in Italy and Sicily Hesiod First Oriental influence Athens		700
		Solon reforms	600
	Persians conquer Anatolia	Persians conquer Anatolia	
	Persian invasions of Greece	Persian invasions of Greece	500
	Herodotos	Herodotos	
	Peloponnesian War	Peloponnesian War	
	Sokrates	Sokrates	400
	Plato, Isokrates	Plato, Isokrates	
	Rise of Macedon	Rise of Macedon	
	Alexander the Great	Alexander the Great	
	Aristotle	Aristotle	

INTRODUCTION

Almost always the men who achieve these fun-
damental inventions of a new paradigm have either
been very young or very new to the field whose
paradigm they change.

(Thomas Kuhn, *The Structure of Scientific*
Revolutions, p. 90)

M Y USE OF THIS QUOTATION from Thomas Kuhn is an
attempt to justify my presumption, as someone trained in
Chinese history, to write on subjects so far removed from my
original field. For I shall be arguing that although the changes of view
that I am proposing are not paradigmatic in the strict sense of the word,
they are none the less fundamental.

These volumes are concerned with two models of Greek history: one
viewing Greece as essentially European or Aryan, and the other seeing
it as Levantine, on the periphery of the Egyptian and Semitic cultural
area. I call them the 'Aryan' and the 'Ancient' models. The 'Ancient
Model' was the conventional view among Greeks in the Classical and
Hellenistic ages. According to it, Greek culture had arisen as the result
of colonization, around 1500 BC, by Egyptians and Phoenicians
who had civilized the native inhabitants. Furthermore, Greeks had
continued to borrow heavily from Near Eastern cultures.

Most people are surprised to learn that the Aryan Model, which most
of us have been brought up to believe, developed only during the first
half of the 19th century. In its earlier or 'Broad' form, the new model
denied the truth of the Egyptian settlements and questioned those of
the Phoenicians. What I call the 'Extreme' Aryan Model, which

flourished during the twin peaks of anti-Semitism in the 1890s and
again in the 1920s and 30s, denied even the Phoenician cultural
influence. According to the Aryan Model, there had been an invasion
from the north – unreported in ancient tradition – which had overwhelmed the local 'Aegean' or 'Pre-Hellenic' culture. Greek civilization is seen as the result of the mixture of the Indo-European-speaking
Hellenes and their indigenous subjects. It is from the construction of
this Aryan Model that I call this volume *The Fabrication of Ancient Greece
1785–1985*.

I believe that we should return to the Ancient Model, but with some
revisions; hence I call what I advocate in Volume 2 of *Black Athena* the
'Revised Ancient Model'. This accepts that there is a real basis to the
stories of Egyptian and Phoenician colonization of Greece set out in
the Ancient Model. However, it sees them as beginning somewhat
earlier, in the first half of the 2nd millennium BC. It also agrees with the
latter that Greek civilization is the result of the cultural mixtures created
by these colonizations and later borrowings from across the East
Mediterranean. On the other hand, it tentatively accepts the Aryan
Model's hypothesis of invasions – or infiltrations – from the north by
Indo-European speakers sometime during the 4th or 3rd millennium
BC. However, the Revised Ancient Model maintains that the earlier
population was speaking a related Indo-Hittite language which left little
trace in Greek. In any event, it cannot be used to explain the many
non-European elements in the later language.

*If I am right in urging the overthrow of the Aryan Model and its replacement
by the Revised Ancient one, it will be necessary not only to rethink the
fundamental bases of 'Western Civilization' but also to recognize the penetration of racism and 'continental chauvinism' into all our historiography, or
philosophy of writing history. The Ancient Model had no major 'internal'
deficiencies, or weaknesses in explanatory power. It was overthrown for external
reasons. For 18th- and 19th-century Romantics and racists it was simply
intolerable for Greece, which was seen not merely as the epitome of Europe
but also as its pure childhood, to have been the result of the mixture of
native Europeans and colonizing Africans and Semites. Therefore the
Ancient Model had to be overthrown and replaced by something more
acceptable.*

What is meant here by 'model' and 'paradigm'? The value of defining such terms is limited, both by an unavoidable looseness in their use and by the fact that words can be defined only by other words, providing no bedrock upon which to build. Nevertheless, some indication of their intended meaning is necessary. By 'model' I generally mean a reduced and simplified scheme of a complex reality. Such a transposition always distorts, as the Italian proverb puts it – *traduttore traditore*, 'translator traitor'. Despite this, like words themselves, models are necessary to nearly all thought and speech. It should always be remembered, however, that models are artificial and more or less arbitrary. Furthermore, just as different aspects of light are best explained as waves or particles, other phenomena can be fruitfully seen in two or more different ways; that is to say, using two or more different models. Usually, however, one model is better or worse than another in its capacity to explain the features of the 'reality' confronted. Thus it is useful to think in terms of competition between models. By 'paradigm' I simply mean generalized models or patterns of thought applied to many or all aspects of 'reality' as seen by an individual or community.

Fundamental challenges to disciplines tend to come from outside. It is customary for students to be introduced to their fields of study gradually, as slowly unfolding mysteries, so that by the time they can see their subject as a whole they have been so thoroughly imbued with conventional preconceptions and patterns of thought that they are extremely unlikely to be able to question its basic premises. This incapacity is particularly evident in the disciplines concerned with ancient history. The reasons seem to be, first, that their study is dominated by the learning of difficult languages, a process that is inevitably authoritarian: one may not question the logic of an irregular verb or the function of a particle. At the same time as the instructors lay down their linguistic rules, however, they provide other social and historical information that tends to be given and received in a similar spirit. The intellectual passivity of the student is increased by the fact that these languages have generally been taught during childhood. While this facilitates learning and gives the scholar thus trained an incomparable *feel* for Greek or Hebrew, such men and women tend to accept a concept, word or form as *typically* Greek or Hebrew, without requiring an explanation as to its specific function or origin.

The second reason for inhibition is the near, or actual, religious awe felt in approaching Classical or Jewish cultures, which are held to be the founts of 'Western' civilization. Thus there is a reluctance to use 'profane' analogies to provide models for their study. The great exception to this has been in folklore and mythology where, since the time of James Frazer and Jane Harrison at the turn of the 19th century, there has been considerable comparative work. Nearly all this, however, has stayed within the bounds set in the 1820s by the man who destroyed the Ancient Model, Karl Otfried Müller. Müller urged scholars to study Greek mythology in relation to human culture as a whole, but was adamantly opposed to recognizing any specific borrowings from the East.[1] When it comes to higher culture, there has been an even greater reluctance to see any precise parallels.

The situation is at its most extreme, however, in the realms of language and names. Since the 1840s Indo-European philology, or study of the relationships between languages, has been at the heart of the Aryan Model. Then, as now, Indo-Europeanists and Greek phil-ologists have been extraordinarily reluctant to see any connections between Greek – on the one hand – and Egyptian and Semitic, the two major non-Indo-European languages of the Ancient East Mediterra-nean, on the other. There is no doubt that if Egyptian, West Semitic and Greek had been the languages of three important contiguous tribes in the modern Third World, there would have been extensive comparative study, after which most linguists would have concluded that they might well be distantly related to each other and that there had certainly been considerable linguistic and presumably other cultural borrowings among the three peoples. Given the deep respect felt for Greek and Hebrew, however, this type of crude comparative work is felt to be inappropriate.

Outsiders can never have the control of detail gained so slowly and painfully by experts. Lacking a full understanding of the background complexities, they tend to see simple-minded correspondences between superficial resemblances. This does not mean, however, that the outsiders are necessarily wrong. Heinrich Schliemann, the German tycoon who first excavated at Troy and Mycenae in the 1870s, made a naive but fruitful conjunction of legends, historical documents and topography, showing that much as academics might like it to be so, the obvious is not always false.

Another tendency among professionals is to confuse what I would call the ethics of a situation with its reality. While it is 'only fair' that the expert who has spent a lifetime trying to master a subject should know better than a brash newcomer, this is not always the case. The latter sometimes has the advantage of perspective; the ability to see the subject as a whole and to bring outside analogies to bear on it. Thus one encounters the paradoxical situation that while amateurs are usually unable to help scholarly advance within a model or paradigm, they are often the best people to challenge it. The two most important break-throughs in Hellenic studies since 1850 – the archaeological discovery of the Mycenaeans and the decipherment of their script, Linear B – were both made by amateurs: Schliemann, to whom I have just referred, and Michael Ventris, who was an Anglo-Greek architect.

Yet the fact that fundamentally new approaches often come from the outside certainly does not mean that all proposals from this quarter are correct or helpful. Most are not, and are rightly rejected as cranky. Discrimination between the different types of radical challenge poses two difficult problems. Who should do it? How should it be done? Naturally, the first group to be consulted should be the experts. They have the knowledge necessary to assess the plausibility and use of the new ideas. If, as with Ventris' decipherment of Linear B, most of them accept one of these, it would be foolish to challenge their verdict. Their negative opinion, on the other hand, cannot be regarded with the same unqualified respect, for, while they have the necessary skills to make a judgement, they have a direct stake in the case. They are the guardians of the academic *status quo* and have an intellectual and often an emotional investment in it. In some cases scholars even defend their position with the claim that the heroic age of amateurs, which in their field was once necessary, is now over. Therefore, although their discipline was founded by nonprofessionals, the latter can no longer contribute to it. However plausible the idea of an outsider may appear, it is inherently impossible for it to be true.

It is because of such attitudes that just as 'war is too serious a matter to be left to military men', informed lay, as well as professional, opinion is necessary to assess the validity of new challenges which have been rejected by the scholars concerned. Although the latter generally know better than the public, there have been cases that show the contrary. Take, for example, the idea of Continental Drift, first proposed by Professor A. L. Wegener at the end of the 19th century. Throughout much of the early 20th century the significance of 'evident fits' between Africa and South America, the two sides of the Red Sea and many other coasts was denied by most geologists. Now, by contrast, it is universally accepted that the continents have 'floated' apart. Similarly the American populists' proposals, in the 1880s and 90s, to abandon the gold standard were denounced by the academic economists of the time as completely unworkable. In such cases it would seem that the public was right and the academics wrong. Thus, although professional opinion should be studied carefully and treated with respect, it should not always be taken as the last word.

How should an informed layperson distinguish between a constructive outside radical innovator and a crank? Between a Ventris who deciphered a Cretan syllabary and a Velikowski who wrote sequences of events and catastrophes completely at variance with all other reconstructions of history? Ultimately, a lay jury has to rely on its own subjective or aesthetic judgement. There are, however, some helpful clues. The crank – that is, someone with a coherent explanation, whose hypotheses do not quickly attract the interest of the academic establishment – tends to add new unknown and unknowable factors into their theories: lost continents, men from outer space, planetary collisions, etc. Sometimes, of course, this type of hypothesis is spectacularly vindicated by the discovery of the postulated unknown factors. For instance, the great Swiss linguist Saussure's mysterious 'coefficients' which he hypothesized to explain anomalies in Indo-European vowels were found in the Hittite laryngeals. Before this, however, the theory remained untestable and to that extent uninteresting.

Less imaginative innovators, by contrast, tend to remove factors rather than to add them. Ventris took away the unknown Aegean language in which Linear B was supposed to have been written, leaving a direct juxtaposition between two known entities, Homeric and Classical Greek, and the corpus of Linear B tablets. Thus he instantly created a whole new academic field.

I maintain that the revival of the Ancient Model of Greek history proposed in these volumes belongs to this second category. It adds no extra unknown or unknowable factors. Instead it removes two introduced by proponents of the Aryan Model: (1) the non-Indo-European-speaking 'Pre-Hellenic' peoples upon whom every inexplicable aspect of Greek culture has been thrust; and (2) the mysterious diseases of 'Egyptomania', 'barbarophilia' and *interpretatio Graeca* which, the 'Aryanists' allege, have deluded so many otherwise intelligent, balanced ˙ and informed Ancient Greeks with the belief that Egyptians and Phoenicians had played a central role in the formation of their culture. This 'delusion' was all the more remarkable because its victims gained no ethnic satisfaction from it. The removal of these two factors and the revival of the Ancient Model leaves the Greek, West Semitic and Egyptian cultures and languages in direct confrontation, generating hundreds if not thousands of testable hypotheses-predictions that if word or concept *a* occurred in culture *x*, one should expect to find its equivalent in culture *y*. These could enlighten aspects of all three civilizations, but especially those areas of Greek culture that cannot be explained by the Aryan Model.

The Ancient, Aryan and Revised Ancient models share one paradigm, that of the possibility of diffusion of language or culture through conquest. Interestingly, this goes against the dominant trend in archaeology today, which is to stress indigenous development. The latter is reflected in Greek prehistory by the recently proposed Model of Autochthonous Origin.[2] *Black Athena*, however, will focus on the competition between the Ancient and Aryan models.

The 19th and 20th centuries have been dominated by the paradigms of progress and science. Within learning there has been the belief that most disciplines made a quantum leap into 'modernity' or 'true science' followed by steady, cumulative, scholarly progress. In the historiography of the Ancient East Mediterranean these 'leaps' are perceived to have taken place in the 19th century, and since then scholars have tended to believe that their work has been qualitatively better than any that has gone before. The palpable successes of natural science during this period have confirmed the truth of this belief in that area. Its extension to historiography is less securely based. Nevertheless, the destroyers of the Ancient Model and the builders of the Aryan believed themselves to be 'scientific'. To these German and British scholars, the stories of Egyptian colonization and civilizing of Greece violated 'racial science' as monstrously as the legends of sirens and centaurs broke the canons of natural science. Thus all were equally discredited and discarded.

For the past hundred and fifty years, historians have claimed to possess a 'method' analogous to those used in natural science. In fact, ways in which the modern historians differ from the 'prescientific' ones are much less certain. The best of the earlier writers were self-conscious, used the test of plausibility and tried to be internally consistent. Furthermore, they cited and evaluated their sources. By comparison, the 'scientific' historians of the 19th and 20th centuries have been unable to give formal demonstrations of 'proof' or establish firm historical laws. Today, moreover, the charge of 'unsound methodology' is used to condemn not merely incompetent but also unwelcome work. The charge is unfair, because it falsely implies the existence of other methodologically sound studies with which to contrast it.

Considerations of this kind lead to the question of positivism and its requirement of 'proof'. Proof or certainty is difficult enough to achieve, even in the experimental sciences or documented history. In the fields with which this work is concerned it is out of the question: all one can hope to find is more or less plausibility. To put it in another way, it is misleading to see an analogy between scholarly debate and criminal law. In criminal law, since conviction of an innocent person is so much worse than acquittal of a guilty one, the courts rightly demand proof 'beyond reasonable doubt' before a conviction can be made. But neither conventional wisdom nor the academic *status quo* has the moral rights of an accused person. Thus debates in these areas should not be judged on the basis of *proof*, but merely on *competitive plausibility*. In these volumes

I cannot, and therefore do not attempt to, *prove* that the Aryan Model is 'wrong'. All I am trying to do is to show that it is less plausible than the Revised Ancient Model and that the latter provides a more fruitful framework for future research.

20th-century prehistory has been bedevilled by a particular form of this search for proof, which I shall call 'archaeological positivism'. It is the fallacy that dealing with 'objects' makes one 'objective'; the belief that interpretations of archaeological evidence are as solid as the archaeological finds themselves. This faith elevates hypotheses based on archaeology to a 'scientific' status and demotes information about the past from other sources – legends, place names, religious cults, language and the distribution of linguistic and script dialects. In these volumes it is maintained that all these sources must be treated with great caution, but that evidence from them is not categorically less valid than that from archaeology.

The favourite tool of the archaeological positivists is the 'argument from silence': the belief that if something has not been found, it cannot have existed in significant quantities. This would appear to be useful in the very few cases where archaeologists have failed to find something predicted by the dominant model, in a restricted but well-dug area. For instance, for the past fifty years it has been believed that the great eruption on Thera took place during the ceramic period Late Minoan IB, yet despite extensive digging on this small island, no sherd of this ware has appeared below the volcanic debris. This suggests that it would be useful to look again at the theory. Even here, however, some pots of this type could still turn up, and there are always questions about the definition of ceramic styles. In nearly all archaeology – as in the natural sciences – it is virtually impossible to *prove* absence.

It will probably be argued that these attacks are against straw men, or at least dead men. 'Modern archaeologists are much too sophisticated to be so positivist', and 'no serious scholar today believes in the existence, let alone the importance, of "race".' Both statements may be true, but what is claimed here is that modern archaeologists and ancient historians of this region are still working with models set up by men who were crudely positivist and racist. Thus it is extremely implausible to suppose that the models were not influenced by these ideas. This does not in itself falsify the models, but – given what would now be seen as the dubious circumstances of their creation – they should be very carefully scrutinized, and the possibility that there may be equally good or better alternatives should be seriously taken into account. In particular, if it can be shown that the Ancient Model was overthrown for externalist reasons, its supersession by the Aryan Model can no longer be attributed to any explanatory superiority of the latter; therefore it is legitimate to place the two models in competition or to try to reconcile them.

At this point, it would seem useful to provide an outline of the rest of this introduction. In a project as large as the one I am trying to realize here, it is obviously helpful to give summaries of arguments, together with some indications of the evidence provided to back them. It is for these reasons that I have included an outline of the chapters that make up this book. The problems involved in explaining my arguments clearly are compounded by the fact that my views on the larger context in which the topics of *Black Athena* are set sometimes differ from conventional wisdom. Therefore, I have written a very schematic historical background which sweeps across the Western Old World, over the last twelve millennia. This broad survey is followed by a historical outline of the 2nd millennium BC, the period with which *Black Athena* is largely concerned. This is provided in order to show what I think *actually happened* as opposed the other people's views on the subject.

Then comes the summary of the *The Fabrication of Ancient Greece* itself, which is followed by rather more detailed descriptions of the contents of the other two volumes of the series. The outline of the second, *Greece European or Levantine?*, is included here to demonstrate that a powerful case can be made for the revival of the Ancient Model in terms of the archaeological, linguistic and other forms of evidence available. I have written a rather more sketchy descripton of the intended contents of Volume 3, *Solving the Riddle of the Sphinx*, in order to show the interesting results one can achieve through applying the Revised Ancient Model to previously inexplicable problems in Greek mythology.

BACKGROUND

Before outlining the topics covered in these volumes, it may be useful to give a general impression of my views on their historical background, especially where they differ from conventional wisdom. Like most scholars, I believe that it is impossible to judge between the theories of monogenesis and polygenesis for human language, though I incline towards the former. On the other hand, recent work by a small but increasing number of scholars has convinced me that there is a genetic relationship between the Indo-European languages and those of the Afroasiatic language 'superfamily'.[3] I further accept the conventional, though disputed, view that a language family originates from a single dialect. I therefore believe that there must once have been a people who spoke Proto-Afroasiatic-Indo-European. Such a language and culture must have broken up a very long time ago. The latest possibility would be the Mousterian period, 50–30,000 years BP (Before the Present), but it may well have been much earlier. The *terminus ante quem* is determined by the far greater differences between Indo-European and Afroasiatic than those within them, and I believe that the break-up of the latter can be dated to the 9th millennium BC.

I see the spread of Afroasiatic as the expansion of a culture – long established in the East African Rift Valley – at the end of the last Ice Age in the 10th and 9th millennia BC. During the Ice Ages water was locked up in the polar icecaps, and rainfall was considerably less than it is today. The Sahara and Arabian Deserts were even larger and more forbidding then than they are now. During the increase of heat and rainfall in the centuries that followed, much of these regions became savannah, into which neighbouring peoples flocked. The most successful of these were, I believe, the speakers of Proto-Afroasiatic from the Rift. These not only had an effective technique of hippopotamus-hunting with harpoons but also possessed domesticated cattle and food crops. Going through the savannah, the Chadic speakers reached Lake Chad; the Berbers, the Maghreb; and the Proto-Egyptians, Upper Egypt. The speakers of Proto-Semitic settled Ethiopia and moved on to the Arabian savannah (map 1; chart 1).

With the long-term desiccation of the Sahara during the 7th and 6th millennia BC, there were movements into the Egyptian Nile Valley from the west and east as well as from the Sudan. I also maintain – but here I am in a minority – that a similar migration took place from the Arabian savannah into Lower Mesopotamia. Most scholars believe that this area was first inhabited by Sumerians or Proto-Sumerians and was infiltrated by Semites from the Desert only in the 3rd millennium. I argue that during the 6th millennium Semitic speech spread with the so-called Ubaid pottery to Assyria and Syria, to occupy more or less the region of South-West Asia where Semitic is spoken today (map 2). I see the Sumerians as having arrived in Mesopotamia from the north-east, at the beginning of the 4th millennium. In any event, we now know from the earliest texts that have been read – those from Uruk from *c.*3000 BC – that bilingualism in Semito-Sumerian was already well established.[4]

Few scholars would contest the idea that it was in Mesopotamia that what we call 'civilization' was first assembled. With the possible exception of writing, all the elements of which it was composed – cities, agricultural irrigation, metalworking, stone architecture and wheels for both vehicles and pot-making – had existed before and elsewhere. But this assemblage, when capped by writing, allowed a great economic and political accumulation that can usefully be seen as the beginning of civilization.

Before discussing the rise and spread of this civilization, it would seem useful to consider the break-up and separate development of the Indo-European languages. In the first half of the 19th century it was thought that Indo-European originated in some Asian mountains. As the century wore on this *Urheimat*, or homeland, shifted west, and it was generally agreed that Proto-Indo-European was first spoken by nomads somewhere to the north of the Black Sea. In the last thirty years, this has been generally identified with the so-called Kurgan Culture attested in this region in the 4th and 3rd millennia BC. Possessors of this material culture seem to have spread west into Europe, south-east to Iran and India, and south to the Balkans and Greece.

The general scheme of expansion from Central Asia or the Steppes was developed before the decipherment of Hittite, the discovery that it was a 'primitive' Indo-European language, and the further recognition that there was a whole Anatolian linguistic family. I should mention that for linguists, 'Anatolian' languages do not include those like Phrygian and Armenian which, though spoken in Anatolia – modern Turkey – are clearly Indo-European. The true Anatolian languages – Hittite, Palaic, Luvian, Lycian, Lydian, Lemnian, probably Etruscan and possibly Carian – present a number of problems for the conventional view of Indo-European origins (map 3). It is generally conceded that Proto-Anatolian split from Proto-Indo-European before the latter disintegrated. However, it is impossible to tell the length of time between the two events, which could be anywhere from 500 years to 10,000. In any event, the difference is sufficient to cause many linguists to make a distinction between Indo-European – which excludes the Anatolian languages – and Indo-Hittite, which includes both families (see chart 2).

If, as most historical linguists suppose, not merely Indo-European but Indo-Hittite began north of the Black Sea, how and when did speakers of the Anatolian languages enter Anatolia? Some authorities argue that this took place during the late 3rd millennium when, Mesopotamian sources indicate, there were barbarian invasions there. These invasions would seem much more likely to have been those of the Phrygian and Proto-Armenian speakers. It is almost inconceivable that a period of a few hundred years, before the first attestation of Hittite and Palaic, would allow for the very considerable differentiation between Indo-European and Anatolian and within the latter family. The archaeological record for the 3rd millennium is extremely spotty, but there is no obvious break in material culture that would fit such a major linguistic shift. Nevertheless, one should not rely too heavily on the argument from silence, and an influx of Anatolian culture during the 5th and 4th millennia cannot be ruled out.

A more attractive possibility is the scheme proposed by Professors Georgiev and Renfrew.[5] According to this, Indo-European – I should prefer Indo-Hittite – was already spoken in Southern Anatolia by the makers of the great Neolithic cultures of the 8th and 7th millennia, including the famous one at Çatal Hüyük in the plain of Konya. Georgiev and Renfrew propose that the language moved into Greece and Crete with the spread of agriculture around 7000 BC, when

archaeology suggests a significant break in material culture there. Thus
a dialect of Indo-Hittite would have been the language of the Neolithic
'civilizations' of Greece and the Balkans in the 5th and 4th millennia. It
would seem convenient to accept the proposal of the American Professor Goodenough that the Kurgan nomadic culture was derived from the
mixed agricultural system of these Balkan cultures and hence derived
its language from them.[6] In this way it is possible to reconcile the
theories of Georgiev and Renfrew with those of orthodox Indo-
Europeanists, by postulating that the Indo-European-speaking Kurgan
culture spread back into the Balkans and Greece over an Indo-Hittite-
speaking population.

The hypothetical expansion of Afroasiatic with African agriculture in
the 9th and 8th millennia BC, and of Indo-Hittite with that of South-
West Asia in the 8th and 7th, would to some extent explain what seem to
be fundamental differences between the north and south coasts of the
Mediterranean. These migrations were largely overland because sea
travel, though possible at least as early as the 9th millennium, was still
risky and laborious. With the improvement of navigation in the 5th and
4th millennia, the situation was largely reversed. Despite the fact that
nomads continued to migrate overland, particularly across plains,
transport and communications from the 4th millennium BC until the
development of railways in the 19th century AD were generally easier by
water than by land. In this long period rivers and seas provided links,
while territories were isolated by riverless deserts and mountains. Such
a pattern of historical layering of first land, then sea, would explain the
general paradox with which this book is concerned: the apparent
contradiction between the striking cultural similarities found among
populations all around the Mediterranean and the fundamental linguistic and cultural division between the peoples of its south and north
coasts.[7]

Civilization spread from 4th-millennium Mesopotamia with great
speed. The idea of writing seems to have been taken up in India and
many parts of the East Mediterranean even before its codification as
cuneiform in its land of origin. We know that hieroglyphs were
developed in the Nile Valley by the third quarter of this millennium,
and despite the lack of attestation it would seem likely that Hittite

hieroglyphs, as well as the prototypes of Levantine, Cypriot and Anatolian syllabaries, were formed before the arrival in Syria, near the beginning of the 3rd millennium, of fully fledged Sumero-Semitic civilization, with its regular cuneiform script.

Egyptian civilization is clearly based on the rich Pre-dynastic cultures of Upper Egypt and Nubia, whose African origin is uncontested. Nevertheless, the great extent of Mesopotamian influence, evident from late Pre-dynastic and 1st-dynasty remains, leaves little doubt that the unification and establishment of dynastic Egypt, around 3250 BC, was in some way triggered by developments to the east. The cultural mix was further complicated by the fundamental linguistic and, I would argue, cultural links between Egypt and the basically Semitic component of Mesopotamian civilization.

The miraculous 4th millennium was followed by the prosperous 3rd. The newly discovered archives from Ebla in Syria, dating from around 2500 BC, portray a concert of rich, literate and sophisticated states stretching from Kurdistan to Cyprus. We know from archaeology that civilization at this time extended still farther – to the Harrapan culture stretching from the Indus to Afghanistan, and the metalworking cultures of the Caspian, Black Sea and Aegean. The Semito-Sumerian civilizations of Mesopotamia were tightly bound by a common script and culture. Those on the periphery, though equally 'civilized', retained their own languages, scripts and cultural identities. In Crete, for instance, there seems to have been a considerable cultural influx from the Levant at the beginning of the ceramic period Early Minoan I, at the turn of the 3rd millennium. Nevertheless, cuneiform did not become the dominant script, and Crete was never fully incorporated into Syro-Mesopotamian civilization. Apart from sheer distance, the most plausible reasons for this would seem to be the resilience of the native culture and the fact that Crete was culturally between the Semitic and Egyptian spheres of influence.

This double relationship with both the Levant and Africa is reflected in archaeological discoveries. Many Syrian and Egyptian objects of this period have been found in Crete and other parts of the Aegean. Around 3000 BC, as in the Near East, copper began to be mixed with arsenic to make bronze; pots started to be wheel-made, and there are striking similarities between fortification systems in the Cyclades and those of the same period found in Palestine. The archaeologists Professors Peter Warren in Bristol and Colin Renfrew in Cambridge ask us to believe that these developments took place independently, unaffected by the fact that the same changes had occurred somewhat earlier in the Near East and by the undoubted contacts between the two regions.[8] I find this very implausible. It would seem much more likely that the Aegean developments took place as the result of contacts through Levantine trade and settlement and local initiatives in response to these stimuli.

We know that most of the bronze-using world of the 3rd millennium was literate, either in cuneiform or in local scripts. There is, however, no trace of writing in the Aegean at this period. How seriously should 'the argument from silence' be taken in this case? There are some cogent points to be made against it. In the first place, the climates of Greece and Anatolia are far less suitable for preserving clay tablets and papyrus than those of the Middle East or North-West India. Even in these dry regions, evidence is often hard to find. Until the discovery of tablets at Ebla in 1975, there was no evidence whatsoever of literacy in Syria during the 3rd millennium. We now know that Syria at that time contained a cultivated literary class and that men travelled from the Euphrates to study at the schools of Ebla.

A further point suggests that there was writing in the Aegean during the Early Bronze Age. Although Linear A, Linear B and the Cypriot syllabaries found from the 2nd millennium seem to share a common prototype, they also show great divergences which, by analogy with historically observed developments of scripts, would take many centuries to come about. Thus the evidence from the scripts' 'dialects' would seem to indicate that the original form existed in the 3rd millennium and would allow for its development in the 4th which, on the grounds given above, would have been a plausible period for this to have taken place. Finally, I have argued elsewhere that the latest the alphabet could have reached the Aegean is the middle of the 2nd millennium.[9] If this is the case, it would seem plausible to suppose that the survival of the syllabaries shows that they were already well rooted in the region. Thus, in this way too, the evidence points to their existence in the 3rd millennium.

Early Bronze Age civilization broke down in the 23rd century BC. In Egypt, it has been marked as the First Intermediate Period. In Mesopotamia there was the Gutian invasion from the north. The whole civilized world was racked by barbarian invasion and social revolt, both of which may have been brought about by sudden climatic deterioration. It was in these years that Anatolia was invaded by groups that I believe should be identified with Phrygian and Proto-Armenian speakers. In Mainland Greece in this and the following centuries there were widespread destructions at the end of ceramic period Early Helladic II, which have been plausibly linked to an 'Aryan' or 'Hellenic' invasion of Greece but could also be the result of Egyptian raids and colonies at the beginning of the Middle Kingdom. Three centuries later there was another, though less devastating, destruction at the end of Early Helladic III, c.1900 BC, for one or both of the two causes mentioned above.

Postulating this degree of contact between the Aegean and the Near East in the 3rd millennium, it is likely that some of the words, place names and religious cults of Egyptian and Semitic origin discussed in this work were introduced into the Aegean at this time. On Mainland Greece these are less likely to have survived the turmoil of the northern invasions or infiltrations. However, in Crete and the Cyclades, which were not affected by such turmoils and may well have been largely Semitic-speaking, these cultural elements are much more likely to have continued.

I must repeat here that the scheme given above is not the topic of these volumes, but my perception of its background. Thus, though I shall discuss many of the linguistic issues in Volume 2, and I have written elsewhere on some other aspects, I cannot provide full evidence here to back up all these contentions.[10]

PROPOSED HISTORICAL OUTLINE

Black Athena is focused on Greek cultural borrowings from Egypt and the Levant in the 2nd millennium BC or, to be more precise, in the thousand years from 2100 to 1100 BC. Some of these may be earlier, and a few later exchanges will also be considered. The reasons for choosing this particular time-span are first that this seems to have been the period in which Greek culture was formed, and secondly that I have found it impossible to discover indications of any earlier borrowings either from the Near East or from legendary, cultic or etymological Greek evidence.

The scheme I propose is that while there seems to have been more or less continuous Near Eastern influence on the Aegean over this millennium, its intensity varied considerably at different periods. The first 'peak' of which we have any trace was the 21st century. It was then that Egypt recovered from the breakdown of the First Intermediate Period, and the so-called Middle Kingdom was established by the new 11th Dynasty. This not only reunited Egypt but attacked the Levant and is known from archaeological evidence to have had wide-ranging contacts further afield, certainly including Crete and possibly the Mainland. The succession of Upper Egyptian black pharaohs sharing the name Menthotpe had as their divine patron the hawk and bull god Mntw or Mont. It is during the same century that the Cretan palaces were established and one finds the beginnings there of the bull-cult which appears on the walls of the palaces and was central to Greek mythology about King Minos and Crete. It would therefore seem plausible to suppose that the Cretan developments directly or indirectly reflected the rise of the Egyptian Middle Kingdom.

Just north of the Greek Thebes there is a large mound, traditionally called the tomb of Amphion and Zethos. One of its latest excavators, the distinguished archaeologist T. Spyropoulos, describes this as an earthen stepped pyramid with a brick top in which there was a monumental – though robbed – tomb. He dates the pottery and few pieces of jewellery found near it to the ceramic period Early Helladic III – generally accepted to be around the 21st century. On the basis of this, of the extraordinarily sophisticated draining of the nearby Lake Kopais – which seems to have taken place at about this time – and of the considerable Classical literature connecting the region to Egypt, Spyropoulos postulates an Egyptian colony in Boiotia in this period.[11] There is further evidence to support his hypothesis, which will be cited in the later volumes of *Black Athena*.

Meanwhile, it is interesting to note that according to an ancient tradition referred to by Homer, Amphion and Zethos were the first founders of Thebes and that its other founder, Kadmos, arrived from the Near East long after their city had been destroyed. Like the Egyptian Pyramids, the tomb of Amphion and Zethos was associated with the sun and, like them, the Greek Thebes had close associations with a sphinx. Furthermore, it was in some way linked to the zodiacal sign Taurus, and many scholars have drawn parallels between the Theban and the Cretan bull-cults. Nothing is certain, but there is strong circumstantial evidence connecting the tomb and the first foundation of Thebes directly or indirectly to 11th-dynasty Egypt.

While Crete kept the bull-cult as central for another 600 years, Egypt abandoned the royal cult of Mont with the rise of the 12th Dynasty soon after 2000 BC. The new dynasty had the Upper Egyptian ram god Amon as its patron. I believe that it is from influence of this period that most of the ram-cults found around the Aegean and generally associated with Zeus were derived, drawing both from Amon and from the Lower Egyptian cult of the ram/goat Mendēs.

Herodotos and later authors wrote at length about the widespread conquests of a pharaoh he called Sesōstris, whose name has been identified with S-n-Wsrt or Senwosret, that of a number of 12th-dynasty pharaohs. Herodotos' claims on this, however, have been treated with especial derision. The same treatment has been given to ancient legends concerning wide-ranging expeditions by the Ethiopian or Egyptian prince Memnōn, whose name could well derive from 'lmn-m-ḥȝt (written Ammenemēs by later Greek writers), the name of other important 12th-dynasty pharaohs. Both legendary cycles now seem to have been vindicated by the recent reading of an inscription from Memphis which details the conquests, by land and sea, of two 12th-dynasty pharaohs, Senwosret I and Ammenemes II. There is also an intriguing resemblance between Ḫpr kȝ Rʿ, an alternative name for Senwosret, and Kekrops, the legendary founder of Athens whom some ancient sources said was an Egyptian.[12]

The next wave of influence, about which tradition was much more clear-cut, took place during the Hyksos period. The Hyksos, whose name came from the Egyptian Ḥkȝ Ḫȝst, 'Rulers of Foreign Lands', were invaders from the north who conquered and ruled at least Lower Egypt from about 1720 to 1575 BC. Although other, possibly Hurrian, elements seem to have been involved, the Hyksos were predominantly Semitic-speaking.

The first revision I propose for the Ancient Model is to accept the idea that there were, during the 4th and 3rd millennia, invasions or infiltrations of Greece by Indo-European speakers from the north. The second revision I want to make is to put Danaos' landing in Greece near the beginning of the Hyksos period, at around 1720 BC, not near its end – in or after 1575 – as set out in the ancient chronographies. Ever since late Antiquity, writers have seen links between the Egyptian records of the expulsion of the hated Hyksos by the Egyptian 18th Dynasty, the biblical tradition of the exodus from Egypt after the Israelite sojourn there, and the Greek legends of the arrival in Argos of Danaos. According to Greek tradition Danaos was either Egyptian or Syrian, but he definitely came from Egypt after or during his struggle with his twin, Aigyptos – whose origin is self-evident. This three-way association would seem plausible and has been reconciled, by some authorities, with the archaeological evidence. However, recent developments in radiocarbon dating and dendrochronology make it impossible to place the new settlements in Greece at the end of the Hyksos period. On the other hand, they and archaeological evidence from Crete would fit in very well with a landing in the late 18th century, at the period's *beginning*.

The ancient chronographers varied in their dating of the arrival of Kadmos and his 'second' foundation of Thebes. I would associate these legends too with the Hyksos, though they could refer to later periods. Greek tradition associated Danaos with the introduction of irrigation and Kadmos with the introduction of certain types of weapons, the alphabet, and a number of religious rituals. According to the Revised Ancient Model, it would seem that irrigation came with an earlier wave but other borrowings, including the chariot and the sword – both introduced to Egypt in Hyksos times – came soon after to the Aegean. In religion, the cults introduced at this stage seem to have centred on those around Poseidon and Athena. I maintain that the former should be identified with Seth, the Egyptian god of the wilderness or sea, to whom the Hyksos were devoted, and with the Semitic Yam (Sea) and Yahwe. Athena was the Egyptian Nēit and probably the Semitic 'Anåt who also seems to have been worshipped by the Hyksos. This is not to deny that other cults of such divinities as Aphrodite and Artemis were introduced over this period.

It is generally agreed that the Greek language was formed during the 17th and 16th centuries BC. Its Indo-European structure and basic lexicon are combined with a non-Indo-European vocabulary of sophistication. I am convinced that much of the latter can be plausibly derived from Egyptian and West Semitic. This would fit very well with a long period of domination by Egypto-Semitic conquerors.

In the mid-15th century the 18th Dynasty established a powerful empire in the Levant, and received tribute from the Aegean. Many 18th-dynasty objects have been found in that region. I believe that this was another high tide of Egyptian influence and that it was probably in this period that the cult of Dionysos – which was traditionally considered to be 'late' – was introduced to Greece. Specifically, I accept the ancient tradition that the Eĺeusinian mystery cult of Demeter was established in this period.[13] At the beginning of the 14th century BC I believe there was another invasion of Greece, that of the Pelopids or Achaians from Anatolia, which introduced new styles of fortification and possibly chariot-racing; but this is not of direct concern to my project.

In the 12th century BC there was a more disruptive historical break. In Antiquity, what is now called the 'Dorian Invasion' was much more frequently termed 'The Return of the Heraklids'. The incomers undoubtedly came from the north-western fringes of Greece, which had been less affected by the Middle Eastern culture of the Mycenaean palaces which they destroyed. Their calling themselves 'Heraklids' is fascinating, as it was a claim not only to divine descent from Herakles but also to Egyptian and Phoenician ancestors of the royal families which had been replaced by the Pelopids. There is no doubt that the descendants of these conquerors, the Dorian kings of Classical and Hellenistic times, believed themselves to be descended from Egyptians and Phoenicians.[14]

In Volume 2, I shall consider what I see to be the 'Egyptianizing' of

Spartan society between 800 and 500 BC, and in Volume 3 I shall also discuss the introduction in the 6th century BC of Egyptian Orphic cults. I have written elsewhere about the Phoenician origin of the *polis* or city-state and of Marxist 'Slave Society' as a whole, in the 9th and 8th centuries. I also hope, at some time, to work on the transmission of Egyptian and Phoenician science, philosophy and theoretical politics by the Greek 'founders' of these subjects, most of whom studied in Egypt or Phoenicia. However, *Black Athena* is essentially concerned with the Egyptian and Semitic roles in the formation of Greece in the Middle and Late Bronze Age.

BLACK ATHENA, VOLUME 1:
A SUMMARY OF THE ARGUMENT

The first volume of *Black Athena* is concerned with the development of the Ancient and Aryan Models, and the first chapter, 'The Ancient Model in Antiquity', treats the attitudes of Greeks in the Classical and Hellenistic periods to their distant past. It considers the writings of authors who affirmed the Ancient Model, referred to Egyptian colonies in Thebes and Athens, and gave details of the Egyptian conquest of the Argolid and the Phoenician foundation of Thebes. I discuss the claims made by various 19th- and 20th-century 'source critics' that the Ancient Model was concocted only in the 5th century BC, and I cite iconographic evidence and a number of earlier references to demonstrate that the scheme existed several centuries earlier.

Chapter I pays special attention to Aischylos' *The Suppliants*, which describes the arrival in Argos of Danaos and his daughters. The argument here, on the basis of a number of etymologies, is that there is considerable evidence of Egyptian influence in the play's peculiar vocabulary, indicating that Aischylos was in touch with extremely ancient traditions. In particular, I claim that the theme itself is based on a pun between *hikes(ios)* (suppliant) and Hyksos; while at another level, the idea that the settlers from Egypt had come as suppliants can be seen as a sop to Greek national pride. A similar attempt to soften the blow can be seen in the *Timaios*, in which Plato admitted an ancient 'genetic' relationship between Egypt and Greece, in general; and Athens and

Sais, the major city at the north-western edge of the Delta, in particular. But, rather implausibly, he claimed priority for Athens.

Like some other Greeks, Aischylos and Plato appear to have been offended by the legends of colonization because they put Hellenic culture in an inferior position to that of the Egyptians and Phoenicians, towards whom most Greeks of this time appear to have felt an acute ambivalence. The Egyptians and Phoenicians were despised and feared, but at the same time deeply respected for their antiquity and well-preserved ancient religion and philosophy.

The fact that so many Greeks overcame their antipathies and transmitted these 'traditions [of colonization] so little accommodating to national prejudice' greatly impressed the 18th-century historian William Mitford, who used it to maintain that 'for their essential circumstances they seem unquestionable.' Before Mitford no one questioned the Ancient Model, so there was no need to articulate a defence of it. Such motives of 'national prejudice' would help explain Thucydides' failure to mention these legends, of which he was certainly aware.

Chapter I goes on to discuss some of the equations made between specific Greek and Egyptian divinities and rituals, and the general belief that the Egyptian were the earlier forms and that Egyptian religion was the original one. Only in this way – the desire to return to the ancient and proper forms – can one explain why, starting in the 5th century at the latest, Egyptian deities began to be worshipped under Egyptian names – and following Egyptian ritual – throughout Greece, the East Mediterranean and later the whole Roman world. It was only after the collapse of Egyptian religion in the 2nd century AD that other Oriental cults, notably Christianity, began to replace it.

Chapter II, 'Egyptian wisdom and Greek transmission from the Dark Ages to the Renaissance', considers the attitude of the Church Fathers towards Egypt. After the crushing of Neo-Platonism, the Hellenic, pagan descendant of Egyptian religion, and Gnosticism, its Judaeo-Christian counterpart, Christian thinkers tamed Egyptian religion by turning it into a philosophy. The process was identified with the figure of Hermes Trismegistos, a euhemerized or rationalized version of

Thoth, the Egyptian god of wisdom; and a number of texts associated with Thoth, written in the last centuries of the Egyptian religion, were attributed to him. The Church Fathers were divided on whether or not Trismegistos antedated Moses and biblical moral philosophy. Saint Augustine's weighty opinion came down firmly in favour of the priority, and hence the superiority, of Moses and the Bible. Following the Classical tradition, however, the Fathers were united in the belief that the Greeks had learnt most of their philosophy from the Egyptians – though the Egyptians might have learnt some of theirs in turn from Mesopotamia and Persia. Thus, throughout the Middle Ages, Hermes Trismegistos was seen as the founder of non-biblical or 'Gentile' philosophy and culture.

This belief continued through the Renaissance. The revival of Greek studies in the 15th century created a love of Greek literature and language and an identification with the Greeks, but no one questioned the fact that the Greeks had been the pupils of the Egyptians, in whom there was an equal, if not more passionate, interest. The Greeks were admired for having preserved and transmitted a small part of this ancient wisdom: to some extent the experimental techniques of men like Paracelsus and Newton were developed to retrieve this lost Egyptian or Hermetic knowledge. A few Hermetic texts had been available in Latin translation throughout the Dark and Middle Ages; many more were found in 1460 and were brought to the court of Cosimo di Medici in Florence, where they were translated by his leading scholar, Marsilio Ficino. These and the ideas contained in them became central to the Neo-Platonist movement started by Ficino, which was itself at the heart of Renaissance Humanism.

Although Copernicus' mathematics was derived from Islamic science, his heliocentricity seems to have come with the revival of the Egyptian notion of a divine sun in the new intellectual environment of Hermeticism in which he was formed. His champion Giordano Bruno, at the end of the 16th century, was more explicit on this and went beyond the respectable Christian Neo-Platonic Hermeticism of Ficino. Appalled by the Wars of Religion and Christian intolerance, he advocated a return to the original or natural religion, that of Egypt, for which he was burnt at the stake by the Inquisition in 1600.

This brings us to Chapter III, 'The triumph of Egypt in the 17th and 18th centuries'. Bruno's influence continued after his death. He seems to have had some contact with the founders of the mysterious and elusive Rosicrucians, whose anonymous manifestos fascinated people in the early 17th century: the Rosicrucians, too, saw Egypt as the fount of religion and philosophy. It is commonly supposed that the Hermetic Texts were discredited in 1614 by the great scholar Isaac Casaubon, who showed to his satisfaction that the Texts did not come from deepest Antiquity but were post-Christian. This view has been accepted as axiomatic since the 19th century, even by 'rebel' scholars such as Frances Yates. However, in this chapter I try to show why I am inclined to the view put forward by the Egyptologist Sir Flinders Petrie that the earliest Texts date back to the 5th century BC. Whatever their actual date, the belief that Casaubon destroyed the credibility of the Texts is wrong. Hermeticism continued to be a major force well into the second half of the 17th century and retained considerable influence even after that. The Texts did, however, lose their appeal with the decline in the belief in magic among the upper classes at the end of the 17th century.

Though the Hermetic Texts became less attractive to the thinkers of the Enlightenment, interest in and admiration for Egypt did not diminish. In general the 18th century was a period of Classicism and one with a desire for order and stability, and so Rome was usually preferred to Greece; at the same time – in order to break away from the feudalism and superstitious Christianity of the European past – there was great interest in other non-European civilizations. By far the most influential of these, for this century, were those of Egypt and China. Both were seen as having superior writing systems representing ideas, not sounds; and both had profound and ancient philosophies. Their most attractive feature, however, seems to have been that they were ruled rationally, without superstition, by a corps of men recruited for their morality and required to undergo rigorous initiation and training.

Egyptian priesthoods had in fact appealed to conservative thinkers at least since the time when Plato had modelled his Guardians on them. In the 18th century this line of thought was taken up by the Freemasons; but even in the Middle Ages, Freemasons appear to have been especially interested in Egypt because, following ancient tradition, they believed it to be the home of geometry or Masonry. With the formation of Speculative Masonry at the turn of the 18th century they drew on Rosicrucianism and Bruno to establish a 'twofold philosophy'. This entailed superstitious and limited religions for the masses but, for the illuminati, a return to the natural and pure original religion of Egypt, from the debris of which all the others had been created. Thus the Masons, who included almost every significant figure in the Enlightenment, saw their religion as Egyptian; their signs as hieroglyphs; their lodges as Egyptian temples; and themselves as an Egyptian priesthood. Indeed, the Masonic admiration for Egypt has survived the country's fall from grace among academics. With some degree of self-deprecation, Masons have maintained the cult until today, as an anomaly in a world where 'true' history is seen to have begun with the Greeks.

The culmination of radical Masonry – and its most acute threat to Christian order – came during the period of the French Revolution. Here the political and military menace was accompanied by an intellectual challenge in the work of the great French scholar, anticlerical and revolutionary Charles François Dupuis. Dupuis's case was that Egyptian mythology – which, following Herodotos, he saw as the same as that of Greece – was essentially made up of allegories for the movements of the constellations, and that Christianity was merely a collection of misunderstood fragments of this grand tradition.

'Hostilities to Egypt in the 18th century' is the topic of Chapter IV. The Egyptian menace to Christianity naturally provoked response and Bruno's immolation, and Casaubon's attack on the antiquity of the Hermetic Texts, can both be seen as early instances of this reaction. However, the situation became acute once more at the end of the 17th century with the reorganization and attempted radicalization of Masonry. The threat posed by this 'Radical Enlightenment' can explain the sharp change in Newton's attitudes towards Egypt. In his early work he followed his Cambridge Neo-Platonist teachers in their respect for the country, but the last decades of his life were spent trying to diminish Egypt's importance by bringing down the date of its foundation to just before the Trojan War. Newton was concerned with a threat to his conception of physical order and its theological and political counterparts – a divinity with regular habits and the Whig constitutional monarchy. The threat was of pantheism, implying an animate universe without need for a regulator or even a creator.

This pantheism could be traced back past Spinoza to Bruno and beyond, to the Neo-Platonists and Egypt itself. The first articulate rejection of the challenge of the Radical Enlightenment – and the earliest popularization of the Newtonian 'Whig' scheme in science, politics and religion – was made in 1693 by Richard Bentley, Newton's friend and a great sceptical Classicist. One way in which Bentley attacked his and Newton's enemies was to use Casaubon's tactics. He employed his critical scholarship to undermine Greek sources on the antiquity and wisdom of the Egyptians. Thus throughout the 18th and 19th centuries we find a *de facto* alliance of Hellenism and textual criticism with the defence of Christianity. The ructions caused by occasional Hellenist atheists like Shelley and Swinburne were trivial compared to the threat of Aegypto-Masonry.

Newton had merely tried to demote Egypt in relation to Christianity; he did not try to raise Greece. By the middle of the 18th century, however, a number of Christian apologists were using the emerging paradigm of 'progress', with its presupposition that 'later is better', to promote the Greeks at the expense of the Egyptians. These strands of thought soon merged with two others that were becoming dominant at the same time: racism and Romanticism. Thus Chapter IV also outlines the development of racism based on skin colour in late-17th-century England, alongside the increasing importance of the American colonies, with their twin policies of extermination of the Native Americans and enslavement of African Blacks. This racism pervaded the thought of Locke, Hume and other English thinkers. Their influence – and that of the new European explorers of other continents – was important at the university of Göttingen, founded in 1734 by George II, Elector of Hanover and King of England, and forming a cultural bridge between Britain and Germany. It is not surprising, therefore, that the first 'academic' work on human racial classification – which naturally put Whites, or to use his new term, 'Caucasians', at the head of the hierarchy – was written in the 1770s by Johann Friedrich Blumenbach, a professor at Göttingen.

The university pioneered the establishment of modern disciplinary scholarship. In the same decade, other professors at Göttingen began to publish histories not of individuals, but of peoples and races and their institutions. These 'modern' projects, combined with exhaustiveness and a critical approach to sources, can usefully be seen as an academic aspect of the new Romantic concern with ethnicity, current in German and British society at the time. 18th-century Romanticism was not merely a faith in the primacy of emotion and a belief in the inadequacy of reason. Clustered around these were feelings for landscapes – especially wild, remote and cold ones – and admiration for the vigorous, virtuous and primitive folk who were somehow moulded by them. These sentiments were combined with the belief that as the landscape and climate of Europe were better than those of other continents, Europeans must be superior. They were championed by Montesquieu and Rousseau, but took firmest root in Britain and Germany.

By the end of the 18th century, 'progress' had become a dominant paradigm, dynamism and change were valued more than stability, and the world began to be viewed through time rather than across space. Nevertheless, space remained important for the Romantics, because of their concern for the local formation of peoples or 'races'. Thus a race was believed to change its form as it passed through different ages, but always to retain an immutable individual essence. Real communication was no longer perceived as taking place through reason, which could reach any rational man. It was now seen as flowing through feeling, which could touch only those tied to each other by kinship or 'blood' and sharing a common 'heritage'.

To return to the theme of racism. Many Ancient Greeks shared a feeling very like what would now be called nationalism: they despised other peoples and some, like Aristotle, even put this on a theoretical plane by claiming a Hellenic superiority based on the geographical situation of Greece. It was a feeling qualified by the very real respect many Greek writers had for foreign cultures, particularly those of Egypt, Phoenicia and Mesopotamia. But in any event, the strength of this Ancient Greek 'nationalism' was negligible compared to the tidal wave of ethnicity and racialism, linked to cults of Christian Europe and the North, that engulfed Northern Europe with the Romantic movement at the end of the 18th century. The paradigm of 'races' that were intrinsically unequal in physical and mental endowment was applied to all human studies, but especially to history. It was now considered undesirable, if not disastrous, for races to mix. To be creative, a civilization needed to be 'racially pure'. Thus it became increasingly intolerable that Greece – which was seen by the Romantics not merely as the epitome of Europe but also as its pure childhood – could be the result of the mixture of native Europeans and colonizing Africans and Semites.

Chapter V, 'Romantic linguistics: the rise of India and the fall of Egypt, 1740–1880', begins with a sketch of the Romantic origins of historical linguistics and the passion at the turn of the 18th century for ancient India largely caused by the perception of a fundamental relationship between Sanskrit and the European languages. It also surveys the decline in the European estimation of China, as the balance of trade between the two turned in Europe's favour and the British and French carried out increasingly large-scale attacks on China. I argue that these factors necessitated changing the image of China from one of a refined and enlightened civilization to one of a society filled with drugs, dirt, corruption and torture. Ancient Egypt, which in the 18th century had been seen as a very close parallel to China, suffered from the same effects of the need to justify the increasing European expansion into other continents and maltreatment of their indigenous peoples. Both were flung into prehistory to serve as a solid and inert basis for the dynamic development of the superior races, the Aryans and the Semites.

Despite the fall in Egypt's reputation, interest in the country continued during the 19th century. Indeed, in some ways this interest even increased with the explosion of knowledge about it that followed Napoleon's Expedition there in 1798; its most important consequence being Jean François Champollion's decipherment of hieroglyphics. In the chapter I look at some of the intricacies of Champollion's motivation and academic career in relation to the Masonic tradition and the triangular relationship between Ancient Egypt, Ancient Greece and Christianity. Here we need simply note that by the time of his death in 1831 his championship of Egypt had antagonized both the Christian political establishment and the newly and passionately Hellenist academic one. Thus, after an initial enthusiasm for it, Champollion's decipherment was neglected for a quarter of a century. On its revival in the late 1850s, scholars were torn between the appeal of Egypt and the brilliance of Champollion's work on the one hand and the intense racism of the age on the other. By the 1880s academics saw Egyptian culture as a static and sterile cultural cul de sac.

During the 19th century a number of mathematicians and astronomers were 'seduced' by what they saw as the mathematical elegance of the Pyramids into believing that they were the repositories of a higher ancient wisdom. They were classified as cranks for this triple offence against professionalism, racism and the concept of 'progress' – the three cardinal beliefs of the 19th century. Among 'sound' scholars the reputation of the Egyptians has remained low. In the late 18th and early 19th centuries, Romantic scholars saw the Egyptians as essentially morbid and lifeless. At the end of the 19th century a new contrary but equally disparaging image began to emerge. The Egyptians were now seen to conform to the contemporary European vision of Africans: gay, pleasure-loving, childishly boastful and essentially materialistic.

Another way of looking at these changes is to assume that *after the rise of black slavery and racism, European thinkers were concerned to keep black Africans as far as possible from European civilization.* Where men and women in the Middle Ages and the Renaissance were uncertain about the colour of the Egyptians, the Egyptophil Masons tended to see them as white. Next, the Hellenomaniacs of the early 19th century began to doubt their whiteness and to deny that the Egyptians had been civilized. It was only at the end of the 19th century, when Egypt had been entirely stripped of its philosophic reputation, that its African affinities could be re-established. *Notice that in each case the necessary divide between Blacks and civilization was clearly demarcated.* Yet despite the triumph of Hellenism and dismissal of Egypt in academic circles, the concept of Egypt as 'the cradle of civilization' never completely died. Moreover, the widespread mystical and cranky admiration for Egyptian religion and philosophy has remained a constant irritation to 'serious' professional Egyptologists. Two strands of this 'counter-discipline', the 'diffusionism' promoted by Elliot Smith and the long tradition of 'pyramidology', are discussed in this chapter.

Chapter VI is entitled 'Hellenomania, 1: The fall of the Ancient Model, 1790–1830'. Although racism was always a major source of hostility to the Ancient Model and became a mainstay of the Aryan one, it was matched in the 18th and early 19th centuries by an attack on the significance of Egypt from Christians alarmed at the threat of the religion or 'wisdom' of Egypt. These Christian attacks challenged Greek statements about the importance of Egypt, and boosted the independent creativity of Greece in order to diminish that of Egypt. Indeed, it is deeply significant that the Ancient Model was first challenged between 1815 and 1830, for these were years of intense reaction against the Masonic rationalism seen to be behind the French Revolution; and years of Romanticism and Christian revival. Further, as Christianity was identified with Europe, the two could come together with the notion of progress in a philhellenic movement which backed the struggle of the Christian, European and 'young' Greeks against the 'old' Asian, infidel Turks.

In the 1820s, the Göttingen professor Karl Otfried Müller used the new techniques of source criticism to discredit all the ancient references to the Egyptian colonizations, and weaken those concerning the Phoenicians. These techniques had also begun to be used to attack the reports of Greeks having studied in Egypt. The Ancient Model had placed a barrier in the way of the new faiths that Greek culture was essentially European and that philosophy and civilization had originated in Greece; this barrier was 'scientifically' removed even before the general acceptance of the notion of an Indo-European language family.

The title of Chapter VII is 'Hellenomania, 2: Transmission of the new scholarship to England and the rise of the Aryan Model, 1830–60'. Unlike the Ancients, the proponents of the Aryan Model were firm believers in 'progress'. Victors were seen as more advanced, and hence

'better', than the vanquished. Thus, despite apparent and short-term
anomalies, history – now seen as the biographies of races – consisted of
the triumphs of strong and vital peoples over weak and feeble ones.
'Races', formed by the landscape and climates of their homelands,
retained permanent essences, even though they took on new forms in
every new age. For these scholars, in addition, it was self-evident that
the greatest 'race' in world history was the European or Aryan one. It
alone had, and always would have, the capacity to conquer all other
peoples and to create advanced, dynamic civilizations – as opposed to
the static societies ruled by Asians or Africans. Some fringe Europeans,
like the Slavs and the Spaniards, might be conquered by other 'races',
but such a rule – unlike the conquest of 'inferior races' by Europeans –
could never be permanent or beneficial.

These paradigms of 'race' and 'progress' and their corollaries of
'racial purity', and the notion that the only beneficial conquests were
those of 'master races' over subject ones, could not tolerate the Ancient
Model. Thus Müller's refutations of the legends of Egyptian colonization in Greece were quickly accepted. The Aryan Model – which
followed his success – was constructed within the new paradigms. It was
encouraged by a number of factors: the discovery of the Indo-European
language family with the Indo-Europeans or Aryans soon seen as a
'race'; the plausible postulation of an original Indo-European homeland in central Asia; and the need to explain that Greek was fundamentally an Indo-European language. Moreover at precisely the
same period, the early 19th century, there was intense historical
concern with the Germanic overwhelming of the Western Roman
Empire in the 5th century AD, and the Aryan conquests in India in the
2nd millennium BC. The application of the model of northern conquest
to Greece was thus obvious and very attractive: vigorous conquerors
were supposed to have come from a suitably stimulating homeland to
the north of Greece, while the 'Pre-Hellenic' aborigines had been
softened by the undemanding nature of their homeland. And although
the large number of non-Indo-European elements in Greek culture
could not be reconciled with the ideal of complete Aryan Hellenic
purity, the notion of a northern conquest did make the inevitable 'racial'
mixing as painless as possible. Naturally the purer and more northern

Hellenes were the conquerors, as befitted a master race. The Pre-Hellenic Aegean populations, for their part, were sometimes seen as marginally European, and always as Caucasian; in this way, even the natives were untainted by African and Semitic 'blood'.

The question of 'Semitic blood' leads us to Chapter VIII, 'The rise and fall of the Phoenicians, 1830–85'. K. O. Müller, writing in the 1820s, had denied that the Phoenicians had had any influence on Greece, but he was extreme in his Romanticism and ahead of his time in the intensity of his racialism and anti-Semitism. In some ways, therefore, the Phoenicians even profited from the fall of the Egyptians, since legends of Egyptian colonization could now be explained as having referred to them. Consciously or unconsciously, all European thinkers saw the Phoenicians as the Jews of Antiquity – as clever 'Semitic' traders. The predominant mid-19th-century view of world history was one of a dialogue between Aryan and Semite. The Semite had created religion and poetry; the Aryan conquest, science, philosophy, freedom and everything else worth having. This limited recognition of the 'Semites' corresponded with what one might call a limited 'window of opportunity' in Western Europe, between the disappearance of religious hatred of the Jews and the rise of 'racial' anti-Semitism. In England, which had mixed traditions of anti- and philo-Semitism, there was considerable admiration of the Phoenicians because their cloth trading, exploration and apparent moral rectitude seemed, to both foreigners and English, to be almost Victorian. The opposing view of the Phoenicians – and other Semites – as luxurious, cruel and treacherous always persisted, and was generally predominant on the continent.

This hatred of the Phoenicians as both 'English' and Oriental was particularly striking in the works of the great French Romantic historian Jules Michelet. Michelet's views on the Phoenicians were spread even more widely in Flaubert's immensely popular historical novel *Salammbô*, published in 1861. *Salammbô* contained vivid descriptions of Carthage at its most decadent which powerfully reinforced the already widespread anti-Semitic and anti-Oriental prejudices. Still more damning was his brilliant and gruesome description of the sacrifice of children to Moloch. The firm and public attachment of this ultimate biblical abomination to the Carthaginians and Phoenicians made it very difficult to champion them, and during the 1870s and 80s their reputation plummeted even faster than that of the Jews.

This leads us to Chapter IX, 'The final solution of the Phoenician problem, 1880–1945'. With this reputation and the rise of anti-Semitism in the 1880s, there was a sustained attack on the Phoenicians which was particularly fierce where it came to their legendary contacts with, and influence on, the Greeks – who had by now been given semi-divine status.

A decade later, in the 1890s, two short but extraordinarily influential articles were published by Julius Beloch, a German who taught in Italy, and Salomon Reinach, an assimilated Alsatian Jew at the centre of Parisian cultivated society and scholarship. Both recognized Müller as a forerunner and claimed that Greek civilization was purely European, while the Phoenicians, apart from their transmission of the consonantal alphabet, had contributed nothing to Hellenic culture. Although many scholars were reluctant to accept this position over the next twenty years, the basis of what I call the Extreme Aryan Model was firmly established by the turn of the 19th century. There was a marked difference, for instance, between reactions to Heinrich Schliemann's discovery of Mycenaean civilization in the 1870s and Arthur Evans' reports of the Cretan one at Knossos in 1900. In the earlier case, several scholars initially suggested that the finds, which were completely unlike those from Classical Greece, could be Phoenician. This was then energetically denied in the following decades. In 1900, by contrast, the culture at Knossos was immediately tagged with the new name 'Minoan' and considered to be 'Pre-Hellenic'; certainly not Semitic, despite the ancient traditions that Crete had been so.

The final elimination of the Phoenician influence on Greece – and its complete dismissal as a 'mirage' – came only in the 1920s with the crescendo of anti-Semitism resulting from the imagined and real role of Jews in the Russian Revolution and the Communist 3rd International. In the 1920s and 30s all the legends of Phoenician colonization of Greece were discredited, as were reports of Phoenician presence in the Aegean and Italy in the 9th and 8th centuries BC. The many previously proposed Semitic origins of Greek names and words were all denied.

Every effort was now made to limit the significance of the only irreducible borrowing from Semitic culture – the alphabet. First, great emphasis was laid on the supposed Greek invention of vowels which, it was argued, were essential to a 'true' alphabet and without which, it was implied, man was unable to think logically. Secondly, the site of the borrowing was shifted to Rhodes, Cyprus and finally to an alleged Greek colony on the Syrian coast. This was partly because it was now seen as more in character for the 'dynamic' Greeks to have brought it from the Middle East than to have received it passively from 'Semites' as the legends had stated, but it was also because borrowing was perceived to involve social mixing, and the racial contamination that this would have entailed in Greece was unacceptable. Thirdly, the date of transmission was now lowered to *c.*720 BC, safely *after* the creation of the *polis* and the formative period of Archaic Greek culture. This opened up a long period of illiteracy between the disappearance of the Linear scripts discovered by Evans and the introduction of the alphabet, which in turn provided a double advantage: it allowed Homer to be the blind – almost northern – bard of an illiterate society, and it established an impermeable seal or complete Dark Age between the Mycenaean and Archaic ages. In this way, later Greek reports of their early history and the Ancient Model were discredited still further.

The 1930s were years in which positivism weakened in 'hard' science but gained strength beyond its borders in such fringe subjects as logic and ancient history. Thus in Classics the solution of the Phoenician problem seemed 'scientific' and final: from now on the discipline could proceed scientifically or, as one would now put it, a paradigm had been established. Any scholar who denied it was outlawed as incompetent, unsound or a crank. The strength of this position is demonstrated by its survival for more than thirty years after the consequences of anti-Semitism were revealed in 1945, profoundly shaking the ideological basis of anti-Phoenicianism. In the long term, however, there has been a retreat from the Extreme Aryan Model, and this process is described in Chapter X, 'The post-war situation: the return to the Broad Aryan Model, 1945–85'.

It is probable that the foundation of Israel has been more influential than the Holocaust in the restoration of the Phoenicians. Since 1949, Jews – or at least Israelis – have been increasingly accepted as full

Europeans, and it has become quite clear that speaking a Semitic language does not disqualify people from military achievement. Moreover, the 1950s also saw a sharp increase of Jewish confidence in their Semitic roots.

In the context of this process – and possibly because they were unable to accept the exclusiveness of either orthodox Judaism or Zionism – Cyrus Gordon and Michael Astour, two great Semitists, began to champion West Semitic Civilization as a whole and to attack the Extreme Aryan Model. Gordon, who knows the languages of the Ancient East Mediterranean better than any other living person, has always seen it as his mission to prove interconnections between Hebraic and Hellenic culture. In this process his bridges have been Ugarit, an ancient port on the Syrian coast, and Crete. He saw connections to both the Bible and Homer in the Canaanite myths recorded in Ugarit in the 14th and 13th centuries and translated in the 1940s and 50s; the monograph he published on the subject in 1955 destroyed his reputation as a 'sound' scholar, but fascinated some general historians and members of the lay public. Soon after this, he offended the orthodox still further by reading the Cretan Linear A inscriptions as Semitic, immediately facing a barrage of objections, nearly all of which have been removed by later research. Most scholars, however, have still not accepted his interpretation. While Ventris' decipherment – a few years earlier – of Linear B as Greek was novel, it was welcome in that it confirmed the geographical breadth and historical depth of Greek culture; but to accept Linear A, and hence Minoan civilization, as Semitic-speaking was to upset all notions of Hellenic, and therefore of European, uniqueness.

The upholders of conventional wisdom have been equally, if not more, disconcerted by *Hellenosemitica*, a major work by Gordon's colleague Michael Astour, which first appeared in 1967. *Hellenosemitica*, a series of studies of striking parallels between West Semitic and Greek mythology, showed connections of structure and nomenclature that were far too close to be explained away as similar manifestations of the human psyche. Apart from the challenge posed by this basic theme, Astour made three other fundamental attacks. First, the fact of his writing the book at all upset the academic *status quo*. While it was permissible for a Classicist, coming from the dominant discipline, to discuss the Middle East in its relation to Greece and Rome, the converse did not hold true. A Semitist was felt to have no right to write about Greece. Secondly, Astour questioned the absolute primacy of archaeology over all other sources of evidence about prehistory – myth, legend, language and names – thus threatening the 'scientific' status of ancient history. Thirdly, he sketched out a sociology of knowledge for Classics, indicating links between developments in scholarship and those in society. He even implied a connection between anti-Semitism and hostility to the Phoenicians and cast doubt on the notion of steady accumulative progress of learning. But the worst threat came from his basic message that the legends of Danaos and Kadmos contained a factual kernel.

So many heresies could not go unpunished. Astour was so battered by his critics that he has stopped work on the field he had so brilliantly opened up. Nevertheless his work, like that of Gordon, has had profound effects: together with the increasing number of finds of Levantine objects in Late Bronze Age and Early Iron Age sites in the Aegean, it has subverted the Extreme Aryan Model. It would seem fair to say that by 1985 the majority of researchers working in the area have retreated to the Broad Aryan Model. That is to say, they accept the possibility of Bronze Age West Semitic settlements not merely on the islands but on the mainland, at least at Thebes. They also believe that Phoenician influence on Iron Age Greece began well before the 8th century BC, and possibly as early as the 10th.

On the other hand, Gordon and Astour, for all their intellectual daring, have not challenged the Aryan Model itself. Neither of them has considered the possibility of a massive Semitic component in the Greek vocabulary; nor, given their Semitic preoccupations, have they investigated the possible Egyptian colonizations of Greece and the hypothesis that Egyptian language and culture played an equal or even more central role in the formation of Greek civilization.

There have been a few attempts to revive the traditions of Egyptian influence on Greece. In 1968, the East German Egyptologist Siegfried Morenz published a major work on the subject and its wider ramifications for Europe as a whole, but this has received very little attention outside Germany. Dr Spyropoulos' postulation of an Egyptian colony in 21st-century Thebes has been buried in decent obscurity. Scholars have sniped at his dating, while avoiding as far as possible any mention of his 'cranky' conclusion.[15] For the most part, the only people to consider major Egyptian influences on Greece have been on or beyond the fringes of academia; men such as Peter Tompkins – who has written on a wide range of journalistic topics as well as his cautiously written but boldly titled *Secrets of the Great Pyramid* – and the Afroamerican scholar G. G. M. James, whose fascinating little book *Stolen Legacy* also makes a plausible case for Greek science and philosophy having borrowed massively from Egypt. The *Fabrication* ends with the prediction that although the Broad Aryan Model will take somewhat longer to overthrow than the Extreme one, a revised form of the Ancient Model will be generally accepted early in the next century.

The following sections of the Introduction contain a considerable amount of technical discussion and are not necessary to an understanding of this volume. I therefore recommend readers whose chief interests are in historiography to go directly to the beginning of Chapter I.

GREECE EUROPEAN OR
LEVANTINE? THE EGYPTIAN AND
WEST SEMITIC COMPONENTS OF
GREEK CIVILIZATION

Volume 2 of *Black Athena* is concerned with comparing the relative fruitfulness of the two models to a number of different disciplines or approaches to historical reconstruction; contemporary documentary sources, archaeology, place names, language and religious cults. The Introduction to this volume is a comparison of the inherent plausibility of the two models.

With the possible exception of knowledge of Ancient Egypt, it is clear that proponents of the Ancient Model had more information about the 2nd millennium BC than do those of the Aryan one. The latter, however, have not based their claims to superiority on quantity of information but on their 'scientific method' and objectivity, both of which are fundamentally questioned in *The Fabrication of Ancient Greece*. On the issue of objectivity it is pointed out that while the Greek writers were torn between their wish to gain additional historical depth for their culture and their desire to be superior in every way to their neighbours, the 19th-century scholars had no such ambivalence. They had every interest in elevating European Greece and in downgrading the African Egyptians and the Semitic Phoenicians. This in itself would make an outsider incline to the belief that the Ancients were more 'objective' than 19th- and early-20th-century historians.

However, better possibilities of access to information and greater objectivity do not in themselves mean that the Ancient Model has a superior explanatory value to that of the Aryan one. As I have argued, and reiterate in the conclusion of this volume, the latter should not be dismissed simply because the motives that inspired its construction are now considered suspect. For example, the fact that the 19th-century scholars revelled in the historical pictures of the Aryan invasion of India and the formation of the caste system on the basis of colour does not remove the scheme's utility as a historical explanation. We should remember, however, that in India, unlike Greece, there were ancient traditions of invasion.

Chapter I of *Greece European or Levantine?* outlines the documentary evidence for the period and area with which we are concerned. The East Mediterranean in the 2nd millennium BC was not illiterate: Egyptians and Levantines had been writing for centuries; Crete was using its own hieroglyphs and Linear A, which was also employed on the Cyclades. Further, it is overwhelmingly likely that Linear B developed on Mainland Greece during the first half of the millennium, and I also maintain that most of the East Mediterranean was using alphabets by the 15th century BC.[16] Thus not only was writing widespread but, unlike the formulators of the Aryan Model, we are able to read most of its various forms.

Having said this, the documentary evidence for relations between the different cultural regions of the East Mediterranean in this period remains scanty. The Mit Rahineh inscription discovered recently on a block under a colossal statue gives details of wide-ranging Egyptian

land expeditions and marine voyages in the 20th century BC.[17] It has
been known for some time that early in the 16th century BC Queen
Aḥḥotpe, the mother of the first pharaoh of the 18th Dynasty, was
supposed to have come from Ḥꜣw Nbw, a foreign region that has been
plausibly identified with the Aegean. The report seems to be confirmed
by the Aegean designs of some of her jewellery. Although her son
Amōsis also seems to have claimed some kind of suzerainty over Ḥꜣw
Nbw, nothing further is heard of this for over a century. Whatever the
nature of the relationship between Amōsis and Ḥꜣw Nbw, it is clear that
at the end of the Hyksos period and the beginning of the 18th Dynasty
there was some interchanging of population. The name Pꜣ Kftỉwy, 'The
Cretan', occurs in Egypt at this time, and Egyptians and Levantines
appear on a list of Cretan names found in a contemporary Egyptian
papyrus. This picture of a thoroughly mixed population in the Southern
Aegean in the 17th century BC is confirmed by frescoes from Thera and
by later personal names found in Linears A and B.

Egyptian documentary evidence of contact with the Aegean is much
more abundant for the 15th and 14th centuries BC. Inscriptions and
tomb-paintings make it clear that after Tuthmōsis III's conquests in
Syria in the middle of the 15th century, the Egyptians felt able to
exercise some form of suzerainty over Crete and beyond, which was
renewed many times over the next hundred years. Soon after the
relationship was established, Egyptian documents and paintings indicate a change of power in Crete, which tallies with archaeological
evidence from Knossos to suggest that there was a Mycenaean conquest of the Minoans at this point. Egyptian texts stopped referring to
Kftỉw in the Aegean, replacing it with Tỉnꜣ or Ta-na-yu. The identification of this with the Danaans and Greece is made almost certain by a
14th-century inscription giving the names of places in Ta-na-yu,
several of which have been plausibly identified with toponyms in Crete
and Greece. Moreover, from the same period there is a letter from the
king of the Phoenician city of Tyre to the Egyptian pharaoh referring to
a king of Da-nu-na, which could well be in Greece.

There are references to contacts between the Levant and the Aegean
in the 14th century in both Ugaritic and Linear B. Ugaritic merchants
were trading with Crete, and I believe that the personal name Dnn

found at Ugarit is 'Danaan' and points to there having been Greeks at that port. The tablets in Linear B show that there was a Greek-speaking palatial society and economy in Crete and the Peloponnese, very much like those in the contemporary Near East. Linguistically, the Linear B inscriptions show that many of the admitted Semitic loan words in Greek were already present in the 14th century. Admittedly, these are generally the 'ideologically sound' semantic areas of luxury goods that could have been brought by Semitic traders. However, they include *chitōn*, the standard word for 'dress', and *chrysos* (gold), a metal that had been of central cultic importance in Greece since the Neolithic, which indicate a great depth of contact by the Late Bronze Age. Furthermore, there are many personal names of the type 'Egyptian', 'Tyrian', and so on. All in all, the documents indicate close contacts and population mixture of a type that would be quite consistent with the Ancient Model. On the other hand they could be accommodated by the Aryan Model, and there is no documentary proof of the legendary colonizations.

Chapter II is on Archaeology. It begins with the possible traces of Middle Kingdom influences in Boiotia at the turn of the 2nd millennium. Much of the chapter, however, is concerned with the dating of the great explosion at Thera, an island seventy miles north of Crete. We know that this eruption of the whole centre of the island was several times the size of the gigantic one at Krakatoa in 1883. Since the Krakatoa eruption broke windows hundreds of miles away, and sent tidal waves across the Indian Ocean – and since the dust it sent around the world helped the development of Impressionism and affected the climate of the whole Northern Hemisphere – the impact of the Thera explosion must have been colossal. Conventional wisdom holds that it took place at the same time as the destructions in Crete which have also been associated with the arrival of the Mycenaean Greeks on the island in around 1450 BC. One difficulty with this scheme, however, is that pottery on Crete before this destruction is of the style Late Minoan IB which, despite intensive search, has not been found below the volcanic deposits on Thera. Some archaeologists have therefore separated the two events, arguing that the eruption was some fifty years earlier than the Mycenaean destruction, that is to say in about 1500 BC.

I believe that the explosion took place even earlier, in 1626 BC, the precision of this date being based on dendrochronology – in this case, the counting of the tree rings of bristle-cone pines in the South-Western United States. Explosions on the scale of Krakatoa leave marks of summer frosts and stunted growth for several years on trees from near the snowline. Now there is no evidence from these aged bristle-cones of a world-shaking eruption in the 15th and 16th centuries BC, but there is for one in 1626. This was also a bad year for oaks in Ireland. Such a 'Krakatoa effect' could have been caused by another massive seismic event anywhere in the world; but, given the problem of finding a record of the Thera eruption, the identification would seem probable.[18] There is, however, other evidence to back the higher or earlier date. Although volcanic gases appear to have distorted some of the carbon dates given for material found just below the destruction level, those from the short-lived plants – which provide the only accurate information – point to a 17th- rather than a 15th-century date for the event.[19]

In China, the fall of Jie, the last emperor of the Xia Dynasty, was accompanied by extraordinary events such as a yellow fog, frosts in summer, a dimming sun, and three suns at a time – all of which have been plausibly explained as resulting from Thera's dust cloud. The next problem, however, is the dating of Jie's fall. It could not have taken place in the 15th century: some historians put it in the 16th century and others before 1700. However, compilations based on ancient – 3rd-century-BC – chronography and archaeological evidence indicate a date in the 17th century.[20]

Further indication of an early date comes from Egypt, where the 15th century BC is very well documented. It would be surprising if an event on the scale of the Thera explosion, which must have affected Lower Egypt, should not have been recorded in some way. Furthermore, as we saw, Crete seems to have been sending tributary missions to Egypt at precisely this time, c.1450. There are, by contrast, virtually no Egyptian records from the 17th century, which would make it easier to explain the absence of any mention of the explosion. The huge scale of the catastrophe allows me to make an exception to my general opposition to the 'argument from silence'. However, I acknowledge that this type of argument is inherently weak. Furthermore, the dendrochronological, the carbon and the 'Chinese' datings are all open to doubt. Nevertheless, given the extreme weakness of the case for a 15th-century date, the four sources together make 1626 BC seem much more plausible.

As there is now very little doubt that the eruption took place during the Late Minoan IA, some adjustment upwards of the absolute dates for a number of periods is required. The *Cambridge Ancient History* gives the chronological scheme using the standard periodization based on changing styles of pottery:

> Middle Minoan III, 1700–1600; Late Minoan IA, 1600–1500; Late Minoan IB, 1500–1450.

The one proposed here is:

> MM III, 1730–1650; LM IA, 1650–1550; LM IB, 1550–1450.

A revision of the Cretan ceramic periods would also require one for those of Mainland Greece, which were based on the Minoan ones and remain more or less correlated with them. In particular it would involve changing the dates of the Shaft Graves – first discovered by Schliemann at Mycenae – from the late to the early 17th century. To do so actually increases the difficulty for the Ancient Model, which maintained that the colonizations that began the heroic age were the result of the Egyptian expulsion of the Hyksos in the 16th century. However, the 16th-century date also conflicts with the absence of Cretan archaeological evidence of a significant general destruction in this period, and it is very unlikely that the colonizers from Egypt would have bypassed the island.

These incongruities with the archaeological evidence explain one of the two major revisions of the Ancient Model proposed in *Black Athena*. The Revised Ancient Model maintains that the Egypto-West Semitic settlements in the Aegean started at the end of the 18th century BC, when the Hyksos first gained control of Lower Egypt, rather than in the 1570s, when their power there collapsed. If, for the moment, one accepts the revision, one is then left with the question of why the

Ancients, with their respect for Antiquity, should have lowered the date
of the landings? One reason could have been the desire to associate
them with the Egyptian expulsion of the Hyksos and the Israelite
Exodus, which probably did take place in the early 16th century.
Another factor could be underestimation through a wish to appear
sober-minded and reasonable, for there is no reason why pressure in
this direction should have been any less in Antiquity than it is today.
Finally, the 'patriotic' feelings and the pun Hikesios/Hyksos could have
been influences. It was less damaging to Greek pride to see the
incomers as refugees or suppliants at the end of the Hyksos period than
as conquerors arriving near its beginning.

There is archaeological evidence that would fit very well with the
hypothesis of a Hyksos invasion of the Aegean soon after their arrival in
Egypt. In the late 18th century BC there was a destruction of all the
palaces in Crete, followed by their rebuilding in a slightly but significantly different way. There is thus a conventional demarcation at this
break between the Early and Late Palace periods; among the changes
are the introduction of swords, shaft graves and the royal motif of
the griffin – all of which existed earlier in the Levant and became
important in Mycenaean Greece. A sealing at this destruction level
at Knossos shows a barbaric, bearded king of strongly Mycenaean
appearance.

Artistically, there are striking resemblances between Aegean objects
of Middle Minoan III/Middle Helladic III, and objects found in Egypt
in the Hyksos period and the early 18th Dynasty. The cultural flow is
generally thought to be from the Aegean to Egypt; however, this is in
some doubt because of the Levantine precedents for many of the most
characteristic Mycenaean objects, techniques and motifs. To my mind,
the most fruitful analogy for the great mixing of – at least – material
cultures around the East Mediterranean in the late 18th and 17th
centuries BC is that of the *Pax Tartarica* in the 13th century AD. In this
the Mongol rulers brought about a mixing of Chinese, Persian and Arab
techniques and art, introducing features of one to another and breaking
their more rigid conventions. In the case of the Hyksos, I postulate that
long-established traditions, like those of Egypt and Crete, quickly
recovered with some slight modification; but that in Mainland Greece,

which lacked such a tradition, the eclectic 'Hyksos international style' lasted rather longer.

The hypothesis of a Hyksos Egypto-Canaanite conquest of Crete, and the establishment of colonies further north at the end of the 18th century, would provide a plausible scheme in which to fit the archaeological evidence I have mentioned. The Shaft Graves at Mycenae, which are full of new weapons and other objects showing foreign, largely Minoan and Near Eastern influence, could well be the tombs of the new conquerors. Indeed, the Cambridge ancient historian Professor Frank Stubbings maintained the same in his article on the Shaft Graves in the *Cambridge Ancient History*, though he accepts a 16th-century date and assures his readers that the Hyksos invaders had no lasting effect on Greek culture.[21] Since the article's publication in the 1960s, more evidence has emerged to strengthen his minority position. Recent archaeological discoveries at Tel ed Daba'a in the Eastern Delta, almost certainly the site of the Hyksos capital Avaris, have revealed a composite West Semitic-Egyptian material culture showing clear resemblances to that of the Shaft Graves.[22]

The continuities in pottery styles in Mycenae from the Middle Bronze Age seem to indicate survival of the earlier culture at a relatively low social level. This is precisely what the linguistic evidence as interpreted by the Revised Ancient Model would suggest. It would also fit descriptions of the native Pelasgians having become Danaans or Athenians on instruction from the newcomers. It must be insisted, however, that this is not the only interpretation that can be given to the archaeological evidence. Even after the finds at Tel ed Daba'a, it is still possible to argue that Mycenaean material culture was the result of native Aegean chiefs becoming rich and powerful and importing foreign objects and craftsmen; or that Greek mercenaries returned from Egypt with wealth and a vision of the new styles. Despite the fact that there is no linguistic evidence or ancient authority to back these interpretations, they are followed by most contemporary archaeologists.

As I have mentioned, there is also a school of thought that sees the radical change in Greek material culture at this point as the result of an invasion without long-term results. In both cases, however, there is little doubt that the archaeologists have been heavily affected by non-archaeological arguments. Inevitably the majority of scholars, who deny that there were any Hyksos settlements, have been influenced by the Aryan Model in which they are working. Similarly, the minority who believe in the settlements have been affected by the legends that make up the Ancient Model. In both cases, it is quite clear that the objects themselves do not impose a single conceptual pattern. In good circumstances, archaeology may be able to provide fascinating and important information on population density, settlement size or local economy, but it is much too blunt a tool to give answers on its own to the questions with which *Black Athena* is concerned.

Chapter III, 'River and mountain names', is the first chapter in *Black Athena* to concentrate on linguistic borrowing. It begins, therefore, with a discussion of the acknowledged phonetic correspondences between Egyptian, Semitic and Greek. Those between Egyptian and Semitic have been worked out in some detail, and a great deal of information about their correspondences with Greek can be deduced from the few admitted loan words and the hundreds of proper names transcribed in the other languages. From all this it is clear that there was an extraordinarily wide range of phonetic correspondences; the wide variety of ways in which, for example, a Semitic or Egyptian word or name could be transcribed in Greek is quite bewildering. This variation can be explained partly by difficulties in hearing and reproducing foreign sounds, and by loaning through different regional dialects or third languages. However, the main source of the divergencies would seem to come from the extraordinarily long time-span over which the borrowing seems to have taken place. In the period from 2100 to 1100 BC – with which we are chiefly concerned – all three languages, and Egyptian in particular, went through radical sound shifts. Thus I argue that the same word or name could have been borrowed two or more times with very different results. The most useful analogy I have found here is with Japanese loans from Chinese over a similar period of about a millennium; in this case, however, the writing system allows one to see what the original word was, and it is the many different Japanese 'readings' or pronunciations of the Chinese character that indicate the different borrowings.

Neither the Egyptian nor the West Semitic writing system indicated vowels. Some attempts at reconstructing them can be made from Coptic and the Masoretic vocalization of the Bible, as well as from cuneiform, Greek and other transcriptions of them. Nevertheless, many etymologies have to be made on the basis of consonantal structure alone. This – with the wide range of equivalences evident among the consonants themselves – creates an extraordinary number of possible phonetic correspondences between Egyptian, Semitic and Greek words and names. On the other hand, the fact that phenomena can be easily imagined has nothing to do with the likelihood of their actual occurrence. Furthermore, there are powerful external arguments in favour of massive linguistic borrowing having taken place. Even without the Ancient Model, there are the geographical and temporal proximities and the documentary and archaeological evidence of close contact. Added to these has been the failure of scholars working in the Aryan model over the last 160 years to explain 50 per cent of the Greek vocabulary and 80 per cent of proper names in terms of either Indo-European or the Anatolian languages supposedly related to 'Pre-Hellenic'.

In these circumstances I think it worthwhile to look for Egyptian and Semitic etymologies of Greek forms, but as rigorously as possible. First of all, I make no attempt to replace generally accepted Indo-European etymologies, even though some of these may well be wrong; the majority of the new ones proposed in this work have no orthodox competition. Even in such cases, however, one should still be extremely cautious. On the phonetic side one should be restricted to consonantal correspondences that are actually attested, even though it is very likely that others do occur. Similarly, there should be no metatheses – or switching of consonantal order. The one exception to this rule is the exchange of liquids – ls and rs between 2nd and 3rd position. This is tolerated because it is extremely common in all three languages, particularly in Egyptian and Greek. Thus it would seem legitimate to derive the Greek *martyr* (witness) from the Egyptian *mtrw* (witness), or *pyramis* (pyramid) from the Egyptian *pꜣ mr* (the tomb) or (the pyramid). The main control to avoid spurious derivations is, however, with semantics, where tight correspondences of meaning are required.

The area of toponyms – place names – is one in which scholars working within the Aryan Model have been particularly lax in this respect. Any loose phonetic correspondence between a Greek and an Anatolian name has been considered sufficient to link the two – regardless of whether they refer to an island, a mountain, a river or a town, let alone their geographical or legendary circumstances. This sloppiness has led the more rigorous to avoid the subject altogether, and nothing in this area has superseded the very sketchy work of the German Classical scholar A. Fick, published in 1905. This startling gap has been the inevitable result of the almost complete inability of Aryanist scholars to explain Aegean toponyms, because only a minute proportion of them are explicable in terms of Indo-European. All the Aryanists can do is to explain why they cannot explain them, and simply call them 'Pre-Hellenic'.

Aryanists place great emphasis on the allegedly 'Pre-Hellenic' place-name elements -(i)ssos and -nthos, which have never been given any meaning. This classification, first made by the German Classical linguist Paul Kretschmer, was developed by the American Classicist J. Haley and the archaeologist Carl Blegen, who argued that the distribution of these place names corresponded with Early Bronze Age settlements; and, further, that as the invaders were supposed to have arrived at the beginning of the Middle Bronze Age, they were indicators of Pre-Hellenic settlements. Archaeologically the theory is very flimsy, as the correspondences would hold as well for Late Bronze Age as for Early Bronze Age sites. The toponymic aspect is equally feeble. Even before Haley and Blegen announced their theory, Kretschmer admitted that the suffixes could be attached to Indo-European roots, and therefore could not in themselves be indicators of the Pre-Hellenes – that is, if one accepts the Aryan Model. As the suffixes also appear at the end of Semitic and Egyptian stems, they are equally unhelpful as indicators of an indigenous substratum when one is working within the Ancient Model.

Given these obvious inadequacies, it might seem surprising that Blegen and Haley's hypothesis continues to be treated with so much respect. The explanation is that not even rubbish can be thrown away in a field so utterly barren as Ancient Greek toponymy. According to the Revised Ancient Model, -nthos has many different origins, the two most common being simple nasalization before dentals and the Egyptian -nṯr (holy); -(i)ssos would seem to be a characteristic Aegean ending, but one that continued to be used at least until the end of the Bronze Age.

As I said, Chapter III is concerned with river and mountain names. These are the toponyms that tend to be the most persistent in any country. In England, for instance, most are Celtic and some even seem to be pre-Indo-European. The presence of Egyptian or Semitic mountain names would therefore indicate a very profound cultural penetration. The chapter cannot treat all my proposals in the area, but those considered include some very widely attested place names. Take, for instance, Kēphisos or Kāphisos, the name of rivers and streams found all over Greece for which no explanation has been offered. I would derive it from Kbḥ, a common Egyptian river name 'Fresh', with the suffix -isos. The semantic fit is excellent: Kbḥ is clearly linked to the words *ḳb(b)* (cool) and *ḳbḥ* (purify). The Greek Kēphisoi were frequently used for purification rituals. *Ḳbḥ* had a subsidiary meaning: 'lake with wild fowl'. This would fit well with the great shallow Lake Kopais, which has many Egyptian connections in Greek tradition and is fed by a river, Kēphisos. As far as I am aware, this etymology has never been proposed before.

That of the Greek river name Iardanos – which is found in Crete and the Peloponnese – from the Semitic Yardēn or Jordan was generally accepted before the onset of the Extreme Aryan Model. Even Beloch and Fick had to admit that the derivation was 'alluring' and could provide no alternatives. Nevertheless, it has been denied throughout the 20th century. Another Semitic etymology widely acknowledged before the late 19th century is that of the Greek toponymic element sam- as in *Sam*os, *Sam*othrace, *Sam*ikon, which always refers to high places, from the Semitic root √smm (high). This too has been neglected or denied. Other derivations proposed in this chapter require rather more discussion.

In Chapter IV I am concerned with city names. These are more commonly transmitted from culture to culture than those of natural features. Nevertheless, the insignificant number of Indo-European city names in Greece, and the fact that plausible Egyptian and Semitic derivations can be found for most of them, suggests an intensity of contact that is impossible to explain in terms of trade. One of the commonest clusters of Greek city names, for instance, is around the stem Kary(at). This could be plausibly explained in terms of the standard West Semitic word for town – *qrt* – vocalized in different city names in many ways, including Qart-, Qårêt or Qiryåh/at. It is, in fact, one of the commonest Phoenician and Hebrew place names, seen in *Cart*hage and many other cities.

I give instances showing a strict parallel between the use of Kary- and that of the standard Greek word for 'city', *polis*. The most striking of these is the placing of the figures of Karyatids around the tomb of Kekrops, the legendary founder of Athens, in a porch of the temple of Athena Polias. Thus, 'Daughters of the City' would seem a more plausible explanation for this name than 'Priestesses of Artemis from Karyai in Lakonia', or 'Nut Fairies', which are the only explanations given today. There are many variants of the stem Kary-, among which I include Korinthos (Corinth).

Near Corinth on the Isthmus was the city of Megara. Pausanias, the Greek Baedeker of the 2nd century AD, explained the name as meaning 'cave' or 'subterranean chamber'. A West Semitic word with exactly this meaning appears in the Ugaritic place name Mǵrt, and the biblical Mᵉʿåråh. These would seem plausible origins for the otherwise un-explained Greek city or city-ward names Megara and Meara.

It is not well known that Ancient Egypt had a long tradition of bull-fighting, that is, of bull fighting bull. The fight – and the arena in which it took place – was called Mṯwn. In Homer the word *mothos* – accusative *mothon* – meant 'battle-din' and 'fight between animals'; while *mothōn* could mean 'licentious dance, a flute tune', or 'a young impudent fellow'. Mṯwn was a common Egyptian place name; Mothōne, Methōne or Methana were almost equally frequent in Greece. These are all set on bays that could well be described as theatrical. It is therefore not surprising to find a coin from Mothone which portrays the port as a theatre, thus tying it clearly to Mṯwn.

The traditional etymology for Mykēnai (Mycenae) is from *mykēs*, 'mushroom'. A more plausible candidate would seem to be from Maḥăneh, 'Camp' or Maḥănayim, 'Two Camps' – a common toponym in West Semitic. Then again, before the advent of the Extreme Aryan Model it was generally accepted that the Greek city name Thēbai came from the Canaanite *têbåh* (ark, chest) which itself came from the Egyptian *tḥ* or *dbt* (box). These two were often confused with another and possibly related word *db3* (wicker float, ark of bulrushes) and *db3t* (coffin, shrine) and hence (palace). Db3, written Tbo or Thbo in Coptic, was an Egyptian city name. Interestingly, however, there is no record of its having been used for the southern capital of Egypt which the Greeks called Thēbai. Nevertheless, it may well have been used for the Hyksos capital at Avaris. If this were the case, Db3/Thēbai could have become a Greek term or name for 'Egyptian capital', which was attached to the Egyptian Thebes when the 18th Dynasty established their capital there. In any event, there is no reason to doubt that the Greek city name came from the West Semitic *têbåh* and the Egyptian cluster mentioned above.

Chapter V is devoted to one city, Athens. In it I argue that both the city name Athēnai and the divine name Athēnē or Athena derive from the Egyptian Ḥt Nt. In Antiquity, Athena was consistently identified with the Egyptian goddess Nt or Nēit. Both were virgin divinities of warfare, weaving and wisdom. The cult of Nēit was centred on the city of Sais in the Western Delta, whose citizens felt a special affinity with the Athenians. Sais was a secular name, the city's religious title being Ḥt Nt (Temple or House of Nēit). This name is not attested in Greek or Coptic, but the toponymic element Ḥt- is transcribed as At- or Ath-. It was also extremely common for Egyptian words to have what are called prothetic vowels before the first consonant. In this case the likelihood that Nt was preceded by a vowel is increased by the name 'Anåt, given to a very similar West Semitic goddess; hence it would seem legitimate to propose a vocalization of *At(h)anait for Ḥt Nt. The lack of i in Athēnē, Athānā in the Doric dialect and A-ta-na in Linear B would

---

* is the convention used to denote hypothesized but unattested forms of a word or name.

seem to be a problem. However, Attic and Doric have the variants Athēnaia and Athānaia, while the full Homeric form is Athēnaiē. And as final -ts were dropped in both Greek and Late Egyptian, the letter's non-appearance in Athēnai and Athēnē should be expected.

If the phonetic fit is good, the semantic one is perfect. As I have said, the Ancients saw Nēit and Athena as two names for the same deity. In Egypt it was normal for a divinity to be addressed by the name of her or his dwelling, and this would explain the Greek confusion between the names of the goddess and her city. Finally there is the statement, by Charax of Pergamon in the 2nd century AD, that 'the Saitians called their city Athēnai', which makes sense only if they saw Ht Nt as a name for Sais.[23]

Chapter V goes on to look at iconographic connections between Nēit and Athena. Nēit had been symbolized since Pre-dynastic times as a cockroach on a stick, from which it developed into a figure 8 shield often associated with weapons. This symbolism would seem to be the origin of the so-called 'Shield Goddess' found in Minoan Crete, which in turn is generally linked to a painted limestone plaque, found at Mycenae, showing the arms and neck of a goddess coming from behind a figure 8 shield. Now this image has been seen as an early representation of the Palladion, a standing suit of armour associated with the cult of *Pallas* Athena, as well as with the goddess herself. In this way, then, one can trace an iconographic development from Egypt in the 4th and 3rd millennia BC, through Crete and Mycenae in the 2nd, to the well-known goddess of the 1st – which corresponds precisely with the legendary association between Nēit and Athena and the etymology here. Furthermore, the high point in the state cult of Athena in Athens was at the same time in the mid-6th century that Amasis, the Saite pharaoh of Egypt, was promoting her worship elsewhere in the East Mediterranean.

Sais was on the frontier of Egypt and Libya and was sometimes part Libyan, which explains Herodotos' detailed description of Athena's association with Libya; it is also clear that this first great Greek historian thought the Egyptians and some Libyans were black. On the other hand, the earliest Greek representation of Athena is that from Mycenae, in which her limbs are painted, in line with the Minoan convention –

taken from Egypt – of representing men as red/brown and women as yellow/white. Nevertheless, it is the conjunction of Nēit/Athena's Egypto-Libyan origins, Herodotos' awareness of the connection, and his portrayal of the Egyptians as black, that has inspired the title of this series.

Chapter VI is exclusively concerned with Sparta. I see this place name as one of a large cluster, including such variants as Spata and Sardis, to be found all over the Aegean basin. I believe that they should all be derived directly or indirectly from the Egyptian toponym Sp(ꜣ)(t) (nome) or 'District and its Capital'. In Old and Middle Egyptian the 'vulture' sign represented here as ꜣ was heard as a liquid r/l; in Late Egyptian it merely modified other vowels. In Egypt the Sp(ꜣ)(t) *par excellence* was one near Memphis dedicated to Anubis the Jackal, messenger of death and guardian of the dead. I maintain that this link persisted in at least Sardis and Sparta, for Spartan or Lakonian culture is full of canine associations. These include the other name for Sparta, Lakedaimōn, which can be plausibly explained as the 'Howling/Gnawing Spirit', an epithet altogether appropriate for Anubis and an exact calque for Kanōb/pos, Kꜣ 'Inpw, 'Spirit of Anubis', the name of the westernmost mouth of the Nile. In Greek myth Kanōpos had close associations with Sparta, and both were seen as entries to the Underworld. Hence I also investigate the religious importance of Anubis' Greek counterpart Hermes in Lakonia and the special Spartan concern with canines, the Underworld and death, all of which I am convinced can be traced back to the Bronze Age.

The last section of the chapter is devoted to Egyptian influences on Iron Age Sparta. The fact that much of the uniquely Spartan political vocabulary can be plausibly derived from Late Egyptian is linked to the tradition that the Spartan lawgiver Lykourgos visited the East and Egypt to study their institutions. Moreover, the notion of Egyptian cultural influence there in the 9th and 8th centuries is strengthened by the strikingly Egyptian appearance of early Spartan art. All these link up with the Spartan kings' belief in their Heraklid – hence Egyptian or Hyksos – ancestry; and would thus explain such anomalies in the Aryan Model as the building of a pyramid at the Menelaion, the Spartan 'national' shrine, and the letter one of the last Spartan kings wrote to the High Priest in Jerusalem, claiming kinship with him.

Chapter VII returns the reader to linguistics, with a survey of the arguments for and against there being a genetic relationship between Afroasiatic and Indo-European languages. Here I come out clearly for the minority position taken by A. R. Bomhard, A. B. Dolgopolskii, Carleton Hodge and the other linguists who believe that there must have been a common proto-language for both families. I also believe that there may well have been loans from Semitic and Egyptian before the disintegraton of Proto-Indo-European at the turn of the 3rd millennium. Both these conclusions complicate my task considerably, however, as resemblances between Egyptian and West Semitic words on the one hand, and Greek ones on the other, cannot simply be attributed to loaning in the 2nd millennium; they could be the result not only of coincidence but of genetic relationships or much earlier borrowings. The best way to control for this is to see whether similar words are found in Teutonic, Celtic and Tokharian – languages remote from the Middle East and therefore relatively unlikely to have borrowed from Afroasiatic. Even with these, however, one can never be certain.

Chapter VIII is entitled 'Common features in Ancient Near Eastern languages, including Greek'. Since the discovery of Indo-European, historical linguistics has been largely concerned with the ramifications and differentiations of language families. Where similarities have been perceived among neighbouring but 'unrelated' languages, these *Sprachbunden* are usually attributed to ancient 'substrates' underlying the later languages. In recent years, however, some linguists have begun to look at linguistic convergence among adjacent, genetically unrelated languages: that is to say, language changes taking place across linguistic frontiers. Take, for instance, the fashionable French r, diffused into German and the upper-class English affected mispronunciation of the sound. Then there is the tendency to replace the simple past tense by a compound one, which seems to have spread from French to adjacent dialects of German, Italian and Spanish. These changes not only indicate close contact but also reflect the high political and cultural prestige of France between the 17th and 19th centuries, when the linguistic changes took place.

Chapter VIII is concerned with the possibility that such processes took place in the Ancient Near East. It is argued, for instance, that although the shift from initial s- to initial h- has happened in many languages, including Welsh, its occurrence in Greek, Armenian and Iranian should be linked to that in the contiguous Anatolian language Lycian, and the Semitic Canaanite and Aramaic. This development seems to have taken place in the 2nd millennium because it is not present in older languages of the region like Eblaite, Akkadian and Hittite. Furthermore, in Ugaritic texts dating from the 14th and 13th centuries the process appears to have begun but is not complete.

Another 2nd-millennium development was that of the definite article, a feature which is not so common among world languages as one might suppose. It is attested only in Indo-European and Afroasiatic languages, and in every case the definite article is a weakened form of a native demonstrative. Still, this does not exclude the possibility of the concept's having been borrowed. The definite article appears first in Late Egyptian, in what seems to be the colloquial of the 16th century BC. It does not exist in Ugaritic or biblical poetry, but is present in Phoenician and biblical prose. Given the Egyptian Empire in the Levant in the 15th and 14th centuries, it would seem plausible to suggest that this – and other characteristically 'Canaanite' linguistic changes – took place then as a result of Egyptian influence.

Greece, for its part, seems to have developed the definite article a little later. There is no trace of it in the Linear B texts and little in Homer; it is, however, present in the earliest Iron Age prose, and the fact that the Greek article is used in a number of ways peculiar to it and to Canaanite suggests that the idea was borrowed from the Levant. As is well known, Latin has no definite article but all its descendants do; so it is likely that it was widespread in vulgar Latin, presumably as a result of its use in Greek, Punic and Aramaic, the next most influential languages in the Roman Empire. Its spread through the Teutonic and Western Slav languages can be traced historically.

It is only with the hypotheses of a genetic relationship between Afroasiatic and Indo-European, and areal features resulting from convergence, that one can explain such 'coincidences' as the remarkable similarity between the Hebrew *ha* (the) and the Greek nominative forms of the word, *ho* and *hē*. Both Afroasiatic and Indo-European had a demonstrative **se*. Both Greek and Canaanite seem to have transformed initial s- into h-, and both developed definite articles out of demonstratives. There may have been a direct influence or 'contamination' from the Semitic to the Greek forms, but the latter is too well-rooted in Indo-European to be considered as a loan.

An even more intricate pattern of convergence can be seen in the breakdown of the long ā or 'a, in many phonetic contexts, which took place in much of the region in the second half of the 2nd millennium. In Egypt and Canaan it shifted to long ō. But in Ugaritic in the Northern Levant, Lycian in Southern Anatolia, and the Ionian of East Greece – but not the other Greek dialects, where the long ā remained – it became long ē. This distribution of ō and ē corresponds well with the known political division of the period between the Egyptian and Hittite empires and spheres of influence. It is particularly interesting because it cuts across the historical and genetic linguistic boundaries of West Semitic and Greek. Such widespread changes in the 2nd millennium BC indicate a degree of contact in the East Mediterranean that is not generally recognized, and indicates the political and/or cultural influence of Egypt and Canaan.

'Labiovelars in Semitic and Greek' is the topic of Chapter IX. Labiovelars are sounds like qu- in which a velar like k or g is followed by a rounding of the lips or a w. It is generally recognized that such sounds existed in Proto-Indo-European, but there is no general recognition that this is the case with Proto-Semitic. However, labiovelars are common throughout the rest of Afroasiatic and in Semitic languages of Ethiopia. In this chapter, I argue that in many respects it is much more useful to reconstruct Proto-Semitic on the basis of some South Ethiopic Semitic languages than from Arabic, as is done at present. In particular, I claim – on the grounds of evidence from these languages themselves – that Asiatic Semitic had labiovelars and that West Semitic retained them well into the 2nd millennium. Since it is generally agreed that the Greek labiovelars broke down during the middle of that period,

I argue that some loans from Semitic into Greek were made when both had labiovelars, some after Greek had dropped them but West Semitic still retained them, and some after they had disappeared from both. Thus, postulating considerable contact between West Semitic and Greek culture before the breakdown of the labiovelars – that is to say, before the middle of the 2nd millennium BC – can resolve a number of otherwise inexplicable problems in Greek etymology. It also illustrates how much the Revised Ancient Model can achieve from using the abundant Greek material to help in the reconstruction of early forms in Egyptian and Semitic.

In this summary I can cite only two examples of this. The first is that of the famous Phoenician city known as Gublu(m) in Eblaite and Akkadian, G^{c}bal in Hebrew, and Jebeil in Arabic. Given my belief in the West Semitic retention of labiovelars, I think it plausible to postulate an early pronunciation *G^{w}eb(a)l, which could explain these variants. By contrast, the Greek name for the city is Byblos or Biblos. This puzzle can be solved by postulating that the name was known in the Aegean before the middle of the 2nd millennium. As it is known that in most dialects the Greek g^{w}i became bi after the breakdown of the labiovelars, it would seem plausible to suggest that the name *G^{w}eb(a)l was in use in Greek as *G^{w}ibl while that language still possessed labiovelars, and then, following the normal sound shifts, became Biblos or Byblos.

The second example is the puzzling name of Demeter. From Ethiopic and West Semitic evidence it is possible to reconstruct the early forms *$g^w e$ and *$g^w ay$, meaning 'land' or 'wide valley'. If this word had been introduced into Greek before the breakdown of the labiovelars and had gone through the regular sound shifts, g^{w}e would have become *de. This could explain why the Greek earth mother goddess was called Dēmētēr and not *Gēmētēr, a problem that has tantalized scholars for two millennia. There are problems with the vocalization, and the fact that the name does not appear in Linear B; nevertheless, in the absence of any alternative it remains a plausible explanation, and one which is reinforced by the existence of the rare word gyēs (measure of land). Gyēs would seem to be a loan from Canaanite into Greek after labiovelars had broken down in Greek, but before the shift had taken place in Canaanite. Finally, after labiovelars had disappeared from both languages, the Greek *gaia* and *gē* (earth), which have no explanation from Indo-European, would seem to have been borrowed from the Canaanite, *gay^e^*, which in the 'construct' or modified form is pronounced *gê'*.

Chapters X and XI are concerned with linguistic borrowings from West Semitic and Egyptian, and here I shall start by discussing the two chapters together. In both, some reference is made to syntax or word order, as for instance the similar uses of the definite article in Late Canaanite – Phoenician and Hebrew – on the one hand and Greek on the other. Elsewhere morphology or word modification is considered; but most of the chapters are devoted to studying lexical borrowings or loan words.

We begin here with morphology, or the modification of words with number, gender, case, tense and so on. With the exception of Hittite Greek is the earliest attested Indo-European language, and this makes the degree of its morphological 'decay' very remarkable. For although the original Indo-European verbal system appears to have been very well preserved in Greek, nouns in Greek had only five cases while Latin, first recorded over 1,000 years later, had six; and Lithuanian, written down only in modern times, has retained all of the eight postulated for Proto-Indo-European. The morphological loss experienced by Greek would suggest intensive contact with other languages; this tallies with the lexical evidence and weakens the Model of Autochthonous Origin. However, it can be explained by both the Ancient and Aryan models which, unlike the first, can explain just such contact.

The major concern of these two chapters, however, is with verbal loans. As I have mentioned, the Indo-European component of the Greek lexicon is relatively small. For instance languages like Old Church Slavonic and Lithuanian, which are first attested 2,000 years later than Greek, have a considerably higher proportion of roots with cognates in other Indo-European languages. Further, the semantic range in which the Indo-European roots appear in Greek is very much the same as that of Anglo-Saxon roots in English. These roots provide most pronouns and prepositions; most of the basic nouns and verbs of family – though not political – life; and of subsistence – though not commercial – agriculture. By contrast, the vocabulary of urban life, luxury, religion, administration and abstraction is non-Indo-European.

Such a pattern usually reflects a long-term situation in which speakers of the language or languages which provide the words of higher culture control the users of the basic lexicon – as in the relationships between Anglo-Saxon and French in English; Bantu and Arabic in the creation of Swahili; or Vietnamese and Chinese in the formation of Modern Vietnamese. A less common pattern is that seen in Turkish and Hungarian, in which the conquerors took over the sophisticated vocabulary of the natives. In these cases, however, Turks and Hungarians retained their own or Mongol words for military technology or organization. In Greek, however, the words for chariot itself, sword, bow, march, armour, battle, etc., are non-Indo-European. Hence Greek, as pictured in the Aryan Model, does not resemble languages of the Turkish type. Thus, to accept the Aryan Model, it is necessary to postulate Greek as a language that is typologically unique. The Ancient Model would place Greek, with English and Vietnamese, in the commonest category of such mixed languages.

To turn now to each of the two chapters. Chapter X looks at Greek borrowings from West Semitic. In this area I can follow not only the scholarship from before the triumph of the Aryan Model, but also that of scholars in the last two decades who have been cautiously and soundly restoring the earlier etymologies and even adding some of their own. Despite this progress, however, we are still far from the situation as it was before the onset of the Extreme Aryan Model. For instance, as I mentioned above, the embargo on Semitic loans never included spices and Oriental luxuries. But the proposals by Semitists of equally plausible etymologies from more sensitive semantic regions, such as *bōmos* from *båmåh* – both meaning 'high place' or 'altar' – are still generally rejected by Classicists.

Other examples of the West Semitic etymologies for religious terms put forward in this chapter include the Greek *haima*, a word that in Homer had overtones of 'spirit' and 'courage', as well as having its standard sense of 'blood'. The first two meanings are reflected in Greek science, where *haima* was seen as the equivalent of air and not – as one might expect – water. It is argued that *haima* derives from the Canaanite *ḥayîm* (life); in Canaanite religion blood was seen as the repository of life. As a second example, there is the extremely well-known Semitic root √qds (sacred); semantically, this tallies very well with the Greek cluster of words around *kudos*, meaning 'divine glory'. Interestingly, too, *qds* in the sense of 'apart, unclean' seems to be reflected in the Greek *kudos* (vile) and *kudazō* (revile). Another cluster of words with religious significance, that around *naiō* (dwell) and *naos* (dwelling, temple or shrine), would seem to come from the Semitic root √nwh, which has the same general and specific connotations. The derivation of *nektar* from a Semitic **niqtar* (smoked or perfumed wine, etc.) was widely accepted before the onset of the Extreme Aryan Model, and has recently been revived by Professor Saul Levin.

Looking at the abstract vocabulary, there is the Greek stem *kosm*, from which we derive not only our 'cosmos' but our 'cosmetics'. Its basic meaning is to 'distribute' or 'arrange'. The Semitic root √qsm covers the semantic range 'divide, arrange and decide'. Then again, Canaanite *sēm* (mark, name) seems to have been borrowed into Greek twice; first as *sēma* (sign, mark, token), and later – probably from the form *šēm* – as *schēma* (form, shape, figure, configuration). In politics, too, there are such word clusters as the Greek *deil-* (wretched) and *doul-* (client) or (slave), which could well come from the Canaanite *dål* or *dal* (dependent, reduced) or (poor); while the Greek *xenos* (stranger) would seem to derive from the West Semitic √śn' (hate, enemy).

In the military sphere we find such etymologies as *phasgan-* (sword) or (blade) from the Semitic root √psg (cleave), and *harma* (chariot) or (tackle), from the Semitic root √ḥrm (net). Finally, there are some basic Greek words which appear to have Semitic etymologies; for instance, *mechri(s)* (up to, as far as) would seem to come from the Semitic root √mḫr (be in front, come to meet). It is true that none of these derivations is certain; but they are all more or less plausible. In the absence of competing Indo-European etymologies, and in the light of all the other evidence in favour of Semitic influence on 2nd- and 1st-millennium Greece, they should be given very serious consideration.

The same is true of the Egyptian etymologies proposed in Chapter

XI. Unlike the study of Semitic etymologies, research into Egyptian loan words in Greek has never been seriously developed. The simple reason for this is that hieroglyphics were deciphered only as the Ancient Model was coming to an end. By the 1860s, when dictionaries of Ancient Egyptian were first published, the Aryan Model was so firmly established that comparison between the two vocabularies was impossible within academia. The only exception to this were the bold and fruitful attempt made by the Abbé Barthélemy in the 18th century to compare Greek words with Coptic. Today, with the three anomalies of *baris* (a type of small boat), *xiphos* (sword) and *makar-* (blessed), no Greek word of any significance has been allowed an Egyptian etymology, and the latter two were widely questioned. Two short articles in 1969 collected and ratified a number of obviously exotic words, with plausible Egyptian origins; but, as with West Semitic, these could easily have been transmitted by trade or casual contact and were therefore acceptable to the Aryan Model. In 1971 an even more negative piece appeared, denying some and casting doubt on others of the few established Egyptian etymologies.[24]

I have stressed the importance of military vocabulary, so the derivation of *xiphos* from the Egyptian *sft* (knife, sword) is therefore very significant. It means that there is one Semitic and one Egyptian etymology for the two Greek words for sword, both admitted to be non-Indo-European – the sword being the new wonder weapon of the 'heroic' Late Bronze Age. Other instances worth mentioning here include *makar-* which comes from the Egyptian *mꜣꜥ ḥrw* (true of voice), the title given to the blessed dead who have passed the test of judgement. Other Greek legal terms would seem to have equally plausible Egyptian etymologies, while we have already come across the derivation of *martyr* from *mtrw* (witness). The stem *tima-* (honour) in both warfare and law probably comes from an Egyptian *dỉ mꜣꜥ* attested in Demotic as *tymꜣꜥ*, meaning (render true, justify).

In politics, while there is a widespread and fundamental Indo-European root √reg meaning 'rule' or 'king' which is found in the Indian *rajah*, the Gaulish *rix*, the Latin *rex*, and the Irish *rí*, the Ancient Greek words for king had nothing to do with this but were *(w)anax* and *basileus*. The former, which will be discussed in Chapter I of this volume, would seem to come from the Egyptian formula *'nḫ ḏt* (may he live for ever!) used after the names of living pharaohs. In early Greek a *basileus* was not a king but an official subordinate to the *(w)anax*. In Egyptian *pꜣ sr* (the official) became a standard title for the vizier. It has been found transcribed in Akkadian as *pa-ši-i-a-(ra)*. As p and b were not distinguished in late Egyptian, and Egyptian r was frequently rendered l in Greek, there is no phonetic difficulty to impede the perfect semantic fit.

The Egyptian origin of the Greek *sophia* (wisdom) is described in Chapter I of this volume. All these etymologies in the areas of power, abstraction and sophistication tally with the pattern suggested by the Ancient Model of Egyptian rulers over a less developed native population. As with Semitic, however, other loan words suggest an even deeper penetration into Greek life. There is no reason to doubt that the Greek *chēra* (widow) comes from the Egyptian *ḫꜣrt* (widow), or that the particle *gar* derives from the Egyptian *grt*, which has the same function and syntactic position. As I have mentioned, final ts were dropped in both Late Egyptian and Greek.

The conclusion of *Greece European or Levantine?* is that while the documentary and archaeological evidence tends to support the Ancient Model over the Aryan one, it is not conclusive. By contrast, that from language and names of all sorts strongly supports the intrinsically plausible case for the ancient tradition, for the scale and centrality of the lexical and nominal borrowing would suggest massive and sustained Egyptian cultural influence on Greece. Although the Japanese case shows that borrowings on such a large scale need not be the result of conquest, conquest or colonization is the usual way in which they arise. The linguistic evidence, then, strongly supports the Ancient Model.

Taking all classes of evidence together, there is no way in which the Aryan Model has superior heuristic value. Given the case – made in Volume 1 of *Black Athena* – that the supersession of the Aryan Model over the Ancient can be explained in terms of the *Weltanschauung* of the early 19th century, there is no need to retain it. In short, as I have said elsewhere in this book, Volume 1 shows that the Aryan Model was 'conceived in sin'. Volume 2 will show that it is bankrupt.

SOLVING THE RIDDLE OF THE
SPHINX AND OTHER STUDIES
IN EGYPTO-GREEK MYTHOLOGY

Volume 3 of *Black Athena* is an attempt to use the Revised Ancient Model to throw some light on previously inexplicable aspects of Greek religion and mythology, and especially on the names of heroic or divine beings. The chapters are set out in what seems to be the chronological order of the various cults that arrived in Greece; like everything in this area, however, the sequence is very uncertain.

The first chapter is concerned with the earliest discernible religious influence – that of the 11th-dynasty royal cult of the hawk/bull god Mnṯw or Mont in the 21st century BC – on the establishment of the Cretan bull-cult at the same time as the foundation of the palaces there in the same century. I argue that the lack of evidence of a bull-cult in Crete in the Early Minoan period, in the 3rd millennium, makes it very unlikely that there is any continuity from the bull-cult found in 7th-millennium Anatolia. Furthermore, mountainous Crete can in no way be considered natural cattle country. Apart from the sudden appearance of the bull-cult there, the coincidence of timing, the known expansion of Egyptian influence during the reigns of the various pharaohs named Menthotpe of the 11th Dynasty, and the archaeological evidence of contacts between Egypt and the Aegean at this time, there is also legendary evidence to suggest Egyptian influence on Crete at this point. I believe that the names of both the god Mnṯw and the pharaoh Menthotpe are reflected in that given in Greek legends to an ancient judge, lawgiver and subduer of the Greek islands, Rhadamanthys, whose name can be plausibly derived from an Egyptian *Rdi M(a)nṯw, 'Mnṯw gives'. Rhadamanthys was also the warlike stepfather of Herakles, who taught the hero how to shoot; Mnṯw was the god of archery. Mnṯw was associated with the goddess Rˁt, whose name we know, from Mesopotamian sources, to have been vocalized Ria. This would then seem a very plausible origin for the name of the goddess Rhea, who played a central role in Cretan religion.

The cult of Mnṯw was not the only Egyptian bull-cult to reach the Aegean. I think it is plausible to associate the legendary figure of Minos, the first king and lawgiver of Crete, with Mēnēs – or Min, as Herodotos called him – the first lawgiver and pharaoh of Egypt, who should be dated to about 3250 BC. Min was credited in Antiquity with having founded the bull-cult of Apis at Memphis. Another Egyptian bull-cult – called Mnevis by the Romans – has been plausibly derived from an Egyptian form *Mnewe. This cult had been associated with 'winding walls' since the Old Kingdom, hundreds of years before the first Cretan palaces were constructed. Thus we have a triple coincidence: in Egypt there were two bull-cults associated with the names Min and Mnewe; the first was the name of the royal founder, and the second was linked to a 'winding wall'; in Crete there was a bull-cult associated with the founder King Minos and a labyrinth! Greek tradition was clear on the point that the labyrinth was copied for King Minos from an Egyptian original by the great craftsman and architect Daidalos. Attempts to derive the name labyrinth from an alleged Lydian word *labrys* meaning 'axe' seem less plausible than the etymology proposed by Egyptologists in the 1860s – and denied by those of the 20th century – from a reconstructed Egyptian place name *R-pr-n-ḥnt, for the site of the great Egyptian labyrinth described by Herodotos and other ancient writers.

Bull-cults deriving not only from that of Mnṯw but also from those of Min, Mnevis, and Apis occurred throughout Greece, but were eclipsed by those of goats and rams. At or near the beginning of the 12th Dynasty, the Egyptian royal cult changed from that of the hawk/bull Mnṯw to one of the ram Amon. As I have mentioned, the 12th-dynasty pharaohs named 'Imn-m-ḥꜣt and S-n Wsrt, who can be plausibly identified with the mighty conquerors Memnōn and Sesōstris of Greek tradition, have now been shown by inscriptional evidence to have carried out wide-ranging expeditions in the East Mediterranean. Thus I argue in Chapter II that the widespread oracular ram/goat-cults found throughout the Aegean basin began to be introduced soon after they rose to prominence in Egypt itself in the 20th century BC. In Egypt the cults were associated with both Amon and Osiris, and in the Aegean with Zeus and Dionysos, who were seen as their Greek equivalents.

The natural confusion between the rams and goats seems to have been compounded by the fact that the oracular cult at the Delta city –

known to the Greeks as Mendēs – was associated with a well-endowed species of ram that – rather embarrassingly for a symbol of fertility – became extinct. In later centuries this was represented in a way that led Herodotos, at least, to describe it alternately as a goat and a ram. Dodona, in North-West Greece, was generally conceded to be the most ancient oracle of this type; according to Herodotos and other Greek writers it had been established from the oracles at Siwa, an oasis in the Libyan desert, and Thebes, with its oracular cult of Amon. Archaeology has confirmed remarkable parallels between Dodona and Siwa. Furthermore, the cult of Amon in Siwa was associated with the deity Ddwn, which would seem to be the origin of the otherwise inexplicable name Dodona.

The confusion between Zeus and Dionysos was particularly great in Crete – where Zeus was supposed to have died – and the northern fringes of Greece, from Dodona in the west to Thrace and Phrygia far to the east. These regions, which on other grounds can be shown to have been particularly conservative, would seem to have preserved an undifferentiated cult that was superseded by the more specific ones that were introduced or grew up later. Nevertheless, many cult centres – like that of Zeus at Olympia – preserved elements of the earlier stratum. At the end of the section on ram/goat-cults I consider the parallels between the acting-out of Osiris' passion or drama in Egyptian religion and the origins of Greek theatre. It is striking to note that in Greece, tragedy, which was essentially religious, was associated with both Dionysos and the goat, *tragos*.

Chapter III of *Solving the Riddle of the Sphinx* is called 'Beauty' and is concerned with the goddess Aphrodite. Her name was traditionally derived from the word *aphros* (foam); no explanation has been offered for the otherwise unknown suffix -*ditē*. The Classical image of the goddess rising from the foam shows that the tradition is ancient. Nevertheless it would seem to me to be a pun or a folk etymology, the true one almost certainly coming from the Egyptian Pr Wȝdyt (House of Wȝdyt). This name, given to two cities – one in the Nile Delta, later known to the Greeks as Boutō/os, and the other in Upper Egypt, called Aphroditopolis – demonstrates the identification of Wȝdyt with

Aphrodite. I have already mentioned the Egyptian association of divinities with their dwellings, in connection with Athena; in this case, however, the use of Pr W₃dyt as a form of address has been attested. Phonetically there are some problems, as there is no other case where the r in *pr* has been preserved; though if it had, the prefixing of a 'prothetic' a/i would be automatic. In any event, the derivation from *aPr-W₃dyt is clearly better phonetically than that from *aphros*.

Semantically, the case for deriving Aphrodite from Pr W₃dyt is very strong indeed. W₃dyt was a goddess of fertility and she was associated with the new growth after the Flood, just as Aphrodite was with spring and youthful love; W₃dyt was also associated with the snakes that emerged in that season. It so happens that one of the most remarkable Egyptian finds from Middle Minoan Crete is the base of a statue of a priest of W₃dyt. What is more, the hieroglyphs are so irregular as to suggest that they may have been engraved locally. In any event, the find suggests that the cult existed on the island at that time. It is striking, therefore, to find several figures from this period of a beautiful and alluring goddess holding two snakes, figures which a number of scholars have tentatively linked to Aphrodite. The cult seems to have flourished towards the end of Middle Minoan, so it would seem plausible to date the goddess's introduction tentatively to the wave of Egypto-Levantine-Minoan influence around the 'Hyksos' invasions at the end of the 18th and the beginning of the 17th century BC.

'Beauty' is followed by Chapter IV: 'and the Beast'. Its topic is Seth or Sutekh, the god to whom the Hyksos were supposed to have been devoted. In Egyptian theology Seth was the divinity of the outside, of the deserts and their wild and unpredictable inhabitants; and, according to Plutarch, he was the god of the sea. There seems every reason to suppose that just as the Hyksos conquest can be identified with the biblical sojourn in Egypt, the Hyksos Seth was the Israelite Yahwe, the god of the wilderness, of volcanos and of the tumultuous seas. In Ugaritic myth, the enemy of the fertility god Ba'al was Yam, 'Sea', who would then appear to be another Semitic counterpart. In Hellenistic times Seth was rendered Typhon but, unlike all the other Egyptian gods, he lacked a Greek divine counterpart. The reason for this seems obvious: by then, Seth as the epitome of evil could not be equated with a respectable divinity.

On the other hand, the only major Greek god lacking an Egyptian counterpart was Poseidon. I maintain that the two loose ends should be tied together. Both deities were concerned with the sea, earthquakes, hunting, chariots and horses, and were generally cantankerous. Just as the Hyksos were devoted to Seth, Poseidon was the god most frequently referred to in the Linear B tablets from Mycenaean Crete and Greece. Alternative forms with a t, such as Poteidōn, have led Indo-Europeanists to identify the name with the root √pot 'power'. However, it is difficult to link the suffix -d(e)ōn to *dios* (divine). To someone working in the Ancient Model the alternation s/t suggests the Semitic letter *ṣade*, which seems to have been a form of ts.

The etymology I propose for Poseidon is pₔ(w) or Pr Sidôn, 'He of' or 'House of Sidon'. Sid, the patron god of Sidon, derived his name from the root √ṣwd, 'to hunt'. He was a divinity of hunting, fishing, chariots and the sea; thus the semantic fit is perfect. The difficulty with the derivation, however, is that it requires an Egypto-Semitic form of a type that has so far not been attested; therefore I can propose the etymology only tentatively. But whether or not it can be accepted, I believe that I can show striking parallels between Seth and Poseidon, and these are particularly interesting precisely because the two were not identified in Classical times. Similarities between the two gods and their cults, therefore, cannot be attributed to later 'Egyptianizing'.

Chapter V, 'The terrible twins', is concerned with the twins Apollo and Artemis. In Egypt the sun was worshipped in many different ways – as Ra, as Aten the solar disc, and as Ḫprr and Tm, the young sun in the morning and the old sun at night, respectively. Phonetically, the only problem with the derivation of Apollo from Ḫprr is that ḫ is very seldom transcribed as ø. Such a borrowing would be possible, on the other hand, if the introduction were late and had come through Phoenician, in which the ḫ merged with the softer ḥ, quite often rendered as ø in Greek. As it happens, there are two indications that this is, in fact, the case. Lateness is suggested by the fact that the name Apollo is not attested in Linear B; and Phoenician transmission by the vocalization

CaCoC, suggesting that the name had passed through the 'Canaanite shift' ā› ō.

Semantically, the derivation of Apollo from Ḥprr would seem very good. Ḥprr was identified with Ḥr m ȝḥt, the Greek Harmachis, 'Horus of the Rising Sun'. Horus had been identified with Apollo at least from the time of the poet Pindar in the 5th century, but this dawning aspect would seem the most appropriate for Apollo, who was always seen as young. The central myth concerning Horus was of his struggle with, and victory over, Seth manifested as a water monster. In Greece a major myth of Apollo was that of Delphi, where the young god, accompanied by his sister Artemis, killed the Python. I argue that Delphi, like *adelphos* (brother), comes from a Semitic word for 'couple' or 'twin'. Thus Apollo's title Delphinios is a doublet of another, Didymos 'twin', and Apollo's 'twinness' seems essential to his nature.

Modern historians of Greek religion are moving away from the idea that Apollo's twin sister Artemis was exclusively a moon goddess. It is now thought that she was a virgin, huntress goddess of the evening and night. In Hellenistic times Artemis was seen as the counterpart of the Egyptian cat goddess Bȝstt, who was identified with the moon. However, Bȝstt also had a fiery aspect and as such was supposed to help in the destruction of Horus' enemies. In this capacity she was seen as a lioness and identified as the female counterpart of Ra and Tm, the god of the evening sun. Ḥprr and Tm together formed the twin aspects of Ḥr ȝḥtwy 'Horus of the (Two) Horizons', who was the equivalent of Ra. Tm's consort Tmt/Bȝstt seems to have had some independence, and from the middle of the 3rd millennium she was connected with the two lion goddesses linked to Horus of the (two) horizons. Horus' greatest monument in Egypt was the Sphinx at Giza. Although the monument is only of a single lion, a dedication inserted near it in the late 15th century, over 1,000 years after its construction, refers to Ḥr ȝḥtwy and to Ḥr(i) Tm, which almost certainly refers to Tm himself. On phonetic grounds, a feminine form *Ḥrt Tmt would provide a good etymology for Artemis. The correspondence of an Egyptian final -t with a Greek final -is is common; the medial t would drop with the normal development of Egyptian; and the vocalization of Ḥr as (Ḥ)ar is amply attested, as is the modification of the Egyptian ḥ to ø. Thus the 'twinness' of

Apollo and Artemis can be seen to be that of Ḫprr and Tm, that between the morning and the evening sun.

Chapter V goes on to investigate the reasons for the sex change, and also the parallels between Apollo and Artemis and Kadmos and Europa, whose names come from the Semitic √qdm (east) and √ʿrb (west) and (evening). The cults and myths of the Greek Thebes are particularly important in this respect because they too are associated with the Sphinx, adding to the intricate network linking them to this aspect of Egyptian solar religion. I argue that the Theban Sphinx can be identified as the savage and leonine nature of Europa and Artemis, but an even tighter connection between the two sphinxes is provided by the riddle posed by the Greek one, 'What being has only one voice, has sometimes two feet sometimes three, sometimes four, and is weakest when it has the most?' Oedipus' answer referred to the life of man, but the riddle belongs to a cluster – found all over the world – many of which refer to the weakness of the sun in the morning and evening and its strength at midday. I think that in the light of the Egyptian Sphinx's dedication to the sun in the morning and evening, the parallel is quite remarkable.

Despite the lateness of Apollo's name, the interplay of Egyptian and Semitic influences leads me to believe that this solar myth cycle was introduced during the Hyksos period. The Eleusinian Mysteries, on the other hand, which are the subject of Chapter VI, seem to have arrived rather later. The ancient chronographers, for their part, were generally agreed that the cult of Demeter and Dionysos arrived in Attica in the second half of the 15th century. This would seem altogether plausible, despite the early-2nd-millennium origin of the name Demeter (see above, p. 57). The late 15th century was a period of great Egyptian power after the conquests of Tuthmōsis III, and one in which the mystery cults of Isis and Osiris seem to have been well established in Egypt and the Levant. Since Egyptian faïence plaques of the type placed under the corners of temples have been found at Mycenae dated to the reign of Amenōphis III (1405–1367), I have no difficulty in accepting the possibility that the Eleusinian cult of Archaic Greece was the descendant of an Egyptian foundation made there 700 years earlier. For

one of the many ways in which this cult was unique in Greece was that –
like Egyptian temples – it had an established priesthood, in this case
made up of two clans whose members in Hellenistic times certainly
believed that they had Egyptian connections.

The Egyptian Osiran mysteries featured Isis' search for her murdered husband/brother, her reassembly of his body, and the triumph of
their son Horus over his father's murderer Seth. At first blush the
Eleusinian story seems very different. In it Demeter searched for her
daughter Persephone, stolen by Hades, god of the Underworld. She
found Persephone but, failing to release her, she went on strike,
preventing any natural seasonal growth. Finally a deal was made,
according to which Persephone should spend half the year with Hades
and half with her mother. These differences are not sufficient to
override the ancient testimony that the Greek mysteries came from
Egypt.

In Egypt, while Osiris was the focus of the cult, its chief protagonist
was Isis; in Greece, there is little doubt that behind Demeter there lay
Dionysos. Furthermore, in the Egyptian mysteries there were in fact not
one, but two women. Isis had a constant companion in her sister/double
Nephthys, who not only searched and mourned for Osiris but was also
married to his murderer, Seth. In this way, she exactly paralleled the
ambiguity of Persephone with her loving and hellish aspects. Above all,
however, the wide variations one finds within these Egyptian and Greek
myth cycles themselves show that too much should not be made of the
differences between them, given the large number of detailed parallels
found between the two mystery cults.

There is also a survey of 20th-century studies of the subject, starting
with the work of Paul Foucart, whose detailed research on Eleusis and
considerable knowledge of Egyptology convinced him that the ancient
tradition of Egyptian origin was irrefutable.[25] In any event, there is no
doubt that the centre of the Eleusinian Mysteries was the search for
immortality, and the paradoxical belief that this could be achieved only
through dying. It was believed that through the initiation of the
Mysteries one could go through a symbolic death to be 'born again' as
an immortal; this conception was current throughout the Ancient Near
East but was overwhelmingly strong in Egypt. Thus the consensus of

ancient writers was that Pythagoras, Orpheus, Sokrates, Plato and others concerned with the immortality of the soul had learnt about it from Egypt.

The concern with personal immortality was central to Orphism, an aspect of Greek religion that appears to have been introduced in the Archaic period, hundreds of years after the end of the Bronze Age with which *Black Athena* is otherwise concerned. Nevertheless, I believe its closeness to the Dionysian and Eleusinian cults justifies its presence in the third volume. The name Orpheus would seem to come from the Egyptian form ('I)rp't (Hereditary Prince), which was transcribed in Greek as Orpais. ('I)rp't was a title given to the Egyptian god commonly known as Geb: the latter was a deity of the good earth – both the flora and fauna that covered it – and the Underworld. This fits both with Orpheus' place as a harmonizer of nature and with his concern with the interior of the earth. Geb had a close relationship with Osiris, who was sometimes supposed to be his son and by whom he was largely replaced as lord of the Underworld. Orpheus and Dionysos seemed in many ways to duplicate each other similarly, but with some hostility between them. Egyptian society appears to have been rather intolerant of homosexuality, and it is hard to find any direct parallel to this aspect of Orpheus' character. Nevertheless, it is interesting to note that the name ('I)rp't is a feminine form. Even more significant is the fact that ('I)rp't was written with an egg as a determinative, which seems to be related to the cosmogenic egg laid by Geb in his form as a goose, often without female intervention. Here, too, there is a striking parallel with Greece, as a primal egg was also the beginning of the Orphic cosmogeny.

Despite Geb's great antiquity, it is probable that the Orphic cult in Greece was a late introduction. There is, for instance, no mention of Orpheus or his cosmogony in Hesiod's *Theogony*, and the vocalization of ('I)rp't as Orpais/Orpheus would seem to be late. It seems likely, therefore – as many Ancients and Moderns have suspected – that although Orpheus may be very ancient, Orphism was established in the 6th century in close conjunction with Pythagoreanism; and that the association with ('I)rp't was an attempt to give a new cult the kudos of antiquity. It is impossible to decide, however, whether the reform began in Greece or in Egypt. The Orphic and Pythagorean emphasis on

metampsychosis – the transmigration of souls – and the linked veg-
etarianism were also current among Egyptian priests in Hellenistic and
Roman times. It is impossible to say how ancient these abstinences
were, but given the general conservatism of Egyptian religion, they
could well date back to the Old Kingdom. They could, on the other
hand, have been promoted by later reforms.

There are also connections between Orpheus and *The Book of the
Dead*. In New Kingdom and later Egypt this served as a guide for the
soul through the perils of the Underworld to immortality, and was
frequently buried with the mummified corpse. In Greece and Italy,
spells and hymns inscribed on gold leaf were placed by the bodies of
devotees of Orpheus. So it is interesting to note in this connection that a
version of *The Book of the Dead* does refer to 'the books of Geb and
Osiris'.

In Classical times it was generally believed the Orpheus was in some
way Thracian, but that he had learnt his mysteries in Egypt. The close
connections between Pythagoras and Egypt were accepted by all in
Antiquity. Thus the striking etymological and cultic similarities between Egyptian forms, and Orphic and Pythagorean ones, seem very
easy to explain in terms of the Ancient Model. I should add, however,
that it would be possible for an Aryanist to admit the Egyptian origin of
such 'late' features without damaging his model as a whole. Nevertheless, I believe it is significant that so few do so.

The conclusion of *Solving the Riddle of the Sphinx* reiterates my
general view that the etymologies and cultic parallels which make up the
volume should be seen in context. The comparisons being made are not
between Greek and, say, Algonquin or Tasmanian religions separated
by vast distances of space and time. They are between two systems
situated at the same end of the Mediterranean during the same
millennia. Furthermore, the Classical and Hellenistic Greeks themselves maintained that their religion came from Egypt, and Herodotos
even specified that the names of the gods were – with one or two
exceptions – all Egyptian. In the absence of any plausible etymologies or
cultic parallels from Indo-European culture, it would seem reasonable
to look for Egyptian ones. The material in Volume 3, taken together
with the sections on Athena and Hermes in Volume 2, shows that

juxtaposing Greek with Egyptian and Canaanite religion makes comprehensible large tracts of what had previously been complete mystery. More importantly, however, it raises many interesting new questions and generates hundreds of testable hypotheses. As I said at the beginning of the overall Introduction to this work, this is precisely what differentiates fruitful radical innovation from sterile crankiness. The scholarly purpose of *Solving the Riddle of the Sphinx* is the same as that of the other two volumes: to open up new areas of research to women and men with far better qualifications than I have. The political purpose of *Black Athena* is, of course, to lessen European cultural arrogance.

CHAPTER I

THE ANCIENT MODEL
IN ANTIQUITY

> *How it happened that Egyptians came to the Pelo-*
> *ponnese, and what they did to make themselves*
> *kings in that part of Greece, has been chronicled by*
> *other writers; I will add nothing therefore, but*
> *proceed to mention some points which no one else has*
> *yet touched upon.*
>
> (Herodotos, *Histories*, VI.55)[1]

THE MAJORITY OF US have been taught to regard Herodotos as the 'father of history', but even those who follow Plutarch and regard him as the 'father of lies' can hardly maintain that Herodotos was lying about the existence of such chronicles. His was not an unverifiable statement about some remote peoples, but one which readers could easily check, if they did not know about it already. Setting aside for a while the problem of what actually happened over a millennium before Herodotos wrote his *Histories*, his statement strongly suggests that in the 5th century BC it was generally believed that Greece had been colonized from Egypt at the beginning of the Heroic Age. In this chapter I hope to demonstrate that Herodotos' views on the Egyptian and Phoenician settlements, though treated with condescension and scorn by most modern Classicists and ancient historians, were conventional not only in his own times but also throughout Archaic, Classical and later Antiquity.

PELASGIANS

Before exploring the views of Greeks in the Classical period on these and other hypothetical invasions, it would be useful to consider their

ideas about the earlier population of Greece. This is because it was the
basis upon which they saw the Near Eastern influences as having acted.
Here we encounter the thorny problem of the most widely known native
population, the Pelasgoi or Pelasgians, a name used differently by
different Greek authors. According to Homer, there were Pelasgians
on both sides of the Trojan War. Some of Achilles' force of Hellenes
and Achaians were supposed to have inhabited 'Pelasgian Argos', which
was clearly seen as being in Thessaly.[2] Fighting for Troy, on the other
hand, were the warriors of Hippothoos the Pelasgian, who came from
Larisa.[3] The probable derivation of the place name Laris(s)a is from the
Egyptian toponym R-ȝḥt, 'Entry into the Fertile Lands', which was
probably used for the Hyksos capital Avaris, in the rich soils of the
Eastern Nile Delta.[4] The semantic fit between Laris(s)a and R-ȝḥ is
excellent. Further, the Homeric epithet for two different Larisai was
eribōlax (deep-soiled).[5] As Strabo, the geographer of the 1st centuries
BC and AD, pointed out, all the many Greek Laris(s)ai were on alluvial
soil.[6]

If we take the Hyksos colonizations as a working hypothesis, it is
striking to note that the akropolis of the Peloponnesian Argos, the city
which Danaos was supposed to have founded and with which he had
many cultic connections, was called Larisa.[7] Furthermore Strabo
maintained, in another part of his *Geography*, that *argos* in Greek meant
'flat land'.[8] This would fit nicely with the etymology of Larisa from
'Entry into the Fertile Lands' as the name of the Hyksos' capital.
However, *argos* also signified 'speed' and 'dog' or 'wolf', both of which
were reflected in the mythology and iconography of the Peloponnesian
city.[9] The core meaning of the word was 'brilliant' or 'silver'. This fits
well with 'Inb ḥd, 'Silver Wall', the most frequently used name for
Memphis, the capital of Lower Egypt.[10] These three-way connections
between Pelasgian, Larisa and Argos are reinforced by the existence of
a Pelasgian Argos in the region of the two Larisai recorded in
Thessaly.[11]

Homer referred to the great and ancient oracle of Zeus at Dodona in
Epirus as 'Pelasgian', an epithet that was used for it by later writers.[12]
Pelasgians appear elsewhere on his list of Cretan peoples which also
included Achaians, Eteocretans, Kydonians and Dorians.[13] Hesiod –

or possibly Kekrops of Miletos – stated that 'Three Hellenic tribes settled in Crete, the Pelasgoi, Achaians and Dorians.'[14] Much later Diodoros Sikeliotes claimed that Pelasgians had settled in Crete after the Eteocretans but before the Dorians.[15]

Even if the earlier quotation does not date back to Hesiod who, according to the Ancient Model, lived in the 10th century BC, it tallies well with the Homeric list. In the latter the Pelasgians are distinguished from the Eteo or 'true' Cretans, who are assumed to be non-Hellenic, possibly Anatolian- but more probably Semitic-speaking.[16] Furthermore, Homer made no mention of Danaans or Argives in Crete. These facts, together with the general connotation of 'native' associated with the name, would make it plausible to suggest that the Pelasgians were the earliest Hellenic or Greek-speaking inhabitants of the island. Thus 'Hesiod's' order would appear to be chronological: the Pelasgians having arrived on the island before the Achaian invasion of the 14th century, and that of the Dorians in the 12th. Thus they would seem on both lists to be equivalent to the Danaans.

A further indication that the Cretan Pelasgians were Hellenic comes from the link, made by several scholars, between the Pelasgians and the Philistines who settled in Palestine in the 12th century BC. According to a substantial biblical tradition, the Philistines were supposed to have come from Crete. The equation *Pelasg and *Pelast has usually been explained by postulating an original 'Pre-Hellenic' final stop that was heard as g by the Greeks and t by Egyptian and Semitic speakers. Apart from my suspicions about the existence of Pre-Hellenes, it is very hard to construct a consonant somewhere between g and t.

There is, however, another way by which one can associate the two. In 1951 Jean Bérard reinforced the links by drawing attention to the variant Pelasgikon/Pelastikon found in the great dictionary of Hesychios of the 5th century AD and in the scholium or commentary to the *Iliad*, Book XVI, verse 233.[17] This shows that it is possible to confuse the written forms of Γ and T. If, as I maintain elsewhere, the Greek alphabet has been in use since the 15th century BC, such an error might explain not only these textual variants but the name Pelasgoi itself. This could have come from *Pelast, the vocalization reconstructed for the Canaanite form.[18] (The development of the name

Hebrides from a misreading of the original Hebudes provides an analogy for this.)[19] Although the nature of the Philistine language or languages is still very uncertain, the most likely candidates are West Anatolian languages like Lydian or Greek. The latter seems to me much more likely.[20] Thus if there is an equation between Pelasgian and Philistine, which is possible, and if the Philistines spoke Greek, which is probable, it would increase still further the likelihood that the Cretan Pelasgians spoke a Hellenic language.

Like Homer, Hesiod seems to have seen Pelasgians in Phthia in Thessaly.[21] He also saw them in Arkadia, where the eponym Pelasgos was described as autochthonous.[22] Akousilaos, in the 6th or 5th century BC, referred to all Greece south of Thessaly as 'Pelasgia'. Aischylos in the 5th enlarged it to include North Greece.[23] Herodotos, meanwhile, wrote several interesting but very confusing passages about the Pelasgians. According to him, although they had lived throughout Greece, they were the ancestors only of the Ionians, not of the Dorians, who were 'Hellenes'. He maintained that the Pelasgian language was not Greek, basing this argument on the observation that in two cities on the Hellespont which were supposed to be Pelasgian, the language was foreign. Thus peoples like the Athenians, who were supposed to have been Pelasgian before becoming Hellenes, would have had to have changed their language.[24]

Apart from Athens, the places Herodotos associated with the Pelasgians were Dodona, the coast of the Peloponnese and Lemnos, Samothrace and the North-Eastern Aegean as a whole.[25] Herodotos' contention would appear to be backed by the modern discovery in Lemnos of a stele in a language resembling Etruscan, and there is every reason to suppose that the cities he referred to on the Hellespont also spoke Anatolian languages.[26]

In general, Herodotos' picture of the Pelasgians seems similar to that given by Thucydides a generation later. According to both, Pelasgians formed the bulk, though not the whole, of the early population of Greece and the Aegean and most of them were gradually assimilated by the Hellenes.[27] Herodotos saw this transformation as having taken place after the invasion by Danaos, which he envisioned around the middle of the 2nd millennium BC, and he described the Egyptian

Danaids as having taught the Pelasgians – not the Hellenes – the worship of the gods. Diodoros referred to Kadmos' having taught the Pelasgians the use of Phoenician letters.[28] Furthermore, the tradition that Kekrops, the founder of Athens, was Egyptian was probably current in Herodotos' day. Thus despite the latter's claims that the Athenians – unlike the Argives and Thebans – were autochthonous – that is to say, aboriginal – one finds the interesting passage:

> When what is now called Greece [Hellas] was occupied by the Pelasgians, the Athenians, a Pelasgian people, were called the Kranaoi. In the reign of Kekrops they acquired the name of Kekropidai. At the succession of Erechtheus they changed their name to Athenians.[29]

The idea that the Pelasgians were the native population, converted to become something more Greek by the invading Egyptians, occurs more clearly in the plays of Aischylos and Euripides, written around the time of Herodotos' *Histories*. According to them the Pelasgians were the indigenes, encountered and somehow overcome by Danaos in the Argolid:

> Danaos, the father of fifty daughters, on coming to Argos took up his abode in the city of Inachos and throughout Greece [Hellas] he laid down the law that all people hitherto named Pelasgians were to be named Danaans.[30]

According to Aischylos the Pelasgians were clearly identified with the later Hellenes, and he refers anachronistically to the practices of the former as Hellenic.[31]

Strabo, in the 1st centuries BC and AD, compiled many of the sources on the Pelasgians, adding a detailed story of a Pelasgian migration from Boiotia to Attica.[32] Pausanias, in the 2nd century AD, referred to Pelasgians at Athens, Corinth, Argos, Lakonia and Messenia, though those in the last were supposed to have come from Thessaly.[33] He stressed, however, the connection between them and the Arkadians. Pelasgos was considered to be the Arkadian ancestor, and Pausanias quoted the 6th-century poet Asios of Samos: 'And black earth produced the god-equalling Pelasgos.'[34]

Can any sense be made of these varied references? It was not only ancient writers like Herodotos and Strabo who had trouble reconciling them. The same difficulty has afflicted modern scholars. 'Their name was probably a national one: at least the Greek explanations of it are absurd', as the 19th-century polymath Niebuhr, the founder of modern ancient history, put it.[35] A century later Eduard Meyer, who dominated ancient historiography at the turn of the 19th century, was equally despairing.[36] Other 20th-century historians have tended to neglect the question and go no further than saying that the Pelasgians were a significant element in the early population of Greece.[37]

It is certainly difficult to accommodate them in the Aryan Model of Hellenic conquest from the north. Some writers, like the 19th-century pioneer of the Aryan Model, Ernst Curtius, saw them as a 'semi-Aryan' people conquered by a minority of superior Aryan Hellenes.[38] This fits quite nicely with Herodotos' reports of Pelasgians in the Anatolian-speaking North-Eastern Aegean. Such a hypothesis, however, makes it difficult to explain why, if the Pelasgians were so well remembered, there should have been no memory of their conquest by the Hellenes. Even Thucydides refers to the Pelasgians and others as having been 'Hellenized' by gradual 'intercourse' with the 'sons of Hellen', who themselves originated in Phthiotis near Thessaly.[39]

One way round this problem is the tack taken by William Ridgeway – who dominated Classical archaeology at the turn of the 19th century – and the 20th-century scholars Ernst Grumach and Sinclair Hood. They claim that the Hellenic conquest was recorded in tradition as the 'Return of the Heraklids' and 'Dorian Invasion', which were indeed tribal movements from north to south in the 12th century BC.[40] Such a scheme jibes well with Herodotos' linking the Dorians to the Hellenes and the Ionians to the Pelasgians.[41] There is a slight problem in reconciling the reported Hellenization of the 'Pelasgian' Athenians with the strong tradition that Athens was never conquered by the Dorians. But this difficulty pales into insignificance next to the 'fact', accepted by most 19th- and nearly all 20th-century historians, that the Pre-Dorian makers of Mycenaean civilization were Greek-speaking. Thus the only way in which the 'Dorian Invasion' can be attached to the 'Aryan Conquest' is to say that it was the last of a series of waves of migration. This, however, gets one no further forward in understanding the first arrival of Greek or 'Proto-Greek' speakers in Greece.

As can be seen from the references to Greek authors made above, the Ancient Model, too, faces difficulties over the Pelasgian question. For a modern proponent of the Revised Ancient Model, the best solution is to follow the mainstream of 19th-century historiography – scholars such as Grote and Wilamowitz-Moellendorf – and say that Pelasgian was a general name given to natives or aboriginals.[42] I would claim, however, that it was predominantly applied to the indigenous Indo-European-speaking peoples colonized and to some extent culturally assimilated by the Egypto-Phoenician invasions. This would fit well with the descriptions of Aischylos and Euripides given above. Thus Danaos' ordering the Pelasgians to become Danaan would represent their adoption of Near Eastern civilization. The idea of assimilation would also tally with the process of the Athenians turning, possibly through the agency of Kekrops and Erechtheus, from Pelasgians to Ionians.

Thus, working in the Ancient Model one does not have the problem faced by scholars following the Aryan one in understanding how Classical writers saw the Pelasgians both as the original 'barbarian' inhabitants of Greece and as in some way Hellenic. It is also striking that in later times the Pelasgians tended to be associated with remote places like Arkadia, Epirus and the edge of Thessaly. In this case they could well be seen as partially unassimilated 'Proto-Greeks'. (An analogy for this would be the blurred distinction between the Vietnamese of the Red River Delta, and the Muong of the mountains to the south whose language and culture are like those of the Vietnamese but with far less of the latter's massive cultural borrowing from China. There is, however, no evidence to back such speculation.) We also know that Arkadians, at least by the end of the Mycenaean Age, were speaking Greek. Arkadia, moreover, seems to have been particularly full of Egyptian and Semitic influence.[43] This could be explained by postulating a slow but complete assimilation there. Thus just as the Welsh, who had resisted Roman rule, preserved many Latin loan words and Roman Christianity, the Arkadians preserved traditions from the higher culture they had previously resisted. Against this, however, one could also argue that they were called 'Pelasgian' simply because of their later traditionalism.

The Arkadians were not the only Greeks to preserve elements of Mycenaean culture into the Iron Age. The same can be said of the Ionians and the Aiolians. The great exception were the Dorians; this raises the problem of the nature of the Dorian culture or that of Northern and North-Western Greece, from which they are plausibly supposed to have come. There is little doubt about the presence of Egyptian and Semitic religious influences throughout Northern Greece and Thrace. There are also the specific links between the most important and probably the oldest oracular centre of the region, 'Pelasgian' Dodona, the Egypto-Libyan oracle of Ammon in the Siwa Oasis and the great oracle of Amon at Thebes, which will be discussed in Volume 3.

Furthermore, the Dorian leaders claimed to be 'Heraklids', that is descendants of the Danaan-Egyptian colonizers, replacing the later Tantalid or Pelopid dynasties which appear to have arrived from Anatolia in the 14th century. It is clear that Dorian kings continued to be proud of their Egypto-Hyksos ancestry well into Hellenistic times.[44] Nevertheless, no Mycenaean palaces have been found in North-West Greece, and it would seem plausible to suppose that in general the region was much less affected by Near Eastern influences than the rest of Greece. In addition the Dorian 'Return of the Heraklids', while claiming Danaan legitimacy, may also have had revolutionary social and national aspects. Several archaeologists have noted a revival of Pre-Mycenaean, Middle Helladic material culture after the destruction of the Mycenaean palaces. Thus it may well by that the Mycenaean Age was ended by invasions of unassimilated Dorians combined – in some areas at least – with support from only partially assimilated peasants living within the palatial economy.[45]

All in all, the references to Pelasgians on Mainland Greece fit the Ancient Model reasonably well. According to it, 'Pelasgian' was simply a name given to unassimilated native Greeks. Such a framework would not be incompatible with the early but Hellenic Pelasgians in Crete.[46] The great difficulty for the Revised Ancient Model, on the other hand, comes from Herodotos' explicit statement that he believed the Pelasgians to have been non-Greek-speaking. He seems to have based this claim entirely on evidence from the North-East Aegean, and it would seem plausible to suggest that in this case 'Pelasgian' was being used in its broad sense of 'native'. It appears to have been the attempt to unify these disparate peoples that has caused such confusion to ancient and modern writers.

IONIANS

The Ionians were one of the two great tribes of Greece, the other being the Dorians. In Classical times the Ionians lived in a band across the central Aegean from Attica to 'Ionia' on the Anatolian shore. They had strong traditions, both of having colonized to the East after the arrival of the Dorians, and of having lived more widely in Greece before the invasions. Herodotos, almost certainly following an older tradition, linked the Pelasgians to the Ionians:[47]

> The Ionians ... according to the Greek account, as long as they lived in what is now known as Achaia in the Peloponnese, before the coming of Danaos and Xouthos, were called Pelasgians of the coast ... The Islanders too ... are a Pelasgian people: they were later known as the Ionians for the same reason as those who inhabited the twelve cities founded from Athens.[48]

The Ionians of Attica and Ionia on the Anatolian coast placed great stress on their ancient native origins. No one denies that I(a)ōn, found in Linear B as ia-wo-ne, is the same as the West Semitic Yåwån, the Assyrian Yawani or Yamani, the Persian Yauna and the Egyptian Demotic Wynn. All mean 'Greek'. All authorities, however, assume the name Ion to be Greek, despite the fact that it lacks an Indo-European etymology.[49] The most plausible origin for the cluster and for the names of the native Aones and Hyantes encountered by the legendary Egypto-Phoenician invaders of Boiotia would seem to be the Egyptian 'Iwn(ty(w)) (bowmen, barbarians).[50] Not only is this word attested well over a thousand years before the others, but it has an obvious etymology from iwnt (bow) and iwn (pillar or tree trunk).

The fact that Egyptian texts tend to apply it to other African peoples and do not use it for Greeks, for whom they had other names, does not seriously weaken the derivation. The indiscriminate use of the English name 'Indian', applied to completely different peoples, shows how easily terms for 'natives' or 'barbarians' can shift. In this case we know that West Semitic speakers were using a strikingly similar term specifically for Greeks at least by the turn of the 1st millennium BC. As has been mentioned in the Introduction, the Egyptian deity of the desert and all the wildness beyond the Nile valley and its inhabitants was St, transcribed as Seth in Greek and Sutekh in Akkadian. It will be argued in Volume 3 that Seth was the equivalent of Poseidon, and it is striking therefore to note that according to conventional wisdom in 5th-century Greece, the father of Ion – the legendary eponym after whom the people were named – was a troublemaker called Xouthos, a name that could phonetically well derive from St. The semantic connection between the two is strengthened by the fact that Poseidon was the patron of the Ionians.[51]

In this way the Revised Ancient Model can provide plausible etymologies for the names Xouthos and Ion, and explanations for the close relations perceived by ancient writers between the Pelasgians and Ionians. Generally it can begin to make some sense of data that have remained a hopeless jumble to the many brilliant scholars who have attempted to understand them in terms of the Aryan Model.

COLONIZATION

When dealing with the Greek traditions of colonization, I think it is useful to put them in three categories. First, there are the vague, not to say incoherent, traditions concerning such legendary figures as King Inachos in Argos and Amphion and Zethos at Thebes. Secondly, there are those concerning Kekrops in Attica or Rhadamanthys in Crete and Ionia which were the subject of debate in Antiquity. Thirdly, there were the reports of Kadmos, Danaos and Pelops, which were generally accepted. As mentioned above, I believe that for reasons of cultural pride Greeks tended to play down the extent of Near Eastern influence and colonization. Furthermore, I am certain that all the legends contain interesting kernels of historical truth, and that the hierarchy of obscurity can be explained in terms of age: the more recent the colonization, the clearer the picture of it. This volume will be largely concerned with the traditions of Danaos and Kadmos, as it was the more recent colonizations that were the battleground during the fall of the Ancient Model and the triumph of the Aryan one.

First, we should consider Kadmos' colonization of Thebes. This was the stronghold of the Ancient Model because it was so vigorously and widely attested, and because respect for the Semitic Phoenicians outlasted that for the African Egyptians by several decades. English-speaking Classical scholarship on Kadmos has been dominated by an article published in 1913 by A. W. Gomme. This author claimed that the Kadmeian and, by implication, the other colonizations had been invented by 'rationalist' historians in the early 5th century, just before Herodotos.[52] Such an extreme position was always difficult to defend, however, and it is now untenable. First of all, there is the intrinsic implausibility of such detailed, varied and unpatriotic legends springing up so suddenly and widely in the intensely nationalistic 5th century. Secondly, there is the pictorial evidence: a 7th-century relief vase fragment depicts Europa in Oriental costume, and there are similar early representations of her and the Danaids.[53]

The central argument, however, comes from literature. While Homer did not mention the colonizations, there is no reason why he should have done. While his epics almost certainly contained earlier materials, they were concerned with the end of the Mycenaean Age, not its beginnings several hundred years earlier. The *Iliad* is full of references to Danaans and Kadmeians, whose eponyms – Danaos and Kadmos – would have been instantly recognized by at least later Greeks as having come from Egypt or Phoenicia. Homer and Hesiod both referred to Europa, who was always seen as a sister or some other close relative to Kadmos, as the 'daughter of Phoinix'. Reluctant to admit that this could have any connection with Phoenicia, Karl Otfried Müller and other source critics have pointed out, correctly, that *phoinix* has many other meanings and need not be directly connected with the Levant.[54]

However, given Homer's frequent use of Phoinix in the sense of 'Phoenician', and the later universal identification of Europa and Kadmos with Phoenicia, this argument seems rather far-fetched, especially when we know that Hesiod described Phoinix as the father of

Adonis, whose Phoenician parentage is as beyond doubt as the origin of his name from the Canaanite 'ådôn (lord).[55] Indeed, since Gomme wrote his article, a fragment of Hesiod's *Catalogue of Women* has been published in which Europa is described as the daughter of the 'noble Phoenician' and her abductor, Zeus, carries her over the 'salt water'.[56] This confirms that the Europa story, which the scholiast on *Iliad* XII.292 attributed to both Hesiod and the 5th-century poet Bakchylides, existed in the time of the former.

For Danaos there is Hesiod's testimony that Danaos and his daughters dug wells for the city of Argos and the strong implication of his relationship with Aigyptos. There is also a fragment from a lost epic, the *Danais*, which describes the daughters of Danaos arming themselves by the banks of the Nile.[57] Thus even if one wants to doubt the antiquity of the sources of Aischylos, Euripides and Herodotos, other evidence makes it overwhelmingly likely that the traditions of Danaos and Kadmos go back to epic times.

In order to know what we are talking about, it would seem useful at this point to consider the different assessments of the dates of the greatest epic writer, Homer, and of his approximate contemporary, Hesiod. The Ancients tended to put Hesiod before Homer and to place them both between 1100 and 850 BC, in any event definitely before the first Olympic Games in 776.[58] Scholars today tend to reverse the order. They place Homer between 800 and 700 BC and Hesiod sometime around the latter. The fundamental basis for this down-dating has been that since the 1930s conventional wisdom has held that the alphabet was introduced only in the 8th century. As the contemporary scholar George Forrest has written:

> Hesiod, like Homer, lived in a period of transition from oral to written composition. Indeed it seems likely that each was the first, or among the first, to commit to manuscript his own version of a long oral tradition.[59]

However, even Classicists now tend to date the introduction of the Phoenician alphabet into Greece to the 9th or late 10th century BC. Some Semitists have put that of the Canaanite alphabet in the 11th, while I argue that the transmission must have taken place before 1400

BC.[60] Thus the alphabetic basis for challenging the ancient chronology would seem unsound. Further reasons for the lowering of Homer's dates are that in the *Iliad* the most refined goods come from Phoenicia, and the *Odyssey* refers to Phoenicians in the Aegean. Hence, as the latter were supposed to have arrived at the earliest in the 9th century, Homer – if there had been such an individual – could not have lived before then.[61] This argument, however, was developed before recent archaeological discoveries indicating that Phoenicians were present in the Aegean from the 10th, if not the late 11th century. This new evidence tallies well with the powerful historical case for the the peak of Phoenician expansion having been between 1000 and 850 BC.[62]

Another reason given for placing Homer in the late 8th or 7th century is that the *Odyssey* is largely set to the west of Greece, and it is argued that the Greeks could not have known about the central Mediterranean before their colonization of Sicily and Southern Italy at the end of the 8th century.[63] I think that it is in many ways useful to look at this epic as a Greek version of the Egyptian *Book of the Dead*, and that in both Egyptian and Greek cosmology the western islands of the sunset were associated with the Underworld and astral realms of the dead.[64] Even without this hypothesis, however, it is clear that there was considerable Mycenaean trade to the west in the Bronze Age and that even if Greeks were not directly involved, they must have been aware of the Phoenician dealings with the West Mediterranean in the 11th, 10th and 9th centuries.

The reasons given for putting Hesiod after Homer are first, that it is supposed that Hesiod

> does not belong with the heroic poets . . . he is always personal and contemporary in his outlook . . . Hesiod is wholly part of the Iron Age of the present, specifically of the Archaic Greek world of the 8th and early 7th centuries BC.[65]

It is also argued that as Hesiod's *Theogony* was clearly based on Near Eastern models of a type that was developed only after 1100, these can have been introduced into Greece only after 800 BC, when it is alleged that a Greek colony was established at Al Mina on the Syrian coast.[66] Hesiod's *Theogony* belongs to a general type which can be traced

throughout the Middle East from the 3rd millennium, and there is little
reason to doubt that some form or forms of it existed in Mycenaean
Greece.[67] Nevertheless Hesiod's version does seem to contain pecu-
liarities that can best be explained in terms of the traditions of the turn
of the 1st millennium.[68] On the other hand, the existence of the Greek
colony at Al Mina is in serious doubt, and it would seem plausible
that Hesiod and his contemporaries were in touch with these later
theogonies through Phoenicia from where, after all, Hesiod seems
to have got his favourite wine.[69]

All in all, the grounds for challenging the ancient traditions for the
dating of Homer and Hesiod seem very weak. It would appear reasonable to accept as a working hypothesis the Classical and Hellenistic
consensus that Hesiod predated Homer, that the former flourished in
the 10th century and the latter around the turn of the 9th. Whatever
dates they are assigned to, however, there seems no reason to doubt that
traces of the legends of colonization from Egypt and Phoenicia appear
in the oldest surviving Greek traditions.

THE COLONIZATIONS IN
GREEK TRAGEDY

Although there are references to Egyptian and Phoenician settlers in
other plays of the period, I shall focus here on the drama in which
settlement on the Greek Mainland is a central theme: Aischylos' *The
Suppliants*. *The Suppliants* is generally considered to be the first play and
sole survivor of a trilogy or tetralogy. The titles of the missing pieces are
believed to have been *The Egyptians*, *The Danaids*, and a satirical play,
Amymone, and from *The Suppliants* and later writings on myth and
legend, the overall theme of the dramas is clear.

Io, the daughter of King Inachos of Argos, was loved by Zeus. Hera,
in one of her many fits of jealousy, turned Io into a cow and tormented
her with gadflies. Io fled to many places and finally settled in Egypt,
where she gave birth to Zeus' child, Epaphos. Epaphos' descendants
and their spouses included Libya, Poseidon, Belos, King Agenor of
Tyre – the father of Kadmos and Europa – and the twin brothers
Danaos and Aigyptos.[70] Danaos had fifty daughters and Aigyptos fifty

sons. The brothers quarrelled but later there was a mass wedding on the night of which, with one exception, Danaos' daughters killed Aigyptos' sons. In some way Danaos then acquired the throne of Argos. The various versions of the story differ greatly, particularly over which of these actions took place in Egypt and which in Argos.

The Suppliants describes one episode of this story, the arrival in Argos of Danaos' daughters as suppliants fleeing from Egypt and the evil intentions of the sons of Aigyptos. There they are given the sanctuary of Zeus Hikesios 'the Suppliant' by the native king, Pelasgos. A herald arrives from Aigyptos and his sons and arrogantly commands that Danaos' daughters be handed back. Pelasgos, with stout Hellenic patriotism, refuses and the play ends with plans for the settlement of Danaos and his daughters with Pelasgos and his people in Argos.

The extent to which modern study of this play and trilogy has been suffused with politics is not generally realized. German Romantic-Positivists and later scholars have insisted that this is the earliest extant play by Aischylos – or, for that matter, by anyone. This dating has in fact been set up as a touchstone of modern Classical scholarship:

> Scholars have hitherto regarded the *Supplices* [*Suppliants*] as the earliest extant play of Aischylos; if we now consent to put it late it makes all attempts to study literature futile.[71]

However, a papyrus published in 1952 now indicates strongly that the trilogy won a prize in 464–3 BC and that it is therefore the product of the tragedian's maturity.[72] This fits well with the high esteem in which the play was held in 5th- and 4th-century Athens. A contemporary Classicist, Dr Alan Garvie, has devastatingly shown the hollowness of the claims made for its early date on grounds of metre, vocabulary and dramatic structure.[73] What then caused the consistent disparagement of its 'immaturity'? The most plausible reason is that it was considered unworthy of the greatest Greek tragedian in his prime to treat a topic that could be understood to suggest that Egyptians had settled in the Peloponnese.

There have been equally persistent attempts to diminish the Egyptian aspects of the play, which in later times became so important a prop for the Ancient Model. For instance, while Io is seen as coming from Argos, most sources agree that she was only the distant ancestor of Aigyptos and Danaos. Thus the brothers and their children were Egyptianized, if not purely Egyptian, and the Danaids are explicitly described as 'black'.[74] The mainstream of German scholarship, however, has preferred the one scholiast who can dubiously be construed to say that the twins were the children of Io herself. The same scholiast also maintains that the whole action of the trilogy took place in Argos. This version has been preferred to all the other sources, some of which held that all the events were situated in Egypt, and all of which – including the lines from the *Danais* mentioned above – had the Danaids arriving from Egypt.[75]

Despite these criticisms of Aryanist scholars, there is no doubt that Aischylos was full of what can usefully be called Hellenic nationalism and wanted to lessen the impact of any invasion. He had lived through the height of the Persian Wars. As an Athenian aristocrat he took part in the critical Battle of Marathon in 492 BC which checked a major Persian invasion. His play *The Persians* directly expressed the xenophobic passions of his generation. In *The Suppliants* they are only thinly disguised:

> Sirrah! What dost thou? What manner of arrogance has incited thee thus to do dishonour to this realm of Pelasgian men? Think'st thou forsooth, 'tis to a realm of women that thou art come? For a barbarian that has to do with Hellenes, thou waxest over-proud.[76]

In such a passionately chauvinist atmosphere, it would seem more plausible to suppose that Aischylos wanted to diminish rather than exaggerate the Egyptian components in the myth cycle. There is considerable evidence from the text to support this contention, but to demonstrate it I shall have to go ahead of my argument and use approaches generally reserved for the second and third volumes of this work.

The elements of any legend can be roughly graded for their historical value. The least useful are motifs common to folk tales everywhere, in this case such elements as the story of the fifty daughters marrying and murdering fifty sons. Other folkloric themes occur elsewhere, but in significant places. The Egyptian informants of Diodoros Sikeliotes told him that Greeks had transferred the site of Io's origin from Egypt to Argos.[77] Michael Astour has shown how the story of Io, Zeus and Hera resembles the Semitic one of Hagar in the Bible. The last, whose name seems to derive from the Semitic √hgr (wander), was loved and impregnated by Abraham and driven by his jealous wife Sarah into the desert. She almost died, but God provided her with rest at an oasis where she gave birth to Ishmael, who was half man, half beast. Astour also cites a striking passage from Jeremiah, 'A beautiful heifer is Egypt, but a gadfly from the north has come upon her', to suggest that the prophet's Israelite audience knew the legend. Astour uses both these to claim that Semitic influence is present in the legends surrounding Danaos' settlement.[78]

However, there seem to be even more indications of the presence of Egyptian mythology. For example, in the *Suppliants* (line 212) Danaos invokes 'the bird of Zeus' and the chorus responds by invoking 'the saving beams of the sun'. Commentators have been obliged to see the striking parallel with the solar hawk of Zeus' Egyptian equivalent Amon-Ra, but they try to diminish its significance by calling it 'Egyptianizing', which gives it the flavour of being somehow late and superficial.[79] Elsewhere, there are references to a 'nether' or 'underground' Zeus who welcomes the dead, and to 'another Zeus' who holds judgement in the Underworld upon men's misdeeds. These look remarkably like the Egyptian trial of the dead by Osiris, and it is not surprising that the latter has been paralleled with passages in the *Odyssey* which are widely accepted as being 'Orphic' and ultimately Egyptian.[80]

These references are suggestive. The 'hardest' historical evidence to be found in legends, however, comes from proper names, and here it is necessary to draw on the recent work of the Classicist and literary critic Frederic Ahl. Ahl has shown the great sophistication of the Classical writers and the need to approach their texts as one would, say, *Finnegans Wake*. His view is that one should avoid imposing – as many Classicists have – a 'monist' or single crude meaning to them. In practice, he argues, one should look for the dense network of puns, anagrams and structural parallels which give the texts multiple and often contradictory meanings or 'readings'. Furthermore, the puns should not be treated lightly but should be considered as revealing deep, if not sacred, connections and truths.[81]

There is no doubt that *The Suppliants* rewards such treatment. Garvie refers to

> the use of words whose sound or form suggests one of the motifs, though its own meaning may be quite different. At *Supplices* 117 βοῦνιν means 'hilly land', but suggests 'land of the cow', [The stem bou- means 'cattle'] while 'Ἀπίαν recalls Apis, the Egyptian equivalent of of Epaphus (cf. 262). This is much more than a play on words. It springs from the idea that a name is not merely a matter of convention, but intimately belongs to the thing it represents.[82]

Garvie then goes on to point out specific parallels between the name Epaphos and the stem *ephap-*, which frequently appears in the play and which itself has the two meanings, 'seize' and 'caress'. There is also *epipnoia*, which means both the gentle breathing of Zeus that impregnates Io and later the storm that threatens the Danaids.[83] Even beyond these and Apia(n), another connection to the name Epaphos has been suggested by Jean Bérard: the name 'Ip.py was that of two or three Hyksos pharaohs and was conventionally rendered in Greek as Ap(h)ōphis.[84] As Astour points out, the difference in vocalization can be explained by the fact that Late Egyptian went through a vowel shift a̱>o towards the end of the 2nd millennium.[85] This would suggest that the name Epaphos was introduced before that time and weaken the argument for late 'Egyptianizing'.

The place name Apia, which is rarely used outside this play, generally means Argos, but it is used elsewhere to cover the whole of the Peloponnese. It has plausibly been linked with *apios* (distant) or *apiē gaiē* (distant land) in Homer.[86] However, this is unlikely to be its origin, and Apia has many other associations. It was obvious to the Ancients – and since 1911 even modern scholarship has recognized – that the name recalls the Apis bull of Egypt and is therefore associated with the cow Io and her Egyptian son Epaphos.[87] The Apis bull-cult in Memphis dated back to the 1st Dynasty but its peak of influence was after the 18th, and the original Egyptian form of the name is Ḥpw.[88] Ḥp or Ḥpy was the name of one of Horus' sons, prominent in *The Book of the Dead*, whose special responsibility was guarding the north.[89] Thus he would, in Egyptian eyes, be associated with Greece. At first sight it might seem too far-fetched to connect him with the Greek Apia; however, in *The Suppliants* there is the passage:

> The ground whereon we stand is Apian land itself, and hath of old borne that name in honour of a leech [doctor]. For Apis, seer and leech, the son of Apollo, came from Naupaktos on the farther shore and purged well this land of monsters deadly to man, which Earth, defiled by the bloody deeds of yore, caused to spring up – plagues charged with wrath, a baleful colony of swarming serpents. Of these plagues Apis worked a cure by surgery and spells to the content of the Argive land . . .[90]

It should be pointed out that, in the Egyptian pantheon, Ḥpy was the guardian of the Canopic jar containing the small intestine, and in *The Book of the Dead* one of his major functions in protecting the dead was to kill demons in the shape of serpents.[91] Apollo was generally equated with Ḥpy's father, Horus. The intricacy of this parallel makes it overwhelmingly plausible. However, unlike the apparently ancient origin of the name Epaphos, that of Apis – at least in this context – seems to have been more recent. The name Apia does not occur in Homer and the story of its eponym told above appears only in this passage and does not seem to have belonged to a more general tradition.

Epaphos and Apia are not alone. Most of the names in *The Suppliants* have strong Egyptian connotations, of which I shall give only a few examples. Inachos, now generally considered to be the most Argive name in the play, is seen as the king of Argos and father of Io. He later became Argos' major river, and as such was often contrasted with the Egyptian Nile. In the 18th century, however, the attitude was very different. The bold and brilliant scholar Nicolas Fréret, for example, maintained – rather dubiously – on the basis of the Christian Church Father Eusebius, that Inachos was an Egyptian colonizer.[92] Fréret argued that the name was a common one in the Middle East, meaning 'men famous for their strength and bravery', and he cited the biblical term ʿănåq, transcribed Enak or Enach in the Greek of the *Septuagint*, and the Greek *anax*, *anaktos* (king).

The name 'ănâq is ambiguous. It was used for the rulers of Qiryat 'Arba', who seem to have been Hittites, but it generally referred to the tall and powerful Philistines, who are widely accepted as having come from the Aegean.[93] As the word *(w)anakt-* appears in Phrygian as well as in Greek, 'ănâq could have been derived from it. Apart from the dubiousness of this etymology, there is the problem of the clear indication that Qiryat 'Arba' was founded in the 17th or 18th century BC.[94] But if, as I believe, the Philistines were predominantly Greek-speaking, the former may well be a loan from the latter.[95]

In any event, Fréret was unaware of the Egyptian root √'nḫ, which very much strengthens his general case. Its basic meaning was 'life', as in the famous symbol of the *ankh*, but it had a wide range of extensions. The formula 'nḫ ḏt (may he live for ever) was the standard formula used after the names of living pharaohs, and this makes a plausible etymology for the Greek *(w)anax, (w)anaktos* (king), which has no known origin in Indo-European.[96] Another use of 'nḫ is as 'coffin', which would seem to be the etymology for the Greek Anaktoron, the sacred reliquary at the centre of the Eleusinian Mysteries.

More relevant to our present concern is the use of 'nḫ in the phrase *mw'nḫ* to describe 'living' water. Anaktos is used in the same way and specifically in the line from the lost epic the *Danais*, ποταμοῦ Νείλοιο Ἄνακτος, 'of the royal/living river Nile'. The Nile was renowned for its fertility and life-giving powers. Furthermore, according to the mythographer Apollodoros, who probably lived in the 1st century AD, the mother of Aigyptos and Danaos, who was the daughter of the Nile, was called Anchinoe. The possibility that this derives from an Egyptian form *'nḫ nwy (living waters or life of water) is increased by the variants of her name as Anchirrhoe or Anchirhoe: *rhoē* means 'stream or flow' in Greek.[97]

The existence of such peculiar semantic clusters – in both Egyptian and Greek – around royalty, coffins and flowing water would seem to lessen the chances of random coincidence very nearly to zero. Also, the triple service of Inachos as king, progenitor and river and the frequent contrasts given between him and the Nile would suggest intricate paranomasia, or punning, in Egyptian and Greek of the type suggested above with Ḥpw/y – Apis/Apia. Here, too, despite the use of

Ἄνακτος in the epic, the facts that neither Homer nor Hesiod uses the name Inachos and that the latter uses another name for Io's father suggests that this Egypto-Greek relation is indeed a later elaboration.

The name of Inachos' daughter Io has been derived from the verb *ienai* (to wander), which would neatly correspond to the etymology of Hagar from √hgr (wander).[98] There are, however, equally clear Egyptian and Semitic etymologies. Modern commentators admit the clear punning going on in the play between ᾽Ιώ 'Io' ῎Ιων 'Ionian' and ῎Ιον 'violet'.[99] The Egyptian origin of Ionian has been suggested above. The double etymology of Io itself would seem to be firstly from the Egyptian *i'ḥ* (moon), which in the Bohairic dialect of Coptic is rendered *iōḫ*.[100] Furthermore, there were traditions that *iō* was a dialect word for 'moon' in Argos. Linked to this – as Ahl points out – are the associations between Io and Isis who, in very late Egyptian religion, was associated with the moon. Ahl further indicates the lunar connections, with the horns and femininity coalesced in the 'cow'.[101] It is here that we find the second and, I believe, basic Egyptian etymologies for Io: those from *iḥt* (cow) – plural *iḥw* – and *iwꜣ* (domestic long-horned cattle).

Among the names of Io's descendants we have considered that of Epaphos. Libya – from the Late Egyptian Rb – is, I believe, a form of Athena.[102] Many scholars have derived the name of their son Belos from the Semitic √b'l, either in the general sense of 'lord' or specifically as the god of that name.[103] The name Phoinix is clearly associated with Phoenicia.[104] Paradoxically, Agenor King of Tyre is the only member of the family to have a Greek name meaning 'manly' or 'bold'. The etymology of the name Aigyptos is obvious. Originally Ḥ(t)-Kꜣ-Ptḥ, 'Temple of the Spirit of Ptah', was a name of the Lower Egyptian capital of Memphis. By the Late Bronze Age, however, it seems to have been in common use for 'Egyptian' throughout the East Mediterranean, and the personal name Ai-ku-pi-ti-jo is mentioned in Mycenaean Greece.[105]

The name of Aigyptos' twin and rival Danaos appears as Da-na-jo in Linear B, but this presents a much more complicated and fascinating problem. No known figure in Egyptian history or mythology has this name. It does, however, have a long association with the Aegean, possibly stretching back into the 3rd millenium.[106] Da-na-ne is attested in Linear A; T'inɜy or ta-na-yu appears as an Egyptian name for Greece from the 15th century, and D₃-in was in use by the 13th.[107] Astour has linked the stem to the Semitic root √dn(n) (judge), seen in such names as Dan'el or Daniel, and he maintains that the Danaans, whose eponym was Danaos, were a Semitic-speaking tribe he sees as having arrived in Greece in the Late Bronze Age, probably from Cilicia in South-Eastern Anatolia.[108] While I accept that there probably were connections between the various peoples called Dani/a or Tani/a in the East Mediterranean, and I believe that both Cilicia and the Southern Aegean were heavily Semitized during most of the Bronze Age, I prefer to follow those scholars who maintain that the Dnnym found later in Cilicia and the biblical tribe of Dan came from the Aegean, rather than the other way around.[109] However, the colonizations with which we are concerned came considerably earlier, and all the legends about these insist that Danaos was an incomer to Greece.

The name Dan- is certainly surrounded by dense and old punning in Egyptian, West Semitic and Greek. Gardiner points out that by the 11th century BC the place name D₃-in or Dene was written with the determinative or pictogram of a bent old man. He associates this with the Egyptian ṯni, later written tni – by this period, d, ṯ, and t were all pronounced in the same way – meaning 'old' and 'tired'. He therefore calls it the 'tired land'.[110] It is interesting to note, therefore, that Danaos' most striking characteristics in *The Suppliants* and elsewhere are his great age and weariness. He was also known as a wise judge and legislator who settled the Argolid, and he and his daughters were especially renowned for their involvement in irrigation. Thus his name could well come from an Egyptian form *dniw (allocator or irrigator), from dni (allocate, irrigate), which is clearly related to the Semitic √dn(n) (judge). It seems to me that the network of punning here is too dense to make it possible to distinguish which came first: the Danaan people of the Aegean or Danaos, the Egypto-Semitic colonial distributor of lands, legislator and irrigator.

If the conclusions to be drawn from Danaos' name are inevitably ambiguous, the legends about his struggle with Aigyptos have been seen, at least since the 3rd century BC, to point unequivocally to his having been a Hyksos chieftain driven out by the Egyptian national revival of the 18th Dynasty.[111] In this connection, we should turn to the Greek name of *The Suppliants*, *Hiketides*. This is clearly linked to Hikesios (the Suppliant), the central byname of Zeus, the god who dominates the play from beginning to end.[112] The rather strange byname or epiclesis Hikesios was occasionally used elsewhere, particularly in Southern Greece, and belongs to a general aspect of the god whereby he protected strangers.[113] It is also interesting to note that the two plays called *Hiketides* both refer to Argos, the city later especially associated with the Hyksos colonization.[114] Hikesios strikingly resembles the Egyptian Ḥḳꜣ ḫꜣst, which in the 3rd century BC was rendered into Greek as Hyksos.

Given the general and pervasive paranomasia or punning in the play shown above, it would seem very likely indeed that Aischylos and his sources were aware of the *double entendre* in a play set in a trilogy about the struggle between Aigyptos and Danaos, and specifically about the arrival of the latter in Argos from Egypt. It would also seem reasonable to suppose that 'Hyksos' was the primary meaning and that the idea of 'suppliant' derived from it. The widespread attestation of Zeus Hikesios, however, would suggest that the pun was an old one, and it is very unlikely that it originated with Aischylos.

There is also little doubt that the portrayal of the arrival as one of refugees who were hospitably received by the natives and who then mysteriously became rulers was much more satisfying to Hellenic nationalism than one of a conquest. It would certainly have helped relieve the tension between ancient tradition and national pride. The question of whether or not there actually was a Hyksos colonization of Argos in the 2nd millennium BC will be discussed in Volume 2. All I argue here is that the theme of *The Suppliants*, and the massive amount of Egyptian material in it, demonstrate that Aischylos and his sources, which go back at least to the writing of the *Danais* in the 7th century or earlier, believed this to have been the case.

Lastly, I should add that *The Suppliants* is not the only tragedy to refer to the colonizations: many of those treating Thebes mention Kadmos' Phoenician origin. In Euripides' *The Phoenician Women*, for instance, the chorus of Phoenician women come – precisely because Kadmos came from Tyre – to see the downfall of his dynasty.[115] There too the evidence points in favour of a general belief in the legends in the 5th century BC.[116]

HERODOTOS

The most striking manifestation of this belief comes from Herodotos, who wrote his great *Histories* in about 450 BC. His major theme was the relationship between Europe – by which he generally meant Greece – and Asia and Africa. He saw this relationship as one of similarities and differences, contacts and conflicts, and he asked many questions on these topics during his wide travels in the Persian Empire from Babylonia to Egypt, and on its northern and western fringes from Epirus and Greece to the Black Sea.

The quotation at the head of this chapter shows that Herodotos did not write any descriptions of the colonizations, because he believed that this had been done elsewhere. Equally, however, the passage makes it clear that he firmly believed they had actually taken place. The *Histories* are full of references to them:

> The temple of Athena there [Lindos in Rhodes] was founded by the daughters of Danaos, who touched at the island during their flight from the sons of Aigyptos.[117]

> Kadmos, the son of Agenor, touched at it [Thera] during his search for Europa and . . . left there a number of Phoenicians.[118]

Herodotos was not so much interested in the settlements themselves, but in how they had been instrumental in introducing Egyptian and Phoenician civilization to Greece:

> I propose to hold my tongue about the mysterious rites of Demeter, which the Greeks call Thesmophoria, though . . . I may say, for instance, that it was the daughters of Danaos who brought this ceremony from Egypt and instructed the Pelasgian women in it . . .[119]

> The Phoenicians who came with Kadmos . . . introduced into Greece, after their settlement in the country, a number of

accomplishments, of which the most important was writing, an art till then, I think, unknown to the Greeks.[120]

Elsewhere he related the introduction of Near Eastern civilization to cultural figures dependent on political and military ones. The process had continued, however, after the initial colonization:

> Now I have an idea that Melampous . . . introduced the name of Dionysos into Greece, together with the sacrifice in his honour and the phallic procession. He did not, however, fully comprehend the doctrine, or communicate it in its entirety; its more perfect development was the work of later teachers. Nevertheless it was Melampous who introduced the phallic procession, and from Melampous that the Greeks learnt the rites that they now perform. Melampous, in my view, was an able man who acquired the art of divination and brought into Greece, with little change, a number of things which he had learned in Egypt, and amongst them the worship of Dionysos . . . Probably Melampous got his knowledge about Dionysos through Kadmos of Tyre and the people who came with him from Phoenicia to the country now called Boiotia. *The names of nearly all the gods came to Greece from Egypt.* [my emphasis] I know from the enquiries I have made that they came from abroad, and it seems most likely that it was from Egypt, for the names of all the gods have been known in Egypt from the beginning of time . . . These practices, then, and others which I shall speak of later, were borrowed by the Greeks from Egypt . . . In ancient times, as I know from what I was told at Dodona, the Pelasgians offered sacrifices of all kinds, and prayed to the gods, but without any distinction of name or title – for they had not yet heard of any such thing. They called the gods by the Greek word *theoi* – 'disposers' . . . Long afterwards the names of the gods were brought into Greece from Egypt and the Pelasgians learnt them . . . then as time went on, they sent to the oracle at Dodona (the most ancient, and at that period, the only oracle in Greece) to ask advice about the propriety of adopting names that had come into the country from abroad. The oracle replied that they would be right to use them. From that time onward, therefore, the Pelasgians used the names of

the gods in their sacrifices, and from the Pelasgians the names passed to Greece.[121]

Moreover, Herodotos did not restrict the introduction of Near Eastern ideas to the colonists. His description of the Egyptian and Libyan origins of the oracle at Dodona in Epirus, based on the reports of priestesses there and priests at the Egyptian Thebes, was in terms of myths that are not in any way related to Danaos or Kadmos.[122]

As I have mentioned, Herodotos was accused by Plutarch, in the 2nd century AD, of being the 'father of lies' and tends today to be treated with indulgent condescension by scholars working within the Aryan Model, who are especially scornful of his 'credulity'. However, he did not rely entirely on legends when he derived Greek customs from the East in general and Egypt in particular:[123]

> I will never admit that the similar ceremonies performed in Greece and Egypt are the result of mere coincidence – had that been so, our rites would have been more Greek in character and less recent in origin. Nor will I allow that the Egyptians ever took over from Greece either this custom or any other.[124]

Thus Herodotos would seem to have been using reason rather than a blind faith in tradition, and the method of competitive plausibility which would seem entirely appropriate for such a subject. We are not concerned here with the rightness or wrongness of his conclusions, however, but merely with the facts that he himself believed in them and that he was being relatively conventional in doing so. The latter claim would seem to be substantiated by the earlier references to the colonizations, and by the acceptance of his ideas on them by the overwhelming majority of later Greek writers. Such an acceptance is particularly impressive in view of the passionate Greek chauvinism of these times, and the Greeks' unease with or dislike of traditions that made them culturally inferior to the Egyptians and Phoenicians, who were still very much around. It may well have been for this kind of reason that Herodotos appears to have been on the defensive, not about the existence of the colonizations but about the extent of Greek cultural borrowings from Egypt and Phoenicia. It is this unease which leads us to the second great Greek historian, Thucydides, who lived from 460 to 400 BC.

THUCYDIDES

The early-19th-century critics made great play of the 'silence' of some authorities on the colonizations, and the historian they clearly had in mind was Thucydides. The latter's introduction to his history does not mention Kadmos or Danaos, although it does mention Pelops' invasion of Greece from Anatolia. Thucydides also stated that at one time 'Carians and Phoenicians inhabited most of the islands', and he referred to the Danaans and to Kadmeis as an old name for Boiotia.[125] He also described the Pre-Pelopid kings of Argos as descendants of Perseus, whom Herodotos had seen either as a 'genuine Egyptian' or as an 'Assyrian'.[126] Nevertheless, there is no mention of Kadmos or Danaos, or of their invasions.

Given the frequent references to the colonizations in Herodotos and the Tragedies in the decades before he wrote, Thucydides must have known the traditions and his omission must be seen as the result of a conscious decision. It is extremely unlikely that this was reached because he possessed evidence disproving them, for in that case he would almost certainly have included it both to bolster his reputation as a historian and also because, as will be argued below, the invasions were offensive to his historical framework. A more charitable explanation would be that as a self-consciously 'critical' historian he was reluctant to deal with unverifiable legends. The force of this argument is weakened, however, by his mention of the still more distant myth of Hellen son of Deukalion – the survivor of the Flood.[127]

One of the reasons Thucydides has had such an appeal during the last three centuries is that his historical view was 'progressive'.[128] According to it, the nearer one came to the present, the greater and more effective political organization became. Hence he tended to play down Mycenaean achievements and to emphasize that society's instability and the chaos of the succeeding 'Dark Ages'. This, for instance, helps to explain his denial that Homer had any sense of the

Hellenes as a single people.[129] According to him, history built up to the unprecedented might of *his* two protagonists, Athens and Sparta, so that his life spanned, and his work described 'The greatest disturbance in the history of the Hellenes, affecting also a large part of the non-Hellenic world, and indeed I might almost say, the whole of mankind.'[130]

This quite extraordinary claim was incompatible with the notion that the Trojan War had involved the Hellenes as a people. Acceptance of the colonizations would have been still more devastating to his historical framework. The distances covered, the scale of operations, and the massive long-term consequences of the legendary invasions would have shown up the essentially trivial nature of the Peloponnesian War, which has been made great only by Thucydides' history of it.

An even more important inhibitory factor than what one might call his 'temporal chauvinism' was his nationalism – a word I use deliberately. Thucydides drew a rigid distinction between Hellene and 'barbarian' and his whole work was a paean to the uniqueness of Greek achievements, even the destructive ones. Thus the idea that the Egyptians, whom Athenians could now conquer, or Phoenicians, who formed the most terrible arm of Persian military power – its fleet – should have played a central role in the formation of Greek culture was clearly disturbing to Thucydides' contemporaries.

Such an attitude would explain why Thucydides, the 'critical historian' who rejected legends, was able to mention Hellen, a purely national figure, but not civilizing foreigners like Danaos, Kadmos or the Egyptian Kekrops. (Whether or not the desire to remove offensive legends can give impetus to the critical approach itself will be discussed in Chapters IV and VI.) This kind of 'nationalism' would seem to be typical in the aftermath of the Persian Wars of the early 5th century and the subsequent expansion of Greek power: from this time on, one finds varying degrees of hatred of and contempt for 'barbarians' among most Greeks. In such an atmosphere one would expect Greek writers, if anything, to play down the legends of cultural indebtedness to the Near East. Hence it would be easier to understand, for example, why any suggestions of Kekrops' Egyptian connections should be replaced by a view of him as autochthonous, or why Thucydides should omit the legends altogether, than why Greeks should invent 'new' stories of foreign colonization and civilization.

ISOKRATES AND PLATO

In the early 4th century, the outstanding spokesman for Panhellenism and Greek cultural pride was the Athenian orator Isokrates. In a famous panegyric given at the Olympian festival of 380 BC he called on Spartans and Athenians to drop their differences and join in a Panhellenic union against Persia and the barbarians. With a new degree of cultural security he proclaimed:

> And so far has our city [Athens] distanced the rest of mankind in thought and in speech that her pupils have become the teachers of the rest of the world. She has brought it about that the name 'Hellenes' suggests no longer a race but an intelligence, and that the title 'Hellenes' is applied rather to those who share our culture than to those who share a common blood.[131]

The arrogance of this statement is surprising when one considers that many cultured Greeks, including Eudoxos, the greatest mathematician and astronomer of the 4th century, still felt obliged to study in Egypt.[132]

Not surprisingly, Isokrates was concerned about the colonizations:

> In former times any barbarians who were in misfortune presumed to be rulers over the Greek cities [for example] Danaos, an exile from Egypt, occupied Argos; Kadmos from Sidon became king of Thebes . . .[133]

It is important to note that despite Isokrates' clear dislike of the invasions, he did not question their historicity. However, he had a still greater ambivalence on the issue. He wrote an extremely flattering picture of Egypt in his *Bousiris*. At one level this speech was merely a rhetorical *tour de force*, the defence of a mythical king chiefly known for his practice of killing foreigners. Nevertheless, to be convincing, the speech had to appeal to conventional wisdom, and it clearly had very serious aspects. The land of Egypt and its people were portrayed in it as the most blessed in the world, but above all the piece was a eulogy to

Bousiris as a mythical lawgiver and to the perfection of the constitution he had devised for Egypt.[134]

Isokrates admired the caste system, the rulership of the philosophers, and the rigour of the Egyptian philosopher/priests' *paideia* (education) that produced the *anēr theōrētikos* (contemplative man), who used his superior wisdom for the good of his state.[135] The division of labour allowed a 'leisure', *scholē*, which allowed for *scholē*, 'learning'. Above all, he insisted that *philosophia* (philosophy) was, and could only have been, a product of Egypt.[136] This word seems to have been used by the Egyptianizing Pythagoreans for some time – possibly since the 6th century – but its earliest extant use comes from *Bousiris*.[137]

There is in fact no logical inconsistency between this deeply respectful attitude towards Egypt and Isokrates' passionate xenophobia. He did not deny the colonization, which at least since Herodotos had been associated with the implantation of Egyptian religion in Greece. Furthermore, his paean to the cultural triumph of Athens and Greece referred only to the present. It made no claims on the past. Nevertheless, there does seem to be a contrast in the two positions. At a superficial level it can be explained by the fact that the 'barbarians' with whom Isokrates was most concerned were the Persians and the Phoenicians, the latter because they formed much of the basis of the Persian fleet and because his patron, the tyrant Evagoras, had seized his territory Salamis in Cyprus from Phoenicians. Furthermore, around 390 BC when *Bousiris* was written, a three-way alliance against Persia was made among Evagoras, Achōris, Pharaoh of Egypt, and Athens.[138]

I believe, however, that the two points of view can be integrated at a much more fundamental level, as part of Isokrates' attempt to unite Athens and Sparta against Persia. There is no doubt that Athenians at the end of the Peloponnesian War, at the turn of the 4th century, were fascinated by the constitution of Sparta, which had been so successful an enemy. This has led scholars like the great 19th-century German Classicist Wilamowitz-Moellendorf, working within the Aryan Model, to postulate the existence of a *Lakedaimonian Politics* which had inspired Isokrates to write his *Bousiris*, and to argue that it was because Herodotos had claimed that the Spartans owed their institutions to Egypt that Isokrates had made Bousiris his ideal.[139] The modern

French scholar Charles Froidefond contests this on the grounds that *Bousiris* looks nothing like the *Lakedaimonian Politics* written by Xenophon because Isokrates specified that the Spartans had borrowed only partially from Egypt, and because the military aspects of Spartan society which most impressed his generation were attributed to Lykourgos. It was only much later, in the 2nd century AD, that Plutarch claimed that Lykourgos had been an imitator of Egypt.[140]

I agree with Froidefond that there is no need to postulate a **Lakedaimonian Politics*. On the other hand, we know that 'Post-War' Athenians were concerned with the secrets of Spartan success. Furthermore, scholars working within the Ancient Model have no doubt that the stories about Spartan, and specifically Lykourgan, institutional borrowings from Egypt were current at the turn of the 4th century because *they were true*. That is to say, the tradition is confirmed not merely by the nature of certain aspects of Spartan society but by the strong Egyptian influences on Spartan Archaic art and the many plausible Late Egyptian etymologies for the names of specifically Spartan institutions.[141]

Isokrates insisted that the Spartans had failed to apply the Egyptian principle of the division of labour and that their constitution fell short of the perfection of the Egyptian model, about which he wrote: 'philosophers who undertake to discuss such topics and have won the greatest reputation prefer above all others the Egyptian form of government . . .'[142]

To whom was Isokrates referring? Froidefond plausibly postulates that it was to the Pythagoreans, and that Isokrates was drawing from their concept of, or even an actual writing on, 'Egyptian Politics'.[143] It takes the greatest Aryanist ingenuity to deny the strong ancient traditions – referred to by Herodotos and given in detail by later writers – that there was such a person as Pythagoras and that his school was established on the basis of his long studies in Egypt. Nevertheless, it has been attempted.[144] In any event, Isokrates was quite explicit about it: 'On a visit to Egypt he [Pythagoras] became a student of the religion of the people, and was the first to bring to the Greeks all philosophy.'[145]

Another less likely possibility is that by 'philosophers' Isokrates meant his great rival Plato and his *Republic*.[146] It is generally thought that the latter was written between 380 and 370 BC, that is after *Bousiris*, *c*.390. It is also believed that the work was the result of many years of thought and teaching, and that there were possibly earlier drafts.[147] The likelihood is, however, that priority should be given to *Bousiris*. Nevertheless, there are striking similarities between it and Plato's *Republic*. In the latter, too, there was a division of labour based on castes ruled by enlightened Guardians produced by careful selection and rigorous education. Plato was sharply hostile to the turbulence of democratic politics in Athens, and this kind of model was clearly comforting.

To what extent can it be related to Egypt? Apart from the resemblance to the explicitly Egyptian *Bousiris* we know that Egypt, where Plato had spent some time, probably around 390 BC, was a central concern of his later works.[148] In *Phaidros*, Plato had Sokrates declare that 'He [Theuth-Thoth the Egyptian god of wisdom] it was who invented numbers and arithmetic and geometry . . . and most important of all letters . . .'[149]

In *Philebos* and *Epinomis* Plato went into more detail on Thoth as the creator of writing, even of language and all sciences.[150] Elsewhere Plato praised Egyptian art and music and argued for their adoption in Greece.[151] Indeed, the only reason for doubting that his *Republic* was based on Egypt is the fact that he does not say so in the text. This omission, however, has an ancient explanation. As his earliest commentator, Krantor, wrote within a few generations of Plato:

> Plato's contemporaries mocked him, saying that he was not the inventor of his republic, but that he had copied Egyptian institutions. He attached so much importance to the mockers that he attributed to the Egyptians the story of the Athenians and the Atlantines to make them say that the Athenians had really lived under this regime at a certain moment in the past.[152]

Faced with all this evidence in favour of an Egyptian derivation, early modern scholars still associated Plato's Republic with Egypt. As Marx put it: 'Plato's Republic, in so far as division of labour is treated in it, as the formative principle of the state, is merely an Athenian idealization of the Egyptian system of castes.'[153]

Popper, who hates Plato, would have loved to tar him with an Egyptian brush. However, he was writing in a more systematically Aryanist age and, though fully aware of Krantor's charge, he has confined it to the footnotes and appears puzzled by Marx's remark.[154] Some scholars favourable to Plato have forcefully denounced the idea that he favoured an Egyptian type of caste system. The majority simply omit any mention of Egypt in connection with the *Republic*.[155]

In his dialogues, *Timaios* and *Kritias*, Plato referred to the wonders of the lost civilization of Atlantis and to its fiery collapse. It will be argued in Volume 2 that this refers to the volcanic destruction of Thera in 1626 BC and that the Atlanteans are an amalgam of northern peoples, the Hyksos who invaded Egypt in the middle of the 2nd millennium, and the 'Peoples of the Sea' who attacked it at the end of that millennium. What concerns us here, however, is Plato's perception of the historic relationships between Greece and Egypt.

As has been mentioned in the Introduction, there was a widespread but only late-attested tradition that Athens had been founded by Kekrops, the Egyptian from the city of Sais on the Western Delta. There was also a recognition that Nēit, the goddess of that city, was the same as Athena.[156] In the famous passage on the myth of Atlantis, Plato attributed to Kritias the story that when the great Athenian lawgiver Solon went to Sais in the early 6th century, when it was capital of Egypt, he was treated as a kinsman because of the special relationship felt by Saitians for Athenians. He was even granted an interview with senior Egyptian priests, one of whom, having condemned Solon with the famous words 'O Solon, Solon, you Greeks are always children. There is no such thing as an old Greek', went on to tell Solon that Athena had founded Athens before Sais, rather than the other way round.[157] He explained that the reason for the Athenians' lack of knowledge about this and the general Greek ignorance about their own past was that Greek culture had been periodically destroyed by disasters of fire and water, leaving no memory of Athens' former glory. In Egypt, however, thanks to her favoured position, institutions had been preserved.[158]

Thus, for Plato, if one wanted to return to the ancient Athenian institutions one had to turn to Egypt. In this way he resembled Isokrates, who both called for a Panhellenic combination of Athens and

Sparta and extolled the Egyptian constitution that was a purer version of the Lakedaimonian one. *The deeper they went towards the true Hellenic roots of Greece, the closer they came to Egypt.* One reason for this was that both Isokrates and Plato maintained that the great lawgivers and philosophers like Lykourgos, Solon and Pythagoras had all brought back Egyptian knowledge. Furthermore, Isokrates and Plato both believed in the colonizations of Pelops, Kadmos, Aigyptos and Danaos and seem to have accepted with Herodotos that the 'barbarians' brought important cultural baggage with them.[159] Even on the issue of the foundation of Athens, Plato was within the Ancient Model to the extent that he accepted that there was a 'genetic' cultural relationship between it and Sais. Thus, despite their ambivalence if not hostility to the ideas, the two leading intellectual figures of the early 4th century BC were forced to admit the critical importance of foreign colonization, and massive later cultural borrowing from Egypt and the Levant, in the formation of the Hellenic civilization they both loved so passionately.

ARISTOTLE

Aristotle was not only the pupil of Plato, he also studied at the Academy under Eudoxos of Knidos, the great mathematician and astronomer who is reported to have spent sixteen months in Egypt shaving his head in order to study with priests there.[160] Aristotle was also heavily influenced by Herodotos on Egypt, and was clearly fascinated by the country. Although at times he stressed the great antiquity of Mesopotamian and Iranian civilization, his considered opinion seems to have been that the Egyptians were the most ancient people.[161] Aristotle was equally contradictory on the issue of diffusionism. At times he stated his belief in independent invention by different cultures, but at others he argued that the Egyptians had created the caste system and hence 'Egypt was the cradle of mathematics because the caste of priests were given great leisure, *scholē*.'[162] According to him, the priests had invented the *mathēmatikai technai* (mathematical arts), which included geometry, arithmetic and astronomy, which the Greeks were beginning to possess.[163] In fact his admiration for Egypt went beyond that of Herodotos in one respect. Where Herodotos believed that the Egyptians had developed geometry, the key science, for practical reasons – to measure land after landmarks had been washed away by the Nile Flood – Aristotle maintained that it had been developed theoretically by the priests.[164]

THEORIES OF COLONIZATION AND LATER BORROWING IN THE HELLENISTIC WORLD

Amongst many other things Aristotle was, of course, the tutor of Alexander the Great.[165] With the extraordinary Macedonian conquest of the Persian Empire in the 330s BC, there was a great surge of Greek interest in all Oriental civilizations, and especially in that of Egypt. It was in the years immediately after the conquest that the Egyptian priest Manetho wrote a history of Egypt in Greek in which he set out the scheme of 33 dynasties which remains the basis of the historiography of Ancient Egypt.[166] It was also at about this time that Hekataios of Abdera set out his view that the traditions of the Egyptian expulsion of the Hyksos, the Israelite Exodus and that of Danaos' landing in Argos were three parallel versions of the same story:

> The natives of the land surmised that unless they removed the foreigners their troubles would never be resolved. At once, therefore, the aliens were driven from the country and the most outstanding and active among them banded together and, as some say, were cast ashore in Greece and certain other regions; their teachers were notable men, among them being Danaos and Kadmos. But the greater number were driven into what is now called Judaea, which is not far from Egypt and at that time was utterly uninhabited. The colony was headed by a man called Moses.[167]

It seems to have been on this basis – and the belief expressed by Herodotos that the ancestry of the Spartan kings went up to the Hyksos colonists – that, sometime around 300 BC, Areios King of Sparta wrote to Jerusalem beginning:

To Onias High Priest, greeting. A document has come to light which
shows that the Spartans and Jews are kinsmen descended alike from
Abraham.[168]

References to the Egypto-Phoenician colonizations in the Hellenistic
period are too frequent to be given in full here. Debates were not on the
existence of the landings but on their specifics: the nationality of the
leaders, their points of departure or their dates.[169]

The tension between Greek cultural pride and respect for the
ancient civilizations seems to have become even more intense with
Alexander's extraordinary conquests before 330 BC. This can be seen,
for instance, in the reactions to Zeno of Kition, the Phoenician
who founded Stoicism at the turn of the 3rd century BC. He was
mocked by his rivals as a 'little Phoenician', yet as a pupil wrote of
him:

> With much toil thou didst found a great new school,
> Chaste parent of unfearing liberty,
> And if thy native country was Phoenicia,
> What need to slight thee? Came not Kadmos thence,
> Who gave to Greece her books and art of writing?[170]

Diodoros Sikeliotes, writing in the 1st century BC, expressed the same
confusion, if not schizophrenia, on the issue of the 'barbarians' who
civilized Greece near the beginning of his massive *Library of History*
when he wrote:

> The first peoples which we shall discuss will be the barbarians, not
> that we consider them to be earlier than the Greeks, as Ephoros has
> said, but because we wish to set forth most of the facts about them at
> the outset, in order that we may not, by beginning with the various
> accounts given by the Greeks, have to interpolate in the different
> narrations of their early history any event connected with another
> people.[171]

In Volume V of his work Diodoros cited the Rhodian historian Zeno
who maintained that Greeks – or the mysterious Heliadai from Rhodes
– had brought culture to the Egyptians but a great flood had wiped out

all memory of it, just as the Athenians had forgotten that Athens was senior to Sais:

> And it was because of reasons such as these that many generations later men supposed that Kadmos, the son of Agenor, had been the first to bring the letters from Phoenicia to Greece.[172]

Presumably still following Zeno, Diodoros went on to detail how both Danaos and Kadmos had left traces on Rhodes while on their way to colonize Greece.[173] Like Plato's belief in the priority of Athens over Sais, Zeno's scheme is an inverted form of the Ancient Model rather than one within the Aryan Model. There is no mention of an invasion from north of Greece and the scheme still maintains a 'genetic' relationship between Greek and Egypto-Phoenician culture and civilization. The view that Greece civilized Egypt has been too much even for the most ardent Aryanists. Diodoros' modern translator, Professor Oldfather, notes at this point:

> Book I, *passim*, presents the claims put forward by the Egyptians for the priority of their civilization; the counterclaims of the Greeks here set forth are empty boasting.[174]

The main thrust of Diodoros' work is his belief in Egypt and, to a lesser extent, other Eastern civilizations as the fount of world civilization:

> And since Egypt is the country where mythology places the origin of the gods, where the earliest observations of the stars are said to have been made, and where, furthermore, many noteworthy deeds of great men are recorded, we shall begin our history with the events connected with Egypt.[175]

Not only did Diodoros frequently refer to the colonizations of Thebes and Argos by Kadmos and Danaos but he devoted considerable space, near the beginning of his work, to Saitian claims that Kekrops and other early Athenian kings had been Egyptians, and their plausible arguments for a special relationship between Athens and Egypt.[176]

This colonization was not generally accepted in Hellenistic and Roman times, but belief in the colonizations of the Western Peloponnese and Thebes seems to have been universal. Pausanias'

Guide to Greece, written in the 2nd century AD, is full of references to them:

> The people of Troizen [in the Argolid] . . . say the first human being to exist in their country was Oros, which looks to me like an Egyptian name, certainly not a Greek one.[177]

> There is another road out of Lerna right down by the sea to what they call the Birthplace; by the sea is a little sanctuary of Poseidon of the Birth. Next to this are the landings, where they say Danaos and his sons first landed in the Argolid.[178]

The linking of the legendary landings with birth is fascinating, as is the fact that Poseidon was the chief god of the Mycenaeans and Seth – whom I see as his Egyptian counterpart – was the chief god of the Hyksos:[179]

> In my opinion the Nauplians were Egyptians at an earlier period who arrived in the Argolid with Danaos' fleet and were settled three generations later by Amymone's son Nauplios in Nauplia.[180]

> When Kadmos marched in [to the Thebaid] with a Phoenician army and they [the Hyantes and the Aones] lost a battle, the Hyantes ran away the very next night, but the Aones made a ritual supplication so that Kadmos let them stay and intermarry with his Phoenicians.[181]

The relation of the names Hyantes and the Aones to the name Ionian and the Egyptian *'Iwn (tyw')* (barbarian) has been discussed above (see p. 83).[182] There is no doubt, then, that Pausanias was convinced of the actuality of the colonizations and believed that there were still many direct signs of them in his time, the 2nd century AD.

PLUTARCH'S ATTACK ON HERODOTOS

The 2nd century AD also saw the closest to what one might call an attack on the Ancient Model. It came in a long essay by the prolific writer Plutarch, entitled 'On the Malice of Herodotos', in which he levelled many charges against Herodotos, one of which was that of being 'philobarbarous':

> He says that the Greeks learnt about processions and national festivals from the Egyptians as well as the worship of the twelve gods; the very name of Dionysos, he says, was learnt from the Egyptians by Melampous, and he taught the rest of the Greeks; and the mysteries and secret rituals connected with Demeter were brought from Egypt by the daughters of Danaos . . . Nor is this the worst. He traces the ancestry of Herakles to Perseus and says Perseus, according to the Persian account, was an Assyrian; 'and the chiefs of the Dorians' he says, 'would be established as pure-blooded Egyptians . . .'; not only is he anxious to establish an Egyptian and a Phoenician Herakles; he says that our own Herakles was born after the other two, and he wants to remove him from Greece and make a foreigner out of him. Yet of the learned men of old neither Homer nor Hesiod . . . ever mentioned an Egyptian or a Phoenician Herakles, but all of them knew only one, our own Herakles who is both Boiotian and Argive . . .[183]

Plutarch clearly believed that his audience would be outraged by Herodotos' ideas on these subjects, but it is interesting to note that he cites only ancient authority on the question of Herakles and that he does not confront the colonizations of Danaos and Kadmos directly. Given the deep knowledge and appreciation of Egyptian religion expressed in his *On Isis and Osiris*, and above all his conviction of its essential identity with Greek religion, there is also serious doubt as to whether Plutarch himself disbelieved Herodotos' claims for the foreign origins of so much of Greek culture. It would seem more likely that Plutarch's assault on Herodotos' 'barbarophilia' was merely a tool to be used in his general attack upon him. It is also fascinating to note that none of the modern detractors of the Ancient Model relied on this essay. One reason for this, as two of his translators have written, is that

> While this essay has offended lovers of Herodotos, it has also disturbed admirers of Plutarch, who have found it hard to believe

that so kindly and good-natured an author could himself write with such fierce malice and thus lay himself open to charges similar to those he levels against Herodotos.[184]

More importantly, the modern scholars have been eager to rely on 'ancient' sources rather than 'late' ones, by which they – living in the 19th or 20th century AD – mean authors writing after the 5th century BC. This preference is influenced by – if not based on – the fact that in Late Classical and Hellenistic Greece the overwhelming weight of testimony is in favour both of the colonizations and of Greek religion having derived from the Egyptian. Before coming to this, however, we should consider the impact of Egyptian religion on Greece in Hellenistic and Roman times.

THE TRIUMPH OF EGYPTIAN RELIGION

The movement among Greeks and other Mediterranean peoples to worship the gods under their Egyptian names began well before Alexander's conquests and the syncretism of Hellenistic times. Early in the 5th century BC the poet Pindar wrote a *Hymn to Ammon*, which opened 'Ammon King of Olympos'. This cult of the Libyan variant of the Egyptian Amon was attached to Pindar's native town of Thebes.[185] However, it was also strong in Sparta, and Pausanias wrote about the sanctuary of Ammon in Aphytis in Sparta:

> The Lakonians seem to have used the Libyan oracle more than anyone else in Greece since the beginning. Ammon is not more honoured by the Libyan Ammonians than he is at Aphytis.[186]

It is impossible to say what Pausanias meant by 'since the beginning'. In any event, it must have been before the end of the 5th century that the brother of the great Spartan general Lysander was called Libys because the family had a traditional relationship with the *basileis* (kings or priests) of the Ammonians, and Lysander himself consulted the oracle.[187] By the 4th century Am(m)on was being worshipped in Athens, and one of its sacred triremes was dedicated to him.[188]

ALEXANDER SON OF AMMON

Alexander the Great clearly considered himself to be a son of Ammon. After his conquest of Egypt he set out into the desert to consult the god's great oracle at the Libyan oasis of Siwa. The oracle told Alexander that he was the god's son, which explains why from then on Alexander's coins portrayed him as a horned Ammon.[189] Modern historians describe as slanders many reports that in the last year of his life Alexander dressed himself and demanded worship in the guise of a number of gods and goddesses and that 'Alexander even desired people to bow to the earth before him, from the idea that Ammon was his father rather than Philip.'[190]

Who, then, was the son of Ammon? According to early Egyptian tradition, Osiris was the son of Ra. With the rise of the cult of Amon in the 12th Dynasty the two came together as Amon-Ra. By the late New Kingdom there was seen to be a mystic union between Ra and Osiris.[191] Thus the thorough confusion between Ammon and Dionysos found in Diodoros Sikeliotes or his source from the 2nd century BC, the Alexandrian Dionysios Skytobrachion, would seem to have precedents in Egyptian theology.[192] In any event Alexander appears to have seen himself as this syncretic divinity, both Ammon and his son.

There is no doubt that the actual conquests of Alexander increased the importance of the myths of the vast eastern civilizing expedition of Dionysos or – as Diodoros named him – of Osiris, traces of which can be found in Egyptian tradition from the 18th Dynasty or even the Middle Kingdom.[193] Even in Greece, as James Frazer pointed out, the scheme had been outlined by Euripides before Alexander was born.[194] Alexander's relationship with Dionysos was strained and he felt some competition with him, at least after his conquests.[195] When he reached Nysa in the mountains of North-West India and was told by the inhabitants of its association with the god, it is reported that

he was very ready to believe the tale about the journeys of Dionysos; he was also ready to credit that Nysa was founded by Dionysos, in which case he had already reached the point which Dionysos had reached, and would go even further than Dionysos.[196]

There are also unreliable reports of his travelling through India 'in mimicry of the Bacchic revelry of Dionysos'.[197] There is no doubt about the political and cultic attention he attached to his many long drinking bouts, and the civilizing mission of Osiris/Dionysos provides a crucial background for Alexander's own activities along these lines. Thus his identification as the son of Ammon, parallel to and rival of Dionysos, was central to his life project. Aryanist historians have preferred to dwell on his reading of Xenophon and his identification and rivalry with Achilles, and there is no doubt that these were significant factors in his decision to invade Asia. But they were less important than his essentially Egyptian religious mission. The fact that his body was buried in Egypt rather than in Greece or Persia cannot simply be attributed to the ruthlessness of his general Ptolemy, who succeeded him as ruler of Egypt. It shows the centrality of that country to Alexander's life and self-image.[198]

Ptolemy and his successors, right up to the Kleopatra of Caesar and Antony, made great use of Egyptian religion both to gain the respect and affection of their Egyptian subjects and to give them cultural power when dealing with the other states that arose from the fragments of Alexander's empire.[199] Nevertheless, this is not enough to explain the huge expansion of Egyptian religion during this period, in what has been called 'the conquest of the Occident by Oriental Religion'.[200]

The Egyptian mother goddess Isis, for instance, had been worshipped in Athens since the 5th century, not merely by resident Egyptians but by native Athenians.[201] By the 2nd century BC there was a temple of Isis near the Akropolis and Athens was officially encouraging its dependencies to take up Egyptian cults.[202] Even on Delos, especially sanctified to Apollo, cults of Isis and Anubis were made official in a move that was in no way connected to the Ptolemaic kingdom which had lost control of the island by that time.[203] Indeed, by the 2nd century AD Pausanias, who made no mention of other Oriental cults, reported Egyptian temples or shrines in Athens, Corinth, Thebes and many places in the Argolid, Messenia, Achaia and Phokis.[204]

It should be stressed that Greece had experienced only part of a wave that had spread throughout the Roman Empire.[205] For instance, the most important shrines discovered at Pompeii from 79 AD – when it was overwhelmed by the eruption of Vesuvius – were 'Egyptian'. Tiberius had banished Egyptian – and Jewish – religion from Rome itself. But the cults were soon restored and later emperors, particularly Domitian and Hadrian, were passionately devoted to the Egyptian gods.[206] The latter even tried to turn his favourite Antinoos into an Egyptian god, and in many ways his extraordinary pleasure garden at Tivoli, east of Rome, is best seen as an Egyptian funerary complex for his divine lover.[207] Marcus Aurelius, Septimius Severus, Caracalla, Diocletian and other emperors visited Egypt and all reports emphasized how respectful they were towards Egyptian religion and culture.[208] Whatever their personal feelings, such an attitude would seem to have been politically necessary given the central role of Egyptian religion throughout the Empire.

Such enthusiasm provoked a backlash. The modern Dutch scholars Smelik and Hemelrijk, who have tried valiantly to scrape up instances of Greek hostility to Egyptian culture, have a rather easier time when it comes to Rome. The weak point in the Egyptian armour was the worship of animals. Cicero, for instance, found this strange 'in that most uncorrupted nation of the Egyptians which preserves written records of events of very many ages'.[209] The later satirists Juvenal and Lucian were unrestrained in their attacks on this zoolatry, and on Egypt as a whole.[210]

Most writers believed this worship to be symbolic and allegorical, a view laid out most clearly by Plutarch in *On Isis and Osiris*. This work is recognized even by scholars working in the Aryan Model as the single most important source on Egyptian religion; furthermore, its interpretations have increasingly been confirmed with the advance of Egyptology.[211]

Plutarch spelled out in detail the general image of Egyptian religion that appears to have been common among cultivated Greeks, at least since the 4th century BC. According to this, the zoolatry and apparent superstition of Egyptian religion were merely an allegorical veneer for the masses: the priests, and/or those who had been initiated, knew that in reality the zoolatry and fantastic myths concealed deep abstractions and a profound understanding of the universe. In *On Isis and Osiris*, Egypt's religious philosophy was principally concerned not with the ephemeral, material world of 'becoming' with its growth and decay, but with the immortal realm of 'being' which was especially manifested in numbers, geometry and astronomy.

All this, of course, strikingly resembled the ideas of Plato, the Pythagoreans and Orphics, not only in content but often in the form of words used to describe them. 19th- and 20th-century scholars have therefore seen Plutarch's work as a prime example of what is called *interpretatio Graeca*, which has been well described as follows:

> The Greek observer was not usually in a position to understand Egyptian religion from the inside; an initial obstacle was his ignorance of Egyptian. Sometimes an equation or an explanation was based on a misunderstanding of an Egyptian phenomenon, or on a modification introduced on a Greek parallel. Each deviation, whether radical or slight, contributed to a remove from the true picture.[212]

A major modern scholar has devoted a whole book to this Greek 'mirage' of Egypt.[213] This *interpretatio Germanica* or axiom – that Egyptian religion and philosophy were necessarily crude and shallow – has difficulties with such superbly intelligent men as Eudoxos who, according to all reports, lived with the priests and learnt Egyptian, and clearly had a great respect and enthusiasm for Egyptian culture. The fundamental weaknesses of the modern scheme, however, are its lack of self-consciousness and the positivist sense of *Besserwissen*, 'knowing better' than the Ancients. This is true even of the beloved Greeks, who were superior in every aspect of their culture except their writing of ancient history and their understanding of Greece's relationships with other cultures.

For Plutarch's contemporaries and later thinkers within the Ancient Model, the striking similarities between Plutarch's description of Egyptian religion and philosophy and those of Plato and the Pythagoreans provided no difficulty whatever. They were simply the result of the fact that – as everyone knew – Plato, Pythagoras and Orpheus had taken their ideas from Egypt. Moreover, Plutarch also maintained that there were more fundamental links between Egyptian and Greek religion. *On Isis and Osiris* was dedicated to Klea, to whom he wrote:

That Osiris is identical with Dionysos who could more fittingly know than yourself, Klea? For you are the head of the inspired maidens [devotees of Dionysos] of Delphi, and have been consecrated by your father and mother in the holy rites of Osiris.

He went on to give details of cultic similarities between Egyptian and Delphic cults.[214] Altogether, Plutarch identified Dionysos with Osiris three times in this work.[215] Although he was not as explicit on the identity of Isis and Demeter, there is no doubt that he was equally certain about it. There are, for instance, many detailed parallels between his descriptions of Isis' troubles in Byblos and those portrayed in Eleusis in the *Homeric Hymn to Demeter*. This is frequently used by Aryanist scholars as a clear example of Plutarch's *interpretatio Graeca*.[216]

It may be so in this case. I would argue, however, that it is probable that the mystery cult at Eleusis, to which the Hymn is clearly linked, originated from Egypt, as the Ancients believed.[217] Even if it were not, there is archaeological evidence to show that Isis was identified with Demeter at Eleusis by the 9th ecentury – that is, before the conventional dating of the Hymn.[218] In any event, there is absolutely no reason to doubt that Plutarch saw the two as manifestations of the same divinity. All in all, it is clear that Plutarch believed both that much of Greek philosophy had been introduced from Egypt and that there was a fundamental unity between Egyptian and Greek religion. He further maintained that the former was purer and older.

This view of Egyptian religion played a central role in the two major 'novels' of the 2nd century AD, Heliodoros' *Aithiopika* and Apuleius' *Metamorphoses* or *The Golden Ass*. In his morally elevating and romantic story with a beautiful and virtuous black heroine, Heliodoros expressed great admiration for the Ethiopians and their gymnosophists (naked philosophers or gurus), but *Aithiopika* is focused on Egypt and the moral superiority of its religion. It also stresses the passionate interest taken in it by Greek priests, who saw it as the key to their own cults. When talking about the priests of Delphi bombarding a visiting Egyptian with questions, the author wrote:

In short, they forgot none of the interesting features of Egypt, for there is no country in the world which Greeks prefer to hear about.[219]

Apuleius' *The Golden Ass*, by contrast, is a satire, but at its serious centre are Egyptian mysteries and the figures of Isis, the mistress of disguises and transformations, and Osiris/Dionysos behind her. At the book's climax the goddess announces to the hero:

> Thus the Phrygians, earliest of all races, call me Pessinuntia, mother of all gods. Thus the Athenians, sprung from their own soil, call me Cecropeian Minerva and the sea-tossed Cyprians call me Paphian Venus, the archer Cretans Diana, Dictynna, and the tri-lingual Sicilians Proserpine; to the Eleusinians I am Ceres, the ancient godess, to others Juno, to others Bellona and Hecate and Rhamnusia. But the Ethiopians, who are illumined by the first rays of the sun-god as he is born every day, together with the Africans and Egyptians, who excel through having the original doctrine, honour me with my distinctive rites and give me my true name of Queen Isis.[220]

The belief that Egyptian religion and rites were the original and 'true' ones made the Greek and other local forms redundant, and this explains the massive turning away from the latter. As the Neo-Platonist philosopher Iamblichos wrote at the end of the pagan period in the 4th century AD:

> Rather think that as the Egyptians were the first of men to be allotted the participation of the gods, the gods when invoked rejoice in Egyptian rites.[221]

The repetition and frequent quotation in this chapter comes from the need I feel to hammer home the conventionality in Antiquity of a picture that is very unconventional in modern Classical studies. The unfamiliarity of this approach itself underscores the fact that proponents of the Aryan Model are unable to quote extensively to back their case. All I claim in this chapter is that after the 5th century BC – the only period from which we have any substantial knowledge of them – the Ancient Greeks, though proud of themselves and their recent accomplishments, did not see their political institutions, science, philosophy or religion as original. Instead they derived them – through the early colonization and later study by Greeks abroad – from the East in general and Egypt in particular.

CHAPTER II

Egyptian Wisdom and Greek transmission from the Dark Ages to the Renaissance

I N THIS CHAPTER I am concerned with the survival of Ancient Egypt after the fall of its high civilization. In the first place we find the survival of Egyptian religion both within Christianity and outside it in heretical sects like those of the Gnostics, and in the Hermetic tradition that was frankly pagan. Far more widespread than these direct continuations, however, was the general admiration for Ancient Egypt among the educated elite. Egypt, though subordinated to the Christian and biblical traditions on issues of religion and morality, was clearly placed as the source of all 'Gentile' or secular wisdom. Thus no one before 1600 seriously questioned either the belief that Greek civilization and philosophy derived from Egypt, or that the chief ways in which they had been transmitted were through Egyptian colonizations of Greece and later Greek study in Egypt.

The Murder of Hypatia

In 390 AD the temple of Serapis and the adjacent great library of Alexandria were destroyed by a Christian mob; twenty-five years later, the brilliant and beautiful philosopher and mathematician Hypatia was gruesomely murdered in the same city by a gang of monks instigated by

St Cyril. These two acts of violence mark the end of Egypto-Paganism and the beginning of the Christian Dark Ages.[1]

It is hardly surprising that scholars working within the Aryan Model prefer to neglect the Christian factor and see these events as representing a resurgence of Egyptian Oriental fanaticism against Hellenistic rationalism.[2] But, if one disregards the absurd implication that Europeans cannot be fanatical, these two explanations – that the fanatical mob was both Christian and Egyptian – are not mutually exclusive. By the 4th century AD, Egypt was a passionately – if not the most passionately – Christian province in the Roman Empire.

THE COLLAPSE OF
EGYPTO-PAGAN RELIGION

What had happened? Egyptian religion had collapsed with remarkable speed between 130 and 230 AD. Why did the heartland of paganism convert to Christianity earlier and more fervently than all the other Roman provinces? This is linked to the larger problem: why did the whole of the pagan world convert to Christianity? For Christian historians this event is a non-problem: naturally, when the Egyptians or any other people saw the light of 'true religion', they left their idolatrous paganism. For historians without this prior commitment, the phenomenon is less easy to explain.

At a broader level it can be argued that with the *anomia* and the breakdown of traditional local structures in the Hellenistic and Roman empires there was a natural tendency towards monotheism, a heavenly reflection of terrestrial world empires. This would be demonstrated first by the enormous expansion of Judaism – largely through proselytizing – throughout the Mediterranean after 300 BC. Indeed, by the middle of the 1st century AD Jews formed between 5 and 10 per cent of the population of the Roman Empire.[3] In 116–17, however, there was a huge revolt in the Diaspora, far greater than the better-known ones of the Zealots and Bar Kokhba in Judaea of 66–70 and 132–5.

The Diaspora revolt was followed by a genocidal repression in Cyprus, Cyrene and, above all, Alexandria which completely destroyed the brilliant culture of Hellenized Jewry.[4] Even before that, although

Jews formed a considerable proportion of the population of Egypt, Judaism was too foreign to absorb Egyptian culture. Like the Indians and Chinese in 19th- and 20th-century colonial empires, or the later Jews in Eastern Europe, the Egyptian Jews were middlemen between the ruling Greeks and the Egyptian people. And, in all these cases, it suited the rulers very well to maintain tension between the natives and the *allogenes*, the foreign middle class. Thus for the rest of the 2nd century and beyond, the elimination of the Jews meant that Christianity – which in any event was more loosely tied to a particular people – had no serious rival as a proselytizing religion.

It would seem plausible to suppose that Egyptian religion collapsed with that of the pharaonic state and Egyptian nationality. This argument has some force, but it also has some problems. Egypt had been ruled by foreigners for most of the time since 700 BC; some, like the Ethiopians and the Ptolemaic Greeks, had ruled their whole empires from Egypt, but the Persians were like the Romans in considering Egypt as a – rather special – province. Most rulers considered good relations with Egyptian religion essential to their control of the country. It is true that the Persians did at times persecute Egyptian religion, but on the whole they too worked with it.[5] The very favourable attitude of their Macedonian successors has been described in Chapter I: Egyptian religion flourished and expanded throughout this period, apparently reaching a peak in the first half of the 2nd century AD. This historical pattern makes its subsequent collapse seem all the more remarkable. For, if foreign persecution had been the crucial factor, the collapse would have been more likely in the 6th or 4th century BC, under the Persians, than in the 2nd century AD when Egyptian religion was basking under Roman imperial favour.

The Ptolemies in Egypt, rather like the Mongols and Manchus in China, were – while posing as its champions – very conscious of the dangers of absorption by the native civilization. They were determined to preserve their own culture and rule through Greeks. Kleopatra VII, the queen of Antony and Caesar, was the first – and last – of the dynasty to learn Egyptian. Thus although the Egyptian priests objectively collaborated with the new foreign rulers, as they had with the earlier ones, they tried personally to stay aloof and to some extent continued to represent Egyptian 'nationalism'. By the 2nd century AD, however, after 400 years of Greek rule, the Roman rulers and the Macedonian and Egyptian upper classes – including the priesthoods – had fused in a common Hellenic civilization with Egyptian religion. The very enthusiasm of the Roman emperors for Egyptian religion and its 'internationalization' seems to have weakened the priests' positions as champions of Egypt.

There is no doubt that by the 3rd and 4th centuries AD there was a definite class basis to hostility to the old religion and that, as elsewhere, the Christians initially represented the poor and then the middle classes against the rich. It is therefore possible that – despite the well-publicized austerity of the priests' lifestyle – the huge wealth of the temples and the priesthood's exploitation of the poor caused resentment.[6] Thus after the 2nd century, despite the fact that Christianity came from Palestine and was consciously international, it came to represent the poor and middle-class Egyptians against the cosmopolitan Hellenized upper classes with their Egyptian pagan religion.

CHRISTIANITY, STARS AND FISH

There is little doubt that these social and national factors played a major part in the destruction of organized Egyptian religion. But they seem to have been slowly-growing, long-term tensions or flaws rather than acute problems, and two new features were present in the 2nd century. First – as conventional wisdom rightly maintains – there was the availability of Christianity, monotheist and universal in a way that Judaism could never quite be, and with an exceptional enthusiasm and capacity for organization. Secondly, there was the general belief that the old world was coming to an end and that a new age was about to begin.

Messianism or millenarianism is the belief in the imminent arrival of a new order or millennium of harmony and justice when the Messiah and the saints 'go marching in'. It is a frequent response to distress of all sorts, but especially to military conquest and economic and cultural domination by foreigners. Indeed, the idea that some outside force will sweep down and overthrow the present illegitimate rulers so that 'the first shall be last and the last shall be first' has been fundamental to Judaism, at least since the captivity in Babylon in the 6th century BC. It is clear, however, that this feeling intensified after about 50 BC and was very prominent for the next 200 years; furthermore, the sense of apocalypse was not restricted to Jews. The crisis can be partially explained by a number of political and economic changes. There were the unprecedented success of the Romans in uniting the Mediterranean, the savage civil wars between the Roman warlords; and finally, in 31 BC, the establishment of the Roman Empire – often portrayed as a new age – under Augustus.

For the Jews, there was the additional factor of the change in Roman policy from friendship with them as allies against their common enemy the Greek Seleukids, who ruled most of South-West Asia; to neutrality, to preserve the balance of power; to hostility, once the Hellenistic kingdoms had been crushed and the whole Empire was turned into a Roman-Greek condominium. Messianism had long been central to Jewish tradition. The first Messiah in the Bible was Cyrus, the king of Persia who released the Jews – at least those who wanted to leave – from Exile in Babylon.[7] Jewish Messianism seems to have retained the hope that deliverance would come from the East and in particular from the Parthians, the new rulers of Persia who also ruled Mesopotamia, with its large Jewish population, and who like the Jews had also fought a war of independence against the Seleukids. There is also little doubt that the risings of 115 and 116, which were clearly seen by their participants in Messianic terms, were connected to the Emperor Trajan's major attack on Parthia in those years.[8]

I should reiterate, however, that the Messianism between 50 BC and 150 AD, and the idea that a new age was dawning, were not restricted to Jews, nor can they be completely explained in terms of the Roman political changes mentioned above. Another element was the astrological change from the age of Aries to that of Pisces. Without getting into the argument over when and by whom the precession of the equinoxes was discovered, there is no disagreement that it was widely known by 50 BC.[9] The significance in this context is that over the period between 50 BC and 150 AD the spring equinox shifted from Aries to Pisces.*

It is only in this concatenation of political, economic, social and astrological changes that one can understand the Roman poet Virgil's Fourth *Eclogue*, written in 40 BC, which states near its beginning:

> Now ... the great line of centuries begins anew ... Only do thou, sweet Lucina, smile on the birth of a child, under whom the iron brood shall first cease, and a golden race spring up throughout the world! Thine own Apollo is now king!

Virgil goes on to greet the child's father, Pollio, who has become Consul, as bringing in 'a glorious age'; but history will repeat itself and there will be a new War of Troy and other great historical events.[10] With modern discomfort at what would seem to be a prefiguration of the advent of Christ, most Classicists have used their monist approach to claim that these are simply poetic conceits around the birth of a friend's child. It would seem much more plausible to suppose that the poet – as a poet – employed several different levels of meaning: the birth of Pollio's child; the beginning of a peaceful age under his and Pollio's patron, Augustus. The words also seem to indicate the coming of a new young divinity. They certainly refer to a cosmic or astral change of age, which can only be the new age of Pisces.

Stars are often associated with great and Messianic leaders, from Cyrus, who founded the Persian Empire in the 6th century BC, to the Chinese rebel leader of the 8th century AD, An Lushan.[11] It is particularly striking to note how often stars appear in association with major leaders during the period of crisis from 50 BC to 150 AD; from the comet seen as representing the spirit of Julius Caesar to the star of Bethlehem and that associated with Hadrian's new god Antinoos; while

---

* The precession is the result of a wobble in the rotation of the solar system which results in the points fixed by that system changing in relation to the stars beyond. In the measure most commonly used, the spring equinox appears 'earlier' and 'earlier' in terms of signs of the zodiac. It is because the equinox shifts from one zodiacal 'house' to the one preceding it approximately every 2,100 years that astrologers are now telling us to prepare for the age of Aquarius a century or two hence, when the spring equinox will occur in that 'house'.)

the last Messianic leader of Jewish resistance was known – at least by his enemies – as Bar Kokhba, 'son of a star'. Indeed, the aged Rabbi Akiba, the cautious and sane founder of modern Judaism who had lived through and accommodated himself to the catastrophic defeat and the destruction of Jerusalem in 70 AD, was so swept away by Bar Kokhba's initial successes that he saw it as the new age and quoted Numbers 24:17 – 'a star hath trodden forth from Jacob'.[12]

From Plutarch's *On Isis and Osiris*, we know the extreme importance attached to astronomical movements as signs of the ideal world of the stars and geometry and the integral relation seen, at least in late Egyptian religion, between the stars and the gods. We also know that astronomers in Hellenistic Egypt were concerned with the precession. During the 2nd century AD the impact of the precession would seem to have been redoubled by an extraordinary astronomical coincidence.[13] To explain: Ancient Egypt had a number of sophisticated calendrical systems. Its two most commonly used 'years' were one based on a civil calendar of 365 days, and the 'Sothic year' tied to the rising of the star Sirius, which was seen to presage the beginning of the Nile Flood.[14] As the astronomical year is a little under 365.25 days, the civil year advanced beyond it at a rate of approximately a day every four years. The two coincided only every 1460 years, and such a coincidence was noted for 139 AD! Thus the Egyptian priesthoods, who were closely tied to the stars, were given a double message of the end of an epoch.

In 130 AD the Emperor Hadrian and his young lover Antinoos had long consultations with the priests of Thoth, the divinity of wisdom and measurement, at his chief cult site of Hermopolis. Soon after that, Antinoos was found drowned in the Nile; a major Egyptian tradition saw Osiris as having drowned.[15] The whole affair was meant to be – and remains – a mystery. However, the consensus today is that it was a voluntary sacrifice, made to avert some sort of catastrophe.[16] It is certain that Hadrian immediately proclaimed Antinoos to be a new Osiris and the cult that he promoted had a success which, though short-lived, seems to have gone beyond its imperial patronage.

Whether or not Antinoos was meant to be the new saviour for the new age can only be a matter for speculation. There is no doubt, however, that the Christians saw their new Osiris, Jesus, in this way. There were,

of course, many other traditional aspects of Christ, but at this point
I should like to raise a new sacred image, that of the fish. Fish were
not prominent in either the Egyptian or the Jewish religious traditions.
In Egypt, certain fish were associated with certain gods, and in some
Egyptian 'nomes' or districts particular species of fish were worshipped
and considered taboo. Furthermore in late times, legends arose that fish
had eaten Osiris' phallus and the word *bwt* (fish), written as such, could
mean 'abomination'. Nevertheless, fish cannot be considered in any
way central to Egyptian religion.[17]

Apart from the dubious case of the Philistine god Dagôn, fish appear
to have had no religious connotations in the Old Testament.[18] In the
New, by contrast, they play a prominent role. Key disciples were
fishermen, and fishing images abound. There is the miracle of the two
fishes and the five loaves of bread. Even more strikingly, in the Gospel
according to St John, Christ gave his disciples fish as the Eucharist.[19]
This theme, and the idea that fish were central to the Last Supper, were
standard in early Christian iconography.[20] In the sense of transubstan-
tiation, Christ was not merely bread or grain like Osiris, he was a fish or
– as was equally often represented – two fishes. As Tertullian, the
brilliant early Christian thinker, wrote around the year 200: 'We little
fishes, after the image of our Ἰχθύς, [Ichthys, the Greek word for 'fish']
are born in water.'[21]

This belief explains the use of the symbol of the fish to represent
Christ and the Christians. The latter is often attributed to the acrostic
on Ἰχθῦς of Ἰησοῦς Χριστὸς θεοῦ υἱὸς σωτήρ (Jesus Christ, Son of
God, Saviour). However, the symbol of the fish is attested, if anything,
earlier than the spelling of the word, and it would seem more likely that
the acrostic was an explanation of the symbol rather than the other way
round. Interestingly, Christian representations of the fish first appear at
the beginning of the 2nd century in Alexandria. All in all, there is very
little doubt that despite the equally strong ram-lamb Arien symbolism
surrounding Jesus, the use of a fish – or, more specifically, two fishes, as
in the sign of the zodiac – shows that the early Christians saw
themselves, and were seen by others, as followers of the new religion of
the new Piscean age.

Let me recapitulate – in the 2nd century AD, in addition to the long-term social, economic and national pressures on Egyptian religion, the extraordinary coincidence of the change from Aries to Pisces and the completion of the cycle of the Sothic and civil years created a powerful self-destructive force at its astronomical heart. Furthermore, not only did Egyptian religion contain a deep cyclical sense but it was centred on the concepts of birth, death and rebirth. It even included the possibility that although the gods were long-lived, they were not necessarily immortal. As Professor Hornung writes:

> We can therefore assume that the possibility of a time without the gods was much more firmly grounded in the Egyptians' awareness than the few clear allusions to it would suggest. A phrase such as *m drw ntrw* 'in the realm of the gods', in the senses of 'so long as the gods are there' is found in Graeco-Roman temple texts . . . otherwise eschatology is . . . the domain of magical spells.[22]

It is in this context that one must read the *Lament* found in one of the *Hermetic Texts*:

> There will come a time when it will be seen that in vain have the Egyptians honoured the divinity with pious mind and with assiduous service. All their holy worship will become inefficacious. The gods leaving the earth will go back to heaven; they will abandon Egypt; this land, once the home of religion, will be widowed of its gods and left destitute. Strangers will fill this country, and not only will there no longer be care for religious observances but, a yet more painful thing, it will be laid down under so-called laws, under pain of punishments, that all must abstain from acts of piety or cult towards the gods . . . The Scythian or the Indian, or some other such barbarous neighbour, will establish himself in Egypt.

However, as in many biblical prophecies and apocalypses, the 'malice' of the enemies of true religion would be destroyed by

> the Lord and Father . . . and by the demiurge of the One God . . . either by effacing it in a deluge or by consuming it by fire, or by destroying it by pestilential maladies . . . Then he will bring back the world to its first beauty . . . That is what the rebirth of the world will

be: a renewal of all good things and most solemn restoration of
Nature herself . . .[23]

This concept of periodicity, of birth and death followed by rebirth, left
an opening for the would-be restorers of Egyptian religion in the
Renaissance and the Enlightenment. In the meantime, however, we
must consider its metamorphosed survival in late Antiquity and under
Early Christianity. In a general sense the passionate religiosity of the
people and the subtle philosophy and theology of the priests attributed
by Greek writers to the Egyptians continued in Early Christian times.
Furthermore, at the level of church organization and doctrine, all
Christianity – not just that of Egypt – was deeply permeated by Egyptian
religion.

The Relics of Egyptian
Religion: Hermeticism,
Neo-Platonism and Gnosticism

Apart from mentioning the striking parallels between Jesus and Osiris
and the Mesopotamian Tamuz, deities of vegetation who are killed,
mourned for and triumphantly resurrected, I will not go into the
fascinating subject of specific survivals of Egyptian and Mesopotamian
religion in Christianity, as it leads us too far from the topic of this
book.[24] Here, we are interested in the remains of institutional Egyptian
religion and their survival on the fringes of orthodox Christianity.

Egypt from 150 to 450 AD was undergoing a period of great political
and religious uncertainty and diversity. Furthermore, the groups we are
concerned with tended to believe that divinity could be reached
individually or in esoteric sects, for which a rigorous and mystical
initiation was necessary. One of the key elements of this was fearsome
oaths of secrecy. These groups also tended to be hostile to explicit
writings or 'publication', believing that true wisdom could be imparted
only directly by the teacher to the disciple, in isolation and over a long
period. They were convinced that it was difficult to describe 'the
ineffable' in words, let alone in writing, and they insisted on the
importance of mystery. It is extraordinarily difficult to describe them

and, even if it were possible, it would be a fundamental betrayal of their thought to make it comprehensible – nevertheless, it is necessary to outline some general patterns.[25]

Late Antiquity was obsessed with the number three: this can be seen in Hermes *Tris*megistos and the Christian Trinity.[26] Among the groups with which we are concerned – the Hermeticists, the Neo-Platonists and the Gnostics – there were trinities of two basic types. The first, to which the Christian form belongs, had a father god, a son who was the activating intellect of the father, and a third force mediating between the two.[27] A second, more common variant was based on the notion of a 'hidden god', behind the demiurge or creator worshipped by the Jews, Christians and others. The two gods were seen either as distinct or mystically united: the Hidden God, 'the Good' or the First Principle of Platonic thought, was the pure thought, as opposed to the creator's action. The third member of the trinity was the most variable – being seen as the 'world soul', the 'mind of god', etc., or even the animated matter of the world or universe – but its essential function was the dialectical one of both mediating between the other members of the trinity and keeping them distinct.

Paradoxically, the fact that the first god was hidden and ineffable was used to justify idolatry. As man could grasp only the finite, and the Hidden God was infinite, it could be only partially perceived. As the 2nd-century Sophist Maximus of Tyre wrote:

> God . . . greater than time and eternity and all the flow of being, is unnamable by any lawgiver, unutterable by any voice, not to be seen by any eye. But we, being unable to apprehend His essence, use the help of sounds and names and pictures, of beaten gold and ivory and silver, of plants and rivers, mountain tops and torrents, yearning for the knowledge of Him.

He continued – in a spirit that can, parenthetically, be directly traced forward to John Locke – to use this as an argument for religious toleration:

> Let men know what is divine, let them know; that is all. If a Greek is stirred to the remembrance of God by the art of Pheidias, an

Egyptian by paying worship to animals, another man by a river, another by fire – I have no anger for their divergences; only let them know, let them love, let them remember.[28]

Hermeticism, Neo-Platonism and Gnosticism were 'twofold' philosophies, with superstition for the masses and true knowledge or *gnōsis* for the elite. *Gnōsis*, however, 'was not primarily rational knowledge . . . we could translate it as "insight", for *gnōsis* involves the intuitive process of knowing oneself.'[29]

Through education and moral and religious exercises the enlightened few could approach the Good, the First Cause, that was hidden to the masses who saw nothing beyond the demiurge. The introspection and elitism were connected to another feature that was completely foreign to orthodox Judaism and Christianity – the belief in the actual, or at least potential, divinity of man. My own view is that this comes from the Egyptian belief that the dead pharaoh became Osiris. In Late Egyptian religion this belief was 'democratized' so that with dedication, good instruction and knowledge of the right procedures every person had the potential to be Osiris and to become an immortal. At a deeper and more vague level, however, I believe this can be traced to a distinction between the transcendent shepherd god of the pastoral Israelites and the sense of Pantheism and immanent divinity among the agricultural Egyptians. In the latter God can be in everything, including man.

The idea that man can become God leads easily from religion, in which the worshipper prays for help, guidance etc., into magic, where he can command such things. As the Neo-Platonist Plotinos said: 'The Gods must come to me, not I to them.'[30] This pattern of thought goes beyond equality with God, to power over him – even to the extent of man making God.[31]

To return now to the stars. Stars played a central role in all these 'power trips'. Although there were a number of different astronomical models, the most influential was that set out by the astronomer Ptolemy, who lived in Egypt in the 2nd century AD, just at the point of transition from the old religion to the new cults. According to Ptolemy the sun, the moon, the planets and the 'fixed' stars circled round the earth on their own spheres. Thus in order to reach the ideal realm one had to transcend them. Hermeticism and Neo-Platonism also contained the very Egyptian and non-Christian notions of the pre-existence of souls and metampsychosis, or the transmigration of souls from one body to the next. This process involved passing beyond the spheres, and the new forms were to some extent moulded by the conjunctions of stars and planets at the point of birth.[32]

In her splendid political treatment of the Gnostics, the contemporary scholar Elaine Pagels is sympathetic to them as champions of freedom and opponents of the rigidity, hierarchy and repression of the orthodox Church. Where the Gnostics had many teachers, texts and gospels, and challenged church authority, the orthodox Church was controlled by the bishops, restricted to approved teachings, and allowed only the four canonical Gospels. Pagels, however, makes less of the fact that the Gnostics seem to have been generally richer than the Orthodox, and that although in principle *gnōsis* was available to everybody, the study needed for it required wealth and leisure.[33] In this context Father Festugière, who dominated Hermetic and Gnostic studies between 1930 and 1980, has distinguished between what he calls *hermétisme savant* and *hermétisme populaire*, by which he was contrasting the philosophy of the Hermetic Texts, on the one hand, with the magic and occult sciences associated with Hermeticism, on the other. However, as other scholars have pointed out, 'astrology, alchemy and magic are arcane disciplines and the practice of them was reserved to the elite.'[34] The extreme example of this was the great Neo-Platonist philosopher and mathematician Hypatia, who could hardly have been more upper-class and elitist. At the theological level, too, the 'twofold philosophy' of the Gnostics – and the Neo-Platonists and Hermeticists – is inherently unequal. Despite its hierarchy, manipulation of authority and repression, the orthodox Church maintained one faith for all believers.

The three schools' lack of formal organization and the necessary individualism of a system of beliefs that emphasized introspection would seem perfectly adapted for the situation after the collapse of institutional Egyptian religion. However, Egyptian polytheistic religion never had the organizational or theological unity of the monotheisms that succeeded it. Furthermore, there are indications that at least a 'proto-Hermeticism' existed well before the 2nd century AD.

To resume the argument so far. The three schools of thought that emerged from the debris of Egyptian religion were Hermeticism, Neo-Platonism and Gnosticism. The Hermeticists remained defiantly Egyptian, the Neo-Platonists were more Hellenized and focused their devotion on the 'divine Plato', while the Gnostics saw themselves as Christians. There was, of course, diversity and rivalry – sometimes intense – both among and within the three schools. Nevertheless, not only did they resemble each other in form but their practitioners associated with each other and read each other's works.[35]

HERMETICISM – GREEK, IRANIAN, CHALDAEAN OR EGYPTIAN?

There is little doubt that Hermeticism was the earliest of the three and had a critical influence on the formation of the other two movements.[36] In addition, everyone agrees that Hermeticism contained Greek, Judaic, Persian, Mesopotamian and Egyptian influences. But because there is heated controversy on the relative extent and depth of these influences, it is necessary to consider the issue in the light of the sociology of knowledge before examining what I see as the mainly Egyptian roots of Hermeticism. The question of its relationship to Ancient Egyptian thought is, of course, highly political. As Bloomfield, a historian of literature and art, wrote in 1952: 'Scholarship has veered from one extreme to the other on this question of the Egyptian elements of Hermeticism.'[37] Related to this is the question of its age. The contemporary expert on Hermeticism, A. G. Blanco, writes: 'those who support the view that the [Hermetic] "Corpus" is of Egyptian origin are also those who tend to push back the dates of the documents.'[38]

In this debate the two key figures have been Reitzenstein and Festugière. Reitzenstein wrote voluminously on Hermeticism at the turn of the century and initially argued that it was Egyptian in inspiration. However, as the century – and the Extreme Aryan Model – progressed, he changed his views until by 1927 he was arguing that it was essentially Iranian, hence Aryan.[39] From the 1930s until quite recently the field has been dominated by Father Festugière, who 'concentrated almost entirely on the Greek influences to the *Hermetica*', and opposed the notion of any connection with an Egyptian mystery cult.[40]

On the face of it, it would seem reasonable to grant considerable Egyptian influence on a tradition whose literature was written by Egyptians, probably in Demotic or Coptic, in Egypt before the collapse of organized Egyptian religion.[41] Furthermore, while ancient sources referred to Iranian-Zoroastrian and Chaldaean-Mesopotamian influences, no one in the Roman period challenged the idea that Hermeticism was essentially what it purported to be – Egyptian.

I want to stress that there is a great deal at stake here. It is not merely that Hermeticism is integrally connected to Gnosticism and Neo-Platonism but that, as Father Festugière has shown, it is closely related to Platonism as a whole. There is also a strong resemblance between Hermeticism, the theology of the Gospel of St John, and some of St Paul's letters.[42] The generally admitted closeness of these connections makes both the date and the 'Egyptianness' of the Hermetic Texts of critical importance. If the Texts antedate Christianity, and are pre-dominantly Egyptian, another possible origin for what have generally been considered to be the Greek, Platonic elements of Christian theology would open up. It would also be very difficult to explain away Plutarch's 'Platonic' and 'Pythagorean' picture of Egyptian religion as a delusion caused by Egyptomania or *interpretatio Graeca*. If the texts were shown to be older still, it would be very hard to deny the ancient view that Plato and Pythagoras took their ideas from Egypt.

Most modern scholarship on the dating of the Hermetic Texts still works in a framework established by the great French Protestant textual critic Isaac Casaubon in the early 17th century. Casaubon attacked the prevailing view of his time that the Texts were an extremely ancient repository of Egyptian wisdom. Using techniques for dating Latin texts developed at the turn of the 16th century, he argued that the theological similarities between the Hermetic Corpus and Saints John and Paul, and the close relation between Hermetic hymns and Psalms, clearly meant that Holy Writ predated the Hermetic Texts. In the same way, the resemblances to Plato – especially to what was then Plato's most widely read work, the *Timaios* – must be the result of borrowing from the latter; in any event, Casaubon pointed out, there was no mention of Hermes Trismegistos in Plato, Aristotle or the other ancient writers.[43]

Modern scholars working in the Aryan Model rather than the Christian framework of Casaubon have made only minor adjustments to his scheme. First, they have no problem in deriving New Testament theology from Platonic thought and, to a lesser extent, they are prepared to admit early Iranian or even Indian influences on Hermeticism. In this way, the Aryan Model allows scholars to raise the date of the Hermetic Texts to the 3rd century BC, that is, any time after Plato. For instance, as Festugière put it:

> These allusions [to the cult of Thoth] do not permit us to conclude that the temples of Egypt under the pharaohs possessed in their archives a collection of works attributed to the god Thoth. Exactly the opposite, it seems that since the Ptolemies there was a Greek Hermetic literature.[44]

Others have not even availed themselves of this opportunity, preferring to date the Texts alongside the Gnostic and Neo-Platonic works in the 2nd and 3rd centuries AD.

Nevertheless many have, in fact, explored the possibility that the Hermetic tradition dates back to the 3rd century BC. The German historian Kroll argued in the 1920s that the society described in Hermetic Texts, supposedly dating from the 2nd century AD, was that of Hellenistic, not Roman Egypt and was definitely one in which the temples were fully functioning.[45] Kroll's view was supported in the 1930s by the great historian of Iranian Mithraism and late pagan religion Franz Cumont, in the light of the discovery and editing of new astrological Hermetic Texts. In addition to backing Kroll, Cumont indicated that astronomical indications from astrological texts pointed to the 3rd century BC, but he also went beyond this to claim:

> The first Graeco-Egyptian astrologists did not invent the discipline they claimed to teach the Hellenic world. They used Egyptian sources going up to the Persian period which were themselves at least partially derived from ancient Chaldaean documents. Traces of

this primitive substratum still survive in our much later texts, erratic blocks transported on to more recent soil. When we find mentions there of 'the king of kings' or 'satraps' we are no longer in Egypt but in the ancient Orient . . . We limit ourselves to noting that in all appearances, the priests who were the authors of Egyptian astrology stayed relatively faithful to the ancient Oriental tradition.[46]

It is true that Cumont was a historian of the Persian religion, and that to some Northern Europeans in the late 19th and early 20th centuries the Iranians were more 'Aryan' than the Greeks. But these facts do not significantly weaken the plausibility of the argument that although the heterogeneous Hermetic Corpus was clearly composed at different times, some of it antedates not merely Alexander the Great in the late 4th century but Plato fifty years earlier.[47] Cumont's argument presents a serious problem to the Aryan Model because it means either that Plato's ideas coincided with the Hermetic Oriental-Egyptian ones or that they came from Egypt, as the Ancient Model maintained.

The notion of Persian origin itself has problems in that the ideas of Solon, Pythagoras and others who are supposed to have visited Egypt before the Persian conquest of that country in 525 BC appear to have been very similar to those of Plato and Plutarch, which makes an Egyptian origin even more likely than a Persian one. On the question of the relative importance of Egyptian and 'Oriental' ideas, it is possible – and indeed probable – that there were considerable Mesopotamian influences on Egypt long before the 6th century BC. These must have intensified during the Persian occupations, and it was probably during these occupations that most Zoroastrian influence came in. Thus I believe that apart from the notorious conservatism and chauvinism of the Egyptian priests, the apparent continuity of Greek views of Egyptian religion before and after the Persian conquests makes it plausible to argue that Cumont exaggerated the extent of 'Eastern' influence on the religion of early Ptolemaic Egypt, which despite foreign conquests seems to have remained fundamentally Egyptian.

Nevertheless, Cumont's arguments for dating the earliest strata of the Hermetic Texts to the Persian period are reinforced in previous work by Sir Flinders Petrie, the brilliant and eccentric founder of modern Egyptology in the late 19th and early 20th centuries. Petrie argued, from historical context, that at least some passages from the Hermetic Texts must date to the Persian period and that the crisis of Egyptian religion began in this period. He maintained that the *Lament* prophesying the proscription of Egyptian religion – quoted on p. 129 – was in circulation long before the Christian prohibition of Paganism in 390 AD, so that it could refer only to the persecutions of the Persian period. He also pointed out that the earlier date would also fit better with the references to Indians and Scythians as typical foreigners. Other Texts refer to foreigners 'newly filling the land'; this could hardly apply to the Greek conquest, let alone the Roman one. They also mention an Egyptian king – the last of whom reigned between 359 and 342 BC.[48]

Petrie's arguments were considered outrageous by scholars who quickly realized that the whole Aryan Model was at stake. As the Hellenist expert in Hermeticism, Professor Walter Scott, wrote in 1924: 'If these dates were proved to be right, there would necessarily result from them an astounding *bouleversement* of all commonly accepted views of the history of Greek thought.' Thus evidence challenging the Aryan Model was not considered in detail on its own merits, but was crushed by the model itself. Petrie's arguments were ruled out of court without any need to answer them: 'But the arguments by which he endeavours to support his datings are not such as to be worth serious attention.' Finally, and with incredible impudence, Scott asserted the superiority of Classics over other lesser disciplines: 'It is to be regretted that a man who has earned a high reputation by good work in other departments has in this case strayed into a field of research in which he does not know his bearings.'[49]

There is no doubt at all that Petrie knew far more Greek than Scott knew Egyptian. In any event, Scott was simply making explicit the hierarchy that had been implicit since the subordination of Egyptology to Indo-European studies in the 1880s. In this case it meant that Egyptologists could have nothing to say about the Hermetic Texts because Hellenists considered them to be Greek. The supposition and the expertise claiming a monopoly were mutually reinforcing.

Aside from Petrie's specific arguments, the central feature pointing to the early dating of the oldest portion of the Texts is that all scholars agree that Hermes is the same as the Egyptian Thoth. Casaubon, the 17th-century debunker of the Texts, did not deny that there might have been an ancient sage called Hermes Trismegistos. Similarly, modern writers can hardly deny the existence of Thoth as the god of wisdom. What is questioned is the antiquity of the Texts and of the figure of the sage Hermes Trismegistos.

It is not so easy, however, to draw clear lines between the traditional worship of Thoth, his allegedly Iranian or Hellenic cult in the Hellenistic period and the philosophy of the Hermetic Texts. Professors Stricker and Derchain have recently shown in detail that the Egyptian element in the Corpus is a good deal more prominent than Festugière and other scholars working at the height of the Aryan Model supposed.[50] Furthermore, the idea of the 'Writings of Thoth' is clearly very old. It occurs frequently in *The Book of the Dead*, which was current in the 18th Dynasty. Father Boylan – who wrote a book on Thoth in the 1920s – mentions a 19th-dynasty reference to 'the writings of Thoth which are in the library'.[51] Plutarch and the early Christian writer Clement of Alexandria refer to the 'Writings of Hermes'.[52] Although the dynastic version may bear very little resemblance to the later Corpus, I believe scholars are too hasty in their denial of any connection with the latter.

Recent discoveries have also pushed back the dates of features of the Hermetic Corpus previously thought to have come in only in the Roman period. The name Dḥwty ꜥꜣ, ꜥꜣ, ꜥꜣ (Thoth Thrice Greatest) has been found at Esna in Upper Egypt from the early 3rd century BC, and Dḥwty pꜣ ꜥꜣ, pꜣ ꜥꜣ, pꜣ ꜥꜣ (Thoth the Thrice Greatest), Hermes Trismegistos, has been read in Demotic texts from Saqqara just outside Memphis, from the early 2nd century BC. This text was among the documents of a priest associated with Thoth. In another item from this collection, *The Treasury of Hor*, there is the tradition that Thoth was the father of Isis, which had previously been attested only in the Hermetic Texts.[53] These two links with the Hermetic Corpus have been found with other writings linking them to the so-called Hermopolitan cosmogony, with its traditional roots and association with the enormously popular cult of Thoth and his sacred bird, the ibis. It has been estimated, for instance, that in any one year there were 10,000 ibises at Saqqara.[54] It is generally believed that Thoth's cult expanded greatly during Ptolemaic times but in *The Book of the Dead*, a thousand years earlier, Thoth was already an extremely powerful and often-invoked deity.[55] All in all, there is no reason whatsoever to doubt that the worship of Thoth in Ptolemaic times was firmly rooted in ancient tradition.

The key reason for making a sharp break between the ancient cult and the later Hermeticism was the latter's abstract 'Platonic' philosophy. The denial that the Egyptians were capable of abstract and philosophical thought has been a linchpin for the Aryan Model and therefore carries a lot of ideological baggage. This can be the only reason why proof that Egyptians could think in terms of abstract religion, which was published eighty years ago, has received so little attention. The proof comes from a text generally called *Memphite Theology*, which dates back to the 3rd millennium. The *Theology* describes a cosmogony according to which Ptah, the local god of Memphis, and his emanation Atum, were the primal beings. Ptah created the world in his heart, the seat of his mind, and actualized it through his tongue, the act of speech. This, though Father Festugière and Father Boylan hasten to deny it, looks remarkably like the Platonic and Christian *logos*, the 'Word' which 'already was, The Word dwelt with God, and what God was, The Word was, The Word then was with God at the beginning, and through him all things came to be . . .'[56]

After translating and publishing the *Memphite Theology* the Egyptologist James Breasted wrote:

> The above conception of the world forms quite a sufficient basis for suggesting that the later notions of *nous* and *logos*, hitherto supposed to have been introduced into Egypt from abroad at a much later date, were present at this early period. Thus the Greek tradition of the origin of their philosophy in Egypt undoubtedly contains more of the truth than has in recent years been conceded.

He went on:

> The habit, later so prevalent among the Greeks, of interpreting philosophically the functions and relations of the Egyptian gods . . .

had already begun in Egypt before the earliest Greek philosophers were born; and it is not impossible that the Greek practice of the interpretations of their own gods received its first impulse from Egypt.[57]

Thoth's role in this cosmogony was as the heart of Ptah, Ptah's tongue being Horus. This tradition of linking Thoth to the heart can still be seen 2,000 years later in the *Treasury of Hor*. Its publisher, John Ray, rightly points out the association of the heart with the intellect of which Thoth was particularly thought to be the master.[58] In other theologies, however, Thoth was the inventor of writing, the originator of mathematics and the master of magic spells; the divine act of speech which related the gods to each other and to men, and even the creator of the world.[59]

The fact that Thoth was a great communicator was a factor in the syncretism between him and Anubis, the Jackal protector of the dead, guide to the soul and messenger of death. Still more important was the fact that Thoth and Anubis played closely intertwined roles in the trial of the dead. The two were closely associated in this function even in the *Pyramid Texts* dating from the 3rd millennium, and a syncretic image of the two deities has been found from the 19th Dynasty or 13th century BC. However, a formal cult of Hermanubis did not appear in Egyptian religion until Ptolemaic times.[60] The relationship of this last development to the existence in Greek religion of Hermes, who combined the roles of Thoth and Anubis, is unclear. Nevertheless, although the original combination seems to have begun in Egypt, there seems little doubt that the Ptolemaic syncretic form derived from Greek religion.

With these multiple aspects, Hermes Trismegistos could play all the roles in the theology or 'twofold philosophy' discussed on p. 132. As father of the gods and the supreme intellect he could be the Hidden God; as activating intellect or act of speech he could be the demiurge; as communicator he could be the Holy Ghost linking and separating the other two. Finally, he could be the messenger or guide who leads souls to immortality and explains the wonders of the universe to them. However, the dominant later tradition made it clear that Hermes was a philosopher and moral teacher.

Here we encounter the question of Hermes' euhemerization, his turning from a god to a sage. Many scholars consider this euhemerization to be another late feature. But here too there are earlier precedents. Plato, in the early 4th century BC, refers to Theuth and Thot as the inventor of writing, numbers and astronomy, etc. Furthermore, Theuth/Thoth appears both as a god and as a sage.[61] Fifty years later, Hekataios of Abdera described Hermes/Thoth as a great human inventor.[62] There are also strong suggestions of his early euhemerization and rationalization from Phoenicia. In the 1st century AD a Phoenician, Philon of Byblos, epitomized and translated into Greek some of the works of an ancient priest, Sanchunation, who he claimed had lived before the Trojan War.[63] After the foundation of Classics, in the early 19th century, Philon's writings on ancient Phoenician religion and myth were dismissed as Hellenistic fantasy. In the 1930s, however, the discovery of striking parallels between Philon's mythology and that of the Ugaritic texts from the 13th century BC led to a sharp change of opinion. Thus Semitists like William Albright and Otto Eissfeldt tended to place Sanchunation in the first half of the 1st millennium and some of his materials as deriving from the 2nd.[64] Still more recently, Professor Baumgarten defied ancient tradition and the two greatest 20th-century authorities in the field to argue for a much later dating. This is firstly because not everything in Philon can be explained by the Ugaritic material, and secondly because Baumgarten takes it as axiomatic that all the rational and scientific thought in Philon has Greek origins. This in turn is because he believes Classicists have *proved* that reason and science began in Greece.[65] In this way, an essentially circular argument – there cannot have been any pre-Greek science or reason, because there was no pre-Greek science or reason – is used to claim that Philon's euhemerism must be Greek and late.

Here I need to draw some distinctions before proceeding. The first type of euhemerism, the non-personalized abstraction of natural forces, seems to have been present in Egyptian thought from the earliest times. It is certainly true of the cosmogony of Hermopolis, which has been linked to Thoth and to the cosmogony of Taautos described by Sanchunation.[66] The abstraction is indicated by the fact that not one of the Hermopolitan Ogdoad – the eight gods of the city of Hermopolis, the four pairs of beings or forces from whom the universe was created – had temples or cults, though they were sometimes equated with divinities which did.[67]

The second type of euhemerism – the turning of gods and goddesses into mortal sages, heroes and heroines – is a worldwide phenomenon, and the widespread tradition of calling the major gods the first kings of Egypt goes back at least as far as the *Turin Canon* of kings from the 13th century BC.[68] In the Levant it would seem to have been associated with the rise of monolatry and monotheism at the turn of the 1st millennium BC; the reason for this is simply that exclusive cults are unable to tolerate even lesser deities. In Genesis, for instance, one finds considerable euhemerism in the turning of what appear to have been deities like Enoch and Noah into patriarchs, and Genesis seems to have been written or compiled early in the 1st millennium BC. Further, scholars from Renan in the 19th century to Albright in the 20th have argued that Phoenician religion lent itself readily to euhemerist analysis.[69] It would therefore appear reasonable to accept – literally or metaphorically – those scholars who link Euhemeros, the original euhemerizer, to Sidon and to agree with Albright and Eissfeldt when they place Sanchunation and Mochos – whose Sidonian cosmogony was preserved by the late Neo-Platonist Damaskios – before the 6th century BC.[70]

Sanchunation's cosmogony was ostensibly based on the lost works of Taautos. However, Taautos was also mentioned in Philon's work as a Phoenician culture hero who had invented letters.[71] Elsewhere in the writings, he appears as Hermes Trismegistos – the earliest mention of the name in Greek – or as the secretary and cunning vizier of the divine hero Kronos, in the thoroughly euhemerized story of the latter's life and adventures.[72]

Thoth also appears in the Bible. In the Book of Job, which dates back to the 6th century BC or beyond, one finds the lines:

Who put wisdom into *ṭḥwt?*
Who gave *śekwî* understanding?

In his authoritative commentary on Job, Professor Marvin Pope writes about this as follows:

J. G. E. Hoffmann was probably right in taking *t̲ḥwt* to refer to the god Thoth himself. The consonantal orthography corresponds rather closely to the form of the name that prevailed in the 18th Dynasty (*d̲ḥwty*), when the worship of Thoth was at its peak and spread to Phoenicia ... Philon of Byblos gives the Phoenician pronunciation as Taaut(os), which would reflect the form *t̲āḥût* ... The suggestion of Hoffmann as to *sekwî*, connecting it to the Coptic name of the planet Mercury (*souchi*), seems preferable to the dubious connection with the 'cock'. The all-knowing, clever-minded Thoth-Taautos, inventor of the alphabet and founder of all knowledge, was identified with the Hermes-Mercury of the Greeks and Romans under the title of Hermes Trismegistos/Tremaximus.[73]

It should be emphasized that *t̲ḥwt* was filled with knowledge by the Lord and was therefore a sage and epitome of wisdom, not a god. Thus unless, like Baumgarten, one takes a principled stand against any pre-Greek rationality, there would seem to be overwhelming evidence that in both Egyptian and Phoenician culture there had been euhemerization of gods into sages and heroes long before the massive Greek influence on Egypt in the 4th century BC. What is more, this is particularly true in the case of Thoth and Hermes Trismegistos.

Let me reiterate my argument up to this point. Neo-Platonism and Gnosticism flourished chiefly in Egypt and among more or less Hellenized Egyptians after the collapse of institutional Egyptian religion. Whether or not there was a Hermetic brotherhood or cult from the 2nd to the 4th centuries AD, Hermetic ideas played a formative role in, and remained central to, these philosophies and heresies and their devotees. The cult of Thoth was always important in Egyptian religion but became increasingly so in the second half of the 2nd millennium. The idea of the 'writings of Thoth' is an ancient one and it is probable that such writings existed by the late 2nd millennium. However, the Hermetic Corpus, as it now survives, seems to represent Egyptian religion in crisis and to contain Iranian and Mesopotamian concepts. It is therefore unlikely that there are any texts from before the first Persian invasion in 525 BC. It is clear that the Corpus is heterogeneous and it probably contains material written over a long period, from the 6th century BC to the 2nd century AD. Despite its relative lateness it is overwhelmingly likely that the Corpus contains many very much older religious and philosophical concepts and that it is fundamentally Egyptian. The Iranian and Chaldaean influences have been mentioned above. There are also undoubted Greek influences, at least on the later texts. I believe, however, that these are difficult to detect because Greek Pythagorean and Platonic philosophy was so heavily dependent on Egyptian religion and thought.

HERMETICISM AND NEO-PLATONISM UNDER EARLY CHRISTIANITY, JUDAISM AND ISLAM

By the end of the 4th century, Gnosticism had been largely extirpated by the orthodox Church. Pagan Neo-Platonism survived rather longer, but it too had disappeared before the Moslem conquest of Egypt in the 630s. The figure of Hermes Trismegistos as the epitome of knowledge, on the other hand, survived in both Christianity and Islam. Euhemerism was now essential; as Jean Seznec, the great 20th-century historian of pagan survivals in the Renaissance, has pointed out, euhemerism enjoyed 'an extraordinary revival' in early Christian times.[74] As with all the descendants of Canaanite monotheism, the Christian Church used euhemerism to diminish and tame the pagan gods at the same time as it allowed them to survive under the new religion. Nēit/Athena was incorporated as St Catherine, Horus/Perseus as St George, and Anubis/Hermes as St Christopher.[75] Significantly, however, Thoth-Anubis/Hermes remained outside the Church, as the sage and epitome of Egyptian and Oriental wisdom Hermes Trismegistos.

Hermes' relationship to Christianity was always delicately balanced, particularly on the question of priority. The 3rd-century Church Father Lactantius maintained that Hermes had lived before Moses; St Augustine, on the other hand, claimed that while Egyptian astronomy and other exact sciences had developed early, there was no moral teaching in Egypt until the time of Trismegistos, who slightly postdated Moses and had learnt from the latter and the biblical Patriarchs. Here, as in so many other areas, Augustine set out the orthodoxy that was to last until the 18th century: that biblical knowledge came before – in both priority and importance – Hermetic Egyptian knowledge, but that the latter was the source of all 'Gentile' wisdom and specifically that of the Greeks.[76]

In Islam, Hermes Trismegistos was euhemerized and identified with Idris, a sincere prophet who appears in the *Qoran*. In this tradition, too, he was seen as the 'father of philosophers' and 'the one who is thrice endowed with wisdom'. In other Islamic traditions he was seen as three sages, one from before the Flood who lived in Egypt and two from after it; one from Babylon and the other again from Egypt. He was seen as the culture hero who had invented all the arts and sciences, especially astronomy, astrology, medicine and magic. Further, although it is plausibly argued that his – or Egyptian – influence in early Islam was largely in these areas, there was an early Islamic philosophical Hermeticism which has not been deeply studied, partly no doubt because of the extreme impenetrability of the texts.[77]

The huge Islamic conquests from Persia to Spain of the 7th and 8th centuries brought great prominence and prosperity to the Jews. Despite its powerful spirit of rationality and equality, Jewish religion had both esoteric cults and a 'twofold philosophy' even before the beginning of Christianity. The Essenes and other sectaries living in the Judaean Desert from the 2nd century BC were convinced that truths had been revealed to them that were unknown to the priests in Jerusalem and to the ordinary people; we know, for instance, that they used the Book of Enoch and other apocalyptic writings. Concerned with astrology and other methods of prediction, they also seem to have shared the mysticism – attested more fully at a later time – around the images of the Throne of God and the Chariot by which Elijah and the mystic could ascend into heaven.[78] The undoubted relationship between these sects and Christianity has been and will be endlessly debated, but less attention has been paid to the parallels and possible causal relations between the Jewish sects' tendencies towards celibacy, communism and desert life and those of early Christian monasticism as it grew up in the Egyptian desert.[79] The two groups certainly shared a common populism, Messianism and tendency to violence.

A much closer parallel to the thinking of the upper-class Hermeticists and Neo-Platonists can be seen in the massive works of Philon of Alexandria. In Philon's wealthy, Egyptian, Hellenized Jewish circle of the 1st century AD there was a desire to syncretize the wisdom of the Old Testament with Platonic-Egyptian thought through allegorical, esoteric and mystical interpretation. Philon even mentioned the existence of a sectarian community of 'Worshippers of God'.[80] Philon himself remained an important figure in the development of Middle and Neo-Platonic thought, and his mixture of Platonism and Judaism has fascinating resonances with that in Christianity. However, the rich, cultivated, Hellenized Jewry he represented was destroyed for ever by the genocide of the Jews within the Eastern Roman Empire in the suppression of their rising of 116 AD.

Even though Philon died before the destruction of the Temple of Jerusalem in 70 AD, his life in the Diaspora was essentially one of the synagogue and thus resembled that of later Jewry. Even in this prosaic, democratic, Pharasaic rabbinic society there were esoteric and mystical tendencies in the early centuries of the Common Era which Professor Gershom Scholem called 'Jewish Gnosticism'. In the writings of these tendencies one finds such specifically Jewish concerns as the Throne and the Chariot and the mystical and numerological significance of the letters of the Hebrew alphabet or the biblical text. Most of the key elements in Hermeticism, Neo-Platonism and Gnosticism are also contained: the concept of man as the measure of all things, the eight spheres or firmaments which can be transcended, and tendencies towards magic.[81]

Mysticism is also attested in Judaism in the 8th and 10th centuries. For instance, a Karaite or Jewish sectarian purist in the 10th century was familiar with quotations from Philon. Professor Scholem, however, warned that

> it should not be deduced from this that there was a continuous influence up to this time, let alone up to the time of the formulation of the Kabbalah in the Middle Ages. Specific parallels between Philonic and Kabbalistic exegesis should be put down to the similarity of their exegetical method, which naturally produced identical results from time to time.[82]

Here, he has raised a general issue that will occur again in this chapter: the possibility of the survival and continuity of secretive mystic sects in the face of general hostility and specific persecution over long periods of time. On the one hand, such groups leave little trace even when they are flourishing; on the other, as Scholem argued, they often use the same texts and similar exegetical techniques. Thus there is often a strong case for independent invention. In this case, the argument for independent invention seems rather extreme. Further, given the transmission of so much else in Jewish culture – not only orthodox religion but also folklore – over these centuries, I see no reason to doubt that there were continuous traditions of mysticism. Scholem himself traces a development of Jewish mysticism from Egypt and Palestine to Babylonia in the 8th and 9th centuries, back to the Mediterranean in Egypt and Italy in the 10th, and in the German Hasidism in the 11th and 12th.[83]

We must continue this sketch of the history of the Kabbalah here because it became closely intertwined with Hermeticism during the Renaissance. Much of the Kabbalistic mysticism of Provence and Spain in the 12th and 13th centuries can be explained in terms of the survival of Hermeticism and its descendants in Christianity and Islam; new developments in these cultures; the peculiar situation of Catalonia and Languedoc; the intensity of persecution experienced by Jews in this period and, as Professor Scholem argued, a mystical reading of the same texts in a period of crisis.

During the 12th and 13th centuries Languedoc was in a state of creative turmoil, having been for centuries a rich and cultivated society on the border of Christianity and Islam and, within Judaism, the conjunction of the Sephardic Jews who lived under Islam with the Ashkenazim from Christian Europe. The inhabitants of Languedoc were able to have a certain objectivity about and transcendence of specific forms of religion. This goes some way to explain why the region should have seen the crystallization of the most radical heresy in European Christendom, that of the Albigensians or Cathars. It was a heresy in which there were two classes of faithful: the ordinary Credentes (believers) and the Perfecti. The Perfecti detached themselves from daily life in the material world for spiritual contemplation, while their ideal was a complete separation from matter and a fast to death. The struggle to preserve Catharism became associated with that of the region to preserve itself from domination by Northern France and the kings in Paris, who claimed to be champions of Catholicism and justified their extension of central power as crusades against the heretics. Nevertheless there is no doubt that there was a great popular attachment to Catharism and to the Perfecti, whose spirituality was felt to benefit the whole community.[84]

Although clearly a religion of two tiers, and sharing some beliefs with the mystical traditions I have discussed above – such as the transmigration of souls – Catharism was much more sharply dualist in a way that is conventionally seen to be Iranian, Zoroastrian or Manichaean. The forces of God and Satan, good and evil, spirit and flesh are cosmic and seen to be equally balanced and in constant conflict. This was very different from the pantheist and anthropocentric vision of the Hermetic traditions.[85] Nevertheless, though both movements existed all over Europe, the flourishing of Albigensianism and Kabbalism in Languedoc and Provence at the same time is striking, and indicates something extraordinary about the social and cultural milieu. It is difficult to believe that the two did not influence each other, and this would seem to be particularly true in social structure. Just as the Perfecti were supported and protected with fierce devotion by the Credentes, the mystical Kabbalist rabbis seem to have been maintained by their communities for the spiritual benefits their holiness brought to them. However, where the Cathars were ruthlessly exterminated by the Catholic French, the enemies of the Kabbalists in Jewry lacked these means and the movement spread into Spain, where it flourished as an esoteric but relatively respectable element in Spanish Judaism until Ferdinand and Isabella's Expulsion of the Jews from Spain in 1492.

Kabbalah is explicitly esoteric – indeed, its study has been generally restricted to good, learned (male) Jews over forty. It rejects both the historicism of the common 'superficial' reading of the Bible and the rationality of orthodoxy in favour of an 'inner' reading of the text which is supposed to reveal a mystic cosmic struggle for the good Jews to reconstitute the primeval light shattered at the moment of creation. In many ways Kabbalism is an extension of the Orthodox Talmudic approach: the mystery is approached through intense study and includes such things as the significance and numerology of the letters of the Bible. But it goes beyond such things into contemplation of the Throne, the Chariot and above all, the Name of God, all of which leads to ecstasy. Kabbalah also contains all the key forms we have seen in Hermeticism and its descendants: trinities, the concepts of the 'absconded' or Hidden God or intellect, the activating *logos* or word and mediating spirit; the eight spheres or firmaments and their transcendence by the well-trained mystic; and man is seen as the measure of all things and sometimes even as the maker of God. In the first centuries of its existence, this led to astrology, medicine and magic, for all of which Jews were renowned throughout Medieval Europe.[86]

Hermeticism in Byzantium and Christian Western Europe

Neo-Platonism, of at least a nominally Christian kind, seems to have survived in the Byzantine Empire, and this was renewed in what has been called the 11th-century Renaissance there. Its leading Neo-Platonic figure, Psellos, was clearly interested in both Hermetic philosophy and magic. The 20th-century scholar Professor Zervos has written:

> We do not know how many works Psellos composed on Hermetic literature. The only one that remains is a gloss on the 'Poimandres' ... After maintaining the influence of 'Genesis' on the formation of the cosmogonic doctrines of the 'Poimandres', Psellos affirms that all Hellenic conceptions of God are influenced by Eastern models. He justifies this superiority of the East over Greek philosophy by pointing out that Porphery [the Neo-Platonist of the 3rd century AD] had gone to an Egyptian priest, Anebon, in order to receive instruction on the first cause.[87]

Here, as with Augustine, one sees the hierarchy – the Bible, Egyptian and Oriental wisdom, and Greece, with interest focused on the second. The fact that some of Psellos' works were taken to Italy in the 15th century means that they had been preserved throughout the troubles of the last 400 years of the Byzantine Empire at Constantinople.

This, in turn, shows the importance with which Neo-Platonism and Hermeticism were treated there.

The belief in Egypt as a powerful, if not the most powerful, centre of magic survived the conversion of Western Europe to Christianity. Both scarabs and a barbaric head of a bull with a solar disc on his forehead, which has been identified with Apis, were found in the pagan tomb of Childeric – the father of Clovis, the first Christian king of France – who died in 481.[88] Three hundred or so years later the great seal of Charlemagne represented the head of the late Egyptian Jupiter Serapis.[89]

Although – like every other cultural activity at this period – interest in the Hermetic Texts was at a low ebb during the Dark and Early Middle Ages, it did not die out completely. However, there is little doubt that medieval thinkers were more interested in Hermetic magic and astrology than in its philosophy. Nevertheless, one philosophic text, *Asclepius*, had remained in circulation ever since its translation into Latin in the 2nd century.[90] The number of copies of that text made in the 11th and 12th centuries indicates that interest in it seems to have increased in what has been called the 12th-century Renaissance of Western Europe.[91] It is also difficult to believe that the increase of humanism in the centuries that followed was not influenced by *Asclepius* and the few Neo-Platonic texts available.

EGYPT IN THE RENAISSANCE

Early-20th-century historians tended to picture the Renaissance as Greek and, though influenced by Plato, as somehow 'pure' until the late 15th century and the introduction of Neo-Platonism.[92] However, the concern with Egypt and the Orient was integral to the whole movement from the beginning. It cannot be emphasized enough that, just as to Shakespeare the Ancient Greeks were quarrelsome Levantines, not demigods, the Italian Renaissance scholars, artists and patrons identified themselves with Greeks but were not centrally concerned with the Greece of Homer or Perikles, or even with the Olympian gods. They were interested in picking up from pagan Antiquity where it had left off. As the philosopher and historian David Hume wrote, with 18th-century sensibility, 'Learning, on its revival, was attired in the same unnatural garb which it wore at the time of its decay among the Greeks and Romans.'[93]

Central to this 'decadence' was a respect for Egypt and the East, an admiration for the 'Oriental' profusion and obscurity of the Neo-Platonists' writings, and a passion for Egyptian and Oriental mystery. However, it is precisely from the Neo-Platonic and Hermetic traditions that the Renaissance drew its most characteristic vision of the infinite potential of man, and the belief that man is the measure of all things. Even in what the 19th- and 20th-century historians have seen as the 'manly' 14th and early 15th centuries, there was an enormous respect for the Egyptians.

By the beginning of the 15th century, Italian scholars had a good idea of the centrality of Egypt and the Hermetic Texts to the ancient learning they wished to revive. Scholars had long known about and read *Asclepius*, and Arabic Hermetic Texts were being translated into Latin. Furthermore, with the increase in contact between Italy and Greece, the Neo-Platonic and Hermetic writings of Psellos and the other promoters of the Byzantine Renaissance became available.[94] In 1419 a copy of *Hieroglyphika*, a late-5th-century work on hieroglyphics by Horapollo, an Upper Egyptian, was brought to Italy and translated.[95] The author had combined a correct interpretation of a number of signs 'with the most grotesque allegorical reasons for those meanings'.[96] The work was enormously popular and confirmed the belief that hieroglyphics was the script of the mysteries, superior to alphabets because one sign was seen to compress rich meaning within it and to be unencumbered with the phonetics of mundane speech. In general, hieroglyphs and the enigmas they were supposed to contain became enormously important in the early 15th century; see, for instance, the famous medal of the explicitly Egyptian winged eye made by the great painter, architect and theorist of art Leone Battista Alberti, who is sometimes regarded as a representatative of the 'uncontaminated' early Renaissance.[97]

The Egyptian priests' use of hieroglyphs was perceived as being linked to their use of allegories and the allegorical significance of the mysteries attributed to them by Plutarch and other Greek writers. As we have seen, 19th- and 20th-century scholars insist that the Greeks 'got it wrong'. They believe that the Renaissance thinkers were equally mistaken. As the early-20th-century art historian Professor Wind wrote about a number of the latter:

> their concern was less with the original mystery cults than with their philosophical adaptation. Good judgement alone did not impose the restriction; it was largely a case of good luck, for it derived from a historical misconception: they assumed that the figurative interpretation was part of the original mysteries.[98]

I believe that the 15th-century interpretation was accurate, at least for late Egyptian religion. In any event, its truth was never questioned by the Italians of the Renaissance.

The Renaissance passion for Egypt came firstly from its ancient reputation of having been the place where the mysteries and sacred initiations were first established. Furthermore, with the possible exceptions of the Persian Zoroastrians and the Chaldaeans, of whom there was only a dim conception, the Egyptians were seen as the origin of all wisdom and arts; for all the sense of progress attributed to them by Romantic historians, Renaissance men and women were fundamentally interested in the past. They were searching for *fontes* or 'sources' – and so they looked behind Christianity to pagan Rome, behind Rome to Greece; but behind Greece there was Egypt, as Giordano Bruno put it in the following century: 'We Greeks own Egypt, the grand monarchy of letters and nobility, to be the parent of our fables, metaphors and doctrines.'[99]

However, lest it be thought that Bruno was atypical, or belonged to a generation that had been 'corrupted' by revived Neo-Platonism, let me quote Frances Yates on the foundation of the new Neo-Platonic school which necessarily reflects attitudes towards Egypt and Greece from *before* this took place:

> About 1460, a Greek manuscript was brought to Florence from Macedonia by a monk, one of those many agents employed by Cosimo de' Medici to collect manuscripts for him. It contained a copy of the *Corpus Hermeticum* ... Though the Plato Manuscripts

> were already assembled, awaiting translation, Cosimo ordered
> Ficino to put these aside and to translate the work of Hermes
> Trismegistos at once, before embarking on the Greek philosophers
> ... Egypt was before Greece; Hermes was earlier than Plato.
> Renaissance respect for the old ... as nearest to the divine truth
> demanded that the *Corpus Hermeticum* be translated before Plato's
> *Republic* or *Symposion* ...[100]

The new translations were used as the centrepiece for the revived
Platonic Academy established by the great translator, scholar and
philosopher Marsilio Ficino in his villa at Carregio outside Florence.
The same was true of the other academies that sprang up in all the
major Italian cities, and later throughout Europe. Although these
academies were consciously modelled on Plato's own in Athens, their
members believed that this had been constructed on the model of an
ideal priesthood in Egyptian temples. All European academies have had
the election of new members as a central *raison d'être*. In the academy of
15th- and 16th-century Rome, for instance, such elections were full of
ritual paraphernalia.[101] The rituals of elevation to the rank of 'immor-
tals' practised in the French Academy and elsewhere can be traced back
to the mysteries and sacred initiations giving immortality concocted in
the Renaissance on the basis of reports from Late Antiquity and
believed – in my opinion rightly – to have derived ultimately from
Ancient Egypt.[102] Moreover, the Renaissance scholars took much more
than their organization from the Neo-Platonists. They looked beyond
them to Plato himself, Pythagoras, Orpheus and Egypt for their
philosophy, science and magic.

In the late 15th century the Neo-Platonic thought was merged with
that of the Kabbalah by the Renaissance thinker and mystic Pico della
Mirandola. Pico's 'spiritual magic' was able to use the two systems in a
way that could even sustain Christianity on a mystical basis of Egyptian
hieroglyphics and Hebrew letters and numbers.[103] Pico had an enormous influence at the time, particularly on the Borgias, who commissioned works of art glorifying Egyptian religion and especially the Apis
bull, whom they took to be their symbol. Much more important in the
long run, however, was Pico's clear articulation of the Egyptian position

that man as a 'magus' could, as Frances Yates put it: 'use ... both Magia and Kabbalah to act upon the world, to control his destiny by science.'[104]

This and similar fusions of the Jewish and Egyptian traditions – which, as mentioned above, were related to each other – appeared again at the turn of the 16th century, notably in the work of the Renaissance philosopher Tommaso Campanella. Kabbalism, too, continued to be a major inspiration for 16th- and 17th-century magic and science.[105] Nevertheless, as Frances Yates has pointed out, Kabbalah was never called a *prisca theologia*, an ancient or primary theology, on the grounds that it belonged to the biblical and not the Gentile tradition. Thus, Renaissance thinkers who wished to transcend Christianity had no alternative to Egypt.[106]

COPERNICUS AND HERMETICISM

Frances Yates, in tune with recent writing on Copernicus, claimed in 1964 that

> Copernicus is not living within the world-view of Thomas Aquinas but within that of the new Neo-Platonism, of the *Prisci Theologi*, with Hermes Trismegistos at their head, of Ficino. One can say, either that the intense emphasis on the sun in this new world-view was the emotional driving force which induced Copernicus to undertake his mathematical calculations on the hypothesis that the sun is indeed at the centre of the planetary system; or that he wished to make his discovery acceptable by presenting it within the framework of this new attitude. Perhaps both explanations would be true, or some of each.[107]

Although, as I have said, the Hermetic Texts tended to work within the geocentric Ptolemaic system, they contained the potential for other cosmologies, including one based on a central fire. Furthermore, there are repeated references to the special sanctity of the sun seen as the source of light and sometimes as the second god which governs the third god, the animate world and all its living creatures.[108] Thus the Texts shared the Ancient Egyptian focus on the sun as the chief divinity and life-giving force.

A great deal has happened in Copernican studies since Frances Yates wrote the text cited above, and there have been attempts to mitigate her upsetting suggestion. Some objections, like those of the historian of science Professor Rosen, have continued to follow the conventional picture of the development of science as a succession of great men's heroic leaps from darkness into light. Hence, for Rosen, Copernicus was 'neither a Platonist nor a Neo-Platonist, nor an Aristotelian, he was a Copernican.'[109] More significantly, a number of recent scholars have shown that Copernicus' mathematical modelling was very largely based on Islamic sources, notably the works, of Naṣīr ad-Din aṭ-Tūsī in the 13th century and Ibn ash Shāṭir in the 14th.[110] These, however, do not include heliocentricity itself, the idea of which came to Copernicus considerably before his mathematical proof of it. It has been argued that Copernicus derived his heliocentricity from the mid-15th-century scholar Regiomontanus. The technical arguments concerned do not diminish the fact that Regiomontanus' opening of the possibility of heliocentricity may well have derived from his being in the thick of mid-15th-century Platonism. Whether or not this is the case, Professor Yates' claim would still seem to hold true.[111]

HERMETICISM AND EGYPT
IN THE 16TH CENTURY

It is generally implied that once the Texts were read, a disillusion set in. This is belied by the bibliographical facts that, as Professor Blanco has put it,

> Between 1471 and 1641 Marsilio Ficino's translation went through 25 editions; that of Patritius went through six; the bilingual edition of Fr De Foix appeared twice; the 'Asclepius' was edited forty times; the commentary of J. Faber Stapulensis on the 'Pimander' appeared in fourteen editions; that of Rosellius in six; the commentary of J. Faber Stapulensis on the 'Asclepius' passed through eleven editions, etc.[112]

Bibliography also tells us something about relative concern with Greece and Egypt. For example, George Eliot, at the height of

Victorian Romanticism, vividly pictured a Renaissance concern with the ruins of pagan Athens.[113] But this is an anachronism. West Europeans from the 15th to the 17th century were far more concerned with travels in Egypt than they were with those in Greece: the editors of a recent collection of reprints maintain that, between 1400 and 1700, there were over 250 descriptions of Egypt by Western travellers.[114]

In some circles, in fact, having travelled to the sources of knowledge in Egypt provided a legitimacy for attacks on conventional wisdom. The clearest example of this in the early 16th century was the great and original doctor and mining engineer Paracelsus, who claimed – probably falsely – to have been to Egypt and called his medicine Hermetic. However, he was only near the beginning of a tradition which continued up to and included Newton, in which scientists justified turning to experiment as a way to retrieve the wisdom of Egypt and the Orient which the Greeks and Romans had failed to preserve.[115]

We have to remember that for the last hundred and fifty years the Renaissance has been seen as one of the twin peaks of European culture, only slightly less elevated than 5th-century Athens. Consequently, 19th- and 20th-century scholars have experienced considerable difficulty and distress in dealing with the Renaissance admiration for Egypt and the Orient. For instance, although the gods were referred to by their Latin names, they were believed to be fundamentally Egyptian. Take Jean Seznec, the leading 20th-century scholar on pagan survivals in Antiquity, writing about the illustrated manuals of the pagan gods:

> But in our manuals [books of illustrations] divinities of the Oriental cults are given extraordinary prominence, especially in Cartari. First of all the Egyptians ... we have already had occasion to note in Picator the same unusual or even disproportionate place given to Oriental divinities; it is due, in our opinion, to a contemporary influence – that of the 'hieroglyphics' which drew the attention of humanists to Egypt and to the Orient in general.[116]

Later on:

> Our manuals, in their manifest preference for the Eastern rather
> than the Olympic divinities – a preference furthered by the contem-
> porary Egyptomania and the taste for enigmas . . . As for Mercury, he
> is a sort of magus capped with a pointed bonnet. Small winged
> beings, who seem to emerge from a well, grasp a stalk of his
> enormous Caduceus, about which are entwined four serpents; other
> similar *puttini* seem to slip and fall back. What is this figure, which
> belongs, as Yriarte remarks, to neither Rome, Greece, Assyria nor
> Persia? It is reminiscent at once of Hermes, the guide of souls to the
> underworld, or *psychopompos* and of the Egyptian Thoth who teaches
> the soul to raise itself by degrees to a knowledge of divine things.[117]

It is not only the conventional historians who prefer to distance
themselves from this 'unfortunate' aspect of the Renaissance. Frances
Yates, who not only opened up but still towers over the study of
Renaissance Hermeticism and championed heresies of all sorts, did not
challenge the full force of the Aryan Model. While detailing the
enormous and fruitful impact of Egyptian Hermeticism on 15th- and
16th-century Italy, she seems to have felt it necessary to reassure her
readers that she was not so unorthodox as to *believe* the men she was
writing about with such sympathy. There are frequent remarks of the
type: 'This huge historical error was to have amazing results.'[118] I think
this is, in fact, far more appropriate as a description of the Aryan Model!

There is no doubt that in the 16th century Hermeticism and concern
with Egypt flourished as a respectable part of high Renaissance culture.
In the view of later history, however, Hermeticism's most important
product of the period was an exception, Copernicus' great champion,
Giordano Bruno. Bruno was acclaimed by 19th- and early-20th-
century historians of science as a pioneer and martyr for science and
freedom of intellectual enquiry, but Frances Yates has firmly situated
him in the Hermetic tradition. Bruno was remarkable in that he went
further than any of his predecessors or contemporaries. For all their
enthusiasm, most early Hermeticists honestly or dishonestly kept
within Christianity and the bounds set by St Augustine that Egyptian
and its derived Gentile philosophies were later than, and inferior to,

biblical wisdom. Bruno, however, went beyond not only Christianity but Judaism to reach Egypto-Paganism:

> Do not suppose that the sufficiency of the Chaldaic magic derived from the Kabbalah of the Jews; for the Jews are without doubt the excrement of Egypt, and no one could ever pretend with any degree of probability that the Egyptians borrowed any principle, good or bad, from the Hebrews. Whence we Greeks [by which he seems to mean Gentiles] own Egypt, the grand monarchy of letters and nobility, to be the parent of our fables, metaphors and doctrines.[119]

The social context of such radicalism was the failure of the Counter-Reformation in the 1570s to overcome the limitations of Catholicism and heal the breach within Western Christianity, and the wars of religion which racked late-16th-century Europe. Bruno tried to attach himself to politically moderate and relatively tolerant rulers who wanted compromise. Paradoxically, this went with his extreme intellectual and theological radicalism. Thus, to bring spiritual and physical peace, Bruno saw it as necessary to transcend Christianity not merely intellectually but politically. As Frances Yates put it: 'Bruno's Hermeticism becomes purely "Egyptian", with the Hermetic Egyptian religion not just as the *prisca theologia* foreshadowing Christianity but actually as the true religion.'[120]

The fact that Bruno had gone beyond the bounds of Christianity and was burnt at the stake for his beliefs by the Inquisition should not lead one to exaggerate his eccentricity in 16th-century Italy. Given the passion for *fontes* (sources) and the belief that priority is superiority, it is not such a great leap from saying that Hermeticism preceded Christianity to claiming that it transcended it. Nevertheless, while the balance between the Bible and Christianity, on the one hand, and Egypt and the Hermetic Texts, on the other, was fine and delicately shifting, the relation between the latter and Ancient Greece was more clear-cut. Erasmus' scepticism about the date of the Hermetic Texts, for instance, seems to have been based on a desire to protect Christianity rather than to assert the priority of Greece.[121] After the Reformation, the Calvinist Lambert Daneau even used the reputation of the Egyptians as teachers of the Greeks to *prove* the superiority of Moses and the biblical tradition in 'natural philosophy', which was more or less what has later been described as 'science'. Quoting ancient sources, Daneau was able to establish the tradition that the Egyptians had learnt astronomy from the 'Syrians'. He was also able to show that the latter had had a learned man called Moschos, whom he then claimed to be Moses. Thus Moses had taught the Egyptians, and hence the Greeks, astronomy. The tradition of identifying Moses with Moschos continued well into the 18th century.[122] Thus there was no question at this stage of challenging the Egyptian superiority of learning over the Greeks.

To conclude this chapter with a familiar example. Shakespeare's portrayal of the Greeks in *Troilus and Cressida* as unreliable and scheming was firmly based in late medieval tradition and was not atypical in his own day. As I have tried to show in this chapter, most Renaissance thinkers believed that Egypt was the original and creative source and Greece the later transmitter of some part of the Egyptian and Oriental wisdom, and the veracity of the Ancient Model was not at issue.

CHAPTER III

THE TRIUMPH OF EGYPT IN
THE 17TH AND 18TH CENTURIES

I N THIS CHAPTER I shall be looking at the continuation of
Hermeticism in the 17th century. While most modern scholars
have maintained that the Hermetic Corpus was discredited by
Casaubon's textual criticism, I believe that this had very little effect on
its reputation. In the short run the texts continued to be believed, and
their eclipse in the 18th century was the result of the general intellectual
shift away from magic rather than of any specific criticism. Furthermore, loss of interest in Hermeticism did not mean any diminution in
respect for Egypt. At the end of the 17th century Ancient Egypt became
associated with the 'Radical Enlightenment' and was used to subvert
Christianity and the political *status quo*. The image of Egypt remained
central to the Freemasons, who dominated intellectual life in the
18th century. Thus Egypt – often linked with the other great
long-lived empire, China – maintained a high reputation for its
philosophy and science, but above all for its political system, until the
break-up of European political and intellectual order in the 1780s
and 90s.

HERMETICISM IN THE
17TH CENTURY

Giordano Bruno was burnt alive in Rome in 1600. His death, however, had a less significant long-term effect on Hermeticism than the work of Isaac Casaubon, the moderate Protestant scholar who attacked the antiquity of the Hermetic Texts in 1614. The surprising feature of Casaubon's work, for Frances Yates, was that the scholarly techniques of textual criticism which had been available since the late 15th century should have been applied so late to the Hermetic Texts. But given the necessary selectivity of the application of such techniques and the political and ideological uses to which they have later been put, I am not so surprised that at the end of the 16th century the threat posed by the Texts, not merely to Catholicism but to Christianity as a whole, should have encouraged a scholar to scrutinize them in a hostile way.[1]

Casaubon demonstrated the philosophical, theological and even textual similarities between the Hermetic Texts, the works of Plato and passages from the New Testament. He argued that the Egyptian texts must be derivative, firstly because there were no references to the texts in the Bible or in Plato, Aristotle or other ancient writers; and secondly because the texts referred to late institutions and cited Hellenistic authors.[2] Casaubon's attack is devastating against its target, the picture of the Corpus as the work of one man writing over a thousand years before the Christian era. Yet Casaubon's scholarly and ideological descendants have not answered the objections made by Ralph Cudworth in the 1670s, that the presence of later material does not make the Texts valueless as sources for Egyptian wisdom because they were written 'before the Egyptian Paganism and their succession of priests were yet extinct'.[3]

Still less have the modern followers of Casaubon addressed themselves to the scheme set out by Flinders Petrie, who argued on specific historical grounds that the Texts form a relatively heterogeneous collection written between the 6th and 2nd centuries BC.[4] Furthermore, the undeniable similarities between the Hermetic Texts, the works of Plato, and the 'Platonic' sections of the New Testament can easily be explained in terms of a common descent from Late Egyptian religion and the Phoenician, Mesopotamian, Iranian and Greek ideas current throughout the East Mediterranean during this period.

The reference to Erasmus at the end of the last chapter (see p. 159) shows that Casaubon's 'Christian Humanist' attack on the idea of Hermeticism as a source of Christianity was not altogether new. Nevertheless, the story of Casaubon's revelation is a perfect philological counterpart to the 19th- and early-20th-century myth of the history of science already mentioned: the heroic and lonely scientific genius standing out beyond his age to turn the darkness of superstition into the light of science and reason.

Unfortunately for this example, however, Hermeticism and the passion for Egypt continued to flourish throughout the 17th century. Moreover, Frances Yates reflected the confusion between myth and reality when she wrote: 'It shattered at one blow . . .' but in the following paragraph continued: 'Casaubon's bombshell did not immediately take effect.' A little later she modified the impact still further by stating:

> Though other factors were working against the Renaissance traditions in the 17th century, Casaubon's discovery must, I think, be reckoned as one of the factors, and an important one, in releasing 17th-century thinkers from magic.[5]

It is true that the early-17th-century philosopher and mathematician Marin Mersenne used Casaubon's dating to attack the Hermetic mysticism of the Elizabethan magician Robert Fludd, but it is hard to argue that this textual criticism had a major impact on society as a whole.[6] It would seem more plausible, and put the horse before the cart, to say that belief in magic dwindled towards the end of the 17th century for large-scale social, economic, political and religious reasons; that this decline was a factor in the gradual loss of interest in the Hermetic Texts; and that to the extent that it did decline, belief in their great antiquity became a victim of the general increase of scepticism.

Whether or not Casaubon's criticism had an impact on 17th-century thought as a whole, it had no effect whatsoever on Hermeticism in that century. Some scholars, like Kircher, ignored Casaubon altogether; others, like the Cambridge Platonists, confronted his criticism but argued that the Texts still contained ancient and valuable material.

The purpose of Bruno's immolation was to preserve the Church from a direct challenge. Catholic interest in Egypt was too powerful to be stifled and Ancient Egypt became the obsession of one of the most influential intellectual and cultural figures in 17th-century Rome: the German Jesuit Athanasius Kircher. Kircher was a Christian Hermeticist concerned with such things as astrology, Pythagorean harmonics and Kabbalah.[7] He had no doubt about the great antiquity of Hermes Trismegistos, believing that he lived about the time of Abraham, and he was perfectly willing to accept Egyptian prefigurations of Christ. As he wrote:

> Hermes Trismegistos, the Egyptian, who first instituted hieroglyphs, thus becoming the prince and parent of all Egyptian theology and philosophy, was the first and most ancient among the Egyptians . . . Thence, Orpheus, Mousaios, Linos, Pythagoras, Plato, Eudoxos, Parmenides, Melissos, Homer, Euripides and others learned rightly of God and of divine things . . .[8]

As well as being interested in Egypt as the place of the *prisca theologia*, Kircher was concerned with it as the home of the *prisca sapientia*, the 'original wisdom' or 'philosophy', most of which the Greeks had failed to preserve. He corresponded with Galileo on the subject of a universal standard of measure which would naturally be that of the Egyptians, and used his powerful position at the papacy to send his agents to Egypt to determine it from the measurements of the Great Pyramid.[9] His greatest effort – to which he devoted his whole life and his extraordinary linguistic talents – was the attempt to unlock the secrets of hieroglyphics, which he saw not merely as the repository of ancient wisdom but as the ideal script. Following Horapollo, Kircher believed the hieroglyphs to be purely symbolic and therefore vastly superior to all alphabets. Although unsuccessful in his attempt to decipher Egyptian inscriptions, he realized that Coptic was a descendant of the ancient language and might – despite the script's supposed lack of phonetic correspondences – provide help in the decipherment. Therefore, just at the point when Coptic was dying out as a spoken language in Egypt, Kircher established its study in Rome on a systematic basis.[10]

ROSICRUCIANISM:
ANCIENT EGYPT
IN PROTESTANT COUNTRIES

Protestants, too, continued to be interested in Egypt and Hermeticism. The elusive Rosicrucians, who sprang up in Germany, France and England in the 17th century, seem, like Bruno – to whom they may well have been connected – to have been promoting a 'true' religion for the elite. It appears to have been designed to avoid the bloody hostility between Catholics and Protestants that erupted so horribly in the Thirty Years War that ravaged Germany from 1618 to 1648.[11] Like the 16th-century Hermeticists, the Rosicrucians, or those who claimed to speak for them, advocated the direction of society by an elite of enlightened men in possession of true, magical and scientific knowledge. In doing this they were following the now familiar succession from the Egyptian priesthoods to the Pythagorean brotherhoods to the Platonic Academy. In this respect Frances Yates makes the plausible claim that it was this Rosicrucian concept that lay behind the 'invisible college' seen by the founders of the Royal Society in England in the 1650s.[12]

With the Commonwealth's freedom of the press, the 1650s saw a striking revival of interest in Hermeticism. As the historian Christopher Hill has written: 'More Paracelsan and mystical chemical books were published in the 1650s than in the whole of the preceding century.'[13] In attacking the linked church and academic establishment, English Hermeticism became allied to political and religious radicalism.[14]

With the Restoration in 1660, however, many thinkers were swept up by the counter-revolutionary current and backed away from their radicalism. What is more, the king prudently took over science by becoming patron of the Royal Society, much as he was head of the established Church. Nevertheless, the Hermetic ferment during the Commonwealth provided an important impetus for the later advances of respectable science. Hermeticism now tended to be associated with a special form of millenarianism that grew up in 17th-century England, focused on the need to perfect or recover all knowledge; this was seen as a necessary precondition for the advent of the new millennium.[15]

The Cambridge Platonists, centred round Henry More and Ralph Cudworth, also came from this Hermetic and millenarian environment.[16] As mentioned above, this group, which flourished from the 1660s to the 1680s, knew all about Casaubon's criticism but still maintained that the Hermetic Texts were valuable because they contained elements of the *prisca sapientia*. Since they saw no reason to attribute the 'Platonic' aspects of Hermeticism to Greece, for them the essential function of the Greeks was as partial transmitters of ancient wisdom. As More wrote:

> Plato's school . . . well agrees with learned Pythagore,
> Egyptian Trismegiste, and th'antique roll,
> Of Chaldee wisdome, all which time hath tore,
> But Plato and deep Plotin do restore.[17]

By far the best-known pupil of the Cambridge Platonists was Isaac Newton, although the degree to which he can usefully be considered Hermeticist continues to be fiercely debated.[18] There is no doubt, however, that he too was, as the modern intellectual historian Frank Manuel puts it, 'unruffled by Isaac Casaubon's revelation'.[19]

Furthermore, whether or not he accepted a Hermetic *prisca theologia*, he certainly believed in an Egyptian *prisca sapientia*, which he saw it as his mission to retrieve. For example, it was essential for Newton's theory of gravitation to have an accurate measurement of the circumference of the world. As far as he knew, there had been no recent, accurate measurement of a degree of latitude. Thus he could rely only on the figures of the Hellenistic mathematician and astronomer Eratosthenes and his followers, and these did not fit Newton's theory. His next assumption was that although Eratosthenes had lived in Egypt he had failed to preserve the ancient measurements accurately. Therefore Newton needed to retrieve the exact length of the original Egyptian cubit, from which he could calculate that of their stadium which, according to Classical authors, bore a relation to a geographical degree.

Earlier in the 17th century Burattini, an Italian working for Kircher, and John Greaves, an English scholar with similar preoccupations, had spent years trying to obain accurate measurements of the Great Pyramid. (From ancient times, it had been believed – quite possibly rightly – that the Pyramid enshrined perfect units of length, area and volume as well as geometric proportions such as π and 'the golden mean' φ.) When Greaves returned to England he published his findings fully and was appointed Professor of Astronomy at Oxford; Newton used Greaves' figures to deduce that the Pyramid had been built on the basis of two cubits. One of these was far closer to the one he needed than that of the Greeks, but it still did not fit his theory. This was possibly because Greaves' and Burattini's measurements of the Pyramid's base were inaccurate, since they were unable to penetrate the accumulated debris around it. Indeed it was not until 1671, when the Frenchman Picard accurately measured a degree of latitude in Northern France, that Newton was able to prove his general theory of gravitation.[20]

This question of measurement is only one example of Newton's faith in the *prisca sapientia* of Ancient Egypt. He was also convinced that atomic theory, heliocentricity and gravitation had been known there.[21] As he wrote in an early edition of his *Principia Mathematica*:

> It was the most ancient opinion of those who applied themselves to philosophy, that the fixed stars stood immovable in the highest parts of the world; that under them the planets revolved about the sun; and that the earth, as one of the planets, described an annual course about the sun . . . The Egyptians were the earliest observers of the heavens and from them, probably, this philosophy was spread abroad. For from them it was, and from the nations about them, that the Greeks, a people more addicted to the study of philology than of nature, derived their first as well as their soundest notions of philosophy; and in the Vestal ceremonies we can recognize the spirit of the Egyptians, who concealed mysteries that were above the capacity of the common herd under the veil of religious rites and hieroglyphic symbols.[22]

In this passage, significantly, we have an epitome of conventional views of the 17th century on the themes that concern us. Newton's admiration and respect for the Ancient Egyptians as the greatest scientists and philosophers are clearly expressed. In view of these earlier attitudes it is striking to find that he spent the last years of his life trying to defend the

argument set out in his *Chronologies of Ancient Kingdoms Amended*. This
was that Egyptian civilization had been founded just before the Trojan
War, and that the Great Sesōstris was only the Shishak of the Bible, who
had invaded Judaea *after* the time of Solomon. From Newton's point of
view this account damned the Egyptians as relative latecomers, making
them inferior to the much older biblical tradition. However, Newton was
concerned only with asserting Israelite priority, and he had no desire to
deny that Egypt was the fount of Greek wisdom. Thus his down-dating
of Egypt led him to scrap all the Greek chronologies and make the
Greeks later still.[23] In the next chapter I argue that this attempt is best
seen as part of the reaction by Christians and respectable deists like
Newton to what the contemporary intellectual historian Margaret
Jacobs has called the 'Radical Enlightenment'.

But before coming to the Radical Enlightenment and the reformation
of Freemasonry, it would seem useful to consider Late Renaissance
beliefs in the significance of the Phoenicians, who have been so
important in Masonic legend, because it was the half-Phoenician
Hiram who built the Temple at Jerusalem which symbolizes the world
and is at the core of Masonic rituals and beliefs. We should remember
that while Egyptian remained a mystery locked in the hieroglyphs, the
boom in Christian studies of Hebrew that followed the Reformation
relatively quickly led to the realization that Hebrew and Phoenician
were mutually intelligible dialects of the same language.[24] Therefore,
long before its alphabet was first read by the Abbé Barthélemy in the
middle of the 18th century, scholars had a relatively clear idea of the
Phoenician language.

Hebrew was, of course, generally believed to have been the original
language of mankind, the speech of Adam and the Tower of Babel.
There was thus an intensive search for Hebrew words in other
languages, especially the European ones, a search which received some
encouragement from what most scholars today would consider to be
remarkable coincidences between words. Some, in fact, may be the
result of pure chance but, as I have said in the Introduction, I believe
that others are the result of the genetic relationship between Afroasiatic
and Indo-European languages, while others come from loaning from
Canaanite or Phoenician into Greek, Etruscan or Latin.[25]

The Phoenicians were seen as a conduit by which Hebrew or other cultures and languages, which we should now call Semitic, were diffused into Europe. The 16th-century political theorist Jean Bodin, for instance, used linguistic evidence to back his claim that all civilization and language had spread outwards from the Chaldaean. He saw the invasions of Danaos and Kadmos as essential steps in this process, and maintained that all the Greeks had originated from Asia, Egypt or Phoenicia.[26] But although Bodin remained a respected political thinker, his and similar philological theories were soon outmoded by the work of scholars like Joseph Scaliger and Casaubon at the turn of the 17th century – men who did not speculate on Hebrew connections and remain within the canon of Classical studies even today. The Huguenot Samuel Bochart, however, an equally learned and cautious scholar, is not there. In the 1640s, working on the correct assumption that Hebrew and Phoenician were essentially the same language, Bochart made an investigation of the plausibly Semitic place names around the Mediterranean that is still unsurpassed. He also conducted serious research on Canaanite loan words in Greek and Latin, which significantly ceased to be authoritative only in the 1820s.[27]

Ancient Egypt
in the 18th Century

Newton is a pivotal figure. Coming from a world of astrology, alchemy and magic, he left a world in which these were no longer respectable. This change, of course, also reflects the social, economic and political transformation of the late 17th century, along with the triumph of capitalism in England and Holland, and statism in France. In this new world there was no place for Hermeticism, at least in its old form, but this did not mean that there was any less enthusiasm for Ancient Egypt. This enthusiasm soared in the century from 1680 to 1780. The best-known novel of the early part of the century, for instance, Fénelon's *Télémaque*, first published in 1699, features a Greek prince – Telemachus the son of Ulysses – as its hero, but it is full of animadversions about the material wealth, great wisdom, philosophy and justice of the Egyptians. These are specifically contrasted with

the inferiority of the Greeks, though the pharaoh Sesōstris favoured
them and had benevolently given them laws.[28]

The middle of the 18th century was a high point of Egyptophilia. As a
French writer put it in 1740:

> The only things talked about are the ancient cities of Thebes and
> Memphis, the Libyan Desert, and the caves of the Thebaid. The
> Nile is as familiar to many people as the Seine. Even the children
> have their ears battered with its cataracts and openings.[29]

The writer was presumably part of the Christian reaction against Egypt
(see Chapter IV). In this period, however, even Europocentric writers
welcomed as pioneers in the 19th and 20th century paid obeisance to
Egypt. The learned Giovanni Battista Vico, who flourished in early-
18th-century Naples and whose Romantic, Europocentric and histori-
cist view of history made him a hero among the 19th-century scholars,
was in many ways hostile to the Egyptians. As a pious Catholic he
explicitly excluded the Jews from profane history, and put their history
back to the Creation. He saw the Egyptians as only one among the
earliest post-diluvian peoples. Nevertheless, they played a central role
in his thinking. He maintained that his world historical scheme of three
ages was based on Egyptian history as narrated by Herodotos: the stages
of the gods, of heroes and of men. These stages he saw as paralleled by
three types of 'language': hieroglyphics, 'symbolic' and 'epistolary'. He
also discussed and accepted the myth of Kadmos, linking it to Egypt.[30]
Montesquieu, too, was forced to concede that 'the Egyptians were the
best philosophers in the world'.[31]

The mainstream of fashionable opinion in England and France
seems to have been – as the French quotation above would suggest –
unequivocally enthusiastic about Egypt. One of the best-known English
playwrights of the mid-18th century, for instance, was Edward Young,
whose series of Egyptian plays have – not surprisingly – received very
little attention in later centuries. In 1752 the fifteen-year-old Edward
Gibbon demonstrated his enthusiasm for Egypt by writing his first
historical essay on 'the Age of Sesōstris'.[32]

This favourable opinion, and the continued conviction that Greek
culture had come from Egypt and Phoenicia, was translated into new

non-mystical scholarship. In 1763 the brilliant Abbé Barthélemy, decipherer of Palmyrene and Phoenician, presented a paper entitled 'General reflections on the relations between the Egyptian, Phoenician and Greek languages'. In this his first correct asumption, based on Kircher – whose other work he considered fantastic – was that Coptic was a form of Ancient Egyptian. He also recognized the language family later known as Semitic, which he called 'Phoenician'. On these two bases, he established that Egyptian, although not a Semitic language, was related to the Semitic family. It is true that some of his lexical evidence can now be seen to have been faulty, as some Coptic words derive from Semitic loans into Late Egyptian. However, the main lines of his argument, based on similarities between pronouns and grammatical features, are irreproachable. In this sense, then, Barthélemy was a pioneer of what we should now call Afroasiatic studies.

Barthélemy admitted that he could see no such grammatical parallels between Coptic and Greek. Nevertheless he believed in the Egyptian colonization and civilizing of Greece and maintained that 'It is impossible that in this exchange of ideas and goods, the Egyptian language did not participate in the formation of Greek.'[33] He then gave a list of etymologies from Egyptian into Greek, several of which – such as the Coptic *hof*, Demotic *hf* to the Greek *ophis* (snake) – would seem plausible today.[34]

Linguists were not the only scholars to maintain the priority and centrality of Egypt. The standard 18th-century work on ancient mythology, that of the Abbé Banier, continued the Classical and Renaissance traditions of deriving the Greek and Roman gods from those of the Egyptians.[35] At the end of the century Jacob Bryant attempted to continue the work of Bochart, but he pointed out that the latter had not been completely successful because he had missed out the Egyptian component in Greek and Roman mythology and language.[36] Bryant thus tried to explain their origins in terms of an 'Amonian' culture that contained both Egyptian and Phoenician elements. Despite the many fantastic aspects of his work, I believe that his approach was fundamentally the right one, but that he failed because Egyptian was still undeciphered and he did not use Coptic. In any event, his *A New System; or an Analysis of Ancient Mythology*, published in 1774, was enormously respected at the turn of the 18th century; it was a major source book for the Romantic poets and above all for Blake.[37]

The same views dominated the history of philosophy. I have already mentioned that Europocentrists like Montesquieu saw the Egyptians as the greatest philosophers. Even Jacob Brucker, whose massive history of philosophy was a sustained attack on Plato, his Egyptian teachers and their esotericism and twofold truth, could not strip the Egyptians of the title 'philosophers'.[38]

THE 18TH CENTURY: CHINA
AND THE PHYSIOCRATS

At the end of the 17th century there was a surge of European self-confidence. The Polish defeat of the Turks outside Vienna in 1683 was followed by the rapid Austrian recovery of Hungary. These, together with the Russian advance to the Black Sea, removed the Turkish threat from Europe. From now on, Europeans were on the advance against Asians by land as well as by sea. With this security, the leaders of the Enlightenment now felt free to show a preference for non-European cultures in their reaction against feudalism and traditional Christianity. By far the most favoured were Egypt and China, which were seen as very similar to each other, if not directly linked. These two civilizations were not seen merely as anti-European utopias – like Turkey, Persia and the land of the Hurons – which could be imbued with some vague general nobility and used to satirize and criticize Europe. Egypt and China had a much greater significance because they provided positive examples of higher and finer civilization.[39] Both were seen to have had massive material achievements, profound philosophies and superior writing systems.

Their most attractive features, however, were their model administrations. These were seen as being carried out rationally and without superstition by a corps of men recruited for their morality and wisdom, and required to undergo rigorous initiation and training. The secular French Physiocrats, on the one hand, felt closer to the Chinese: they liked to see Louis XV as a Chinese emperor and themselves as literati. Under their auspices China made a major cultural impact on France, and many if not most of the centralizing and rationalizing political and economic reforms of the mid-18th century followed Chinese models.[40]

THE 18TH CENTURY: ENGLAND,
EGYPT AND THE FREEMASONS

While the Physiocrats turned to China, the more mystical Freemasons, on the other hand, who included most of the major figures of the Enlightenment, preferred the Egyptians. All Masonic history is vague and that from before the reorganization of the craft in the early 18th century is doubly so, because it has to be gleaned from later writings that were deliberately distorted to create a mythological development. Nevertheless, a certain amount can be agreed. The Freemasons were originally secret societies of masons working on cathedrals and other major buildings in medieval Europe. In most parts of the continent they died out after the Reformation and the Wars of Religion; they survived in Britain but took on a very different character, with the entry of gentlemen members and the beginning of what was called 'speculative masonry'.[41] However, even before this change, which took place in the late 17th century, the Freemasons had a special attachment to Egypt.

The Christian encyclopaedist and historian Isidore of Seville's *Originum sive Etymologiarum*, written in the 620s, contained Herodotos' and Diodoros' statements that geometry had been invented by the Egyptians to measure land after the disappearance of boundary markers in the Nile Flood. For Isidore geometry was only one of the seven arts, but for masons it was centrally important as it was equated with masonry itself.[42] Then again, several medieval Masonic manuscripts refer to Euclid's having founded masonry in Egypt for the Egyptian lords.[43] Before dismissing this quaint story it should be remembered that Euclid seems to have lived all his life in Egypt.[44]

The Phoenicians, who were firmly linked to the Egyptians in the Bible – both are listed as sons of Ham – were at the core of Masonic mythology. Hiram Abif, the half-Phoenician craftsman of Solomon's temple, was probably part of Masonic legend by the 16th century.[45] Supposedly murdered after the completion of the temple, he was certainly a central figure of an Osiran type by the time the craft was re-formed at the beginning of the 18th.

I have already mentioned that Frances Yates saw a connection, through Bruno, between the Renaissance Hermeticists and the 17th-century Rosicrucians. She also saw one between the latter and the Freemasons in the person of Elias Ashmole – founder of the Ashmolean Museum at Oxford – who petitioned to join the Rosicrucians and is also known to have been initiated as a Mason.[46] Frances Yates further showed the fundamental similarities between the Rosicrucians and the Freemasons in their use of the measurements and proportions of buildings – Solomon's temple or the Great Pyramid – to symbolize the structure of the universe and the desire to create a band of illuminati who could lead the world to a better, more peaceful and more tolerant way of life.[47] On the other hand, she did not make the link established by later scholars between this tradition and the widespread millenarianism in the same circles. Many millenarians believed that knowledge had to be reassembled before the coming of the millennium.[48] Therefore the scholar could be the midwife of eschatology. It is from these schools of thought that the English 'scientific revolution' of the late 17th century seems to have evolved.

Gentlemanly interest in Masonry increased in the 1670s and 80s. As well as contingent factors such as the massive rebuilding of London after the Great Fire of 1666, the growth of Freemasonry – like the contemporary rise of coffee houses and men's clubs – reflects changes in the urbanized commercial and landowning upper classes and the beginning of what one could call 'sub-political' activity outside the Restoration Court. During the reign of the Catholic James II from 1685 to 1688, and after the Glorious Revolution of the latter year, there was a revival of radicalism which even brought back some of the survivors of the Commonwealth of the 1650s. However, in this movement which Margaret Jacob, as I have said, has called the Radical Enlightenment, the Puritanism and crude millenarianism of the earlier period was replaced by more modern ideas including deism, pantheism and atheism.

In the 1660s and 1670s atheism was largely associated with Thomas Hobbes. Hobbes' political idea of the Leviathan was less shocking than his atheism, which was based on the atomism and materialism of Demokritos and drew on the Epicurean tradition expressed most fully in the works of the great Latin poet Lucretius. At the same time atheism had been growing in Holland. In the long run, however, the most influential philosophy to emerge from there in the mid-17th century was the pantheism of the great Jewish philosopher Spinoza, which was influenced both by the Kabbalah and by Bruno.[49]

By the 1680s a new, equally radical intellectual force had emerged in England from the Hermetic and Rosicrucian traditions. The new movement argued for a twofold philosophy, for transcendence by the elite of the religious squabbles of the masses. The masses should be given toleration to practise their particular superstition, but political and intellectual power should be firmly in the hands of the enlightened few.

This general attitude was perfectly compatible with 18th-century English society. The Radical Enlightenment, however, contained thinkers like John Toland, who not only drew from the Rosicrucian and Masonic traditions the notions of a *prisca theologia*, but also read Bruno. Toland had absorbed many of Bruno's cosmological Hermetic and Egyptian ideas of animate matter and a world spirit, ideas which lead to pantheism or even atheism. Long before this Newton himself had hesitated, in private, on the question of the activity or passivity of matter, but Newtonianism was not merely scientific. It had a consequent political and theological doctrine which depended on the passivity of matter, with motion coming only from outside. Otherwise, theologically, the universe would need no creator or 'Grand Architect', let alone a 'clock-minder'; while politically, England would need no king – Toland was fully aware of the republican implications of his ideas.[50]

John Toland was a central figure in the establishment of the legends, rituals and theology of speculative Masonry, much of which was standardized and canonized by the fusion of various Masonic and Rosicrucian groups in 1717.[51] By that time, however, the movement had been taken over by respectable Newtonians. Even bold figures like Newton's deputy and successor at Cambridge, William Whiston, who unlike his mentor openly proclaimed his Arianism – disbelief in the divinity of Christ – 'despised and actively combated' Toland and his ideas.[52] Nevertheless, some of the aspects of the Radical Enlightenment survived in respectable Masonry, which retained the essential elitism of the twofold philosophy and – in a new form – its Neo-Platonism. As in that tradition, ordinary people, and even most Masons, followed a partial faith, but the higher ranks transcended Christianity.

For the Masons, as for the Hermeticists, the name of the Hidden God was too sacred or magically powerful to be revealed even to the lower grades, the craft. This name was Jabulon, and – not surprisingly – it is a triple name, its first two syllables being Ja for Yahwe, the God of Israel, and Bul for the Canaanite Ba'al.[53] The last name came from 'On, the Hebrew name of the Egyptian city 'Iwnw, known in Greek as Heliopolis and now a suburb of Cairo. According to Classical writers, Heliopolis had been a major centre of learning where, for instance, Eudoxos had studied.[54] For the Freemasons, it was thus the epitome of ancient esoteric wisdom.[55] Even more significantly, the city was a major centre of the sun-cult and was associated particularly with Ra, who – as mentioned on p. 115 – became associated with Osiris by the 18th Dynasty. The Hermetic Texts refer repeatedly to the perfect city founded by Hermes Trismegistos which is closely associated with the sun; while Città del Sole, City of the Sun, was a term used by Bruno, it was better known in the utopia written by his contemporary Campanella.[56]

Campanella's city is populated by white-robed, pure and religious Solarians who are transparently Egyptian, and its buildings form an ideal model for the universe or a heliocentric system of planets.[57] Here it should be remembered that Masonic ideology was built around the notion of sacred buildings symbolizing the universe. In the City of the Sun Moses, Christ, Mahomet and other great teachers were revered as magi, but the city was ruled by Hermes Trismegistos as sun priest, philosopher, king and lawgiver.[58] In this case, then, the Masonic claim of drawing their traditions from Ancient Egypt has a basis in fact. Through the Hermetic Texts, Bruno, Campanella, Toland and/or his friends, one can trace a line from the final syllable of the name of their ineffable God to 'Iwnw, the cult centre of Ra in Lower Egypt.

The ascending mystery of Jabulon – from Judaeo-Christian to

Canaanite-Phoenician, to Egyptian and the Osiran rituals for the upper grades – does not mean that the centrality of Egypt to the Freemasons was hidden. Masonic temples have frequently been built in an Egyptian style – architecture is naturally of great significance to the craft – showing that the 'Lodges' are to be seen as Egyptian temples. Their symbols are the 18th-century conception of purely logical hieroglyphs. (Some, like the pyramid and eye still to be seen on the Great Seal of the United States and the dollar bill, were taken direct from Egypt.) There is thus no doubt that the Masons have seen themselves as the successors to the Platonic Guardians and the latter's own model, the Egyptian priests.

If the impetus to identify with Egypt and some religious symbols came from earlier traditions, general knowledge of Egypt among 18th-century Freemasons came from contemporary scholarship. However, before examining these new sources of information I want to look at intellectual developments in this area in France.

France, Egypt and 'Progress':
the Quarrel between
Ancients and Moderns

The concept of 'progress' had existed in Europe since the 16th century, when people began to realize that they now possessed products and inventions that the Ancients had lacked – sugar, paper, printing, windmills, the compass, gunpowder, etc. – all of them introductions from Asia. But during the devastating Wars of Religion from 1560 to 1660, it was difficult for such a view to spread or even to take firm root. The century from 1670 to 1770, however, was one of great economic expansion, scientific and technical development, and increased concentration of political power. The popular writer Perrault and the 'Moderns' in France were not merely fawning when they compared the age of Louis XIV to that of Augustus, and considered both the splendour and morals of their own times greater than those of the Ancients – especially those of the barbaric Homeric heroes.[59]

The cult of Louis XIV as Le Roi Soleil, the Sun King, appears to have been instituted at his coming of age in 1661 and seems to have formed part of an attempt to create a national cult to which all the French, whether Catholic or Protestant, could rally.[60] Indeed, as the triple godhead of Apollo, Herakles and God the creator, the cult or conceit clearly profited from Louis's youth and the end of the civil wars of the Fronde. The cult became central to the splendour and cultivation of Versailles, and served the political purpose of 'buying off' the nobility with the spectacles and pleasures of what was thought to the most splendid court on earth.[61] As the young Apollo Louis was patron of the arts, and as Herakles he was mighty in war. He was a traditional sun with his ritual *Journée*, 'day', beginning with a ceremonial *lever* (rising) and ending with an equally formal *coucher* (going to bed or setting); but at the same time a Copernican sun, around which the planets circled. The cult also had alchemical aspects. The modern historian Louis Marin has shown that the use of fireworks and projecting dust into the air, over water in a blaze of light, which was central to his spectacles, demonstrated Louis's ability as the Sun to mix and transcend the four elements.[62]

Nevertheless, although this combination of alchemy, sun worship and a divinized monarch associated with the sun looks very Egyptian, I have not been able to find any direct connections between them. On the other hand, we do know from Voltaire that Louis was identified with Sesōstris, among other monarchs of Antiquity.[63] Thus when describing the splendours of Ancient Egypt French writers during the reigns of Louis XIV and Louis XV must have had some *arrière pensée* of their own society.

This leads us back to the quarrel which dominated European intellectual life during the 18th century: that between the Ancients and the Moderns. As mentioned above, the crux was the issue of whether the Moderns were now morally and artistically superior to the Ancients, and its centre was on the moral and artistic qualities of the Homeric epics; it should be remembered that Homer was seen by the Ancient Greeks as a cultural 'founding father'. From the 15th to the early 17th century the Egyptians had represented true Antiquity, but at the same time the authority of Egypt had been used by innovators to challenge the ancient authorities of Aristotle, Galen, etc. In this respect, then, it had what one might call a double image. In late-17th- and early-18th-century France, the progressive aspect was dominant: Egypt, with its identification with the France of Louis XIV, was clearly on the side of the Moderns.

Fénelon, the author of *Télémaque*, was too slippery a character to allow himself to be seen on one side or the other. He loved Homer and admired the simplicity of the Greeks but, as I have said, his praise of the vast wealth and cultural superiority of the civilization of the Egypt of Sesōstris, compared to that of Homeric Greece, clearly distanced him from Madame Dacier, the translator of the *Iliad* and champion of Homer's eternal artistic and moral perfection.[64]

The Abbé Terrasson, on the other hand, was much more committed to the Moderns. He was born into a talented Catholic family, and his father seems to have shared the millenarian preoccupations which dominated 17th-century English science. The father had his sons educated 'to accelerate the end of the world'. Jean Terrasson became a priest and a leading figure in French intellectual life from the 1690s until his death in 1750.[65] As Professor of Greek and Latin at the Collège de France, and in key positions in both the Académie Française and the Académie des Inscriptions et Belles Lettres, he dominated the study of ancient history in early-18th-century France. A major attack on the *Iliad*, published in 1715, put him in the forefront of the Moderns.[66]

Terrasson also achieved fame as the translator of Diodoros Sikeliotes, the detailed and favourable commentator on Egypt and the colonization of Greece. But he was best known for a novel which first appeared in 1731: *Sèthos, histoire ou vie tirée des monuments: anecdotes de l'ancienne Égypte*. With a relatively shallow pretence, Terrasson claimed that his work was that of an unknown Alexandrian of the 2nd century AD. Although a fake the novel incorporated, with references, a mass of material largely from the ancient writers from Herodotos to the Church Fathers, as well as from the novel *Aithiopika*, which really does seem to have been written in the 2nd century AD.

Terrasson's hero, Sèthos, is an Egyptian prince born a century before the Trojan War. There were in fact two pharaohs named Sety – rendered Sethōs in Greek – in the 13th century BC, while the traditional date of the Trojan War was 1209 BC. Terrasson seems to have taken the name from the Ptolemaic Egyptian historian Manetho, who used the name for the Great Pharaoh Ramessēs II, the son of Sethōs I. The fact that the name and date are reasonably accurate shows that the 18th-century scholars could at times make profitable use of Classical sources for the reconstruction of Egyptian history.[67] The structure of the novel, however, is fictional and resembles that of Fénelon's *Télémaque* in that it is concerned with the adventures and education of a noble young prince. But it also reflects Diodoros' stories of the civilizing conquests of Osiris. After going through various mysterious initiations, Sèthos travels around Africa and Asia setting up cities and establishing laws, later retiring to join a college of initiates.[68]

Like *Télémaque*, *Sèthos* contained many animadversions on the glories of Egyptian civilization and, even more strongly than the former work, it insisted on the great superiority of Egypt over Greece. Terrasson described the academy at Memphis as far finer than that of Athens, giving details of all the arts and sciences in which the Egyptians excelled the Greeks. Using Classical quotations, he demonstrated that the founders of Greek politics, astronomy, engineering and mathematics had all studied in Egypt. Further, he also maintained that there were close parallels between Greek and Egyptian mythology and ritual and that the Greeks had derived their forms from Egypt.[69] He saw the main cultural transmission as having come through Greek study in Egypt. Nevertheless, he also mentioned the colonizing activities of Kadmos and Danaos, and it is significant that he firmly attached the Phoenicians to the glories of Egyptian civilization.[70]

Sèthos immediately became the standard Masonic source of information about Egypt. As Masonry spread throughout Europe and North America the book was translated into English and German and was published in numerous editions throughout the 18th century. It became the source of many plays and operas, most of them Masonic, of which the best known is *The Magic Flute*. Both Schikaneder's libretto and Mozart's score are crammed full of Masonic-Egyptian symbolism.[71] For more than a century the novel was openly used as a source for Masonic history, and *Sèthos* still remains the mainspring of its legend and ritual. The tradition of the primacy of Egypt has remained so important to the craft that Masonry has been unable to bow to popular or academic fashion on this issue. As a Masonic writer put it in the extremely philhellenic 1830s:

> All the ancient and modern historians agree that formerly Egypt was the cradle of sciences and arts and that contemporary peoples draw their religious and political principles from it. As the learned Dupuis has shown: 'Resembling a tree as ancient as the world, Egypt has lifted her magnificent head in the chaos of eternity and has enriched all parts of the world with her products. She has pushed her roots towards posterity under different forms and varied appearances but with a constant essence reaching up to us with her religion, her morality and her science.[72]

MYTHOLOGY AS ALLEGORY
FOR EGYPTIAN SCIENCE

The idea that mythology is an allegorical interpretation of historical events or natural phenomena to the masses, who are capable of grasping only a partial truth, was well established in Antiquity. It is part of the general scheme of the twofold truth or philosophy, referred to so frequently above. Thus it was the dominant mode of understanding myth from the Renaissance to the end of the 17th century.

Frank Manuel has sensitively described the way in which this approach was rejected and overthrown in the 18th-century swing towards common sense. Some 18th-century mythographers, like Fréret and the Abbé Banier, did as the Greek euhemerists had done 2,000 years earlier and tried to interpret myths as the clumsy telling of literal truths.[73] Myths were now supposed to have been taken at face value by the Ancients, just as the contemporary peoples of other continents appeared to take theirs.

The change was linked to the growing sense of 'progress' and the increasing tendency, beginning with the 17th- and 18th-century writer Fontenelle, to revive an analogy – stated in Antiquity by St Augustine – between human history and the growth of a child to maturity.[74] In a complete reversal of the previous view of myth as the hidden signs of a higher civilization, it was now seen as the poetic expression of the childhood of mankind, to be valued not for its truth content but as a source of information about human psychology.

Despite all this activity, however, the allegorical interpretation of myth as an expression of the ancient wisdom of the Egyptian priests survived and flourished among Freemasons and Rosicrucians. Manuel has shown how it was revived in print in the immense and immensely dull works of Court de Gebelin.[75] We, however, are far more concerned with the works of the scholar and revolutionary Charles François Dupuis.

As the great 20th-century historian of science Giorgio de Santillana has pointed out, it is not accidental that Dupuis is so little known today. His beliefs continue to form a coherent challenge to both Christianity and the myth of Greece as a cultural beginning; thus he and his work had to be buried.[76] Dupuis was a brilliant scientist and the inventor of semaphore, and was also active in politics during the French Revolution. His great reputation as a scholar and his dedication to moderate revolutionary principles made him a natural choice for director of cultural events during the Directory from 1795 to 1799, and he became president of the legislative body during the Consulate under Napoleon that followed.

Dupuis's most famous work was the massive *Origin of all Cults*, which appeared in 1795. In it he argued that all mythologies and religions could be traced back to one source, Egypt. Furthermore, he believed that nearly all myths were based on one of two principles: the miracle of sexual reproduction, and the intricate movements of the stars and other heavenly bodies. Although myth was couched in spectacular and fantastic terms, he argued that it concealed an inner scientific truth which could be explained only in terms of science. Much of his gigantic work was in fact a detailed matching of myth to astronomy, which – unfortunately for proponents of the Aryan Model – he knew much better than any later Classicist. Dupuis had two major themes. One of his thrusts was against Christianity, and he showed with massive detail the Near Eastern mythological background of the Gospels. For him the religion was built from the debris of the misunderstood priestly alle- gories. His second major theme was the explanation of Greek myths – which, following Herodotos and the ancient tradition, he took to be fundamentally Egyptian – in terms of astronomy. Here again he produced a series of astounding correspondences, or coincidences, between such myths as the twelve labours of Herakles and the annual stellar movements through the twelve houses of the zodiac.

Frank Manuel sees Dupuis as interesting, but ultimately absurd.[77] De Santillana, by contrast, had a completely different view of him:

> Dupuis's work contains practically everything that has been found out since on Archaic astronomy. He had only the Classical sources to work with, practically no correct Oriental texts, and about other parts of the world only the occasional reports of travellers . . . with these insufficient instruments, he worked out what seems to elude modern researchers. His knowledge of the pre-Sokratics is far more extensive than what can be derived from Hermann Diels, that bible of current scholarship, yet it remains this side of wrong guesses. His *Origine* may be judged extreme, but it is sound, coherent and impressive.[78]

In the twenty years following their publication Dupuis's views were enormously influential, and were seen as the ideological and theological parallel to the political challenge of the French Revolution. The Christian response to his attack will be examined in Chapter V, as well as the linked Hellenist challenge to his view of Greece as an appendage of Egypt, seen for instance in the statement that 'Egypt can be regarded as the mother of all theogonies and the source of all the fictions which the Greeks received and embellished, for it does not appear that they invented much.'[79]

THE EXPEDITION TO EGYPT

Whether or not Dupuis played a direct role in the decision to go to Egypt, there is no doubt that his presence as an important intellectual-political figure reflects the general Egyptophil atmosphere in Napoleonic circles before 1798, when the great Expedition there was launched. It is known that he influenced its further penetration of

Upper Egypt, which he believed to have been the source of Egyptian and hence world culture.[80]

Plans for the colonization of Egypt had in fact been made long before the Revolution, in the 1770s at the height of French Masonic enthusiasm for Egypt. While there were important political and economic reasons for the Expedition, there is no doubt that the ideas of France reviving the 'cradle of civilization' that Rome had destroyed, and the desire to understand the Egyptian mysteries, also provided important motivation.[81]

It is uncertain whether or not Napoleon was a Mason himself. There is, however, no doubt that he was deeply involved in Masonic affairs, that there were many members of the craft in the higher ranks of his army, and that Masonry 'flourished exceedingly' under his rule.[82] It is also clear that he took his imperial symbol of the bee from Egypt and probably through Masonic sources.[83] His initial behaviour in Egypt also indicates this influence: he tried, for instance, to transcend Christianity and appear as a champion of Islam and Judaism, and he dutifully went into the Great Pyramid and had a mystical experience.[84]

The whole Expedition is a fascinating turning point in European attitudes to the East. In many ways the elaborate surveys, maps and drawings, and the stealing of objects and cultural monuments to embellish France, was an early example of the standard pattern of studying and objectifying through scientific enquiry that became a hallmark of European imperialism and a basis of the 19th-century 'Orientalism' described so well by Edward Said.[85] On the other hand, there were still many traces of the older attitude towards Egypt, and among the scientific members of the Expedition there was the belief that, in Egypt, they could learn essential facts about the world and their own culture and not just exotica to complete Western knowledge – and domination – of Africa and Asia.

For instance, the mathematician Edmé-François Jomard made detailed measurements of the Pyramids and surveys of Egypt on the basis of ancient sources that maintained that the Egyptian measures of length were based on a detailed knowledge of the world's circumference; and that – as mentioned on pp. 166–7 in connection with Newton – the Great Pyramid incorporated specific fractions of latitude. When Jomard published his findings in 1829, at a time of passionate Hellenism, the astounding correspondences which he discovered were quickly rejected on grounds of alleged inaccuracies. His conclusions seem much more credible in the light of recent and more precise measurement.[86]

Even in 1798 Neo-Hellenism and Romanticism were already major forces. Despite his Masonic concerns, Napoleon was very much a child of his age: he clearly imagined himself as Alexander – seen in a very Greek way – and he took Plutarch's *Lives* with him to provide Classical models. He also had a copy of the *Iliad*, whose hero Achilles had been an inspiration to Alexander. More directly relevant was the copy of Xenophon's *Anabasis*, depicting a succession of episodes in which European Greeks cut their way through much larger numbers of assorted Asiatics. This suitable text became a 'bible' for 19th- and early-20th-century imperialism, although it took some decades for it to replace the democratic orations of Demosthenes and the *Iliad* as the standard text for beginning Greek.[87]

Napoleon's other reading provides a perfect sample of contemporary Romantic taste. There were the poems of *Ossian*, the central significance of which to the Romantic movement will be discussed in the next chapter. Finally, there were the Bible and the Sanskrit *Vedas* representing the new Romantic craze for Ancient India, to be described in Chapter V.[88]

Napoleon's position was, as usual, dramatic but his situation as someone living within the Ancient Model but caught up in the new paradigm of 'progress' and Romantic Hellenism was quite typical of the age. Schikaneder and Mozart might still be celebrating Egyptian wisdom in *The Magic Flute*, written in 1791, but that was in remote Vienna. Things were different in Western Europe. By 1780 Edward Gibbon was referring in a staged progressive way to 'Egyptian theology and the philosophy of the Greeks', and before this he had burnt his 'juvenile' essay on Sesōstris, arguing that 'at a riper age I no longer presume to connect the Greek, the Jewish and the Egyptian antiquities, which are lost in a distant cloud.'[89]

In the same decade another distinguished scholar made a move in the same direction. Abbé Barthélemy's work on the decipherment of Phoenician and the comparison of Coptic, Hebrew and Greek has already been mentioned; in 1788, near the end of his long life, he published what was to become his best-known work, *The Voyage of the Young Anacharsis*. This story of the journey of a young Scythian prince through 4th-century Greece was an erudite and heavily annotated novel in very much the same style as *Sèthos*, which, along with *Télémaque*, was one of its inspirations.[90] *Anacharsis's* success equalled that of *Sèthos*: it came out in more than forty editions in French and was translated into eight languages.[91] But the reversal it gives to the situation of Greece is fascinating. Where Fénelon's innocent young northerner Télémaque came from Greece to sophisticated Egypt, Anacharsis comes from virtuous Scythia to Greece in a period of sophistication and decadence, with Greece nevertheless the site of a great civilization.

While glorifying Greece, Barthélemy was too firmly rooted in the Ancient Model to neglect the civilizing roles of Egypt and Phoenicia. In his introduction to the novel, he saw the Egyptians as arriving as legislators for the primitive Greeks. Following Fréret, he dated this arrival not merely to Kekrops, Kadmos and Danaos, but to 300 years earlier in the 20th century BC with Inachos and Phoroneus – whom Greek tradition tended to regard as Pelasgian or autochthonous.[92] Further, he interestingly anticipated the argument put forward seventy years later – in the 1850s – by the great Semitist Ernest Renan that the harsh Semitic character and its harsh monotheism were created by the desert sun. Barthélemy argued that the blazing Egyptian sun and contrasting deep shade produced a severe simplicity of thought and art, while the sparkling light of Greece had produced something that was lighter and more vital:

> Thus the Greeks, emerging from their forests, no longer saw objects under a frightening and sombre veil. Thus the Egyptians in Greece softened bit by bit the severe and proud expressions in their paintings. The two groups, now making a single people, created a language that sparkled with vivid expressions. They clothed their old opinions with colours which changed their simplicity but made them more seductive.[93]

This view puts Barthélemy in what we can now see as a transitional phase. That is, he accepted Winckelmann's Romantic Neo-Hellenist view of the Egyptians as stiff, formal and somehow dead, while the Greeks were seen as laughing children. On the other hand, he did not see things as people in the 19th century did, in terms of the absolute need for Greek racial and linguistic purity. Thus he appears to have had no difficulty with the Ancient Model's descriptions of the colonizations.

Not only was *Anacharsis* a major route for escapism during the French Revolution, but it was probably the most influential history of Greece during the peak of Philhellenism in France. The most influential English book, a massive *History of Greece* written by Gibbon's friend William Mitford, was more straightforwardly academic. Mitford was much less impressed by Greece than Barthélemy had been. As a consistent conservative he rejected the idea of 'progress' and was not at all sure that Greece had surpassed Egypt and the Near East; in fact, he generally preferred the latter. As he wrote in the first volume of his *History*, which remained the standard work on the subject from its publication in 1784 until the 1830s:

> Assyria was a powerful empire, Egypt a most populous country governed by a very refined polity, and Sidon an opulent city abounding in manufactures and carrying an extensive commerce when the Greeks, ignorant of the most obvious and most necessary arts, are said to have fed upon acorns. Yet it [*sic*] was Greece the first country in Europe that emerged from barbarism; and this advantage it seems to have owed intirely [*sic*] to its readier communication with the civilized nations of the East.[94]

Mitford also maintained the Ancient Model's view of the colonization of Greece:

> It appears that in a very remote period some revolutions in Egypt, whose early transactions are otherwise little known to us, compelled a large proportion of the inhabitants to seek foreign settlements. Crete probably owed its civilization and polity to this event. **Some of the best-supported of Ancient Grecian traditions relate to the establishment of Egyptian colonies in Greece; traditions so little accommodating to national prejudice and so perfectly consonant to all known history, that for their essential circumstances they seem unquestionable.** [my emphasis][95]

The argument that traditions or legends are plausible if they are widespread, fit other historical patterns and outside information, and go against the interests of those who report them remains very powerful. However, it is interesting to note that there are no earlier defences of the Ancient Model. This is because the owl of Minerva flies only at dusk – that is, traditional beliefs are articulated only when they are under challenge. As with many embattled defenders of the *status quo*, Mitford argued that all serious scholars agreed with his position and believed with him in the Oriental origins of Greek civilization. He did, however, admit that a 'shallower' scholar, Samuel Musgrave, had argued that Greek culture was autochthonous.[96] It is to this kind of thinking that we must turn our attention in Chapter IV.

CHAPTER IV

Hostilities to Egypt in the 18th Century

W E ARE NOW APPROACHING the nub of this volume and the origins of the forces that eventually overthrew the Ancient Model, leading to the replacement of Egypt by Greece as the fount of European civilization. I concentrate on four of these forces: Christian reaction, the rise of the concept of 'progress', the growth of racism, and Romantic Hellenism. All are related; to the extent that Europe can be identified with Christendom, 'Christian reaction' is concerned with the continuation of European hostility and intensification of the tension between Egyptian religion and Christianity.

On the question of 'progress', I argue that its rise as a dominant paradigm damaged Egypt for two reasons. The country's great antiquity put it *behind* later civilizations; while its long and stable history, which had been a source of admiration, now. became reason to despise it as static and sterile. In the long run we can see that Egypt was also harmed by the rise of racism and the need to disparage every African culture; during the 18th century, however, the ambiguity of Egypt's 'racial' position allowed its supporters to claim that it was essentially and originally 'white'. Greece, by contrast, benefited from racism, immediately and in every way; and it was rapidly seen as the 'childhood' of the 'dynamic' 'European race'.

Racism and 'progress' could thus come together in the condemnation of Egyptian/African stagnation and praise of Greek/European dynamism and change. Such assessments fitted perfectly with the new Romanticism, which not only emphasized the importance of geographical and national characteristics and the categorical differences between peoples but saw dynamism as the highest value. Moreover, Greek states were small and often quite poor and their national poet was Homer, whose heroic epics fitted splendidly with the 18th-century Romantic passion for Northern ballads, most of which were extremely gory, like the *Iliad*. Here, as with language, a special relationship was seen between Greece and Northern Europe which was marred only by Greece's geographical position in the South-Eastern Mediterranean and the Ancient Model, which emphasized her close association with the Middle East. All in all, while Egypt, along with China and Rome, were the models of the Enlightenment, Greece became allied to the lesser, but growing 18th-century intellectual and emotional current of Romanticism.

CHRISTIAN REACTION

Here it should be emphasized that for most of the almost 2,000 years with which we are concerned, the tension or 'contradiction' between Christianity and the Egyptian 'twofold' philosophy was not – in the Leninist or Maoist sense – an 'antagonistic' one. As movements confined to the elite, Hermeticism and Masonry did not fundamentally threaten the social, political or even the religious *status quo*. However, the exclusive claims of Judaeo-Christian-Islamic monotheisms make any kind of unconformity difficult to tolerate, and there have been periods of bitter rivalry between the two traditions.

The ruthless and bloody destruction of Gnosticism and Neo-Platonism by the early Church was mentioned in Chapter II. In the 15th and 16th centuries, however, the Church generally tolerated or even encouraged Platonism and Hermeticism. The execution of Bruno was not surprising, given his blatant attacks on the Judaeo-Christian tradition and his call for a return to Egyptian religion. Moreover, the burning was followed not by a ban on the study of Egypt but by the encouragement and massive funding of what Frances Yates calls Athanasius Kircher's 'reactionary Hermeticism' or, to put it more charitably, a Church-sanctioned 'Egyptology' which included Kircher's establishment of Coptic studies.[1] Although Hermeticism and Rosicrucianism were often influential in Northern European intellectual circles, they did not loom large in the violence of the Thirty Years War in Germany, the Fronde revolts in France and the anti-monarchical struggles in England and Holland. The religious struggles between Catholic and Protestant or High and Low Church had little or nothing to do with Hermeticism.

Neo-Platonism and Hermeticism, as I have said, were often philosophies espoused by moderates as attempts to transcend the raging political and religious battles of the time. Similarly, the atomist atheism associated with Thomas Hobbes grew up in an atmosphere of despair at competing brands of religion. Thus in England in the 1660s and 1670s moderate men like Ralph Cudworth, who were concerned with two main foes, Catholic superstition and Puritan Enthusiasm, saw Platonism as an antidote to both.[2] Apart from its transcendence over sectarian squabbles, its doctrine that there was a light or life immanent in the world weakened the Enthusiasts' – or inspired believers' – claims to have a monopoly of holy spirit. Furthermore, Cudworth believed that the dangers of atheism from the Egypto-Platonic identification of spirit with matter, or the Creator with the Creation, was less acute than that from Hobbesian mechanical, atomist atheism.[3]

Newton was intellectually formed in this atmosphere and it is in this context that his early admiration for the Egyptians, referred to in the last chapter, must be seen. However, his attitude towards Egypt changed drastically in the 1690s and the last years of his life were spent on chronological works, of which the most important was *The Chronology of Ancient Kingdoms Amended*. Here, as mentioned on p. 168, Newton *proved*, on the basis of the Bible and astronomy, that the claims for antiquity made by the Egyptians and other peoples had been grossly exaggerated, and that the Israelites had existed long before all the others.

Newton's most recent biographer, Professor Westfall, describes this as 'a work of colossal tedium' and believes that in it Newton had 'produced a book with no evident point and no evident form'. The only explanation Westfall can give for it is that it had a concealed deist message.[4] But the same could be said for most of Newton's works, and I do not think it provides a sufficient motive for the immense labour he put into his *Chronology*. Indeed, it could be argued that it was the most orthodox work Newton ever wrote: William Whiston, who can be described as Newton's deist conscience, fiercely attacked *The Chronology*, as did the French atheist Fréret.[5] Furthermore, as Westfall points out, Newton had effectively been co-opted by the Establishment by the end of his life. Thus I think it more useful to see *The Chronology* as the result of what the modern intellectual historian Professor Pocock describes as 'a complete reversal in Cudworth's attempt to demonstrate that ancient thinking was naturally in accord with Christian theology'.

Pocock attributes this partly to the 'impact of Spinoza', an attribution that has problems because, as the historian Professor Colie has shown, Cudworth was fully aware of Spinoza's thinking by the 1670s, and his great work *The True Intellectual System of the Universe* contained an attack on Spinoza's position.[6] This is not to deny that Spinoza's pantheism continued to weaken the possibility of a Christian Platonism after the publication of Cudworth's work in 1679. However, the new factors after the 'Glorious Revolution' of 1689 were Toland and the Radical Enlightenment. All in all, I think Newton's later work and his lowering of the antiquity of the Egyptians and other ancient peoples should generally be seen as a 'respectable' deist and Christian defence against the Radical Enlightenment and the latter's use of the antiquity of Egypt and the Orient. As with Bruno in the 16th century, the peaceful coexistence between Christianity and esoteric Egyptian religion and philosophy, which had lasted through most of the Renaissance, broke down in the 1690s and the Christians struck back.

THE 'TRIANGLE':
CHRISTIANITY AND GREECE
AGAINST EGYPT

The defence of Newtonianism brought Greek studies into alliance with Christianity, and this brings us to a central concern of this volume, which is less with the binary conflict between Egypt and the Bible than with the triangular relations between Christianity, Egypt and Greece. During the first centuries of the Christian era the main struggle was between Christians and pagans. As the dominant culture of the East Mediterranean during this period was Hellenic with a religion based on Egypt, both Christians and pagans – of whom the most influential were the Neo-Platonists – saw the distinctions between Egypt, the Orient and Greece as relatively unimportant. Jews like Josephus and Church Fathers like Clement of Alexandria and Tatian, on the other hand, scored points against the Greeks by pointing out the lateness and shallowness of Greek civilization in comparison with those of the Egyptians, Phoenicians, Chaldaeans, Persians and so on and, of course, the Israelites. They also stressed Greece's heavy cultural borrowings from the more ancient peoples.[7]

The possibility of pitting Greeks against the Egyptians, Chaldaeans and others, in the defence of Christianity, did not occur until the Renaissance. I have already pointed out that Erasmus' hostility to Hermeticism in the early 16th century was essentially linked to his defence of Christianity and religion against magic. Erasmus, however, was also a champion of pure Latinity and the study of Greek.[8]

During these same decades, Germans were becoming aware of striking similarities between their language and Greek. The nouns of both had four cases rather than the five of Latin. Both Greek and German used the definite article and made massive use of particles and of prepositions with verbs. After the Reformation, and the break away from *Roman* Catholicism, the relationship became much stronger, with the new image of Greek and German as the two languages of Protestantism. Luther fought the Church of Rome with the Greek Testament. Greek was a sacred Christian tongue which Protestants could plausibly claim was more authentically Christian than Latin. With the spread of the Reformation to England, Scotland and Scandinavia, a feeling developed that the Teutonic-speaking peoples were 'better' and more 'manly' than the Romance-speaking nations of France, Spain and Italy and that their languages as a whole were superior to Latin and on a par with Greek. As a 17th-century English writer put it:

Our language was a dialect of the Teutonick, and although then but in her infancie, yet not so rude as hopefull, being most fruitfull and copious in significant and well-founding rootes and Primitives and withall capable and apt for diffusion from those her rootes into such a Greek-like ramosity [sic] of derivations and compositions, beyond the power of Latine and her off-spring dialects . . .[9]

Greek studies flourished in Protestant schools and universities throughout the 16th and 17th centuries. It is striking, for instance, how many of the major French Hellenists of the 17th century – including Isaac Casaubon and Mme Dacier, who will be discussed when I come to the cult of Homer – were brought up as Huguenots.[10] From using Greek to attack Roman Catholic superstition, it was not such a long step to employing it against Egyptian magic. Nevertheless, Casaubon's criticism of the antiquity of the Hermetic Texts was not juxtaposing a rational Greece to a magical and superstitious Egypt. It was using critical methods of approach to Greek texts to discredit the age, and hence the value, of Egyptian wisdom.

A similar approach was used seventy years later by Richard Bentley. Known in his lifetime as the hated and tyrannical Master of Trinity College Cambridge, Bentley is, however, a hero in the history of Classics as the discoverer of the *digamma*, or rather of the fact that the w sound represented as F in some Greek alphabets had existed in Homeric and other Greek dialects, in which it was not written. This Bentley did with extreme ingenuity by observing that in certain cases words beginning with vowels did not elide or come together with the preceding syllables. He is even more respected for his rigorous critical scholarship which, though not particularly appreciated in his own day, has given him the later reputation as the greatest English Classicist of all time.[11]

Richard Bentley was also the first man to popularize Newtonian physics and to spell out its theological and political implications: that, as matter could not move itself, a god – of generally regular habits – was needed to create and maintain the universe, just as a king was necessary to a Whig constitutional monarchy. Bentley put this scheme forward in 1692, when he preached the first series of sermons or lectures set up by the famous Anglo-Irish chemist Sir Robert Boyle against 'notorious infidels, namely, Atheists, Theists, Pagans, Jews and Mahometans'.[12] Bentley hardly mentioned the last two. His concern was clearly with the first three, and most of all with the Radical Enlightenment. He seems to have been especially concerned with the radical thinker and pioneer of Freemasonry John Toland's use of Bruno's Egyptian notion of animate matter, which the radical had used to attack Newtonian physics. Bentley and his circle also seem to have known about Toland's republicanism. Toland was fully aware of the interconnections between his physics and his politics.[13] Bentley used his own formidable intelligence and Classical scholarship not only to expound the Newtonian system and its implications, but also to cast doubt on the reliability and age of the Greek sources referring to Egyptian and Oriental wisdom and astronomy.[14] Thus he tried to deprive Toland and the radicals of one of their most powerful sources of legitimacy.

What most concerns us here, however, is the alliance between Newton and Bentley and the combination of the new science and critical Classical scholarship to defend the *status quo*. It is ironic that these two men, who were always on, if not over, the brink of Arianism or deism became two of the most effective defenders of the Christian Establishment.[15]

THE ALLIANCE BETWEEN
GREECE AND CHRISTIANITY

A more orthodox alliance between Christianity and Greece was present in the work of John Potter, a younger contemporary of Bentley at Wakefield Grammar School and later Archbishop of Canterbury. In 1697 Potter brought out four volumes on Greek political institutions and religion which, with new editions, remained standard until replaced by Dr Smith's *Dictionary* in 1848.[16] Working in a tradition that went back at least to Lucretius, Potter maintained not only that Athens, unlike the rest of Greece, had never been conquered by barbarians but also that Greek culture and institutions had come from Athens.[17] In this way he was able to detach Greece from the Near East without challenging the ancient authority for the invasions.

This tension is also present in his treatment of Greek religion. Here, though he tried to raise Thrace to equal status, he admitted that the religion had come from Egypt but went on to treat it as if it were purely Greek.[18] Throughout the 18th century one finds similar attempts, especially among Christian apologists, to reconcile a desire to play down Egypt and elevate Greece with an inability to confront the Ancient Model.

'PROGRESS' AGAINST EGYPT

While the proponents of the Radical Enlightenment in England used the antiquity of Egypt and Mesopotamia to bolster their position, they, like the French Moderns, seem to have felt themselves to be 'progress-ive'. In the long run, however, Egypt was bound to lose from the establishment of the new paradigm of 'progress'. The transformation this brought about can be seen in the contrast between Newton's attack in the 1710s on the antiquity of Egypt and the East, and Bishop William Warburton's very different approach in the 1730s. Warburton saw his *The Divine Legation of Moses* as part of the struggle against deists, Spinozists and pantheists, whose opposition to Christianity he traced back to the Neo-Platonists.[19] Thus, in attacking the Radical Enlighten-ment, Warburton gave defence of Christianity a progressive edge. As Pocock describes his position:

> far from seeing modern philosophy as threatening religion with its scepticism, he was much inclined to the view that only in modernity had philosophy attained to the sanctity and moderation compat-ible with belief. Even the irreligion of modern times – which he identified with Jacob's Radical Reformation [Enlightenment] – seemed to Warburton an archaistic revival of 'ancient' modes of philosophizing.[20]

Warburton's view of Egyptian religion itself was regressive, and not so far from that of Newton. Writing in the 1730s, he could not deny that Egyptian religion had once been a sublime monotheism, but he argued that it had fallen into appalling idolatry. In what Frank Manuel has described as a bishop's 'sense of solidarity with the priesthood of

Egypt', he blamed this corruption on the politicians.[21] In Warburton's eyes, however, priority was no advantage. He savaged Newton's chronology, even though this put him alongside such notorious deists as William Whiston and atheists like Nicolas Fréret.[22]

For Warburton, the fact that the Greeks came later made them better. They had excelled their teachers. While he was obliged to admit that the Greeks had learnt the names of the gods and their rituals from the Egyptians, he emphatically denied that they were the same.[23] He also maintained that while Pythagoras had studied in Egypt for twenty-one years he had set out his theorems only on his return to Greece. On this basis, he argued that the Egyptians had been unable to hypothesize – a canon that survives today.

A similar ambivalence towards Ancient Egypt was expressed by Jacob Brucker, the great German historian of philosophy of the mid-18th century.[24] Unable to deny the massive ancient tradition that the Egyptians had been philosophers, Brucker nevertheless argued that they should more properly be called 'theogonists' who had invented and manipulated allegories. According to him, true philosophy had begun with the 'Pre-Sokratic' Ionians, but the real break with theogony had come with Sokrates himself. Sokrates' triumph, according to Brucker, was that, as Professor Pocock puts it, he

> abandoned the attempt to know nature, regarding it instead with reverent scepticism, and had focused philosophy on its proper object, the discovery of moral truths leading to the apprehension of the true god.[25]

This anti-scientific 'philosophy', however, was betrayed by Plato, who had unluckily studied with Pythagoreans in Sicily and priests in Egypt. According to Brucker, Plato had reimported the allegory, poetry and esotericism from which the Ionians and Sokrates had tried to break away.[26] Thus – by making a rather improbable categorical break between Sokrates and his devoted disciple and biographer, Plato – Brucker was able to claim superiority for the Greeks, at the same time retaining the ancient view that all types of Platonism were integrally bound to the Egyptian tradition.

EUROPE AS THE
'PROGRESSIVE' CONTINENT

The Turkish defeats of the 1680s and the general acceptance of Newtonian physics transformed Europe's self-image. In the post-Newtonian world writers like Montesquieu, whose reference to the Egyptians as the greatest philosophers has been noted above, began to contrast Oriental 'wisdom' with the 'natural philosophy' of Europe.[27] Montesquieu wrote this in 1721; as the century continued, the notion of European superiority increased with European economic and industrial progress, and expansion into other continents.

The position was far from that produced with the triumph of imperialism in the 19th century, however, for no European of the 18th century could claim that Europe had created herself. Nevertheless, it was argued that Europe was now further advanced than any other continent, and here there was a close parallel with the situation in 4th-century and Hellenistic Greece *vis-à-vis* the older civilizations. For instance, there is the frequently quoted passage in *Epinomis*, by Plato or one of his students, after a laudatory description of Egyptian and Syrian astronomy: 'And let us note, that whatever the Greeks acquire from foreigners is finally turned by them into something finer.'[28]

The claim that some ineffable quality is added to imported techniques, concepts or aesthetic styles often occurs in culturally peripheral nations like England, Germany, Japan, Korea or Vietnam. Cultural pride needs to be maintained in the face of foreign borrowing that is so massive that it cannot be denied, or where borrowings run counter to a hierarchy of cultural or 'racial' superiority.[29] As the popular writer Oliver Goldsmith wrote – in 1774 in his *History of the Earth* – strikingly paraphrasing *Epinomis*: 'Those arts which might have had their invention among other races of mankind have come to their perfection there [in Europe].'[30]

'PROGRESS'

It is frequently said that the clearest 18th-century statement of the idea of 'progress' was that of Condorcet's *Sketch of a historical table of the progress of the human spirit*, written in 1793. However, most of the ideas

Condorcet propounded there had been set out earlier in a speech *On the Successive Progress of the Human Spirit*, given in 1750 by the nineteen-year-old Anne Robert Turgot. Turgot, who later became a finance minister of Louis XVI, was close to the leading Physiocrats and was a promoter of Chinese economic ideas. He was subsequently described as the founder of political economy. From the speech and unfinished draft histories, his ideas on 'progress' are quite clear.[31]

These ideas are important in themselves and because of their bearing on the views held by Turgot and his contemporaries on the Egyptians, Phoenicians and Greeks. According to the new paradigm, these civilizations had to be seen in ascending order as the human spirit 'progressed'. But, as in all schemes of historical evolution – notably the Hegelian and the Marxist – each stage was seen as having started out beneficially 'progressive' but as having later slipped into decadence and opposition to the new forces. Thus Turgot saw Egypt and China as initially pioneering: 'they advanced with great strides towards perfection.'[32]

The Egyptians and Chinese were perceived as having been mathematicians, philosophers and metaphysicians. Unfortunately, in both civilizations these 'sciences' had been sapped by superstition and priestly dogmatism. Just as Bishop Warburton had tried to exculpate the priests on this issue out of 'clerical solidarity', so intellectuals like Turgot and Condorcet were delighted to have yet another stick with which to beat them, for here, as in the modern world, priests could largely be blamed for the decadence.[33] However, Turgot differed from the Physiocrats, who admired contemporary China, by condemning the country to the past; and this part of the 'progressive' scheme brought him – or kept him – very close to the old, regressive picture of the Egyptians as having been in possession – probably from the Israelites – of a pure and true religion, but as having lost it.

Turgot also saw the decadence as the result of the despotism of Egyptian and Chinese government. Like Montesquieu, however, who had attributed it to the morally improving effects of irrigation, Turgot maintained that Egyptian and Chinese governments were not as bad as their hot climates would seem to determine, or as the Mahometan forms actually were.[34] Like Brucker and most 18th-century thinkers,

Turgot included the Pythagoreans, Neo-Platonists and, by implication, Plato himself among the decadent Asiatic metaphysicians.[35] For him, the higher stages of the progress of the human spirit began with Aristotle's logic and continued directly to Bacon, Galileo, Kepler, Descartes, Newton and Leibniz.[36] As far as Greece was concerned Turgot, although encouraged by the country's disunity and liberty, believed that 'it was only after many centuries that one saw the appearance of philosophers in Greece.'[37]

For Turgot the real Hellenic glory was in poetry, which derived directly from the richness of the Greek language. This richness had come about because

> The Phoenicians, inhabiting an arid coast, made themselves the agents of exchange between peoples. Their vessels spread throughout the Mediterranean. They began to reveal nation to nation, astronomy, navigation and geography perfected each other. The coasts of Greece and Asia Minor were filled with colonies . . . From the mixtures of these independent colonies with the ancient peoples of Greece and with the remains of successive barbarian invasions the Greek nation was formed . . . by these multiple mixtures this rich language was formed, expressive and sonorous, the language for all the arts.[38]

The liberal denial of the Egyptians in favour of the Phoenicians was an indication of future attitudes on their relative importance. Otherwise, Turgot's statement reflects the contemporary linguistic research already mentioned in connection with Barthélemy, and Turgot's scheme also seems to reflect the origin of French from a mixture of Celtic, Latin and Germanic languages.[39] This does not, however, affect its competitive plausibility against the equally subjective image of Greek as a language that was somehow 'pure', like the idealized German. The picture of purity is extremely improbable, not only on geographical and historical grounds but also, as Turgot pointed out, on linguistic ones too.

While Turgot and his contemporaries proclaimed and articulated the new vision of 'progress', they retained respect for the Egyptians and Phoenicians and never questioned the legends of their having colonized

and civilized Greece.[40] Nevertheless, the introduction of the 'progressive' paradigm was ultimately fatal to the reputation of the Egyptians.
Their antiquity – which had previously been one of their major assets –
now became a liability.

The obverse to the fall of the Egyptians was a rise in the status of the
Greeks. Before coming to this, however, we must consider the two
forces that aided Christian reaction and the 'progressive' paradigm in
the overthrow of the Ancient Model: racism and Romanticism.

RACISM

All cultures have some degree of prejudice for, or more often against,
people whose appearance is unusual. However, the intensity and
pervasiveness of Northern European, American and other colonial
racism since the 17th century have been so much greater than the norm
that they need some special explanation.

It is difficult to say whether or not racism was unusually strong before
the 16th century, the first in which Northern Europeans came into
frequent contact with peoples from other continents. In the early
anti-Semitic ballads about the alleged murder of Little Sir Hugh, the
evil Jews do not appear to have been seen as particularly dark.[41] It is
even possible that with the influx of French and Italians after the
Norman Conquest, dark colouring had high status, and early ballads do
sometimes contrast the poor fair girl with the rich brown one. On the
other hand, there is no doubt that the 'fair maid' is seen as morally
superior and the ballads of two sisters, which appear to have very old
Norse antecedents, lay emphasis on the wicked dark sister as opposed
to the good fair one.[42]

By the 15th century, too, there is no doubt that clear links were seen
between dark skin colour and evil and inferiority, when the newly
arrived Gypsies were feared and hated for both their darkness and their
alleged sexual prowess.[43] Whether or not this concern with and dislike
of the dark 'other' was exceptionally intense in medieval Northern
Europe, it is generally accepted that a more clear-cut racism grew up
after 1650 and that this was greatly intensified by the increased
colonization of North America, with its twin policies of extermination

of the Native Americans and enslavement of Africans. Both these presented moral problems to Protestant societies, in which equality of all men before God, and personal liberty, were central values which could be eased only by strong racism.

The Classical writer most often appealed to to justify slavery was Aristotle, who had argued at length in its favour. The appeal was linked to the fact that his work was shot through with the belief that Greeks were inherently superior to other peoples:

> The races that live in cold regions and those of Europe are full of courage and passion but somewhat lacking in skill and brainpower; for this reason, while remaining generally independent, they lack political cohesion and the ability to rule others. On the other hand, the Asiatic races have both brains and skill but are lacking in courage and willpower; so they have remained both enslaved and subject. The Hellenic race, occupying a mid position geographically, has a measure of both. Hence it has continued to be free, to have the best political institutions and to be capable of ruling others given a single constitution.[44]

In this way Aristotle linked 'racial superiority' to the right to enslave other peoples, especially those of a 'slavish disposition'.

Similar perceptions of 'racial' differences appear to have been central to the thought of John Locke, the philosopher of the late-17th-century Whigs. There is no doubt that Locke, who was personally involved with slave-owning American colonies, was what we should now call a racist, as was the great 18th-century philosopher David Hume. Whether or not these attitudes affected their philosophies is more debatable, but Harry Bracken and Noam Chomsky's arguments for this connection seem very plausible.[45]

Locke's consistent disparagement of Native Americans was essential to his politics, because the land the indigenous population inhabited was needed to provide a wilderness available for English and other settlers. The possibility of such colonization was necessary to the argument that men had a choice as to whether or not they joined the Social Contract, with all its manifest inequalities.[46] Locke refused to justify the enslavement of people of the same nationality, and called what might appear to be slavery of this kind mere 'drudgery'. For him, as for most thinkers of the time, slavery was justified only when it was the result of capture as an alternative to a deserved death in a just war.[47] Christian European attacks on heathen Africans and Americans, for instance, were classed as 'just wars' because the latter were not defending their property, but merely 'waste land'. Furthermore, Locke had the curious but convenient belief that Africans and Americans did not practise agriculture and, according to him, the only entitlement to land came from cultivation.[48] The general scheme allowed for the taking of black slaves by Europeans. Moreover, the very existence of large numbers of African slaves led to the belief that they were 'natural slaves' in the Aristotelian sense.

By the 1680s there was in fact a widespread opinion that Negroes were only one link above the apes – also from Africa – in the 'great chain of being'.[49] This type of thinking was made easier by Locke's nominalism: his denial of the objective validity of 'species' and view of them as subjective concepts. He was particularly sceptical of the inconvenient category of 'man':

> And I imagine none of the Definitions of the Word *man*, which we yet have, nor Descriptions of that sort of Animal, are so perfect and exact, as to satisfy a considerate inquisitive person; much less a general consent . . .[50]

This position is in sharp contrast not only to the biblical 'God made man in his own image' but also to Descartes's insistence on a categorical distinction between unthinking animals and thinking man. Empiricism thus seems to remove an (admittedly flimsy) barrier against racism; however, there is no necessary connection between empiricism and racism.[51]

To recapitulate: it is certain that Locke and most 18th-century English-speaking thinkers like David Hume and Benjamin Franklin were racist: they openly expressed popular opinions that dark skin colour was linked to moral and mental inferiority. In Hume's case, racism so transcended conventional religion that he was a pioneer of the view that there had been not one creation of man but many different ones, because 'Such a uniform and constant difference could not happen in so many countries and ages, if nature had not made an original distinction betwixt these breeds of men.'[52] The centrality of racism to European society after 1700 is shown by the fact that this 'polygenetic' view of human origins continued to grow in the early 19th century, even after the revival of Christianity.

Racism was not so clear-cut in 18th-century France. Nevertheless, the Aristotelian – and pseudo-Platonic – scheme of climatic and topographic determinism of races that had permeated the work of Jean Bodin in the 16th century was revitalized by Montesquieu in the 18th.[53] Montesquieu became famous in 1721 through his *Persian Letters*. At one level he was using distinguished Persians to criticize and satirize Europe; at another, he was setting up the image of Europe as the 'scientific' and 'progressive' continent. This primacy was explained as the result of her beneficent, temperate climate. His pro-European views and hostility to Asia and Africa came out more clearly in his *Spirit of Laws*, which was published in 1748.[54]

Rousseau, in his *Social Contract*, published in 1762, violently attacked any justification of slavery. On the other hand, he followed the school of geographical determinism, believing that a people's virtue and political capacity depended on climate and topography. He was Europocentric and showed remarkably little interest in Egypt and China. This was a trait which persisted among later Romantics, whose predilections were nearly always for the misty and mountainous North of Europe, which was seen as the true repository of human virtue.

ROMANTICISM

After the defence of Christianity and the idea of 'progress', racism was, I believe, the third major force behind the overthrow of the Ancient Model; the fourth was Romanticism. To put it crudely, Romanticism maintains, against the Enlightenment and the Masonic tradition, that reason is inadequate to handle the important aspects of life and philosophy. Romanticism is concerned with the local and particular, rather than the global and general. There is also an oversimplified, but useful, contrast to be made between the 18th-century Enlightenment, with its interest in stability and the ordering of space, and the Romantic passion for movement, time and 'progressive' development through history. Outstanding examples of Enlightenment achievement are the accurate mappings of the world's coasts, Linnaeus' systematic arrangement of natural species, and the American Constitution, which is supposed to last for ever.

Apart from the extraordinary achievements of natural science during the period of Romantic dominance from 1790 to 1890 there was an enormous interest in history, and in both the chief model used was that of the 'tree'. Trees, which are to be found in Darwinian evolution, Indo-European linguistics and most 19th-century histories, provide the ideal Romantic image. They are rooted in their own soils and nourished by their particular climates; at the same time they are alive and grow. They progress and never turn back. Like the image of history as biography mentioned above, trees have a simple past and a complicated and ramified present and future. Nevertheless, the image of the tree had disadvantages in the description of European and Greek history, and I shall return to this theme later.[55]

It should be borne in mind that despite the enormous influence of Rousseau, Romanticism was never as strong in France as it was in Britain and Germany, and it is in these regions that one should look for the movement's further development.

First, Germany: during the early part of the 18th century, Germany went through one of its most acute crises of national identity. In striking contrast to France, Holland and England, for more than a century following the end of the Thirty Years War in 1648 there was continued military devastation, political fragmentation and economic backwardness. The same period saw the military and cultural rise of France to a point where it seemed about to become a 'New Rome', capable of absorbing all Europe.[56] The language and culture of the German courts, including that of Frederick the Great in Prussia, was French; most of the books published in Germany in the first half of the century were in Latin and French. Thus there was a reasonable fear, voiced by the late-17th-century philosopher and mathematician Leibniz and later patriots, that German would never develop into a language capable of being used for cultural and philosophical discourse; it might even, like the Germanic Frankish language spoken by the early rulers of

France, disappear altogether in the face of French. German culture and the German people were seen as being in mortal danger.[57]

The most significant response to this crisis on the part of the German Romantics was the attempt to return Germans to their cultural roots, and to create an authentic German civilization from the German soil and the German people. According to the new Romantic and progressive views, peoples now had to be seen in their geographical and historical contexts. The racial genius or spirit belonging to the land and *its* people changed its forms according to the spirit of the age or, to use a term developed in the 1780s, its *Zeitgeist*; but a people always retained its immutable essence. The most powerful figure concerned with this aspect of the Romantic movement was Johann Gottfried Herder, who was also important in relation both to Neo-Hellenism and the development of linguistics. Herder himself stayed within the universalist bounds of the Enlightenment, maintaining that all peoples, not merely Germans, should be encouraged to discover and develop their own genii.[58] Nevertheless, the concern with history and local particularity, and the disdain for rationality or 'pure reason' apparent in his views and those of other late-18th- and early-19th-century German thinkers including Kant, Fichte, Hegel and the Schlegels, provided a firm basis for the chauvinism and racism of the following two centuries.

OSSIAN AND HOMER

The two purest essences of a 'race' were seen as being its language and folksong. As sounds they were temporal, not spatial. They were not stable but moving, if not 'living', and they were seen as communicating feeling, not reason. Furthermore, they were felt to be expressions not merely of the whole race but of its most characteristic and vital period, its 'childhood' or primitive stage. At this point, then, we focus on folksong and ballads.

In the concern with songs and epics and their relation to a people, the main impetus behind the German movement came from Britain or, more precisely, Scotland. The Act of Union with England in 1707, the defeats of the Old Pretender and his son Bonnie Prince Charlie in 1715 and 1745 and the destruction of the Gaelic culture of the Highlands forced a major realignment of the old nationalism. Upper-class English-speaking Scots very quickly developed a safe literary sublimation of nationalism, in which there was a cult of the simple, the backward and the remote combined with a nostalgia for a lost innocence.[59] The chief artistic expressions of this were genuine or newly manufactured ballads or folksongs.

By far the most influential product of this movement was Robert MacPherson's forgery of a Gaelic epic cycle, allegedly by the 3rd-century poet Ossian, about the heroic deeds of his father. *Ossian* was published in 1762 and, although soon shown to be a forgery, remained the most widely read poem in Europe for the next fifty years. It has been mentioned above (see p. 185) as being among Napoleon's books in Egypt. Even before *Ossian*, Bishop Percy had brought out his *Reliques of Ancient English Poetry*. This collection of genuine Scottish and English Border ballads also had a powerful influence throughout Europe, especially in Germany, where it inspired Herder to promote a new movement to collect and publish folksongs.[60] The folksong movement became integrated with the 'storm and stress' school started by Goethe around novels (*Romane* in German – from which '*Roman*ticism' gets its name).

For most of the later 18th century, Ossian was considered to be better than Homer. This does not mean, however, that Homer was unpopular. He had held a very special position in Ancient Greece: he was 'the Poet' and his epics were central to all Greek education and to the sense of being Greek.[61] In Rome, a Greek education always began with Homer. In the Renaissance – despite the dominance of the Platonic-Egyptian tradition – there was considerable concern for Homer, especially among Protestant scholars, with their attachment to Greek as a sacred and non-Roman language. As Tanneguy Le Fèvre, a leading Huguenot scholar and the father of Anne Dacier, wrote in 1664:

> The Ancients – geographers, poets, rhetoricians, theologians, doctors of medicine, moral philosophers, and even army generals – regarded Homer as an ultimate source of wisdom in each of their professions.[62]

Madame Dacier herself translated Homer into French and championed him against the Moderns and the general public, whom she believed to be prejudiced against him. She and her husband made a well-paid and opportune conversion to Catholicism just before Protestantism was banned, a conversion which is difficult to reconcile with her concern with morality and high principles. However, the tension seems to have been eased by her continued loyalty to her father's secular passion for Homer.

In 1714 Madame Dacier published her extremely influential *On the Causes of the Corruption of Taste*. In this she attacked the Moderns like Terrasson, who had criticized Homer and the Greeks as being too primitive and crude for civilized peoples like the modern French and the Ancient Egyptians. She saw Homer as the earliest poet who had expressed the feelings of an uncorrupted age, but to make him the earliest she had to deny the importance not only of Egyptian but of 'Hebraic' civilization.[63] However, Madame Dacier and the Ancients were not successful in promoting the Greeks in France, the centre of the Enlightenment. As Voltaire wrote in the middle of the century: 'It seems to me that the Greeks are no longer fashionable and that was true from the times of M. and Mme Dacier.'[64]

Things were different in other countries. The Italian scholar and visionary Giovanni Battista Vico, writing in the 1720s, saw Homer as the epitome of 'poetic wisdom' in the first two 'divine' and 'heroic' stages of his historical scheme.[65] Then in the 1730s an Aberdonian, Thomas Blackwell – the teacher of MacPherson, creator of Ossian – saw Homer as the poet of the primitive age, and the Greeks as the childhood of Europe.[66]

The new concept of 'childhood' that developed with such speed in the 18th century comes at the intersection of 'progress' and Romanticism. Childhood was seen as a period of emotion and feeling before rationality, but also as one that was without the sexuality and corruption of adulthood. Furthermore, it was a period of potential – looking towards the future and not tied to the past. Thus the growth of childhood went hand in hand with the growth of Romanticism and 'progress'. Classical authority for the image of Greeks as children came from Plato's *Timaios*, in which, as I have already mentioned, Plato reports an aged Egyptian priest as telling Solon: 'You Greeks are always children: there is no such thing as an old Greek . . . You are always young in soul, every one of you. For . . . you possess not a single belief that is ancient . . .'[67]

For ancient, medieval and Renaissance scholars such a statement was utterly damning. Even the 18th-century Moderns were able to condemn the Greeks as childish and trivial. With the rise of the concept of 'progress' this could be, and was, turned to the Greeks' advantage.

ROMANTIC HELLENISM

It is often assumed that as the country was part of the Classical world, study or admiration of Greece should be seen as a form of Classicism. In the 18th century, however, Hellenism is far more usefully seen as belonging to the Romantic camp. The gentlemen of the Enlightenment were concerned with order, regularity and stability over wide regions. In the contemporary world they tended to be concerned with the 'big ones', concentrating their efforts at reform on France, Russia and Prussia. In Antiquity they preferred powerful states that had lasted over long periods of time, like China, Egypt and Rome. As Classicists they read most of the Latin authors, but little or no Greek. By the 1790s, however, the upper classes were beginning to read Homer in the original. Thus the shift from reason to sentiment was associated with a shift of attention from Imperial Rome to Classical and Homeric Greece.

Romantics longed for small, virtuous and 'pure' communities in remote and cold places: Switzerland, North Germany and Scotland. When considering the past, their natural choice was Greece. It clearly qualified in terms of smallness, and its states could, with some stretching of the imagination, be described as virtuous. Its lacks in the other respects could be temporarily overlooked, although in the long run it was more difficult to do this. In many ways the destruction of the Ancient Model and the establishment of the Aryan one can best be seen as attempts to impose these Romantic ideals of remoteness, cold and purity on this most unsuitable candidate.[68]

Romanticism had existed from the beginning of the Enlightenment, and in the very cosmopolitan 3rd Earl of Shaftesbury, Locke's pupil, 'sensibility' – combined with a cult of beauty and form – was associated with a Neo-Hellenism.[69] Then in the 1730s, British Romantic Philhellenism increased with Blackwell's association of Homer with Scotland, mentioned on p. 208. In the same decade, the Society of Dilettanti was founded. The Society, as its name suggests, started as a social club for rich young men, but it became more serious in the import of Classical statues from Italy to decorate the houses and parks of the British nobility. In 1750 it extended its activities, commissioning a thorough and accurate survey of the surviving works of ancient art in Athens. The commission reflected a great new enthusiasm for Greek art, which West Europeans had so far seen only in Roman copies. At the same time daring noblemen began to extend their Grand Tours from Italy to the Levant, which included Greece.[70] Enlightened scholars could study the general truths of the world by reading books in the comfort of their studies.

But this was not good enough for Romantics, with their concerns for feeling and particular locality. They wanted to confront, and if possible even smell, the original documents and other remains of the period and place they wished to study.[71] In the 1750s, for instance, Robert Wood went to the Troad – the region around Troy – and read the *Iliad in situ*. In his *Essay on the Original Genius and Writings of Homer*, which appeared in 1775, Wood saw Homer as the product of a particular people in a particular landscape. Although – unlike later Romantics – he still maintained that Homer was one man, he drew on the ancient tradition that Homer had been blind to stress his illiteracy. Wood's picture of Homer was very 'Ossianic' – that is, it was of a primitive and almost Northern bard, the poet of the childhood not only of Greece but of all Europe.[72]

By the middle of the century the Romantic mood, Europocentrism, and the concept of 'progress' were creating a considerable enthusiasm in Britain for the Greeks, who seemed to fit all these criteria. James Harris, the English grammarian – who, it is important to note, was concerned with spoken language – hated Orientals and saw the Romans as culturally inferior. By contrast he adored the Greeks, and in 1751 he wrote of them:

In the short space of little more than a century, they became such statesmen, warriors, orators, historians, physicians, poets, critics, painters, sculptors, architects, and (last of all) philosophers that one can hardly help considering that Golden Period as a Providential event in honour of human nature to show to what perfection the human species might ascend.[73]

Thus the concept of the 'divine Greeks' was already formed. The lateness and rapidity of their development were now seen not as signs of shallowness but as marks of extraordinary greatness. By 1767 Britons were even beginning to assert Greek superiority over the Egyptians. As another Aberdonian, William Duff, wrote in that year:

In Greece the sciences made rapid progress and reached a very high degree of improvement . . . if the Egyptians were the inventors, this proves them to be ingenious, but the Greeks shewed themselves to possess superior genius . . . Arts and sciences have been known to the Chinese for many ages . . . yet they have not . . .[74]

The Classicist Samuel Musgrave led a disreputable life, and – as has been mentioned in the last chapter – Mitford called him a 'shallower' scholar. Nevertheless, Wilamowitz-Moellendorf gave him an honourable mention in his *History of Classical Scholarship*.[75] In 1782 Musgrave published a 'Dissertation on Greek Mythology' in which he argued that Greek culture was autochthonous, and even denied the massive tradition that Greek religion had been derived from Egypt. He did this on the basis of an oblique reference from Lucian, a prolific sophist and satirist of the 2nd century AD, and from the dissimilarities between the best-known names of the Egyptian and Greek gods.[76] However, as we have seen, Musgrave's arguments were crushed by Mitford, and the Romantic breakthrough on this aspect of the Ancient Model was made in Germany.

WINCKELMANN AND
NEO-HELLENISM IN GERMANY

The greatest champion of Greek youth and purity in the mid-18th century was the German Johann Joachim Winckelmann. This hardworking and obsessional man had taught himself Greek in a period when the Hellenic scholarship of the 16th and 17th centuries had virtually disappeared. In order to get near the Greek works of art he loved, but had never seen, he converted to Catholicism and spent most of his life in Rome as a priest and an art expert for exquisite cardinals.

Winckelmann specifically rejected the idea that the Greeks had a monopoly on philosophy.[77] Their triumph was in something that for him was far more important: aesthetics. As early as 1607, the great Renaissance scholar Scaliger had tried to establish a periodization of four stages for Greek art and poetry, to which Winckelmann acknowledged his debt.[78] In many ways, however, his scheme seems closer to the contemporary notions of a staged history and in particular to Turgot's *Progress of the Human Spirit*, according to which there were three stages, very similar to those set out eighty years later by Auguste Comte as the theological, the metaphysical and the scientific.[79] Winckelmann's *History of Ancient Art*, published in 1764, was the first attempt to integrate the history of art into that of society as a whole. According to Winckelmann, Egyptian art had only reached the primitive stage, in which the artist was forced to concentrate his attention on what was strictly essential.[80]

Egyptian art, the argument ran, was imperfect because it could not have been otherwise. Its development was blocked by unfortunate natural and social circumstances: in a very early example of modern racial discrimination against Ancient Egyptians, Winckelmann followed Aristotle's claim that they were mostly bandy-legged and snubnosed.[81] Thus they had no beautiful artistic models. Going against all Classical sources, and to some extent even against Montesquieu, he maintained that Egypt's geographical situation was unfortunate and not conducive to high culture. He also claimed – in the teeth of Herodotos, Plutarch, Diodoros and other ancient writers who had emphasized their passionate joy and grief – that the Egyptians were pessimistic and unenthusiastic.

At one level this conviction reflected the prevailing view that the reason so many peoples of other continents gave up in the face of the European advances was that they had been debilitated by their environments, and were naturally weak and passive.[82] At another it was an appreciation of the very real Egyptian concern with death which could be interpreted, within the 'progressive' paradigm, as reflecting the fact that Egypt had always been doomed to be surpassed by more 'vital' civilizations.[83]

Winckelmann did not approve of Greek art merely because it came later in the historical sequence. A Philhellene of extraordinary passion, he loved every aspect of his image of Greece, seeing its two dominant essences as liberty and youth.[84] According to him Greece epitomized freedom, while Egyptian culture had been stunted by its monarchism and conservatism and was the symbol of rigid authority and stagnation – which also happened to be non-European. In his mind, the Greek city-states contained the liberty without which it was impossible to create great art. Winckelmann, and his followers, loved this liberty and youth for their freshness and vitality. Yet he insisted upon the soft gentleness of Greek art, and the 'noble simplicity' and 'serene greatness' of Greek culture as a whole, which he saw as the result of the equable Greek climate. Moreover, central to his love of Greece was his appreciation of Greek homosexuality. Winckelmann himself was homosexual, and the major homosexual strand which has persisted in modern Hellenism has continued to be associated with him.[85]

While Winckelmann's interpretation of the Greeks as liberal, serene and youth-loving has remained a central theme in later Hellenism, even in the 18th century there were other images of Greece. The belief in the tragic and 'Dionysian' qualities of Greek culture, which culminated in the works of Nietzsche at the end of the 19th century, was already apparent among 18th-century thinkers, as well as in the poets Hölderlin and Heine at the beginning of the 19th.[86] Admiration for the austere and authoritarian Dorians was another strand of Hellenism. Nevertheless, all these late-18th- and 19th-century schools of thought were united in their perceptions of the relationship between Egypt and

Greece. Egypt represented an earlier, lower and strangely dead stage of human evolution which had been raised by the European genius of Hellas to a qualitatively higher and more vital level.

The effect of Winckelmann's work on Germany was electric. As the historian of Classics Rudolph Pfeiffer has written:

> A break was made with the Latin tradition of humanism and an entirely new humanism, a true new Hellenism, grew up. Winckelmann was the initator, Goethe the consummator, Wilhelm von Humboldt, in his linguistic, historical and educational writings, the theorist. Finally, Humboldt's ideas were given practical effect when he became Prussian Minister of Education and founded the new university of Berlin and the new humanistic gymnasium.[87]

Goethe, himself generally credited as the founder of Romanticism, exuberantly called the 18th century 'the century of Winckelmann'.[88] In the 1930s, in a grimmer mood, the brilliant English Germanist Miss Butler saw Winckelmann as the first figure in what she called 'the tyranny of Greece over Germany'.[89]

The second major response to the German crisis of identity in the 18th century, along with the desire to return to authentic German roots, was Neo-Hellenism. I have already discussed the long-standing perception of the 'special relationship' between Greek and German, and Greek's position as the Protestant religious opponent to Catholic Latin. In the 18th century the threat to Germany was from Paris, a 'new Rome', and from French, a Romance language. In addition to the revival of this old cultural alliance between Greek and German, there was a new motive for the identification of Germany as the New Hellas. By the 1770s it was becoming clear that Germany had the potential to be a major cultural centre; however, this was not reflected politically. The wars of Frederick the Great convinced contemporaries that Prussia could not unite Germany and that the Austrian Empire was equally incapable of this. The combination of cultural strength with political weakness and disunity seemed to indicate that, while Germany could not become a new Rome, she could be the new Hellas.

The leading dramatist of the age, C. M. Wieland, wrote several plays about the Greeks during the 1760s and 1770s.[90] Goethe was completely captivated by the Greeks, and in his middle age he made frequent, though not very successful, attempts to learn Greek.[91] Herder, too, had a passionate admiration for the liberty and artistic creativity of Athens, writing about Greek poetry and persuading Goethe to renew his study of the language.[92] These thinkers and artists were not as obsessed by Greece as Winckelmann and the 19th-century Neo-Hellenists; but there is no doubt that Ancient Greece and its perceived intimate relationship with modern Germany were becoming increasingly central to German cultural life, including the newly formed 'academia'.

Göttingen

Winckelmann is generally recognized as the founder of the discipline of art history, and Goethe certainly accepted him as a scholar. Nevertheless he was not acceptable to the new kind of 'professional' academics beginning to emerge in late-18th-century Germany, particularly at Göttingen. Göttingen can well be considered the embryo of all later, modern, diversified and professional universities. It was established in 1734 by George II, King of England and Elector of Hanover, was well endowed, and as a new foundation was able to escape many of the medieval religious and scholastic constraints that persisted in other universities. With its British connections it was a conduit for Scottish Romanticism as well as for the philosophical and political ideas of Locke and Hume, whose racism has been mentioned above (see pp. 202–4).[93]

It is true to say that while exclusive professionalism was the distinctive form of Göttingen scholarship, the chief unifying principle of its content was ethnicity and racism. This, of course, was the result not merely of the English scholarly contacts but, much more importantly, of prevailing opinion in German cultivated society as a whole.[94] Despite the Göttingen professors' insistence on their academic high standards and detachment, they were inevitably influenced by such 'popular' writers as Winckelmann, Goethe and Lessing.

Europocentricism was strikingly apparent in the views of one of the university's founders, Kristophe August Heumann. As a pioneer of the new professionalism Heumann established a scholarly journal, *Acta Philosophorum*, in the first issue of which, in 1715, he argued that although the Egyptians were cultivated in many studies they were not 'philosophical'. This claim – which his contemporaries Montesquieu and Brucker, as we have seen above, did not dare to make – was both striking and daring in the light of the strong ancient association between *philosophia* and Egypt.[95] Heumann's categorical distinction between Egyptian 'arts and studies' and the Greek 'philosophy' is rather difficult to comprehend, as his definition of the latter was 'the research and study of useful truths based on reason'.[96] Nevertheless its very imprecision made, and makes, the claim that the Greeks were the first 'philosophers' almost impossible to refute.

It is true that there is one ancient assertion that only the Greeks were capable of philosophizing, that attributed to Epicurus by Clement of Alexandria; Clement went on to demonstrate the extreme implausibility of the claim.[97] There is also the statement on the Greeks' making everything 'finer' from *Epinomis*, quoted on p. 198.[98] These should not, however, detract from Heumann's daring in impugning the massive ancient and modern tradition which saw Egypt and the Orient as the seats of wisdom and philosophy.

There is little doubt that Heumann's views on this were linked to his German nationalism and his Europocentrism. He advocated, and tried to practise, writing philosophy in German when this was almost unheard of; he was also a climatic determinist even before Montesquieu.[99] According to Heumann, philosophy arose in Greece because it could not flourish in climates that were too hot or too cold; only the inhabitants of temperate countries like Greece, Italy, France, England and Germany could create true philosophy.[100]

Heumann's views on the Greek origin of philosophy, like his views on the philosophical capacity of the German language, were more than fifty years ahead of his time. His work on the history of philosophy was eclipsed by Brucker's massive works in which, as we have seen, the author took a compromise position but did not deny the Egyptians the title of 'philosophers'.[101] Nevertheless, Heumann's influence persisted at Göttingen and it is not surprising that Dietrich Tiedemann, the first of a new wave of historians of philosophy of the 1780s, had studied at that university.[102] For this ethnic and 'scientific' school, as for all subsequent writers on the subject, it became axiomatic that 'true' philosophy had begun in Greece.

By this decade historical studies were being revolutionized, especially at Göttingen. One professor there, Gatterer, started a project of writing histories not of kings and wars but as 'biographies' of peoples. Another, Spittler, studied institutions as expressions and moulders of particular peoples.[103] Still more important was the work of the historian and anthropologist Meiners, later to be honoured by the Nazis as a founder of racial theory. Between 1770 and 1810 Meiners introduced and developed the concept of the *Zeitgeist*, or spirit of the age.[104] Possibly unaware of Vico's earlier work along these lines, Meiners argued that each age and place had a special mentality determined by its situation and institutions.[105]

The extent to which this approach was lacking among earlier historians has been exaggerated, but there is no doubt that after the 1780s it became impossible for serious historians to judge an action or statement without taking into account its social and historical context. Closely linked to this development was another of Meiners' innovations – 'source criticism'. This involved the historian assessing the value of different historical sources according to their author and social context, and basing his interpretation largely or solely on the reliable ones. Meiners attacked earlier writers like Brucker for having accepted historical sources uncritically and indiscriminately, instead of choosing those that revealed 'the spirit of the age' in which they were written.[106]

This was an approach which fitted well with the new 'scientific' spirit of Göttingen and the tradition already apparent in Galileo, who argued that 'one necessary reason once found destroys utterly a thousand merely probable reasons.' The measure has proved extremely useful in experimental sciences; however, as Giorgio de Santillana has pointed out,

> as soon as we leave the territory of direct and continuous check – what Galileo expressly called the ordeal – and take it as a philosophical guide to explanation, dangers begin to arise.[107]

Meiners' procedures, which have come to dominate 19th- and 20th-century historiography, do seem to be essential to a historian as opposed to a chronicler: it is inevitable that one should give different weight to different sources. The danger arises from a lack of self-consciousness and the awareness that by neglecting or rejecting certain sources because they are supposed to be 'out of tune' with the age concerned, the historian can impose almost any pattern he chooses. This increases the element of the history that merely reflects the age and concerns of the historian. In the case of the late 18th century, the situation was made worse by the 'modern' historians' confidence that they 'knew better'. They were convinced that, unlike earlier scholars, *they* were writing objectively. Furthermore, Meiners and his colleagues insisted on trusting what they confidently saw to be the 'quality' of their sources, rather than their quantity or even their analogical plausibility.

When dealing with the areas with which *Black Athena* is concerned, these historians' refusal to accept the information contained in the number, spread and plausibility of historical reports opened the door to the denial of the Ancient Model. The many ancient references to the Egyptian and Phoenician colonization and the later cultural borrowings could now be dismissed as 'late', 'credulous', or simply 'unreliable'. What is more, scholars could now use the facts that many ancient texts contradicted each other, or went against the newly established canons of natural science, to discredit anything they disliked. Nevertheless, the reason why the Model did not fall for another forty years is partly that it retained its formidable traditional hold on people's minds, and partly the fact that there were no ancient sources of good quality that challenged it. When the Ancient Model was overthrown, the new scholars were forced to rely on what they saw as the 'tacit dissent' and 'refutation by silence' of those ancient authors who, for whatever reasons, had failed to mention the colonizations.[108]

Despite the links between 'source criticism' and the new scientific spirit, it is important to note that the method did not arise in positivist France or empirical England but in Romantic Germany. For example, Meiners himself used the new scholarly techniques to write 'progress-ive' Romantic histories of peoples whom he divided categorically into the white, courageous, free, etc., and the black, ugly, etc. The spectrum ranged from chimpanzees through Hottentots and others to Germans and Celts.[109]

A more cautious and systematic racial hierarchy was established by J. F. Blumenbach, a professor of natural history at Göttingen. His *De Generis Humani Varietate Nativa*, published in 1775, was the first attempt at a 'scientific' study of human races of the type Linnaeus had written for natural history a few decades earlier. Blumenbach could not, however, apply Linnaeus' definition of a species, a population that can breed and produce fertile offspring, to human beings. He was not a progressive or a believer in polygenesis, the denial of the biblical tradition of a single creation of man and the assertion that different 'races' had been created separately. Blumenbach believed in a unique creation of a perfect man. In fact, Blumenbach's explanation for what he perceived as important 'racial' differences followed the Europocentric pattern set out earlier in the century by the naturalist Buffon. Buffon had argued that the *normal* type of species found in Europe had degenerated in other continents because of unfortunate climatic conditions there: individuals became too big, too small, too weak, too strong, too brightly coloured, too drab, etc.[110]

Blumenbach was the first to publicize the term 'Caucasian', which he used for the first time in the third edition of his great work in 1795. According to him the white or Caucasian was the first and most beautiful and talented race, from which all the others had degenerated to become Chinese, Negroes, etc. Blumenbach justified the curious name 'Caucasian' on 'scientific' and 'racial' grounds, since he believed the Georgians to be the finest 'white race'. However, there was much more to it than that. There was firstly the religious belief – given publicity by Vico in the 18th century – that man could usefully be seen as coming after the Flood and, as everyone knew, that Noah's Ark had landed on Mount Ararat in the Southern Caucasus.[111] There was also the increasingly important German Romantic tendency to place the origins of mankind – and therefore of the Europeans – in Eastern Mountains, not in the river valleys of the Nile and Euphrates, as the Ancients had believed. As Herder put it: 'Let us scale the mountains laboriously to the summit of Asia.'

Herder placed human origins in the Himalayas, while the general belief that mankind – at least in its purest form, the Aryans – came from the highlands of Asia remained dominant in the Romantic search for origins until the end of the 19th century.[112] One advantage of the scheme of Asiatic origins was that it placed Germans closer to the pure beginnings of mankind than the West Europeans; this was, however, far more effectively exploited in the 19th century.

Blumenbach was conventional for his period in that he included 'Semites' and 'Egyptians' among his Caucasians. However – although I have been unable to trace it precisely – it seems clear that there was already some sense in which the Caucasus was linked specifically to the Aryans, another new term that was coming into use from the 1790s.[113] The Caucasus was the traditional site of the imprisonment and cruel punishment of Prometheus, who was considered the epitome of Europe. Not only was he the son of Iapetos, plausibly identified as the biblical Japhet, third son of Noah and the ancestor of the Europeans; but his heroic, beneficial and self-sacrificing action – of stealing fire for mankind – soon came to be seen as typically Aryan. Gobineau saw him as the ancestor of the principal white family and by the 20th century the ultra-Romantic Robert Graves was even suggesting that the name Prometheus meant 'swastika'.[114]

In the 1780s yet another Göttingen professor, A. L. Schlözer, tried to set up a 'Japhetic' linguistic family which included most of the languages later subsumed under the name Indo-European. He failed in this but succeeded in establishing a 'Semitic' one.[115] Semitic studies at Göttingen were, however, dominated by his teacher, J. D. Michaelis, who combined being the greatest Hebrew scholar of his day with strong anti-Semitism.[116]

As must by now be clear, Göttingen, in the period from 1775 to 1800, not only established many of the institutional forms of later universities, but its professors established much of the intellectual framework within which later research and publication within the new professional disciplines was carried out. In this very distinguished company, there is no doubt that the centre of the intellectual ferment was in Classical Philology, later to be given the more imposing and modern name *Altertumswissenschaft* or 'science of Antiquity'.[117]

The field was dominated by Christian Gottlob Heyne, who married into the professorate of the town and was a brother-in-law of Blumenbach. From his appointment in 1763 to his death in 1812, Heyne was the central figure in both the town and the university. He ran the library, which rapidly became one of the best in Europe, and he was one of the chief proponents of 'modern' professional scholarship.[118] Heyne promoted the secular Seminar, taken from the Sokratic method, and source criticism was developed in this.

Not surprisingly, one of the most frequent targets of source criticism was the Ancient Model and favourable references to Egypt in Greek texts.[119] Source criticism can helpfully be compared to the use of factor analysis in demography and the measurement of intelligence, about which Stephen Gould writes:

> virtually all its procedures arose as justifications for particular theories of intelligence. Factor analysis, despite its status as pure deductive mathematics, was invented in a social context, and for definite reasons. And, though its mathematical basis is unassailable, its persistent use as a device for learning about the physical structure of the intellect has been mired in deep conceptual errors from the start.[120]

Heyne had known Winckelmann when he had been a young librarian at Dresden. As a 'professional' academic he made criticisms of Winckelmann's writings, but there is no doubt that Heyne was heavily influenced by his passionate Neo-Hellenism.[121] As Rudolf Pfeiffer wrote:

> It was precisely the influence of Winckelmann that distinguished the scholarship of Heyne and his friends and pupils from that of other contemporary scholars.[122]

The contemporary historian of science Steven Turner enlarges on this point in his important work on the transformation of the traditional German *érudits Gelehrte* into 'professional' academics:

> Through Heyne, Neo-Humanism had a similar invigorating effect upon Classical scholarship and its 'public image'. Throughout his career Heyne strove to forge new links between traditional

philological scholarship of the school and the academies and the currents of aesthetic Neo-Hellenism and Weimar Classicism building up outside academia.[123]

Heyne epitomized what one may usefully call 'Romantic Positivism'. As Frank Manuel has written about him:

> His scholarship was impeccable, his editing of texts in the great tradition, but for all the appurtenances of learning, the spirit that animated him and generations of German *Gelehrte* was the same Romantic Hellenism which possessed his literary compatriots in the 18th century.[124]

Heyne was fascinated by overseas travel and by exotic peoples. Given the importance, in German academic life, of marrying the professor's daughter, the fact that Blumenbach was his brother-in-law was less significant than the fact that both Heyne's sons-in-law were concerned with extra-European travel. One of them, Heeren, will be discussed in Chapter VI; the other, who was much better known in the 18th century, was Georg Forster. Forster had sailed with Captain Cook and wrote a description of sailing round the world. His political radicalism and his dislike of exploitation – even of non-Whites – went together with a refusal to discount the possibility of polygenesis. Heyne and Forster adored each other and they had an extensive correspondence, much of which was concerned with tropical climes and anthropology.[125]

Heyne was not particularly concerned about Christianity. However, when issues were polarized after 1789, he became passionately involved in preserving the *status quo*. His vehement denunciations of the French Revolution cannot be explained away simply as rage against Georg Forster, even though Forster had not merely gone to Paris to take part in the Revolution but had left his wife – Heyne's daughter – for the love of her best friend Caroline, the daughter of the Semitist Michaelis.[126]

The explanation for Heyne's fury also needs to be based on his profound involvement with the Hanoverian and German *status quo*, which is in no way diminished by his ability to work with the French occupying forces to protect his beloved university. Thus it is altogether appropriate that so many of Heyne's students and followers should have worked for Prussia in the struggle against France and revolutionary ideas. Altogether, it is clear that the acknowledged ancestor of *Altertumswissenschaft*, later transposed to Britain and America as the new discipline of 'Classics', was a typical product of Göttingen – with its desire for reform rather than revolution, its profound concerns with ethnicity and race, and its exhaustive scholarship. Furthermore, both the ancestor and the discipline itself shared the reaction against the French Revolution and its challenge to traditional order and religion and the concern with the differences and inequalities between different races. They also shared the passionate Romanticism and Neo-Hellenism of progressive German circles of the late 18th century.

CHAPTER V

ROMANTIC LINGUISTICS
The rise of India
and the fall of Egypt, 1740–1880

WE NOW TURN TO the fall of the Ancient Model which, although affected by a similar background and many of the same social and intellectual forces, should be distinguished from the rise of the Aryan Model some twenty years later. The chapter begins with the fascination of Sanskrit and other Indian languages that grew in the last quarter of the 18th century, and the impact this had on the understanding of relationships between European languages. By the 1830s this had led to a general perception of the Indo-European language family which, in the racist atmosphere of the time, developed quite quickly into the notion of an Indo-European or 'Aryan race'. The passion for India also meant that it replaced Egypt as the exotic ancestor of Europe. This time, however, the ancestry was not seen in terms of the transmission of philosophy and reason but as a Romantic one of 'blood' and kinship.

To return now to the Ancient Model. After the 1780s, the intensification of racism and the new belief in the central importance of 'ethnicity' as a principle of historical explanation became critical for perceptions of Ancient Egypt. The Egyptians were increasingly detached from the noble Caucasians, and their 'black' and African nature was more and more emphasized. Thus the idea that they were the cultural ancestors of the Greeks – the epitome and pure childhood of Europe – became unbearable. There was also a new crisis between Egyptian mythology and Christianity with the works of Dupuis, which represented the ideological or theological counterpart of the French Revolution's attack on European social order. It is only with this background that one can make sense of the tormented career of Champollion during the years of reaction between 1815 and 1830. Although Champollion was an avowed revolutionary and an enthusiastic Bonapartist, one of his earliest discoveries discredited some of the theories of Dupuis's supporters, and he and his decipherment were therefore welcomed by the Church and the Restoration nobility. On the other hand, his championing of Egypt over Greece combined with his political beliefs to infuriate Hellenist and Indianist scholars, who continued to do all they could to block his academic career.

Just before his premature death in 1831, Champollion challenged Christian orthodoxy by his high dating of Egyptian Antiquity. Thus by the time of his death he had antagonized both Christians and Hellenists, and Egyptology, despite a popular fascination with Egypt as well as some continuation of the Masonic respect for it, went into a sharp decline for the next twenty-five years. Its slow recovery began only in the late 1850s. Between 1860 and 1880 there was a period of tension between the spirit of Champollion and the prevailing racism and the passion for Greece; after 1880, however, Egyptology tended to conform and subordinate itself to the dominant discipline of Classics.

Since then, there have always been some discordant voices and claims that Egyptian civilization really had possessed at least some of the high religion, philosophy and science claimed for it by the Ancients. Nevertheless, the predominant view has been maintained that although the Egyptians were technically proficient they were not 'truly civilized', and the Greek respect for their culture was based on delusion. The discrepancies between this 'official line' and the surviving monuments and the ancient reports has led to the emergence of a number of counter-cultures or counter-disciplines.

Two of these are discussed at the end of the chapter: the first is the theory of 'diffusionism' promoted by the anatomist and physical anthropologist Elliot Smith, according to which Asian immigrants had established Egyptian civilization and spread it to Europe and the rest of the world. The second is the school of 'pyramidologists', the more cautious members of which maintain that the Great Pyramids were built according to the plans of architects with a very sophisticated understanding of astronomy and mathematics. The chapter ends with a discussion of the possibilities of a future meeting between these 'heresies' and orthodox Egyptology.

THE BIRTH OF INDO-EUROPEAN

Language has always been a central concern to Romantics. According to them, languages are peculiar – that is, they are attached to a particular place, landscape and climate. They are therefore seen as the individual expression of a specific people, to be treasured as such. Herder was obsessed by language, and especially by speech. Following the English enthusiasm for Homer, Blackwell and the German mystic philosopher Hamann, Herder denied the priority of thought and reason over words; in this way he opposed the Enlightenment predilection for visual signs, Egyptian hieroglyphics or Chinese characters, which were thought to express universal ideas untrammelled by particular phonetics. For Herder and the Romantics, the chief purpose of language was not to transmit reason but to express feeling, and it was for this that both German and Greek were admired. As we have seen, Greek was valued in the mid-18th century not as a vehicle of philosophy but for its poetic qualities.[1]

This concern with language on the part of Herder and the other Romantics was important in the formation of historical philology. Furthermore, Romantic influence can be seen in the discipline's two chief models – the tree and the family – which, with their enormous aesthetic and progressive appeal, became widely popular throughout 19th-century scholarship and science. In historical linguistics, the assumptions of simple beginnings and later ramification and divergence – through regular, though specific, shifts that can be charted – proved extremely useful in the early stages of the new discipline. On the other hand, the tree and the family do not allow for 'backtracking' or mixing and convergence and they have a tendency to teleology, the assumption that each language has an ultimate nature inbuilt in its beginnings which are not fundamentally affected by later contacts.[2] Anticipating discussion in Chapters VII and VIII, we can just note here that it was largely for these reasons that historical philology was moribund by the end of the 19th century.

Before this, however, philology was one of the most exciting areas of intellectual life. Schlözer's establishment of the Semitic language family has already been mentioned, in connection with both the work of the Abbé Barthélemy and developments at Göttingen. By 1820, scholars – notably the Dane Christian Rask and Herder's disciple Franz Bopp – had systematically traced the relationships between the phonetics and morphology of most European languages.[3]

This endeavour was clearly related to the new systematic racial taxonomy. As the Caucasians had come from Asian mountains, the European languages were supposed to have had the same origin. It is significant that, just as the Germans were supposed to be purer Caucasians because they were the latest to leave the *Urheimat* or original homeland, German was thought to be purer and more ancient than other languages in the family. Hence the German name for the newly defined language family became *Indogermanisch* (Indo-Germanic) – a term coined by the German Indianist H. J. Klaproth in 1823.[4] Franz Bopp himself, however, sided with scholars from other countries who preferred 'Indo-European', a title first used by Thomas Young in 1816.[5]

THE LOVE AFFAIR
WITH SANSKRIT

The 'Indo-' was linked to the new passion for India and for Sanskrit. In his fascinating book *The Oriental Renaissance*, first published in 1950, the early-20th-century French intellectual Raymond Schwab traced the growing interest in ancient Indian and Iranian cultures and languages that accompanied French and British penetration of the subcontinent. As with so many 19th-century artistic and intellectual developments, the first man to introduce the idea of an 'Oriental Renaissance' was the linguist and ardent Romantic Friedrich

Schlegel. In *The Speech and Wisdom of the Indians*, Schlegel wrote that

> The study of Indian Literature requires to be embraced by such students and patrons as in the 15th and 16th centuries suddenly kindled in Italy and Germany an ardent appreciation of the beauty of Classical learning, and in so short a time invested it with such prevailing importance that the form of all wisdom and science, and almost of the world itself, was changed and renovated by the influence of that reawakened knowledge.[6]

Schwab's title, *The Oriental Renaissance*, is that of a chapter heading from a book by Edgar Quinet published in 1841. Quinet and, later, Schwab had two very similar bases. The first was the claim that the new Orientalism had overtaken Neoclassicism.[7] A modification of this – the claim that Orientalism, in alliance with Medievalism, was surpassing Classicism – was a possible, though not very plausible, view in the 1840s. With the triumph of Greece and Rome and the abandonment of ancient India at the end of the 19th century, however, it became completely untenable and its revival by Schwab is merely antiquarian.

The second concept behind the Oriental Renaissance belongs to the category of the myths of the history of science in which heroic men create light, order and science out of darkness, confusion and superstition. It assumes that before the Romantic age men and women did not know, or even care, about 'the Orient', and that it was first *discovered* in the late 18th century. It is true that Egypt, during the Enlightenment, was sometimes thought of as belonging to the West and not the Orient.[8] On the other hand, as I have tried to show in earlier chapters, there was intense interest in Egypt and in China, and considerable knowledge about them, well before 1750. Though less central to the concerns of Enlightenment thinkers than Egypt and China, even India was known about in the 17th and early 18th centuries. The Indian Brahmins were less admired than the Egyptian priests or the Chinese literati, but they were in some ways their functional equivalents in the general criticism of European institutions and religion.

Indian scholars had, of course, always known their Classical language, Sanskrit, and there had been knowledge of it in the West since the late 17th century.[9] With this came the general impression, explicitly stated by Sir William Jones in 1786, that Sanskrit, in relation to Greek and Latin,

> bears a stronger affinity, both in the roots of verbs and in the forms of grammar, than could possibly have been produced by accident; so strong, indeed, that no philologer could examine all three without believing them to have sprung from some common source, which perhaps no longer exists; there is a similar reason, though not quite so forcible, for supposing that both the Gothick and the Celtick, though blended with a very different idiom, had the same origin with the Sanskrit.[10]

19th-century German and British scholars rejected the idea that their languages could be the result of impure mixture. Apart from that, however, this admirable and concise statement – which, it should be noted, is based on plausibility – has been the basis of Indo-European and all other historical philology ever since.

The linguistic relationship meant that Indian language and culture could now be seen as both exotic and familiar, if not ancestral. This idea came about because, despite Jones' prudence on the subject – he argued that Sanskrit and the European languages probably had a common unknown ancestor – it was generally thought that Sanskrit itself was the original Indo-European language. This tie – and the knowledge, through the Indian tradition, that the Brahmins were the descendants of 'Aryan' conquerors who had come from the highlands of Central Asia – fitted wonderfully with the German Romantic belief that mankind and the Caucasians had originated in the mountains of Central Asia.[11] This was a great force behind the extraordinary enthusiasm for all aspects of Indian culture that raged from the 1790s to the 1820s. In the short run, however, Jones had an even greater impact through literature than through linguistics, and his translations of Indian poetry were received rapturously all over Europe.[12] The English Lake poets were all moved by Indian poetry, while in 1791 Goethe wrote: 'When I mention *Shakuntala* [an Indian poem translated by Jones] everything is said.'[13] It will be remembered, too, that in 1798 Napoleon had a copy of the *Vedas* with him on his Expedition to Egypt.[14]

The academic results of this enthusiasm were the establishment of many chairs of Sanskrit and the creation of a disciplinary base which, in alliance with Germanic studies as *Indogermanisch*, could threaten the monopoly of Latin and Greek as the only ancient languages.[15] This is not to say that Sanskrit and Germanic studies were a serious challenge to the latter, though some scholars, like K. O. Müller in the 1820s and Salomon Reinach in the 1890s, perceived them as such.[16]

To begin with, the new academic studies were centred in Britain and France, both of whom had colonial interests in India. However, the British effort soon faded, and even the French study of Sanskrit and ancient India was overwhelmed by the German Romantic response to them. The dominant figures in this were Friedrich von Schlegel and his brother Wilhelm, who became the first Professor of Sanskrit at Bonn. Even a less passionate man like Wilhelm von Humboldt thanked God for having allowed him to live long enough to become acquainted with the *Bhagavad Gita*.[17]

SCHLEGELIAN
ROMANTIC LINGUISTICS

Twenty years earlier, in 1803, Friedrich Schlegel's passion for India had been even less restrained: 'Everything, absolutely everything, is of Indian origin.'[18] Schlegel was also the first to insist, against the biblical tradition of the Tower of Babel and most later thinkers, on linguistic polygenesis. Specifically, he argued that there was a categorical distinction between the Indo-European family and other languages, and he attacked William Jones and his contemporaries for having seen relationships between Indian and Semitic languages.[19]

Although he did not spell it out, the concept of an Aryan race can also be traced back to Schlegel. His Romantic passion and conviction of the superiority of the Ancient Indian Race were sufficient to surmount the total lack of evidence and provide a simple answer to what had now become 'the Egyptian problem': how could Africans have produced such a high civilization? According to Schlegel, the answer lay in the fact that Egypt had been colonized and civilized by Indians. So confident was he of this scheme that he cited the magnificence of Egyptian architecture as proof of the greatness of the Indian race.[20] This notion of Egypt's Indian origin was to remain powerful throughout the 19th century, and we will encounter it again in Gobineau.

Despite his interest in race, Schlegel never lost sight of the centrality of language. He distinguished between two kinds of language – the 'noble', inflected languages, and the less perfect ones that were not inflected. The former had a spiritual origin, while the latter were originally 'animal'.[21] Only with the inflection of the Indian-based languages, he believed, could there be clear and penetrating intelligence or high and universal thought.[22]

Somewhat surprisingly, Schlegel did not get high marks from the Nazis. The reasons for this were that he was not anti-Semitic in his political views – he advocated Jewish emancipation – or personally, in that he married the daughter of the famous Jewish philosopher Moses Mendelsohn.[23] He also praised the 'lofty power and energy of the Arabic and Hebraic languages'. But, he continued, 'they indeed stand on the loftiest point of their particular branch.'[24] At times he even maintained that they were hybrids between the 'spiritual' and 'animal' languages.[25] This, however, did not save them from their position in the lower category. Schlegel also supposed that Jewish culture had been influenced by the Egyptians – who, you will recall, had received their high civilization from the Indians.[26] Furthermore, as Friedrich Schlegel was one of the first men to link language to race, his views on the polygenesis of language were clearly linked to contemporary attitudes to the polygenesis of man.[27]

By paving the way for the Aryan and Semitic races, Schlegel was definitely ahead of his time. These ideas were not taken up seriously for another forty or fifty years: externally, the forces of racial anti-Semitism were still not strong enough, while internally, there was a great inconsistency in his approach.[28] Schlegel insisted that there was a categorical distinction between affixing – the external addition of suffixes or other particles to a word – and *in*flection, in which the 'root' was modified internally in what he saw as an organic way.[29] Unfortunately for Indo-European superiority, the Semitic languages are modified in precisely this way, and the term 'root' itself is taken from Hebrew grammar.[30] Thus later scholars were obliged to place Semitic along with Indo-European in the top rank. At the same time the suggestion made by Barthélemy in the 1760s, that there was a fundamental and exclusive relationship between the 'Phoenician' and Coptic languages, was seldom taken up seriously in the 19th century. Further, the idea of a Semito-Hamitic or Afroasiatic linguistic 'superfamily', including Semitic and Egyptian and other African languages, was not generally accepted until after the Second World War.[31]

The other great modification of Schlegel's scheme made by mid-19th-century linguists was on the matter of 'progress'. He played an important role in transforming philology from being the history of languages into becoming the interpretation of language as a force in the making of history. He also partially incorporated 'progress' into his thinking. Nevertheless, Schlegel's views were old-fashioned in that he saw the 'spiritual' Indian languages as regressive. That is to say, having been formed as perfect, they had undergone more or less decay. Among the 'animal' languages, on the other hand, there was 'progress' as they became more complex.[32] Here, too, later scholars who were more thoroughly steeped in the 'progressive' paradigm had to modify his ideas and explain superiority and inferiority of languages in terms of their relative places in evolution.

English and French scholars were equally confident that Indo-European languages were superior to any others. However, as they themselves spoke languages with relatively little inflection, they did not show much enthusiasm for Schlegel's ideas in this area, with their implication that Sanskrit, Greek, Latin and German were the only languages suitable for philosophy and religion. By contrast – and despite the modifications mentioned above – German scholars shared or accepted his new scheme. Wilhelm von Humboldt, for example, tended to see a progress from affixing or agglutinative languages to inflected ones, and he too saw the differences between the two as categorical.[33]

Wilhelm von Humboldt was a wide-ranging genius who established, among many other things, the bases for both Basque and Malayo-Polynesian linguistics. Nevertheless, as has already been mentioned, he had a passion of a different order for Sanskrit. For instance, he thought that with its massive and intricate inflection, Sanskrit was a far better language than Chinese, which is 'isolating' and has even less inflection than English. In his brilliant essay on Chinese written in the 1820s, Humboldt was forced to admit that, despite its unmodified words, Chinese was the equal to the best Indo-European languages as a vehicle of logical thought.[34] On the other hand, he maintained that its lack of inflection 'prevented the free soaring of thought', which needed grammatical forms to guide it.[35] Thus not merely was the Chinese script static, but the spoken language itself was seen to lack the full emotional power now demanded of language by German Romantics. Presumably because of their own languages' lack of inflection, English and French Romantics do not seem to have made this point.

The equation of inflection with freedom neatly epitomized the distinction perceived by the Romantics between the rigid Sinophilia of the Enlightenment and their own free love for their Indian kin.[36] By the 1820s, even his limited admiration for Chinese and his studies of other non-Indo-European languages marked Humboldt out as a member of the older generation. Younger men cut off from the Enlightenment were more rigorous: they were almost exclusively concerned with Indo-European.

THE ORIENTAL RENAISSANCE

Quinet and Schwab claimed that this breakthrough in Indian studies was only the centre of a general 'Oriental Renaissance' – which Schwab rightly sees as integrally linked to Romanticism – and they linked this movement to the great decipherments of the 19th century.[37] It is true that the decipherment of cuneiform was begun in 1800 by the Göttingen Romantic scholar G. F. Grotefend by reading the names of Persian kings, but I will try to show in this chapter that the much more impressive decipherment of hieroglyphics came not from Romanticism and the Oriental Renaissance but largely from the Egypto-Masonic tradition and the scientific spirit of the French Revolution.[38]

Schwab's claim that the Oriental Renaissance was linked to the establishment of 'Orientalism' as an academic discipline, on the other hand, does seem partly justified. Arabic, having been a language of high culture in Early Medieval Europe, had been taught there from time to time ever since. However, its regular position as a modern academic study was established in 1799 with the appointment of Sylvestre de Sacy as the first teacher in the newly founded École de Langues Orientales Vivantes, in a move that was associated with the Expedition to Egypt. There is no doubt that de Sacy, both as a teacher of the new aracane Orientalism and as a supporter of the monarchy, fits the Romantic and conservative pattern of the Oriental Renaissance very well.[39] While France needed Arabic, both for the Egyptian Expedition and for the conquest of Algeria which began in 1830, Germany did not, and there was very little interest in Arabic in that country. Furthermore, as Edward Said has pointed out, Orientalism inherited much of the traditional hatred of Islam as *the* enemy of Christendom.[40] In this context, it is important to note that the 1820s, a crucial decade in the formation of Orientalism, were dominated by the Greek War of Independence between Christian Greeks and Moslem Turks and Egyptians. There were, however, religious and linguistic senses in which the Semitic cultures were considered to be if not the equals, at least on the same plane as those of the Aryans (see Chapter VII).

The Oriental Renaissance did not include China. Many Jesuits had known Chinese well since the 16th century and by the turn of the 18th, through their translations and scores of travellers' reports, Europeans knew about China in some detail.[41] The language had been taught intermittently at Paris since then, but it was only in the late 19th century that regular chairs were established elsewhere in Europe. It is particularly striking that while the first chair of Sanskrit was established at Berlin in 1818, Chinese studies remained in a parlous state in Germany until the end of the century. As a French Sinologue wrote in 1898: 'Germany and Austria have not occupied in Sinology the brilliant place that belongs to them in some branches of Oriental studies.'[42]

Although German scholars came to dominate Egyptology after the 1880s, in the period of the Oriental Renaissance the mainstream of German academics would have nothing to do with the new discipline. The French Orientalists' hostility towards Champollion will be described below. Here, it is sufficient to point out that Raymond Schwab calls one of his sections 'The Prejudice for Egypt' and writes in it: 'This view of Egypt as the first and the essential Oriental influence on the West is totally erroneous. In point of fact, the Egypt of the scholars was a relative latecomer, arriving only in the 19th century.'[43] In a footnote Schwab makes it clear that what he means by this is that 'the 19th-century infatuation with Egypt replaced its infatuation with India.'[44]

These statements are misleading in so many directions that it is difficult to know where to begin. First there was the Orientalists' hostility to Egypt and the slowness of the establishment of Egyptology. Secondly, as we have seen, Egypt had been perceived as 'the essential Oriental influence on the West' since Antiquity, far longer than there had been any comparable interest in India. Thirdly, although there was considerable curiosity about Egypt in the first half of the 19th century, the country was seen then as exotic and alien – that is to say, very differently from Egypt's earlier position as the ancestral culture of Europe. It was precisely from the latter niche that it was replaced by the Romantic view of India.

All in all, it is clear that academic Orientalism, most strikingly in Germany but elsewhere as well, began with quite definite limits. The only regions of the Orient for which the early Orientalists showed respect were Central Asia, seen as the mountainous European *Urheimat*, and India, seen as the home of kin from whom Europeans could learn about themselves. By the end of the 19th century, even the respect for these had disappeared.

Edward Said and R. Rashed have shown that Orientalism, at a fundamental level and from the beginning, has combined interest in Asian societies with a contempt for them and the conviction that 'Orientals' were unfit to analyse and arrange their own cultures.[45] Orientalist scholars concurrently tried to emphasize the ancient civilizations of other continents, and to play down their medieval and modern continuations and developments.[46] Other ancient civilizations could be completely appropriated by Western scholarship because the modern inhabitants, it was argued, were either new interlopers themselves or, in their decadence, had 'lost' the high culture of their ancestors. The later civilizations, which could not be taken over in this way, were dismissed and ignored – even though, in nearly every case, the Europeans had been able to learn about the ancient ones only through them.[47] It was asserted above all, and despite overwhelming evidence to the contrary, that only Europeans had a true sense of history.[48]

There is no doubt about the extraordinary efforts of the early Orientalists, and of their great and lasting achievements. Nevertheless, the growth of Orientalism did not simply go with a broadening of horizons, as Quinet and Schwab claimed. In many respects it involved a narrowing of the imagination and intensified feelings of the innate and categorical superiority of European civilization. It has served to distance and objectify non-European cultures, lumping their very different characteristics into a general category of 'Oriental' merely because they are not European. These have been seen as 'exotic', and viewed as inert or passive in the face of European dynamism. Indeed, since the 19th century it has become literally unthinkable to Europeans that peoples of any other continent could be 'scientific' in the way they themselves are, or that Asians or Africans could have contributed in any profound way to the making of Europe.[49] The only apparent exceptions here were ancient Iran and India, but these, of course, were seen as part of the Indo-European family. As such they filled the niche of 'exotic ancestors' that had previously been occupied by Egypt and Chaldaea. Gobineau, for instance, was sure that 'the nations of Egypt and Assyria took a place behind the men of Hindustan.'[50]

Naturally, the institutional rise of Orientalism must – at least in England and France – be associated with the huge expansion of colonialism and other forms of domination over Asia and Africa taking place at the same time. Not only was a systematic understanding of non-European peoples and their spoken languages needed to control these peoples but a knowledge of their civilizations, by seizing and categorizing their cultures, ensured that the natives themselves could learn about their own civilizations only through European scholarship. This provided yet another rope to tie the colonial elites to the metropolitan countries, which has been an increasingly important factor in the retention of European cultural hegemony since the decline of direct colonialism in the second half of the 20th century.[51]

Raymond Schwab has brilliantly shown how frequently Oriental-Romantic themes appear in 19th-century culture. His implication, however, that this was a new phenomenon in European art is entirely misleading. Interest in other continents long antedates the 18th-century enthusiasms for Egypt, Abyssinia and China described above. Furthermore, the establishment of arcane Orientalist academic disciplines in the 19th century relieved the cultured generalist of the distasteful duty of coming to grips with Oriental civilizations and treating them with respect. Unlike the 17th- and 18th-century artists and politicians, who took Egypt and China very seriously indeed, those of the 19th could simply collect china or introduce exotic romantic themes into their literature and art.

These intellectual and educational changes can be related to specific national configurations of European colonization and expansion into other continents. For instance, the initial development of ancient Indian studies in the 17th and 18th centuries grew out of the East India Company's need to understand their subjects and 'native' allies. It is equally significant that the romanticizing of India was carried out by Germans, who had no direct interest in the subcontinent. Even in England the dominant Indianist of the second half of the 19th century was Max-Müller, who was appointed at the instigation of the Prussian ambassador Baron Christian Bunsen and who remained very German throughout his fifty years as Professor of Indian Languages at Oxford.[52]

THE FALL OF CHINA

The historiographic fall of Indian culture, like that of the ancient Semites, took place only at the end of the 19th century. Here we are concerned with the beginning of the century and the degradation of the Chinese and the Egyptians. The complete triumph of racism and 'progress' and the Romantic 'return' to Europe and Christianity took place as European manufacturers began to replace Chinese luxury goods such as furniture, porcelain and silk with their own products. Europe's gain from this was not merely cultural satisfaction. As Britain began to penetrate the Chinese market with Lancashire cottons and Indian opium the balance of trade tipped against China, and Europe's commercial advantage was soon followed by military initiatives.

From 1839 – when the British went to war to protect their opium trade from an official Chinese ban – until the end of the century, Britain, France and the other 'powers' made successive attacks on China to extract more and greater concessions. The need to justify these actions and exploitation, the real social breakdown in China – itself largely the result of European pressure – together with the general racism and 'return to Europe', were the forces that led to a transformation of the Western image of China. From being a model of rational civilization China became seen as a filthy country in which torture and corruption of all sorts flourished. With obscene irony, the Chinese were especially blamed for their consumption of opium. De Tocqueville, writing in the 1850s, found it incomprehensible that the 18th-century Physiocrats should have had such an admiration for China.[53]

The fall in China's reputation can also be traced in linguistics. As an isolating language, Chinese – together with Coptic and to some extent even English – was difficult for Humboldt to fit into his evolutionary progress from agglutinative to inflected languages. He toyed with, but rejected, the idea that Chinese was a baby talk and therefore the language of the babyhood of mankind.[54] By the middle of the century men like the great Indo-European linguist August Schleicher had no such qualms. Schleicher saw a three-stage evolutionary hierarchy from isolating Chinese, to agglutinative Turanian (Turkish and Mongol), culminating in inflected Semitic and Indo-European.[55]

Baron Christian Bunsen, whose ambivalence about Egypt was agonized, had no hesitation about the linguistic and hence the historical position of Chinese. According to him, Sinism (China) was the most primitive stage in world history; it was followed by Turanism and then Khamism (Egypt). After that came the Flood and the beginning of true history, which consisted of the dialectic between the Semites and the Indo-Germans.[56] Thus, on the 'scientific' basis of historical linguistics, both Egypt and China were kicked out of history into the antediluvian past. As I have stressed, relations between race and language were extremely close during the 19th century. Thus the fall in the linguistic position of Egypt and China was paralleled by one in their anatomical and racial one.

RACISM IN THE
EARLY 19TH CENTURY

The extraordinary growth of racism in the early 19th century included the increasingly pejorative 'racial' classifications of the Chinese and Egyptians. With the reaction to the French Revolution and the revival of Christianity, one key area of doctrine in which Christianity was not able to restore its position was on the unity of mankind. Even polygenesis somewhat revived after a setback in the Evangelical 1820s, while the period from 1800 to 1850 in general was one of intense activity to find anatomical bases for the racial differences which every cultivated European 'knew' existed.[57] The lack of clear-cut results of this research did not affect general opinion on the matter; it may, however, have been a factor in making a number of more cautious scholars continue to use language to explain what they saw as the obvious inequalities between different peoples. Whatever form it took, the new principle of ethnicity pervaded all areas of life and scholarship.[58]

A Renaissance traveller, Andrea Corsalis, described the Chinese as 'of our quality'.[59] For the most part, 17th- and 18th-century writers considered them to belong to a distinct but not necessarily inferior race.[60] By the period of the Opium Wars in the middle of the 19th century, however, the Chinese were racially contemptible. As a jingle published in *Punch* put it in 1858:

John Chinaman a rogue is born,
The laws of truth he holds in scorn;
About as great a brute as can
Encumber the earth is John Chinaman.
   Sing Yeh, my cruel John Chinaman,
   Sing Yeo, my stubborn John Chinaman.
   Not Cobden himself can take off the ban
   By humanity laid on John Chinaman.

With their little pig-eyes and their large pig-tails,
And their diet of rats, dogs, slugs and snails,
All seems to be game in the frying pan
Of that nasty feeder John Chinaman.

Sing lie-tea, my sly Chinaman,
No fightee, my coward John Chinaman,
John Bull has a chance – let him, if he can
Somewhat open the eyes of John Chinaman.[61]

19th-century scholars were only slightly less damning. However many divisions of humanity the new anthropologists envisioned, the 'yellow' races came out in the middle, below the white and above the black. What is more, the Chinese were now condemned for what the Enlightenment had considered admirable, their stability. According to Baron Cuvier, the great naturalist of the early part of the century: 'This race has formed mighty empires in China and Japan ... but its civilization has long appeared stationary.'[62] For the racist pioneer the Comte de Gobineau, the yellow tribes

> have little physical vigour and tend towards apathy ... feeble desires, a will that is obstinate rather than extreme ... In everything they tend to mediocrity. They have an easy enough understanding of what is not too elevated or too profound ... The Yellows are a practical people in the strict sense of the word. They do not dream or enjoy theories. They invent little, but they are capable of appreciating and adopting what they can use ...[63]

It should be remembered that Gobineau became notorious only as an antecedent of Hitler; during the 19th century, although some might disagree with him, he was accepted as an eccentric but reputable scholar. The new racial position of the Chinese was quite sufficient to exclude them from the Romantic picture of dynamic world history, and there was no doubt in anyone's mind that racially the 'Chinaman' was mediocre.

WHAT COLOUR WERE THE
ANCIENT EGYPTIANS?

The racial position of the Ancient Egyptians was much more precarious than that of the Chinese for two reasons: scholars differed greatly on their 'race', and the Egyptians themselves were balanced between the white acme of mankind and its black pit. For Cuvier,

The Negro race ... is marked by black complexion, crisped or woolly hair, compressed cranium and a flat nose. The projection of the lower parts of the face, and the thick lips, evidently approximate it to the monkey tribe: the hordes of which it consists have always remained in the most complete state of barbarism.[64]

While for Gobineau,

The black variety is the lowest and lies at the bottom of the ladder. The animal character lent to its basic form imposes its destiny from the moment of conception. It never leaves the most restricted intellectual zones ... If its faculties for thinking are mediocre or even nonexistent, it possesses in its desire and as a consequence in its will an intensity that is often terrible. Many of the senses are developed with a vigour unknown in the other two races: principally taste and smell. It is precisely in the greed for sensations that the most striking mark of its inferiority is found ...[65]

If Europeans were treating Blacks as badly as they did throughout the 19th century, Blacks had to be turned into animals or, at best, sub-humans; the noble Caucasian was incapable of treating other full humans in such ways. This inversion sets the scene for the racial and main aspect of the 'Egyptian problem': *If it had been scientifically 'proved' that Blacks were biologically incapable of civilization, how could one explain Ancient Egypt – which was inconveniently placed on the African continent?*[66] *There were two, or rather, three solutions. The first was to deny that the Ancient Egyptians were black; the second was to deny that the Ancient Egyptians had created a 'true' civilization; the third was to make doubly sure by denying both. The last has been preferred by most 19th- and 20th-century historians.*

To what 'race', then, did the Ancient Egyptians belong? I am very dubious of the utility of the concept 'race' in general because it is impossible to achieve any anatomical precision on the subject. More-over, even if one accepts it for the sake of argument, I am even more sceptical about the possibility of finding an answer in this particular case. Research on the question usually reveals far more about the predisposition of the researcher than about the question itself. Nevertheless I am convinced that, at least for the last 7,000 years, the population of Egypt has contained African, South-West Asian and Mediterranean types. It is also clear that the further south, or up the Nile, one goes, the blacker and more Negroid the population becomes, and that this has been the case for the same length of time. As I stated in the Introduction, I believe that Egyptian civilization was fundamentally African and that the African element was stronger in the Old and Middle Kingdoms, before the Hyksos invasion, than it later became. Furthermore, I am convinced that many of the most powerful Egyptian dynasties which were based in Upper Egypt – the 1st, 11th, 12th and 18th – were made up of pharaohs whom one can usefully call black.[67]

The actual African nature of Egyptian civilization, however, is not relevant to our present discussion, which is concerned with the ambiguities in the *perceived* 'racial' position of the Egyptians. In Classical times the Egyptians were seen as both black and white or yellow; Herodotos referred to them as having 'black skins and woolly hair'.[68] On the other hand, portraits of Bousiris on vases tend to show him as Caucasian, though he has black as well as white attendants.[69]

Professor Jean Devisse has expressed surprise at how many Blacks there appear to have been in early Christian portrayals of Egyptians.[70] He has also shown how the Egyptians were 'blackened' in the 15th century, when they were very much admired. There also appears to have been a relation between blackness and Egyptian wisdom. Many medieval and Renaissance paintings portray one of the *magi* – presumably an Egyptian – as a Black.[71] On the other hand, representations of Hermes Trismegistos from the Renaissance picture him as a European, though sometimes with vaguely Oriental features.[72]

In England, the fact that the name Gypsy (or Egyptian) was given to people from North-West India shows that in the 15th century the Egyptians were seen as an archetypally dark people.[73] The Talmudic interpretation that 'the curse of Ham' (the father of Canaan and Mizraim, 'Egypt') was blackness was widespread in the 17th century.[74] On the other hand, with the late-17th-century combination of increased racism and growing respect for the Ancient Egyptians, their image tended to be whitened. Bernier, the author of *New Division of the*

Earth by the Different Species or Races who Inhabit it, published in 1684, maintained that the Egyptians were part of the White Race.[75]

There is little doubt that many Masons have been racist. The facts that they were directly or indirectly involved with the slave trade and were less tied to monogenesis than orthodox Christians tended to override their anthropocentric tradition and the Masonic tenet that 'all mankind are brothers plighted'. With their focus on Egypt, they needed to make a drastic separation between the 'animal' Blacks and the noble Egyptians. In *The Magic Flute*, for instance, Mozart made a striking contrast between the lustful Moor Monostatos and the Egyptian philosopher Sarastro.[76] Indeed, if we note the stress on the benefits of Egyptian colonization, which was a central theme of *Sèthos*, and the stark contrasts drawn in it and in many other 18th-century writings between the 'acorn-eating' Pelasgians before the Egyptians' arrival and the glories of Greek civilization after it, we can suggest that these were, to some extent at least, justifications of contemporary European activities.

In the second half of the 18th century, however, there were also tendencies to pull the Egyptians back to Africa, tendencies linked to an enthusiasm for Ethiopia reflected in Dr Johnson's translation of the 17th-century travels of Father Lobo in that country and his novel *Rasselas*.[77] Although the medieval legend of the Kingdom of Prester John, Europe's Christian ally beyond Islam, had been applied to various regions of Asia and Africa, Ethiopia as an exotic, remote mountain and Christian kingdom was an admirable candidate. Furthermore, Ethiopia could very plausibly be linked to Ancient Egypt.

It should, however, be made clear that the name 'Abyssinia' was used precisely to avoid 'Ethiopia', with its indelible associations with blackness. The first American edition of Johnson's work, published in Philadelphia in 1768, was entitled *The History of Rasselas Prince of Abissinia: An Asiatic Tale*! Baron Cuvier equated Ethiopian with Negro, but categorized the Abyssinians – as Arabian colonies – as Caucasians.[78] Nevertheless, this was too fine a distinction to be effective. The great Scottish explorer James Bruce, who was inspired by the vision of Abyssinia/Ethiopia and the quest for the sources of the Nile, learnt better. For him the inhabitants of the Ethiopian mountains were black and – on the whole – beautiful. His fascinating discoveries encouraged admirers of Egypt like Bruce himself, the traveller and *savant* the Comte de Volney, Dupuis and Champollion to stress the importance of Upper Egypt or even Ethiopia as the sources of Egyptian civilization.[79]

Despite its obvious Romantic charm, Germans did not get swept up in the Ethiopian craze. Their extra-European fantasies were always fixed on Asia, and when they linked Egypt to black Africa it was to denigrate it. Winckelmann's dislike of the appearance of the Egyptians has been mentioned; the following quotation illustrates how damning he believed an African connection could be to Egypt:

> How can one find even a hint of beauty in their figures, when all or almost all of the originals on which they were based had the form of the African? That is they had, like them, pouting lips, receding and small chins, sunken and flattened profiles. And not only like the African but also like the Ethiopian, they often had flattened noses and a dark cast of skin . . . Thus all of the figures painted on the mummies had dark brown faces.[80]

Similar attitudes were held in England and France. Charles de Brosses, for instance, writing at almost the same time as Wickelmann, argued that the Ancient Egyptians resembled contemporary Blacks in that their zoolatry – which the Masons, following a tradition at least as old as Plutarch, saw as allegorical – was simply 'Negro fetishism'.[81] Nevertheless, at the end of the 18th century the predominant view was that of Mozart and his librettist Emanuel Schikaneder in *The Magic Flute*: that the Egyptians were neither Negro nor essentially African. Similarly Herder, with his great admiration for the East, saw them as an Asian people.[82] The anthropologist and pioneer of racial studies Lord Monboddo, who is famous for having included the oran-gutan with humankind, had a great admiration for the Egyptians.[83] Blumenbach placed the Egyptians, together with the Arabs and Jews, as members of the Caucasian race.[84] A few decades later, Cuvier saw them as 'probably' white.

The dominant Ethiopian languages are Semitic, and it seems to have been on these grounds that the position of the Abyssinians as members of the superior race was actually more secure than that of the Egyptians.[85] With the huge increase of pictorial representations of Ancient Egyptians available to Europeans during the first half of the 19th century, which showed them to have been a thoroughly mixed population, the Egyptians tended to be seen as increasingly African and black.

By the middle of the 19th century, Gobineau was reviving the biblical – or to be more precise, the Talmudic – scheme, and categorizing the Egyptians as Hamites and virtually black. He thus found it useful to accept Schlegel's theory that Egyptian 'civilization' – to the extent that Gobineau conceded that it had existed – derived from the implantation of Indian 'Aryan' colonists.[86] Before then, two compromises between the blackness of the Egyptians and their high civilization were reached, with the help of the long stretches of time seen to be involved. The first was the same as that generally agreed for India – that the original 'pure' Egyptians had been white but that there had later been considerable mixture from other races, and this mixture or miscegenation had been the major cause of their decadence.[87]

The second compromise, advanced by the early-19th-century anthropologist W. C. Wells, was just the opposite. Wells was linked to the humanitarian movement and opposed extreme racism and polygenesis, and he argued for the improvement of the black race. While he accepted the correlation between colour and degree of civilization, he maintained that it tended to be civilization that determined colour, rather than the other way round. He noted, for instance, that Ancient Egyptian art showed people who were clearly Negroid, yet the modern Egyptians were not Negroes. Thus, he argued, it was possible that their skins had become lighter with the advance of civilization.[88]

Wells, writing in 1818, shows how completely the intellectual atmosphere had changed since the Enlightenment. The notion of a higher Ancient Egyptian civilization was dismissed in the face of a completely triumphant 'progress' which could even transcend the biblical epitome of permanence: 'can the Ethiopian change his skin, or the leopard his spots?'[89] However, Wells was right in two ways. In the first place, the perception of the early Egyptians in the late 18th and early 19th centuries was as Negro – see, for instance, the famous representations of the Sphinx being measured by the French scientists of the Expedition.[90] Secondly – whether or not Wells was aware of it – Egypt, in 1818, was at the beginning of a 'national renaissance'.

The National Renaissance of Modern Egypt

Here we come to a subject that appears to be a non-issue in the history of the reputation of Ancient Egypt. However, as with 'the dog that did not bark in the night' in the Sherlock Holmes story, the failure of the Egyptian renaissance to affect scholars' racial stereotypes of the Ancient Egyptians tells us something very significant about them.

Egypt had been part of the Turkish Empire since the 16th century. However, the Turks continued to rule through the previous rulers, the Mamelukes, a corps of slaves largely from the Caucasus, who made up the most formidable section of the army and had controlled Egypt since the 13th century. Mameluke history is extremely bloody, and power at the top shifted frequently. By the end of the 18th century, however, commercial agricultural production, trade and manufacture had reached a level that made Egypt wealthy by world standards.[91]

Mameluke rule and Turkish suzerainty were then severely weakened by Napoleon's conquest in 1798, which had largely been carried out by manipulating class, religious and ethnic divisions in Egyptian society. By 1808 – after great confusion following the French withdrawal and British intervention – the British had been driven out and power had been seized by Mohamed Ali, the Albanian general of the Turkish forces. Some years later he had the Mamelukes massacred and became viceroy, virtually independent of the Turks.

Mohamed Ali began a state-led modernization of the Egyptian economy and society that can be compared only to those of Peter the Great in Russia and the Meiji Emperor in Japan. The land of the Mamelukes and tax farmers was seized and distributed directly to peasants, who now paid a combination of rent and tax to the state. Huge irrigation projects were set up, and the commercial cropping of cotton and sugar was established on a large scale. Furthermore, with the help of foreign experts modern factories were built to process these crops but, as in Russia and Japan, the industrial centrepieces were the arsenals established to supply the modern army and to make it independent of foreign weapons.[92] It can be claimed, with some justice, that there were harmful effects of this programme in that it made the country too dependent on cotton and built up a class of rich commercial landowners whose influence became very detrimental to national development. In the short term, however, the programme had a startling success. By the 1830s Egypt was second only to England in its modern industrial capacity.[93]

With these economic and political bases, Mohamed Ali began to create an Egyptian empire overseas. His modern army subdued many of the Turkish dependencies in Western Arabia, and by 1822 his generals had conquered the Sudan. He also looked towards the north, to Syria and Greece: as common subjects of the Ottoman Empire, many Greeks lived in the Delta and they became particularly involved in the new commercial sectors of the economy. After Mohamed Ali's rise to power more Greeks came both to join his new army and to take part in the economic boom.[94]

With the beginning of the Greek War of Independence in 1821 the Turkish Sultan, in desperation, gave Mohamed Ali the *pashaliks* or provincial governorships of Crete and the Morea (the contemporary name for the Peloponnese) with a commission to exterminate the rebels. For four years the Egyptians were unable to invade because of the skilful and ferocious Greek fleet. In 1825, however, the Egyptians took advantage of the Greek fleet's mutiny over lack of pay, and landed a disciplined army under Mohamed Ali's son Ibrahim. This force was able to crush the ferocious resistance of the Greek guerrillas, but only with increasingly savage repression. Ibrahim then moved north to Missolonghi, where the Greek patriots were being besieged by the Turks.

The arrival of the superior Egyptian army tipped the balance in favour of the Turks, and this centre of the Greek Revolution was taken, but only after a heroic defence which, with Byron's death there, was critical in bringing the governments of Europe round to the position of the Philhellene students and artists supporting the Greek cause. The

Rising now became a continental struggle between Europe on the one hand, and Asia and Africa on the other.[95] To some, declining Turkey was seen as less of a threat to Greece and Europe than Egypt. As the Austrian chancellor Metternich wrote, when considering the possibility of Egypt's gaining complete independence from Turkey, 'In this way one would see the realization of what has so often been announced as the most redoubtable danger to Europe – a new African power . . .'[96]

To counter such a possibility, the British and French governments tried to split Egypt from Turkey. They also attempted to persuade Mohamed Ali to withdraw from Morea and to force the Turkish government to grant him the *pashalik* of Syria in compensation. In 1827 squadrons of the British, French and Russian navies destroyed the Turkish and Egyptian fleets at Navarino, and Greek independence was assured. An agreement was made by which the Egyptians withdrew from the Peloponnese and released their Greek slaves. Despite this humiliation and defeat Mohamed Ali was granted Syria, and continued with his economic and military expansion.

During the 1830s the Egyptians controlled Syria and began a modernization of the country and an establishment of a new power base there. At the same time, Mohamed Ali and his son Ibrahim were able to establish colonial rule over Crete. The island's population had suffered huge casualties during the savage fighting between Greeks and Turks during the Greek War of Independence: the only relative truce had been that established by Ibrahim's army when it controlled Crete for eighteen months as a stepping stone to the Peloponnese.[97]

After the defeat at Navarino in 1827, the Christian Cretans rose again under the protection of the European fleets. England, however, did not wish to tip the balance too far, and in 1829 Mohamed Ali was allowed to re-establish his government over the island. After three years of relative quiet Christian Cretans, dissatisfied with their subjection to Moslems while other Greeks were independent, rose in another revolt, but this was brutally suppressed. After 1834 strict colonial rule in which no favouritism was given to the Moslems was imposed, and connections with the large Greek population of Egypt were established. The economy was restored, and developed for the mutual benefit of Mohamed Ali and the Cretans. Diseases were controlled and both the wealth and the population greatly increased in what – after decades of Turkish misrule – later seemed to have been a golden age for the island.[98]

In 1839 Mohamed Ali declared his independence from the Porte and invaded Turkey. Five days later the Sultan died, and soon after this the Turkish fleet mutinied and joined the Egyptians. The threat of the East Mediterranean under the control of non-Europeans was too terrible to contemplate, and in a show of unity not paralleled until the Boxer Rising in China, some sixty years later, Austria, England, France, Prussia and Russia came to the aid of Turkey. Mohamed Ali was forced – under threat of blockade – to hand back North Syria and Crete and, once more, to become a vassal of the Turks.[99]

The new settlement dealt an even more severe blow to the Egyptian economy than that imposed after Navarino. During the 1830s Mohamed Ali's state-centred autarky had been weakened by European commercial penetration; after the new settlement in 1839, the Egyptian economy was forced to go back in the direction of the traditional Turkish pattern. This reversal laid it completely open to the European manufactures which weakened and often destroyed Egyptian industry.[100] Nevertheless, Mohamed Ali's descendants retained considerable wealth and power until their political and military defeat by the British. Indeed, a further and much more severe collapse of the modern economy came only after the British takeover in 1880.[101]

The fact that this episode of modern history is so little known is not at all surprising. It does not fit the paradigm of active European expansion into a passive outside world. The Egyptian Empire of the 19th century was like the equally obscure, short-lived success stories of the Cherokees in the Appalachians, the Maoris in New Zealand and the Chinese in California. It was an example of non-Europeans beating Europeans at their own games and therefore being coerced into giving them up.[102] Where the racial stereotype of natural European superiority failed, artificial intervention was necessary to preserve it.

Where these events fit with our concerns is that no mention of the greatest Egyptian Empire since the time of Ramessēs II appears in the contemporary writing about ancient history. It is still more remarkable that at precisely the time when Egyptians were controlling large areas of

Greece, the invasion of Danaos the Egyptian should have been denied, at least partly, on grounds of 'national character'.[103] To some extent, the failure to see any anomaly in this can be explained in terms of contemporary 'media coverage'. Although official reports noted the relative efficiency and benevolence of the Egyptian rule, in popular reports Egyptian involvement in massacres was assimilated to the much more widespread killings by both Turks and Christian Greeks. Furthermore, the image of Blacks on the soil of Greece was seen as particularly appalling.[104]

The failure on the part of contemporary ancient historians to mention the contemporary Egyptian successes in general, and conquests in Greece in particular, cannot be entirely explained away on the grounds that recent events are no concern of the professional historian, or that there had been a complete rupture in Egyptian history with the coming of Islam. Early-19th-century historians were at the heart of the Romantic age, in which peoples were supposed to have permanent essences and characteristics. There was no hesitation at that time, for instance, in associating the pagan Goths and Vikings with Christian English and German triumphs of the 19th century. The reason for the double standard is obviously racist. It was inconvenient at the time, and even in retrospect, for historians who were convinced that Africans were racially and categorically inferior to admit that – even when led by renegade Europeans like Mohamed Ali and Ibrahim – Egyptians could form heroic conquering armies on a par with those of Napoleon, Wellington or Blücher.

Dupuis, Jomard and Champollion

Racism was, from the beginning, an important factor in the downplaying of the Egyptians and the dismissal of the Ancient Model, and after 1860 it became the overriding one. In the 1820s and 30s, however, the old rivalry between Egyptian religion and Christianity continued to play a significant role. I have already discussed the threat posed to Christianity by Charles François Dupuis, both as a cultural adviser to revolutionary regimes and through his *Origin of All Cults*, which set out, with massive corroborative detail, the claim that Christianity had arisen from the misunderstood debris of Egyptian astronomical religious allegory.

Such thinking became anathema after the French Revolution and the revival of Christianity as a necessary bastion of social order. It was not only crude reactionaries but 'critical apologists' for Christianity who were distressed by Dupuis. Coleridge declared himself to be a 'Berkeleyan' after reading him; Berkeley's defence against challenges to the historicity of the Gospels was to argue, from the position that all history is myth, that they were as reliable as any other texts.[105] Just as Newton, Bentley and Whiston had been frightened by Toland and the Radical Enlightenment, even the enlightened in the early 19th century felt threatened by Dupuis. Ex-President John Adams, for instance, was obsessed by him. In 1816 he wrote to his friend Thomas Jefferson to say that, instead of spending money on missionaries, 'we should project a society to translate Dupuis into all languages, and offer a reward in diamonds to any man or body of men who should produce the best answer to it.'[106] The diamonds should have gone to Jean François Champollion.

The intensity of the dread of Dupuis and Egypto-Masonry with their links to the French Revolution, together with the complicated triangular relations between Christianity, Greece and Ancient Egypt, appear in the tortuous career of Champollion. The antithesis of the Oriental Renaissance, Champollion should in many ways be seen as the culmination of the Masonic Enlightenment. He seems to have discovered his mission to decipher the hieroglyphs at very much the same point in his adolescence at which he became a Mason, and by the time he was twenty he had mastered Hebrew, Arabic and Coptic to prepare himself for the task.[107]

A decipherment was now made possible by the availability of copies of new texts, including the newly discovered Rosetta Stone on which the same text was inscribed in Greek, Demotic and hieroglyphics. However, as Gardiner put it, Champollion was 'always inclined to hark back to his incompatible theory of the purely symbolic character of the hieroglyphics'.[108] The fact that he overcame this illustrates that while his decipherment required the Masonic impulse, it could have succeeded only when the Egyptian ideal was starting to crack and Romantic linguistics beginning to triumph. Only at this point could he discard the central Masonic tenet that hieroglyphs were purely symbolic and without phonetic function.

A further irony was that Champollion's first substantive discovery, in 1822, was to date to Roman times the zodiac at Dendera, which Edmé-François Jomard, a follower of Dupuis and a leading scholar on Napoleon's Expedition, had claimed to have come from many thousands of years BC.[109] The help that this was seen to give Christianity appears in a report made by the French ambassador to Rome on the attitude of the Pope, who was reported as having said that

> [with this] ... important service rendered to religion: 'He [Champollion] has ... humbled and confounded the pride of this philosophy which claimed to have discovered in the zodiac of Dendera a chronology earlier than that of the Holy Scriptures.' The Holy Father has therefore requested that M. Testa, a man most learned in the studies of Antiquity, set out in detail for him the arguments whereby M. Champollion establishes: (1) that this zodiac was constructed under Nero; and (2) that no monument exists from before 2200 BC, dating back, that is, to the time of Abraham, so that, in accordance with our faith, there remain approximately eighteen centuries of darkness through which interpretation of the Holy Scriptures alone can guide us.[110]

This help against the threat of Dupuis explains the striking change of attitude exhibited after 1822 by the Ultra nobles, as well as Louis XVIII and Charles X, towards Champollion and his elder brother, whom they had detested for their Jacobinism and support for Napoleon, and the considerable patronage the younger brother received from a regime he despised. Champollion prudently restricted his historical discoveries to the post-Hyksos dynasties, then dated to 2200 BC, thus allowing biblical primacy. While this gained him support from the defenders of Christianity, his drawing attention to Egyptian triumphs from long before the earliest Greek civilization roused the hatred of the Hellenists. So for a time he split the alliance between Christianity and Hellenism.

Champollion had many enemies in academic circles including rival

Egyptologists like Jomard, whose dating of the zodiac he had discredited, and the Romantic and conservative founder of Orientalism, Sylvestre de Sacy. The backbone of the resistance that kept him out of the Academy and the Collège de France, however, was made up of Hellenists like Jean Antoine Letronne and Raoul Rochette, who by this time were passionately anti-Egyptian.[111] Nevertheless, by 1829 royal patronage and the plausibility and use of his decipherment won enough of them over, and Champollion received long-overdue recognition. Then, in the liberal atmosphere after the July Revolution in 1830, Champollion felt free to publish his conclusion that the Egyptian calendar, and hence Egyptian civilization, went back to 3285 BC. This reunited the Christians and the Hellenists against him and after his death in 1831 Egyptology virtually disappeared for a quarter of a century, while his Hellenist and Orientalist enemies went on to dominate the French Academic Establishment. Indeed, the ultimate irony was that his eulogy was read not by Champollion's friend and patron Dacier, the permanent Secretary of the Academy, but by Dacier's successor, Champollion's arch-enemy de Sacy.[112]

It was not until the late 1850s that translations of Egyptian texts were considered reliable by ancient historians. This absence of any serious consideration of Egyptology between 1831 and 1860 is of great importance to the theme of this book, as it was precisely during this period that the Egyptian-based Ancient Model was destroyed and the Indian-based Aryan Model erected. A good example of this process and of the general decline in the reputation of Ancient Egypt can be seen in George Eliot's *Middlemarch*, which, though written in the 1860s, was a careful reconstruction of intellectual life around 1830. In the novel the old scholar Casaubon's interest in Ancient Egypt was made to typify his obscurantism. Young Ladislaw, by contrast, fresh from the centre of Romanticism, the German community in Rome, did not criticize Casaubon for his failure to take Champollion's new decipherment into account. He was scornful of his failure to read the new German scholarship and for being interested in Egypt at all.[113]

The official heads of the German community in Rome during the teens and twenties were Barthold Niebuhr – the great historian of Rome and, for a time, the Prussian Minister at the Vatican – and his secretary and successor Christian Bunsen. Both were fully in favour of the new Romanticism and passion for ethnicity. Nevertheless, together with Alexander and Wilhelm von Humboldt, they were among the handful of German scholars who were convinced by Champollion's decipherment in the 1820s. Even they, however, had serious reservations about Egyptian culture. In 1833, as organizer of the new national museum in Berlin, Wilhelm von Humboldt insisted that while Egyptian objects were valuable to scholars – including himself – they should not be given equal status in a national museum which, for the public improvement, should be devoted to *Kunst*, by which he meant Greek and Roman antiquities and Renaissance art.[114]

Christian Bunsen had studied at Göttingen, and later became the Prussian ambassador to Britain at a critical time in the 1840s. He learnt hieroglyphics and championed Egyptology in the 30s and 40s against the 'resolute mistrust and indifference of his countrymen', keeping the discipline alive during its doldrums, but only at the price of having Ancient Egypt turned into an alien object of study.[115] When he first contemplated working on Egyptian he wrote to Niebuhr that he had 'a kind of shrinking from it'.[116] Describing a trip to the Villa Albani outside Rome, he recorded: 'nothing beautiful or Grecian could be looked at but everything Egyptian was sought out.'[117]

Bunsen's support of the German Egyptologist Reichardt Lepsius and the English Egyptologist and Assyriologist Samuel Birch have earned him a permanent place of honour in the history of Egyptology. Birch's short *Dictionary of Hieroglyphics* – the first of its kind in any language – was published in 1867 only as an appendix to the second edition of the fifth volume of Bunsen's massive *Egypt's Place in Universal History*. Indeed, it was for these volumes that this Egyptological aspect of Bunsen's many-sided career was chiefly known during and immediately after his lifetime.

Although he wrote the work in the 1840s, Bunsen claimed that his basic ideas on the subject had in fact been developed long before the decipherment, when he was a student at Göttingen in 1812. Thus they can be traced back to the intellectual world of Heyne, whom Bunsen met, and Blumenbach, under whom he studied. Nevertheless, there are clearly traces of later intellectual developments in his scheme, according to which the Egyptian was an African version of the common root of both the Aramaic (Semitic) and Indo-Germanic races. Bunsen maintained that

> The civilization of the human race is principally due to two great families of nations whose connection is a fact which is as beyond the possibility of mistake as is their early separation. What we call universal history necessarily appeared to me as the history of two races . . . of these the Indo-Germanic seemed to me the mainstream of history; the Aramaic crossed it and formed the episodes of the divine drama.[118]

Elsewhere he made this point in another form: 'If the Hebrew Semites are the priests of humanity the Helleno-Roman Aryans are, and ever will be, its heroes.'[119]

This perceived inequality between the two 'master races' will be discussed further, but here it is worth emphasizing that despite Schlegel's earlier claim that the two language families were absolutely distinct, the idea of a common origin for the Aryans and the Semites was still acceptable in the 1840s. It became less acceptable as the century wore on, but persisted until the climax of anti-Semitism in the 1920s and 30s.[120] Bunsen, maintaining that his framework fitted the new information coming from Champollion's work, saw clear links between Egyptian and Semitic, and significant ones between them and Indo-European.[121]

Much of *Egypt's Place* is concerned with chronology. For this Bunsen added new Egyptian and astronomical data to the Classical and biblical sources. His conclusion followed that of Champollion – that the Egyptian calendar had begun in 3285 BC. By contrast, the dates he used for universal history bore no relation to this system and would today be considered utterly fantastic. Bunsen belonged to the new generation of fervent Christians, and maintained that world history had gone through three stages before the Flood: Sinism, 20–15,000 BC; Turanism, 15–14,000 BC; and Khamism, 14–11,000 BC.[122]

The historical sequence – from China to Central Asia, to Egypt and finally to Europe – was rather different from that set out in his first draft, which consisted of three stages: the East, then the Greeks and Romans and finally the third stage, that of the Teutonic nations. The two schemes, put together, look very like Humboldt's 'progress' from agglutinative to inflected languages or Hegel's grand sweep of the 'Phases of World History', both of which were made at very much the same time. With Hegel, just as the sun moves from east to west, so the *state* or Universal Idea moved from the intuitive, 'theocratic despotism' of Mongolia and China, to the 'theocratic aristocracy' of India and the 'theocratic monarchy' of Persia; while Egypt was a point of transition between east and west. All these comprised the first phase of humanity, which Hegel explicitly likened to childhood.[123] The second phase, humanity's adolescence, was that of Greece, when there was ethical freedom for the first time. The third was that of Rome and the final climax was in the Germanic World.

It is noticeable that Hegel wrote exceptionally little about Egypt in this scheme, and his placing it above India seems to have been a shallow device to keep the overall direction of the Universal Idea from east to west. In his *Lectures on the History of Philosophy*, given between 1816 and 1830, he wrote at some length on Chinese and Indian thought, but touched on Egypt only when dealing with the origins of Greek philosophy.[124] Staged histories in which Oriental cultures were surpassed by European ones were thus all the rage in early-19th-century Germany.

To return to Bunsen. His Aryo-Semitism and his belief in Egypt as a remote source of civilization place him firmly in the early 19th century; such ideas lost ground during his lifetime (1791–1860), and became unacceptable in academic circles after 1880. Although Bunsen and his contemporaries saw the Chinese and Egyptians as pioneers of civilization, Bunsen kicked them far downstairs into the antediluvian past. For him, as for nearly all mid-19th-century historians, true history consisted of the dialogue between Aryans and Semites. Hence Bunsen flatly denied the Greek legends of Egyptian settlements in the Aegean.

Like most of his contemporaries he admitted that Greek mythology contained some Semitic influences; however, following the latest German scholarship, he believed that these were indirect. According to his scheme, the Semitic Hyksos had been called Peleset or Pelasgoi when they were expelled from Egypt in the 16th century BC. Some had settled in Crete and the South Aegean, driving out the Aryans who had lived in the islands. These Aryan islanders took the names of their expellers and moved to Mainland Greece, where they became the ancestors of the Ionians. It was they who, having been subjected to Semitic influence, introduced fragments of Near Eastern culture into Greece.[125]

In this intricate and cumbersome way – for which there was no ancient authority – Bunsen tried to incorporate both the Greek legends about Phoenician settlement and the apparent Semitic influences in Greece, while at the same time preserving Hellenic Aryan purity. Here, however, we are going into the age of anti-Semitism which is discussed in Chapters VIII and IX, where these differentiations between Egyptians and Phoenicians on the one hand, and Ionians and Dorians on the other, will be treated at length.

At this point it is important to note that knowledge of Egyptian as a language became available for comparative purposes only many decades *after* scholars had given up any idea that Egyptians had colonized Greece, or that Egyptian culture had had any significant impact on the Archipelago. Hence while Renaissance and Enlightenment scholars longed to make comparative studies with Egyptian, they were unable to do so. By contrast late-19th-century scholars, who possessed the tools, were convinced that any detailed comparison would be futile. By the 1840s Egyptian language and culture were seen as the products of a categorically inferior and more backward race, inherently incapable of having made contributions to the great Aryan civilization and the noble languages of India, Greece and Rome.

EGYPTIAN MONOTHEISM OR
EGYPTIAN POLYTHEISM

It is sometimes suggested that a major reason for the fall in Egypt's reputation was disillusion with the content of Egyptian texts once they were read. This, however, does not hold for Champollion, whose enthusiasm for Egypt increased as his life went on. With the revival of the study in the late 1850s, Egyptologists were torn between their admiration for Champollion – the acknowledged founder of their

discipline – and acceptance of his reverence for Egypt, and the
prevailing Romantic-Positivist ethos and contempt and condescension
towards the culture. Although the congruence between the two is not
exact, the key issue over which this tension was manifested was on the
nature of Egyptian religion. As the historian of religion Karl Beth wrote
in 1916:

> Monotheism or polytheism? This has been the great issue in
> Egyptology since the discovery of the first Egyptian texts. The survey
> I have given here shows that both answers have their justification; it
> also shows that the proponents of both use these concepts like
> slogans, yet neither concept can characterize the true individuality of
> Egyptian religion.[126]

If, as he plausibly argued, the corpus of Egyptian texts can be read in
either sense, what was – and is – the argument about? Its essence would
seem to be a continuation of the old struggle between Egyptian religion
and Christianity. If Egyptian religion were monotheist, it could be seen
as the basis or origin of Christianity. In the late 19th century, however,
the racial question was more salient. If Egyptian religion were
monotheist, it would impinge on the Aryo-Semitic monopoly of
civilization.

Emmanuel de Rougé and Heinrich Brugsch, the leaders of the
second wave of Egyptology in the 1860s and 70s, both followed
Champollion, and the Hermetic and Platonic tradition behind him, in
believing that the pure Egyptian religion was sublime and essentially
monotheist, as de Rougé said: 'one idea predominates, that of a single
primeval God; everywhere and always it is One Substance, self-existent
and an unapproachable God.'[127]

Brugsch was appointed to the chair of Egyptology at Göttingen in
1868, the first professor of the subject since the death of Champollion.
He too maintained that the Egyptians had originally been monotheist,
as initially did Sir Peter le Page Renouf, the leading Egyptologist in
England.[128] However, by the time the second edition of his *Lectures on
the Origin and Growth of Religion* appeared in 1880, Renouf had changed
his mind, denying that he had stated: 'the Egyptians commenced with
monotheism.'[129] Internalists like the modern Egyptologist and historian

of Egyptology Erich Hornung argue that this change of opinion came from increased knowledge of Ancient Egypt.[130] I find it more useful to see the denial of Egyptian monotheism as part of the process in which the racism and Romantic Hellenism that prevailed in Classics and ancient history as a whole took over in Egyptology.

The intermediate stage in this process can be seen in a passage from the work of Professor Lieblein. In a passage written in 1884, Lieblein attempted to fit the old view of monotheism into the new linguistic and historical schemes, and came up with the compromise that the Egyptians might have only had a proto-God or no God at all:

> All things considered it is possible, even probable, that the idea of God has developed itself in an earlier period of languages than the Indo-European. The future will perhaps be able to supply evidence for this. The science of languages has been able partly to reconstruct an Indo-European prehistoric language. It might be able also to reconstruct a prehistoric Semitic, and a prehistoric Hamitic, and of these three prehistoric languages, whose original connection it not only guesses, but even commences to prove, gradually, [sic] it will, we trust in time, be able to extract a still earlier prehistoric connection, which according to analogy might be called Noahitic. When we have come so far, we shall most likely, in this prehistoric language, also find words expressing the idea of God. But it is even possible that the idea of God has not come into existence in this prehistoric language either.[131]

Thus for Lieblein the Egyptians were relegated to the distant and primitive past. The last traces of the Platonic, Hermetic and Masonic respect for Egypt were being expelled from academia, and a full-scale attack on the older Egyptology was launched a few years later by the French Egyptologist Maspero. As he described the situation in 1893:

> I believed at the beginning of my career, which will soon be twenty-five years ago, and I maintained for a long time like M. Brugsch that the Egyptians arrived during their earliest period at the notion of divine unity and they took from this an entire religious system and symbolic mythology . . . this was the period when I had

not myself tried to decipher religious texts and when I limited myself
to reproducing the texts of our great masters. When I was forced to
tackle them ... I had to admit that they did not show any of the
profound wisdom that others had seen in them. I cannot be accused
of wanting to depreciate the Egyptians and I am convinced that they
were one of the great people of humanity, one of the most original
and the most creative, but they always remained semi-barbarians ...
They invented, produced and above all, promised much in art, in
science, and in industry, but their religion presents the same mixture
of coarseness and refinement that one finds in the rest.[132]

What is significant about this statement by a liberal Frenchman and
heir to the Enlightenment is not the description of the Egyptians, most
of which would seem eminently fair. It is the implication that there were
other, presumably Indo-European and Christian civilizations that were
entirely refined and lacking in barbarism.[133] Elsewhere in the same
passage, however, Maspero showed his racist colours quite clearly:

Time, which has done so much harm to other nations, has shown
itself most favourable to the Egyptians. It has spared their tombs,
their temples, their statues, and the thousand small objects which
were the pride of their domestic life, and it has led us in such a way
that we judge them by the most beautiful and the prettiest of the
things which they made, and has at length caused us to place their
civilization on the same footing as that of the Romans or the Greeks.
But if it be looked at more nearly, the point of view changes; to speak
quite shortly, Thothmes III and Rameses II resemble Mtesa of
Central Africa more than they do Alexander or Caesar ...[134]

The argument that one should not be deceived by mere appearances
into breaking the 'scientific' laws of racism is also interesting as an
indication of the complete rupture between the scientific and prescientific period seen by late-19th-century scholars. For Maspero and
his contemporaries, Ancient Egypt was a modern discovery. Anything
written about it before Napoleon's Expedition and Champollion's
decipherment had no relevance whatsoever.

Moreover, Maspero continued:

Most of its myths it holds in common with the most savage tribes of the Old and the New Worlds. The Egyptian possessed the spirit of a subtle metaphysician, a fact which he proved when Christianity furnished him with a subject worthy of his subtle powers.[135]

One might think that having been stripped of civilization, religion and philosophy, the Egyptians might be allowed the shred of metaphysics. However, the tidal wave of racism could not even tolerate this. Ten years later, in 1904, the English Egyptologist Wallis Budge added:

The Egyptians, being fundamentally an African people, possessed all the virtues and vices which characterized the North African races generally, and it is not to be held for a moment that any African people could become metaphysicians in the modern sense of the word. In the first place, no African language is suitable for giving expression to theological and philosophical speculations, and even an Egyptian priest of the highest intellectual attainments would have been unable to render a treatise of Aristotle into language which his brother priests, without teaching, could understand. The mere construction of the language would make such a thing an impossibility, to say nothing of the ideas of the great Greek philosopher, which belong to a domain of thought and culture wholly foreign to the Egyptian.[136]

Here, as well as using the common 19th-century strategem of justifying his racism on linguistic grounds, Budge was being subtle! It is true that nothing like Aristotle is attested in Egyptian thought, but Budge used this absence to imply that there was a categorical distinction between Greek and Egyptian thought as wholes. He could not, for instance, have used Plato as an example.

Elsewhere Budge attacked Brugsch's argument that the commonest Egyptian word for 'divine', *ntr*, was identical with the Greek φύσις and the Latin *natura*:

It is difficult to see how the eminent Egyptologist could attempt to compare the conception of God formed by a half-civilized African people with those of such cultivated nations as the Greeks and Romans.[137]

There is no doubt that this contempt is at some level related to the British occupation of Egypt and dislike of the inhabitants of that country. Indeed, after 1880 Egypt became – with the exceptions of Ireland and Somaliland – the most troublesome British possession. Budge's own identification with imperialism is typified by the dedication of his great work *The Gods of the Egyptians* to Lord Cromer, who presided over the destruction of the Egyptian manufacturing economy, as 'The Regenerator of Egypt'.

German scholars were not behind the British and French in their scepticism about the Egyptians. Lieblein's questioning of their monotheism was followed by forthright criticism and scorn for any idea of their having had an ancient wisdom.[138] Moreover, by the 1880s some Egyptologists shared the Indo-Europeanists' concepts of Aryan linguistic purity. As Professor A. Bezzenberger, editor of the leading journal in Indo-European studies, *Beiträge zur Kunde der indogermanischen Sprachen*, described the situation in 1883:

> It is maintained by many that Egypt had a very significant influence on Ancient Greece. However, this assumption has up to now never had the least proof from the point of view of language. Given the seriousness of the question, such a proof is definitely called for. I therefore directed myself to Herr Dr Adolph Erman [later to become the doyen of German Egyptology] and asked him to collect and treat the true and supposed Egyptian loan words in Greek.
>
> Erman, who had a good – though heavy – sense of humour, replied: 'In theory I should be delighted to go along with your proposal – but it appears to me that the most important requisite is lacking: the loan words themselves. One can find enough "supposed" ones in Egyptological works. But as far as my understanding reaches I cannot see a single one that is sure.'[139]

Erman admitted that some Egyptian words for Egyptian objects had been used in Greek, but these were not true loans. In the next issue of the journal Erman was challenged on this. His response to the challenge was to make two concessions:

I never claimed that there were no Egyptian loan words in Greek. I merely stated that I did not know of any secure cases. I do not believe that the names of Egyptian objects that appear here and there in the Greek authors should be seen as accepted Greek loan words.[140]

His second concession was to admit that the word βᾶρις (small boat), which clearly came from the late Egyptian and Demotic *br* (small boat), had been assimilated into Greek. He ended defiantly, however:

After this all that remains is essentially negative; there are a few 'culture words' and probably one true loan word, βᾶρις, and that is all; the conventional view of a deep Egyptian influence on Greece does not reach the same results. I do not doubt that broad-minded colleagues could find substantially more, as I could have. I must in this case remind them that in a script in which the vowels are unmarked, and with a vocabulary in which the meanings are very precarious, with some good will, one can find an Egyptian origin for every Greek word . . . This is a sport that I happily leave to others.[141]

Although this attitude was typical among Egyptologists of the time and later, it must be admitted that Erman's attitude of condescension towards the Ancient Egyptians was notorious among Egyptologists. Alan Gardiner reported the following story about him:

Once Erman asked Maspero to get collated for him a passage in the *Pyramid Texts*, of which a set of squeezes existed in Paris. On reception of the collation Erman wrote to Maspero: 'What a pity it is that even at this early period the Egyptians could not write correctly!' On which Maspero's caustic comment – not communicated to Erman, needless to say – was: 'What a pity that the Egyptians of the Old Kingdom had not read M. Erman's grammar!'[142]

Nevertheless, despite Erman's extremism on this, I think it is fair to say that this essentially racist attitude of scepticism about, and scorn for, Egyptian achievements was predominant in Egyptology throughout the high tide of imperialism between 1880 and 1950. It would, however, be oversimplifying to say it was the only one. Resistance to this view on or beyond the fringes of academia will be touched on later in this chapter, but there were exceptions to it even in the heart of the discipline. It was precisely at the peak of racism in the first decade of the 20th century, for instance, that Professor James Henry Breasted published the *Memphite Theology*, which I discussed in Chapter II. Its conception of the world, he concluded,

> forms quite a sufficient basis for suggesting that the later notions of *nous* and *logos*, hitherto supposed to have been introduced into Egypt from abroad at a much later date, was present at this early period. Thus the Greek tradition of the origin of their philosophy in Egypt undoubtedly contains more of the truth than has in recent years been conceded.

He continued:

> The habit, later so prevalent among the Greeks, of interpreting philosophically the functions and relations of the Egyptian gods . . . had already begun in Egypt before the earliest Greek philosophers were born; and it is not impossible that the Greek practice of the interpretations of their own gods received its first impulse from Egypt.[143]

This conclusion would seem to have been forced on him by the text itself, however, and seems to have been anomalous even in Breasted's own thinking. Later on, in his *The Development of Religion and Thought in Ancient Egypt*, he wrote in the standard linguistic racist terms:

> The Egyptian did not possess the terminology for the expression of a system of abstract thought, neither did he develop the capacity to create the necessary terminology, as did the Greek. He thought in concrete pictures.[144]

A still more striking exception to the prevailing fashions in academia at the turn of the 19th century was the work of the French Classicist Paul Foucart, who knew a considerable amount about Egypt and whose son Georges was an Egyptologist. Foucart's detailed work on the mystery cult at Eleusis led him not only to the conclude that the cult had been introduced from Egypt but also to make an articulate defence of the Ancient Model which will be discussed in the next chapter.

From the point of view of the 20th-century orthodoxy, however, the difficulty with Foucart has been that his work on Eleusinian inscriptions was so superb that later scholars working in the field have found it indispensable. Hence, subsequent workers have tended to distinguish the brilliant epigrapher from the cranky theorist. As one put it: 'One can only be sincerely sorry that such a significant scholar should hold this error.'[145]

Despite these aberrations or heresies, there is no doubt that during the first two-thirds of the 20th century most 'sound' scholars did not take the Egyptians too seriously. Interestingly, however, there was a significant change in their pejorative image. Most 19th-century scholars accepted the view, propounded by Winckelmann and others, that the Egyptians were an old and strangely dead people. With the firm establishment of the paradigm of 'progress', and with the analogy between history and biography, the Egyptians were pushed into precisely the opposite position. They now began to be thought of as children, and came to occupy a rather similar niche to that of Winckelmann's carefree Greeks. In his *Egyptian Grammar*, published in 1927 and generally accepted as the 'bible' of modern Egyptology, Alan Gardiner wrote:

> Despite the reputation for philosophic wisdom attributed to the Egyptians by the Greeks, no people has ever shown itself more averse from speculations or more wholeheartedly devoted to material interests; and if they paid an exaggerated attention to funerary observances, it was because the continuance of earthly pursuits and pleasures was felt to be at stake, assuredly not out of any curiosity as to the why and whither of human life.

He later described the Egyptians as 'a pleasure-loving people, gay, artistic and sharp-witted, but lacking in depth of feeling and idealism'.[146]

Thus both the ancient reputation of profound wisdom and the old one of passivity and gloom were stood on their heads. Nevertheless, the Egyptians remained categorically inferior to Europeans. Elsewhere, however, Gardiner admitted that Egyptologists were under some constraints: 'Classical scholars have not in the past taken very kindly to the idea of Hellenic dependence on Egyptian civilization.'[147]

Given the centrality and strength of Classics within the universities, there was nothing the Egyptologists in a small peripheral discipline could do about the denigration of Egypt, even if they wanted to. Few, if any, did. Nearly all of them had had a thorough Classical education before beginning their own subject. Thus Gardiner was clearly reflecting the views of most of his colleagues when he wrote: 'The supposed Greek dependence on Egyptian philosophy proves on examination to be the merest moonshine.'[148]

The denial of Egyptian philosophy and suspicion of Egyptian religion dominated Egyptology until the 1960s. Hornung, for instance, refers to 'half a century of abstinence' from considering the problem of the fundamental nature of Egyptian religion.[149] There were, in fact, one or two other scholars like Margaret Murray who continued to take Egyptian religion seriously, but they were considered by 'sound' scholars to be on the fringes of Egyptology.[150]

However, cracks in the orthodoxy began to appear after the Second World War. In 1948 Abbé Etienne Drioton, Director General of the Egyptian Antiquities Service, began to see genuine religion in the Egyptian Wisdom Literature and to consider the possibility of an earlier monotheism.[151]

Since the 1960s this more open attitude has begun to establish itself, especially in France and Germany. In these countries the possibility of real Egyptian spirituality and originality began to be considered once more. Some Egyptologists, like the German Hellmut Brunner, are even calling for a 'new picture of Egypt', and Brunner maintains that there was a qualitative intellectual and spiritual leap in Egypt around the turn of the 3rd millennium.[152] Despite this new flexibility, however, there is still a considerable gap between the discipline of Egyptology and what one could call its 'counter-cultures'.

POPULAR PERCEPTIONS OF ANCIENT EGYPT IN THE 19TH AND 20TH CENTURIES

Before going on to examine the counter-currents on the periphery of academia to this prevailing view of Egyptian intellectual and spiritual life, I want to consider attitudes towards Ancient Egypt in society at large. It is commonly believed that as a result of the Napoleonic Expedition there was a period of Egyptomania in the early 19th century. Indeed, this picture fits the general pattern best articulated by Raymond Schwab, according to which the Romantic-Positivists were the first Europeans to be truly aware of the outside world. This view in turn derives from and reinforces the notion that the only proper relationship between Europe and other continents is one of clear-cut superiority, which did not exist until the 19th century. Nevertheless, the conventional view of a period of Egyptomania does contain an element of truth and there was, in fact, great curiosity about Egypt in the early 19th century.

However, as we have seen, there was considerable interest in, and knowledge about, Egypt long before that period.[153] Furthermore, Egypt exerted much more influence on Europe from the 15th to the 18th century than it did in the 19th. There is also no doubt that 19th-century 'Egyptomania' was weaker than 'Indomania', and trivial in comparison to the 'Hellenomania' or passion for Greece that swept Northern Europe and America in the same period. What is more, Greece was seen, in the eyes of most people, as a revered and beloved ancestor, while Egypt was now perceived as essentially alien or exotic.

It remains true, however, that there was intense interest throughout Europe in the publications of the French Expedition and the results of further explorations and discoveries.[154] Not surprisingly these focused on pyramids and tombs, and in the second half of the century there were translations of the Egyptian guide book for the soul, *The Book of the Going Forth by Day*, generally known as *The Book of the Dead*. All this increased the by now well-established impression of Egypt as a gloomy and dead kingdom, and as such it was given one domain that was very important in the middle and late 19th century – that of death. Egyptian styles appeared in all the cemeteries of Europe and North America.[155] What is more, mummification became widespread in the United States during the 1860s and 70s. Although this development is often attributed to the higher requirements of hygiene in urban societies, it is still interesting to contrast the American (Egyptian) way of death with the spread of cremation – the Greek form of disposal – adopted in much of Northern Europe at the same time.[156] Was this because of the much greater influence of Freemasonry in the USA?

Masonry remained the great repository of respect for Egypt. Indeed, Masonic architecture, symbols and rituals continued – and continue – to follow their Egyptian traditions rather than the dictates of academic fashion.[157] In the USA Masonry, Egypt and hieroglyphics were central to the foundation of Mormonism in the 1820s, and had a major influence on mid- and late-19th-century American writers. Melville's novels – especially *Moby Dick* – are full of Egyptian symbols and hieroglyphs, while Hawthorne's *The Scarlet Letter* bears the same stamp.[158]

Although Masons were very influential in Europe as well, there the craft's concern with Egypt was almost completely confined to its inner or spiritual life. Like the rest of the European upper and middle classes, Masons were much more taken up with the prevailing Hellenomania. Other, much smaller groups also retained a central position for Egypt in their beliefs: the Rosicrucians, both as an inner ring of the Masons and as a separate spiritual organization, kept and keep Egypt as the centre and origin of their beliefs. The mystical Swedenborgians of the 18th and 19th centuries and the later Theosophists and Anthroposophists also placed Egypt in a central position.[159]

In the first half of the 19th century, however, the St Simonians were a much more influential group. These disciples of the pioneer 'socialist' and proto-Positivist Claude Henri Comte de St Simon followed a typical tripartite view of world history, in which the third and final 'epoch of the positive system' involved the unification of the world. Such a unification required opening up communications throughout the world and for St Simon, as for Napoleon and most thinkers of the time, Egypt was the bridge between east and west.[160] Thus he and his successor Prosper Enfantin were particularly concerned with the country, not just from the spiritual and but also from the practical point of view.

Enfantin arrived in Egypt in 1833 with a number of disciples including engineers, doctors, businessmen and writers. He had official approval from the new French regime of Louis Philippe for what he saw as the second French intellectual and scientific expedition; however, he also had a mystic mission as 'the father', to marry the mysterious 'mother' in the Orient. The mission, in turn, was linked to the practical project of building the Suez Canal. Articulating the imagery of piercing a canal, and in a travesty of the general belief that European domination of non-Europeans was somehow a heterosexual sexual act, Enfantin wrote: 'Suez is the Centre of our life work. We shall carry out the act for which the world is waiting to proclaim that we are male!'[161] The canal was built by a member of this group, Ferdinand de Lesseps, but not until the 1860s. In the meantime St Simonians played key roles as engineers, doctors, teachers and so on in Mohamed Ali's state-led modernization of Egypt, and the image of their project was very much like that of Napoleon's Expedition – that of France reawakening Egypt, the ancient source of civilization.[162]

It was in this St Simonian atmosphere that Mohamed Ali's grandson Ismail commissioned Verdi, the composer of the Italian *Risorgimento*, to create an Egyptian national opera, *Aïda*. The opera's plot – devised by the French Egyptologist Auguste Mariette, who was employed by the Egyptian government – glorified Ancient Egypt in a Western manner. However, the difference from the 18th century is clear: where Mozart glorified the priests who possessed Egyptian wisdom and morality, Verdi placed his priests in opposition to Aïda and her lover Radames.[163]

Aïda became a great success all over Europe. This continued acceptance of a favourable view of Egypt – as essentially white and as a fount of civilization – was especially widespread in France and Italy, but it can also be seen in the art of England and the United States.[164] Together with the Egyptophilia of the second generation of Egyptologists of the 1860s and 70s, it explains the defensiveness or defiance noted above in the statements of the scholars of the 1880s, like Maspero and Erman. They, like the Classicists but unlike the general public, had an overall and systematic view and could see the threat that too favourable a picture of Egypt could pose to the uniqueness of Greek civilization and that of Europe as a whole.

ELLIOT SMITH AND
'DIFFUSIONISM'

There were, however, two other threats to the new conventional wisdom from within academia itself. We will first consider the one that arose later because so far, at least, it has had a less serious impact on Egyptology; it came from the 'diffusionist' ideas of Elliot Smith. Born in Australia in 1871, Smith qualified as a doctor and went to England, where he became a distinguished anatomist. In 1901 he was appointed Professor of Anatomy at Cairo, where he set up a medical school. During his next eight years there he became fascinated by early Egypt – not only its physical anthropology, but its culture.[165] It was in this period that he became convinced that Egypt had been the source of Near Eastern and European culture.

Elliot Smith was a man of his racist times. Thus, while he could not avoid the fact that the bulk of the Egyptian population had always been very much like that of the rest of East Africa, he was convinced that in the 'Pyramid Times' – the Old Kingdom – there had been a critical influx of broad-skulled – non-Semitic – Asiatics.[166] According to him, this mixed race had migrated around the Mediterranean and on into Northern Europe, bringing the megalithic culture whose impressive monuments he saw as reflections of the Pyramids. This part of Elliot Smith's theories is now completely untenable, as carbon dating has shown that the European megalithic culture began over 1,000 years before the Pyramid Age.[167]

Elliot Smith's views were received with interest by the British public because 'diffusionism' fitted so well with contemporary Imperialism; because his Egyptians were not African; and because he was an anatomist. Anatomy was considered to be a 'hard' science, whereas the disciplines of history and archaeology did not have that status. Professional ancient historians and Egyptologists were naturally much more wary. As far as I am aware, there was no attempt to incorporate his theories into their academic disciplines. Nevertheless, he did not get into serious trouble until he expanded his scope to claim that Egypt had been the source not only of European culture, but also that of the rest of the world. He found Egyptian origins for the Pyramids of Mexico, and for the mummification techniques of Peru and the Torres Strait Islands near New Guinea.

Paradoxically, this part of his theories stands up today rather better than does that about the megalithic cultures of Europe. On the one hand, increased archaeology and carbon dating have shown that the metal-using cultures of South-West Asia and the Neolithic cultures of Europe were considerably older than those of Egypt, thus invalidating his theories in these areas. On the other, the increased evidence of African influence on Pre-Columbian America after about 1000 BC, and discoveries such as the fact that the Meso-American Pyramids were not merely bases for temples but could contain burials, strengthen the possibility of indirect Egyptian influence on these much later civilizations.[168]

At the time, however, Elliot Smith's second great book in this field, *The Ancient Egyptians and the Origin of Civilization*, published in 1923, led to attacks from conservatives who retained the Romantic views of local peculiarity, and hardline racists who saw all civilization as stemming from the pure Aryans. There were even more violent struggles with the liberals, who were beginning to turn anthropology from a racist stronghold – whose practitioners were used to maintain empires cheaply – into one that could bring cultural relativism home to Europe. Nevertheless, during the 1920s the battle was not uneven. Elliot Smith had the backing of most in his own discipline, and his students gained important positions in physical anthropology. He even converted W. H. R. Rivers, one of the founders of social anthropology, to his beliefs. Furthermore, there were at that time no senior social anthropologists who had been trained in the discipline who could outrank Smith.[169] Even more important, he had good connections with the Rockefellers, whose foundations provided massive funding for both Egyptology and anthropology in the 1920s and 30s. With all these resources Elliot Smith had considerable clout inside academia.[170]

Even so, the combination of forces arrayed against him proved too strong. Rivers died prematurely in 1922, and Elliot Smith himself in 1937 at only sixty-six. Even if they had lived longer, the connection between his ideas and racism could never have survived the revulsion against the latter during and after the Second World War. Neverthe-less, the threat to anthropology that Elliot Smith represented at a vulnerable stage in the discipline's development can still be seen: it is in the shudder or grimace at the mention of his name or the word 'diffusionism' that is still a necessary sign of orthodoxy or 'competence' in the field.

JOMARD AND THE
MYSTERY OF THE PYRAMIDS

Although they generally disliked an interloper trampling over their territory, Egyptologists and ancient historians were much less involved in this struggle than anthropologists. This was possibly because Elliot Smith never even approached language, the *sanctum sanctorum* of Romantic-Positivism. They were, however, much more concerned with the second threat to Egyptology, which was far longer-lasting than 'diffusionism'. This academic heresy had its ultimate origin in the ancient view that the Egyptians had been the possessors of an superior wisdom, which the Greeks had been unable to learn and preserve in its entirety.

This was revived in the early 19th century by the work of Cham-pollion's bitter and lifelong rival Edmé-François Jomard, the math-ematician and surveyer attached to Napoleon's Expedition whom we have already encountered. Jomard put together the results of his own surveys of the Great Pyramid at Giza and its precise geographical position, with ancient descriptions of the mathematical significance of its measurements. He became convinced that the Ancient Egyptians must have had an accurate knowledge of the earth's circumference and based their units of linear measurement upon it, which, of course, put him firmly in the camp of Dupuis. There were criticisms of details in his work, but in the Masonic atmosphere of the Napoleonic Empire his views were treated very seriously; having become a member of the French academic Establishment before the Restoration, he was able to survive it.[171]

Despite the blow to Jomard's reputation over the dating of the zodiac at Dendera, his ideas survived or were frequently rediscovered and developed throughout the 19th century.[172] Differences between this heterodox school and academic Egyptology became sharp after the discipline's establishment in the 1860s, and acute in the 1880s after it accepted the dominance of Classics. At no stage, however, were there formal debates between the two. This was firstly because of the general principle that no group holding academic power will willingly 'dignify' outsiders in this way; and secondly because the two groups were speaking different scholarly languages. In fact, they reflected the differences between Champollion and Jomard. The Egyptologists were primarily philologists applying the new techniques of linguistics to the Egyptian written material. The heretics, however, were mathematicians, surveyors and astronomers, few of whom gained any fluency in Egyptian. On the other hand, 19th-century Egyptologists were unable to follow, let alone refute, the heretics' technical arguments.

The struggle was unequal from the start, for the heretics were fighting against the two principal paradigms of the 19th century – 'progress' and racism. If they were right, an ancient African or semi-African people had had better mathematics than any European until the 19th century itself. At a more mundane level the heretics, lacking the discipline and sanctions of formally organized academic knowledge, sometimes slipped into religious fantasy. The tendency to do this was increased by the genuine difficulty the heretics had in accounting for the astounding achievements they found in the ancient mathematics and astronomy, which led them to explanations in terms of divine revelation. This in turn sometimes encouraged beliefs that the Pyramids contained divine prophecies.[173] All this served to discredit such 'Pyramidiocy', as it came to be called.

Another grave disadvantage for the heretics was the fact that Classics and linguistics had a higher status in 19th-century Germany and England than mathematics. In France, with its *Polytechniques*, the situation was more finely balanced, and here Egyptologists seem to have been under some pressure to consider arguments in the tradition of Jomard. In the 19th century, for instance, Maspero was forced to concede that he had been convinced by the astronomer Sir Norman Lockyer's detailed arguments for the case that the Egyptian temples had been very carefully built for astronomical purposes.[174] What is striking, however, is that so many men – including such distinguished and well-established astronomers as Professor Piazzi Smyth, the Astronomer Royal for Scotland, and Sir Norman Lockyer – should have risked or given up their careers to pursue these ideas. In the case of Piazzi Smyth it can partly be explained in terms of religious enthusiasm, but here, as with Lockyer, sheer excitement over the mathematical elegance of the correspondences seems to have been the major motivation.[175]

The 'pyramidologists' received their biggest setback with the defection of Flinders Petrie, mentioned on p. 138 for his early dating of the Hermetic Texts. Petrie had an engineering and surveying background, as well as an enthusiasm for the ideas of Smyth and other successors of Jomard, and in 1880 he was able to go to Egypt with the latest surveying equipment to check for himself the accuracy of previous measurements.

His conclusions were inconclusive. On the one hand, he agreed that the Great Pyramid had been aligned to the cardinal points of the compass with more accuracy than any later building, and that the measurements of the inner chamber demonstrated a knowledge of π as 22/7 and of Pythagorean triangles. In general, too, he was astounded by the technical and mathematical skills that had gone into the Pyramids' construction. On the other hand, he disagreed with Piazzi Smyth on the length of the cubit used in the construction, and he did not accept Smyth's claim that the building incorporated the precise length of the year.[176] Moreover, given the changes taking place within Egyptology in the 1880s and the general professionalization in academia and elsewhere between 1880 and 1960, 'pyramidologist' theories were pushed into the new category of crankiness or pseudo-science.

With his superb surveying and his development of typologies for the ordering of different styles of pottery, Petrie became the founder not only of Egyptian but of all modern archaeology. Later knighted, he was incorporated into academic Egyptology and provided it with essential support. Nevertheless, the relationship was never easy.[177] He had to be given a chair by an outside donor, and remained a maverick until the end of his long life in 1942.

Petrie's defection did not stop the investigation of the Pyramids and other Egyptian constructions in the belief that they could reveal a higher ancient wisdom. Lockyer continued to develop his ideas on the sophisticated astronomical knowledge demonstrated in Egyptian buildings, and these were taken up in the 20th century by a number of scholars, most notably by the brilliant amateur Schwaller de Lubicz. De Lubicz's books, published in the 1950s and 60s, have had a wide success particularly in mystic circles, but also among the public at large.[178]

Meanwhile, a new and still more accurate survey of the Pyramids had been made by the engineer J. H. Cole in 1925. This survey confirmed many of the claims made by earlier 'pyramidologists' – even those of Jomard, who appears to have arrived at relatively accurate estimates for lengths for the Egyptian units of measurement as the result of two countervailing errors. The imprecision of his measurement was counterbalanced by his failure to realize that the Great Pyramid must have had a peak or pyramidion on its top. Moreover, since the 1920s there have even been two significant defections to the 'pyramidological' position from 'straight' academia. The first of these was Livio Catullo Stecchini, an Italian who studied in Germany and gained a doctorate in ancient mensuration at Harvard. In a number of studies published in the 1950s and 60s Stecchini demonstrated, with some plausibility, that the Egyptians had had a very precise knowledge of global measurement and that this knowledge had been applied in Egypt and elsewhere with extraordinary exactitude.[179]

The second conversion to the belief in a higher ancient wisdom was much more spectacular: it was that of one of the greatest, if not the greatest, historians of Renaissance science, Giorgio de Santillana. Having written a major book on Galileo, de Santillana became interested in the Hermetic Egyptian tradition; then, late in life, he read Dupuis's *Origine de tous les cultes*, and was convinced by its argument that much of ancient mythology was indeed allegory for scientific astronomy. However, de Santillana went beyond Dupuis and Egypt to claim an even earlier knowledge, traces of which could be found in myths from all over the world and which, by using the precession of the equinoxes, he dated to before 6000 BC.

Despite de Santillana's enormous reputation, *Hamlet's Mill* – the book in which he and a younger German colleague set out this scheme –

was not accepted by any university press and was published commercially. This means that respectable scholars are not obliged to take such work into account.[180] In addition, de Santillana's having stuck his neck out so far lessened his effectiveness as a proponent of the school of Dupuis and Jomard. Furthermore, his work – like that of Stecchini and Tompkins – could be lumped together with a more or less 'lunatic fringe'; this allowed or even compelled orthodox scholars to ignore it.

Through the influence of archaeology, Egyptologists and ancient historians tend to be more numerate now than they were fifty or a hundred years ago. Nevertheless, few of them have the combination of time, effort and skill necessary to take on the very technical arguments of Schwaller de Lubicz, Stecchini or de Santillana. Rather, over the last thirty years the tendency within these disciplines has been to rely on the refutations by another grand old man of the history of science, Professor Otto Neugebauer, whose name has almost tantric power among defenders of the *status quo*.

Neugebauer's range is astounding. He has already been mentioned in connection with Copernicus, but his best-known work has been on science in Antiquity. Here he has been more broad-minded than most and, just as he has been prepared to concede the Islamic science behind Copernicus, he has demonstrated some significant Mesopotamian influences on Greek mathematics and astronomy.[181] He has also published several works on Egyptian astronomy in collaboration with orthodox Egyptologists, but in these, in sharp contrast to his treatment of Mesopotamia, he shares his collaborators' condescending and contemptuous attitude towards Egypt and Hermeticism.[182] Indeed, in all his works Neugebauer has insisted that the Egyptians had no original or abstract ideas. The accurate alignments of the Pyramids and temples, and the use of π, are all explained as the results of practical knacks rather than of profound thought; an example of this being the following: 'It has even been claimed that the area of a hemisphere was correctly found in an example of the Moscow papyrus, but the text admits also of a much more primitive interpretation, *which is preferable*' (my italics).[183] Interestingly, however, Neugebauer does not take on the Pyramid school. He simply denounces them:

Important mathematical constants, e.g. an accurate value of π and deep astronomical knowledge, are supposed to be built into the dimensions and structure of this building. These theories contradict flatly all sound knowledge obtained by archaeology and by Egypto-logical research about the history and purposes of the Pyramids.[184]

He then recommends that those interested in what he admits to be 'the very complex historical and archaeological problems connected with the Pyramids' read the books by Edwards and Lauer on the subject.[185]

The Egyptian archaeologist Edwards does not involve himself with the 'pyramidologists' and their calculations. The surveyor and archae-ologist Lauer did, in the face of opposition from Egyptologists, who were 'astonished that we should give so much importance to the discussion of theories which have never had any credit in the Egyptological world'.[186]

All told, Lauer's work had a certain contradictory quality. On the one hand, he admitted that the measurements do have some remarkable properties; that one can find such relations as π, ϕ, the 'golden number' and Pythagoras' triangle from them; and that these generally corre-spond to what Herodotos and other ancient writers claimed for them.[187] On the other, he denounced the 'fantasies' of Jomard and Piazzi Smyth; attacked, rather implausibly, Jomard's reconstructed cubit; and claimed that the formulae and the extraordinary degree of sidereal accuracy with which the Pyramids were aligned were purely the result of 'intuitive and utilitarian empiricism'.[188]

The contradiction between an acceptance of the extraordinary mathematical precision of the Great Pyramid and a 'certainty' that the Greeks were the first 'true' mathematicians runs throughout Lauer's many writings on the subject. The tension is made still more unbearable by the facts that the Greeks had been told about many of the Pyramid's extraordinary features and that they believed the Egyptians to have been the first mathematicians and astronomers. Finally, there is the problem that so many of the Greek mathematicians and astronomers had studied in Egypt. Lauer's honest attempt to deal with these difficulties was the following:

Even though up to now no esoteric Egyptian mathematical document has been discovered, we know, if we can believe the Greeks, that the Egyptian priests were very jealous of the secrets of their science and that they occupied themselves, Aristotle tells us, in mathematics. It seems, then, reasonably probable that they had been in possession of an esoteric science erected, little by little, in the secrecy of the temples during the long centuries that separate the construction of the pyramids, towards the year 2800, to the eve of Greek mathematical thought in the 6th century BC. As far as geometry is concerned, the analysis of buildings as famous as the Great Pyramid would take a notable place in the researches of these priests; and it is perfectly conceivable that they could have succeeded in discovering in it, perhaps long after their erection, chance qualities that had remained totally unsuspected to the constructors.[189]

Lauer was a discoverer of the actual existence of the 3rd-dynasty architect Imhotep, previously dismissed as a late Egyptian legend, and he excavated some of the latter's superb buildings at Saqqara. He also spent a lifetime admiring the extraordinary achievements of the Pyramids. It is difficult to see why he should then baulk at the simplest solution, believe the Greeks and accept, with the German Egyptologist Professor Brunner, that there was an *Achsenzeit* or 'axial age' around 3000 BC. Thus one or two centuries later, in the 3rd and 4th Dynasties, there was a sophisticated knowledge of mathematics, some features of which were built into the Great Pyramid. Traditions of this were retained by later Egyptians and hence told to visiting Greeks.[190]

Why – if one discards racist and crudely 'progressive' arguments – should this be any more improbable than the Greeks having achieved a qualitative intellectual breakthrough in the 4th century BC? Indeed, there is nothing to back the second hypothesis, approximating to the actual achievements of the Pyramids and the consistent ancient tradition of a superior Egyptian mathematics.

However, such a perspective was not available to conventional scholars at the height of imperialism. It is nevertheless clear that Lauer was anguished on the issue and ultimately seems to have been constrained by social forces. To accept the simplest answer would have made him a crank, like Jomard and Piazzi Smyth. Thus he preferred to attribute the exquisite mathematical relationships in the Great Pyramid and their place in ancient tradition to mere chance which Egyptian priests had later discovered and exploited.

However, even Lauer's solution still allowed some later Egyptians to have been capable of some relatively advanced thought. He continued:

> For the whole length of the 3,000 years of her history, Egypt thus, little by little, prepared the way for the Greek scholars who – like Thales, Pythagoras and Plato – came to study then even to teach, like Euclid, at the school in Alexandria. But it was in their philosophic spirit, which knew how to draw from the treasure amassed by the technical Positivism of the Egyptians, that geometry came to the stage of a genuine science.[191]

How could Lauer be sure, against the ancient writers who insisted on the spirituality and unworldliness of the Egyptian priests, that the Egyptian secret wisdom – about which he had no evidence – was merely 'technical Positivism'? It is hard not to see this simply as an article of faith for all who work in the Aryan Model.

The nameless Egyptologists who disapproved of Lauer's discussion of the 'pyramidologists'' theories were quite right to do so. By fighting the 'pyramidologists' he came to resemble them – or at least to accept so many of their arguments as to make his own defence of the orthodoxy seem hopelessly cumbersome.

Lauer was not alone in his difficulty. The Abbé Drioton, who has been mentioned above for his acceptance of Egyptian spirituality, wrote: 'one should pay no attention to the ... renewed delusions of Charles Piazzi Smyth that the measurements of the Great Pyramid reveal a mysterious science of the Ancient Egyptians.'[192] Elsewhere, however, he wrote that because they fail to pay attention to the 'pyramidologists', Egyptologists are being treated like 'naif, blind, refractory dabblers in a science whose quiet routines have been disturbed'.[193] There have been other hints that a number of 'respectable' Egyptologists feel pressure from the outside – or the material they handle? – and have toyed for more or less long periods of time with the heresies.[194] In this important skirmish between an Ancient and an

Aryan Model, I believe that the Ancient will – with some modifications – prevail. In the meantime, however, there is no doubt that the field as a whole still basically follows the linguistic tradition of Champollion as transformed by Maspero, Erman and the other scholars of the late 19th and early 20th centuries who brought their discipline into line with the predominant Romantic-Positivism, and that the mathematical and surveying school of Jomard is still very much on the outside.

CHAPTER VI

HELLENOMANIA, I
The fall of the Ancient Model,
1790–1830

THIS CHAPTER IS ALMOST entirely concerned with social and intellectual developments in Protestant North Germany during a period of forty years. The time-span may be short but it covers the French Revolution, the Napoleonic conquests, the crescendo of German nationalism against the French, the years of reaction, and the establishment of Prussia as the dominant German state and the focus of all German nationalism.

It is precisely at this critical period that the new discipline of *Philologie* or *Altertumswissenschaft* (Science of Antiquity) was established as the pioneer discipline in the modern sense. It was the first to establish clear-cut meritocratic networks of student–teacher relationships, Seminars or departments capable of manoeuvring to secure as large a portion of state funding as possible, and journals written in a professional jargon designed to maintain barriers between the practitioners of the discipline and the lay public.

I argue that the intellectual and academic developments have to be seen together with the social and political ones. It is striking to note that some of the key leaders on linguistic and historical issues, like Humboldt and Niebuhr, played active roles not only in setting up the new discipline but in the establishment of the new university system as a whole. They were also important politicians on the national scene.

It is extremely significant that the period of their greatest political influence was during the reforms which the Prussian government felt obliged to make after its catastrophic defeat by Napoleon's armies at Jena in 1806. The development and widespread promotion of the new *Altertumswissenschaft*, which Humboldt put at the centre of his *Bildung* (educational formation), should be seen as one of these reforms. He and his friends saw study of 'Antiquity in general and the Greeks in particular' as a way in which to integrate students and the people as a whole, whose lives they saw as being fragmented by modern society. More immediately, Humboldt and the others saw the study as a way of promoting an 'authentic' reform, through which Germany could avoid revolution of the type that so horrified them in France. From the beginning, then, *Altertumswissenschaft* in Germany – like its equivalent, Classics, in England – was seen by its promoters as a 'third way' between reaction and revolution. In actuality, however, its effect was to shore up the *status quo*. The educational institutions and the Classical *Bildung* that infused them became pillars of 19th-century Prussian and German social order.

At the core of *Altertumswissenschaft* was the image of the divine Greek, both artistic and philosophical. Greeks also had – like the idealized image of the Germans themselves – to be integrated with their native soil, and pure. Thus the Ancient Model, with its multiple invasions and frequent cultural borrowings and the implicit consequences of racial and linguistic mixture, became increasingly intolerable. It is only within this political and social context that one can understand the attack by one of the first products of the new system, Karl Otfried Müller, on the overwhelming ancient authority of the Ancient Model.

In 1821, the year after the publication of *The Minyans*, the book in which he set out his arguments, the Greek War of Independence broke out and Western Europe was swept by Philhellenism. In such anti-Asian and African Hellenomania, defence of the Ancient Model became almost unthinkable; paradoxically, its only major champion was the great ancient historian Barthold Niebuhr, who had done so much to introduce Romanticism and racism into the writing of history. After

Niebuhr's death in 1831 it became hard, if not impossible, for 'sound' scholars to argue that Egyptians had colonized Greece or played an important role in the formation of Greek civilization.

FRIEDRICH AUGUST WOLF
AND WILHELM VON HUMBOLDT

Having considered the 'fall' of Egypt, we should now turn to the 'rise' of Greece. Christian Gottlob Heyne's best-known student, Friedrich August Wolf, studied at Göttingen only for the two years 1777–9. But from this experience, and from the *Zeitgeist*, he became in many ways the epitome of Romantic-Positivism.[1] He was a disciple of Winckelmann, a believer in staged history and a lover of Greece. A German patriot, he was deeply influenced by the movement for authenticity, with its emphasis on folksong. He also saw himself in the Romantic tradition of Homeric studies that we encountered in the discussion of Mme Dacier and Vico, and in this connection Wolf believed that he had an especial affinity with Bentley.[2]

Wolf brought all these strands together. Setting his work in a context of detailed textual analysis, he envisioned the *Iliad* and the *Odyssey* as coming from the childhood of the Greek and, by implication, the European race. Basing himself on these feelings, and on the ancient tradition that Homer had been blind, Wolf was convinced that the epics had been composed orally, long before the Greeks had possessed an alphabet.[3] According to him, the epics were too long to have been the work of one illiterate bard. Hence they must have been created by a number of folk poets and put together only when they were edited or, as he supposed, first reduced to writing in 6th-century Athens. With these hypotheses Wolf arrived at the perfect Romantic conclusion. The Homeric epics should now be seen not as the work of a single author but as the product of the childhood of the Greek/European *Volk* as a body.[4]

Many of these ideas came from the Scottish writers and from Robert Wood, the Romantic dilettante who – it will be remembered – had read the *Iliad in situ*. With his textual expertise and his status as a professor, however, Wolf gave them an academic authority which was essential in the new world of 'professional' knowledge.[5] On the other hand, we should not overlook the fact that on paper at least, Wolf's scholarship seems rather shallow. Although extremely stimulating, his *Prolegomena to Homer* has been regarded as a 'hurried piece' and his written works as a whole 'make little show in a library'.[6]

Wolf's achievement was in the tradition of *Altertumswissenschaft* that he established. On his matriculation at Göttingen in 1777 he had called himself a 'student of philology', considered a radical step at the time.[7] Later, however, he called the study of ancient texts – rounded out with Classical art and archaeology – *Altertumswissenschaft*, or 'science of antiquity'. Wolf has been called its founder, though he clearly derived the disciplinary form from his teacher Heyne and the content ultimately from Winckelmann, while the name was drawn from the new vocabulary of science and progress promoted in Germany by Kant.[8] Wolf's forte was teaching, and as a professor at Halle in the 1780s he promoted both the new discipline and the seminar as a teaching method and as an institutional basis for research. Wolf's fame was secured by his connection with the young Prussian aristocrat Wilhelm von Humboldt.

Before examining their friendship and its extraordinary scholarly and institutional results, however, I want to consider for a moment the political positions of both Romantic Hellenism and Göttingen Positivism. These, as I have been arguing, were closely related. The proponents of both considered themselves 'progressive' and were in favour of small 'free' states. However, there was considerable ambiguity on the meaning of 'free'. Furthermore, when the test came with the French Revolution, nearly all holders of these views and sentiments recoiled from it because of its threat to privilege, its violence and what they saw as its 'unnatural' or 'inorganic' approach to 'freedom'. It is with this background in mind that one should view the reforms they planned and later carried out.

Wolf and Humboldt became close friends during 1792–3, at the height of the Revolution. From their discussions Humboldt produced a *Skizze* or sketch, 'On the Study of Antiquity and of the Greeks in Particular'.[9] Although not published in his lifetime, it was read and criticized by Wolf and the great poet, playwright and philosopher Schiller. The sketch also became extremely important because it expressed the ideas which Humboldt was later to try to put into practice as Prussian Minister of Education.

Humboldt gave two justifications for making the study of Antiquity central in general education. There were obvious aesthetic reasons for studying the Greeks, he argued, but far more important was his faith that learning about the unalienated men of Antiquity would create a new society of better men today. Such a study would be the centre of *Bildung*, or educational and moral formation. With the Romantic concern for growth and formation through time, Humboldt valued the study of the Ancients not so much as a goal but as a process. He believed that grasping the complex organic development of Antiquity would somehow stretch and strengthen the creative powers of the student.[10]

It is possible that Humboldt originally intented this *Bildung* for the whole population. In the event, however, it became the stamp of a meritocratic elite.[11] As such, it challenged the nobility. Its purpose was to reform Prussia within German culture, avoiding the horrors of the French Revolution. For 'On the Study of Antiquity' was written during the trial of Louis XVI, about which Humboldt wrote at the time: 'this execution and horrible trial have left stains that can never be obliterated.'[12] In France the upper classes read Barthélemy's *Anacharsis* as an escape from the tensions and horrors of the Revolution, and there is no doubt that study of the Greeks also provided an escape for Humboldt and his friend Schiller.[13] However, it was much more than that; they saw study and imitation of the Greeks as a way of transcending the extremes of revolution and reaction. Similarly, in Schiller's famous series of letters on the *Aesthetic Education of Man* the fifth letter, concerning the chaos of the French Revolution, was followed by the sixth, on the harmonizing function of studying the Greeks.[14]

HUMBOLDT'S
EDUCATIONAL REFORMS

Objectively, whatever their subjective political positions, Humboldt and Schiller helped defend the *status quo*. It was precisely to this kind of safe radical that the Prussian monarchy turned after the humiliation of the traditional government and its beloved army after their catastrophic defeat by Napoleon at Jena in 1806. In 1809, among other reforms undertaken to face the French Revolutionary challenge, Humboldt was entrusted with the reorganization of the educational system. He based the new structure on *Bildung*, which he believed would reanimate the German people after their crushing defeats. In higher education he consciously rejected the French *Polytechniques*, with their emphasis on mathematics and natural science, in favour of schools teaching the much broader concept of *Wissenschaft*. Ostensibly the new Prussian curriculum was to contain the three disciplines of mathematics, history and languages. Humboldt's priorities, however, can be seen from the fact that no mathematics was taught for the first five years at his chief creation, the new university at Berlin.[15]

The leading scholar Humboldt recruited to Berlin was Wolf, who, as we have seen, introduced the Seminar, which spread from there to Prussia, then to Germany and then beyond. This system, with its insistence that students learn actively through their own research, would seem to give the students far more freedom and scope for originality than do traditional lectures. Over the past 180 years, however, while the form has produced great scholarly achievements, it is apparent that it can be and is used as a very effective tool to control both the choice and the treatment of topics of academic concern.

Wolf's practice of *Altertumswissenschaft* followed that of Heyne and the Göttingen school. He rejected what he saw as the conceptualizing and abstract search for universals of the Enlightenment, in favour of direct confrontation with particulars and detailed source criticism. Completely oblivious to what can be seen, with hindsight, as his own intense Romanticism, he was able to write: 'All our research is historical and critical not of *things* to be hoped for but for *facts*. Arts should be loved but history revered.'[16]

This simple-minded approach has dominated the practice of most history and Classics ever since. Humboldt, at least by the end of his life, was far more sensitive. In his essay 'The task of a historian', he recognized that comprehension of the past required far more than external description. What was needed was a balance between 'rational observation' (*beobachtender Verstand*) and 'poetic imagination' (*dichtende*

Einbildungskraft). The historian, however, unlike the poet, must subordinate his imagination to the investigation of reality, and 'must of necessity yield to the power of form, while keeping constantly in mind the ideas which are its laws.'[17] In the 19th century these ideas certainly included the 'scientific laws of race'.

Humboldt also tried to wrestle with the difficulties of the relationship between subject and object in historical enquiry, which he believed required some feelings of kinship such as those existing between Germany and Ancient Greece. It was thus possible to write a history of Antiquity. At the same time, however, the Greeks were seen to transcend history. As he wrote in another piece:

> Our study of Greek history is therefore a matter quite different from our other historical studies. For us the Greeks step out of the circle of history. Even if their destinies belong to the general chain of events, yet in this respect they matter least to us. We fail entirely to recognize our relationship to them if we dare to apply the standards to them which we apply to the rest of world history. Knowledge of the Greeks is not merely pleasant, useful or necessary to us – no, in the Greeks alone we find the ideal of that which we should like to be and produce. If every part of history enriched us with its human wisdom and human experience, then from the Greeks we take something more than earthly – almost godlike.[18]

Humboldt's view of the transcendent quality of Greek history was matched by his view of its language. He saw Greek not as an *Ursprache*, or 'original language' like Sanskrit, but as a perfect balance between youthful vitality and philosophical maturity – reflecting the double qualities of aesthetics and philosophy that had been attributed to the Greeks since the 1780s.[19]

The central importance of language, its fundamental relationship with nation and national character, and the Romantics' fascination with all three have already been touched on.[20] Humboldt, who though many-sided was fundamentally a linguist, tended to regard language as an essentially independent fixed variable.[21] For him the nature of the Greek language was of paramount importance. Furthermore, as always – or at least since the 15th century – concern with Greek paralleled that with German.[22] Thus with the crescendo of German nationalism towards the climax of the War of Liberation against Napoleon in 1813–14 came an increasing glorification of the German language; its chief virtue was seen to be that it was, unlike French, somehow *echt* (authentic) and *rein* (pure).[23]

Well before this, in his *Skizze* of 1793, Humboldt had argued that the excellence of Greek lay precisely in its being uncontaminated by foreign elements.[24] Thus the superb linguist, who was particularly fascinated by the complexities of linguistic mixing, suspended his critical faculties when it came to Greek, holding it as an article of faith that the language was 'pure'. This inherently implausible notion would have been considered absurd before the triumph of Romantic-Hellenism but, with certain provisos, it now became canonical in *Altertumswissenschaft* and modern Classics. Since then only the names of clearly Oriental luxury goods have been exempted from the otherwise complete embargo on Afroasiatic loan words.

While Humboldt and other Romantics insisted on the infinite variety of societies, and the absence of the universals proclaimed by the Enlightenment, they saw a general direction provided by an inner order, supreme force or being.[25] The Greeks were perceived as having transcended mundane chaos and being closer to the ineffable best. In some sense, then, they were themselves the human universal.

It was precisely this and their supposed transcendence of historical and linguistic laws that made the Greeks the central concern of *Bildung*, through which the young leaders of Germany were to understand and remake themselves. It was for equivalent purposes that *Altertumswissenschaft* and Classics spread to the rest of Europe and its offshoots beyond: despite its scholarly trappings, its role in the ideological formation of the ruling class has continued to be more important than historical or linguistic enquiry. Thus, while early-19th-century Philhellenism – though consistently racist – had both radical and reactionary aspects, the discipline of Classics was conservative from the start. The educational reforms of which it formed the centrepiece were systematic attempts to avoid or prevent revolution.[26]

THE PHILHELLENES

To make some sense of the fall of the Ancient Model in the 1820s, we should start by considering the general political and ideological environment in which the change took place. Central to it was the philhellenic movement which, in the 19th century, occupied what might be called the 'radical wing' of the Romantic movement. Philhellenism tended to share the Romantic rejection of urban industrialization, the universalism and rationality of the Enlightenment, and the French Revolution. On the other hand, while the mainstream of Romanticism turned towards the medieval past and Christianity – especially Catholicism – Philhellenes were sometimes religious sceptics or atheists, and political radicals.[27] As young men, for instance, Hegel and Friedrich Schlegel loved the Greeks, but as they grew older and increasingly conservative they turned to Christianity.[28] The Left Hegelians, including Marx, preserved the young Hegel's passionate interest in Greece.

The reason for the radicals' enthusiasm seems obvious. Compared to Rome – or, for that matter, Egypt or China – the Greek states were indeed models of liberty. Moreover, this tension within the Romantic movement has persisted. Both the revived public school system, in which the future leaders of England were supposed to become 'Christian gentlemen' by studying the pagan Classics, and the movement to create an Indo-Germanic or Hellenic Christianity, can usefully be seen as attempts to bring together these two wings of the Romantic movement.[29]

The experience of the French Revolution and the triumph of reaction after 1815 caused much bitter disillusion among upper-class Romantics. However, the love of freedom revived – if only in an alienated form – with the outbreak of the Greek War of Independence in 1821, and the Germans were the nationality most quickly and deeply involved.[30] Indeed, their movement in support of the struggle provided the only important centre for liberalism in the country: over 300 Germans went to fight in Greece, but they were only the tip of the iceberg in a movement that involved tens of thousands, mostly students and academics.[31] Many French and Italians also went, supported by numerous philhellenic committees; and the movement was even powerful in the United States. Though only sixteen North Americans reached Greece, the widespread philhellenic feelings arising from the War provided a big boost for the 'Hellenic' – Greek letter – fraternities in the United States. The other chief influence on the American student organizations came from the book-burning German student fraternities revived between 1811 and 1819, by the eccentric teacher and promoter of exercise 'Father' Jahn, to support the Romantic nationalism of the War of Liberation. Fraternities in both countries have preserved this chauvinism with the strong physical and anti-intellectual bias envisaged by their founders.[32]

Britons, too, were deeply involved in the Greek cause. We have seen that the English and Scottish poets had been passionately concerned with Greece since the mid-18th century. When the Parthenon or 'Elgin' Marbles were exhibited in London in 1807 there was a craze for pure Greek art, which had never before been seen there.[33] Henry Fuseli saw the Marbles and shouted: 'De Greeks were godes. De Greeks were godes!'[34]

Fuseli, né Füssli, was a Swiss artist and art historian living in London, where he promoted the ideas of Winckelmann. His passion for Greece and hatred of Egypt seem to have been equally intense. For him, Greece was 'that happy coast, where, free from an arbitrary hieroglyph, the palliative of ignorance, from a tool of despotism or a ponderous monument of eternal sleep, art emerged into life, motion and liberty.'[35]

It should be noted, however, that the idea of Greece emerging from Egypt implies an acceptance of the Ancient Model which later Phil-hellenes were unwilling to concede. Although Fuseli was foreign, his ideas on Greece were not that far from general cultivated opinion in the first quarter of the 19th century.

With the beginning of the War in 1821, enthusiasm for Greece rose to fever pitch. As Shelley wrote:

> We are all Greeks. Our laws, our literature, our religion, our arts all have their roots in Greece. But for Greece . . . we might still have been savages and idolators . . . The human form and the human mind attained to a perfection in Greece which has impressed its

images on those faultless productions whose very fragments are the despair of modern art, and has propagated impulses which can never cease, through a thousand channels of manifest or imperceptible operation, to enable and delight mankind until the extinction of the race.[36]

Hellenomania was well and truly launched!

Despite Shelley's passionate eloquence and his dramatic drowning just when he was about to go to Greece, the most famous philhellenic poet of the Romantic age was Byron. It was no coincidence that he was from Scotland: the 18th-century links between that *northern* country and Romanticism have already been noticed. In the early 19th century they involved not only Byron but Sir Walter Scott, the herald of the medieval revival, and the invention of a fictitious sentimental national tradition at which even Scott baulked.[37] Although a coarse Regency rake, Byron linked Scottish Romanticism to Greece. He had called for the country's independence a decade before the revolt broke out, and to crown it all – with mixed but essentially Romantic motives – he joined the War in order to die in it.[38]

Throughout Western Europe, the Greek War of Independence was seen as a struggle between European youthful vigour and Asiatic and African decadence, corruption and cruelty:

> The barbarians of Genghis Khan and Tamerlane are revived in the 19th century. War to the death has been declared against European religion and civilization.[39]

Even in the 18th century, Turkish rule in Greece and the Balkans had begun to be seen as unnatural, the result of the conquest of a superior race by an inferior one. It will be remembered that Christian Bunsen placed the 'Turanians' or Turks between the Chinese and the Egyptians in his historical hierarchy of races; in the 19th century rule by this race was seen as bound to fail in the end, and could certainly never result in any advance of civilization.

By the end of the century this principle was being applied systematically throughout history, and perceptions of the Arab and Berber rule of Spain provide a clear example of the change. Before 1860, English and

North American writers were sympathetic towards the Moors because Islam was less pernicious to them than Catholicism. By the end of the century, 'racial' considerations had transcended the religious ones; hence Arab rule of Spain was seen as sterile and 'doomed' throughout its 800 generally flourishing years.[40]

The intensification of these racial feelings with the Greek War of Independence thus had a direct effect on the Ancient Model. As first the Egyptians and then the Phoenicians were increasingly perceived as 'racially' inferior, the Greek legends of their having not only colonized but civilized 'sacred Hellas' became not merely distasteful but paradigmatically impossible. Like the stories of sirens or centaurs, they had to be dismissed because they offended against the biological and historical laws of 19th-century science. Objections to this picture were made still greater by another aspect of the change from the Enlightenment to Romanticism. Since the Enlightenment placed much emphasis on cultivation and improvement, it was no great slur on the Greeks for their civilization to be attributed to Egyptian and Phoenician colonization. Romantics, on the other hand, stressed nature and distinct, permanent national essences, so that it was now intolerable to suggest that the Greeks had *ever* been more primitive than Africans and Asians.

DIRTY GREEKS AND THE DORIANS

The Philhellenes were more concerned with the Classical Greeks than with their heroic, but superstitious, Christian and dirty 'descendants', whom some tried to explain away as 'Byzantinized Slavs'.[41] Philhellenes sought the pure essence of Greece before it had been tainted by Oriental corruption, and with their apotheosis – as we have seen in Humboldt and Shelley – even the Ancient Greeks themselves began to fall short of the new exalted standards. These standards increasingly began to call for cultural, linguistic and finally 'racial' purity, and such new paragons had been found as early as the 1790s by Friedrich Schlegel in the Spartans or the larger tribal grouping to which they belonged, the Dorians. Elizabeth Rawson, the modern historian of the image of Sparta, has described Schlegel's writing about them:

From the start, however, language reminiscent of Winckelmann on the Greeks in general is used for the Dorians; we are told of their *milde Grossheit*, 'serene greatness', and indeed in contrast to the more easily Orientalized Ionians they form the older, purer and more truly Hellenic branch chiefly responsible for those two essential procedures for the Greek spirit, music and gymnastics.[42]

Notice that Schlegel and many other later writers took these two nonverbal, irrational and – dare I say it – 'German' aspects of Greek culture as the essential ones. Nietzsche's *Birth of Tragedy*, published in 1872, in which music and Dionysian tragic passion are emphasized over Apollonian reason, is often seen as a radical break away from Winckelmann's view of the 'serene greatness' of the Greeks. In fact it belongs to a German tradition which goes back through the poems of Heine in the 1840s, to Heyne and the playwright Wieland in the 18th century.[43]

During the 19th and 20th centuries the German cult of, and identification with, the Dorians and Lakonians continued to rise until it reached its climax in the Third Reich.[44] By the end of the 19th century some *völkische* (populist, nationalist) writers saw the Dorians as pure-blooded Aryans from the north, possibly even from Germany, and they were certainly seen as very close to the Germans in their Aryan blood and character.[45]

Such enthusiasm was not restricted to Germans. As John Bagnell Bury wrote in his *History of Greece*, first published in 1900 and still considered standard,

The Dorians took possession of the rich vale of the Eurotas, and, keeping their own Dorian stock pure from the mixture of alien blood, reduced all the inhabitants to the condition of subjects ... The eminent quality which distinguished the Dorians ... was that which we call 'character' and it was in Lakonia that this quality was most fully displayed and developed itself, for here the Dorian seems to have remained most purely Dorian.[46]

It is interesting to note that Bury – like many of the leading British Classicists of the turn of the 19th century, including John Pentland

Mahaffy and William Ridgeway – came from the Protestant Ascendancy in Ireland. All three men were enthusiastic about the pure
northern, and possibly Germanic, blood of the Dorians. Thus, apart
from participating in the general racism of the period, it is clear that they
saw an analogy between the Teutonic English relationship with the
Irish, whom they saw as 'marginally European', and that between the
Dorians and their subject populations, the Pelasgian native inhabitants
and the Helots.[47] Ridgeway was an altogether consistent racist who,
though his family had lived in Ireland for 200 years, boasted that he had
'not a drop of Gaelic blood in his veins'.[48] By 1900, then, the Spartans –
the 'true' Greeks – were seen as racially pure and somehow northern.
The situation was not so extreme in early 19th century, but the
pressures were building up.

<h2 style="text-align:center">TRANSITIONAL FIGURES, 1:
HEGEL AND MARX</h2>

Another prerequisite to examining the full-out attack on the Ancient
Model in the 1820s is to look at thinkers who straddled the changes. To
do this I have taken three examples: Hegel and Marx; A. H. L. Heeren;
and Barthold Niebuhr.

Hegel was born in 1770 and was at the height of his power and
influence in the 1820s, but he was not accepted by the philologists,
whose power kept him out of the Prussian Academy for many years.
Nevertheless, not only was he central to German philosophy of the
time, but he also had a profound effect on the Romantic historians.[49]
There is also no doubt that Hegel was typical of his age. He loved
Europe or, as he put it, the temperate zone; he respected the Asian
mountains and India; he hated Islam and had complete contempt for
Africa.[50] His trajectory of the World Spirit from east to west obliged
him to claim that being further to the west, Egypt was more advanced
than eastern India.[51]

Hegel's true feelings seem to emerge in his *Lectures on the History of
Philosophy*, given between 1816 and 1830. In these he wrote at some
length on Chinese and Indian thought, but touched on Egypt only when
dealing with the origins of Greek philosophy:[52]

From Egypt Pythagoras thus without doubt brought the idea of his Order, which was a regular community brought together for purposes of scientific and moral culture . . . Egypt at that time was regarded as a highly cultured country, and it was so when compared with Greece; this is shown even in the differences of caste which assume a division amongst the great branches of life and work, such as the industrial, scientific and religious. But beyond this we need not seek great scientific knowledge amongst the Egyptians, nor think that Pythagoras got his science there. Aristotle (Metaph.I) only says that 'in Egypt mathematical sciences first commenced, for there the nation of priests had leisure.'[53]

Elsewhere Hegel wrote:

The name of Greece strikes home to the hearts of men of education in Europe, and more particularly is this so with us Germans . . . They [the Greeks] certainly received the substantial beginnings of their religion, culture . . . from Asia, Syria and Egypt; but they have so greatly obliterated the foreign nature of this origin, and it is so much changed, worked on, turned round and altogether made so different, that what they – as we – prize, know and love in it is essentially their own.[54]

Thus, following the tradition from *Epinomis*, he admitted the massive borrowings but argued that the Greeks had qualitatively transformed them.[55]

Hegel's argument that the Orient was the childhood of mankind and Greece its adolescence strongly resembles, of course, the views of the Young Hegelian Karl Marx.[56] Marx argued that it was only in Greece that the individual had cut the umbilical cord from his community, and had changed from a *Gattungswesen* (species being) to a *zōon politikon* (political animal/city-dweller). With his lifelong love for the country, he completely accepted the prevailing view that in every aspect of its civilization Greece was categorically different from – and superior to – all that had gone before.[57] However, Marx went beyond this to claim – just as clearly as Shelley had done – that Greece towered over its posterity. Such a claim then caused a problem, in that it made Greece go against the stream of progress. In an attempt to deal with this Marx wrote in the introduction to his sketched outline for *Das Kapital*, the *Grundrisse*:

> In the case of the arts, it is well known that certain periods of their flowering are out of all proportion to the general development of society, hence also to the material foundation . . . For example, the Greeks as compared to the moderns or also Shakespeare.

He nevertheless saw the paradox that 'in their world-epoch-making classical stature . . . certain . . . forms . . . of the arts are possible only at an underdeveloped stage of artistic development.'

Marx went on to argue that mythology was impossible once it had been overtaken by reality, as with the triumphs of capitalist industry. However, he was adamant that mythology could be produced only by a given society, with its distinctive social forms:

> Greek art presupposes Greek mythology, i.e. nature and the social forms already reworked in an unconsciously artistic way by the popular imagination. This is its material. Not any mythology whatever, i.e. not an arbitrarily chosen unconsciously artistic reworking of nature . . . Egyptian mythology could never have been the foundation or womb of Greek art.[58]

My interpretation of this opaque passage, inasmuch as it concerns the theme of this book, is this: even in the 1850s when he wrote the *Grundrisse*, Marx was still sufficiently aware of the Ancient Model to have to face the possibility that Greek mythology – hence art – did not come from Greek social relations but from Egypt. To accept this would, of course, make nonsense of his scheme.[59] And he was living in an age when everybody felt in their bones that Greece was categorically apart from, and above, Egypt. Thus the destruction of the Ancient Model gave his generation a freedom on this question that was not available to Hegel. Marx was able to deny Egyptian influence on Greece outright.

TRANSITIONAL FIGURES, 2:
HEEREN

A. H. L. Heeren was born in 1760, ten years earlier than Hegel, but he outlived him by eleven years, dying only in 1842. Heeren was a son-in-law of Heyne, and was a distinguished Professor of History at Göttingen in the 1820s and 30s. His scholarship, which focused on economic and technical developments, was exhaustive in the approved Göttingen fashion. Like his father in-law Heyne and his brother-in-law Georg Forster, Heeren was fascinated by the 18th-century explorations and his *magnum opus, Reflections on the Politics, Intercourse, and Trade of the Principal Nations of Antiquity*, combined these explorations of Africa and the Near East with ancient writings on the subjects. His conclusions stressed the importance of Carthage, Ethiopia and Egypt, and – somewhat apologetically, because he admired Greece greatly – he felt obliged to retain the Ancient Model to explain the striking parallels he saw between these cultures and that of Greece.[60]

Heeren was not treated well by those of his contemporaries who have had an influence on posterity. Humboldt considered him a 'rather dull man', and he is best known today for the poet Heinrich Heine's merciless caricature of Heeren in his *Pictures of Travel*.[61] Heeren was punished by the Romantics not merely for his choice of subject but for staying with the Ancient Model too long. Only black historians read him today.[62]

TRANSITIONAL FIGURES, 3:
BARTHOLD NIEBUHR

Niebuhr's reputation has fared much better than that of Heeren. He is generally and rightly recognized as the founder of modern ancient history. But from the point of view of this book, the interesting thing about him is that he remained within the Ancient Model. I treat Niebuhr in some detail because he represented advanced German thinking at the turn of the 18th century, and because of his enormous influence on 19th-century understanding of ancient history and good historical 'method'. Through him we can realize how saturated both were in Romanticism and racism.

However, I have also included Niebuhr as a transitional figure, for although he provided massive help to the intellectual and ideological forces that overthrew the Ancient Model, he himself was still maintaining it at the end of his life. It is possible that he did so out of his intense conservatism at this stage, or for reasons of personal or professional rivalry. The cogency with which he argued in favour of the Ancient Model, however, suggests otherwise.

Barthold Niebuhr, born in 1776, had a wide Teutonic background. His family were Frisians of German culture living in Holstein, then in Denmark. His father, Carsten Niebuhr, was a famous traveller in the East employed by the Danish court and Göttingen. He was also an Anglophile and the boy's first foreign language was English while, almost alone in his generation, Barthold studied in Britain. Carsten Niebuhr also encouraged his son to read not only Latin and Greek, but Arabic and Persian as well. Thus Barthold had an exceptionally broad scholarly background. As a *Wunderkind* he was taken up by cultivated neighbours, including the Homeric scholar Voss and the Romantic poet M. C. Boie, both products of Göttingen.[63]

Barthold was in correspondence with Heyne, and both wanted him to study at Göttingen. Carsten Niebuhr, however, preferred to send Barthold to the University of Kiel, which was then Danish; this could lead to official posts in Denmark. From Kiel he went for a year to Edinburgh; he then spent six years in Copenhagen as an extremely successful civil servant specializing in finance and continued his studies, now focused on Roman history. In 1806 he joined the Prussian government at its lowest ebb, working for the reforms that helped the monarchy survive. Here too he made time for scholarship and in 1810–11 wrote his *History of Rome*, quickly recognized as being the foundation of modern and 'scientific' ancient history. Then in 1816 he was sent as the Prussian representative to Rome, where he remained until 1823. After that Niebuhr went into semi-retirement at Bonn where, though still deeply concerned with politics, he devoted most of his time to scholarship until his death at fifty-four, early in 1831.

Niebuhr was primarily a historian of Rome. The reason for this concern has been explored by the intellectual historian Zvi Yavetz. Yavetz points out that the picture painted by the early-20th-century literary historian Miss E. M. Butler, in her great book *The Tyranny of Greece over Germany*, needs some qualification. Although, Yavetz admits, there had long been the special association with Greece, and the country had obsessed late-18th-century Germans and its image continued to dominate 19th-century poets and 'progressives', the great conservative and liberal German historians concentrated on Rome – its rise and not its fall – which they identified with Prussia.[64] Nevertheless, Niebuhr was also passionately concerned with Greece.

It is worth spending some time considering Niebuhr's general ideological position. The Finnish scholar Seppo Rytkönen describes Niebuhr as a man who 'found his own way between the Enlightenment and Restoration'; however, Rytkönen's definition of 'the Enlightenment' is so broad as to include not only Montesquieu but Burke and the German conservative Möser.[65] His notion of 'Restoration' is proportionately narrow. It seems to be restricted to the poetic and Indophiliac absurdities of Heidelberg, ruling out the much more formidable Göttingen tradition to which Niebuhr so clearly belonged.

The great Classicist Professor Momigliano, who towers over the history of Classical studies, is always eager to dissociate his discipline from Romanticism and German nationalism. He claims that the basis of Niebuhr's thinking came from English – not even British – economists.[66] Momigliano cites Niebuhr's *protégé* F. Lieber to the effect that Niebuhr had told him that most of his British friends were Whigs and that Whigs had saved England in 1688.[67] As most of Barthold Niebuhr's friends in Britain were men from the East India Company who had known his father Carsten, their political persuasion is not surprising.

Furthermore, the Glorious Revolution of 1688 was, for Niebuhr, the model of political change with minimal disorder. In his youth he had believed that this kind of event could take place only among superior northern races; by middle age, however, he despaired even of these. Frances Bunsen, the wife of Niebuhr's secretary, Christian – later Baron – Bunsen, who knew Niebuhr intimately after 1816, described him as the most rigid reactionary and as 'ultra-Tory'. She wrote that in general it was his 'inclination to trust government rather than the nations governed'.[68] Niebuhr acted on these principles, and his contempt for Southern Italian 'Polcinellos', when he went beyond the call of duty as a Prussian official to help the Austrians crush the Carbonari rising in Naples in 1821.[69] It also seems very likely that his early death was hastened, if not caused, by his terror at the French and Belgian Revolutions of 1830.[70] Thus there is no doubt that after 1817 Niebuhr was reactionary even by the standards of the counter-revolutionary age, and that this affected his later historiography.

Does this mean that he was already a conscious conservative in 1811 when he first wrote his *History*? Rytkönen believes that Niebuhr's ideology seemed more conservative than it actually was, while Professor Momigliano refers to Niebuhr's early 'democratic sympathies' and his support for the liberation of serfs in Denmark and Prussia.[71] In fact, Niebuhr's sympathies for the French Revolution were remarkably shallow and short-lived at a time when such sympathies were all the rage.[72] Indeed, the idea that his conservative ideas were always fundamental is strengthened by the fact that they were those of his father. Carsten Niebuhr always disliked the French, and political disturbances of any sort. The combination of the two appalled him. Coming from peasant stock himself, Carsten had great sympathy with that class in his native Dithmarsch, which of course fitted the Romanticism of the times; in Barthold such feelings were reinforced by Carsten's friend Boie, who combined activity in poetic circles with passionate support for authentic 'German' freedom and opposition to the French Enlightenment.[73]

Momigliano sees Niebuhr's ideas as containing a 'mixture of conservative and liberal attitudes quite unusual on the continent', this being 'a consequence of his British experience'.[74] These ideas, however, appear to have been the same as those of his father and his circle, and were perfectly Romantic. As a young man, Niebuhr seems to have believed not only that northern peasants were worthy of authentic traditional freedom, but that they could be a bastion against revolutionary and Catholic forces.[75] This combination of ideas occurred in Britain, but it was equally German and Scandinavian; hence there would seem no reason to challenge mainstream historiography, which labels Niebuhr as a Romantic and a conservative.[76]

No one has ever compared Niebuhr to Adam Smith, Bentham or James Mill. The Briton he turned to was Burke. As he wrote in the introduction to the third edition of his *History of Rome*: 'Not one of the bases of the political judgement in my work cannot be found in Montesquieu or Burke.'[77] The close parallels between Niebuhr and Burke have been accepted by virtually all writers – with the exception of Momigliano – from Baroness Bunsen and the conservative German nationalist of the late 19th century Heinrich von Treitschke, to the modern historians Witte and Bridenthal.[78] Thus, as an example of Niebuhr's enlightened spirit, Professor Momigliano argues that he went to Edinburgh because, unlike London, it had a university. This practical reason may well have played a role in his decision, but Niebuhr told a friend that he was going to Scotland to learn the language of Ossian![79]

While consistently Romantic Niebuhr was, until about 1810, a reform-conservative, arguing for reform to save Denmark and Prussia from revolution. (It is in this context that his promoting the abolition of serfdom should be seen.) For these ideas he was sometimes attacked by the whole-hog reactionaries with whom he later sided.[80] Rytkönen, for instance, maintains that Niebuhr was linked to the Enlightenment by his lack of historical relativism, and belief in an ahistorical human nature. At other points, however, he sees Niebuhr as having had a concept of Romantic growth later overshadowed by a *Traditionalismus*, a 'stasis' very different from the permanent rational order to which the Enlightenment aspired.[81]

Niebuhr's cross-cultural comparisons were, moreover, within strict bounds. His central one – between early Rome and his beloved native Dithmarsch – was possible only because he viewed both peoples as purely authentic and the products of their environments. Thus here too he was in the mainstream of Romanticism. At no point did he accept the universalism, deism or atheism and belief in reason of the Enlightenment, let alone the liberty, equality and fraternity of the Revolution. Furthermore Niebuhr's promotion of Romanticism was not restricted to his history. As mentioned in Chapter V, he presided over the German community in Rome when it was the seedbed of the new Romantic movement.[82]

How did Niebuhr's conservatism and Romanticism affect his writing of history? Firstly, like Humboldt, he saw the broad study of Antiquity – which he still called *Philologie* – as a way of providing *Bildung* and so promoting the fatherland.[83] His method was that of the Göttingen source critics, a 'combination of rational criticism and imaginative reconstruction from text analysis, analogy and intuition'.[84] Or, as the very favourable article on him in the 11th edition of the *Encyclopaedia Britannica* described it: 'He brought in inference to supply the place of discredited tradition and showed the possibility of writing . . .'[85] How these traditions had been 'discredited' was not specified, but clearly the least reliable were those that broke the canons of early-19th-century science – including its racial branch. This aspect of Niebuhr's method is linked to the crucial point, made by Momigliano, that Niebuhr was the first to challenge the great ancient historians on their own turf. Even Gibbon had only begun where Tacitus left off, but Niebuhr wrote on early Rome, which was well covered by Livy and others.[86]

Niebuhr took Humboldt's views on the necessity of inference and imagination a step further. He is cited by the early-20th-century intellectual historian G. P. Gooch as having written: 'I am an historian, for I can make a complete picture from separate fragments and once I know where the parts are missing and how to fill them up, no one believes how much of what seems to be lost can be restored.'[87] Though cast in positivist terms, Niebuhr's is an honest confession and would seem to fit all historians. Even so, it is difficult to see how, if his method contained so much subjectivity, one can proclaim Niebuhr as the first 'scientific' historian and claim that he raised his discipline to a categorically higher plane, above such 'prescientific' historians as Herodotos, Thucydides, Sima Qian, Tacitus, Ibn Khaldun, Voltaire, and Gibbon! All these, at least, wrote clearly!

What were Niebuhr's specific contributions? At the time, and since, the best-known aspect of his work has been – *pace* Rytkönen and Momigliano – the hypothesis that Roman history had been taken from lost 'lays' or epic poems. As many writers have pointed out, Niebuhr's idea clearly derives from the Romantic belief in the centrality of folksong at the origins of nations.[88] Given his view of Niebuhr as essentially a product of the Scottish Enlightenment, it is not surprising that Professor Momigliano downplays the significance of the 'lays'. For him the most important innovation in Niebuhr's work was on a second topic: the nature of early Roman land law and the *Ager Publicus* (Public Field). He demonstrates that Niebuhr gained his ideas on this from information about India, which he learned from his father's Scottish friends.[89] Momigliano admits, however, that Niebuhr's motive for studying the topic was what he saw as the misuse of Roman precedents by the French Revolutionaries in their – very mild – land reform. As Niebuhr himself put it, he wrote to refute 'the mad and detestable sense given to the agrarian law by a criminal gang'.[90]

For Niebuhr Rome, like Britain, was a model of how internal conflicts could be worked out in a gradual and constitutional manner. In the development of this idea he introduced his third major new theory, which was that the Patricians and the Plebeians were not merely different classes but different races. The idea that class differences originated from race differences – which Niebuhr applied to other situations as well – had been used earlier in France; there the belief that the nobility were the descendants of the Germanic Franks, while the Third Estate were native Gallo-Romans, had played a significant role in the development of the Revolutions of 1789 and 1830. Still another pattern that is likely to have influenced Niebuhr is the Indian caste system, which is supposed to have originated from the Aryan conquest and to have been an attempt to maintain the purity of the conquerors.

It was Niebuhr, however, who gave this theory academic *cachet*, and he was credited with having introduced it. The great Romantic French historian Michelet saluted Niebuhr for having discovered the ethnic principle of history 'as early as 1811'.[91] This was also the message taken from Niebuhr by his English disciple Dr Arnold, the famous head-master of Rugby.[92] Despite doubts about the 'lays', the *Ager Publicus*, the racial origin of the Roman classes and another theory on the Northern origin of the Etruscans, the anonymous writer on Niebuhr in the 1911 edition of the *Encyclopaedia Britannica* wrote:

if every positive conclusion of Niebuhr's had been refuted, his claim
to be the first who dealt with the history of Rome in a scientific spirit
would remain unimpaired, and the new principles introduced by him
into historical research would lose nothing of their importance.

One of these 'new' principles was the Romantic-Positivist one, championed at Göttingen, of studying peoples and their institutions rather
than individuals. However, Niebuhr was even more admired for his
introduction of race into history:

> By his theory of the disputes between the Patricians and the
> Plebeians arising from original differences of race, he drew attention
> to the immense importance of ethnological distinctions and contri-
> buted to the revival of these divergences as factors in modern history.

In addition, Niebuhr was adamant about the desirability of national and
racial purity:

> It seems to be the course of the history of the world that conquest and
> divers intermixtures are to fuse numberless original races together
> ... Seldom will a particular people be the gainer by such an
> intermixture. Some sustain the irreparable loss of a noble national
> civilization, science and literature. Even a less cultivated people will
> hardly find that the refinements thus imported – which, moreover, if
> they are suited to its genius, it might have attained for itself – will
> make amends for the forfeiture of its original character, its national
> history and its hereditary laws.[93]

It is no surprise, then, that ancient historian Ulrich Wilcken – who
flourished under the Nazis – was able to celebrate Niebuhr as a
'founder of critical-genetic historiography'.[94] In a letter written to his
parents in 1794, when he was eighteen, Niebuhr described the deleterious effects of racial mixture, and there is no doubt that this Romantic
ethnicity was based on what he saw as physical and fundamental racial
differences. At this stage, at least, he believed in polygeny:

> I maintain that we must make very cautious use of differences of
> language as applied to the theory of races and have much more
> regard for physical conformation ... [race is] one of the most

important elements of history still remaining to be examined – that which is, in truth, the very first basis upon which all history is reared and the first principle upon which it must proceed.[95]

Niebuhr's preference for physical rather than 'linguistic' racism may well have come from his father, and through him from the British in the East. It put him beyond Humboldt and the tradition later upheld by Niebuhr's own secretary Bunsen and the great French Semitist and historian Ernest Renan, which insisted that the manifest differences between peoples were caused not by physical conformation but by adequacy of language.[96] Physical racism was essential to Niebuhr's principle of the racial nature of class, given that different classes and even castes speak the same languages. It is remarkable to note how constant he was to this principle, and also on the undesirability of racial mixture.

Niebuhr brought together the Romanticism and the racism of the 1790s. The alliance was an easy one. In many ways *Rasse* (race) or *Geschlecht* (kind) were merely the 'scientific' terms for the Romantic *Volk* (people) or *Gemeinschaft* (community). In his classic statement of historicism and progressive relativism *Also a Philosophy of History*, published in 1774, Herder insisted that the *Volk* was the source of all truth.[97] This notion appears in the 19th century as the 'racial truth' which supersedes all others.[98]

Despite the fundamental congruence between Romanticism and racism, there is a contradiction between the Romantic ideal of racial authenticity and the racialist right of a master race to conquer. Niebuhr's early belief in the desirability of backward peoples – that is, Germans – developing autochthonous cultures did not extend to lesser, non-European breeds. In 1787, at the age of eleven, he supported the Austrians – for whom he otherwise had no great love – against the Turks, and in 1794 the worst insult he could devise for Revolutionary France was 'New Tartary'.[99] In 1814 he called for European and Christian unity to fight Islam, and in lectures given near the end of his life he is recorded as having said:

European dominion naturally supports science and literature, together with the rights of humanity, and to prevent the destruction of a barbarous power would be an act of high treason against intellectual culture and humanity.[100]

The occasion for this defence of imperialism was a future European conquest of Egypt. Like the Humboldt brothers and Bunsen – but unlike most German Classicists and Orientalists – Niebuhr accepted Champollion's decipherment. This led him to attack the great F. A. Wolf, who had, he said, 'investigated the antiquity of writing among the Greeks completely independently of the art in the East'; this one-sided view Niebuhr attributed to Wolf's 'prejudice against the high antiquity of writings in the East'.[101]

Niebuhr, himself in touch with Rome, followed Champollion's compromise with the Church on the dating.[102] Thus he put Egyptian history back to 2200 BC, the date then assumed for the Hyksos. However, showing the cultural, racial and temporal arrogance or *Besserwissen* of the critical method, which has been a bane to the writing of ancient history ever since, he claimed that the thirteen dynasties reported before the Hyksos had been invented by the Egyptians, who 'ought to have been contented with possessing a history as far backwards as the age of Abraham, but they wanted to ascend still higher in accordance with the spirit of Eastern nations.'[103]

Niebuhr was also in the Romantic-racist mode when he made a categorical distinction between the free and creative Greeks and the Egyptians, who, 'like many oppressed people, were very far advanced in their arts while their intellectual culture remained behindhand.'[104] He also attacked the Phoenicians for their rootlessness. This cardinal sin against the Romantic canon was, of course, used against the Jews until the triumph of Romantic Zionism, and there is no doubt that Niebuhr shared the growing anti-Semitism of his social circles.[105]

Nevertheless, as I have said, Niebuhr remained within the Ancient Model. In his attack on Wolf, he wrote:

> Admitting that . . . intolerable abuse has been made of the influence exercised upon the Greeks by the Eastern nations . . . Wolf too much ignores the fact that relations did exist between Greece and the East and that, though afterwards they were independent, in earlier times the Greeks were influenced and instructed by Eastern nations.[106]

Niebuhr believed that the myth of Kekrops' Egyptian settlement at Athens in some way reflected Egyptian influence there, as did the legends of Danaos and Aigyptos for the Argolid. He had no doubt whatever about Kadmos' foundation of Thebes.[107] There is, on the other hand, a tone of defensiveness in these assertions that must be attributed to the influence of Wolf and his ideas and, in the 1820s, of Wolf's follower Karl Otfried Müller. I shall return to Müller after considering the first 19th-century attack on the Ancient Model, that of the Abbé Petit-Radel.

PETIT-RADEL AND THE FIRST ATTACK ON THE ANCIENT MODEL

Petit-Radel was a scholar greatly interested in art and architecture. In 1792 he emigrated to Rome, already the centre of Romantic aesthetics, and while in Italy he became fascinated by the country's pre-Roman ruins. Following an ancient tradition he called these 'Cyclopean', seeing them as irregular and hence 'free' in a way that Egyptian and Oriental architecture was not.[108] On the basis of the occurrence of these buildings, he became convinced that a common European civilization had been established in both Italy and Greece before the arrival of the Egyptians and Phoenicians.[109]

In 1806 Petit-Radel presented a paper, 'On the Greek origin of the founder of Argos', to the *Institut de France* in Paris. His argument was based on the early dating by Dionysios of Halikarnassos, a Greek historian of the 1st century BC, of an Arkadian settlement in Italy which Petit-Radel linked to the Cyclopean buildings. The Frenchman attacked Fréret and Barthélemy, as exponents of the Ancient Model, regarding the cultural level of the native Greeks when the Egyptians had settled. He backed this view with his contention that the Cyclopean architecture antedated the arrival of the Egyptians, and his Romantic faith that the glorious Greeks could *never* have been so backward.

In addition, Petit-Radel specifically challenged the traditions that kings Inachos and Phoroneus of Argos had been Egyptian.[110] He showed how weak this tradition had been in Antiquity – and it is true that even among the shadowy figures of the legendary period, these two are outstandingly murky. The tone of the paper casts some doubt on the extent of his boldness, as there are suggestions that what he was saying was welcome to his Parisian audience.[111] The paper appears to have been well received, and Petit-Radel went on to play a distinguished role in Restoration academic life.

Karl Otfried Müller
and the Overthrow
of the Ancient Model

Where Petit-Radel tried to bypass ancient authority and the Ancient Model, the first direct challenge to them came from Karl Otfried Müller. In general terms, there is no doubt about the Romanticism of Müller's scholarship and life. The early-20th-century historian of Classics Rudolf Pfeiffer saw him as the 'radiant figure of a happy young scholar', while to the otherwise sober English intellectual historian G. P. Gooch he was 'the Shelley of the modern renaissance, the young Apollo in the historical pantheon'.[112]

Müller was one of the first generation to be trained in Humboldt's educational system. Born in Silesia in 1797, he studied at its capital, Breslau, attending the new Seminar which had been established on the Berlin model. His teacher, Heindorf, was an estranged pupil of Wolf, and Müller himself worked for a year under Wolf in Berlin. Although Müller thoroughly disliked him, his writings are, nevertheless, permeated with Wolf's influence.

For both men, the key words were the Kantian *Prolegomena* and *Wissenschaft*.[113] Adopting Wolf's progressive and scientific mode, Müller stressed the pioneering nature of his own studies, which he believed would be superseded by the collective labours of later scholars. But, while deferential to the future, he was arrogant towards the past. The only previous works he considered worthy of favourable note were publications from Göttingen and the writings of French Royalist scholars like Petit-Radel and Champollion's great enemy, the Classicist Raoul Rochette. In this contempt, Müller was a perfect example of the professional 19th-century philologists who despised the generalist *érudits* or *Gelehrte* of the 18th century whom they were replacing.[114]

Müller's thesis was a local history of the island of Aigina. Though partly inspired by the marbles recently brought to Germany from there, the project was a perfect example of Romantic-Positivism. First, as Gooch pointed out, this first local history of Ancient Greece resembled the first German one: that of Osnabrück by the Romantic conservative Justus Möser.[115] Secondly, Aigina is an island – the perfect finite space and convenient for exhaustive study. Still more significant is the fact that it was inhabited by Dorians and faced Athens, the chief city of the 'corrupt' Ionians.

On the strength of this work, and at an astoundingly young age, Müller was appointed to a chair at Göttingen. This, in a surprisingly Hebrew turn of phrase, he called 'the place of places for me'.[116] From then on his academic position – unlike that of many of his contemporaries – was secure. He received money and recognition from the governments of Hanover and other German states until his untimely, but Romantic, death from fever in Athens in 1840.[117]

Despite his professionalism, Müller's scholarly range was prodigious. He was able to round out philology in the approved new manner, and as well as producing a major work on the Etruscans he wrote voluminously on ancient art and archaeology.[118] The works that became the pillars of *Altertumswissenschaft*, however, were his *History of Greek Tribes and Cities*, published between 1820 and 1824, and his *Introduction to a Scientific System of Mythology*, published in 1825. His attack on the Ancient Model was explicit in both. The first volume of his *History of Greek Tribes and Cities, Orchomenos and the Minyans*, began with a quotation from Pausanias:

> Greeks are terribly prone to be wonderstruck by the expense of home-products; distinguished historians have explained the Egyptian Pyramids in the greatest detail and not made the slightest mention of the treasure house of Minyas [at Orchomenos] or the walls of Tiryns, which are by no means less marvellous.[119]

The quotation is pivotal: it directs the readers' attention both to the Minyans, whom Müller saw as an invading northern tribe related to the Dorians; and it denounces what he believed to be the besetting sin of the Greeks, later given the pathological names 'Egyptomania' and 'barbarophilia'.[120] These disorders were manifested in the 'delusion' that Egyptians and other non-European 'barbarians' had possessed superior cultures, from which the Greeks had borrowed massively.

Müller had enemies on two fronts: the Ancient Model and the uses made of it by the Masons and Dupuis; and the Indophilia of Schlegel and the Romantic Heidelberg group around the mystical philosophers and mythologists Creuzer and Görres. Where Schlegel had seen Egypt as an Indian colony, Creuzer – seeing otherwise inexplicable similarities between Indian and Greek religion, especially in their symbolism – went on to argue, completely without evidence, that Indian priests had somehow brought their philosophy to Greece.[121] Although – unlike the champions of the Ancient Model – they were certainly more influential in Germany after 1815, the Indophils could provide no specific evidence of transmission for Müller to attack.[122]

In dealing with the Ancient Model, Müller frequently referred to the *Verbindungen* (combinations) and *Verknüpfungen* (liaisons) between Greek and barbarian priesthoods. These, he maintained, had suggested fundamental relationships between the various religious systems and myths. According to Müller, it was these 'late' contacts that had created the false impression that Greece had derived its religion, myths and civilization as a whole from the Near East, and here his main technique for removing what he saw as these late accretions was the 'argument from silence'.[123] In principle, he recognized that genuinely ancient traditions sometimes appeared only in 'late' sources – indeed, he himself sometimes relied on such evidence. Thus, to deny the authenticity of a legend he required an additional criterion: that there must have been a strong contemporary reason for fabricating it.[124] In practice, however, lack of attestation alone was seen as damning, especially when Müller was attacking the Ancient Model. Indeed, he and his successors have employed Homer and Hesiod not as broad-ranging poets but as encyclopaedias. In this way the common phrase 'unknown to H.' was used not in the sense 'unattested in the surviving corpus of H.', but to mean 'did not exist in the time of H.'.

Müller's second technique for demolishing the Ancient Model was dissection or analysis: he maintained that this was rectifying what he saw as a general tendency in Antiquity towards syncretism.[125]

Championing Romantic particularism against Enlightenment universalism, he argued that 'Separation, therefore, is one main business of
the mythologist.'[126] Reduced in this way to local specifics, the earliest
myths could be viewed as rooted in the soil of Greece. Nevertheless,
Müller maintained that there was need for 'combination' not of
the 'late' or priestly kind already mentioned, but through tracing
cultic and mythological patterns that had spread with conquering
races.

The prime example of this process was what Müller saw as the
association between Apollo and the Dorians – that the cult of the god
had spread with the Dorians' conquests. Such an interpretation was
typical of the general Romantic belief that vitality flows from north to
south and not vice versa.[127] In this way, Müller maintained that if
similar cults, myths or names were found in Greece and the Near East,
they must be Greek; while if they had existed in Greece and Thrace or
Greece and Phrygia, which were to the north-east of Greece, they
originated from the latter.[128] The same was true within Greece,
according to Müller: if similar features were found in both the north
and the south of the country, they nearly always came from the former.
Furthermore, if cults or names were widespread in Greece or the
Aegean, they had to be indigenous and not the result of foreign
introduction.

Müller's first attack was against the legends surrounding Kekrops
and his supposed colonizations of Athens and the region of Lake
Kopais in Boiotia, which included Orchomenos, the city after which the
first volume of his *History* was named.[129] These traditions were only
attested 'late', thus fulfilling Müller's first condition of spuriousness.
There were also close relations between Greeks in general and Athens
in particular and the Egyptian 26th Dynasty, 664–520 BC, whose capital
was Athens' sister city Sais, thus satisfying his second. Furthermore,
Müller pointed out that the main sources of the legend were a book
claimed by Pausanias to have been a forgery, and stories told to
Diodoros by Egyptians, whose manifest self-interest discredited
them.[130] What is more, Herodotos, who firmly believed in foreign
settlements elsewhere, saw Kekrops as autochthonous.[131] Finally,
Müller quoted Menexenos, in one of Plato's dialogues, to the effect

that the Athenians were pure-blooded, unlike the Thebans and the Peloponnesians, who had been colonized by Easterners.[132]

Müller did not refer to this passage when challenging the legends surrounding Danaos' acquisition of the Argolid; he did this by showing genealogical discrepancies in the mythic cycle. He also maintained that Danaos could not have been Egyptian because he was the eponym of the Danaans, who were clearly Greeks.[133] However, he admitted that 'While Kekrops' Egyptian origin is merely historical sophism, that of Danaos is genuine myth.'[134] Müller could hardly avoid the concession, since he knew about the lines referring to Danaos' daughters from the *Danais* epic.[135] This, however, did not grant the legends historical status, given the 'facts' of the general north–south direction of cultural flow and 'the Egyptian abhorrence of all travel and seafaring'.[136]

Müller conceded that the legends surrounding Kadmos presented even more difficulties. In the first place they concerned the Phoenicians, whom he saw as an 'active merchant people [who] were more ancient than the ... xenophobic and bigoted Egyptians'.[137] Nevertheless, convinced of the permanence of national characteristics, Müller thought it inconceivable that seafaring merchants could have *conquered* inland Thebes. He attacked the legends around Kadmos by separating the alleged Phoenician colonies in Boiotia from those in the Aegean. He then dismissed the legends of ancient as opposed to 'later' Phoenician settlements on Samothrace and Thasos in the Northern Aegean, because Herodotos had seen the ancient cult of the Kabeiroi there as Pelasgian.

Here, although he did not admit it, Müller was in difficulties, because 17th- and 18th-century scholars knew that the name Kabeiroi came from the Semitic *kabir* (great) – the Greeks called them Megaloi Theoi and the Romans Dei Magni, meaning 'Great Gods'.[138] Müller preferred to derive the name from the Greek *kaiō* (burn), linking it to the undoubted associations between the cult and metalwork. He also pointed out a connection between Kadmos and Kadmilos, one of the Kabeiroi, and noted that the latter was worshipped near Thebes. However, instead of seeing the cult in both places as Near Eastern, he used the 'proof' that the Aegean one was Pelasgian to argue that the cult and the name Kadmos at Thebes came from the same 'substratum' and therefore had nothing to do with Phoenicia.[139]

At the time, this confused and confusing argument was no more successful than Müller's attack on the Indophils and, as on the latter, his views on the Phoenicians became predominant only in the 20th century. In 1882, for instance, the great Classicist and Indo-Europeanist Hermann Usener attacked Müller's denial of the 'now obvious influence of the Middle East'.[140] Müller did better with the Egyptians. F. C. Movers in his *The Phoenicians*, published in the 1840s, tried to salvage the legends of Danaos on the grounds that Danaos' Hyksos connections made him Semitic, not Egyptian; but he was largely discredited, and by 1840 it became impermissible to accept any story of Kekrops' Egyptian origin.[141] Thus, after Müller, all 'reputable' scholars have worked in what I call the 'Broad Aryan Model', believing that while there may or may not have been Phoenician settlements on Mainland Greece, there were certainly no Egyptian ones.

Most later historians, and some of his contemporaries, have regarded Müller as essentially Romantic in maintaining a categorical distinction between Greek and other cultures. In *Orchomenos* he denied the charge and, after apologizing for having treated Greek mythology as if it were all mythology, he claimed that Greece was part of the world, and that therefore Greek mythology had the same basis as that of the rest of mankind.[142] What he objected to was the belief in colonial bonds and the wholesale borrowing of Greek religion and mythology from the East. He was convinced that he had shown these to be unhistorical, though illusions about them had led all previous research astray.

In *Prolegomena*, Müller made an eloquent appeal for scholars to do what he had failed to do, and investigate all mythologies for insights into the Greek one.[143] The 'anthropological' school of the Cambridge Classicists James Frazer and Jane Harrison, which flourished at the beginning of the 20th century, in no way overstepped these bounds.[144] What Müller outlawed was any special relationship between Greek and Eastern myth. Indeed, as he put it, 'the entire book is opposed to the theory which would make the majority of myths importations from the East.' He continued with a splendid example of Romantic-Positivism:

In order to assume this just for one [myth] even, distinct proof is required either of so great internal agreement as only to be explained by transplantation or, secondly, that the mythos is absolutely without root in the soil of local tradition, or, lastly, that transplantation is expressed in the legend itself.[145]

A demand for 'distinct proof', as opposed to competitive plausibility, is dubious in any branch of knowledge. It is absurd in such a nebulous region as the origins of Greek mythology.

Müller's second sleight of hand was to switch the onus of such 'proof' on to proponents of the Aryan Model. As the early-20th-century scholar Paul Foucart argued, it would be more reasonable to require proof from those who challenge the ancient consensus that there had been Near Eastern colonization than from those who defend it.[146] The fact that Müller's bluff was so successful only shows how much his audience, during and after the Greek War of Independence, wanted to hear it. With Müller's capture of the academic 'high ground' from which he could demand 'proof' from challengers, the destruction of the Ancient Model was secure.

Müller admitted that one of the best ways of distinguishing the historical elements of myth or legend was through etymology, especially the etymology of names.[147] He himself was able to make very little headway with this in the case of Greece, and after some feeble attempts he exclaimed:

But alas! Etymology is still a science in which blind guesswork is more practised than methodical investigation; and in which because we wish to explain everything too soon, our labours more frequently result in confusion than elucidation.[148]

This failure explains why, as two of Müller's modern admirers put it, 'philology in Müller's work is usually subordinate to mythology.'[149] Typically, however, Müller had faith in the advance of science: 'yet . . . there is no folly in hoping for still more important solutions from this quarter'.[150] Unfortunately for the Aryan Model, however, Indo-European philology has failed, over the last 160 years, to be of any help in explaining Greek myth and religion. This state of affairs is in striking contrast to the hundreds of plausible etymologies from Semitic and Egyptian.[151] Many of these, including those for Thebes, Kadmos, Kabeiroi and the element Sam – in Samothrace – were known to Müller, but he seldom confronted them directly, preferring to dismiss them out of hand.[152]

Now we come to the later reception of Müller and his ideas. He was admired in his own time; his was the first memorial tablet erected in Göttingen in 1874, and by the end of the 19th century he was considered a pioneer of 'modern' ancient history.[153] In his *History of Classical Scholarship*, published in 1921, the great Wilamowitz-Moellendorf said, after mentioning Müller's name, 'We have at last arrived at the threshold of the 19th century, in which the conquest of the ancient world by science was completed.'[154]

We should note that this statement – apart from the colonizing image it conjures up – casts Müller as the heroic figure in the conventional history of science, who turns chaos and dark into order and light and creates a new scientific field. And in the field of mythology, this image of him was well established during his lifetime. Thomas Keightley's *The Mythology of Ancient Greece and Rome*, published in 1831, and William Smith's *Dictionary of Greek* and *Roman Biography and Mythology*, which appeared between 1844 and 1849, both took on his new methods. The historian of Classics F. M. Turner refers to Keightley and Smith as 'serious British commentators on Classical myths',[155] while the mainstream of students of mythology continue to accept Müller's self-definition as 'scientific', and consider him a 'serious' and 'scrupulous' founder of their discipline.[156]

In the past twenty years, however, knowledgeable Classicists have tended to be more sensitive to his more questionable aspects. Rudolf Pfeiffer, for instance, admitted that Müller's massive two volumes on *The Dorians* were 'more an impressive hymn on the excellence of everything Doric than a narration of history'.[157] Momigliano, in seeking to stress the rational aspects of his discipline, emphasizes the importance of Niebuhr, whose Romanticism he tries to deny, but omits Müller from his many portraits of 19th-century Classicists.[158]

The most striking feature of Müller's work for us is that it was based entirely on traditional material that had always been available to scholars. None of the 19th-century extensions of knowledge was involved. Naturally he could not take into account the reading of cuneiform or Schliemann's archaeological discoveries – these took place after his death. However, unlike Heyne and Heeren, he was not particularly interested in the 18th-century explorations; and unlike Humboldt, Niebuhr and Bunsen he disregarded the sensational scholarly developments between 1815 and 1830. There is no indication that he paid any attention to Champollion's decipherment, and his hostility to India meant that despite his close contact with the Grimm brothers and other Indo-Europeanists, he did not apply the new Indo-European linguistics to his work. All this means that the destruction of the old model took place entirely for what historians of science call 'externalist' reasons. The Ancient Model fell not because of any new developments in the field but because it did not fit the prevailing world-view. To be more precise, it was incompatible with the paradigms of race and progress of the early 19th century.

CHAPTER VII

HELLENOMANIA, 2
Transmission of the new scholarship to England and the rise of the Aryan Model, 1830–60

T HE FIRST HALF of this chapter is concerned with the transmission of Müller's work to England. This has to be seen in the context of the introduction of *Altertumswissenschaft* to England and the establishment of the discipline of Classics, in which contemplation of all aspects of Greek and Roman life was supposed to have a beneficial educational and moral effect on the boys who were to be the rulers of Britain and the Empire.

Classics became the centre of the reformed public school system, and dominant in the universities. These reforms were led by Dr Arnold and other early Victorian reformers who saw in German education and scholarship a 'third way' that broke away from the stagnation of Tory and Whig England while avoiding French radicalism. However, as with Humboldt and his colleagues in Germany thirty years earlier, there is no doubt that the English reformers were much more afraid of revolution than of reaction. This did not, however, save them from attack by conservatives.

Connop Thirlwall and George Grote, the two men who challenged Mitford's defence of the Ancient Model, belonged to slightly different factions of this reforming elite. Both were very impressed by Müller's work, but both shied away from his iconoclastic radicalism. Thirlwall

refused to reject the Phoenician settlements, while Grote cut the
Gordian knot and completely refused to speculate about the veracity of
the Greek legends about their past. Despite the differences in their
approaches, the net effect of their work was to discredit the traditions of
colonization and to enhance the independent creativity of the Greeks,
who were now looked upon as semi-divine. This, of course, was
very welcome to public opinion, which was becoming increasingly
Philhellene and contemptuous of all non-European cultures.

The second part of Chapter VII is concerned with the reconciliation
of Indophilia and Indo-European studies with Philhellenism and
Altertumswissenschaft. After Müller's demolition of the Ancient Model,
it was relatively easy to fill the vacuum with the model of Indo-European
conquest from the north. In this case, unlike the destruction of the
Ancient Model, there was a good internalist explanation for the change:
the need to explain the Indo-European basis of Greek. Nevertheless,
there is no doubt that German and English scholars were particularly
attracted to ideas of northern invasion, which fitted so well with the
prevailing racism and with Niebuhr's scheme of ethnic history. There is
also no doubt that the contemporary passion for India drew Europeans'
attention to the Aryan invasions of the subcontinent from the north. It
took very little imagination to transpose from these invasions – which
are attested in Indian tradition – to Greece, where there were no extant
records of such a conquest.

THE GERMAN MODEL
AND EDUCATIONAL REFORM
IN ENGLAND

Just as Isokrates had viewed the Athenians and Greeks in the 4th
century BC, so by the beginning of the 19th century AD Germans were
convinced that they were the 'intellectual instructors of mankind'.[1] It
was a self-assessment accepted by most 'progressive' Europeans and
North Americans. German philosophy and education provided a
middle way between bankrupt traditions and the French Revolution
and atheism. As the contemporary literary historian Elinor Shaffer
writes about one aspect of it:

The German criticism was learned and technical, unsuitable to serve as the handbook of a working-class movement ... moreover, it was susceptible of many interpretations, among them a revisionist reform from within that left ecclesiastical and political institutions apparently intact, and real power where it was before. From the 1830s in England knowledge of the most advanced continental scholarship was a stick to beat the Anglican academic establishment ... The nature of this mode of thinking tells us much about the double face of political Romanticism and even more about the nature of Victorian compromise. From one point of view it might be seen as a major intellectual monument to bourgeois hypocrisy.[2]

In France this Germanic trend is best represented by the popular philosopher and politician Victor Cousin, who flourished under the *grand bourgeois*, compromise regime of Louis Philippe. Cousin established French primary education on the Prussian model, and like Humboldt, whom he greatly admired, he reserved a special place in the whole educational system for the Ancients, and for the Greeks in particular. He was also an ardent believer in the categorical distinction between the primitive, 'spontaneous' philosophy of the East and the 'reflective' philosophies of the pagan and Christian worlds.[3]

While some English reformers were ready for the Prussian *Bildung* almost as soon as it was articulated, the power of conservatism held back the 'Germanizing' of education for many decades. In fact, it could begin only in the second third of the century, after nonconformist and industrialist pressure had forced the establishment of new universities, and the need for reform of the public schools and Oxbridge became blatant. Even after the university reforms, however, Seminars did not take root, and professors at Oxbridge were prevented by the Colleges and liberal feelings among the reformers from establishing an autocracy of the German type.[4] Furthermore, in England, the *Bildung* of the German system was taken much more seriously than its research. It is striking that Jowett, the leading Classicist in the second half of the 19th century, left a lasting impression on his students but was much less competent as a scholar than many of his unreformed predecessors.[5]

The production of research from the English universities was negligible compared to that of the formidable German professorate.[6]

Study of Latin as a language and reading of the Ancients had been central to the basic curricula of medieval universities. In England the relative importance of these aspects of education grew during the 18th century with the decline of the interest in religion and theology and the disdain for mathematics shown by the increasingly aristocratic students. Moreover, as we have seen, after 1780 more attention began to be paid to Greek. Knowledge of Latin had always marked the upper classes; now Greek became the inner or first circle. Nevertheless, the first use of Classics – the study of all aspects of Antiquity as moral and intellectual training for the elite – emerged only in the first half of the 19th century, directly or indirectly following the German pattern.

The most prominent figure in its promotion was Thomas Arnold, best known as the promotor of that improbable hybrid, the 'Christian-Gentleman'. As headmaster of Rugby and with a keen interest in university reform, he became immensely influential in the last ten years or so of his life, between 1832 and 1844. Like Humboldt and Cousin, Arnold belonged to what one might call the pugnacious middle, hating both revolution and reaction.[7] Central to all his ideas of reform for the purpose of preserving the best of tradition was his love of Germany: he had met Bunsen in Rome in 1827 and the two became fast friends; and, though somewhat concerned about Niebuhr's historical scepticism, he became a fervent admirer and wrote a popular digest of his *Roman History*.[8] Arnold also shared Niebuhr's enthusiasm for race as the primary principle of historical explanation, and his inaugural lecture as Regius Professor of Modern History at Oxford in 1841 was devoted to this theme.[9] Dr Arnold and his son Matthew are especially significant because of their 'trendiness'; they articulated and reinforced feelings already present in fashionable opinion.[10]

A much more original group of scholars emerged from Cambridge. Indeed, the possibility of reform in this slightly more flexible Whig university is shown by the fact that the Classical Tripos of the modern, 'all-round' type was established there in 1822; and it was through Cambridge that the new German scholarship and *Altertumswissenschaft* were introduced into England. The key figures in their transmission were two close friends at school and university, Julius Hare and Connop Thirlwall. Hare had spent time as a child in Germany, where he learnt German and developed a lifelong enthusiasm for its culture, which he passed on to Connop Thirlwall. Together with the mathematician William Whewell, they were active in the first attempt to found the Cambridge Union and after the student debating society was closed down in 1817 as subversive, Whewell and Thirlwall devoted themselves to learning German from Hare. By the time he went down the following year, Thirlwall had not only learnt German but had read Niebuhr's *History*. He soon went to Rome, where he attached himself to the German community and established a friendship with Bunsen that 'had a most important influence on his life'.[11]

On his return to England Thirlwall translated *St Luke*, a difficult theological treatise by Schleiermacher, a Romantic and 'Aryanist' theologian who was a favourite of Humboldt and Bunsen.[12] This caused a mild scandal among conservative clerics opposed to all German theology, but it did not prevent Thirlwall's returning to his college, Trinity, and taking the required holy orders. In 1827 he and Hare began the translation of Niebuhr's *History*; one volume appeared in 1828, a second three years later, but their extraordinary patience and dedication were exhausted and the third was left unfinished.

By 1830, Thirlwall and Hare had come into contact with a small exclusive and secret student society, the Apostles, which had been founded as a Christian social club ten years earlier. They helped to transform it and give it the distinctive metaphysical liberal character that – with some deviations – has lasted ever since. The two encouraged the younger 'brethren' to revere the Romantic poets and German scholarship.[13] According to a member elected in 1832, 'Coleridge and Wordsworth were our principal divinities and Hare and Thirlwall were regarded as their prophets'; another source claimed that 'Niebuhr was for them a god who for a lengthy time formed their sentiments.'[14] The Romantic ethos of the group was intensified in 1833 by the death of Hallam, a brilliant young man loved by Thirlwall and many of the brethren; his cult, symbolizing their own lost youth and beauty, was immortalized in Tennyson's *In Memoriam* and remained central to 'the Society' for the next forty years.

There is no doubt that Thirlwall saw himself as the Sokrates of the group, consciously training the best minds of the younger generation to feel Romantically and think sceptically. Thus from the Apostles in particular, and the *Zeitgeist* in general, Romantic-scepticism became the ethos of what the contemporary social historian Noel Annan has called the 'intellectual aristocracy' or the 'new intelligentsia'.[15] Indeed, Thirlwall's Sokratic reputation was increased by his principled stand for the admission of dissenters to Cambridge degrees. Let down by Hare and betrayed by Whewell, he was forced to resign his fellowship. His hemlock, however, was not so bitter since he had Whig friends in high places: he immediately received a rich living in the East Riding which gave him the leisure to write his *History of Greece*.

In 1840 Thirlwall was appointed Bishop of St Davids, the most ancient see in Wales. This must be seen as one of a series of pro-German moves that included the appointment of Dr Arnold to the Regius Professorship and Bunsen's special mission from the Prussian government to England to further his great religious scheme – which had strong Teutonic racial overtones – to unite the Lutheran and Anglican Churches. The scheme took tangible form in the foundation of the joint Evangelical bishopric at Jerusalem, and it was this move that finally drove the future Cardinal Newman to Catholicism. His conversion provides a good illustration of the division within the Romantic movement between the 'progressive' lovers of Greece and Germany, and the 'reactionary' passion for Christian ritual and the Middle Ages that could lead the unwary to Rome.

As a bishop, Thirlwall championed the liberalism of the 'new intelligentsia' and its ecclesiastical wing, the 'Broad Church'. In this he was often alone, and his first action astounded his peers. He was the only bishop to vote in favour of civil rights for Jews. His motives for making this brave stand were mixed. They combined genuine liberalism with the belief that assimilation would be the fastest road to conversion. (Conversion of the Jews was in fact a major purpose of the Evangelical bishopric at Jerusalem.)[16] For the rest of his life, Thirlwall continued to combine this principled liberalism with unpleasantness to all around him, apart from children and pets.

Through all his courageous reformism – culminating in an extraordinarily eloquent speech in which he routed the champions of anti-
disestablishmentarianism – it must be emphasized that Thirlwall
remained a Romantic and a counter-revolutionary. His *Primitiae*,
essays written at the age of eleven, were fulsomely praised by the
Anti-Jacobin Review and were dedicated to Bishop Percy, whose *Reliques
of Ancient British Poetry* we saw as having been central to the Romantic
interest in ballads in both Britain and Germany. Then, during the
1820s, he and Hare revered Wordsworth and Coleridge in the poets'
extreme reactionary phases. Thirlwall was also terrified of the revolution he thought he detected in the Daughters of Rebecca – Welshmen
who dressed up as women to burn hated tollbooths – and during the
American Civil War, much as he deplored slavery, he found still more
alarming the prospect of an 'ascendancy of a military democracy in
which the basest bear rule'.[17] Furthermore, he had what his friend
Thomas Carlyle described as 'almost frantic apprehensions of the
French menace'.[18] All in all, Thirlwall's political views seem to have
been close to those of Bunsen, Thomas Arnold and the young Niebuhr.

Thirlwall's eight-volume *History of Greece*, which began to appear in
1835, was the first major work in English to incorporate the results of
the new German scholarship. It was also the first to replace Mitford's
massive *History*, published between 1784 and 1804. However, the
attack on the conservative Mitford, who was very sceptical of Greek
achievements, had begun ten years earlier during the Greek War of
Independence in reviews appearing in 1824 and 1826. The first, by
Thomas Babington Macaulay, was a ferocious critique on the extremely
reactionary anti-Athenian and pro-Spartan views he attributed to
Mitford. Above all, however, Macaulay objected to Mitford's having
treated the Greeks as just another people: like Shelley, or Schiller and
Humboldt in Germany, Macaulay was convinced that the Greeks were
above such forms of analysis. As he put it, when thinking about Greece,
he loved to 'forget the accuracy of a judge in the veneration of a
worshipper'.[19]

The second attack, in 1826, came from George Grote, a young
radical banker. Grote had read Mitford more carefully than Macaulay
and conceded that Mitford was not pro-Spartan and – like Aristotle –

had actually favoured mixed constitutions. What Grote objected to was what he saw as Mitford's pro-English bias and his failure to recognize the special nature of Greece which he, Grote, derived from its free institutions: 'It is to democracy alone (and to that sort of open aristocracy which is, practically, very similar to it) that we owe that unparalleled brilliance and diversity of individual talent which constitutes the charm and glory of Grecian history.' He went on to make the circular argument that Greece should be given special treatment because its special position was already institutionalized. He stressed 'the extraordinary interest which the Classical turn of English education bestows on all Grecian transactions . . .'[20] Thus both critics agreed that Ancient Greece should be placed beyond the normal bounds of scholarship. Macaulay went on to other things, but Grote pursued his mission, and twenty years later produced his own massive history of Greece.

Before that, however, Thirlwall's had appeared. The usual comparison made is that while Mitford's conservative scorn for Greek democracy made his work a 'five-volume tract' for the Tory Party to which Grote's *History* was a Radical challenge, Thirlwall's is supposed to have held the balance.[21] On the issue that concerns us, however, the contrast is between Thirlwall's and Grote's attack on the Ancient Model, and Mitford's defence of it. As we saw in Chapter III, earlier scholars, accepting the Model without question, had never needed to justify it. By the 1780s, however, Mitford had felt obliged to articulate a defence of the orthodox view that Greece had been colonized by Egyptians and Phoenicians. There was every reason to believe the Greek reports of colonization, he had argued, because they were so detailed and widespread, and because the Greeks would have been unlikely to invent stories that were against their own interest.[22]

Against this plausible case Thirlwall summarized Müller's arguments, though without mentioning him by name. He also added a fascinating note on Müller's motivation:

In a comparatively late period – that which followed the rise of historical literature among the Greeks – we find a belief generally prevalent, both in the people and among the learned, that in ages of very remote antiquity, before the name and dominion of the Pelasgians had given way to that of the Hellenic race, foreigners had been led by various causes to the shores of Greece and there planted colonies, founded dynasties, built cities, and introduced useful arts and social institutions, before unknown to the ruder natives. The same belief has been almost universally adopted by the learned of modern times . . . It required no little boldness to venture even to throw a doubt as to a truth sanctioned by such authority and by prescription of such a long and undisputed possession of the public mind, and perhaps it might never have been questioned, *if the inferences drawn from it had not provoked a jealous enquiry into the grounds on which it rests.* (my emphasis)[23]

Thirlwall did not specify what these inferences were but, given Müller's work, it is hard to see any alternatives to Romantic and racial ones. This statement by someone in close contact with the German scholars is important, because it suggests that the criticism was applied not because there were formal inconsistencies – as Müller himself claimed in the case of Danaos – but because the legends' content was objectionable. Thirlwall continued:

When, however, this spirit once awakened, it was perceived that the current stories of these ancient settlements afforded great room for reasonable distrust, not merely in the marvellous features they ex-hibit but in the still more suspicious fact that with the lapse of time their number seems to increase and their details [seem] to be more accur-ately known and that the further we go back the less we hear of them, till, on consulting the Homeric poems, we lose all trace of their existence.[24]

Like Müller before him, Thirlwall was unable to find any explicit challenge to the Ancient Model among the early Greek writers and was forced to make do with the 'argument from silence'. Thus he claimed to detect a 'tacit dissent' from Greek authors, and believed that the legends were 'refuted by the silence of the older Greek poems and historians'.[25]

In true Apostolic spirit, Thirlwall could usually see two or more sides to any question, and on this one he seems to have been torn between

Müller's radical yet satisfying conclusions, and the orthodoxy which Niebuhr had defended. Thus he wrote: 'it seems possible and even necessary to take a middle course between the old and the new opinions.'[26] His compromise was the standard one – Egyptians no! Phoenicians maybe? – and he denied the truth of the legends surrounding the Egyptian Kekrops and Danaos on racial grounds: 'settlers of purely Egyptian blood, crossing the Aegean and founding maritime cities, appears inconsistent with everything we know about national characters.'[27] Note the 'purely' and the 'maritime'! Thirlwall chose his words very carefully, to avoid contradiction by the contemporary actions of Mohamed Ali and Ibrahim, but this systematic racism shows how easily ideology can transcend mere facts.[28]

On the other hand, Thirlwall did accept the legends concerning Kadmos and the Phoenicians, not only in the islands but in Boiotia too. Another reason for distinguishing him from the late-19th- and 20th-century racists and anti-Semites is that, although a true Romantic who talked in terms of 'blood' and 'race', he was insisting in the 1830s that

> It is in itself of very little importance whether a handful of Egyptians or Phoenicians were or were not mingled with the population of Greece. All that renders this enquiry interesting is the effect which the arrival of these foreigners is supposed to have produced on the state of society in their new country.[29]

Such a lack of concern with purity was much less acceptable eighty years later.

GEORGE GROTE

Thirlwall's *History* was soon eclipsed by that of George Grote, which appeared in 1846. The two men had been near-contemporaries at school at Charterhouse, and Grote claimed that he would never have begun his project if he had known about Thirlwall's. Thirlwall, for his part, accepted his supersession with striking cordiality.[30] Momigliano has pointed out the similarities between Thirlwall's circle and that of Grote's banking Radicals: 'Both societies disliked Mitford, read German, and were attacked by the *Quarterly Review*. Both aimed at liberalization of English political and intellectual habits and wanted them to be founded on firm philosophical principles.'[31]

Yet Momigliano went on to claim a fundamental difference: while Thirlwall and Hare wanted to introduce a Romantic philosophy of history and replace the empirical studies carried on at Oxbridge, Grote was himself an empiricist and a positivist.[32] In fact the distinction between the two should not be taken too far. Many Utilitarians shared the Romantic passion for Greece, which by the 1830s and 40s was held by women and men of all shades of opinion, except for extreme reactionaries. (Momigliano cites John Stuart Mill on Greece, but the Hellenic passion of Mill's Utilitarian father – who had his son taught Greek at three! – is still more telling.)[33] Grote's admiration for the Greek *polis*, for instance, seems in many ways similar to that of Rousseau. Indeed, as Momigliano points out, Grote's 'sympathy for small states . . . led him later to make a close study of the politics of Switzerland.'[34] On the other hand, as a Radical and a Utilitarian, Grote was naturally in sympathy with the scientific spirit which, in the 1830s, was being articulated in France in the positivism of Comte. Grote was thus able to demand 'proof' from ancient history with more consistency than either Niebuhr or Müller, and he deplored what he saw as the 'German licence to conjecture'.[35]

Momigliano maintains that Grote, by making a sharp distinction between legendary and historical Greece, 'broke with K. O. Müller and his English admirers'.[36] However, Müller began his *Prolegomena* with the statement that there was 'a tolerably distinct boundary' between the two.[37] Also, both Müller and Grote followed Wolf in believing that writing had not existed in Greece before the 8th century and that there had been no priestly instruction, as there had been in the East. Thus the links with earlier times were extremely tenuous.[38] Furthermore, both men agreed that while myth could contain historical elements, it was not useful to think of a nucleus of pure reality upon which mythical elements had been imposed; rather, the two elements should be seen as having been integrated from the beginning.[39] Here too, then, the distinction between Grote and the Romantic historians does not seem to be as great as Professor Momigliano supposes. There was, however, one important difference between Grote and the German Romantics, who were concerned with Greece as the infancy of Europe: as a Radical rather than a conservative he did not regret the passing of the mythopoeic age. Like James Harris the grammarian a century earlier, Grote's passion was for the late and sudden flowering of Athenian democracy and, as we have seen, his main concern was to refute Mitford's Tory scepticism about Greek institutions.[40]

Momigliano also argues that Grote was strictly neutral on the question of the historicity of Greek myths: it was simply that he demanded 'collateral evidence' before accepting them.[41] Apart from the inappropriateness of this requirement of 'proof', Grote's neutrality on this issue is in serious doubt, because the tone of his discussion of historicity is sceptical, if not scoffing. Thus he approvingly cited the late-18th-century historian and mythographer Jacob Bryant, who had argued that it was impossible to take seriously the accounts of people who believed in centaurs, satyrs, nymphs and horses that could speak.[42]

Byrant's argument would seem plausible. It should, however, be remembered that every period has general beliefs which in later times are considered absurd. I maintain that in this case, what we now believe to be the mistaken beliefs in centaurs and other mythical creatures are less misleading – on the issues with which we are concerned – than the 19th-century myths on race, unchanging national characteristics, the productiveness of purity and the deleterious effects of racial mixture – and, above all, the semi-divine status of the Greeks, which made them transcend the laws of history and language. Thus, while we should be wary of the ancient reports, we should have a still greater suspicion of 19th- and early-20th-century interpretations of them.

Momigliano claims that because of his 'neutrality', Grote's views on mythology have in no way been invalidated by later archaeological discoveries that would seem to confirm legendary accounts.[43] This excuse does not apply if, as I maintain, his views were sceptical. Moreover, such scepticism seems more justifiable in Grote than in his 20th-century successors: having been bitten over Troy, Mycenae and Knossos and so on, one would expect them to give the benefit of the doubt at least to those traditions that were uncontested in Antiquity. It would have seemed prudent, for instance, to have retained as working hypotheses the idea that Boiotia had a special relationship with

Phoenicia, or that the lengendary Sesōstris and Memnon – the Egyptian pharaohs called Senwosret and Ammenemes – had made widespread expeditions around the East Mediterranean in the 20th century BC rather than denying them as absurd, only to be humiliated when archaeological or inscriptional evidence is found to confirm both traditions.[44]

Nevertheless, Grote's contempt for tradition's failure to satisfy the requirements of 'proof' has been immensely influential. His insistence – added to that of Müller – that Greece must be assumed to have been isolated from the Middle East until proven otherwise has been useful as a tool to expel heretics from the Aryan Model out of the academic fold.[45] Similarly, by starting Greek history with the first Olympiad in 776 BC, Grote powerfully reinforced the impression that Classical Greece was an island in both space and time. Greek civilization was seen to have come from nothing, springing up almost fully armed in a way that was rather more than human.

Grote's history immediately became standard for scholars, not only in England but in Germany and elsewhere on the continent.[46] Exhilarating as Grote's procedure on myth might have been, however, it did not satisfy other historians, who still felt obliged to present some opinion on early Greek history. In general they seem to have followed Thirlwall's compromise position: that while Greek legends maintained that there had been both Egyptian and Phoenician invasions, the 'scientific' evidence of linguistics now suggested that the Greek language was pure and autochthonous. Sir William Smith's *History of Greece*, the standard English textbook on the subject from its first publication in 1854 until the 1880s, demonstrated the difficulties of this position:

> The civilization of the Greeks and the development of their language bear all the marks of home growth, and were probably little affected by foreign influence. The traditions, however, of the Greeks would point to a contrary conclusion. It was a general belief among them that Pelasgians were reclaimed from barbarism by Oriental strangers, who settled in the country and introduced among the rude inhabitants the first elements of civilization. Many of these traditions, however, are not ancient legends but owe their origin to a later age.[47]

Given the ideological roots of the notion of the 'purity' of the Greek language, discussed in Chapter VI, it is fascinating to note that language, several decades later, was being used as the 'scientific' basis for the denial of the Ancient Model. Like Thirlwall, Smith had made the compromise of accepting the Kadmeian Phoenician settlement of Thebes while rejecting any stories of Egyptian colonization.

While Romantics had toyed since the 18th century with the idea of a northern origin for the Greeks, scholarly attacks on the Ancient Model, from Samuel Musgrave to Karl Otfried Müller and Connop Thirlwall, had insisted on the autochthony of the Greeks and on the affinities between Hellenes and Pelasgians. By the 1850s, the Indo-European language family and the Aryan race had become established 'facts'. With a coherent racial theory, and the concept of an original Aryan homeland somewhere in the mountains of Central Asia, the picture of Greek origins was transformed.

Aryans and Hellenes

Niebuhr, Müller and the Indo-Europeanists had, between them, provided all the elements necessary for the construction of the Aryan Model. Niebuhr had made it legitimate to reject ancient sources, and had introduced the French and Indian models of northern conquest into Antiquity. Müller had removed the Ancient Model from Greece. More powerful than either of these, however, had been the work of linguists in relating Greek to Sanskrit, and making it clear that Greek was an Indo-European language. Some historical explanation of this relationship was necessary, and the model of northern conquests from Central Asia fitted well. Thus a clear distinction has to be made between the fall of the Ancient Model, which can be explained only in externalist terms – that is, through social and political pressures – and the rise of the Aryan one, which had a considerable internalist component – that is to say, developments within scholarship itself played an important role in the evolution of the new model.

I also want to emphasize that the Ancient and Aryan Models are not necessarily mutually exclusive. In fact, for much of the 19th century the two coexisted in what I call the Broad Aryan Model. This held that the early Greeks, who emerged as the result of Indo-European conquest of Pre-Hellenes, had been conquered again by Anatolians and Phoenicians, and the latter left significant cultural traces. I myself argue, in my Revised Ancient Model, that there may well have been early invasions or infiltrations by Indo-European speakers into the Aegean basin before the Egyptian and West Semitic colonizations.[48] On the whole, however, the supporters of the Aryan Model have been concerned with racial hierarchy and racial purity, and the idea of Egyptian and Phoenician colonization always seems to have been distasteful to them.

There was one great drawback to the new Aryan Model: the lack of ancient attestation. Thucydides had mentioned tribal movements in which the Hellenes from northern Greece had moved south and absorbed other peoples. His dating of this process is obscure, but he emphasized that it had not been completed at the time of the Trojan War; this left the origins of the Danaans, Argives, Achaians and many other Greeks unexplained.[49] Similar problems of lateness mar the other possible tradition of northern conquest – the Return of the Heraklids or the Dorian Invasion – in which tribes from the north-west of Greece swept south and captured most of the Peloponnese and much of the South Aegean.

These events were consistently reported to have happened after the Trojan War, which took place around 1200 BC. Thus – if one accepted them as constituting the 'Aryan Invasion' – Agamemnon, Menelaos and most of the Homeric heroes could not have been Greeks. This was a price few Hellenists were willing to pay, even before the decipherment of Linear B proved that Greek was being spoken in Greece long before the Trojan War.[50] Hence the only possibility has been to argue that the Dorian Invasion was only the last in a series of invasions – but this still leaves the initial conquest unreported.

Ernst Curtius, Müller's devoted junior colleague, admitted that there was no ancient authority for the Aryan conquest and, as he put it, 'the notion of autochthony is developed among them [the Greeks] in the greatest variety of traditions.'[51] However, *Philologie* was now a 'scientific' discipline and was above such things; lack of ancient authority did not bother the new historians. As Theodor Mommsen, the great

historian of Rome of the mid- and late 19th century, is reported to have
written: 'History must first make a clean sweep of all these fables which,
though purporting to be history, are little more than improvisations.'[52]

Given the rise of Indo-European studies, the saliency of the Indian
Model of Aryan conquest, and Müller's destruction of the Ancient
Model, the application of an Aryan Model for Greece was so obvious
that it appears to have occurred generally in the 1840s and 50s. It is,
therefore, difficult to know to whom to credit it. The most likely
candidates, however, are the Curtius brothers, and breaking the rule of
primogeniture we will consider Georg the younger first.

Georg Curtius was born in Lübeck in 1820, studied at Bonn and
Berlin and was a professor at Prague (already a great centre of
linguistics), Kiel and Leipzig. His many books were applications of the
new principles of Indo-European linguistics to Greek. He worked on
comparative grammar and on the Indo-European component in Greek,
in both of which he set out the elegant and regular sound shifts
according to which much of Greek can be derived from the hypothetical
Proto-Indo-European.[53] During the 1850s Georg Curtius established
a firm basis beyond which it has been hard to go. The early-20th-
century lexicographer H. Stuart Jones described the situation in the
1920s in his preface to the 9th edition of the standard Greek–English
dictionary of Liddell and Scott:

> After careful consideration, it was decided that etymological infor-
> mation should be reduced to a minimum. A glance at Boisacq's
> *Dictionaire étymologique de la langue grecque* will show that the specu-
> lations of etymologists are rarely free from conjecture; and the
> progress of comparative philology since the days of G. Curtius
> (whose *Griechische Etymologie* was the main source drawn upon by
> Liddell and Scott) has brought about the clearance of much rubbish,
> but little solid construction.[54]

This is as true today as when he wrote it in 1925. Much of the
'rubbish' was, of course, Semitic, which was impossible to tolerate in
the 1920s.[55]

If Georg Curtius linked Greece to the Indo-Europeans linguistically,
his older brother Ernst did so historically. Ernst Curtius was born in

1814. He studied at Bonn and at Göttingen, where he became attached to Müller. He spent the years from 1836 to 1840 in Greece and was with Müller when he died. Curtius wrote a detailed historical description of the Peloponnese and gained a post at Berlin; he was next a professor at Göttingen from 1856 to 1868; he then took up a chair at Berlin and spent the last twenty-eight years of his life there.[56]

Ernst Curtius shared Müller's passion for the landscape of Greece and for its monuments, archaeology and art. His was thus the first major history of Greece to be written by someone who had actually been to the country. Moreover, Curtius always maintained his mentor's romantic view of Greece. As Wilamowitz-Moellendorf points out, he 'never outgrew his faith in that ideal conception, but proclaimed it to his dying day.'[57] Unlike Müller, however, Curtius was swept up in the new enthusiasm for Indo-Europeans and Aryans, and his Romanticism was extended to them.

Such a vision permeates his *History of Greece*, the first volume of which was published in 1857. Curtius accepted the linguists' idea of an Indo-European *Urheimat* somewhere in the mountains of Central Asia; it was from there that, just as the Aryans had swept south to conquer India, the Hellenes had descended into Greece. Unlike the Ancients and his predecessors, however, Curtius emphasized the distinction between Pelasgians and Hellenes: 'The Pelasgian times lie in the background – a vast period of monotonony: impulse and motion are first communicated by Hellen and his sons; and with their arrival history commences.'[58]

This view would seem to parallel the distinction between Aryan and non-Aryan. In fact, however, Curtius saw the Pelasgians as a first wave of inferior Aryans who came through Anatolia and over the Hellespont to Greece, leaving traces in Phrygia. The later Hellenic invasions were smaller, but 'though less in number they were, by their superior mental powers, rendered capable of collecting scattered elements . . . advancing it to a higher development.'[59] The analogies between the pre-Dorian natives of Sparta and Messenia and the 'off-Aryan' Irish have been mentioned on p. 294.[60] Curtius' historical scheme of Aryan Hellenes conquering semi-Aryan Pelasgians has the advantage of combining two ideologically desirable features – northern conquest by a master race, and the preservation of essential racial purity.

The new invaders were thoroughly northern. One of their groups 'took the land way through the Hellespont's ancient portal of the nations: they passed through Thrace into the Alpine land of Northern Greece, and there, in mountain cantons, they developed their peculiar life in social communities ... under the name of Dorians.'[61] The reason for this picturesque description of isolated mountain life in 'cantons' – making them almost Swiss – seems to have come from the long-standing Romantic need to derive a people's character from the landscape of its homeland. It was an embarrassment for proponents of such a view to find that the 'soft' Ionian Athenians were formed in rugged Attica, while the Spartans lived in the lush valley of the Eurotas.

Curtius was much more brief on Ionian origins, noting simply that the Ionians had come straight from Phrygia to the east coast of the Aegean.[62] Greek tradition stated clearly that Anatolian Ionia was settled by Ionians from Greece only in the 11th century, but Niebuhr had defied the Ancients on this point. In this way Curtius had the authority of the new scholarship behind him when he denied the tradition and claimed that Greeks had lived there much earlier. In conclusion to this section he argued that their separate migrations had differentiated the Dorians from the Ionians: hence 'the first foundations had been laid of the dualism which pervades the whole history of this people.' They were, however, racially united: 'an inner sense of kinsmanship attracted them to one another.'[63]

Above everything else, Curtius' mystic feelings about the Aryan Hellenes were concerned with language:

> The people which knew in so peculiar a manner how to develop the common treasure of the Indo-Germanic language was ... the Hellenes. Their first historic deed is the development of this language, and this deed is an artistic one. For above all its sister-tongues the Greek must be regarded as a work of art ... if the grammar of their language were the only thing remaining to us of the Hellenes, it would serve as a full and valid testimony to the extraordinary natural gifts of this people ... The whole language resembles

the body of a trained athlete, in which every muscle, every sinew, is developed into full play, where there is no trace of tumidity or of inert material, and all is power and life.[64]

This 'pure' language had to be fully formed in northern mountains before the descent into Greece. Curtius saw this early completion as especially necessary, for he believed that languages were directly related to landscapes: 'One class of sounds is wont to predominate on the hills, another in the valleys, and again another on the plains.'[65] It was unthinkable that such an object of beauty and purity as the Greek language could have developed on the Mediterranean; still less could it be the result of Hellenes mixing with Egyptians and Semites.

Curtius did admit that in early times, Phoenicians had traded in Greece and had introduced certain new inventions. He maintained, however, that they had soon been driven out by the more dynamic Ionians. And he was convinced that the legends of Egyptian and Phoenician settlement had been demonstrated by 'racial science' to be absurd:

It is inconceivable that Canaanites proper, who everywhere shyly retreated at the advance of the Hellenes, especially when they came into contact with them, when far from their own homes; and who as a nation were despised by the Hellenes to such a degree as to make the latter regard intermarriage with them in localities of mixed population, such as Salamis or Cyprus, as disgraceful; it is inconceivable, we repeat, that such Phoenicians ever founded principalities among a Hellenic population.[66]

The anti-Semitic implications of this passage, and the very different attitudes towards the Phoenicians held in Britain at the time, will be discussed in the next chapter. For his part, Curtius explained away the references to the Phoenicians in a manner similar to and equally as cumbersome as Bunsen's. According to Curtius, the Greek traditions of Phoenician settlement had arisen either from a natural confusion between Phoenicians and Ionians who had been abroad and learnt some foreign ways, or from the 'facts' that Caria had been called Phoinikē and the Carians seem to have been a type of Eastern Greek.[67]

The only exception he allowed was Crete, where he admitted the actual Phoenicians might have settled in larger numbers, although they never displaced the native Pelasgians there.[68] In the 1850s, with the island still under Turkish rule, this did not seem improbable; it was only after Evans' discovery of 'Minoan' civilization on the island in 1900 that Crete became a territory too valuable to be conceded to the Phoenicians.

I should like to conclude this chapter with a vignette. The formidable and bigoted William Ridgeway has been mentioned above, in connection with the image of Spartans as Ulstermen. He was the dominant figure in early Greek history at Cambridge at the beginning of the 20th century.[69] In his *Early Age of Greece*, published in 1901, he gave his intellectual pedigree when he referred to: 'four historians whose scepticism or sober-mindedness no one has yet called into question – Niebuhr, Thirlwall, Grote and E. Curtius'.[70] No one can doubt their scepticism towards theories they did not like. On the other hand there is also no doubt that all – with the possible exception of Grote – were racist and that all were Romantics with a passionate love for their images of Greece. It must now be clear that I should like to call their sober-mindedness, balance and objectivity into question.

CHAPTER VIII

THE RISE AND FALL OF THE PHOENICIANS, 1830–85

W E NOW COME to an intermediate stage in the establishment of the Aryan Model: Egyptian involvement in the formation of Greece had been dismissed, while that of the Phoenicians was still generally admitted. I argue in this and the following chapters that the essential force behind the rejection of the tradition of massive Phoenician influence on early Greece was the rise of racial – as opposed to religious – anti-Semitism. This was because the Phoenicians were correctly perceived to have been culturally very close to the Jews.

In the intermediate period with which we are concerned, however, the situation was complicated by another parallel seen between past and present – that between the English and the Phoenicians, the proud manufacturing and merchant princes of the past. This identification was accepted both by the English and by their enemies – the French at the beginning of the 19th century and the Germans at its end. Thus there were distinct differences in the historical treatment of the Phoenicians on the opposite sides of the Channel: the English tended to admire them, while the continentals were more or less violently hostile. French interest in the Phoenicians increased with their colonial and military involvement in both Lebanon (the old Phoenicia) and North Africa (the new one). French hostility to the Phoenicians came to a climax in Flaubert's enormously popular historical novel *Salammbô*, which vividly portrayed the luxury and cruelty of Carthage in the 3rd century BC.

Salammbô also spectacularly raised the issue of the horrible ritual of Moloch and the sacrifice of the first-born that is mentioned so often in the Bible. Flaubert's spectacular reminder of the association of the Carthaginians and the Phoenicians with this ultimate abomination made it difficult even for British and Jewish scholars to champion them.

The last three sections of the chapter are concerned firstly with Gobineau's views of Greece as a largely Semitized and hence corrupt culture; and secondly with Schliemann's discovery of Bronze Age 'Mycenaean' civilization and the discussions about the racial and linguistic nature of its rulers and inhabitants. I am particularly concerned, here, with the widespread belief that the whole culture was heavily 'Semitized'.

The third and final topic is the influence on historiography of the East Mediterranean of the decipherment of cuneiform and the discovery first of the Semitic-speaking Assyrians and Babylonians, and then of the non-Semitic Sumerians. By attributing all aspects of Mesopotamian civilization to the Sumerians, the anti-Semites who by the 1890s dominated much of the writing of ancient history were able to maintain their general tenet that Semites were essentially uncreative.

PHOENICIANS AND
ANTI-SEMITISM

There has always been considerable overlap between religious hatred of the Jews and ethnic hostility to them. Nevertheless, it is equally true that there was a shift in emphasis during the 19th century from the traditional Christian *Judenhaß* (hatred of the Jews) to a modern 'racial' anti-Semitism. The transition was a complicated process, however, and it took place at various speeds in different places. In Germany, for instance, the gap between the two hatreds was minute, and existed only in Enlightened and Masonic circles before the French Revolution. *Judenhaß* revived, and the seeds of anti-Semitism grew rapidly, in the early 19th century with the return to Christianity and the terror of the revolutionary consequences of the Enlightenment; the latter was closely related, in the minds of reactionaries, to Jewish rationalism.

Changes taking place among the most cultivated of the elite represent the tip of the iceberg for the German ruling classes as a whole. Thus Wilhelm von Humboldt and his wife Caroline moved in Jewish circles before the Revolution, but by the end of her life Caroline's vehemence against Jews gained her recognition by the Nazis as a pioneer anti-Semite. Humboldt himself still advocated giving the Jews civil rights, but he wrote in 1815: 'I like the Jews *en masse*; *en détail*, I very carefully avoid them.'[1] There is also no doubt, however, that the situation became far more acute in the 1870s and 80s, and many distinguished liberals like Wilamowitz-Moellendorf and Mommsen, and others like Nietzsche, vehemently opposed the new intensification of anti-Semitism.

In France – with many fewer Jews – the double links between Jewish rationalism and the Enlightenment, and the Revolution's having given civil rights to Jews, have firmly associated Jews with the Republican strand of French politics ever since. It has also meant that Jews have been more violently hated by Royalists and Catholics in France than anywhere else in Europe. On the other hand, while liberals and 'progressives' often shared the new racism and anti-Semitism, they did at times see Jews as the outer bulwark of the Republic; thus Jews had important allies in French society, and frequently in French government.

In England, from which Jews had been expelled until the 1650s, there were theoretically philo-Semitic tendencies as well as the anti-Semitic ones. There was a medieval tradition of the English as having descended from Noah's son Shem – the ancestor of the Jews – rather than from Japhet, forefather of the Europeans. There was also the Puritan vision of England as the new Jerusalem, which survives today in Blake's moving hymn.[2] These traditions – and the important role played by Jews in establishing Britain's financial and colonial supremacy in the late 17th and 18th centuries – meant that here, as in France, the transformation from *Judenhaß* to anti-Semitism was slow, and opened an extraordinary 'window of opportunity' in the middle of the 19th century. Converts like Disraeli could reach the highest office in a way that was impossible both before and after, and practising Jews gained civil rights and a social acceptability which did not return until the 1950s or 60s.

WHAT RACE WERE THE SEMITES?

Although we have seen how the name 'Caucasian' was related through Prometheus to Japhetic, as opposed to Semitic, its inventor J. F. Blumenbach introduced the term only in the third edition of his great *De Generis Humani Varietate Nativa*, in 1795. We know that his first conception of the superior White Race included both Arabs and Jews, and this was the sense in which many English writers took the word Caucasian until the end of the 19th century.[3] In the 1840s, for instance, Disraeli described Moses as 'in every respect a man of complete Caucasian model', while he wrote that the European Jews could not have borne all their suffering if they had not been 'of the unmixed blood of the Caucasus'; later, in the 1870s, George Eliot referred to Jews as 'purer Caucasians'.[4] Even in Germany the violently anti-Semitic Christian Lassen, a pupil of the Schlegels, did not refuse the Jews Caucasian status.[5]

In the same decades, however, new attitudes were developing. Professor Robert Knox, the anatomist, became infamous as the employer of the grave-robbers Burke and Hare. It is alleged that he asked for fresh corpses, complaining that the bodies they brought him for dissection were too old and scrawny. In any event, he was happy to accept the victims of their murders. Burke and Hare were hanged but Knox, though banned from anatomy, went on to become a pioneer pampleteer of racism. Paraphrasing the wise Sidonia in Disraeli's *Tancred*, who had said: 'all is race, there is no other truth', Knox maintained in 1850 that 'the race is everything, is simply a fact, the most remarkable, the most comprehensive, which philosophy has ever announced. Race is everything: literature, science, art – in a word, civilization depends on it.'[6]

Knox gloried in the opportunities for white men to commit genocide: 'What a field of extermination lies before the Saxon Celtic and

Sarmatian [Slav] races!'[7] He described 'the Jew' as a 'sterile hybrid', accusing the people of having always been uncreative parasites:

> But where are the Jewish farmers, Jewish mechanics [and] labourers? Why does he dislike handicraft labour? Has he no inventive power, no mechanical or scientific turn of mind? . . . And then I began to enquire into this and I saw . . . that the Jews who followed any calling were not really Hebrews, but sprung from a Jewish father and a Saxon or Celtic mother: that the real Jew had never altered since the earliest recorded period; . . . that the real Jew has no ear for music, no love of science or literature, pursues no enquiry, etc. . . .[8]

Knox had clearly passed from religious hatred of the Jews to modern racial anti-Semitism. Although – as the modern historian of anti-Semitism Poliakov has pointed out – such racial arguments were novel in Great Britain, advanced thinkers like Darwin and Herbert Spencer (the creator of Social Darwinism) were working along very similar lines, and the former quoted Knox with approval.[9]

Let us return to France. In 1856 the great Semitist Ernest Renan complained that 'France believes very little in race, precisely because race has almost disappeared from her breast . . . all this [concern with race] can only be born in a people like the Germans, who still keep to their primordial roots.'[10] The comparison between France and Germany may be just, but the French, too, were concerned with race. By the 1850s, the idea of a 'Semitic race' had long been incorporated into the new racism of France. I have already mentioned the linguistically based theory of history as a dialogue between Aryans and Semites; Niebuhr's French disciple Michelet, on the other hand, saw this as a racial struggle to the death. As early as 1830 he wrote in his *Roman History*:

> It is not without reason that the memory of the Punic Wars has stayed so popular and so alive. The struggle was not merely to decide the fate of two cities or two empires; it was to settle which of the two races, the Indo-Germanic or the Semitic, was to rule the world . . . On the one side the genius of heroism, of art and of law; on the other

the spirit of industry, navigation and commerce ... The heroes
fought – without ceasing – their industrious and perfidious neighbours. They were workers, smiths, miners, magicians. They loved
gold, hanging gardens and magic palaces ... They constructed
towers with titanic ambition, which the swords of the warriors broke
up and effaced from the earth.[11]

This passage must be seen at two levels, both of which were to
become very important. First, there was the surface level of the racial
struggle between Aryans and Semites. Secondly, at another level, the
words 'perfidious neighbours' point to 'perfidious Albion', the French
name for England. There is no doubt that when writing about the Punic
Wars, Michelet was thinking about the Napoleonic Wars of his own
day. Thus, although heroic France had been beaten by the English
Industrial Revolution, the parallel with the Punic Wars gave the
promise of revenge. This analogy reflected the perception of a close
relationship between England and the Semites in general – and the
Phoenicians in particular – which to some extent explains the positive
English images of Jews just mentioned, and to which we shall frequently
return.

We shall see Michelet's ideas on the Phoenicians in Gobineau and
Flaubert. For the moment, however, we shall continue to look at the
development of racist anti-Semitism in France, the clearest example of
which comes in the work of Émile Louis Burnouf. Émile Burnouf was a
distinguished Hellenist, – he was director of the French School at
Athens – a Sanskritist, and an enthusiast for Indo-European connections. He was also the cousin of Eugène Burnouf, one of the founders of
Indian studies in France and the hero of Schwab's *The Oriental
Renaissance*. Émile Burnouf, writing in the 1860s, described the Semitic
race as follows:

A real Semite has smooth hair with curly ends, a strongly hooked
nose, fleshy projecting lips, massive extremities, thin calves, and flat
feet. And what is more, he belongs to the occipetal races: that is to
say, those whose hinder part of the head is more developed than the
front. His growth is very rapid, and at fifteen or sixteen it is over. At
that age the divisions of the skull which contain the organs of

intelligence are already joined, and in some cases even welded together. From that period the growth of the brain is arrested. In the Aryan races this phenomenon, or anything like it, never occurs, at any time of life . . .[12]

According to Burnouf, the Semitic race was a mixture of the white and the yellow races. His contemporary Gobineau, the ferocious reactionary later acknowledged as the father of European racism, had an even more complicated view of Jews and Semites. The Comte de Gobineau was torn between his conservative support for the Church and his excitement at the new theory of racism. This conflict led to all kinds of difficulties, the most fundamental of which centred on the question of a single or multiple creation of man. Poliakov rightly describes him as 'a monogenist in theory and a polygenist in practice', for Gobineau did see the three races – white, yellow and black – as separate species.[13] Personally torn between a rigid noble father and an 'adventuress' mother, Gobineau was explicit in his sexual imagery of race.[14] According to him, the 'Whites' were essentially 'male' while the 'Blacks', on the other hand, were 'female'. Despite his disgust for them, he saw 'the black element . . . [as] . . . indispensable for developing artistic genius in a race, for we have seen what outbursts of . . . vivacity and spontaneity are intrinsic to its soul and how much the imagination, that mirror of sensuality, and all cravings for material things, prepare it . . .'[15]

The same tension was reflected in Gobineau's overall historical view, a hybrid of the Bible and the new Indo-Europeanism. According to him, the three races represented by the sons of Noah – Ham, Shem, and Japhet – had all originated in Sogdiana, or some such region in Central Asia, and, rather like the Three Little Pigs, they had all set out to seek their fortunes.[16] The first to head south were the Hamites. After founding some civilizations and attempting to keep their blood pure, the Hamites had become hopelessly mongrelized by the native and inferior Blacks.[17] The next to leave were the Semites. Though these too had made attempts to preserve their purity of line, they were heavily polluted with black blood; this was partly from direct contact with the Blacks, but more from that with the 'mulatto' Hamites.[18] Only the Japhetites, or Aryans, had stayed in the north and retained their purity.

Although Gobineau's whole work was a lament for a lost purity, the mixture was essential to his scheme. Only if a race were mixed could one explain both its good and its bad features. Thus Gobineau attributed what he liked about the Jews – their prowess in fighting and their good cultivation of land – to their Semitic blood, but their skill in trading, their love of luxuries, cruelties, use of mercenaries and so on were due to Hamitic influence.[19]

In 1856 Gobineau's patron Alexis de Tocqueville wrote to console him about the slow response to his great work in France. Like their mutual friend Ernest Renan, de Tocqueville thought that the book would have a better reception in Germany, with its 'enthusiasm for abstract truth . . .', and he reassured his protégé that the work would 'return to France, above all by way of Germany'.[20] The book was, in fact, immediately reprinted after the German conquest of France in 1940.

The Linguistic and Geographical Inferiorities of the Semites

Jews and Phoenicians had long, and rightly, been seen as closely related. Well before the decipherment of the Phoenician alphabet by Barthélemy in the middle of the 18th century, scholars like Samuel Bochart in the 17th had been fully aware that Hebrew and Phoenician were dialects of the same language.[21] By the 1780s the two had been subsumed with Arabic, Aramaic and Ethiopic under the title 'Semitic'. Many early-19th-century scholars, reacting against the biblical picture of Hebrew as the language of Adam and the speech of all mankind until the fall of the Tower of Babel, fiercely denied that it was perfect or original. Hebrew was now felt to be primitive. Humboldt, for instance, urged that it be taught in the gymnasia just for that reason.[22] We saw in Chapter V how Friedrich Schlegel defined the Semitic languages as the highest form of 'animal' language, but since inflection was considered to be the touchstone of the superior 'spiritual' languages, there was no way of avoiding the fact that the Semitic languages were the inflected languages *par excellence*.[23] Thus, as Humboldt and others created more or less 'progressive' linguistic hierarchies, Semitic had to be put on the same top rung as Indo-European. This situation, which reflected the relative toleration of Jews in early-19th-century Europe, was used as a basis for the academic view of 'true' history as a dialogue between Aryans and Semites.

Physiological racists perceived the Semites as both 'female' and 'sterile' – superficially intelligent and imaginative, but fundamentally incapable of creative thought or action. Ernest Renan, disagreeing with his friend Gobineau, followed the older strand of the Romantic tradition, which maintained that there were essentially linguistic reasons for the incapacities of particular peoples. Generally acknowledged to be the leading French expert in Semitic languages, and the 19th-century founder of Phoenician studies, Renan was greatly concerned with what he saw as the inadequacies of Semitic. Expressing himself with the long-windedness of the German scholars he so much admired, he wrote:

> The unity and simplicity of the Semitic race is found in the Semitic languages themselves. Abstraction is unknown to them, metaphysics impossible. Language being the mould necessary for the intellectual operations of a people, an idiom almost denuded of syntax, lacking any varieties of construction, without the conjunctions which establish such delicate relations between the elements of thought, painting all objects with their exterior qualities, it ought to be eminently suitable for the eloquent inspirations of *seers* and the painting of fugitive impressions, but it ought to refuse all philosophy and all purely intellectual speculation. Imagine an Aristotle or a Kant with a similar instrument . . .[24]

The other reason for the Semitic inferiority was, for Renan, geographical. Europeans, living in a rainfall climate (he was a Breton), had been given a subtle and multiform nature. Semites, coming from the desert with its pitiless sun and sharp distinctions between light and shade, had been made simple and fanatical:

> The Semitic race appears to us as incomplete through its simplicity. It is, dare I say it, to the Indo-European family what drawing is to

painting or plainsong to modern music. It lacks that variety, that scale, that superabundance of life that is necessary for perfectibility.[25]

On the other hand, this simplicity and intensity had been the sources of religion, which the Semites had given to the world; and Renan saw it as his mission to bring science, which was Aryan, to religion, which was Semitic.[26] Hence his philological and racial studies of the origins of Christianity. Religion, however, should not be thought of as giving the Semites equality:

> Thus the Semitic race is to be recognized almost entirely by negative characteristics. It has neither mythology, nor epic, nor science, nor philosophy, nor fiction, nor plastic arts, nor civil life; in everything there is a complete absence of complexity, subtlety or feeling, except for unity. It has no variety in its monotheism.[27]

Renan's attitude is crucial, not only because his extraordinary public recognition indicates that he was articulating commonly held views but also because of his dominant position in Semitic, biblical and Phoenician studies. The combination meant that he both reflected and focused popular opinion and scholarly attitudes in these disciplines.[28] Indeed, there are striking parallels between Renan's relations with the Semitic languages and those of Humboldt, Niebuhr and Bunsen in their promotion of Egyptology. In both cases the scholars appear to have feared the charge of having too much sympathy with the object of their study. Any implication of treachery to Europe was of course unjustified, as the very act of 'scientific' study of a non-European culture made that culture qualitatively inferior, exotic and inert.[29] Renan, however, insisted that the Semites were not like the other non-Indo-Europeans, about whom there was nothing good to be said. The Semites had good qualities which, he maintained, they shared with the English; and his hostility to both, unlike that of Michelet, was tempered. According to him, both peoples possessed 'a great uprightness of mind and an enviable simplicity of heart, an exquisite sentiment of morality . . .'[30]

THE ARNOLDS

The contrasts between Thomas and Matthew Arnold provide an instructive example of the changes that were taking place in English racism in the 19th century. Dr Thomas Arnold was preoccupied in the 1820s and 30s with the conflicts between Teuton and Gael – including Gallo-Roman – and notably those between the English and the French and Irish. He was proud to be known as 'that Teuton of Teutons, the Celt-hating Dr Arnold'.[31] His son Matthew in the 1850s, 60s and 70s favoured both the Irish and the French, believing that he had transcended his father's narrow-mindedness.[32] Fully aware of the new linguistic advances, he was a systematic supporter of Indo-Europeans and Aryans. He loved them all. Indeed, leading another school of mid-19th-century English thought, he was even enthusiastic about the Gypsies or Bohemians. These Indo-European speakers were now seen, rather like Winckelmann's Greeks, as gay, charming, feckless, childish – yet somehow philosophical – Aryan cousins. They were the lighter side of Indo-European culture.[33]

Matthew Arnold recognized that Renan, after his own father, was the greatest intellectual influence on his life.[34] He had accepted Renan's belief – shared by most advanced thinkers of the time – that the fundamental divide in world history was between Hellene and Hebrew, between Aryan and Semite.[35] However, he was faced with a problem which did not affect the continental racists: he was forced to recognize the validity of their charge that the English shared qualities with the Semites. Furthermore, as I have mentioned, Britain had a philo-Semitic tradition which became particularly strong with the rise of the bourgeoisie in the mid-19th century. Thus many Victorians saw themselves as biblical patriarchs, priding themselves on their diligence, thrift, discretion, respect for forms and – above all – their sense of rigid righteousness.

Arnold was tormented by this affinity, which cut across linguistic and racial lines. His explanation for the anomaly was that the English 'Hebraic' spirit was chiefly the result of the Reformation and of Puritanism. That is, the division between Hellene and Hebrew was that of the Civil War, the continuing struggle between High and Low

Church, Church and Chapel, and between the industrialized north and
the agricultural south.[36] Like Renan, Matthew Arnold claimed to
recognize many virtues in the 'Hebraic' tradition; nevertheless, he
called upon England to turn away from the bourgeois philistinism of the
latter-day Puritans and look towards the Greeks. The Greeks –
following the major tradition, that of Winckelmann – he saw as
spontaneous, light, artistic and serene. But – as a man of the 19th
century – Arnold also added clear thinking and a unique capacity for
philosophy. By turning towards the Hellenic spirit, England could join
the progress of her European neighbours. Arnold's ultimate appeal,
made in his famous *Culture and Anarchy*, was to race: 'Hellenism is
of Indo-European growth. Hebraism is of Semitic growth, and we
English, a nation of Indo-European stock, seem to belong naturally
to the movement of Hellenism.'[37]

Although Victorian Hellenism was a vital and complex movement
with many facets, there is no doubt that all images of Greece after
Matthew Arnold published *Culture and Anarchy* in 1869 were developed
in relation or reaction to his restatement of German Neo-Hellenism.
Where Dr Arnold's love of Greece meshed with his Protestantism,
Teutonism and anti-Semitism, his son's Hellenism was explicitly
linked to the vision of the Indo-European or Aryan race in a perpetual
struggle with the Semitic one, or to the conflict between 'cultivated' and
bourgeois values. And in this, of course, he was following a well-beaten
path. In theory – like Michelet, Renan and others – he accepted, as
Bunsen put it, that 'If the Hebrew Semites are the priests of humanity,
the Helleno-Roman Aryans are, and ever will be, its heroes.'[38] All, however, clearly felt that in granting the Semites religion they were granting
them too much. As Matthew Arnold noted in a letter to his mother:

> Bunsen used to say that our great business was to get rid of all that
> was purely Semitic in Christianity and to make it Indo-Germanic,
> and Schleiermacher that in the Christianity of us Western nations
> there was really much more of Plato and Sokrates than of Joshua and
> David; and on the whole Papa worked in the direction of these ideas
> of Bunsen and Schleiermacher and was perhaps the only powerful
> Englishman of his day who did so.[39]

Without wishing to detract from Dr Arnold's pioneering spirit on this issue, it will be remembered that in 1825 Thirlwall had translated Schleiermacher's *St Luke*, which contained many of these ideas. What is more, in France Victor Cousin had been proclaiming the Hellenic nature of Christianity as early as 1818.[40]

While one cannot always blame fathers for the sins of their sons, it is interesting to note that during the 1870s Bunsen's son Ernst invented a form of Aryan sun worship, based on biblical tradition, in which Adam was Aryan and the serpent Semitic![41] By the end of the century there had been a number of different attempts to found an Aryan or Germanic Christianity. The most successful of these was created by the fringe academic Semitist and passionate German nationalist Paul Lagarde. Lagarde argued that Jesus had been an 'Aryan Jew' from Galilee who had been crucified by the 'Semitic Jews' of Judaea. To make matters worse, Christianity had been taken over and perverted by another Jew, Paul, and there was thus a need to strip the true Aryan religion of its Semitic excrescences. Lagarde was a passionate anti-Semite who called repeatedly for the destruction of Judaism and the exile of the Jews in Madagascar, which later became one of Hitler's schemes. Lagarde's movement in general has been convincingly described as one of the sources of Nazism.[42]

In England, things were never so crude. Even so, towards the end of the century there was a desire to strip the Semites of their one contribution to humanity. One of the chief themes of Hardy's *Tess of the d'Urbervilles*, first published in 1891, is the conflict between the true, ever-vital Saxon England in its heartland of Wessex, and the decadent French descendants of the conquerors. However, Hardy's Germanism was also linked to Hellenism, which he saw as battling with the Semitism and the philistinism of the new bourgeoisie. The hero, Angel Clare, wants to return to the land and wed a pure Saxon maid. At the same time, he has the Dionysian qualities of one of Winckelmann's Greeks: he likes dancing, eating and drinking and generally frolicking in the blissful countryside. Angel's father and brothers are archetypal Semites: moral, upright, and completely out of touch with nature and life. Hardy describes the crucial moment of their conflict in these terms:

Once upon a time Angel had been so unlucky as to say to his father
... that it might have been better for mankind if Greece had been the
source of religion for modern civilization and not Palestine, and his
father's grief was of that blank description which could not realize
that there might work a thousandth part of truth, much less a half
truth or a whole truth, in such a proposition.[43]

Here, then, though he did not share their love of the Gaels, Hardy
aligned himself with Matthew Arnold and Renan.

PHOENICIANS AND ENGLISH, 1:
THE ENGLISH VIEW

Despite the association between the English and the Semites, no one
compared the English to the Arabs or the Ethiopians. The 'Semites'
they had in mind were Jews and/or Phoenicians, and in this part of the
chapter we will concentrate on the identification with the Phoenicians.
While Michelet's discussion of the perpetual war between the Indo-
Europeans and Semites focused on the conflict between Rome and
Carthage, the parallels between Carthage and England were very clear
for 19th-century readers on both sides of the Channel. Many Victorians
had a positive feeling towards the Phoenicians as sober cloth merchants
who did a little bit of slaving on the side and spread civilization while
making a tidy profit. Thus William Gladstone, who came from very
much this kind of mercantile background, was an ardent champion of
the Phoenicians.[44] This many seem surprising in view of his passion for
Homer's aristocratic values, his love for European Greece, and his
hatred for Asiatic Turkey.[45] Such enthusiasms, however, were quite
compatible in the 1840s, when Gladstone's future rival, Disraeli, was
proclaiming the superiority of the Semitic race. And as late as 1889, the
respected historian G. Rawlinson produced a very favourable history of
Phoenicia in which he described the Phoenicians as 'the people who of
all Antiquity had the most in common with England and the English.'[46]
    There was also a widespread – and quite reasonable – belief that the
Phoenicians had come to Cornwall to trade for tin, and Matthew Arnold
seems to have seen this as an early source of English Hebraism. In his

famous poem beginning 'Some grave Tyrian trader . . .', the Phoenician slips shyly away from the new Greek master race, 'the young light-hearted masters of the wave'. The Phoenician is then driven out of the Mediterranean to the Atlantic and Britain, and the same sympathy for the doomed Phoenician appears over fifty years later in 'Death By Water' in T. S. Eliot's *The Waste Land*:

> Phlebas the Phoenician, a fortnight dead,
> Forgot the cry of gulls and the deep sea swell
> And the profit and loss.
>   A current under sea
> Picked his bones in whispers. As he rose and fell
> He passed the stages of his age and youth
> Entering the whirlpool.
>   Gentile or Jew
> O you who turn the wheel and look to windward,
> Consider Phlebas, who was once handsome and tall as you.[47]

The Waste Land belongs to the 'post-Bérard' era, which I shall discuss in the next chapter. Nevertheless, it is indicative of longer-term Anglo-Saxon attitudes as well, in its relating Phoenicians to their own activities on the sea and in banking. Its ambiguity on the Phoenicians' Semitic nature is also telling, for if Semites were the epitome of parasitism and passivity, then the Phoenicians – who were active in sailing, manu-facture and trade rather than the Jewish 'financing' – could not have been truly Semitic.

In extreme old age, Gladstone felt the need to defend his beloved Phoenicians from the now crippling charge of being Semitic: 'I have always believed that the Phoenicians were at bottom a non-Semitic stock.'[48] Indeed, by the beginning of the 20th century Britain was quickly catching up with the rest of Europe in its anti-Semitism, and attitudes to the Phoenicians became even more complicated. Belief that Britain could have a special connection with even marginal Semites became increasingly suspect. So to look for it, as Sherlock Holmes intended to do during his retirement in Cornwall, was now considered the epitome of crankiness. On the other hand, even the attribution of crankiness implies a certain fondness for the notion and for the

Phoenicians; very different attitudes towards them had developed elsewhere in Europe.

PHOENICIANS AND ENGLISH, 2:
THE FRENCH VIEW

Michelet's implicit – and ultimately comforting – analogy between the French and the Romans, and the English and the Carthaginians, has been mentioned above. Elsewhere, however, he was explicit:

> Human pride personified in a people, that is England. What happens when the barbarians (Normans and Danes) are transplanted to this powerful island, where they become fat on the richness of the land and the tribute of the ocean? Kings of the sea, of the world without law and without limit, uniting the savage hardness of the Danish pirate and the feudal arrogance of the 'Lord' son of the Normans . . . How many Tyres and Carthages would one have to pile up to reach the insolence of titanic England?[49]

The ferocity behind this analogy can be seen from his references to the Phoenicians: 'The Carthaginians, like the Phoenicians from which they came, appear to have been a people who were hard and sad, sensual and greedy, and adventurous without heroism.' After this splendid example of having it both ways, he continued with the view that 'at Carthage too the religion was atrocious and full of frightful practices.'[50]

The damning parallels between the English and the Phoenicians in general, and the Carthaginians in particular, remained a strand in French thinking throughout the 19th century. This contrast can be seen from the fact that when Gladstone said that the Phoenicians were not Semites, he meant that they were better than Jews. For most French and German writers, on the other hand, they were much worse, and here it would be useful to consider Gobineau's attitudes towards the Phoenicians. Gobineau is important for two reasons: he had a considerable influence on French and German thought as well as on Matthew Arnold, and he seems to have expressed, in extreme form, many views that friends of his like de Tocqueville and Renan held, but did not dare publish.

The position of the Phoenicians in Gobineau's scheme of the three invasions of the Hamites, Semites and Japhetites, or Aryans, was complicated. The Bible clearly placed them as descendants of Ham but, as we saw in Chapter III, scholars have known about the extremely close relationships between Phoenician and Hebrew at least since the 17th century.[51] For Gobineau in the 19th century, this linguistic affiliation was both crucial and distressing. The powerful combination of biblical tradition, his reluctance to have the holy language too closely related to that of the Phoenicians, and his mixed – but in many ways positive – attitude towards the Jews impelled him to portray the Phoenicians as Hamites and not as Semites. Thus the only way for Gobineau to reconcile the biblical and linguistic sources was through outright falsehood. In 1815, the great German Semitist Wilhelm Gesenius had divided the Semitic languages into three subfamilies: (1) Aramaic and Syriac; (2) Canaanite, including Hebrew and Phoenician, from which came Punic; and (3) Arabic, from which he derived Ethiopic.[52] At another point, however, Gesenius had mentioned that Phoenician had been spread to the widespread Phoenician colonies and markets, and Gobineau cited this page to claim that Gesenius had classified the Semitic languages into four categories:

> The first contains Phoenician, Punic and Libyan, from which the Berber dialects are derived; the second Hebrew and its variations; the third . . . Aramaic . . . the fourth, Arabic . . .[53]

Apart from the separation of Phoenician and Hebrew, the linguistic outrage in this classification is Gobineau's derivation of Phoenician from the Berber languages. No Semitist, then or now, would accept these as Semitic. However, both violations were essential to his scheme in order to define the Phoenicians as Hamitic, according to the biblical pattern. That is, their initial 'white' nature had allowed them to establish a certain degree of civilization, but by the time the Semites arrived from the north-east the Phoenicians had become virtually 'black' and were therefore responsible for the corruption of the Jews: 'At the time of Abraham, Hamite civilization was in a full bloom in its perfection and in its vices.'[54]

Gobineau spent much more time on the vices than on the perfection.

Near the beginning of the whole work, and using the images of rats and disease that the Nazis applied to the Jews, he asked the rhetorical question: 'Did the Phoenicians owe their downfall to the corruption that gnawed at them and which they spread everywhere? No, quite the contrary, their corruption was the chief instrument of their power and their glory.'[55] To what extent, then, did Gobineau have England in mind when he wrote this? Gobineau knew English well and frequently cited English sources, and he dedicated his *Essay on the Inequality of Human Races* to the English-born king of Hanover. Nevertheless, it is interesting to note that in all his travels around the world, from Scandinavia to Persia, Brazil and many other places, he never went across the Channel to England. Furthermore, Gobineau is strangely silent about the country that dominated the world of his time – and here there is a striking contrast with his bubbling enthusiasm for Germany.

Following his patron de Tocqueville, Gobineau obviously approved of the Anglo-Saxon sense of categorical superiority over the native Americans and Blacks in North America; he was equally scathing about the hypocrisy surrounding slavery.[56] He was much more concerned with and appalled by American immigration policies, and in this connection he compared New York unfavourably to Carthage, which had at least been settled by noble Canaanite families. Furthermore: 'Carthage gained everything that Tyre and Sidon lost. But Carthage has not added a jot to Semitic civilization, nor did it prevent its eventual fate.'[57] Elsewhere Gobineau compared the mercantile functions of Tyre and Sidon to London and Hamburg, and the manufacturing ones to Liverpool and Birmingham.[58] The analogy between the Anglo-Saxons and the Canaanites, and his dislike of both, would seem clear. Nevertheless, it is obvious that he detested the Hamites and the impure Semites in their own right. He saw the later Phoenicians as the result of a mixture of 'mulatto' Hamites and Semites, in which of course the latter, being more 'white', were superior. Yet, with the tragic irony which he found throughout history, the 'black' and inferior 'female' races conquered and corrupted the 'white', 'male' ones. Thus the Phoenicians created cities in which incredible luxury and splendour were mixed with barbarous customs; and above all there were the hideous religious rites, including prostitution and human sacrifice, which, he assured his readers, 'the white race has never practised'.[59]

In their government, the Phoenicians were not noble and free like the 'Whites', but ruled either by despots or by democratic mobs.[60] Worst of all was Carthage – without a history and founded after the Hamites had completely degenerated, and then exposed to still more African influence.[61] Gobineau saw the arrival of the Semites as a great step forward, but they too were seduced by 'black' culture, and in general he was torn in his attitudes towards the Jews. At times he argued that they had preserved some of their white nature; at others he maintained that the Hebrews changed from martial herdsmen into effeminate merchants.[62] But worst of all, they hired other peoples as mercenaries. About this practice Gobineau wrote:

> One of the principal characteristics of the degradation of the Hamites and the most apparent cause of their fall . . . was their loss of warrior courage and the practice of no longer taking part in military activities. This scandal, profound in Babylon and Nineveh, was hardly less in Tyre and Sidon . . .[63]

SALAMMBÔ

Michelet gave the same message in 1830, when describing the revolt of the Carthaginian mercenaries after their defeat in the First Punic War in 241 BC. Basing himself on Classical sources – mainly the Greek historian Polybios – Michelet gave a vivid report of this mutiny of an army that was extraordinarily mixed ethnically and was led by a Black, Matho, and a Greek, Spendios. It was defeated after campaigns of extraordinary violence and cruelty in which both the mercenaries and a number of their Carthaginian opponents were put to death in scenes of exceptional horror.[64]

Michelet's text became the basis for Gustave Flaubert's novel *Salammbô*. Flaubert had long been fascinated by the exoticism of the 'Orient'. He had been to Egypt, and after the success of *Madame Bovary* he had wanted to write a novel about that country called *Anubis*.[65] At some point before March 1857, however, he changed his mind and

decided to use the plot that eventually became *Salammbô*. The Italian
scholar Benedetto suggested that he dropped *Anubis* because
Théophile Gautier brought out a novel on Ancient Egypt in the same
year. But neither he nor other 'Flaubertians' have been able to
determine what caused Flaubert to choose his new topic.[66]

Despite the fact that it does not appear in his correspondence, the
answer would seem to be the 'Indian Mutiny' which broke out in
February that year. Britain – the great empire of the modern Phoenicians – had succeeded, through its greed and brutality and by its use of
beef and pork fat on cartridges which had to be licked by the soldiers, in
the difficult task of uniting its Hindu and Moslem mercenaries in revolt
against it. Even at its outbreak it became clear that the 'Mutiny' was
being fought on both sides with exceptional ferocity and cruelty. Thus
the parallel between England and Carthage was in *Salammbô* from its
inception.

In May 1861, when Flaubert felt that his book was ready for his
friends, he invited the famous Parisian literary figures the Goncourt
brothers to come to a reading with the following programme:

> 1. I begin to shout at 4 o'clock punctually, sometimes about 3
> o'clock.
> 2 At 7 o'clock, Eastern dinner. You'll be served human flesh,
> bourgeois brains, tigress's clitoris fried in rhinoceros butter.
> 3. After the coffee, a resumption of the Punic bawling until after the
> listeners croak.[67]

Baudelaire, the poet of decadence, was a particular friend while
Flaubert was writing the novel, and *Salammbô* is a study in decadence.[68] From the viewpoint of the French upper class in the 1850s,
Flaubert had chosen the most decadent aspect (mercenaries) of the
most decadent city (Carthage) and of the most decadent people (the
Phoenicians). Or, to put it another way, he pictured the accumulation of
all the opposites of decent masculine white society: the ethnic potpourri
of mercenaries led by a Black on the one hand and a Greek who was
a traitor to his race on the other; against the Carthaginians, who
were themselves seen as a hideous mixture of Negroes, Hamites and
Semites; with a luxurious subtropical background containing priests,

eunuchs and sensuous, corrupting women; all locked in cruel and frightful conflict.

There was, as I have said, genuine historical material with which to build up such a case. Flaubert reinforced his reading of Michelet and Polybios with a trip to the site of Carthage; but also, and much more importantly, he used material from the latest French Orientalist scholarship, notably that of Renan. Following this, he became fully aware of the close cultural relations between all Canaanite speakers, and used biblical information about the Israelites and their neighbours to eke out the meagre material available about the Phoenicians and Carthaginians.[69]

Benedetto, writing in 1920, showed that Flaubert's reconstruction had stood the test of later scholarship quite well.[70] Despite the fact that Benedetto was associated with the exceptionally anti-Semitic School of Classics in Rome and was writing at a period of intense racialism and general anti-Semitism, much of what the Italian claimed would still seem true today.[71] Where I do think Flaubert was fundamentally misleading, however, was in two of his implications. One was that Carthage in the 3rd century BC was in some way typical of Oriental culture; hence not only did it deserve the genocide it received from the Romans ninety years later, but there was little moral objection to the colonial destructions of non-European civilizations in the 19th century. (Here, moreover, we have another reason why Flaubert dropped his scheme of writing on Ancient Egypt, which was far too lacking in vice and cruelty for his purposes.)

Secondly, Flaubert implied that Europeans – with the possible exception of the English – were incapable of such things. In fact, the Romans outdid the Carthaginians in virtually every luxury and outrage, while the Macedonians were not far behind. And in specifics, the Carthaginian Mercenary War in the 3rd century BC, with its social revolutionary component, was comparable to the Roman War – less than 200 years later – against the armies of slaves led by Spartacus, which were fought and exterminated with equal horror.[72] Flaubert's own society, the France of the Second Empire, was inflicting incredible outrages on the populations of China and Indo-China and, even more to the point, on those of Algeria. In some ways, furthermore, the exploitation, luxury and corruption of *Salammbô*'s Carthage were very similar to the same features in Flaubert's Paris, as described so vividly in the novels of Émile Zola.[73]

Salammbô was an immense success. When Flaubert had tried to portray French bourgeois life realistically in *Madame Bovary*, his book had been mutilated by the publisher and he was put on trial for 'outraging public morals'. *Salammbô* was far more scabrous in every respect, but this time it made Flaubert the lion of Parisian high society and enabled him to become a friend of the Imperial family.[74] Flaubert had hit a literary jackpot; his 'realism' applied to the 'Orient' allowed readers to get their sexual and sadistic thrills, while maintaining their sense of innate and categorical superiority as white Christians. It also increased the urgency of France's *mission civilisatrice* to save the peoples of other continents from their own cruelty and wickedness.[75]

MOLOCH

Flaubert made much of one horrific aspect of Carthaginian culture shared by neither the Romans nor the 19th-century Europeans. It was the special sacrifice of children either through cutting the throat, or burning, or both. Following the exegetical tradition of the time, he referred to it as a sacrifice to the terrible god Moloch. It has since been established that the root √mlk in this case refers not to a divinity but to the name of the sacrifice itself.[76] In Carthage the victims were meant to be the sons of the ruling families but Flaubert, following Classical sources, recounted that some of the rich obtained substitutes from the children of the poor or of slaves.[77] Here, though he added gruesome details of his own, he was following Greek and Roman historians; and here too the later excavation, at Carthage and many of its colonies, of hundreds of urns full of burnt children's bones and dedicated to the God Ba'al would seem to confirm his reconstruction.[78]

There is no doubt that in both the Jewish and Christian traditions, this child sacrifice was felt to be the ultimate abomination. The huge success of *Salammbô*, in France and in the rest of Europe – which partly resulted from its depiction of Moloch – reopened the biblical horror with extraordinary force. For many this feeling extended to a complete condemnation of the society that practised it, and provided powerful ammunition for all those who hated Carthage and the Phoenicians with their Jewish and English associations.

Furthermore, there is no doubt that such feelings extended into academia. Nearly all 20th-century historians of Carthage and Phoenicia have had to take Flaubert into account.[79] On the Jewish side, *Salammbô* and its emphasis on Moloch would seem to have revived and intensified the biblical and religious hatred of the Canaanites and their abominations, and to have led even non-religious and assimilated Jews to keep their distance from the Canaanites and Phoenicians.

In 1870, the chief enemy of Carthage and England changed. France went into the Franco–Prussian War as an empire and emerged as a republic, while the King of Prussia came out of it as the Emperor of Germany. Many Germans now believed that the mantle of the Holy Roman Empire and of Rome itself had fallen upon them. Even in the 18th century, Herder is reported as having said that Carthage was so flawed by its abominations that it should be compared to a jackal which the Roman she-wolf should destroy; by the late 19th century the deserved destruction of the city was a platitude.[80] Great stress was laid upon the finality of the Roman Destruction of the city. The sentence 'Carthage, which was destroyed by the Romans, was never rebuilt' – incidentally, completely untrue – appears to have been a commonplace expression.[81]

This principle – of a final solution – was extended in propaganda towards England in the two World Wars, and in actuality towards the Jews in the Holocaust.[82] In this, however, I am going ahead of myself into the period of intense 'racial' anti-Semitism after the 1880s, and here we should consider mid-19th-century attitudes towards the idea of Phoenician settlement in Greece.

THE PHOENICIANS IN GREECE: 1820–80

K. O. Müller, who denied the Phoenician role in the formation of Greece, was probably anti-Semitic.[83] As we have seen, however, his attack on Kadmos was not generally accepted at the time. In fact, with

the decline of admiration for the Egyptians there was increased interest
and respect for the Phoenicians. The change was reflected in F. C.
Movers' *The Phoenicians*, which appeared during the 1840s, whose huge
volumes were based on the compilation of every Classical and biblical
reference to the people. Like Julius Beloch in the 19th and Rhys
Carpenter in the 20th century – whose careers we shall consider in the
next chapters – Movers tended to attribute Phoenician dynamism to
northern influences, and especially those from the Assyrians.[84] Like
many later historians he had a great admiration for this brutal culture,
which is often portrayed as in some way less 'Semitic' than its purely
Semitic language would suggest. In the 19th century, Assyrian military
prowess was credited to 'white' influences.[85] On the other hand, if the
Semites lost credit to the north and east, they gained it to the south. As
far as the presence of Phoenicians in Greece was concerned, not only
did Movers accept all the credit given to the Phoenicians by the
Ancients, but he also annexed that of the 'Egyptian' Danaos. This
position can to some extent be justified by the real complexity of the
mixed culture of Lower Egypt in the Hyksos period. However, as his
admirer Michael Astour puts it, Movers had grasped this point by
'intuition rather than with the aid of the evidence at his disposal'.[86]
Thus we should judge his conclusion historiographically – and in this
way it fits the era following the fall of the Egyptians, but before that of
the Phoenicians.

GOBINEAU'S IMAGE OF GREECE

This is also the period in which we should situate Gobineau's attitude to
the origins of Greece. Gobineau, as we saw, was working within the
Aryan Model, but in the 1850s the model was still very 'broad' and
allowed for Semitic influences. He analysed the Greeks in the following
way:

1. Hellenes – Aryans modified by yellow principles, but with a great
preponderance of white essence and some Semitic affinities.
2. Aborigines – Slav/Celts saturated with yellow elements.
3. Thracians – Aryans mixed with Celts and Slavs.

4. Phoenicians – Black Hamites.
5. Arabs and Hebrews – very mixed Semites.
6. Philistines – Semites, possibly more pure.
7. Libyans – almost black Hamites.
8. Cretans and other islanders – Semites similar to the Philistines.[87]

It is enough to make even the most stout-hearted racist throw up his hands in despair! Gobineau, however, persisted, though he found it impossible to be consistent in such a complex situation.

To say this of him is not to disparage him entirely. If one translates from 'race' to culture there is no doubt of the reality of some of the shifting mixtures involved. Gobineau was quite right to say: 'no country presents, in primitive epochs, such ethnic convulsions, such sudden displacements and multiple immigrations.'[88] Furthermore, his scheme has far greater explanatory value than the Extreme Aryan Model. He believed that the Greek Aborigines had been invaded from the north by the Aryan 'Titans' sometime in the 3rd millennium; at around the same time, however, they had been invaded from the south by Canaanites, whom he saw both as Semitic Arabs and Hebrews and as black Phoenicians.[89] He followed Movers in seeing the Phoenicians as having gained their civilization from Assyria, which had white elements.[90]

Given the corruption of Greek blood by black Phoenicians, the issue of whether or not there had been Egyptian colonies was not very important to Gobineau. Nevertheless, he accepted the recent scholarship that had denied the existence of Egyptian colonies in Greece.[91] While he followed Schlegel's theory that the greatness of Egyptian civilization had come from Indian colonization, he also believed that the racial mongrelization of the Egyptian population – which included considerable black and even Negroid elements – had given the country a static and passive nature.[92] For Gobineau saw Greek history as a struggle between the Aryan Greek spirit based to the north of Thebes, and the Semitic spirit of the south, both being reinforced by their racial cousins from outside the country.[93] In this way he had no problem with the traditions of Kadmos and Danaos or with the excellence of the Dorians.[94]

It must be noted, however, that despite his enthusiasm for the

character and institutions of the Aryan Hellenes, Gobineau was convinced that Ancient Greece as a whole had been thoroughly 'blackened'
and 'Semitized'. He was among those who maintained that the modern
Greeks were so mongrelized that they could no longer be considered as
descendants of the Ancients.[95] Indeed, his belief in the Phoenician
influence on Greece was part of his general belief that Southern Europe
had been irredeemably 'Semitized' and that only the Germanic peoples
of the north had retained their 'white' purity.[96] In this, however, he was
clearly in the minority. While they were coming to share his views on
Aryan superiority, most Northern Europeans were not prepared to give
up Greece and Rome.

All in all, there was increasing reluctance to believe in the Phoenician
settlements. We have seen in the last chapter how Grote avoided the
issue; how Bunsen and Curtius wriggled around the legends; and
how William Smith and George Rawlinson equivocated on them.[97]
Others, however, though they would not go as far as Gobineau, still
saw no reason to doubt the Ancient Model where it touched on the
Phoenicians. As Gladstone wrote in 1869:

> . . . a further prosecution of the subject with respect to the Phoeni-
> cians has brought out much more clearly and fully what I had only
> ventured to suspect or hint at, and gives them, if I am right, a highly
> influential function in forming the Greek nation. The detection, if it
> be a real one, of these powerful Semitic influences, both in the
> Greece of Homer and as they had operated before his time, opens a
> new perspective into the ancient history of the world.[98]

SCHLIEMANN AND THE DISCOVERY
OF THE 'MYCENAEANS'

Of course Gladstone was primarily a politician and not an academic;
therefore his views were not completely up to date. However, it is
noteworthy that his remarks came just before Heinrich Schliemann's
startling discoveries at Mycenae and Tiryns in the 1870s. Schliemann
himself insisted that he had 'gazed upon the face of Agamemnon', and
that the remains were those of the Homeric heroes, who were of course

Greek. Initially, however, his finds had exactly the opposite effect. They strengthened the hands of those who maintained that there had been significant Phoenician influence in Greece.

The Mycenaean finds were certainly very unlike any previous notion of Greek art, and it was generally agreed that they were ugly. Therefore it was variously assumed that they were Byzantine, Gothic, or – most commonly of all – Oriental; and in the last case either imports or made in Greece by Eastern craftsmen or their Greek apprentices.[99]

The obvious conclusion, then, was that these were traces of the Phoenician colonists of the Greek tradition. As the eminent German ancient historian Max Dunker wrote in 1880:

> The examination of the most ancient monuments on the soil of Greece has afforded proof of an extensive commerce of the Phoenicians on the coasts of the country; not only the objects found within the monuments, but the monuments themselves, spoke incontestably in favour of the influence, and therefore of the presence, of Phoenicians in Greece. There are further traces, signs, and remains of Phoenician settlements on Greek soil, and of Phoenician influence on the Greeks. The Greek tradition itself tells us of the city and dominion which a Phoenician king's son founded in their land. This is the only settlement of which it speaks: but *we are in a position to prove that there existed a whole series of Phoenician colonies on the coast of Hellas*. (my emphasis)[100]

Other German scholars, like the historian of Greece Adolf Holm, disagreed. Holm, who avowedly saw the Greeks as an 'exceptionally high type of humanity', followed Ernst Curtius' 'most recent scientific revision of the traditionary epoch'. Writing in the 1880s, he set out his own view of the scholarly dilemma:

> Of late a decided reaction has set in against the popular theory of the great influence exercised by the Phoenicians on Greece, which is perfectly justifiable, but it is not always to the point. *The real reason why people contest the existence of Phoenicians in Greece is that they object to make the Greeks indebted to Phoenicia for anything of importance.* We believe we have proved that the widespread influence ascribed to

them ... originates solely in caprice. But why should there be a reluctance to admit the existence of mere settlements of Phoenicians in Greece, *when supported by historical criteria which are considered valid in other cases? Phoenicians were once there, but their influence was inconsiderable.* (my emphasis)[101]

Holm's words show with wonderful clarity the outside pressures on the ancient historians, and the reason for the compromise taken by scholars like Connop Thirlwall in the 1830s and Frank Stubbings in the 1960s.[102] However, it was not acceptable in the high tide of imperialism and anti-Semitism from 1885 to 1945, which was also the period of the professionalization of Classical archaeology.

The tone that was to predominate throughout that period had already been set. As a writer put it in the first issue of *The American Journal of Archaeology* in 1885:

> The Phoenicians, so far as we know, did not bring a single fructifying idea into the world ... their arts ... hardly deserve to be called arts; they were for the most part only traders. Their architecture, sculpture, painting were of the most unimaginative sort. Their religion, so far as we know it, was entirely an appeal to the senses.[103]

BABYLON

By the 1880s, however, there was a new type of less objectionable 'Semite'. Since the beginning of the century there had been considerable interest in the ancient ruins of Mesopotamia, while the sympathy of men like Movers and Gobineau for the Assyrians, who conquered and slaughtered in a very 'unSemitic' way, has been mentioned above. Furthermore, the 1840s and 50s saw the gradual decipherment of the cuneiform scripts in which Old Persian, the Assyrian and Babylonian dialects of Akkadian, and the ancient non-Semitic language Sumerian were written. The decipherment generated great scholarly excitement, which intensified over the following decades as Akkadian texts with striking biblical parallels began to be read.[104] With the increasing secularization of the 1870s and 80s, these texts were welcomed as providing a background for the Old Testament. They could also be used to confirm the belief that the culture of the West Semites – the Jews and Phoenicians – was, as one would expect from Semites, essentially derivative, and had come from the much older Babylonian civilization. This tendency became greater still in the 1890s, when it was established to everyone's satisfaction that Mesopotamian civilization had been created not by Semites but by the Sumerians, and that 'when the Semites appeared in Babylonia, civilization was fully developed.'[105]

Scholars who, for various reasons, wanted to avoid giving credit to the Phoenicians began to attribute irreducible Semitic elements in Greek and other European cultures to the Assyrians and Babylonians.[106] Even here, however, there was the problem that the normal route of transmission would be by sea, through Phoenicia – or at least North Syria. Indeed, from the late 19th century there has been a tendency to attribute Oriental influences on Greece to Anatolia, whose 'Asianic' populations were not Semitic-speaking. Ancient tradition does refer to Greek contacts with Asia Minor, and it was from there that Pelops was supposed to have conquered much of Southern Greece. According to the Ancient Model, however, this conquest was consistently placed after those of Kadmos and Danaos, and Pelops was not given the credit for any cultural innovations – apart from chariot-racing. After the language of the ancient Anatolian empire of the Hittites was discovered to be related to Indo-European in 1912, it was taken up with much enthusiasm by German Orientalists. Both they and Classicists have attempted to give Anatolians as much credit as possible for 'Oriental' influence on Greece. For instance, the British Classicist and historian P. Walcot, whose important work *Hesiod and the Near East* was published in 1966, devotes his first chapter to the Hittites, and his second to the Babylonians; however, neither of these – in striking contrast to the Egyptians and Phoenicians – are mentioned in Antiquity as sources of Greek mythology and religion.[107] Indeed, in the years with which the next chapter is concerned – 1885 to 1945 – what little scholarly attention there was on Oriental influences on Greece concenrated on the transmission of Babylonian influence to Greece overland, avoiding Syria and following the German preference for land rather than sea transport and communication. It is to this period that we shall now turn.

CHAPTER IX

THE FINAL SOLUTION
OF THE PHOENICIAN PROBLEM,
1885–1945

THIS CHAPTER IS CONCERNED with the consolidation of the Aryan Model and the denial of both Egyptian and Phoenician influence on the formation of Greece. The denial of Phoenician influence is clearly related to the strong anti-Semitism of the period, and in particular to its two climaxes or paroxysms – in the 1880s and 90s and the 1920s and 30s. The first of these followed the mass migration of East European Jews into Western Europe and crystallized around the Dreyfus Affair; the second came after the critical role of Jews in international Communism and the Russian Revolution and during the economic crises of the 1920s and 30s.

In the 1890s in scholarship, initial salvos against traditions of Phoenician colonization were fired by an. assimilated French Jew, Salomon Reinach, and a German exile in Italy, Julius Beloch. These were followed by a lull during which the great French scholar Victor Bérard had a great success in promoting his ideas of a fundamental Semitic penetration of Greece among the lay public – but not among his Classical colleagues.

In the same period, however, Arthur Evans' sensational discoveries in Crete, and his differentiation of the 'Minoans' from the Semitic speakers who had previously been thought to have been the native

population of the island, encouraged great interest in the 'Pre-Hellenic'
populations of the Aegean. All aspects of Greek culture that could
not be explained in terms of Indo-European were attributed to this
mysterious 'Minoan' people, allowing Greece to be culturally self-
sufficient and removing any need to explain developments in terms of
influences from the Near East.

In the 1920s this rejection of any Semitic influence in the Aegean
included a strikingly successful attempt to diminish the importance of
the one Phoenician borrowing that could not be denied: the alphabet.
Indeed, by 1939 supporters of the Extreme Aryan Model dominated
the field to such an extent that for someone to suggest that the legends
about the Phoenicians in Greece contained a kernel of truth meant an
immediate loss of scholarly status.

THE GREEK RENAISSANCE

It was only in the late 1880s that Schliemann's views on the nationality
of the 'Mycenaeans' began to be accepted, and their remains began
to be labelled as European; the most active proponent of the new
classification was the Greek archaeologist C. Tsountas.

Since the establishment of independence, Greek intellectuals had
made a heroic effort to return their country to its 'Hellenic' past.
Classical place names were revived and Turkish, Venetian and even
Byzantine buildings were levelled to reveal ancient ruins. At the same
time, 19th-century Greeks could not claim that Greeks had always been
like the idealized image of 5th-century Athenians. Thus the Hellenic
genius, though constantly shaped by its past and by the Greek climate
and landscape, was seen to have taken many forms, while preserving its
national essence. With this background, then, it is not surprising that
Tsountas was excited by the new discoveries, which could be interpreted as showing that Greek genius was not limited to its Classical
form, but could have others which were equally genuine.

Tsountas was convinced that the Mycenaean remains were traces of
Greek antecedents of Classical civilization, and strongly denied that they
had anything to do with the Orient. 'This indigenous art, distinct and
homogeneous in character, must have been wrought out by a strong and

gifted race. That it was of Hellenic stock we have taken to be self-evident.'[1] At other points, however, he did attempt to prove his case. In 1891 the *American Journal of Archaeology* published a summary of one of his articles:

> Dr Tsountas' conclusions are unfavourable to the Asiatic origin of Mycenaean civilization. His main points are as follows: (1) The representation of divinities may be explained according to Greek ideas; (2) At Mykenai and Tiryns, there are no remains of eatable fishes but there are oysters, and the Greeks of Homer were not ichthyophagous, while there is one word in the Arian tongues to designate the oyster; (3) The Mycenaeans are connected on the one hand with the Italiotes and other Arians, and, on the other, with the Greeks of the historic period whose civilization is a continuation of theirs; (4) The type of Mycenaean house is adopted for a rainy climate and was imported from the north.[2]

The error in the first point has been touched on in the Introduction, and will be treated at length in the other two volumes. The second is too tenuous to assess. The third is circular, and in any event was completely outdated by the discovery of 'Minoan' civilization in Crete. It is difficult to say what the fourth was based upon, as pitched roofs occur throughout Syria and flat ones appear to have been the most common in the Bronze Age Aegean. All in all, very few ancient historians or archaeologists would take these arguments seriously today, though nearly all would accept the conclusions Tsountas ostensibly drew from them.

Support for Semitic influence on Greece did not disappear immediately. More common sense prevailed at the popular level. An American textbook published in 1895 contained the following:

> The nucleus of fact in all these legends is probably this – that the European Greeks received the primary elements of their culture from the East, and this in two ways: first, directly through the settlement in Greece in prehistoric times of Semitic races, particularly the Phoenicians; and secondly indirectly, through Oriental Greeks who, settled on the shores of Asia Minor, in Crete and

Cyprus, and possibly lower Egypt, came into contact with peoples of Semitic or semi-Semitic race . . . and transmitted these germs of culture to their kinsmen in European Greece.[3]

By 1898, the independent scholar Robert Brown was fully aware of the issues involved. He attacked the 'Aryanists', who for a century had 'almost wholly ignored or denied the existence of that great mass of Semitic influence, which the Aryo-Semitic School hold is to be found throughout the length and breadth of Hellas.'[4] It is interesting that Brown's point of view, which had in fact been acceptable through much of the 19th century, now seemed eccentric and his whole book, read today, gives a sense of embattlement.

SALOMON REINACH

From the 1880s onwards the intellectual atmosphere of Europe was transformed by the triumph of racial anti-Semitism in Germany and Austria, and its sharp rise elsewhere. This change clearly had many causes, the most significant of which was the mass migration of East European Jews to Western Europe and America. They were used as a scapegoat for the sufferings of the urban workers, in building up an identification of the urban workers and the peasants with the capitalists and landowners against these 'aliens'. Anti-Semitism also gained from the secularization and loss of faith after the late 1850s, and the success of other types of racism.

The surge of racism was linked to imperialism and the sense of national solidarity built up in the metropolitan countries against the barbarous non-European 'natives'. Paradoxically, the 1880s and 90s were also the decades in which Europe and North America gained complete control of the world. The indigenous peoples of America and Australia had been largely exterminated, and those of Africa and Asia were totally subdued and humiliated; there was no reason for 'the White Man' to take them into any political account. In this respect anti-Semitism can be seen as a European luxury, to be indulged in only when there are no outside enemies.

This, then, was the situation in 1892 when the French polymath

Salomon Reinach wrote of Tsountas' writings: 'these ideas are in the air.'[5] The following year he himself published a key article along the same lines. The fact that Reinach should champion 'these ideas' shows that they were no longer the sole preserve of Romantics. Salomon Reinach and his distinguished brothers could hardly have been less Romantic. They came from a rich, assimilated Jewish family living in Paris, and Renan and other fashionable intellectuals were frequent visitors to their father's house. The brothers' attitude towards Judaism was complicated. Without religious education themselves, they believed that both it and Christianity were outdated superstitions. On the other hand, Salomon was concerned with preserving Jewish culture and was a patron of the *Revue des Études Juives* for many years. With his brother Joseph he was active in the Dreyfus case, being diametrically opposed to the Catholic Royalist forces behind the new anti-Semitism in France.[6]

Salomon Reinach was a scholar of extraordinary breadth and depth. His central interests, however, were in the new disciplines of archaeology and anthropology. Although he was knowledgeable about India and the Near East, his greatest concern was with the explosion of archaeological information coming from Northern, Central and Western Europe. Since he was always adamant that language could not be linked to physical type, his writings in the early 1890s were a double declaration of independence: of Europe from the *mirage oriental*, and of 'scientific' archaeology and anthropology from philology and its Romantic associations. In Reinach one can see both the virtues and the vices of 20th-century archaeology and Classics: the virtues are common sense and scepticism, while the vices are the requirement of proof – when it concerns your opponents – low dating, and contempt for the Ancients.

His long article 'Le mirage oriental' was a two-pronged attack on both India and the Semitic Near East. To use a military analogy of the type favoured by Reinach himself, the demotion of China, Egypt and the Turks had been achieved by an Indo-European–Semitic alliance. In the 1820s only K. O. Müller, whom Reinach described as 'always in advance of his times', had had the courage to discard Europe's allies.[7]

By 1885 Europe's conquest of the world was so complete that this courage had become commonplace and could now cast the Indians and the Semites aside.

When the history of the evolution of the historical sciences of the 19th century is told, it will be rightly emphasized that it was in the period from 1880 to 1890 that – timidly at first, but later with an assurance that was better and better justified by the facts – a reaction against the '*mirage oriental*' was set in motion; the revindication of the rights of Europe against the claims of Asia in the obscurity of the first civilizations.[8]

Reinach attacked the Indianist Romantics on three scores. First, he demonstrated that the attempts to link Indian to Greek mythology had failed. Secondly, on language, he cited the young linguist Ferdinand de Saussure, who had developed one of the ideas of the so-called Neo-Grammarians, who had seen themselves in general revolt against the older generation of scholars. Reinach maintained that Saussure had dethroned Sanskrit from its position as the oldest and purest Indo-European language; Saussure now identified 'Proto-Indo-European' as European and, specifically, with Lithuanian. Connected with this was the general shifting of the *Urheimat* of the Proto-Indo-European language family to the steppes of the Ukraine, or even to the Baltic.[9] In any event, and as his third point, Reinach insisted that the Indo-European speakers, if they ever had been a 'race', had been physically absorbed by the indigenous peoples of Europe and that the impressive prehistoric cultures of Western Europe were essentially autochthonous.[10]

The externalist reasons for Reinach's hostility to Aryan racism and his belief in the assimilative capacities of Europe are obvious. His attack on Semitic influences is more complicated. This would seem to be related to a desire to assure his own cultural identity as an assimilated European, with a consequent lack of Semitic cultural baggage. It may also have been partly derived from the new secular desire to distance European Jews from the Phoenicians and Carthaginians that we saw above in connection with Moloch. Apart from an assertion of his integrity, his support of Judaic studies should be seen as serving the double function of 'preserving for science by killing' that permeated all 19th-century natural science.

Reinach denied 'absolutely' that there had been any Semitic or 'Cushitic' (Egyptian) influence on Europe up to the later 'Metallic Age'. He did, however, admit that from the beginning of Phoenician commerce, which he put in the 13th century BC, 'Occidental civilization became . . . to a certain extent . . . tributary to that of the Orientals.'[11] Nevertheless, he maintained that the basis of the civilization had remained resolutely indigenous. Furthermore, he believed that the great prehistoric civilizations of Europe had influenced those of the Orient, and if scholars tried boldly enough this 'passage from the defensive to the offensive' would be successful.[12] Reinach agreed with Tsountas that Mycenaean civilization was European, as, he maintained, were similar cultures found around the Mediterranean and Black Sea; and he saw temporal and local differences as the results of superpositions of different tribes 'of the same stock which had reached different degrees of culture'.[13]

JULIUS BELOCH

Despite his radicalism, by admitting Semitic influence after 1300 BC Reinach had not returned all the way to K. O. Müller. This was achieved in the following year, 1894, by Julius Beloch in a short but immensely influential article, 'The Phoenicians on the Aegean Sea'.[14] Beloch was yet another German living in Rome. He taught at its university for fifty years, from 1879 to 1929, and like Humboldt, Niebuhr and Bunsen, he loved travelling in Italy and cataloguing its monuments; like them he remained 'impervious to Italian culture'.[15]

For all his success as a teacher and the massive volume of his publications, Beloch seems to have regarded himself as a failure condemned to exile. He appears to have been kept out of German academic life by the great German historian of Rome, Mommsen. Another reason for Beloch's inability to find a satisfactory position in Germany was that he was suspected, rightly or wrongly, of being Jewish. Despite – or more probably because of – this suspicion, he was not only a passionate German nationalist but also a virulent anti-Semite.[16]

Furthermore, he extended his anti-Semitism into his writing of history: 'A Negro who speaks English is not for that reason an Englishman, and a Jew who spoke Greek was as little a Greek as a Jew who speaks German passes today for German.'[17]

Julius Beloch wrote prodigiously on both Greek and Italian history, and he is best remembered and respected for his introduction of modern statistical methods into ancient history.[18] This application of hard treatment to soft – if not liquid – data went with a rigid requirement for proof, an ultra-critical approach to ancient sources and a passion for low dating. It also went with what I described in the Introduction as 'archaeological positivism', an absolute faith in archaeology as the one 'scientific' source of information on Antiquity. This in turn is related to the punning belief that dealing with objects somehow makes one 'objective', and Beloch and his successors have shown little sensitivity to the fact that archaeological interpretations can be just as susceptible to subjective influences as the interpretation of documents, linguistics and myths.

Professor Momigliano, in his essay on Beloch, refers to 'the implicit conflicts between his liberalism and his nationalism ... between his racism and his cult of numbers'.[19] While not denying the implicit contradictions, I believe that they are usually 'non-antagonistic'. If one broadens 'cult of numbers' to a positivist requirement of proof, these 'implicit conflicts' have been the staple of 19th- and 20th-century Classics. They make up the 'critical-genetic writing of history' for which the right-wing ancient historian Wilcken rightly praised Niebuhr.[20] Although Beloch was attacked by more liberal colleagues like Mommsen and Wilamowitz-Moellendorf – as he is now by Momigliano – his views were only an extreme version of those held by the discipline as a whole. Leaving aside for the moment his treatment of the Semites, few Classicists would disagree with his notion that 'science has nothing to do with mere possibility', which, like him, they combine with frequent use of the word 'probably'.[21]

Like most 20th-century Classicists, Beloch knew no Semitic language. Nevertheless, citing recent German scholarship, he felt able to deny Phoenician loans into Greek language and place names, however 'alluring' the correspondences might appear. For instance, he even denied the previously widely recognized relationships between the Jordan and the river name Iardanos, found in Crete and Elis; or between Mt Tabor in Israel and Mt Atabyrion in Rhodes.[22] He found Eduard Meyer – himself a stalwart German nationalist – useful in this respect. Meyer was like Adolf Holm in that while radical in his purging of Semitic influences from Greece, he did not deny the Phoenician settlements in the Aegean. Thus he could be cited as objective on the issue.[23] Beloch followed K. O. Müller in attributing the Greek and Near Eastern references to common cultic origins to contacts in late Classical or Hellenistic times.[24]

Beloch took from another scholar the idea that the Phoenicians could not have taught the Greeks to make ships, because there were supposed to be no Semitic loans among Greek nautical terms. Hence they could not have arrived early in the Aegean.[25] This argument is doubly misleading. In the first place, the presence of Phoenicians in the Aegean in, say, the 2nd millennium does not mean that the Proto-Greeks before then lacked ships; secondly, there are, as it happens, a number of quite plausible Semitic etyma for Greek nautical terms which have no known Indo-European roots. Although everybody had conceded the Egyptian origin for *baris* (skiff), Beloch and his contemporaries did not consider the possibility of other Egyptian roots in this semantic area. In actuality these can explain an equally large number of the terms, which would tally well with the fact that the earliest detailed representations of boats from the Aegean, those from the mid-2nd-millennium murals at Thera, are clearly of Egyptian types.[26]

Beloch also maintained that Phoenician boats had been too small and inexpertly sailed to brave the open sea. Thus, while they might have been able to creep along the coast to North Africa, they could not have reached the Aegean before the 8th century. Apart from the massive ancient tradition to the contrary, there is now overwhelming archaeological evidence to suggest that they did.[27] Here, like most Extreme Aryanists, Beloch naturally preferred to attribute any unavoidable Oriental influences to, or at least through, Anatolia and the land route.

In general, one way of distinguishing Broad from Extreme Aryanists is by their attitude to Thucydides. While the Broad Aryanists are uncomfortable with Herodotos' 'Egyptomania' and 'interpretatio

Graeca', they deeply respect Thucydides. Thucydides did not mention any Egypto-Phoenician colonies on mainland Greece; he did, however, refer to Phoenician settlements on the Greek islands and all around Sicily. Beloch utterly denied their existence, demanding archaeological 'proof' for the 'unsubstantiated' though widespread ancient testimony about them.[28] His chief concern, however, was over Homer's relatively frequent references to Phoenicia(ns) and Sidon(ians). Like Müller, Beloch tried to diminish the former by pointing out that *phoinix* had many different meanings in Greek; he dealt with the irreducible references to Phoenicians by postulating that they belonged to the latest layer of the epics which, following Wolf and Müller, he saw as accretive rather than as single creative acts. Beloch firmly denied that there were any references to Phoenicians at the epics' core, and justified this belief by citing the absence of Phoenicians from the list of Troy's barbarian allies in the *Iliad*, which he took to be exhaustive for the Aegean and Anatolia.[29] Thus he was able to maintain that Phoenicians could not have come to the Aegean before the end of the 8th century and therefore could not have played a significant role in the formation of Greek civilization.

The modern Belgian scholar Guy Bunnens has written about the men who founded Extreme Aryanism:

> In reading their work, one cannot help thinking that these authors were not always ruled by scientific objectivity alone. Reinach and Autran [a French scholar with similar views] insisted on reserving a place in the most distant past for the peoples who dominated world politics in their own period: that is to say, for the Europeans. They maintained that it was unbelievable that nations so important today should have played no role in the past. It was therefore necessary to 'assert the rights of Europe over the claims of Asia'. The historical background at the end of the 19th and the beginning of the 20th centuries explains these new theories. For this was the epoch when the colonialism of the European powers was triumphant . . . There was another non-scientific factor. The end of the 19th century saw a great current of anti-Semitism in Europe, particularly in Germany

and France . . . this hostility against the Jews extended in history against those other Semites, the Phoenicians.[30]

VICTOR BÉRARD

Interestingly, the pattern Bunnens describes was visible to the perceptive at the time. In 1894, the year in which Beloch published his article, Victor Bérard brought out his much more substantial *On the Origin of the Arkadian Cults*; this had precisely the opposite interpretation of Greek relations with the Phoenicians.

Bérard, born in the mountains of the Jura near the Swiss border, made his way by scholarships to a *lycée* in Paris and the *École Normale*. In 1887 he went to the French school at Athens and for three years he was involved in excavations in Arkadia, the archetypal rustic and archaic mountainous province in the centre of the Peloponnese; he travelled widely in this remote province, and throughout Greece and the Balkans as well. Bérard was a man of extraordinary energy and determination – not only did he continue with his academic career, but he published many books on the contemporary Balkans, Near East and Russia and for some years edited a political journal, the *Revue de Paris*. He was later elected senator for the Jura. Although radical in politics, he became closely attached to the French navy and developed a fascination for the sea.[31]

He attributed the themes of his first book on Arkadian cults to two revelations that came to him while living in the province. The first was the extraordinary accuracy of Pausanias, wherever it was possible to check his work by surveying or archaeology. It may seem rather strange that Bérard should have been surprised at this discovery when the 2nd-century guidebook had just been so spectacularly vindicated by Schliemann's discoveries in Mycenae and Tiryns, precisely where Pausanias had indicated that there would be significant sites. However, the academic spirit of *Besserwissen* epitomized by Reinach and Beloch was not so easily disconcerted. Pausanias, like other ancient historians and geographers, continued to be treated with the affectionate condescension considered appropriate for children. In any event, Bérard was convinced that Pausanias had visited the sites he said he had, and had described them accurately, and this encouraged the Frenchman to believe other ancient writers too.[32]

Bérard also saw that the Arkadian cults were unHellenic. This was not controversial, because Arkadia had always been associated with the Pelasgians. What did surprise him, and outrage his colleagues, was his conclusion that they were Semitic. For by the late 1880s it was axiomatic that the Phoenicians, as a seafaring people, could not go inland, and Beloch was only systematizing a general belief that Phoenician influence in Greece was very late. Both these suppositions were violated by the idea of substantial Semitic influences in an inland province proverbial for its archaic customs.

Bérard fully realized the incongruities. Convinced of his conclusions, he began to question the orthodoxy against which they offended, and to look for modern analogies. It led him to make a statement which I shall quote in full, because it beautifully summarizes the main theme of *Black Athena*. When justifying the Phoenician presence in poor, remote and inland 'Pelasgian' Arkadia, he wrote:

> ... many Europeans today go to Pelasgians, who are no less distant or savage, and for equally slight gains, to discover African Arkadias. The taste for voyages and adventures is not the monopoly of any one period or any one race, and the extraordinary dispersion of Semites in the contemporary world ... It is true that modern travellers have two motives that the Sidonians do not appear to have possessed, at least to the same degree: scientific curiosity and religious zeal. Furthermore, this comparison between the Pelasgians and the modern Congolese may be surprising. However, one should be on guard against two preconceived ideas, or rather two little-reasoned and almost unconscious feelings: ... our *European chauvinism* and also what one could call, without too much irreverence, our *Greek fanaticism*.
>
> From Strabo [the 1st-century geographer] to [Carl] Ritter [the early-19th-century geographer trained at Göttingen], all the geographers have taught us to consider *our* Europe as a land favoured above all others, unique and superior to all the others in beauty ... in elegance of forms and power of civilization ... This way of looking at

the world perhaps can influence a large number of our most habitual thoughts, despite ourselves or almost without our knowledge. We put Europe on one side and Asia or Africa on the other – and between the two, an abyss. When we talk about Asiatic influences on a European country we cannot imagine . . . that barbarians could have dared to come to us. Harsh reality forces us to admit that they have sometimes flooded in. Certain people even maintain that the cradle of our first ancestors was far from our Europe, in the centre of Asia. But for our Aryan fathers we have the indulgence of good sons in that even if they came from Asia, they were not Asiatics, they were for all eternity Indo-Europeans. By contrast, an invasion from Semitic Asia to our Aryan Europe is repugnant to all our prejudices. It seems really as if the Phoenician coast was further away from us than the Iranian plateau. It also appears that the Arab invasion throughout the Mediterranean was only a unique fluke, an unfortunate chance . . . which one should not for an instant suppose could be repeated. That the Phoenicians occupied Carthage and possessed half Tunisia only concerns Africa. That the Carthaginians in their turn conquered Spain and three-quarters of Sicily is [all right because they are] only, as we say, Africa. But when we find Phoenician traces at Marseilles, Praeneste, Kythera, Salamis, Thasos and Samothrace, in Boiotia and in Lakonia at Rhodes and in Crete we do not want, as in Africa, real occupations; we only talk about temporary landings or simple trading posts . . . If we go as far as pronouncing the words *fortresses* or *Phoenician possessions* we hasten to add that they were only coastal establishments . . . This European chauvinism becomes a veritable fanaticism when it is not in Gaul, Etruria, Lucania or Thrace but in Greece that we meet the stranger. At the beginning of this century, all Europe rose up . . . the generous Philhellenism of 1820 is no longer fashionable. But one can say that the sentiment has not greatly changed . . . We can only conceive of Greece as the country of heroes and gods. Under porticos of white marble . . .

In vain does Herodotos tell us that everything comes from Phoenicia and Egypt. We know what we should think of *dear old* Herodotos. After twenty years of Archaeology have provided us, every day and in all the Greek states, with indisputable proofs of Oriental influence, we are still not allowed to treat Greece as an Oriental province like Caria, Lycia or Cyprus because of this. If in our geography we separate Europe from Asia, in our history we separate Greek history from what we call ancient history. We see, nevertheless, from their material and tangible monuments that the Greeks ... were the pupils of Phoenicia and Egypt, and we see that they borrowed from the Semitic Orient right up to their alphabet; yet we recoil with some shock at the sacrilegious hypothesis that their institutions, their customs, their religions, their rituals, their ideas, their literature and all their primitive civilization could also be inherited from the Orient. (his italics)[33]

It is interesting to note that for all his boldness, Bérard did not – unlike his contemporary, Foucart – seriously propose Egyptian influence; nor did he challenge the holy of holies, the Greek language.

I found it very moving to discover this articulate statement of the beliefs behind my own work written at the height of imperialism and the beginning of the Extreme Aryan Model. However, this fact itself appears to pose a challenge to my method of explaining these scholarly developments in externalist terms – that is, as being heavily influenced by outside social and political developments and the overall intellectual atmosphere. To overcome this challenge, I think it would be useful to look at three tiers of scholarship: the thoughts of individual scholars; their ability to teach and publish; and the general developments in scholarship. I believe that the sociology of knowledge can make only approximate predictions of attitudes and behaviour at the first level. It can do rather better at the second, but it comes into its own only at the third and most general level.

This case belongs to the first and second levels. I believe that a German Bérard would have been impossible and an English one unlikely. Schliemann gives a neat example of the Romantic confines within which even the most creatively radical German could think on these matters. Gladstone, Frazer and Harrison show the relatively broader bounds possible in Britain. Only the professional heretic and brilliant anthropologist of Semitic religion Robertson Smith could begin to go beyond them. It was solely in France – with its post-1870 suspicion of German Aryanism – and among republicans – with their hatred of Catholic Royalist anti-Semitism – that such thoughts could be thought. One might even say, in a Romantic way, that Bérard's regional origin was important in that there was a strong tradition of secular and socially radical individualism in both the French and Swiss Jura which made it the model for the 'big three' social anarchists, Proudhon, Bakunin and Kropotkin.[34] Another important factor was that Bérard was not a 'pure' academic: he had his outside, journalistic and political worlds to give him a wider perspective, and we should note similar features in Schliemann and Gladstone.

This last factor is crucial at the second level. It is only when he or she has a wider, public status that the academic heretic can have any hope of publishing their 'unsound' ideas. In the 19th and early 20th centuries conformist academia did not have the near monopoly on 'respectable' publication now available to the orthodoxies through university presses, which allows academics to ignore arguments published elsewhere. Even then, however, it was difficult for nonconformist scholars and outsiders to obtain a hearing.

Going beyond the bounds of orthodox academia has another disadvantage in that it is difficult for the scholar without a discipline, 'going it alone', to know where to stop. On the principle that one might as well be hung for a sheep as for a lamb, there is a great temptation to 'tell it like it is', regardless of the preconceptions of one's audience. The scholar can easily go beyond not only the bounds of what is possible for the most broad-minded of the orthodox to accept, but also of what is useful to the rigorous development of his or her ideas.

Bérard, for instance, developed the theory that as there was a Phoenician Mediterranean behind the Greek Mediterranean, there was a Phoenician *Odyssey* behind the Greek one.[35] This wild hypothesis provided 'sound scholars' with an ideal weapon to discredit him and all his ideas. Nevertheless, in the course of his massive and detailed researches on the topic he discovered a large number of plausible Semitic etymologies for Greek place names, and he also established the useful principle of the toponymic 'doublet'. This referred to situations where two apparently different place names were used for the same or nearby places. In such cases he argued that the names were simply Greek and Semitic words for the same thing.

Take, for example, the Island of Kythera, to the south-east of the Peloponnese. A Mesopotamian inscription dating back to the 18th century BC had been discovered there in 1849; Herodotos wrote that the temple of Aphrodite Ourania was founded there by the Phoenicians; Aphrodite was frequently portrayed as wearing a crown.[36] Bérard noticed that the name of the island's chief harbour was Skandeia, which the earliest extant Greek lexicographer, Hesychios, said meant 'a kind of head-dress'. Bérard then pointed out that Kythera, the name of the island and its chief city, which had no Indo-European etymology, could be plausibly derived from the Semitic root √ktr found in the Hebrew *keter* or *kōteret*, 'crown or tiara'.[37]

Despite the very plausible nature of this and many other toponymic and cultic parallels, the orthodox were able to dismiss Bérard and all his works because of the evident impossibility of Odysseus' being a Phoenician. By the time of Bérard's death in 1931 his name had become a byword for crankiness in scholarly circles, but it should be noted that an underground movement continued to hold such ideas 'in the closet'. Furthermore, his books were widely read and appreciated by the public at large, among whom there seems to have been the feeling, expressed by Gobineau fifty years earlier, that Odysseus was in some way Semitic. Bérard was particularly well received in Britain, with its remaining identification with and affection for the Phoenicians, and his influence has left a permanent mark on literature in James Joyce's *Ulysses*, which is about Jews, not Greeks.

Nevertheless, Bérard was unable to stop the steamroller of Extreme Aryanism in scholarship, and at this third and most significant level the sociology of knowledge can be used with some accuracy. I am convinced that European politics and society from 1880 to 1939 were so steeped in racism and anti-Semitism, and Classics was so central to the educational and social systems, that – regardless of the historical and archaeological evidence – it would have been impossible to change the image of Ancient Greece in the way Bérard wanted to. It was not until after the decline of colonialism and the official delegitimization of racism and anti-Semitism between 1945 and 1960 that any dent could be made in the models of ancient history based upon them.

AKHENATON AND THE
EGYPTIAN RENAISSANCE

Neither Bérard nor Foucart refers to each other in their works. Although one can only speculate, it is almost as if they felt that one heresy was enough – that it would have been too much to champion both the Egyptians and the Phoenicians at the same time. Nevertheless, it is clear that with the rise of anti-Semitism and hostility to the Phoenicians, there was increasing room for toleration of the Egyptians. Professional Egyptologists now preserved the orthodoxy of the Egyptians' categorical inferiority, but among lay people they were now seen as so exotic as to pose no threat to European civilization.

The figure of the heretic king Akhenaton was particularly admired. As Amenophis IV, this 18th-dynasty pharaoh of the 14th century BC broke away from his family's and dynasty's worship of Amon and the other gods, and tried to establish a monotheism based on the sun disc *itn*, Aton. From Aton he took the new name Akhenaton. He moved from the traditional capital at Thebes to a new one, built at a site now known as El Amarna. Soon after his death, however, the reform was ended, the worship of Amon was re-established and the capital returned to Thebes. The destroyed and deserted El Amarna was left as a perfect site for archaeology and when, in the 1880s, the site was excavated by Flinders Petrie and the outline of the events around the attempted reform was established, a great European enthusiasm for Akhenaton developed.

Egyptologists paid particular attention to giving him and his new religion Aryan, or at least northern, credentials. Petrie claimed that the religion had originated in the Hurrian-speaking northern kingdom of Mitanni, from where, he alleged, Akhenaton's grandfather, mother and wife had all come.[38] These beliefs – or modifications of them – remained very popular for the next fifty years, as in the following statement by an Egyptologist who was able to turn the reforms into a racial matter: 'It must always be remembered that the king had much foreign blood in his veins. On the other hand those with whom he spoke, though highly educated, were but superstitious Egyptians . . .'[39]

It is generally, and reasonably, agreed today that if the members of the royal family of the 18th Dynasty were foreign, they were Nubian. It is equally probable, however, that they were Upper Egyptian, and from their portraits they would seem to have been Blacks.[40] On the question of the new religion, it was argued that the cult of '*itn* came from a Semitic cult of '*dn*, '*adōn* (lord). Nevertheless, here too the consensus is that the religious reforms can be more plausibly explained as a native Egyptian development, and the schema of Mitanni origin was clearly designed to explain the racial 'impossibility' of 'static' African Egyptians having made a drastic reform – in what Christians had to admit was a positive direction.[41]

On the other hand, the enthusiasm for Akhenaton and his reforms – even on the part of those who were reconciled to his being Egyptian – would seem to indicate that other forces were involved. One of these was a revival of the old belief that the Jews as a people, or Moses as a man, had learnt their religion from Egypt. Scholars were cautious on the issue, but the existence of a monotheism in the 14th century BC in a neighbouring country made it altogether natural to derive the Israelite form from there. Some writers even believed that worship of Aton was superior to Judaism: 'By no other religion in the world is Christianity so closely approached as by the faith of Akhenaton.'[42] Thus Christianity, either spiritually or historically, could be ultimately derived not from the Semites but from an actual or honorary Aryan, and this is the context in which one should view Freud's *Moses and Monotheism*, written in the late 1930s. Freud, however, wanted precisely the opposite of Akhenaton's Christian admirers. In order to alleviate the intense anti-Semitism of the times he appears to have hoped to excuse Judaism and Jews from responsibility for the repression of Christian monotheism, and put the blame on Akhenaton and the Egyptians.[43]

ARTHUR EVANS AND THE 'MINOANS'

Soon after the beginning of the 20th century, scholarly discussions had to include a new factor: the 'Minoan' civilization of Crete. Evidence of it came from Arthur Evans' sensational discoveries at Knossos in the 1890s, and the other excavations quickly undertaken elsewhere on the island. With the realization that the Mycenaean culture was in many ways simply a debased form of the Cretan one, the linguistic identification of ancient Cretan culture naturally became critically important. In Classical times, the Egyptian use of the name Kftiw seems to have shifted from 'Cretan' to 'Phoenician', and the Greeks seem to have referred to 'Minoans', as well as Phoenicians, as Phoinikes.[44] This would suggest a Semitic connection. In any event, it seems to have been accepted, at least in Hellenistic times, that the chief language of early Crete was Phoenician. Lucius Septimius, for instance, wrote in the 4th century AD that when an earthquake in 66 AD had revealed ancient Cretan documents, the Emperor Nero had called in Semitists to interpret them.[45] Then, as we saw in Chapter VII, Ernst Curtius was willing to concede that there had been considerable Semitic settlement in Crete, while denying that the local Pelasgians had ever been completely overcome.[46] Arthur Evans himself believed that there was a relationship between ancient Cretans, whom he now called the 'Minoans' – after the legendary king Minos of Crete and the commonplace name Minoa – and the Phoenicians; though we should remember that he agreed with Gladstone that the Phoenicians were not purely Semitic, and had received Aegean influence.[47]

Evans was born in 1851 and, though educated at Oxford and Göttingen, belonged to the older and more broad-minded generation. Thus he accepted the possibility of Semitic, and even Libyan, influence on Crete, and hence on the Aegean as a whole. Nevertheless, his coining of the name 'Minoan' encouraged people to think of Crete as a unitary culture which was completely detached from the civilizations of the Middle East. It was easy, therefore, for the academic consensus to come to the conclusion that the Minoan language was neither Hellenic nor Semitic; nor, despite the huge number of Egyptian objects found at every level in Crete, was it thought to be Egyptian. 'Minoan' was generally considered to be related to various Anatolian languages; therefore it was or was not Indo-European, according to one's definition of the latter.

There was an equal determination to show that the Minoans were 'racially' not Semites. As one scholar wrote in 1911, describing a well-known Minoan fresco:

> The cupbearer may indicate their physique, black curly hair, straight nose, long skull; and I, for one, decline to believe that this fine fellow is a Semite or Phoenician, as has been suggested. We know that these people were extraordinarily gifted, especially in the sense of form, and that they were capable of very rapid development.[48]

By this time the Minoans were seen as the most civilized Pelasgians, and the prevailing line was spelled out by two historians of Western Asia:

> Probably no discovery of more far-reaching importance to our knowledge of the history of the world generally, and of our own culture especially, has ever been found than the finding of Mycenae by Schliemann, and the further finds that have resulted therefrom, culminating in the discoveries of Mr Arthur Evans at Knossos. Naturally, these discoveries are of extraordinary interest to us, for they have revealed the beginnings and first bloom of the European civilization of today. Our culture ancestors are neither the Egyptians nor the Assyrians, nor the Hebrews, [note the omission of the Phoenicians even as a possibility!] but the Hellenes; and they, the Aryan Greeks, derived most of their civilization from the Pre-Hellenic people whom they found on the land before them.[49]

Everything now depended on the Pre-Hellenes!

I have mentioned the old compromise that Phoenicians may have come to Greece but that it did not matter, because they had had no effect on the development of Greek civilization. Despite the growing strength of the Extreme Aryan Model, there were still holdouts from the Broad Aryan Model who took this line, and these included Evans; Schliemann's old colleague, the brilliant architect and surveyor Wilhelm Dörpfeldt; and the great polymath Eduard Meyer. They maintained, with Thucydides, that there had been genuine Phoenicians in the islands, and possibly even at Thebes.[50] Such thinking was intolerable to the younger generation who had come to maturity after 1885. As the leading early-20th-century British historian of Greece – and a leading liberal – J. B. Bury put it in 1900, in his *A History of Greece*, which remains standard today: 'The Phoenicians, doubtless, had marts here and there on coast and island; but there is no reason to think that Canaanites ever made homes for themselves on Greek soil or introduced Semitic blood into the population of Greece.'[51] Note the use of the two key Romantic and racist words 'soil' and 'blood'! Such attitudes survived up to and beyond the Second World War.

THE PEAK OF ANTI-SEMITISM, 1920–39

The atmosphere became even harsher in the 1920s. Anti-Semitism intensified throughout Europe and North America following the perceived and actual centrality of Jews in the Russian Revolution. There had always been Jewish bankers and financiers to blame for economic crises and national frustrations; now in the Bolshevik party the previously vague image of a Jewish conspiracy to subvert and overthrow Christian morality and order seemed to have taken visible form.[52]

Such feelings were not restricted to Germany, or to vulgar extremists like the Nazis. All over Northern Europe and North America, anti-Semitism became the norm in 'nice society', and 'nice society' included the universities. The contemporary social historian Professor Oren has recently provided detailed background to the imposition of tight quotas to reduce the number of Jewish students at Yale and at associated professional schools during the 1920s, and there is no reason to suppose that what he describes there did not apply to other colleges and universities in the US, and – in a more disorganized way – in Britain too.[53]

It is true that in the 1930s there were a number of very distinguished anti-Fascist Classicists whose love of Greek liberty went with their opposition to Nazi and Fascist tyranny. But we have seen that Philhellenism has always had Aryanist and racist connotations, and Classics its conservative bias. Thus there is no doubt that the discipline as a whole shared the prevailing anti-Semitism, if it did not go beyond it. An example of the atmosphere of the times in Classics can be seen in the following letter, found in 1980 on the desk of Professor Harry Caplan of Cornell, who was for many years the only Jewish tenured professor of the subject in the Ivy League:

> My dear Caplan: I want to second Professor Bristol's advice and urge you to get into secondary teaching. The opportunities for college positions, never too many, are at present few and likely to be fewer. I can encourage no one to look forward to securing a college post. There is, moreover, a very real prejudice against the Jew. Personally, I do not share this, and I am sure the same is true of all our staff here. But we have seen so many well-equipped Jews fail to secure appointments that this fact has been forced upon us. I recall Alfred Gudeman, E. A. Loew – both brilliant scholars of international reputation, and yet unable to obtain a college position. I feel it is wrong to encourage anyone to devote himself to the higher walks of learning to whom the path is barred by an undeniable racial prejudice. In this I am joined by all my Classical colleagues, who have authorized me to append their signatures with my own to this letter. (signed) Charles E. Bennet, C. L. Durham, George S. Bristol, E. P. Andrews [27/3/1919] Ithaca.[54]

In this atmosphere, it is hardly surprising that scholarship should emphasize both the complete separation of Greece from the Near East, and scepticism about Phoenicia's ever having played a positive cultural role in the Mediterranean.

20TH-CENTURY ARYANISM

Despite the beginnings of a new attack on racism, there was an increase of Aryan racism not only among the extreme and disreputable right, typified by the Nazis, but in regular academic circles. Even the great Marxist prehistorian Gordon Childe shared in it, devoting a whole book to *The Aryans*, the preface of which linked language and physical race: 'The Indo-European languages and their assumed parent speech have been throughout exceptionally delicate and flexible instruments of thought . . . It follows then that the Aryans must have been gifted with exceptional mental endowments, if not in the enjoyment of a high material culture.' Childe also referred to the 'certain spiritual unity' of those who share a common tongue. He explained the superiority of the Aryan spirit with the following example: 'Anyone who doubts this would do well to compare the dignified narrative carved by the . . . (Aryan) Darius on the rock at Behistun with the bombastic and blatant self-glorification of the inscriptions of the (Semitic) Ashurbanipal or Nebuchadrezzar.'[55]

An equally crude racism pervades the first edition of the *Cambridge Ancient History*, published under the editorship of Bury and his colleagues in 1924. Intended as a model of the 'new', 'objective' history written collectively by experts about their own particular fields, it quickly succeeded in gaining canonical status, and the same model of 'Cambridge History' has now been applied to many regions and cultures in the world. The introductory section of the entire *Ancient History* is dominated by race. In its first chapter, John Myres, Professor of Ancient History at Oxford, proclaimed his position in the Niebuhrian ethnic tradition of ancient history:

> Ancient peoples come upon the stage of history . . . in a certain order . . . each with a make-up congruous with the part they will play . . . history presupposes the formation of that character, . . . in the greenroom of the remoter past: and the sketch which follows . . . is intended . . . to describe how men came by these qualities of build and temperament . . .[56]

Accepting the common tripartite view of human races, Myres described 'the Mongol' as 'parasitic', 'infantile' and like 'a quadruped seen from behind'! Having made this jocular reference to their cowardice, Myres proceeded to have his cake and eat it, stating that their group psychology was of a 'peculiar' type which did not 'set much value on human life . . . Almost inhuman in his normal apathy, the Mongol can display almost equine savagery when provoked by panic or ill-usage.'[57] Blacks came off surprisingly lightly, though 'the Negro' was described as having a 'carnivorous-looking jaw' and 'great physical strength'.[58]

Professor S. A. Cook, in his chapter on 'the Semites', also reflected the attitudes of the times. Since Semites were fundamentally different from Aryans, there was something very wrong about them. Cook accused them of extremes of optimism and pessimism, of asceticism and sensuality. They possessed great energy, enthusiasm, aggressiveness and courage, but no perseverance, little civic or national loyalty, and little concern about the ethical value of actions: 'Personal feeling is the source of action, not common sense, or plan or morality.'[59]

There is a striking contrast between Cook's 'unethical' Semites and Renan's 'moral' Semites sixty years previously. This would seem to reflect both the additional impact of the Arabs on the amalgam of 'Semites', and of the fear of the Jewish-led, Bolshevik hordes following their Hebrew prophet, Marx. Cook was, on the other hand, closer to Renan when he argued that discursive thought was lacking among the Semites: 'In the Hebrew prophets and in Mohammed's Koran we have enthusiasm, eloquence and imagination rather than logical exactness, sustained thought and sweeping comprehension . . . The thought does not proceed step-wise, nor is it detached or objective.'[60]

This type of thinking continued well beyond the Second World War, forming the basis for the archaeologist, art historian and philosopher of ancient history Henri Frankfort's distinction between the 'mythopoeic' thought of the Ancient Egyptians, Semites and 'modern savages' as opposed to the 'rational' thought of the Greeks and later Europeans.[61] A categorical distinction of this kind, of course, plays down the huge extent of 'mythopoeic' thought in modern society; but more than this, it is invalidated by the 'objective accuracy' achieved by Mesopotamians and Egyptians in their measurement of space and time, and the extent to which they allowed measurement to dominate their lives.

To return now to Cook's vision of the Semites in the *Cambridge Ancient History* as 'middlemen, copying foreign models . . . , reshaping what they adopt . . . and stamping themselves on what they send out.'[62] Here, paradoxically, we have something that sounds remarkably like the tradition of *Epinomis*, according to which the Greeks had 'perfected' everything they took from other cultures.[63] For Cook, however, the Greeks – together with the Pre-Hellenes – were no longer seen in this way. They were the originators of their own culture.

The basic views of the scholars who started the *Cambridge Ancient*

History can be seen from these introductory chapters. They made it clear that everything now hinged on the Pre-Hellenes, and during the 1920s they and other 'modern' scholars made a determined effort to find out as much as possible about these Pre-Hellenes and their relations with the Hellenes themselves. It was in this decade that the great Swedish scholar Martin Nilsson began to demonstrate the links between Classical Greek mythology and the iconography of the Mycenaean and Minoan civilizations. With this link established, he could no longer accept the easy-going attitudes towards Minoan and Mycenaean contacts with the Middle East held by Evans and the older generation. Fundamental contacts across the East Mediterranean in the Bronze Age were now impossible. The difficulties posed to this denial by the manifest similarities between the architecture and material cultures of Crete, Egypt and Syria were insignificant when compared to the issues at stake, which were nothing less than the integrity and purity of Greek civilization itself.[64]

We have seen that since the late 19th century there had been a widespread belief that the language or languages of the Pre-Hellenes were in some way 'Asianic' or Anatolian. By the 1920s, however, as Hittite was beginning to be read and Lydian, Lycian and Carian inscriptions became available, the hypothesis was increasingly difficult to sustain, as it was impossible to find parallels with the non-Greek elements in Greek. Nevertheless, this seemed to be the only possible lead, and in 1927 it was used in an attempt to pin down the Pre-Hellenes geographically. In an article written in the new approved collaborative 'scientific' fashion in two parts by an archaeologist, Carl Blegen, and a Classicist, J. Haley, the authors took from the German linguist Paul Kretschmer the hypothesis that there were two Pre-Hellenic place-name elements, -i(s)sos and -nthos, which could be seen as related to the elements -ssa and -nda found in Anatolia. This suggested, they argued, that all these place names came from the ancient pre-Indo-European stratum. Their further claim – that the distribution of these and other non-Hellenic Greek place names corresponded with that of Early Bronze Age settlements – was seen to fit nicely with the hypothesis that the Indo-Europeans had invaded at the beginning of the Middle Bronze Age.[65] (The consensus has since developed that the invasion came not at this point but with the archaeological break seen in material cultures between Early Helladic II and Early Helladic III.)

The two authors' evidence for toponymic and archaeological correspondence is not impressive. They themselves admitted that the place names also fit closely with the area of Late Bronze Age Mycenaean culture.[66] Their linguistic arguments were even more shaky. First of all, toponymic suffixes usually have meanings: -ville (town), -ham (village), -bourne (stream), -ey (island), etc. However, -s(s)os and -nthos refer to all kinds of geographical features, suggesting heterogeneous origins. Secondly, as the contemporary Anatolian linguist Professor Laroche has claimed, the suffixes -ssa, etc., can be explained as Hittite or Luvian and not as Pre-Hellenic.[67] Now this argument can be overcome if one sees a close similarity between these Anatolian languages and Pre-Hellenic – though difficult, it is just possible. There is, however, an insuperable obstacle, raised by Paul Kretschmer in later work, which was available before Blegen and Haley published theirs. This was the fact that the suffixes were sometimes attached to Indo-European stems.[68] Thus, even though they might in certain circumstances be very old, they could not be taken as indicators of the language and culture of the Aegean population before the arrival of the Indo-European-speaking Greeks.[69] It says something for the weakness of Ancient Greek toponymic studies that Blegen and Haley's fundamentally flawed article could become a classic study, to which students interested in such subjects are still referred.

Blegen and Haley's work illustrates the inabilities of scholars to get to grips with the 'Pre-Hellenes', despite the fact that so much depended on them. They remained essential if it was absolutely impossible that Egypt or Phoenicia had had a fundamental influence on the formation of Greece, and so the late 1920s and early 1930s saw an intensification of attacks on Phoenicians. The non-Semitic nature of the Minoans was by now so secure that the ancient identification of the Minoans with the Phoenicians could be reversed along the lines suggested by Bunsen and Curtius in the 19th century; now it was claimed that when Greek myths mentioned the Phoenicians, they were really referring to Minoans.[70]

TAMING THE ALPHABET:
THE FINAL ASSAULT
ON THE PHOENICIANS

The leading figure in the climax of the Extreme Aryan Model was the American archaeologist Rhys Carpenter, who was a great admirer of Julius Beloch and an opponent of the *mirage oriental* throughout his long life. By 1930 legends of Phoenician settlement in Greece were largely discredited, and nearly all the Semitic etymologies for Greek names and words had been ruled out. There remained only the Phoenician alphabet. The poet and novelist Robert Graves could claim an Aryan origin for it but, try as they did, scholars could not ignore the fact that the Greek letters looked like Semitic letters, sounded very similar, and most had corresponding names: *alpha/'alep* (ox); *bēta/bêt* (house), and so on. These had obvious meanings in Late Canaanite, but made no sense in Greek.[71] Thus, even though the new scholars would have felt free to dismiss the massive and unanimous ancient testimony that the Greeks had been given their alphabet by the Phoenicians, they could not avoid admitting its Semitic origin.

According to a great range of ancient writings on the subject, the introduction of the alphabet was attributed to Danaos from Egypt or Kadmos from Tyre. This put it in the middle of the 2nd millennium BC. However, there was also a passage in the writings of Josephus, the Jewish apologist, in which he asserted – in an anti-Greek tirade specifically attacking the Greeks for their lack of cultural depth – that the Greeks were only boasting when they claimed that they had learnt letters from Kadmos. In fact, according to him, they had been illiterate at the time of the Trojan War.[72] Not surprisingly, Josephus' version was preferred by the Romantic Hellenists when considering their imge of Homer the illiterate bard. Nevertheless, most scholars preferred to accept the ancient consensus, for the authenticity of the legends surrounding Kadmos' foundation of Thebes was not seriously challenged until the end of the century.

This early date, however, was not acceptable to Reinach and Beloch. Reinach lowered the period of transmission to the 13th or 12th century, at which time he believed Phoenician influence had begun.[73] Beloch suggested the 8th century as his date for the first contacts, and he supported this with four arguments. In the first place, he maintained that there were no datable Greek inscriptions from before the 7th century; secondly, he stated that the only reference to writing in Homer was obscure, and it was possible that the poet and his audience did understand reading; thirdly, he claimed that the way from Phoenicia to Greece went through Cyprus, which did not use the alphabet until Alexander's time; and fourthly, he argued that the names of the letters resemble Aramaic, not Phoenician, forms; thus the alphabet must have been borrowed after Aramaic became dominant in the Levant in the late 8th century.[74]

The dubiousness of Beloch's first point, the argument from silence, has been and will be discussed elsewhere in *Black Athena*. On the second point, despite the assurances of Beloch and many later scholars that the reference is of no consequence, there is no doubt that Homer did once refer to *sēmata lygra* (baneful signs) which were 'written'.[75] The lack of an alphabet in Cyprus was the result of local conditions which meant that the island failed to respond at the time when the alphabet was transmitted from the Levant to the Aegean. It gives us no indication, one way or the other, of when the transmission took place. Finally, we have already seen that Beloch knew no Semitic languages, and he was wrong when he claimed that the Greek letter names reflect Aramaic pronunciations. The ō in the letters *iōta* and *rhō* reflect a sound shift which took place in Canaanite, but not in Aramaic.

In any event, Beloch's ideas on the alphabet were not taken seriously by his contemporaries, and the debate on the dating of the alphabetic introduction was even more fluid during the first quarter of the 20th century than that between the Broad and Extreme Aryan Models as a whole. A likely cause for this openness was the relative influence of Semitists and Jews in the study of Semitic epigraphy, which was essential for any serious dating. In general, however, there is no doubt that the tendency was for the date of the transmission to be lowered, for the same reasons that brought the Extreme Aryan Model at power; not forgetting the now familiar and increasing 'positivist' desire for 'proof', as well as the desire to give archaeology and ancient history what was thought to be the certainty of natural sciences.

The lowering process culminated in 1933 when Professor Rhys Carpenter, an archaeologist and an avowed outsider to epigraphy, proposed a date around 720 BC for the date of the introduction of the alphabet to Greece. The reasons he gave for doing this were twofold: that the earliest Greek letters resembled those of 8th-century Phoenician; and that no Greek alphabetic inscriptions had been found from before that date, 'the argument from silence'.[76] This lowering of the date was only one of three attempts Carpenter made to diminish the importance of the introduction of the alphabet and to make it less likely that it could have been accompanied by any other significant cultural borrowings. Another attempt took the form of making a categorical distinction between consonantal and vocalized alphabets. The invention of vowels was attributed – in my opinion wrongly – to the Greeks.[77] Making it clear that he thought vowels were beyond the capacity of Semites, Carpenter referred to 'that brilliantly Greek creation of the vowels', thus crediting the Greeks with having invented the first 'true' alphabet.[78]

Carpenter's third attempt was to remove the place of borrowing as far as possible from Mainland Greece. He suggested Crete, Rhodes and later – most implausibly, for the reason I have given above: that it did not use an alphabet – Cyprus. In the late 1930s, however, the archaeologist Sir Leonard Woolley showed to his satisfaction that there had been an 8th-century Greek colony at Al Mina on the Syrian coast, and suggested that the Greeks could have learnt the alphabet there.[79] Despite the tenuousness of this claim – and the complete lack of early Greek inscriptions within 500 miles of the site – Classicists and archaeologists, including Carpenter, enthusiastically accepted this as the point of transmission.[80]

Why should Carpenter, who made such a fetish of the need for attestation when it came to time, have been so lax in regard to place? One reason was that he saw it as more befitting the 'dynamic' Greek culture to have brought the alphabet home rather than to have received it passively. His second reason was still more sinister. His leading successor in the field of epigraphy, Professor Lilian Jeffery, has summarized the case:

The second point was well brought out by Professor Carpenter: that only in an established bilingual settlement of the two peoples, not merely a casual Semitic trading post somewhere in the Greek area, will the alphabet of one be taken over by the other.[81]

This imaginative reconstruction takes it as axiomatic that 'Semitic' colonization was categorically more 'casual' than that of the Greeks, a contention for which there is little ancient authority, and for which see Bérard's discussion on pp. 378–80.[82] However, the reason for insisting on the small scale and transitory nature of Phoenician settlements has a powerful ideological aspect: they had to be so if Greece was to remain the racially pure childhood and quintessence of Europe. Lest anyone should think that this is exaggerated, I should like to repeat the passage from Bury, which was written in connection with the transmission of the alphabet:

> The Phoenicians, doubtless, had marts here and there on coast and island; but there is no reason to think that Canaanites ever made homes for themselves on Greek soil or introduced Semitic blood into the population of Greece.[83]

Alphabetic transmission had to have taken place outside Greece; otherwise it would have required substantial Phoenician settlement, and hence 'racial' mixing.

To return to the question of the time of transmission. Why did Rhys Carpenter insist on a late-8th-century date which could be – and has been – so easily falsified by later discoveries? Its first advantage was that it could explain why the essentially 'passive' Phoenicians had sailed west; they had been directed by the Assyrians, who had a major impact on the Phoenician coast only in the mid-8th century. We saw the preference for only 'partially Semitic' Assyrians when discussing Movers and Gobineau.[84] What is more, the late date meant that what Phoenician influence there had been in Greece had come not in the country's formative period, but only *after* the establishment of the *polis* and the beginning of colonization – two institutions that could otherwise be construed as Phoenician.[85]

When challenged, Rhys Carpenter acknowledged that his late dating required a uniquely rapid spread and diversification of the alphabet throughout not only the Aegean but Italy and Anatolia as well. Nevertheless, he responded:

> I hold it worse than absurd. I hold it unGreek and hence unthinkable that it [the alphabet] should have lingered for any considerable lapse of time among this intensely active people, in passive abeyance, known but unutilized. Truly the Greek climate does miracles to a young alphabet; we can almost see it growing.[86]

Apart from the Romantic images of climate, trees, youth and growth, the passage illustrates the power and the continuity of the tradition, already present in Humboldt, that all normal laws and analogies are suspended when it comes to the Ancient Greeks and that it is inappropriate – if not improper – to judge them as one would other people.

Not all scholars were swept away by Carpenter's rhetoric. Hans Jensen, for instance, the broadest alphabetic scholar of the 20th century, continued to maintain a 10th- or 11th-century date.[86] But the only direct challenge to Carpenter came from the American Semitist B. J. Ullman, who – in an article Carpenter did not cite – had previously proposed a date of the 12th century or earlier. Ullman agreed that many Archaic Greek letters deviated from the forms on the 9th-century Phoenician or Moabite inscriptions; but he saw them as deriving from earlier Levantine types, not as resembling later ones, and insisted that an alphabet was as old as its oldest letter. Ullman identified the letters of the earliest datable Phoenician inscription, that on the sarcophagus of Ahiram King of Byblos, as being very similar to the 9th-century ones, but said that where the letters differed, the earlier ones were closer to the Greek forms.[88]

In his rejoinder to Ullman, Carpenter implicitly took the opposite position – that an alphabet should be seen as being as recent as its latest letter. That is, he focused on K and M, the Greek forms of which do resemble the later Phoenician ones.[89] Even though this did not address Ullman's arguments about the 'older' letters, Ullman could not withstand Carpenter's vigorous forensic style, the anti-Semitic *Zeitgeist* and the relative power of Classics and Semitic studies. Indeed, Classicists welcomed Carpenter's conclusions enthusiastically. They confirmed the belief at the Romantic heart of the discipline that Homer(s) had been illiterate. For there had been some disconcertion at Evans' discovery of writing on Crete and evidence pointing in the same direction from the Mainland. However, the linear scripts could plausibly – if wrongly – be said to have died out with the destruction of the Mycenaean palaces; hence Carpenter's low date was very welcome in that it established a long 'Dark Age' of illiteracy in which folkish Homer or Homers could have sung with barbaric northern vigour. It is interesting to note that it was during the 1920s that Professor Milman Parry began his study of Serbian folk epics to show that the *Iliad* and *Odyssey* could have been composed without writing.[90]

Carpenter's securing of an illiterate and impermeable 'Dark Age' held another attraction for upholders of the Aryan Model. The break in cultural continuity it imposed allowed people to discount what Greeks of the Classical and Hellenistic periods had written about their distant past. This completed the discrediting not only of the Ancient but of the Broad Aryan Model.

In the spirit of the age, then, Classicists were won over by Carpenter. Where Beloch had failed in the 1890s, Carpenter – using very much the same arguments – succeeded in the 1930s. Most Semitists made accommodations to the line laid down by the hegemonic discipline, but some – particularly the Jewish ones – were less happy. Ullman remained unconvinced, and he and others – notably Professor Tur-Sinai in Jerusalem – continued to see it as obvious that the Greek alphabet could not have derived from Iron Age Phoenicia but must have originated from an earlier Canaanite script.[91]

From 1938 to 1973 there was no serious challenge to Carpenter's ultra-low dating of the Greek borrowing of the alphabet. The reduction of the alphabet removed the last serious obstacle to the establishment of the Extreme Aryan Model, and by the outbreak of the Second World War Classicists and ancient historians were convinced that their disciplines had entered the scientific age. To put it in modern terms, a paradigm had been established. It was no longer tolerable for a 'scholar' to suggest that there had been any significant Egyptian or Phoenician influences on the formation of Greece. Anyone who now did so was – if possible – expelled from the academic community, or at least labelled 'cranky'.

CHAPTER X

THE POST-WAR SITUATION
The return to the
Broad Aryan Model, 1945–85

W ITH THIS CHAPTER we have come full circle. I started this
volume with concerns about the present, but since then have
tried to make them intrude as little as possible. At this point, I
hope the reader who is essentially interested in the world today will gain
some reward for her or his hard work with the last nine chapters. I hope
too that she or he will have been convinced of the contemporary
relevance of history and historiography.

This chapter contains two stories. I believe that the first is close to a
happy ending: it is the movement, led mainly by Jewish scholars, to
eliminate anti-Semitism in the writing of ancient history, and to give the
credit due to the Phoenicians for their central role in the formation of
Greek culture. In the terms used here, these scholars are close to
re-establishing the Broad Aryan Model.

Without going into the internalist factors involved in this shift, we can
say that from an externalist point of view, the successful restoration of
the Phoenicians' reputation required two preconditions, both of which
have been fulfilled. The first was the reincorporation of Jews into
European life; the second has been the great emphasis, within Jewish
culture, on intellectual pursuits and the respect for academia. The
former has removed the conceptual barriers of anti-Semitism that

made it impossible to recognize the Phoenician and Canaanite achievements; the latter means that even the tiny number of Jewish scholars
concerned with these issues can have a powerful effect on the academic
status quo.

The second story contained in Chapter X concerns the rejection of
the tradition of Egyptian colonization in Bronze Age Greece; its end is
not so clearly in sight. One or two German scholars are trying to
reinstate the tradition of Egyptian colonization, but there is no broad
movement within academia for the restoration of the reputation of
Ancient Egypt in this respect. Moreover, the Ancient Egyptians, unlike
the Phoenicians, have no 'natural' champions. Islamic Egyptians have a
deep ambivalence about Ancient Egypt, made more acute by the uses
made of its image by corrupt and pro-Western governments to promote
a non-Arab idea of modern Egypt. Possibly because of this – but more
likely because of an acceptance of the massive power of Western
scholarship – Egyptian scholars have not challenged the orthodoxy on
the world role of Ancient Egypt or investigated its influence overseas.

The only people to champion Ancient Egypt have been small groups
of West African and American Blacks. Even they, however, are much
more concerned with proving that Egypt is truly African and black than
with its influence on Greece. And where they are concerned with this
influence, they have focused on transmission through Greeks' studies
in Egypt, and what they see as the wholesale plundering and appropriat-
ing of Egyptian philosophy and science after the Alexandrian conquest.

An even more powerful inhibitory factor to the restoration of the
Egyptian aspect of the Ancient Model has been the fact that, unlike the
champions of the Phoenicians, these black scholars have been outside
academia. Thus most of the writing on what G. G. M. James called the
Stolen Legacy – Egyptian cultural achievements stolen by the Greeks –
has been circulated among friends or published in very small editions;
rapidly sold out to a passionately concerned public, but not considered
as scholarship by academics, and not even stocked by libraries. An
illustration of this is the fact that I had been studying these issues for
eight years before I became aware of this literature.

After making this contact, I found myself very torn. On the one hand,
my training made me recoil at the lack of so many of the outward

trappings of scholarship; on the other, I found that my intellectual position was far closer to the black literature than it was to orthodox ancient history.

I believe that my feelings are significant. There must be other scholars who have been shaken by the revelation of the Phoenician role in the formation of Greece and the political aspects of its suppression, and have begun to question not only the Extreme Aryan Model but the Broad one too. And from the hundreds of discussions I have had on this subject, I know that the ideological objections to the Ancient Model can no longer be stated in public. In private they may still be believed in, but I am convinced that even this attitude – though common in society at large – is not very frequently found in liberal academia.

It seems, then, that the Aryan Model is being maintained very largely by its own tradition and academic inertia. Neither of these forces should be underestimated; nevertheless, they have been considerably weakened by a number of startling internal developments – all of which show that the Bronze Age civilizations were much more advanced and cosmopolitan than had been thought, and that in general the ancient records are more reliable than more recent reconstructions. Given these externalist and internalist contexts, I am convinced that even the Broad Aryan Model is untenable and that the Ancient Model will be restored at some point in the early 21st century.

THE POST-WAR SITUATION

The Second World War and the public revelation of the Holocaust removed the legitimacy of anti-Semitism and racism, but the new stated value of racial equality took a long time to be institutionalized. In practice, in both Europe and North America, anti-Semitism remained prevalent throughout most of society, including academia, despite the distinguished role played by Jewish scholars who had fled to Britain and the United States. Many American universities continued to exclude Jews or to impose strict quotas on them until the late 1950s or early 1960s.[1] As with the anti-Semitism between the Wars, the British institutions are less easy to pin down, but it would seem likely that a similar situation existed there. From the late 1950s, however, Jewish students and academics became completely accepted in the leading universities. This process also took place in Classics, and by the 1970s many of the dominant figures in the field were Jewish.

Racial prejudice against Africans and Asians was – and is – a far more formidable barrier. The American Supreme Court did not begin to move against legal racial discrimination until the mid-1950s, and it was not until the 1960s that most – though by no means all – US Blacks gained the right to vote. These legal and political reforms have not changed other aspects of the situation of Blacks and South Asians. Some Blacks and non-European immigrants in industrial countries gained economically during the sustained boom from 1945 to 1973, but the differentials between races remained the same, or worsened. With the slump of the 1970s and 80s non-Europeans have lost more, and lost it faster, than Whites throughout Europe and North America.

The writing of history has also been affected by events in the Third World, which I shall discuss below. Here it would seem fair to say that the foundation and military expansion of Israel after 1949 did more to reduce anti-Semitism than the revelation of anti-Semitism's consequences in the Holocaust. For their part, Whites were generally not impressed by Indian independence in 1947 or the 'wind of change' of the 1950s, in which Britain and France found it expedient to grant political independence to their tropical colonies. In any event, neo-colonialism maintained the economic power of the metropolitan countries. Moreover, real problems in the quasi- or newly independent countries and the media's racist treatment of them continued to sustain the dogma that only Whites had the capacity for self-rule. However, even more important from our point of view was the maintenance of European cultural hegemony: there was no real change in the understanding and teaching of history. The 'European chauvinism' denounced by Victor Bérard still flourished. As late as the 1960s, for instance, the only course on the Third World taught in the Cambridge History Tripos was on 'The Expansion of Europe'.

There were, however, significant changes – first, the extraordinary economic success of Japan. This was coupled with the reunification of China and its becoming a major power which, after 1970, the West courted as an ally against the Russians. Hitler had given the Japanese 'honorary Aryan' status in the 1930s, and his view became generally accepted by 1960. During the 1970s, the Chinese too began to receive this accolade, and there would now seem to be a general Western perception of East Asians as somehow different but equal. Indians, too, received slightly more respect as the subcontinent recovered from the horrors of partition. On the other hand, the image of the Romantic Arab sheikh has changed into one of bloated oil princes and Palestinian 'terrorists'. All the old Christian hatred of Islam has been revived and turned against Arabs, and – unlike the 19th-century European admiration of the Persians – Islamic Iran is portrayed in diabolical terms. Moreover, despite independence, Africa and its diaspora are still seen as hopeless, and Blacks are thought of as the lowest form of humanity.

I have listed these crude stereotypes not because most academics accept them – though some clearly do – but because all of us, except for Moslems but including many Asians and Africans, are at some level influenced by them. Many of the Third World movements, of which Negritude is an example, have accepted the European conceit that only Europeans can think analytically; as a result of this many black and brown intellectuals have tended to deny their own analytical intelligence and retreat into the 'feminine' qualities of community, warmth, intuition and artistic creativity – which, interestingly, Gobineau was prepared to concede to the Blacks. In other words, it has not only been white Gentiles who have found it easy to accept the myth of the 'Greek miracle' and the consequent categorical superiority of 'Western' civilization. Nevertheless, there has been some peeling away from this consensus, and we shall look at it later in this chapter.

DEVELOPMENTS IN CLASSICS, 1945–65

Even in the 19th century, cautious historians had often opened their work by stating that linguistic and racial boundaries did not always coincide – before going on to treat them as if the two were identical.[2] After 1945 this became the only acceptable approach, and scholars always referred to linguistic divisions rather than racial ones. On the other hand, while racism was damaged by the War, science came out of it triumphant. Thus the passage of time gave the Extreme Aryan Model increasing legitimacy, as almost no one doubted that it was the 'scientific truth' arrived at by archaeology and other modern methods. The Ancient Model, no longer seen as a coherent scheme to be confronted and overcome, had disintegrated into a collection of ludicrous legends which 'no one today' could begin to take seriously.

The debates on early Greek history, which were fought with great passion, took place almost entirely within the Extreme Aryan Model. There was great discussion as to when the Hellenes had arrived in Greece: until the 1950s a significant minority of scholars maintained, in the legends about the 'Return of the Heraklids' and the Dorian Invasion, that the Aryans had swept south only at the end of the Bronze Age. Despite the overwhelming discrediting of this view by Michael Ventris' decipherment of Linear B as Greek, a number of diehards continued to hold these views until the 1970s.[3]

This decipherment is accepted as being the greatest internal development in the field since the discoveries of Schliemann and Evans and, as with Schliemann, it was made by an amateur. Michael Ventris, an architect, had attempted to crack the published corpus of Linear B texts cryptographically, assuming that they were written in a language of the mysterious Pre-Hellenes. In 1952, however, he tried to match them with Greek, and with that combination he succeeded in deciphering them.

I want to return to a theme raised in my Introduction to this volume. Why should both these breakthroughs have been made by outsiders? In Schliemann's case there was his simple-mindedness and his faith in the Ancients, both of which scholars of his period had been taught to avoid at all costs. Ventris, too, was 'simple-minded' in his juxtaposition of the Linear B corpus with Greek, rather than with some abstruse and scarcely understood Anatolian language or some concoction made from 'Pre-Hellenic' elements in Greek.[4] Furthermore, there was the fact that Linear B represented Greek in an extremely crude way: to read it as Greek did violence to all the refinements that Classicists have spent their lives striving for.

The view that no Classicist could have done it is strengthened by a comparison with the Cypriot syllabary: this was used to represent Greek

on Cyprus until Hellenistic times and was almost equal to Linear B in
the roughness of its approximation of Greek phonetics. It was deciphered by George Smith, who knew little Greek, and Samuel Birch
who, though a competent Hellenist, was essentially an Egyptologist and
an Assyriologist, and therefore used to the looseness of connections
required for such work.[5] This argument – that Hellenists are too
refined for such work, at least in its initial stages – will come into play in
the second volume of *Black Athena*, when I shall try to establish Egyptian
and Semitic loans in Greek with correspondences that would be
acceptable to most comparative linguists but appallingly crude to
Hellenists.

Given the threat he posed to professionalism, it is remarkable how
rapidly and warmly Ventris' work was accepted.[6] This can partly be
explained by his personal charm; his astuteness in asking a sound and
essentially conservative Classicist, John Chadwick, to be his collaborator; and the discovery of corroborative evidence to support his interpretation from newly discovered tablets. On the other hand, there is no
doubt that when they came to consider the matter, Classicists saw the
new decipherment as supporting the Extreme Aryan Model, because it
extended both the time depth and the geographical range of the Greeks.
There were, however, some flies in the ointment. The first of these was
that the name of the god Dionysos was found on a Linear B tablet. In the
Greek tradition, Dionysos was generally supposed to be a latecomer;
therefore Classicists had argued about his cult having arrived or
developed in the 6th or 7th century BC. His appearance in the 13th
century pushed things back almost to the date suggested by the
Ancients – the 15th. However, this has been all too confusing and
although no one could deny the attestation, most scholars continue to
argue along the old lines.

More serious than this, however, was the discovery in Linear B of
Semitic and Egyptian personal names and many of the admitted
Semitic loan words for allegedly exotic goods – spices, gold, and so on –
which had been thought since the 1920s to have been introduced by the
Phoenicians after their supposed arrival in the late 8th century. Here
too the incongruity with the Extreme Aryan Model was not noted by
Hellenists until Semitists confronted them with it. In general, the

decipherment strengthened the Extreme Aryan Model and encouraged scholars to continue looking to the north for origins by invasion. During the 1950s a consensus developed that Indo-European-speaking Proto-Greeks had arrived in the Aegean basin at the end of the Early Helladic II ceramic period, in approximately 2200 BC.

THE MODEL OF
AUTOCHTHONOUS ORIGIN

The only scholars who both accept the reading of Linear B as Greek and reject the idea of this Hellenic invasion are the proponents of what they call 'the model of autochthonous origin'. Led by the grand old man of ancient history in Bulgaria, Vladimir Georgiev, and the distinguished but ultra-isolationist archaeologist Colin Renfrew, they deny that Indo-European was brought to Greece from a homeland north of the Black Sea. Instead they argue that Proto-Indo-European was never anything but a congeries of dialects spoken over Anatolia and the Balkans, of which the Greek spoken in Greece was one.[7] This model belongs to the isolationist or anti-diffusionist paradigm which has been dominant in archaeology and anthropology since the 1940s; its dominance seems to be related to a reaction against colonialism, of which diffusionism is clearly an academic reflex.[8] Linguists and Classicists tend to be less ready than these other scholars to abandon the concept of diffusion, however, because it frequently provides a satisfactory explanation for the relationships within known language families. They have also used the powerful argument that diffusion through conquest and migration has played an important role in recorded history, and there is no reason to suppose that prehistory was significantly different in this respect.

The Model of Autochthonous Origin represents a return to the position of Karl Otfried Müller in the 1820s and 30s, before the development of the Aryan Model. As with Müller, however, its proponents are very much in the northern and European modes of thought, and if anything they are more hostile than the Aryanists to the traditions of colonization from the Near East at the end of the Middle Bronze Age. But this denial and its lack of a Pre-Hellenic substratum leaves the

Model of Autochthonous Origin without any explanation for the non-Indo-European elements in Greek, a weakness that is exploited by defenders of the Aryan Model.[9] Nevertheless, probably because they are working within the dominant paradigm in archaeology, proponents of the Model of Autochthonous Origin feel able to neglect this apparently fundamental flaw. And since both it and the Aryan Model exclude the possibility of Near Eastern settlement, the clash between them is not directly relevant to the topic of *Black Athena*, where the focus has been on the conflict between the Ancient and Aryan models.

EAST MEDITERRANEAN CONTACTS

Up to the mid-1960s, hatred of the Phoenicians seems, if anything, to have increased. Rhys Carpenter pressed on with his campaigns to lower the dates of alphabetic transmission and to limit the extent of Phoenician colonization, and his proposals were generally accepted.[10] The possibility of colonization at Thebes was generally dismissed. In fact, the most determinedly Aryan interpretation of the Kadmeian legend, that by the French scholar F. Vian, appeared in 1963.[11] Many writers continued to deny or at least minimize the extent of contact around the East Mediterranean; in 1951 the English ancient historian R. Meiggs felt able to write, in his revision of Bury's history,

> There would seem to be a coherent body of literary evidence that there were close relations in the Bronze Age between the Mycenaeans and the Phoenicians, or other Semites. Unfortunately this evidence is less coherent and less cogent than it appears to be . . . More serious is the increasing doubt whether any of the Near Eastern peoples came into the Aegean or the Western Mediterranean during the Bronze Age.[12]

As increasing archaeological evidence of contacts between the Aegean and the Levant accumulated, it was assumed that these must have been the result of Greek initiative: '. . . after the close of the MM [Middle Minoan] II period, and throughout the later part of the 2nd millennium, only the sailors, merchants and craftsmen of Mycenaean Greece can justifiably lay claim to the honour of forming the links connecting the Aegean with the Orient.'[13] For the reasons touched on in Chapters VIII and IX, many Semitists seem to have been unwilling to study Phoenician history, which until the 1960s was largely left to Classicists and Philhellenes. In 1961 the Lebanese scholar D. Baramki revived the theory – put forward by Evans at the turn of the century and Woolley in the 1920s and 30s – that what success the Phoenicians did have came from an infusion of Aryan blood; while the Classically trained D. B. Harden, in his *The Phoenicians*, published in 1962, accepted the idea of Mycenaean control of the sea during the Bronze Age.[14]

In the face of new archaeological discoveries of contacts, and the fact that the flow of influence would appear to have been from east to west, there were reactions not only against the theories that denied all contacts, but also against those that attributed these contacts entirely to the activity of the Mycenaeans and later Greeks. The great American scholar William Foxwell Albright, doyen of Semitic studies until his death in 1963, argued for the 9th or even 10th century for Phoenician colonization.[15] The Australian ancient historian William Culican, in a strikingly bold work, stressed the centrality, originality and influence of the Levant in the 2nd millennium, but he studiously avoided the Ancient Model and the question of whether or nor the West Semites had had a profound and/or long-lasting impact on Greek civilization.[16]

Furthermore, the denial of the tradition of Kadmos, the weak link in the Extreme Aryan Model, continued to provoke doubt. The great Marxist Classicist George Thomson in 1949, and his colleague R. F. Willetts in 1962, maintained that the Kadmeioi were a Semitic tribe who went from Phoenicia to Crete and on to Thebes.[17] Also in the 1960s, the Lebanese historians D. Baramki and Nina Jidejian also believed that there had been a Phoenician settlement at Thebes, though they maintained that this had taken place during the Iron Age.[18] Some historians went beyond this, accepting not only the Kadmeian legends but those concerning Danaos too. The Classicist G. Huxley argued for these propositions in his *Crete and the Luvians*, published in 1961; as his title suggests, however, he was more concerned with the respectable Anatolian connection than he was with those to Egypt and the Levant. It is also interesting to note that the book was published privately.[19] A much more startling development was the publication the following year of the Classical archaeologist Dr Frank Stubbings' chapter on 'The rise of Mycenaean civilization' in the 3rd edition of Volume 2 of the *Cambridge Ancient History*.[20] Here, Stubbings accepted the Ancient Model to the extent that he argued for an invasion from Egypt and that Hyksos principalities had been established in Greece; he also claimed that this interpretation was backed by recent archaeological evidence to prove that there had been Near Eastern and Egyptian influence in Greece at the beginning of the Mycenaean period.[21]

Another Classical archaeologist went even further. Emily Vermeule, Professor of the subject at Harvard, suggested that Mycenaean civilization had retained contacts with Egypt and Phoenicia throughout its existence. In 1960, when describing the causes of its collapse, she wrote as follows:

> ... it is clearly not the Mycenaeans who disappeared, but Mycenaean civilization. The strength of that civilization depended greatly upon invigorating contact with Crete and the East, from the time of the Shaft Graves [the earliest tombs discovered by Schliemann at Mycenae] onward. When contact was broken, Mycenaean culture drifted so far in sterility that it is hard to recognize.[22]

But we should remember that these views were, and are, by no means typical. Most modern British archaeologists and historians of Mycenaean Greece – Chadwick, Dickinson, Hammond, Hooker, Renfrew and Taylour, for instance – maintain that Mycenaean civilization was the result of indigenous development. The evident Greek cultural borrowings from the Near East and Africa have been seen as introductions through Greek initiative: the return of mercenaries, trade, or even tourism in the Middle East.[23]

Having absolutely ruled out the possibility of Egyptian or Canaanite influence on Greek culture or language, the academic Establishment could use this 'fact' to attack invasion hypotheses based on Greek tradition or archaeological parallels. Dr Stubbings tried to get around this in connection with the Hyksos:

That their arrival is not accompanied by any more wholesale Egyptianizing is perfectly compatible with what we know of the Hyksos in Egypt. There they had introduced little but new military techniques and organization, they do not represent a mass movement of population, rather they were a warrior caste ... They introduced no new language ...[24]

I think there are real problems with his analysis of the impact of the Hyksos in Egypt. We know very little directly about the Hyksos period there. In the long term, however, there is no doubt that despite the resurgence of Egyptian nationalism and culture in the 18th Dynasty, a major cultural transformation took place during the period of foreign rule. Dr Stubbings does seem to be right in seeing the Hyksos as a warrior caste; but like the Mongols, who churned up the cultures of Eurasia, the Hyksos seem to have been culturally formative in transmitting other civilizations – Semitic into Egypt, 'Minoan' and Egyptian into Greece, etc. Greece, however, lacking the massive tradition of civilization of Egypt, was much more susceptible to change; therefore the Hyksos were likely to have had an altogether greater influence in the Aegean.

Historiographically, on the other hand, Stubbings' position was a return to the argument of Connop Thirlwall in the 1830s and Adolf Holm in the 1880s: that though there may have been Egyptians and Semites in Greece, it did not matter because they had had no long-term effects. Although breaking with the crude racism of the period 1885–1945, Stubbings, like his predecessors, firmly rejected the Ancient Model.

The 'recent' archaeological evidence upon which Stubbings had based his claim was not enough to shake the well-entrenched Extreme Aryan Model. During the 1960s, however, a number of new finds did have a significant bearing on the relative importance of Levantines and Greeks in the East Mediterranean. In 1967, the marine archaeologist George Bass published his report on the only Late Bronze Age ship then excavated in the region. Although he maintained that this trading vessel, sunk off Cape Gelidonya in Southern Turkey, was Syrian, Bass did not go on to claim that this indicated that all shipping at this period was Canaanite. However, from this and other evidence he argued that it was clear that Levantine trade had been centrally important during the Late Bronze Age.[25] This undercut the widely accepted but unbased claims for non-Semitic Minoan and Mycenaean thalassocracies or sea kingdoms and finally destroyed the argument, used by Beloch, that Phoenician boats were incapable of reaching the Aegean before the 8th century.

In 1963 and succeeding years a large number of Near Eastern objects, including thirty-eight cylinder seals, were found in a stratum dating to about 1300 BC in the Kadmeion or royal palace at Thebes.[26] Most archaeologists were cautious, but this find, in a city so closely linked by tradition to Phoenicia, naturally reopened the possibility that the legends around Kadmos might contain some truth. It also provided ammunition for a radical challenge to the anti-Phoenician aspects of the Aryan Model.[27] Then, again, in the 1960s work by art historians on the many motifs and techniques common to the Near East and the Aegean in the Late Bronze Age demonstrated close contact; while the direction of influence in the earlier part of the period seemed to indicate that they have travelled westward.[28]

Interestingly, Classical and Aegean archaeologists were not overtly hostile to this work.[29] On the other hand, there is no doubt that archaeological indications of Near Eastern influence in the Aegean have generally been played down. And, by contrast, the large amounts of Mycenaean pottery found in the Levant from the end of the Late Bronze Age have been widely interpreted as indicating Greek presence, if not colonization, in the region.[30] While Michael Astour and some of the Semitist critics object to this, I accept that there does seem to have been considerable Greek cultural influence on the Levant in the 14th and 13th centuries. But I still think it right to draw attention to the double standards applied when scholars maintain this influence but deny that of the West Semites on the Aegean.[31]

MYTHOLOGY

It should be emphasized that Hellenists have found evidence of contacts in material culture between the two civilizations less disturbing than those in what are seen as the more fundamental areas of mythology and language. In mythology, there were two ways of dealing with the increasing evidence of striking parallels between Near Eastern and Aegean forms, while staying in the Extreme Aryan Model. The first and most satisfactory of these was the 'anthropological' approach advocated by Karl Otfried Müller and pioneered by the Cambridge Classicists of the turn of the century, James Frazer and Jane Harrison: this entailed seeing the parallels as coincidental manifestations of the human psyche. The similarities between Greek myths and cults and those of the Middle East could also be obscured by flooding works on the subject with parallels from all over the world.[32] The other major approach was the one mentioned on p. 365, adopted by the modern Classicists Professors Walcot and West. This consisted of attributing Oriental influence to the Indians, Iranians, Hittites, Hurrians and Babylonians, in descending order of desirability.[33]

A third technique, that of the American Classicist and mythographer Professor Fontenrose, was to combine the two and postulate both universals and borrowings over the land route.[34] Yet another approach, attempting to deal with the problems posed by the close parallels seen between Greece and the West Semitic culture of Ugarit, was to postulate Greek colonies in the Syrian city and the transmission home by the colonists of Semitic myths and stories.[35] In all these approaches, the trick was to explain the parallels in any way except for that set out in the Ancient Model – the Egyptian and Phoenician colonization of Greece.

LANGUAGE

Throughout this volume I have been stressing that language is the *sanctum sanctorum* of the Aryan Model. Not only is there the Romantic belief that language is the fundamental expression of the unique spirit of a people; there is also the position of language at the core of an academic discipline. Ability to use the language is the *sine qua non* for making any statements in the area, and it is largely through the necessarily authoritarian process of language teaching that students are inculcated with the bounds of the discipline. Thus it is not surprising

that while there has been considerable relaxation of the ban on Near
Eastern influences in the area of material culture, and some movement
on mythology, when it comes to language the prohibition on fundamental Afroasiatic influences is still rigidly maintained. Here again,
'respectable' scholars attributed the irreducibly 'Oriental' items in the
Greek vocabulary to Indian, Iranian, Hittite, Hurrian, Babylonian,
West Semitic and Egyptian sources, in the same descending order of
desirability.[36]

There are, however, two modern American scholars with equal
facility in Greek and Hebrew, Saul Levin and John Pairman Brown,
who have worked with great caution and soundness to re-establish a
number of Canaanite loans into Greek. In so far as Classicists are aware
of their work, Levin's is dismissed because he maintains that there are
genetic links between Semitic and Indo-European languages, a position that became anathema at the same time as the establishment of the
Extreme Aryan Model – and for very much the same reasons.[37] Brown's
work, which is largely published in journals of Semitic studies, is simply
ignored.[38] This is, in fact, the traditional way of dealing with such
irrefutable work.

There had also been the forced recognition that the admitted loan
words found in Linear B had been introduced in the Bronze Age.
Despite this, the most widely acknowledged and praised work on
Semitic loaning into Greek was a booklet by the French linguist E.
Masson which restricted confirmed loans to words for material objects
attested in the minute corpus of Phoenician inscriptions, excluding
those found in Ugaritic or the Bible.[39] Thus the already exiguous
number of admitted loans was lessened.

UGARIT

Nevertheless, a reaction to this Aryanism was emerging. Before we
come to it, however, we should briefly consider the major internalist
development weakening the Extreme Aryan Model: the discovery of
Ugaritic civilization. Ugarit, a port on the Syrian coast, was excavated
with great thoroughness after its discovery in 1929. Almost immediately, in the first archaeological season, large numbers of baked clay

tablets were unearthed in strata dating to the 14th and 13th centuries BC. Some were in Akkadian, the *lingua franca* of the Late Bronze Age; others, however, were in an unknown cuneiform script. This was deciphered with great speed, for two reasons: first, because unlike other forms of cuneiform, which are syllabic, this writing was alphabetic; and secondly, because the language was a previously unknown form of West Semitic very close to Canaanite.

This 'new' language has been extremely valuable to linguists. Most of the texts are economic and provide precious information on the structure and trade of a major entrepôt. Others concern legends and ritual, and these have been of outstanding importance because of their striking parallels to both Bible stories and Greek mythology. This causes immense problems for the Extreme Aryan Model, with its central belief in a categorical separation between the Aryan Greeks and the Semitic Levantines.

Scholarship and
the Rise of Israel

Hellenic scholarship was not directly affected by the foundation and military expansion of Israel, even though they provided a clear-cut demonstration that Canaanite speakers were not *ipso facto* incapable of conquest or the establishment of overseas colonies. The immediate effect on most Jewish historians was to narrow the focus of their studies to Palestine and to neglect the Diaspora. Equally, there was an increasing tendency to emphasize the distinctions rather than the similarities between the Israelites and their Canaanite and Phoenician neighbours, thus limiting extremely important comparative studies.[40]

The indirect impact of the foundation of Israel was critically important. It renewed Jews' pride in secular Jewishness. Furthermore, by providing two poles – the religious and the secular nationalist – it allowed more room for manoeuvre within the Jewish tradition. A few scholars were able to make use of this new scope to become independent, and in the area with which we are concerned the two most outstanding of these, Cyrus Gordon and Michael Astour, are working in America. Both men are self-consciously Jewish, but outside the mainstreams of religion and Zionism. The major motive behind Gordon's work appears to be a drive for assimilation. This is not the assimilation of scholars like Reinach, who wanted Jews to conform to Christian or Hellenic culture. Gordon seems to see assimilation as a partnership in which both sides, aware and proud of their roots, create a richer civilization.[41] Astour's views are similar, but there seems to be a stronger element of pan-Semitism in his work and a reluctance to concede any creativity to Indo-European or Egyptian speakers.

CYRUS GORDON

Cyrus Gordon is a brilliant linguist and one of the greatest living Semitists. Despite attempts by his enemies to replace it, his pioneering *Ugaritic Grammar* remains the standard work on the first new Semitic language to be discovered this century. Nevertheless, for the past thirty years he has been on the fringes of academia and most scholars consider him to be a crank. This is partly because his sins or errors are not ones of omission – towards which academia is extremely lenient – but of commission, which are considered irredeemably heinous. Moreover, his attempts to demonstrate the existence of Phoenician or even early Jewish influence on America are so far from conventional wisdom as to make him appear ludicrous. This means that all his original work can be, and has been, brushed aside with contempt.[42]

A much more serious and immediate threat to the academic *status quo* has come from Gordon's attempts to link Semitic and Greek cultures. He sees two bridges between them in Ugarit and Crete, and it was on the basis of his massive work on Ugarit that he wrote a monograph, published in 1955, which he entitled *Homer and the Bible*. He concluded at the end of this that 'Greek and Hebrew civilizations were parallel structures built on the same East Mediterranean foundations.' Although this was relatively similar to Evans' ideas at the beginning of the century, it was not tolerable to scholars working in the Extreme Aryan Model. As Gordon describes it, the reaction to this work was

sharp: some of the reviewers were lavish in their praises, while others were scornful. But this much was clear: I was no longer a sedate scholar whom specialists accepted as another quiet specialist. I had become a disturber of the academic peace, and at the same time a scholar whose writings and lectures had become of interest to a wider public.[43]

Here, as with Victor Bérard fifty years earlier, there was a division between lay opinion, with its 'lumper' preferences for simple and large combinations, and professional opinion with its 'splitter' ones. The professional needs narrow, unrelated topics suitable for individual research and 'private ownership' of knowledge. In responding to Bérard and Gordon other specialists felt threatened, precisely because of the plausibility of the case made against the academic *status quo*.

To a layperson, the idea of close connections between Homeric Greece, Ugarit and biblical Palestine seems perfectly plausible in view of their historical and geographical proximity, especially after the Nazis had discredited the notion that Aryans were categorically distinct and superior. For the professional, things were 'not so simple', and laymen, who had no idea of the details of the situation contained in the scholarly literature, had no right to challenge the experts. Unfortunately, however, much as academics would like it to be so – because their status and livelihood depend on it – *the obvious is not always false*! Sometimes it is possible to say in retrospect that members of the lay public have known better than the professionals: I mentioned the case of Continental Drift in the Introduction.

Crete, Gordon's second connection between the Semites and the Greeks, was still more upsetting. Excited by Ventris' decipherment of Linear B, Gordon proceeded on the assumption – criticized at the time, but now generally conceded – that its signs had the same phonetic values as its predecessor Linear A, the linear writing system of at least later Minoan civilization.[44] Following this principle, Gordon was able to read several Semitic words and discern Semitic sentence patterns in the earlier script. To do this, he assumed that as in Linear B there was little distinction made between voiced and unvoiced stops (ps and b̲s; t̲s and d̲s and k̲s and g̲s). He also drew, for his vocabulary, from both West Semitic and Akkadian. Gordon published preliminary results of his reading of Linear A in the very respectable journal *Antiquity* in 1957; in the 1960s he developed his ideas on this and on Semitic readings for later Eteocretan inscriptions written in the Greek alphabet.[45] The procedures he adopted were generally considered illegitimate, but they were spectacularly vindicated by the discovery in 1975 of Eblaite, a West Semitic language of the 3rd millennium BC. Eblaite combines Akkadian archaisms with features found in Ugaritic and Canaanite.[46]

Gordon's work on Homeric and biblical parallels, like his work on Linear A, has been considered 'controversial'. Interestingly, however, Gordon received immediate support from two white 'English' South African scholars and this, I believe, can be explained by externalist or ideological forces. Whereas after 1885 most Northern Europeans and Americans felt free to indulge in anti-Semitism, the Afrikaners, because of their fundamentalist tradition, felt both love and hate towards the Jews.[47] The combination turned to anti-Semitism with the systematization of their racism and their alliance with the German Nazis.[48]

On the other hand, 'English' South Africans could never neglect the threat of non-Europe, and they preserved the 19th-century ambivalence towards the Jews. Furthermore, they had a specific need to explain away the massive stone ruins of Zimbabwe, after which the country is now named. Even before the carbon dating of these remains in the 1960s to the 15th and 16th centuries, it was pretty clear that they had been built by the Shona people, who still live in the region. Such a conclusion was impossible, however, because racial stereotypes forbade Africans to carry out such undertakings; so the buildings were attributed to the Phoenicians.[49] Thus in Southern Africa the positive feelings of the Victorian period towards the Phoenicians had been preserved, and would seem to be a factor in the open-mindedness of South African Classicists on this issue.

However, both scholars withdrew their support and took more orthodox positions on Linear A in favour of agnosticism and Anatolian connections. The change must be seen in the light of the harsh reactions against a Semitic connection among European Hellenists, notably from Ventris' collaborator John Chadwick, the doyen of Mycenaean linguistic studies. In neither his article on Linear B for the *Cambridge Ancient History*, nor his massive *Documents in Mycenaean Greek*, does Chadwick make any mention of Gordon's work on Linear

A, much of which is published in standard journals. Interestingly, Chadwick specifically claims that omission from his bibliography 'must not be construed as criticism'. Neverthless, the importance of Gordon's hypothesis – not only to the interpretation of Linear A but also to the nature of Mycenaean script, language and society – makes the failure to refer to it very significant.[50]

So far at least, Gordon has suffered the fate of many radicals. Even now that the Extreme Aryan Model, against which Gordon had offended in the 1950s, is beginning to crumble; and although it is now acknowledged that Linear A can be read with the sound values of Linear B; that 'mixed' Semitic languages have existed; that there are Semitic words in Linear A and Eteocretan, and that there is no inherent reason why they should not be Semitic; it is still denied that they are Semitic and that Gordon deserves any credit for having suggested this.[51]

Although Cyrus Gordon is in many ways an academic pariah, his language and teaching skills have meant that his pupils are the best equipped of their generation, and they have now become a major force in American Semitic studies. One of the lessons they have learnt is the high cost of stepping out of line, and only one of them has published on Crete.[52] Nevertheless, most retain a basic sympathy with his views and the conviction that the role of Canaanites and Phoenicians has been systematically neglected.[53] There is no doubt that their influence is sapping the academic *status quo*, and in the United States is leading to a refusal to accept the previously unquestioned dominance of Classics over Semitic studies.

ASTOUR AND *HELLENOSEMITICA*

In the short run, however, Gordon's colleague Michael Astour has had a much greater impact. Astour was in Paris in the 1930s, where he was a student of the French decipherer of Ugaritic, Charles Virolleaud; Virolleaud had been influenced by Bérard and privately believed in the basic truth of the Phoenician references in the Kadmeian myths. From 1939 to 1950 Astour was in Soviet prison camps; he spent the next six years in a Siberian city, where he was able, in his free time and overcoming great difficulties, to continue research on Greek–Semitic relations. In 1956 he left the Soviet Union for Poland and there, a year later, he read Gordon's first article on Linear A. Soon after this he went to the United States, where he was given a post by Gordon in the latter's department at the great Jewish university of Brandeis.[54] In 1967 he published *Hellenosemitica*, a book containing major studies on the myth cycles of Danaos, Kadmos and what he called the 'healer heroes', who included Jason and Bellerophon. In these he tried to show detailed similarities between Greek, Ugaritic and biblical myths in both structure and nomenclature, and here he followed and went beyond the work of Bérard.

As I have mentioned, other scholars during the late 1950s and the early 1960s, like Fontenrose and Walcot, had traced detailed parallels between Greek and Near Eastern mythology, never doubting that the Greek forms were derivative.[55] Why was Astour's work considered so much more offensive? First, it offended at a formal level, because it challenged the academic hierarchy; this was a reflection of the relative power of the two disciplines. Although Classicists had previously discussed Eastern parallels to Hellenic mythology, it was entirely different and unacceptable for Orientalists to pronounce on Greece.

There were also fundamental objections to the content of Astour's work. Scholars like Fontenrose and Walcot had made broad sweeps of world mythology – including India, Iran and so on – and they gave preference, if possible, to the less offensive sources. By contrast, Astour's derivation of Greek names from Semitic not only poached on the sacred ground of language, but also made the connections between West Semites and Greeks disturbingly close and specific. Furthermore, two of the myth cycles he treated – those of Kadmos and Danaos – were concerned with Near Eastern colonization in Greece, and he made a plausible case for their having a historical kernel of truth. The fourth section of *Hellenosemitica* was even more provocative in that it went into the sociology of knowledge, and its sketch of the history and ideology of Classics and Classical archaeology has been the basis of all later writings on this subject, this volume included. In doing this Astour injected relativism into subjects that had previously been impervious to the forces of probabilism and uncertainty that have transformed other disciplines since the 1890s.

Astour has proved – *pace* Ruth Edwards *et al.* – that there were fundamental links between West Semitic and Greek mythology.[56] But this is clearly only part of his aim. Like Movers and the other mid-19th-century scholars who maintained the Broad Aryan Model, Astour believes that the Ancient Model's picture of colonization is substantially correct, except that the latter attributed to the Egyptians what were essentially West Semitic conquests. In general he maintained that 'Not only was Phoenician spoken in several parts of Mycenaean Greece, but the entire Mycenaean civilization was essentially a peripheral culture of the Ancient East, its westernmost extension.'[57]

Although he pointed out the presence of the loan words in Linear B, proving significant Semitic influence before the 14th century BC, Astour did not look for any further examples at other stages in the development of Greek. Moreover, he never considered the possibilities of Egyptian cultural influence; or of a general Near Eastern influx capable of explaining most of the non-Indo-European elements in the Greek language, toponyms and mythological nomenclature which would thus do away with the need for the hypothetical substratum of the Pre-Hellenes. Nevertheless, Astour has permanently changed the historiography of the ancient Mediterranean.

Hellenosemitica has sold exceptionally well. The reviews, however, were so hostile that Astour has given up work on the subject. The critics were led by one of the few scholars with the necessary skills to debate him – J. D. Muhly, an American archaeologist with a knowledge of both Greek and Akkadian. Muhly claimed that '*Hellenosemitica* is a profound disappointment. Instead of a fresh treatment of the problem, based upon the wealth of new material, the reader is served with a *réchauffage* of the theories of Victor Bérard.'[58] According to Muhly, Astour had proved nothing about Greek relations with the Levant during the Bronze Age. Muhly also claimed that in attacking the anti-Phoenician excesses of scholars like Beloch in the 1890s, Astour was setting up a straw man whose views were unlike those of modern Classicists. However, the force of this argument was weakened by another of Muhly's statements: 'I do not propose to defend the absurdities which have been published and *are still being published* about Near Eastern Civilization by eminent Classicists' (my emphasis).[59]

Muhly's second statement should be allowed to stand, because Beloch is still widely respected in some quarters of his discipline and because there is very little to choose between his anti-Phoenicianism in the 1890s and that of Rhys Carpenter in the 1950s.[60] Muhly was undoubtedly right, on the other hand, to point out that the majority of modern Classicists do not share the racism and anti-Semitism endemic among their teachers or their teachers' teachers. But he was still asking his readers to swallow the implausible idea that the Extreme Aryan Model grew up pure and uncontaminated by the *Zeitgeist* in which it was formed or the views – which would now be considered unacceptable – of those who created it.

Three years later, in 1970, Muhly returned to the attack in an article entitled 'Homer and the Phoenicians'. In this he argued along the lines of the conventional wisdom that has been outlined earlier in this chapter – that there was no archaeological proof of Phoenician presence in the Mediterranean before the 8th century, and that Levantine objects found in Bronze Age levels there had been brought by Greeks through mercenary service, trade or even as tourists' bric-à-brac. He asserted that Homer's Phoenicians were those of Homer's own period, which Muhly saw as the 8th century; they were not contemporary with the Trojan War or the Late Mycenaean period. Muhly was clearly and passionately maintaining the arguments of Beloch and Rhys Carpenter that Phoenician influence on Greece was late and shallow.[61] We shall return later to Muhly's partial change of heart in the 1980s.

ASTOUR'S SUCCESSOR?
J. C. BILLIGMEIER

Although Astour did not have much immediate impact on Classics, his work did elicit some response among ancient historians. In 1976 a short PhD thesis by J. C. Billigmeier, entitled *Kadmos and the Possibility of a Semitic Presence in Helladic Greece*, was approved at the University of California, Santa Barbara. In fact the thesis was more daring than its title suggests, for not only did it accept Astour's work on the Kadmeian and Danaan legends but it went beyond him to consider, favourably, the traditions of Danaos' Egyptian origin. Billigmeier also reiterated a number of the accepted Semitic etymologies for Greek words and place names and revived several of those that had been discarded in the 19th century.[62]

Seven years later, in 1983, it was announced that a small Dutch publisher was going to bring out Billigmeier's work as a book. However, the promised book was withdrawn at the last moment and it has not appeared since. Without knowing the specifics of the case, it is impossible to say anything definitive – on the other hand, the sequence would appear to fit a general pattern by which publishers are 'discouraged' from publishing books advocating this particular academic heresy.[63] Saul Levin, for instance, wrote:

> The search for a willing publisher proved to be slower than the actual research had been, and as disagreeable as the research had been exhilarating. Experience taught me to wait for a year or more for nothing better than a letter of rejection with a brief explanation or none.[64]

This is a good description of my own experience too, while Cyrus Gordon has published all his later books with a small press owned by a family member. Ruth Edwards, whom I come to next, thanks her publisher 'for accepting this work for publication at what proved to be a difficult time'.[65] This pattern shows the way in which control of university presses, and major influence over the commercial ones, allows academics supporting the *status quo* to 'maintain standards' – as they would express it – or, in other words, to repress opposition to orthodoxy.

An Attempt at Compromise: Ruth Edwards

No Classicist has felt it worthwhile – or perhaps been able? – to make a full-scale defence of their position against the challenge coming from Gordon and Astour. On the other hand, one scholar has tried to establish a compromise by which the positive aspects of the Semitists' work could be incorporated into 'respectable' scholarship. This was Dr Ruth Edwards, a pupil of Dr Stubbings, who was mentioned on p. 410 for his belief in the Hyksos conquests. Ruth Edwards' thesis was completed in 1968, but her book only appeared over ten years later. Her work *Kadmos the Phoenician* is of central importance to the topics with which we are concerned.

Her attitude to Astour is critical. She savagely attacks his linkages through mythological parallels because, she argues, many are loose; based on dubious readings of Ugaritic texts; come from different periods; or are simply the result of common folkloric motifs.[66] She is also sceptical about his etymologies, because of the laxity that is inevitable when dealing with purely consonantal West Semitic alphabets. On the other hand, she is equally scathing about the source-critics' denial of the antiquity of the Kadmeian and Danaan legends: as no early Greek writer attacked them, she points out, the source-critics had to rely on the dubious 'argument from silence'. She goes on to prove that the legends of Phoenician colonization are indeed very old.[67]

In general Dr Edwards maintains that all legends should be treated with extreme caution and that, as far as possible, common folkloric motifs should be factored out. But she is convinced that the legends about Kadmos and Danaos contain genuine Mycenaean elements and, moreover, she follows Astour in his argument that evidence from legends is no more subjective than that from other sources. As she puts it:

> It is sometimes assumed by those who urge us to disregard legend and concentrate on these other sources that they are in some way more *objective* than the traditions. But we must emphasize that archaeology, language and documents are objective only within a very restricted compass, in fact only so long as they are concerned with mere observation and description of data. Once they aspire to interpretation, a subjective element enters in. This is particularly worth illustrating in regard to archaeology: the same assemblage of artefacts, the very same destruction levels, may be interpreted in different ways by different archaeologists. There is, moreover, a

tendency for archaeological interpretations to run in fashions. Thus in British prehistory it was customary in the first part of this century for certain changes in material culture to be explained by invasion; today this view is generally rejected in favour of explanations through indigenous development. Similarly in Greek prehistory we can see how up to the 1890s there was a tendency to interpret many Bronze Age achievements as the work of Phoenicians or other Orientals . . . how shortly afterwards the Cretan hypothesis became almost universally accepted, and how at the present time the independence of Mainland Greece is generally stressed. The other sources, then, are not in themselves objective *for the purpose of reconstructing prehistory*; they are subject to limitations of precisely the same order as the legendary tradition. The prehistorian is always working from imperfect and ambiguous material and there is . . . nothing basically illogical or unsound about using legendary evidence, provided one recognizes what one is doing.[68]

Thus, while she accepts that there is a historical kernel to the Kadmeian legends – and, by implication, to the Danaan ones too – Dr Edwards is uncertain whether they refer to a 16th-century Hyksos colonization or to a 14th-century trading settlement. She also believes that the legends allow for a Kadmeian foundation at Thebes coming from either Crete or the Near East, and prefers the latter.[69] But – following her teacher, Dr Stubbings, and the 'Thirlwall tradition' that 'while there may have been Semitic invasions, it did not make any difference' – she makes it clear that the only thing about which she is nearly certain is that there was no large-scale migration to Greece:

If settlement on a *large scale* from the Orient had occurred in Mycenaean Greece, one would expect either more specific traces of it in the archaeological record, or some record of it in the Oriental documents. But evidence of this sort is lacking, and no good support is given by linguistic material, since (*pace* Astour) the Semitisms which occur in Greek are comparatively few and explicable as loan words.[70]

One should note here the use of 'the argument from silence' for archaeology and the circularity of the linguistic argument, which runs something like: 'It is pointless looking for Near Eastern etymologies for Greek words because there is no evidence of sustained contacts between the two cultures. As there are so few loan words, there cannot have been significant contacts . . .'

Nevertheless, despite her caution and her desire to keep them at arm's length, there is no doubt that Ruth Edwards has been profoundly influenced by the work of Gordon and Astour. It is striking that Billigmeier, who was completely unaware of her thesis, should have worked along such similar lines. Taken together, they indicate to me that the Extreme Aryan Model is crumbling. Edwards and Billigmeier both accepted without question that contemporary anti-Semitism had affected historical writing about the Phoenicians. Futhermore – and here Edwards was also following her teacher, Dr Stubbings – both maintained that legends were a legitimate source of information about prehistory.

THE RETURN OF THE
IRON AGE PHOENICIANS

While Astour and his successors have been reviving the Bronze Age Phoenicians or Canaanites, there have also been moves to reinstate the Phoenicians in the Early Iron Age Aegean. The Belgian Classicist D. Van Berchem's articles on 'The sanctuaries of Hercules-Melqart: contributions to the study of the Phoenician expansion in the Mediterranean', published in 1967, showed the extent, depth and high dating of Phoenician influence in the Mediterranean in the early 1st millennium BC.[71] Then, in 1979, a major work on Phoenician expansion by another Belgian scholar, Guy Bunnens, appeared. In this the author combined the Francophone philo-Phoenician tradition of Bérard with the academic self-consciousness of the 1960s and Astour's political analysis of Classics.[72]

By 1980 even Muhly's bailiwick, the University of Pennsylvania, had been infected. A thesis by one of his students, P. R. Helm, lists the considerable amount of recent archaeological evidence suggesting a

Phoenician presence in the Aegean as early as the 10th century BC. And in a paragraph which shows signs of the difficulties involved when a student comes to conclusions that run counter to the strongly held views of his professor, he writes:

> All of this is not to suggest that the theory of a Near Eastern maritime monopoly – rejected as a model for Aegean–Oriental commerce in the Late Bronze Age – should be revived to describe conditions in the Early Iron Age. Nor is it proposed to resurrect the 'days when scholars saw Phoenician traders everywhere in the 8th-century Aegean, bringing their goods to Greece and instructing the Greeks in the higher arts of civilization', even if Phoenician traders are now to be dubbed 'Cypro-Phoenicians'. There is abundant evidence to demonstrate that Athens and the other Greek states regularly engaged in maritime enterprises at this period. *What is suggested is that the Oriental trade was largely, if not exclusively, in the hands of merchants from Cyprus (and probably the Levantine coasts as well)* [elsewhere he writes that Cypriot wares were 'actually of Phoenician origin'] *who traded regularly with the South-Eastern Aegean and occasionally with the Cyclades, Euboea and Attica.* (my emphasis)[73]

Now, in the mid-1980s, Muhly himself is shifting ground. In a paper published in 1984 – and apparently overwhelmed by the archaeological evidence – he sees massive West Semitic influence on Mycenaean Greece.[74] However, despite this volte-face and Helm's conclusions, he remains obdurate on the issue of Phoenicians in the Aegean during the Early Iron Age.[5]

NAVEH AND THE TRANSMISSION OF THE ALPHABET

It is not surprising that the 'revolt' of the Semitists has been most successful at the weak point of the Aryan Model, the alphabet; for we have seen how the attacks on the Extreme Model of the 1950s and 60s were clearly linked to the rise of Jewish self-confidence after the establishment of Israel. Moreover, on the alphabet the challenge came from Israel itself. During the 1940s, the Semitist and epigrapher

Professor Tur-Sinai at Jerusalem had continued to oppose Rhys
Carpenter's ultra-low dating; then in 1973 a new start came with a
path-breaking article by an archaeologist turned epigrapher, Joseph
Naveh, entitled 'Some Semitic epigraphical considerations of the
Greek alphabet'.[76] Working purely from epigraphy, Naveh argued that
the uncertain direction of the early Greek inscriptions resembled not
the regular right to left of the Phoenician alphabet, but the irregularities
of the Canaanite one that had preceded it. Similarly, the stances of a
number of Greek letters, notably A and Σ, were not those of Phoenician
but paralleled those of the earlier period. Naveh further maintained that
the early Greek H and O were identical to the Canaanite, not the
Phoenician, forms and that Δ,E,N,Ξ,Π,Q,P and possibly Θ, though
not identical to the earlier Semitic shapes, could be much more
plausibly derived from the Late Canaanite forms than from the Phoenician ones.[77]

Naveh could see that his scheme faced difficulties over K and M, the
earliest examples of which seemed to resemble Phoenician forms from
around 850 BC rather than the earlier ones. He had rather cumbersome
explanations for these, and despite the complications was convinced
that the older letters and the bulk of the evidence pointed conclusively
to a date from before the standardization of the Phoenician alphabet. As
he – wrongly, in my opinion – accepted Albright's low dating of the
Aḥiram inscription of just after 1000 BC, according to the validity of 'the
argument from silence' he cautiously postulated this date as the time of
standardization, and put the date of transmission fifty years earlier, at
about 1050.[78]

Naveh's article appeared in *The American Journal of Archaeology*, in
which Carpenter and Ullman had published their pieces. Even so, as so
often happens with fundamental challenges to academic orthodoxies,
his argument met with almost no response. Rhys Carpenter's leading
successor, the Oxford Classicist and specialist in early Greek alphabets
Dr L. Jeffery, has limited her criticisms to short comments of the type:
'Naveh, an article deserving serious attention by Greek epigraphers,
though the blank on the Greek side before the 8th century remains a
problem (and his argument is wrong in assuming that the tailless forms
of *mu* and *psi* are early).'[79] On the whole, she and her colleagues have

continued to base themselves on 'the fundamental work of Rhys Carpenter'; though now, since the discovery of datable Greek inscriptions from the 8th century, they tend to think in terms of around 800 rather than 700 BC.[80] Incidentally, this concession removes one of the main props of Carpenter's argument – the need for the Assyrians to propel the Phoenicians westward. It also takes away one of his main motivations to show that Phoenician influence came after the formation of the Greek *polis*.

The situation has been rather different among Semitists. The biblical scholar and epigrapher Professor Kyle McCarter, a pupil and colleague of the great Albright's successor, Professor Frank Cross, the leading Semitic epigrapher at Harvard, tried to find a compromise between Naveh and Carpenter, concluding with the uncertain declaration:

> While the Greeks may have begun to experiment with Phoenician writing as early as the 11th century BC, they did not, for whatever reason, develop a true independent tradition until the beginning of the 8th century. The Greek system, therefore, is best described as descended from a Phoenician prototype of *c.* 800 BC . . .[81]

I believe that Professor McCarter is right to stress two periods of borrowing. Where he is transparently misleading, however, is in his protestations of orthodoxy and his apparent acceptance of Carpenter. McCarter did, in fact, concede Naveh's argument – for what can an alphabetic 'experiment' be, if not an earlier borrowing of an alphabet? On the other hand, McCarter's dilemma has been a general one, and many Semitists have increasingly blurred their dating of the transmission, putting it somewhere between 1100 and 750 BC.[82]

Other Semitists, however, have been moving towards a higher date. Professor Cross is becoming increasingly assertive towards the Classicists. As he put it in 1975, beautifully demonstrating the integral relationship between the low dating of the alphabetic transmission and the Extreme Aryan Model:

From the standpoint of the Orientalist, certain standard arguments
of the Classicists for a late date of borrowing no longer carry weight:
(1) The argument that the Phoenicians were not in the west until the
8th century or later is simply wrong, a classic instance of the fallacy of
argumentum e silentio. The Phoenicians were in contact with the
islands and shores of the West Mediterranean from the 11th century
on . . .
(2) The theory of the prolonged Dark Age of Greek illiteracy
appears to be crumbling . . . To the Orientalist this theory . . .
appears most precarious . . .
(3) The widely held view that the Greek script was borrowed
immediately before the earliest extant Greek inscriptions (now dated
to the second half of the 8th century BC) is wrong . . . We must posit a
considerable time-span between the time the script was borrowed
and its appearance in the earliest known Greek inscriptions to
explain the distance between the earliest Greek scripts and any point
in the sequence of the Proto-Canaanite and Linear Phoenician
script types . . .
(4) No theory of the Greek script will long stand which does not
offer an adequate explanation of archaic features (i.e., typologically
old) in the alphabet of Crete, Thera and Melos. I am strongly
inclined to believe that Phoenicians in the West rather than Greeks
in the East were the primary agents in the initial spread of the
alphabet.[83]

Professor Cross's convictions have been still further strengthened by
recent discoveries in Israel; notably of a 12th-century abecedarium or
complete alphabet found at the village of Izbet Sartah outside Tel Aviv,
the letters of which look far more like those of Greek and Roman than
the later Phoenician ones.[84]

However, there are still Semitic epigraphers who are frightened by
such boldness and they have leapt with some glee upon the recent
discovery of an inscription at Tell Fekheriye, some 200 kilometres
inland on the Syrian-Turkish border. Because the letters of this
inscription – which has tentatively been dated on non-epigraphic
grounds to the mid-9th century – have many 'pre-Phoenician' features,

it has been argued that the archaic characteristics found in the early Greek alphabet could have been transmitted at a much later date.[85] But even these scholars admit that the Levantine coast and its immediate hinterland were writing with standard Phoenician letters by the 9th century. Thus for an alphabet of the Tell Fekheriye type to have reached Greece would have required a leapfrog over Phoenicia, the richest and most prestigious region in the Near East of the time. The implausibility of such an argument only underlines the power of conservatism and the vested interests involved.

Despite this eddy, however, there is no doubt that the general trend for the date of the transmission is now upward, and dates of the 10th century are now relatively common even from those who claim to be opposed to Naveh.[86] There have even been attempts to raise the date beyond the 11th century. In 1981, Gordon's pupil Robert Stieglitz published an article which argued that Naveh had been too minimalist in assuming that the alphabet had been transmitted only at the last possible date before the formation of the Phoenician alphabet. In any event, Stieglitz showed that evidence from late Ugaritic writing indicated the presence of a Phoenician alphabet of the 22-letter type on the Levant by 1400 BC. Furthermore, he demonstrated that there were strong Greek traditions pointing to their having had an alphabet before the Trojan War. Thus he maintained that the alphabet had been transmitted through a Semitic-speaking Eteocretan population in Crete in the 14th century.[87]

In 1983 I proposed a still earlier date for the transmission, based on a new find at Kāmid el Lōz, in the Bek'a valley in Lebanon, that firmly placed the so-called South Semitic Alphabet in the 14th century BC.[88] Inscriptions in the South Semitic scripts, of which the Ethiopian alphabets are the sole survivors today, occur throughout the Arabian and Syrian deserts. One of their most significant differences from the 22-letter Canaanite alphabet and its descendants – which include Phoenician, Aramaic and Aramaic's derivative, the modern Arabic alphabet – is that the South Semitic scripts have up to 30 letters for all the consonants of Arabic and Proto-Semitic. Indeed, the German Semitists and epigraphers Professors Röllig and Mansfeld have plausibly argued, on the basis of the find at Kāmid el Lōz, that the Canaanite alphabet was derived from an earlier one of the South Semitic type.[89]

In 1902 the German Semitist Praetorius pointed out the striking visual and phonetic correspondences between letters from Thamudic and Safaitic – two of the most archaic South Semitic alphabets, but not present in Canaanite – and the so-called 'new letters' Φ, Χ, Ψ, and Ω at the end of the Greek alphabet. These occur in many of the earliest Greek inscriptions, but no origin for them has been discovered. Praetorius went on to argue that these letters were derived from an earlier alphabet of the South Semitic type. Although a number of scholars, including Sir Arthur Evans and the great French Semitist René Dussaud, acknowledged the similarities, the hypothesis was dropped in the 1920s and 30s.[90] The reasons for this seem to have been the incompatibility of these ideas with the Extreme Aryan Model and the archaeological positivism of these decades, which led scholars to demand *proof* of the early existence of the South Semitic alphabets.

Now that there is early attestation, I believe the time is ripe to reopen the debate. I have proposed that the Anatolian, Aegean and other alphabets – and alphabetically derived syllabaries from around the Mediterranean – originate from one in use in the Levant from *before* the development of the 22-letter Canaanite one in the Phoenician cities in the 15th or 14th century BC.[91] To accept this would merely return us to the Ancient Model; to the position of Herodotos and the other ancient writers – with the exception of Josephus – who argued that the alphabet had been introduced to Greece by Kadmos or Danaos, sometime in the middle of the 2nd millennium BC. This return would also destroy the concept of an illiterate Dark Age; while the survival of alphabetic literacy from before the Trojan War would in turn strengthen confidence in the reliability of the Classical Greeks' reports of their Bronze Age past – notably the traditions of colonization.

The assault on the low dating of the transmission of the Semitic alphabet to Greece is only one aspect of the general attack on the Extreme Aryan Model as a whole. There is no doubt that with the tergiversation of Professor Muhly, the active heart of opposition to an early West Semitic presence in the Aegean has collapsed. This is not to say, however, that there is not still considerable inertia working for the maintenance of the Extreme Aryan Model. It is striking, in this context, that the latest edition of the *Cambridge Ancient History*, Volume 3, Part 1 – *The Middle East and the Aegean World, Tenth to Eighth Centuries BC* – has chapters on Assyria, Babylonia, Urartu, the Neo-Hittite states of Syria and Anatolia, Israel and Judah, Cyprus and Egypt – but none on Phoenicia, which was the dominant power in the Mediterranean of the time.

However, although this volume was published in 1982, its planning represents scholarship from well before the rethinking that began in the late 1970s. The bibliography on Eastern influences on Greece, for instance, compiled by the Oxford Classicist Oswyn Murray in 1980 shows how pathetically little work has been done on this crucial subject. And, as one would expect, most authors refer loosely to Babylonia and prefer the 'land bridge', thus avoiding Phoenicia. Murray himself represents the trend away from the Extreme Aryan Model, and seems much more open on the subject of Phoenician influence. However, even he dates that influence to the period after 750 BC; whereas both the heyday of Phoenicia, and the apparent Greek adoption of such Phoenician institutions as the city-state and colonization, began to take place before then.[92]

THE RETURN OF THE EGYPTIANS?

Whether or not these ideas, or those of Naveh and Cross, are accepted, the fact that they are being debated means that the paradigmatic monopoly of the Extreme Aryan Model has been shattered. I believe, therefore, that despite the conservative tide and revived racism of the 1980s, the attack on the Extreme Aryan Model is likely to succeed relatively quickly. The battle to restore the Ancient Model and the position of the Egyptians, on the other hand, will take rather longer. Indeed, the only accepted academic to back the claims that there had been Egyptian colonies, and significant later borrowings from Greeks studying in Egypt, has been the East German Egyptologist Siegfried Morenz. Morenz, a recognized and extremely productive scholar who is best known for his works on Egyptian religion, published in 1969 a very important work on *Europe's Encounter with Egypt*.

This work covers several of the areas approached in this volume. However, it fundamentally differs from *Black Athena* in a number of important ways: it does not set up a scheme comparable to the Ancient and Aryan Models; and it specifically rejects spelling out a sociology of knowledge, though the author is apparently aware of some of the forces involved.[93] Furthermore, Morenz does not consider the possibility of significant linguistic borrowing; nor does he mention Greek borrowings from West Semitic culture. Nevertheless, he does maintain that there was significant cultural contact between Greece and Egypt, especially through Crete.[94] He also explicitly claims that the legends around Danaos contain 'a historical kernel'.[95] He insisted that 'the Greeks did not only learn about the Egyptian gods in Egypt (for example as craftsmen and merchants in Naukratis) [a Greek colony established in Egypt in the 6th century] but also early in their own territory.'[96] He is also convinced that Plato studied in Egypt and that he had learnt from the experience.[97]

Given the social, intellectual and academic forces involved, it is not surprising that Professor Morenz's powerful combination of boldness and detailed scholarship has had so little response. The work was written in conjunction with Swiss scholars, and has been published in the West. Nevertheless, it does not seem to have had a major impact on the mainstream of West German Egyptology as represented by Professor Helck, the intellectually and academically powerful specialist in Ancient Egypt's relations with the outside world. This work of Morenz has not been translated into English or French, and as far as I am aware it is scarcely known outside German-speaking *Mitteleuropa*.

Europe's Encounter with Egypt has had no effect whatsoever on the only other group of scholars who believe that Egypt had a major cultural influence on Greece: black Americans. While the – mainly Jewish – Semitists fought against the Extreme Aryan Model from the fringes of academia, the American champions of the Egyptians, who are largely Blacks, have challenged the Aryan Model from outside the system altogether.

A very small number of black academics, notably Frank Snowden, the leading professor in the field at the chief black university, Howard, have been successful within Classics. They have concentrated on gleaning what little credit the Aryan model allows to Blacks while accepting both its prohibitions: the non-acceptance of a black component of Egyptian culture, and the denial of the Afroasiatic formative elements in Greek civilization.[98] Other scholars, more keenly aware of the degree to which racism has pervaded every nook and cranny of 19th- and 20th-century European and North American culture, have been more sensitive. The pioneer in this effort was George G. M. James, a professor teaching at a small college in Arkansas. In 1954 he published a book entitled *Stolen Legacy: The Greeks were not the authors of Greek Philosophy, but the people of North Africa, commonly called the Egyptians*. *Stolen Legacy* was not concerned with the Bronze Age foundations of Greece but, relying heavily on ancient sources, showed the extent to which the Greeks admitted they had borrowed their learning from the Egyptians during the Iron Age.[99] In a rather looser way James claimed that the Egyptians had been Blacks, and the work ended with a moving appeal calling for a change in black consciousness:

> *It really signifies a mental emancipation, in which the black people will be liberated from the chain of traditional falsehood*, which for centuries incarcerated them in a prison of inferiority complex and world humiliation and insult. (his emphasis)[100]

I had to try twice to have a copy of *Stolen Legacy* accepted by the university library at Cornell before it was finally placed in a smaller branch library. It is not recognized as a *proper book*. Nor has it been read outside the black community.[101] Within intellectual circles in this community, however, it is highly prized and very influential.

Stolen Legacy is generally linked in people's minds to the school of thought pioneered by the late Senegalese nuclear physicist Cheikh Anta Diop. Diop wrote prolifically on what he saw as the integral relationship between black Africa and Egypt, and in the course of this generally assumed the Ancient Model of Greek history and James' theories in *Stolen Legacy* to be true. However, what most concerned him was the great achievements of Egyptian civilization; the systematic denigration of them by European scholars; and his faith that the Egyptians were, as Herodotos had specified, black.[102]

In an interesting analytical essay, the contemporary black scholar
Jacob Carruthers has divided black scholars on this subject into three
schools. The first are 'the old scrappers', who

> without any special training, but with a sincere dedication to ferret-
> ing out the truth about the black past and destroying the big lie of
> black historical and cultural inferiority, took whatever data were
> available and squeezed enough truth from them as circumstances
> allowed.[103]

The second group, which includes George Washington Williams,
W. G. B. Dubois, John Hope Franklin, Anthony Noguera and Ali
Mazrui, have

> argued only that Blacks had a share in building the Egyptian
> civilization along with other races. This strain . . . is completely
> enthralled to European historiography . . . also demand a black share
> in Greek Antiquity which properly understood is true, but for the
> most part these 'Negro Intellectuals' have no grasp of the true
> meaning.[104]

Carruthers sees the third group as an extension of the 'old scrappers'.
They include Diop, Ben Jochannan and Chancellor Williams. He sees
these as having 'developed the multidisciplinary skills to take command
of the facts of the African past which is a necessary element for the
foundation of an African historiography . . .'[105]

There is no doubt, however, that the time for the 'old scrappers' is
past and that most Blacks will not be able to accept the conformity to
white scholarship of men and women like Professor Snowden. However, despite calls for unity, made necessary by the embattled position of
black intellectuals, I suspect that the battle between Carruthers' second
and third groups will continue for a long time.

Thus, at the end of the 1980s, I see continued struggle among black
scholars on the question of the 'racial' nature of the Ancient Egyptians.
On the other hand, there is no serious division among them on the
question of the high quality of Egyptian civilization and of its central
role in the formation of Greece. Furthermore, there is a general
hostility among them to Semitic culture, especially when it is supposed

to have affected Egypt. Meanwhile, where white scholars – with the exception of Morenz – are increasingly prepared to admit that West Semites played a substantial part in the creation of Greek culture, there is still a far greater reluctance to admit fundamental Egyptian influence upon it.[106] One aspect of my work is an attempt to reconcile these two hostile approaches.

THE REVISED ANCIENT MODEL

Interestingly, I find it easier to place myself and my promotion of the Revised Ancient Model in the spectrum of black scholarship than within the academic orthodoxy. I see myself in Carruthers' second class, whom he damns as 'Negro intellectuals'. I am happy to be in the excellent company of Dubois, Mazrui and the others who, while they do not picture all Ancient Egyptians as resembling today's West Africans, do see Egypt as essentially African.

This is an indication of the isolation within academia of the ideas which form the background to this volume. However, I believe that the outrage the Revised Ancient Model causes among Classicists and some ancient historians today is a temporary phenomenon. Why do I think so? First, I believe that the disintegration of the Extreme Aryan Model and the introduction of externalism and relativism into ancient history are having generally subversive effects on the *status quo* as a whole. However, the fundamental reason I am convinced that the Revised Ancient Model will succeed in the relatively near future is simply that within liberal academic circles the political and intellectual under-pinnings of the Aryan Model have largely disappeared.

Since the 1940s both racism and anti-Semitism have lost their respectability with the 'racial' and 'anti-Semitic' policies of Nazi Germany. Since then anti-Semitism has had to become more compli-cated and subterranean. Racism, too, has had to become more devious since the emergence of the Third World. Equally important have been the liberal loss of faith in the mystic of 'science' and the deep suspicion of positivism since the 1960s. Thus – except possibly in the field of language – the Extreme Aryan Model's claim to be *proven scientifically* by *experts* no longer suffices to protect it from common sense.

As I have gone on with my research, people outside the fields concerned have frequently told me that they find my historical schemes more convincing than those provided by the academic Establishment. They cannot see why the colonizations reported by tradition should be so improbable; why the Greek language should not be treated like any other language and why it should not have been heavily influenced by Egyptian and West Semitic; why the Greeks should not have taken their religion from Egypt, as Herodotos and other Ancient Greeks maintained, or why Greek scientists and philosophers should not have learnt much of their science and philosophy in Egypt? In short, the racist and scientistic *raisons d'être* of the Aryan Model no longer provide respectable props. Without them, it will fall. This, however, is a matter for the Conclusion.

CONCLUSION

I T IS ABSURD to try to summarize this book in a dozen paragraphs, when even the previous hundreds of pages in which I have attempted to set out some of the complications of this vast and extraordinarily ramified theme can best be described by the Chinese expression 'looking at flowers from horseback'.

In the Introduction I set out the general way in which I see Western Asian and Northern African history over the past 10,000 years, and – in some more detail – my vision of cultural exchanges across the East Mediterranean in the 2nd millennium BC. In this conclusion, I want to concentrate on the theme of Volume 1, *The Fabrication of Ancient Greece*; which is the change in the models through which the origins of Greek civilization have been perceived. Before I go any further, however, I should like to repeat that the Ancient and Aryan Models are not necessarily incompatible. Indeed, while the Revised Ancient Model which I propose is, as its name states, a form of the Ancient Model, it accepts a number of features from the Aryan one, including the central belief that at some time a significant number of Indo-European speakers came into Greece from the north. On the other hand, there is no doubt that in practice there has been considerable rivalry between the two models, and it is this that I have tried to investigate here.

The main body of the book began with a description of the ways in which Classical, Hellenistic and later pagan Greeks from the 5th century BC to the 5th century AD saw their distant past. I attempted to trace their own vision of their ancestors' having been civilized by Egyptian and Phoenician colonization and the later influence of Greek study in Egypt. I tried to show the ambivalent relationship between Christianity and the Jewish biblical tradition on the one hand and Egyptian religion and philosophy on the other: despite all the centuries of potential and actual rivalry, there was no doubt on either side that up to the 18th century, Egypt was seen as the fount of all 'Gentile' philosophy and learning, including that of the Greeks; and that the Greeks had managed to preserve only some part of these. The sense of loss that this created, and the quest to recover the lost wisdom, were major motives in the development of science in the 17th century.

I went on to show how at the beginning of the 18th century the threat of Egyptian philosophy to Christianity became acute. The Freemasons, who made much use of the image of Egyptian wisdom, were at the centre of the Enlightenment in its attack on Christian order. And it was in opposition to this 18th-century notion of 'reason' on the part of the Egyptophils that the Greek ideal of sentiment and artistic perfection was developed. Further, the development of Europocentrism and racism, with the colonial expansion over the same period, led to the fallacy that only people who lived in temperate climates – that is, Europeans – could really think. Thus the Ancient Egyptians, who – though their colour was uncertain – lived in Africa, lost their position as philosophers. They also suffered through the establishment of the new 'progressive' paradigm because they had lived so far in the past.

In this way, by the turn of the 18th century the Greeks were not only considered to have been more sensitive and artistic than the Egyptians but they were now seen as the better philosophers, and indeed as the founders of philosophy. I suggested that as the Greeks were now viewed as such paragons of wisdom and sensitivity, intelligent counter-revolutionary intellectuals saw the study of them as a way of reintegrating people alienated by modern life; and even of re-establishing social harmony in the face of the French Revolution. Classics as we know it today was created between 1815 and 1830 – an intensely conservative period. The same period also saw the Greek War of Independence, which united all Europeans against the traditional Islamic enemies from Asia and Africa.

This War – and the philhellenic movement, which supported the struggle for independence – completed the already powerful image of Greece as the epitome of Europe. The Ancient Greeks were now seen as perfect, and as having transcended the laws of history and language. Thus it was now thought profane to study any aspect of their culture as one would the culture of other peoples. Moreover, with the rise of a passionate and systematic racism in the early 19th century, the ancient notion that Greece was a mixed culture that had been civilized by Africans and Semites became not only abominable but unscientific. Just as one had to discount the 'credulous' Greeks' stories about sirens and centaurs, so one had to reject legends of their having been colonized by inferior races. Paradoxically, the more the 19th century admired the Greeks, the less it respected their writing of their own history.

I see this destruction of the Ancient Model as entirely the result of social forces such as these, and the requirements put upon the Ancient Greeks by 19th-century Northern Europeans. My belief is that no internalist force – or advance in the knowledge of Ancient Greece – can explain the change. Having said this, I accept that the establishment of the Aryan Model was greatly helped by the working out of the Indo-European language family, which – though inspired by Romanticism – was an internalist achievement; and by the undoubted fact that Greek is fundamentally an Indo-European language. But here, too, the same social and intellectual forces that had brought down the Ancient Model in the 1820s were even more intense in the 1840s and 50s, and they clearly played a role in the increasingly 'northern' picture of Ancient Greece that developed in the late 19th century. At the same time, the sense that only 19th-century men knew how to think 'scientifically' gave the – mainly German – scholars the confidence both to dismiss ancient descriptions of early Greek history and to invent new ones of their own without any regard to the Ancients.

With the intensification of racism in the 19th century there was increasing dislike of the Egyptians, who were no longer seen as the cultural ancestors of Greece but as fundamentally alien. A whole new discipline of Egyptology could thus grow up, to study this exotic culture and at the same time maintain and reinforce Egypt's distance from the 'real' civilizations of Greece and Rome.

The status of Egypt fell with the rise of racism in the 1820s; that of the Phoenicians declined with the rise of racial anti-Semitism in the 1880s and collapsed with its peak between 1917 and 1939. Thus, by the Second World War, it had been firmly established that Greece had not significantly borrowed culturally or linguistically from Egypt and Phoenicia and that the legends of colonization were charming absurdities, as were the stories of the Greek wise men having studied in Egypt. Indeed, these beliefs survived the years between 1945 and 1960, even though their ideological underpinnings of racism and anti-Semitism were generally being discredited in the academic community.

Since the late 1960s, however, the Extreme Aryan Model has been under heavy attack, largely by Jews and Semitists. The important role of Canaanites and Phoenicians in the formation of Ancient Greece is now being increasingly acknowledged. However, the traditional attribution of much of Greek civilization to Egypt is still denied; and in Greek language studies – the last bunker of Romanticism and the Extreme Aryan Model – any talk of significant Afroasiatic influence on Greek is ruled absurd.

The main point I have been trying to make throughout this book is that the Ancient Model was destroyed and replaced by the Aryan Model not because of any internal deficiencies, nor because the Aryan Model explained anything better or more plausibly; what it did do, however, was make the history of Greece and its relations to Egypt and the Levant conform to the world-view of the 19th century and, specifically, to its systematic racism. Since then the concepts of 'race' and categorical European superiority which formed the core of this *Weltanschauung* have been discredited both morally and heuristically, and it would be fair to say that the Aryan Model was conceived in what we should now call sin and error.

However, I insist that its conception in sin, or even error, does not necessarily invalidate it. Darwinism, which was created at very much the same time and for many of the same 'disreputable' motives, has remained a very useful heuristic scheme. One could perfectly well argue that Niebuhr, Müller, Curtius and the others were 'sleepwalking' in the sense in which Arthur Koestler used the term – to describe useful 'scientific' discoveries made for extraneous reasons and purposes which are not accepted in later times. All I claim for this volume is that it has provided a case to be answered. That is, if the dubious origin of the Aryan Model does not make it false, it does call into question its inherent superiority over the Ancient Model. It is for this reason that the next volume in this series is concerned with the competition between the two models as effective tools for understanding Ancient Greece.

WERE THE PHILISTINES GREEK?

T HE PLAUSIBILITY OF A LINK between the two ethnic names Pelasgoi and Peleset or Philistine was discussed in Chapter I, so it would be useful to consider the connections between the Philistines and Crete.[1] No one doubts that the people the Egyptians called the Prst came from the north-west, but there is considerable debate as to whether they came from Crete and the islands or from Mainland Anatolia.

The British archaeologist Dr Sandars argues that Egyptian texts indicate that the Prst (Philistines) came to the Levant by land. This would indicate an Anatolian invasion rather than an Aegean one. Furthermore, the Prst were associated in an Egyptian text with the Trš, who would seem to be the Trojans or Tyrsēnoi from North-Western Anatolia.[2] In the Bible the Philistine princes were known as $s^e r \mathring{a} n \hat{\imath} m$, a title that could come from the Neo-Hittite Sarawanas/Tarawanas or the Greek *tyrannos* (from which comes our tyrant), which was supposedly borrowed from the Lydian. The helmet of the Philistine giant Goliath was called a *qôbaʿ*, which may come from the Hittite *kupaḫḫi* with the same meaning.[3] The name Goliath itself has been linked to the Lydian name Alyattes.[4] Finally, the Lydian historian Xanthos related that a Lydian hero, Mopsos, went from Lydia to Philistia.[5] All these pieces of evidence are used to indicate that the Philistines came from Anatolia rather than Crete.

These arguments, however, are not as strong as they appear. Given the activities of Greeks in Cyprus and in Pamphylia and Cilicia in Southern Anatolia at this time, the late 13th and 12th centuries BC, there is no reason why some of them should not have come overland. According to the poet Kallinos, writing in the 7th century BC: 'Peoples led by Mopsos [a Greek hero of the Trojan War] passed over the Taurus, and that though some of them remained in Pamphylia, the others were dispersed in Cilicia, and also in Syria as far even as Phoenicia.'[6] This account looks remarkably similar to the inscription of Ramessēs III written early in the 12th century BC:

> ... as for the foreign countries, they made a conspiracy in their islands. All at once the lands were on the move, scattered in war. No country could stand before their arms: Hatti [Hittite Central Anatolia], Qode [Cilicia], Karkemesh [Upper Euphrates], Arzawa and Alashiya [Cyprus]. They were cut off, a camp was set up in Amur [Syria] . . . Their league was Prst, Ṯkr, Šklš, Dnn and Wšš.[7]

Note that Ramessēs III saw the conspiracy as having begun 'in their islands', which suggests the Aegean, Sicily or even Sardinia. It would also seem to indicate the presence of the Prst in this last campaign of the 'Sea Peoples'.

It should be noted, too, that the Prst are linked here to the Ṯkr, who also settled in Palestine and who may have been associated with the Greek hero Teukros. The name Šklš is almost certainly connected to Sicily, and Dnn to Danuna and the Danaans. The Trš were not listed on this occasion.[8]

The word Srnm meaning 'princes' appears in Ugaritic texts showing that whether or not it had Anatolian links, the word sᵉrānîm was current on the Levant before the invasions and cannot be directly related to Anatolians among the invading 'Sea Peoples'.[9] Qôbaʿ may be related to the Hittite kupaḫḫi, but Hittites appear frequently in biblical Palestine and there is little doubt that Hittite influenced the Canaanite dialects spoken there.[10] Wearing qôbaʿ, moreover, was not restricted to Philistines. Astour has pointed out that this headgear was also worn by Saul,

Egyptians, Babylonians, Tyrian mercenaries and even Yahwe himself.[11] A connection between Goliath and Alyattes is possible, but according to the Book of Samuel, Goliath belonged to the Rᵉpåʾîm of Gath, who may have been Canaanite in the opinion of J. Strange, a modern student of the subject.[12] This suggestion seems unlikely to me. It would seem more probable that, like the West Semitic Ditanu and the Greek Titans, the Rᵉpåʾîm were the giant spirits of the dead.[13] Hence the title Rᵉpåʾîm may merely have referred to Goliath's size, and the connection Goliath/Alyattes is a possibility.

The strongest argument in favour of an Anatolian migration remains the Lydian tradition that Mopsos the Lydian went from Lydia to Ashkelon in Philistia. However, as we have seen, there were also traditions of expeditions led by a Greek Mopsos, and by other Greek heroes, through Anatolia and Cyprus to the Levant. Apparent confirmation of the Greek Mopsos legends came with the discovery at Karatepe in Cilicia of an 8th-century bilingual inscription in hieroglyphic Hittite – or Luvian – and Phoenician. This refers to a kingdom of Dnnym and to an ancestor called Muksas in Luvian and Mps in Phoenician.[14] Confusingly, the ethnic name points to a Greek settlement, while that of the founder of the dynasty indicates an Anatolian one, which would give support to the Anatolian legend. Thus there are indications that Anatolian elements were involved in the Levant at the time of the 'Invasions of the Sea Peoples' in the 13th and 12th centuries BC.

Evidence for the involvement of Greek speakers is even stronger. Firstly, there is the consistent biblical tradition that the Philistines came from Kaphtôr, Crete or the southern Aegean.[15] There are also references to mercenaries called Kᵉrētî and Pᵉlētî, who are always mentioned together and sometimes paralleled to the Philistines; it is generally thought that these are Cretans and Philistines. They are usually associated with David, who fought not only against Philistines but for them.[16] It should be noted that Hebrew contained perfectly adequate names for Anatolian peoples: Ḥittî, Hittites who appear frequently, Tŭbal, Mešek and Tîrås – the last may well be the same as the Egyptian Tršᵛ and the Trojans. Nevertheless, the Philistines were linked to none of these, but repeatedly and specifically to Kaphtôr;

thus there seems no reason to doubt the biblical links between the Philistines and Crete.

From the archaeological point of view it is striking that the so-called 'Philistine pottery', found largely in the areas associated with the biblical Philistines, is locally made but resembles the style known as Mycenaean III C IB. The closest parallels come from Tarsus in Cilicia, Cyprus, and Knossos in Crete. There is no question, however, that the style originated in the Aegean and that the other regions where it has been found correspond well with the reports of Greek settlement at this period.[17] The fact that the culture of Philistia from the 12th to the 10th century BC shows strong Egyptian influence is not surprising in view of its closeness to Egypt, and the fact that many Sea Peoples served as mercenaries for the Egyptians. Thus the written and the archaeological evidence connecting the Philistines to the Aegean agree to an extent that is rare, if not unique. Despite this, however, the Israeli archaeologist Dr Dothan admits in her massive work on the Philistines that their material culture came from the Aegean, but insists that the Philistines were Illyrians, Thracians or Anatolians; anything, in fact, other than Greeks.[18]

Working on the probable assumption that the bulk of the Philistines originated from Crete and the Aegean and made Mycenaean pottery, it becomes extremely likely that they spoke Greek. Although a non-Hellenic Eteocretan survived in Crete until Hellenistic times, as mentioned above, we know from Linear B that Greek was the dominant language on the island well over a century before the earliest reference to the Prst.

There are other indications, too, that the Philistines were associated with Greece. Assyrian texts refer to a certain Ia-ma-ni or Ia-ad-na, two different forms both meaning 'Greek', who seized the throne of the Philistine city of Ashdod and rebelled against Assyria in 712 BC. There has been considerable debate as to whether this man was a Greek or a local leader.[19] But although it has been clearly established that the Philistines were rapidly Semitized, the problem of Ia-ma-ni could be resolved by following the hypothesis that some influential 8th-century Philistines were of Greek descent.

After the Scythian invasion of the 7th century and the Neo-

Babylonian deportations of the 6th, the name 'Philistine' seems to have been partially replaced by Gazan (*'azzâtî*) and Ashdodite (*'ašdôdî*), from the two chief cities of the region. In about 400 BC Nehemiah condemned Jewish marriage to the women of Ashdod and referred to the 'language of Ashdod', *'ašdôdît*, as a threat to the 'language of the Jews', *Y^ehûdît*.[20] The meaning of the latter term is uncertain but, because both Aramaic and Hebrew were spoken by Jews at this time, it is unlikely that Nehemiah was concerned about a West Semitic language. On the other hand, Greek, which was expanding rapidly throughout the East Mediterranean, would seem to be a much more likely threat. There is no biblical word for 'Greek' as a language. Therefore it would seem plausible to propose that by *'ašdôdît* Nehemiah meant 'Greek' – yet another indication of links between Greeks and Philistines.

A further indication of contacts between Philistia and Greece at this period is that in about 400 BC Gaza was the only city east of Athens minting coins according to Attic weights. It should be noted, however, that they were inscribed with Phoenician letters – some even with an inscription reading either Yhd (Jew) or Yhw (Yahweh) – and a depiction of a seated figure who would seem to be the god of Israel.[21] Other coins from the town have the inscription MEINΩ, which is supposed to be related to Minos of Crete.[22]

Despite the fierce defences of Jaffa and Gaza against Alexander, subsequent Hellenization of the region was far more complete than in either Phoenicia or Judaea. As Victor Tcherikover, the great historian of the Hellenistic period, implies, this would seem to indicate a propensity to Greek culture.[23] Stephanos of Byzantium, for instance, writing in the 5th century AD, stated that the god Marna, worshipped at Gaza, was Zeus Kretogenes, 'born in Crete'.[24]

To sum up: the closest analogy to the invasion of the 'Sea Peoples' would seem to be that of the Crusades. Waves of northern invaders came by land and sea in a period of great confusion; bands crisscrossed each other in their search for plunder and land to settle. The Crusaders were largely Romance-speaking but of different dialect nationalities, and they also included Germans and English. Similarly, the Sea Peoples seem to have been made up of different linguistic groups, including both Greek and Anatolian speakers. The likelihood is that although other groups may have been largely made up of Anatolian speakers, the Philistines were predominantly Greeks. Until the decipherment of Linear B as Greek, however, the Philistines' Cretan connection provided no embarrassment; it was easy to see them as Pre-Hellenes. The failure of scholars since 1952 to recognize the powerful evidence linking the Philistines to the Greeks can be explained only in terms of the 19th- and 20th-century view of 'Philistines' as the exact opposite of the Hellenes – as enemies of culture.

Notes

Introduction

1. See ch. VI, Notes 143–4.
2. See below and ch. X, Notes 7–9.
3. For a discussion of this literature see p. 54 below and vol. 2.
4. Bernal (1980). For the Uruk tablets, G. Pettinato (personal communication, Cornell, 3 Dec. 85).
5. See below, ch. X, Notes 7–9.
6. Goodenough (1970).
7. Bernal (1987b).
8. Warren (1965, p. 8; Renfrew (1972, pp. 345–8).
9. Bernal (1983a, 1983b; see also 1987b).
10. Bernal (1980).
11. Spyropoulos (1972; 1973).
12. Bernal (1986a, pp. 73–4).
13. See vol. 3.
14. Herodotos, VI.53–5.
15. Buck (1979, p. 43) refers to Spyropoulos' hypothesis but dismisses it. Symeono-glou (1985) fails to cite the former's articles containing it in his massive bibliography. Without mentioning the pyramidal form or any Egyptian connections, he snipes at Spyropoulos' dating (pp. 273–4). Helck (1979) neglects Spyropoulos' work altogether.
16. Bernal (1987b).
17. Farag (1980).

18. La Marche and Hirschbeck (1984, p. 126). For the Irish oaks: personal communication M. G. L. Baillie to P. Kuniholm, Athens, April 1985.

19. Michael and Weinstein (1977, pp. 28–30).

20. For the correlation with China, see Pang and Chou (1985, p. 816). For the Shang date, see Fan (1962, p. 24). For a low revisionist date, see Keightley (1978); for a high one, see Chang (1980, pp. 354–5).

21. Stubbings (1973, pp. 635–8).

22. Bietak (1979).

23. C. Müller (1841–70, vol. III, p. 639).

24. Hemmerdinger (1969); McGready (1969); Pierce (1971).

25. For Foucart and the responses to him, see below, ch. V, Note 45.

Chapter I

THE ANCIENT MODEL IN ANTIQUITY

1. Trans. A. de Selincourt, 1954, p. 406. The text refers to the kingships of Argos and Sparta. For the later Spartan kings' belief in their Hyksos ancestry, see vol. 2.

2. *Iliad*, II.681. For an almost complete list of Classical references to the Pelasgians, see F. Lochner-Hüttenbach (1960, pp. 1–93).

3. *Iliad*, II.841; X.429 and XVII.290.

4. The tentative identification was made from inscriptional evidence by Professor Bietak, the excavator of Tel ed Daba'a (Avaris) (1979, p. 255). The phonetic problems with the derivation of Laris(s)a from R-3ht are not great. The Egyptian initial r was usually rendered as l in Greek. In Middle Egyptian 3, the double 'aleph, was transcribed in Semitic as r. Medial laryngeals like ḥ often disappeared and there are many instances of the Egyptian final t being rendered as *-is* in Greek. For the details and phonetic parallels, see vol. 2.

5. *Iliad*, II.841 and XVII.301.

6. Strabo, XIII.621.c, cited with other references to the connections of Laris(s)ai with mud, rich soil and Pelasgians by K. O. Müller (1820, p. 126).

7. For Danaos' associations with the Larisa and Argos, see Pausanias, II.19,3 (see Frazer, Levi in Bibliography).

8. Strabo, VIII.6.9.

9. See Ahl (1985, pp. 158–9).

10. For 'Inb ḥd, see Gauthier (1925, vol. I, p. 83) and Gardiner (1947, vol. II, pp. 122–6). The Hittite capital Hattus or Hattusas also meant 'Silver'. Whether the Greek and Anatolian names are calques for the much older Egyptian one or whether they come from the actual colour of the city or citadel walls is impossible to say.

11. *Iliad*. II.681.

12. *Iliad*. XVI.233. For further discussion of Dodona, see vol. 3.

13. *Odyssey*. XIX.175.

14. *Aigimios*, fr. 8, in White (1914, p. 275).

15. V.80.1.

16. On the whole I accept the arguments of C. Gordon (1962a, 1963a–b, 1966, 1967, 1968a–b, 1969, 1970a–b, 1973, 1975, 1980, 1981), *pace* Duhoux (1982, p. 232). For implausible attempted etymologies of 'Eteocretan' see Duhoux, pp. 16–20. The word **eteos* itself has no Indo-European etymology. A plausible derivation would be from the Egyptian i̓t found in Demotic and as *eiōt* in Coptic meaning 'barley'. i̓t m i̓t in Middle and Late Egyptian, literally 'barley in barley', means 'really barley' – presumably referring to the grain or kernel. In Greek one finds the term *eteokrithos* (good or genuine barley). For the centrality and seriousness of wordplay in ancient civilization, see below. Whether or not Eteokrētes is a pun on eteokrithos, i̓t would seem a plausible etymology for **eteos*. There is probably, however, some contamination from the Egyptian i̓t(y), Coptic *eiōt*, 'forefathers'. This would seem to be the origin of the clan-name Eteoboutadēs, the hereditary priests of the temple of Athena Polias in Athens.

17. J. Bérard (1951, p. 129) and Lochner-Hüttenbach, p. 142. For the Cretan origin of the Philistines, see the Appendix.

18. W. F. Albright (1950, p. 171); for the early transmission of the alphabet, see Bernal (1987a).

19. For the influence of writing on spoken languages, see Lehmann (1973, pp. 178 and 226) and Polomé (1981, pp. 881–5).

20. See the Appendix.

21. Fr. 16, *The Great Eoiai* (White, p. 264).

22. Strabo. V.2.4.

23. Akousilaos, fr. 11, quoted in Ridgeway (1901, I, p. 90). At another point, however, he restricted the meaning to the Peloponnese, as did Ephoros in the 4th century. See Apollodoros, II.1.1. For Aischylos, see his *The Suppliants*, 251–60.

24. Herodotos, I.58 and II.50.

25. Herodotos, II.50–5; IV.145; VII.94. For other surveys of his views on Pelasgians, see Abel (1966, pp. 34–44) and A. B. Lloyd (1976, pp. 232–4). For the early Athenians as 'Pelasger und Barbaren', see Meyer (1892, vol. 1, p. 6).

26. M. Pallotino (1975, pp. 72–3).

27. Thucydides, I.3.2.

28. Herodotos, II.50–5 and Diodoros, III.61.1.

29. Herodotos, VIII.44. For Kekrops as an Egyptian, see vol. 2. For this belief of Erechtheus, see Diodoros, I.29.1 and schol. Aristeides, XIII.95, quoted in Burton (1972, p. 124). The predominant view was that he was indigenous.

30. Euripides, *Archelaos*, (lost) fragment, quoted in Strabo, V.2.4.

31. *The Suppliants*, 911–14.

32. Strabo, V.2.4. and IX.2.3.

33. Pausanias, I.28.3; III.20.5; IV.36.1; VIII.1.4–5 and 2.1.

34. Pausanias, VIII.1.4.

35. Niebuhr (1847a, vol. 1, p. 28).
36. Meyer (1928, vol. 2, Pt 1, p. 237, n.).
37. For a survey of modern views, see Abel (1966, pp. 1–6).
38. See ch. VII, Note 59.
39. Thucydides, I.3.2.
40. Ridgeway (1901, vol. 1, pp. 280–92); Grumach (1968/9, pp. 73–103, 400–30); Hood (1967, pp. 109–34).
41. Herodotos, I.58.
42. See Grote (1846–56, vol. 2, p. 350, etc.); Gobineau (1983, vol. 1, p. 663); Wilamowitz-Moellendorf (1931, vol. 1, pp. 60–3).
43. V. Bérard (1894); ch. IX, Note 33.
44. See below and vol. 2.
45. Sandars (1978, p. 185); Snodgrass (1971, pp. 180–6); Wardle (1973).
46. See the Appendix.
47. Herodotos, I.58. Abel (1966, p. 13) points out that the fact that this information is introduced by the particle *gar* (for) indicates that Herodotos was referring to conventional wisdom and not to a discovery of his own.
48. Herodotos, VII.94–5 trans. p. 473.
49. Chantraine (1968–75, vol. 1, p. 475b); T. Braun (1982, pp. 1–4).
50. The Greek letter upsilon required an initial 'breathing', or h. Thus it would have been impossible to have a form *Yantes. Further confirmation of the Egyptian etymology would seem to come from yet another Greek name for primitive people – which is also particularly associated with Attica – Paiōn. Scholars are generally agreed that it is cognate with Iōn or Iaōn but they cannot understand the supposedly 'Pre-Hellenic' mechanism by which the two are related; see the bibliography in Cromey (1978, p. 63). The source could simply be explained as the Egyptian *p3 iwn* (the barbarian).
51. For Xouthos, see Herodotos, VII.94; VIII.44 and Pausanias, VII.1.2. For Poseidon as patron of the Ionians, see Farnell (1895–1909, vol. 4, pp. 10–11, 33–4, etc.). The uncertainty of the initial sibilant in Xouthos and Zethos, which is probably also a variant of Seth, may well come from confusion with the Canaanite Sid – the god of the sea and hunting – and the Semitic root √swd (hunt), an activity which was of central importance to both Seth and Poseidon, whose name was sometimes written Poteido/an. See vol. 3.
52. Gomme (1913). For a description of his continuing influence, see Muhly (1970, esp. p. 40) and R. Edwards (1979, p. 65, n. 63).
53. See R. Edwards (1979, p. 77, n. 70).
54. K. O. Müller (1820–4, vol. 1, pp. 113–21).
55. R. Edwards (1979, p. 77, n. 70); Chantraine (1968–75, vol. 1, p. 21). The West Semitic root first found in the Eblaite *adana* would seem to come from the Egyptian *idn(w)* (deputy, governor).
56. Merkelbach and West (frs 141 and 143).

57. *Catalogue of Women*, fr. 16 and that quoted in Strabo, VIII.6.8 and fr. 17. For the fragment of the *Danais*, see Kinkel (1877, fr. 1) and R. Edwards (1979, p. 75).

58. Parian Marble, 1.11.44–5 and Herodotos, IV.53. For an ancient survey of estimates see Tatian, I.31. For a study of the ancient datings of both poets, see Jacoby (1904, pp. 152–8).

59. Forrest (1982, p. 286). For good surveys, and a bibliography on modern literature on Hesiod and his dates, see G. P. Edwards (1971, pp. 1–10, 200–28. For more on Homer, see ch. VI, Note 3 below. For discussion of the low dating of the transmission, see ch. IX, Notes 74–91.

60. For all these dates and their political implications, see Bernal (1987a; 1988).

61. For this widespread argument, see Finley (1978, pp. 32–3). The references to the Phoenicians have led some scholars to claim that the *Odyssey* was composed considerably later than the *Iliad* (Nilsson, 1932, pp. 130–7; Muhly, 1970). Muhly (p. 20, n. 6) points out that this theory had already been proposed in Antiquity (Longinus, *De Sublimitate*, IX.13).

62. See Albright (1950, pp. 173–6; 1975, pp. 516–26); Cross (1974, pp. 490–3; 1979, pp. 103–4; 1980, pp. 15–17; Sznycer (1979, pp. 89–93); Naveh (1982, pp. 40–1); Helm (1980, pp. 95–6, 126).

63. Finley (1978, p. 33).

64. See vol. 3.

65. Finley (1978, p. 33).

66. Forrest (1982, pp. 286–7).

67. Walcot (1966, p. 16) accepts this possibility.

68. Walcot (1966, pp. 27–53). It should be pointed out that while Zeus was never confused with Marduk in Greece, he was frequently identified with Am(m)on. Therefore it is quite possible that theogonies focusing on him may well have been taken from 2nd-millennium Egypt. For the significance of Walcot's playing down of Egypt and Phoenicia, see ch. X, Note 33.

69. *Works and Days*, p. 589. There is no reason to doubt that Biblinos means from Bi/yblos.

70. The idea that *The Suppliants* belonged to a trilogy was first suggested by A. W. Schlegel in 1811. See Garvie (1969, p. 163). For its themes, see Apollodoros, II.1.3 and III.1.1, Nonnos (*Dionysiaka*, II.679–98, III.266–319), and the Scholiast on Euripides' *The Phoenician Women*. All these are neatly summarized in R. Edwards (1979, pp. 27–8). See also Garvie (1969, p. 163). For references to the story of Amymone, see Frazer (1921, vol. I, p. 138, n. 2).

71. F. R. Earp (1953, p. 119), cited by Garvie (1969, p. 29).

72. Garvie (1969, pp. 1–28).

73. Garvie (1969, pp. 29–140).

74. *The Suppliants*, 1.154. For a discussion of this, see Johansen and Whittle (1980, vol. 2, p. 128).

75. Scholiast on *Hekabe 886*. See the article in *Pauly-Wissowa*, IV, 2, 2094–8. For its ambiguity, see Garvie (1969, p. 164, n. 3).

76. *The Suppliants*, 1s. 911–14, trans. Weir Smyth pp. 89–91.

77. Diodoros, I.24.8. His informants clearly identified Io with Isis.

78. 46.20. Astour (1967a, pp. 86–7, 388).

79. Johansen and Whittle (1980, vol. 2, p. 171).

80. ls. 155–8, 228–34, 822–4. See Johansen and Whittle (1980, vol. 2 p. 184).

81. See Ahl (1985, especially pp. 17–63).

82. Garvie (1969, pp. 71–2). Herodotos, IV.199, wrote that *bounos* (hill) – which, although the standard term for mountain in modern Greek, is rare in the Classical language – came from Cyrene in what is now Libya. See Garvie (p. 71) and Johansen and Whittle (1980, vol. 2, pp. 105–6). It would seem to me legitimate to link it, at least at a punning level, to the Egyptian root √ bn, found in the words *wbn* (rise like the sun) and *bnbn* (point or peak) or the (primeval hill). See A. B. Lloyd (1976, pp. 318–19).

83. Garvie (1969, p. 72).

84. J. Bérard (1952, p. 35).

85. Astour (1967a, p. 94). Johansen and Whittle, (1980, vol. 2, p. 45) cite, without giving reference, an objection by J. R. Harris to the quantity of this vowel which, given the distortions caused in the shift and the putative loaning, seems a very weak case. Johansen and Whittle themselves refer to the 'disregard of quantity in Aeschylaean etymologizing' (p. 105). Harris's main charge, however, is made on the purely ideological grounds that a connection between Epaphos and Aphophis 'makes no sense'.

86. *Iliad*, 1.270; 3.49 and *Odyssey*, 7.25; 16.18, cited in Johansen and Whittle (1980, vol. 2, p. 105).

87. For the ancient knowledge see, for example, Fréret (1784, p. 37). For the modern, see Sheppard (1911, p. 226).

88. Vercoutter (1975, cols 338–50).

89. Van Voss (1980, cols 52–3).

90. *The Suppliants*, 260–70 (trans. Weir Smyth, 1922, vol. 1, p. 27).

91. Van Voss (1980, cols 52–3); Budge (1904, vol. I, p. 198).

92. Castor, cited in Eusebius, 1866, p. 177. For the complications of Eusebius' text, see A. A. Mosshammer (1979, pp. 29–112). See also Fréret (1784, p. 20). See above, Notes 8–10, for the many different meanings of the name Argos itself.

93. Num. 13:22–33; Deut. 1:28, 2:10–21, 9:2; Josh. 11:21–2, 14: 12–15, 15:14 and 15:13–14; Judg. 1:20. For the Philistines, see Appendix. Gobineau (1983, vol. 1, p. 663) saw Inachos and *anax* as coming from the Semitic *'ānâq*.

94. In Num. 13:22 it is specified that Hebron – which was probably the *later* name of Qiriat 'Arba – was founded seven years before Zoan, which seems to have been the Hyksos capital Avaris, founded in the 17th century BC or earlier.

95. Fréret (1784, p. 37). The derivation from √'nq ('necklace', or possibly 'neck') would seem to be a folk one.

96. The detailed phonetics of the loan will be argued in vol. 2.

97. Apollodoros, II.1,4. For the variants see Frazer (1921, vol. 1, pp. 134–5). The idea of water of 'life', or 'living' or flowing water, is, of course, natural. It occurs in later Greek thought as ὕδωρ ζῶν, and even more strongly in the Jewish and Christian traditions. One finds it, for instance, in the Hebrew מַיִם חַיִּים (Leviticus 14:5, 6, etc.). See also Daniélou (1964, pp. 42–57). For further Latin complications of Io's relationships to her father Inachos (river water), flumen and the fulmen (thunder) of her ravisher, Zeus, in Ovid's Metamorphosis, see Ahl (1985, pp. 144–6).

98. See Astour (1967a, p. 86).

99. Johansen and Whittle (1980, vol. 2, p. 65).

100. I accept the point made by T. T. Duke (1965, p. 133).

101. Ahl (1985, pp. 151–4). For the Egyptian and Greek roots of the identification of Isis with the moon, see Hani (1976, p. 220).

102. The Egyptian origins of Athena, like those of Libya's husband Poseidon, have been touched on in the Introduction and will be discussed in more detail in vol. 2.

103. Meyer (1892, vol. 1, p. 81) cited in Astour (1967a, p. 80). Meyer claims that the vocalization of Bēlos indicates that the name could not have come from the Canaanite ba'al but must come from the Aramaic bᵉ'ēl; it must therefore be late. It could equally, however, have changed from *Bālos to Bēlos in Greek.

104. The great intricacies of the Egypto-Semitic roots and the word phoinix will be discussed in vol. 2.

105. Astour (1967a, p. 81).

106. In two parallel texts dating to around 2500 BC, one from the Syrian city of Ebla and the other from the Mesopotamian site of Abu Salabikh, one finds the two names Am-ni and DA-ne^ki in matching places in what seems to be the western region (G. Pettinato, 1978, p. 69, no. 186). The author has suggested to me (personal communication, March 1983) that the former could be related to the Cretan city of Amnisos, the name of which is now attested in both Linear B and Egyptian from the 2nd millennium. In this case – or even if Am-ni were merely a generic term for 'the west', which in Egyptian is 'imn – the land of Da-ne could well refer to Crete.

107. See Helck (1979, pp. 31–5; Gardiner (1947, vol. I, pp. 124–6). For more on these problems, see vol. 2.

108. Astour (1967a, pp. 1–80).

109. See Gordon (1962b, p. 21); Yadin (1968); Arbeitman and Rendsburg (1981) for a survey on the literature on this and some important new points.

110. Gardiner (1947, vol. I, p. 126); Morenz (1969, p. 49). The root ṯni (to grow old) would seem to be the origin, through the common euphemisms surrounding

death, of the Greek root √θν found in *thanatos* and elsewhere, meaning 'die' but with connotations of ageing. For Egyptian confusion of old age and death, see Hornung (1983, pp. 151–3).

111. For doubts about this tradition see above, pp. 43–5.

112. Johansen and Whittle (1980, vol. 2, p. 5).

113. Farnell (1895, vol. 1, pp. 72–4); A. B. Cook (1925, vol. 2, pt 2, pp. 1093–8).

114. The other being that by Euripides.

115. *The Phoenician Women*, 202–49. For other plays, see *The Bakchai*, 170–2, 1025 and *Phrixos*, frs 819 and 820.

116. For a general survey, see R. Edwards (1979, pp. 45–7).

117. Herodotos, II.182 (trans. p. 201).

118. Herodotos, IV.147 (trans. p. 319).

119. Herodotos, II.171 (trans. p. 197).

120. Herodotos, V.58 (trans. p. 361).

121. Herodotos, II.49–52 (trans. pp. 149–51). For recent detailed attempts to explain this all away, see Froidefond (1971, pp. 145–69); A. B. Lloyd (1976, vol. 2, pp. 224–6).

122. Herodotos, II.55–8.

123. Plutarch, *De Malig*. For the seriousness with which some modern scholars have begun to treat Herodotos in the last fifteen years, see A. B. Lloyd (1976).

124. Herodotos, II.49 (trans. p. 149).

125. Thucydides, I.8.

126. Herodotos, VI.53–4.

127. Thucydides, I.3.2.

128. See, for instance, Snodgrass (1971, p. 19).

129. Thucydides, I.3.2; for a discussion of this, see Strabo, VIII.6.6. The formula καθ Ἑλλάδα καί μέσον Ἄργος, (through Hellas and Middle Argos) is frequently used for Greece in the *Odyssey*, I.343–4; IV.726, 816; XV.80.

130. Thucydides, I.1.

131. *Panegyrikos*, 50 (trans. Norlin, p. 149). For the context of the speech, see Bury (1900, pp. 540–1, 568–9). See also Snowden (1970, p. 170), who welcomes it as a sign of the Greek lack of racialism.

132. Diogenes Laertius, VIII.86–9; de Santillana (1963, pp. 813–15).

133. *Helen*, X.68 (trans. p. 226).

134. *Bousiris*, 30. *Pace* Smelik and Hemelrijk (1984, p. 1877), who wear their anti-Egyptian colours clearly on their sleeves.

135. *Bousiris*, 16–23.

136. *Bousiris*, 28.

137. See Cicero, *Tusculanae Disputationes*, V.3.9; the derivation of the word *sophia* from the Egyptian *sb3* (teaching, learning) will be discussed in vol. 2.

138. Bury (1900, p. 541); Gardiner (1961, p. 374) and Strauss (forthcoming, ch. 6).

The name Salamis – which was given to sheltered harbours in both Cyprus and the Salamis, just west of Athens – clearly comes from the Semitic *salam* (peace), found today in the Arabic toponym Dar es Salam (Harbour of Peace). Athens proved to be the alliance's weak reed.

139. Wilamowitz-Moellendorf (1919, vol. 1, pp. 243–4; vol. 2, p. 116, n. 3).

140. Plutarch, *de Iside*, 10; *Lykourgos*, 4; Froidefond (1971, pp. 243–6). In footnote 77 he confesses that Strabo – 1st century – also referred to Lykourgos' indebtedness to Egypt.

141. See vol. 2.

142. *Bousiris*, 18 (trans. p. 113).

143. Froidefond (1971, p. 247).

144. Herodotos, II.81. For a later affirmation, see Diogenes Laertius, VIII.2–3. For an attempt to deny it, see Delatte (1922, p. 152 and elsewhere).

145. *Bousiris*, 28. Isokrates, p. 119.

146. See, for instance, Norlin's trans., p. 112, n. 1.

147. See the discussion in Froidefond (1971, pp. 240–3).

148. For surveys on the controversies among Aryanist scholars as to whether or not Plato went to Egypt, see Froidefond (1971, p. 269, n. 24) and Davis (1979, p. 122, n. 3). It should be noted, however, that as Davis points out: 'the tradition [is] never explicitly contradicted by any of our Classical authorities.' It should also be noted that some of the greatest scepticism about Plato's visit came in the work of T. Hopfner, especially in his *Plutarch über Isis und Osiris*.

149. *Phaidros*, 274 D (trans. H. N. Fowler, p. 563).

150. *Philebos*, 16C; *Epinomis*, 986E–987A.

151. Davis, 1979, pp. 121–7.

152. Cited in Proklos, *In Tim.* LXXVI (trans. Festugière, 1966–8, vol. 1, p. 111). Plato's telling of the legend of Atlantis will be referred to below.

153. Marx, *Kapital*, vol. 1, Pt 4 (1983, p. 299).

154. Popper (1950, pp. 495, 662).

155. For the former, see A. E. Taylor (1929, pp. 275–86). For the latter, see for instance Lee (1955, Introduction).

156. Herodotos, II.29, 62; Plato, *Timaios*, 21E. For details on the *real* relationship between Sais and Athens, see vol. 2. See also Bernal (1985a, pp. 78–9).

157. *Timaios*, 22B (trans. Bury, 1913, p. 33).

158. *Timaios*, 23A. It is possible that Plato really is recording an old tradition here. The content of legends of disaster will be discussed in vol. 2. It is also possible that there was a sacred paranomasia, or pun, in that by Athens the priest meant Ḥt Nt, the religious – and hence the earlier – name of Sais. See the Introduction and vol. 2. See also Bernal (1985a, p. 78).

159. For Isokrates, see Note 133 above. For Plato, see *Menexenos*, 245D.

160. See Note 132 above.

161. *Meteorologika*, I.14.351b, 28.

162. *Metaphysika*, I.1.981b.

163. *De Caelo*, II.14.298a. For modern attempts to remove astronomy from the list, see Froidefond (1971, p. 347. n. 35).

164. Froidefond (1971, p. 350, n. 61).

165. G. G. M. James (1954, pp. 112–30) claims that this position gave him acess to Egyptian libraries, which in turn could explain the almost incredible quantity and range of Aristotle's writings. This argument, and the general one that the Greek conquest of the Middle East was similar to that of the Arabs a thousand years later – in that they took over and Hellenized/Arabized much of the earlier culture and lost the rest – though extremely hard to test, is worthy of serious examination.

166. H.-J. Thissen (1980, cols 1180–1).

167. Quoted in Diodoros, XL.3.2, trans. F. R. Walton and R. M. Geer, vol. XII, p. 281.

168. This letter is quoted in both I Maccabees XII:20–2 and Josephus, *Antiquities*, XII.226. Professor Momigliano, who believes in the authenticity of most of the documents contained in I Maccabees, maintains that this letter is apocryphal. Working within the Aryan Model, he naturally treats the idea of a relationship between the Jews and the Spartans as absurd (1968, p. 146). E. Rawson (1969, p. 96) is equally incredulous. Neither refers to E. Meyer's thoughtful work on it (1921, p. 30), in which he accepts its genuineness and links it to the work of Hekataios. J. Klausner (1976, p. 195) has no doubts about its authenticity. See also Astour (1967a, p. 98).

169. For a debate on whether Kadmos was an Egyptian or a Phoenician, see Pausanias, IX.12.2. For the competing dates of the ancient chronographers for his landings, see R. Edwards (1979, p. 167).

170. Zenodotos, quoted in Diogenes Laertius, VII.3 and 30 (trans. Hicks, vol. II, p. 141).

171. Diodoros Sikeliotes, I.9.5–6 (trans. Oldfather, vol. I, pp. 33–5).

172. Diodoros Sikeliotes, V.57.1–5 (trans. Oldfather, vol. III, pp. 251–3).

173. Diodoros Sikeliotes, V.58.

174. Oldfather, vol. III, pp. 252–3.

175. Diodoros Sikeliotes, I.9.5–6 (trans. Oldfather, vol. I, pp. 33–5).

176. Diodoros Sikeliotes, I.28–30 (trans. Oldfather, vol. I, pp. 91–7).

177. Pausanias, II.30.6 (trans. Levi, vol. I, p. 202).

178. Pausanias, II.38.4 (trans. Levi, vol. I, pp. 222–3).

179. The identification of Poseidon with Seth has been touched on in the Introduction and will be discussed in detail in vol. 3.

180. Pausanias, IV.35.2 (trans. Levi, vol. II, p. 187).

181. Pausanias, IX.5.1 (trans. Levi, vol. I, p. 317).

182. See Note 50 above.

183. *De Malig.* 13–14 (trans. Pearson and Sandbach, pp. 27–9).

184. L. Pearson and F. H. Sandbach, p. 5.
185. Pausanias, IX.16.1 (trans. Levi, vol. I, p. 339, n. 75).
186. Pausanias, III.18.3 (trans. Levi, vol. II, p. 62). This oracle will be discussed in vol. 3.
187. Pausanias, III.18.3 (trans. Levi, vol. II, p. 62 and Levi's note 153).
188. F. Dunand (1973, p. 3); S. Dow (1937, pp. 183–232).
189. Arrian, *Alexander*, III.3.2; Lane-Fox (1980, pp. 202, 207. For the horns, see the striking similarities between an Alexandrian coin and an earlier one of Ammon from Cyrene, a Greek colony on the Libyan coast, in Lane-Fox (1980, pp. 200–1). Cyrenian coins sometimes portrayed Ammon in such a way as to suggest 'a touch of Negro blood'. See Seltman (1933, p. 183).
190. Arrian, IV.9.9; Lane-Fox (1980, pp. 388–9).
191. Hornung (1983, pp. 93–5).
192. Diodoros Sikeliotes, III.68–74. See vol. 3 for a discussion of this very important syncretism in Greek, and especially Cretan, religion.
193. Diodoros Sikeliotes, I.17.3–I.20. For the link between Osiris, the voyaging civilizer, and Dionysos, see also Plutarch, *De Iside* . . . 13, 365B. Helck (1962, col. 505) denies that the legend of Osiris' conquests has any basis in Egyptian tradition. As J. Hani (1976, p. 44) writes, 'it is curious to note' that Helck has omitted the *Hymn to Osiris* of the Louvre, which refers to the tradition. This kind of omission does not surprise me in that bastion of the Aryan Model, the encyclopaedia of Pauly Wissowa.
194. *Bakchai*, 13–20. See the discussion in Frazer (1921, pp. 324–5).
195. Arrian, IV.9.5, 10.6; VII.20.1.
196. Arrian, V.2.1 (trans. Robson, vol. II, p. 7).
197. Arrian, VI.27.2 (trans. Robson, vol. II, p. 191).
198. Lane-Fox (1980, pp. 121–3; for the Egyptian style of his funeral cortège see pp. 408–9).
199. See Parke (1967, pp. 222–30). For a much more extreme Aryanist view, see Wilcken (1928; 1930). For Wilcken's successful career under the Third Reich, see Canfora (1980, p. 136).
200. See also Hani (1976, p. 8), for a bibliography of this process. A long series of volumes edited by M. J. Vermaseren is devoted precisely to this topic (*Études préliminaires aux religions orientales dans l'empire romain*. Leiden: 1961).
201. Zucker (1950, pp. 151–2); Froidefond (1971, p. 228); Dunand (1973, p. 5).
202. Pausanias, I.41.4; Dunand (1973, pp. 13, 99).
203. Dunand (1973, p. 89).
204. Pausanias, I.41.4; II.3.3; II.32.6; III.9.13; III.14.5; III.18.3; IV.32.6; VII.25.5; X.32.9.
205. For the spread of the cult of Isis, for instance, see the massive but incomplete bibliography by J. Leclant (1972, 1974).
206. Smelik and Hemelrijk, 1984, pp. 1931–8.

207. See R. Lambert, 1984, esp. pp. 121–7 and 157–60.
208. Smelik and Hemelrijk (1984, pp. 1943–4).
209. *De Republica*, III.9.14 (trans. Smelik and Hemelrijk, 1984, p. 1956).
210. Smelik and Hemelrijk (1984, pp. 1965–71).
211. See – as one example among many – Plutarch's reference to hymns calling Osiris him 'who is hidden in the arms of the sun' (54.372B) and Ancient Egyptian allusions to the embrace of the spirit of Re and the spirit of Osiris. Hani (1976, p. 219) writes of this: 'Here again one can note the reliability of Plutarch's information.'
212. Gwyn Griffiths (1980, col. 167). It should be pointed out that Griffiths disapproves of discounting the Greek sources on Egyptian civilization as strongly as other scholars such as Froidefond.
213. Froidefond (1971).
214. Plutarch, *On Isis* . . . 35.364.E (trans. Babbit, p. 85). There are many other sources indicating an especially close connection between Delphic and Egyptian religion in this work and elsewhere. See Jeanmaire (1951, p. 385); Hani (1976, p. 177). See also Heliodoros, II.28.
215. 13,356B; 28,362B.
216. Griffiths (1970, pp. 320–1).
217. See Clement of Alexandria, *Protreptikos*, II.13.
218. Snodgrass (1971, pp. 116–17).
219. Heliodoros, II.27.3.
220. Apuleius, XI.5 (trans. Griffiths, 1975, p. 75).
221. Iamblichos, VII.5.3 (trans. T. Taylor, 1821, p. 295).

Chapter II
EGYPTIAN WISDOM AND GREEK TRANSMISSION
FROM THE DARK AGES TO THE ENLIGHTENMENT

1. Gibbon (1776–88, vol. 3, pp. 28, 199–200; vol. 5, pp. 109–10). It should be pointed out that the first library of the Ptolemies had been destroyed accidentally by Julius Caesar's army. The second, however, was still the greatest in the world of its time.
2. See, for example, Baldwin Smith (1918, p. 169).
3. Juster (1914, vol. 1, pp. 209–11, 253–90).
4. Juster (1914, vol. 1, p. 211); Baron (1952, vol. 2, pp. 93–8, 103–8).
5. Herodotos, III.27–43.
6. For the great wealth of the Egyptian temples and their many slaves, see Cumont (1937, pp. 115–44).
7. Ezra 1: 2–4.
8. Neusner (1965, vol. 1, pp. 70–3).

9. For two opposed views on this, see de Santillana (1969); Neugebauer (1950, pp. 1–8).

10. Virgil, *Eclogues*, IV. lines 4–10 (trans. Fairclough, 1932, vol. 1, p. 29).

11. Pulleybank (1955, pp. 7–18).

12. See Finkelstein (1970, p. 269).

13. See especially chs 41–45, 367C–369C. Hipparchos, who lived in Egypt in the 2nd century BC, is conventionally supposed to have discovered the phenomenon.

14. Gardiner (1961, pp. 64–5); von Bekarath (pp. 297–9).

15. See Griffiths (1970, p. 34). Coptic has an interesting term, *hasie*, which Černy derives from the older *ḥsi* (praised drowned person). This is clearly linked to these legends. The Greek stem *hosio-* (sacred, free from pollution) would seem to derive from this rather than from the Indo-European root √es (be). This will be discussed in more detail in vol. 3.

16. Lambert (1984, pp. 126–42).

17. Gamer-Wallert (1977, pp. 228–34); Griffiths (1970, pp. 342–3, 422–3).

18. Although Dâgôn would seem to be related to the Greek *drakōn-*, (fish) or (dragon), it has been traditionally identified with the Hebrew *dåg* (fish). However, *dågån* means 'grain', and there is an old Semitic god Dagan, who in fact seems to have been pre-eminent in 3rd-millennium Ebla (Pettinato, 1981, pp. 246–8). Clearly, punning went on between the two. In any event, the Israelites considered fish as neither sacred nor taboo.

19. John 21:1–14.

20. Baldwin Smith (1918, pp. 129–37).

21. *De Baptismo*, I. For more on the fish in 'living water' in early Christian thought, see Daniélou (1964, pp. 42–57). Tertullian may, at another level, have been alluding to the fact that Pisces follows or comes out of Aquarius, the 'Water Carrier'.

22. Hornung (1983, p. 163).

23. *Corpus Hermeticum*, II.326–8 (trans. F. Yates, 1964, pp. 38–9).

24. For what is still an excellent survey of this, see Dupuis (1822, vol. 1, pp. 75–322). Aspects of the parallels are discussed in Chapter VIII.

25. The attempt to reduce Hermeticism and surrounding philosophies to one system has been made by several scholars – notably J. Kroll – with infinitely greater knowledge of the field than me. However, as modern scholarship generally depends on making finer and finer distinctions, the splitters have so far defeated the lumpers here. See Blanco (1984, p. 2268).

26. For a survey of the concept of 'three' in late Antiquity and the Renaissance, see Wind (1980, pp. 41–6).

27. Des Places (1984, p. 2308).

28. Hobein (vol. 2, p. 10, trans. Murray, 1951, p. 77. n. 1); cited in Wind (1968, pp. 219–20).

29. Pagels (1979, p. xix).

30. Porphery, *Vita Plotini*, X.
31. Des Places (1975, pp. 78–82).
32. See Plato, *Republic*, XI.
33. The prominence of women in their theology, and among the Gnostics them-selves, fits well with the freedom gained by upper-class women in late Antiquity. See Pagels (1979, pp. 48–69). Equally, there is no doubt that the social status of women was traditionally far higher in Egypt than in either Canaan or Greece. Pagels (pp. 63–4) cites Professor Morton Smith as saying plausibly that Christian attitudes to women hardened as the predominant social class within the religion shifted from the lower class – in which, because women were necessary to the economy of the family, they had a certain equality – to the middle class, where they were secluded at home.
34. Blanco (1984, p. 2242).
35. See, for instance, the well-read Hermetic literature – sometimes bound in the same volume – found in the Gnostic library at Nag Hammadi (Blanco, 1984, pp. 2248–9, 2252). For a recent bibliography on Hermeticism and its relations to other schools, see Blanco, pp. 2243–4. For examples of Neo-Platonic relations with Hermeticism, see Des Places (1975, pp. 336–7); Dieckmann (1970, pp. 18–25).
36. For a bibliography on the influence of Hermeticism on Gnosticism, see Blanco (1984, p. 2278, n. 102). For influence on Neo-Platonism, see Des Places (1975, pp. 76–7; 1984, p. 2308).
37. Bloomfield (1952, p. 342), cited in Yates (1964, p. 2, n. 4).
38. Blanco (1984, p. 2264).
39. Blanco (1984, p. 2272). It is interesting to note that while Elaine Pagels does not mention the influence of Egyptian, or even Hermetic, thought on Gnosticism in her excellent popular book on the subject, she finds space to speculate – on the basis of tiny scraps of evidence – on the possibility of Indian influence (1979, pp. xxi–xxii). See also Schwab (1984, p. 3).
40. Yates (1964, p. 3). For surveys of Hermetic studies in the 20th century and a bibliography of Festugière's works on the subject, see Dieckmann (1970, pp. 18–19); Blanco (1984, pp. 2268–79).
41. For the Gnostic Texts' having been written originally in Coptic, see Doresse (1960, pp. 255–60).
42. Blanco (1984, p. 2273).
43. For summaries of Casaubon's work, see Yates (1964, pp. 398–403); Blanco (1984, pp. 2263–4). The technique of denying a thing's existence because it is not attested in surviving literature will be discussed below.
44. Festugière (1944–9, vol. 1, p. 76).
45. Kroll (1923, pp. 213–25).
46. Cumont (1937, pp. 22–3).
47. For Cumont's historical role and achievement, see Beck (1984, pp. 2003–8).

48. Petrie (1908, pp. 196, 224–5; 1909, pp. 85–91). Petrie's argument and my acceptance of it are based on plausibility rather than certainty. It is possible that writers in the 2nd century AD deliberately set their writings in the Persian period, just as Heliodoros appears to have done in his novel *Aithiopika*. However, the lack of ostentation, the intricacy and consistency of the setting of the Hermetic Texts, the universal attribution to them of antiquity and the clear ideological purpose of those who have wished to down-date them, make the earlier date more likely.

49. Scott (1924–36, vol. 1, pp. 45–6).

50. Stricker (1949, pp. 79–88); P. Derchain (1962, pp. 175–98). See Griffiths (1970, p. 520) and Morenz (1969, p. 24).

51. T. G. Allen (1974, p. 280); Boylan (1922, p. 96 – he does not give a date). See also Baumgarten (1981, p. 73).

52. Plutarch, 61, 375F. Clement, *Stromata*, VI.4.37. For a discussion of Plutarch on this, see Griffiths (1970, pp. 519–20).

53. For the Esna inscription, see M.-T. and P. Derchain (1975, pp. 7–10). For Saqqara, see Ray (1976, p. 159). See also Morenz (1973, p. 222).

54. Ray (1976, pp. 136–45).

55. T. G. Allen (1974, p. 280).

56. John I:1. For the denials, see Festugière (1944–9, vol. 1, p. 73); Boylan (1922, p. 182).

57. Breasted (1901, p. 54). G. G. M. James (1954, pp. 139–151) is fully aware of the significance of the *Memphite Theology*. The Greek νόος (mind as employed as in thinking and perceiving) would seem to come from the Egyptian *nw* or *nw3* (see, look), which is also the origin of νοέω (perceive, observe).

58. See the epithet *p3 nb n p3 ḥ3ty* (the lord of the heart), which Ray finds 'enigmatic' (1976, p. 161). Thoth was also seen as the heart of Ra (Budge, 1904, vol. 1, pp. 400–1).

59. Budge (1904, vol. 1, pp. 400–1).

60. *Pyramid Texts*, 1713 C. See Griffiths (1970, p. 517). For the earlier attestation, see Hani (1976, pp. 60–1).

61. For a compilation of these references, see Froidefond (1971, pp. 279–84).

62. Jacoby (1923–9, vol. 3, p. 264); frags 25, 15, 9; 16, 1.

63. Fragments of Philon's work were quoted by the Church Father Eusebius in the 3rd century AD in his *Praeparatio Evangelica*, I.9.20–29 and I.10.

64. Albright (1968, pp. 194–6, 212–13; Eissfeldt (1960, pp. 1–15). The mixed Semitic and Egyptian roots of the cosmogony of Taautos will be discussed in vol. 3.

65. Baumgarten (1981, pp. 1–7, 122–3). In vol. 3 I shall try to show that many of the names in Philon that cannot be explained in terms of Ugaritic and Semitic have plausible Egyptian etymologies.

66. Albright (1968, p. 225). Baumgarten (1981, pp. 108–19) also sees close parallels between the two cosmologies.

67. Budge (1904, vol. 1, pp. 292–3); Hani (1976, pp. 147–9). Derchain (1980, cols 747–56).

68. Gardiner (1961, pp. 47–8).

69. Renan (1868, p. 263); Albright (1968, p. 223). For others, see Baumgarten (1981, p. 92, n. 94).

70. Albright (1968, p. 193); Eissfeldt (1960, pp. 7–8). See also Baumgarten (1981, pp. 107–10). For euhemerism in Canaanite culture and its influence on Greece, see G. Rosen (1929, p. 12).

71. Jacoby (1923–9, vol. 3, p. 812, 15–17). See also Baumgarten (1981, p. 69).

72. Jacoby (1923–9, vol. 3, p. 810, 2–5). See also Baumgarten (1981, p. 192).

73. Pope (1973, p. 302). I do not accept his monist ruling out of the cock, which in Late Egyptian religion does seem to have had some associations with the cult of Thoth. The crucial link between Thoth, Anubis and Hermes and the planet Mercury will be discussed in vol. 2.

74. Seznec (1953, p. 12).

75. See Devisse (1979, pp. 39–40); Morenz (1969, p. 115).

76. *City of God*, 18.39.

77. Blanco (1984, pp. 2253–8).

78. Scholem (1974, p. 11). For the scrolls, see Gaster (1964).

79. Festugière (1961–5, esp. vol. 1).

80. Scholem (1974, p. 9); see also Sandmel (1979).

81. Scholem (1974, pp. 8–30).

82. Scholem (1974, p. 9).

83. Scholem (1974, pp. 30–42).

84. Lafont *et al.* (1982, pp. 207–68).

85. Scholem (1974, p. 45).

86. Scholem (1974, p. 31).

87. Zervos (1920, p. 168, trans. in Blanco, 1984, pp. 2258–9). See this work also for a later bibliography on Psellos.

88. The story of these scarabs gives a nice illustration of the Aryan Model at work. The very richly furnished tomb of Childeric was found in 1653, and although some of the objects rapidly disappeared, the bulk were soon published with illustrations by Jean-Jacques Chiflet, an eminent doctor interested in archaeology. In the 19th century the objects went through many vicissitudes. Thus, although some of the treasure is now in the Cabinet des Médailles in Paris, modern scholars have had to rely on the 17th- and 18th-century publications. On the whole – and where they still have the objects for comparison – modern scholars are very much impressed by the accuracy of their early observations. However, Dr Dumas, the latest writer on the subject, rejects Chiflet's attribution of the bull's head to Apis and writes that there is no need to look for Egyptian or

even Roman origins, as one can find them among the Scythians, Persians and Hittites. She rightly points out that there are 'more or less similar' Scythian parallels (1976, pp. 42–3). The reasons for mentioning the Hittites, whose Anatolian culture had died out over 1,000 years earlier, can only be the barbaric heaviness of their art and the fact that they were Indo-European speakers. Given the facts that Childeric was for most of his life a client of the Romans and spent some time at the court of Attila in Hungary, and that Egyptian religion had been influential in the Northern provinces of the Late Empire in what are now Germany, Austria and Hungary well into the 5th century (Selem, 1980; Wessetzky, 1961), as well as the fact that the Christian Charlemagne considered Serapis of importance, there is nothing outrageous in the idea that there could have been Egyptian influence.

However, this outrage also appears when she considers Chiflet's report of Egyptian scarabs in the tomb. As she explains this 'howler':

> Dealing with silver coins, some of which were pierced, Chiflet had reproduced, as a comparison, certain examples from his collection, but also scarabs. In the 18th century, the learned Benedictine Bernard de Montfaucon (one of the greatest scholars of the time) inadvertently included these scarabs, considered as Frankish coins ... this error was repeated because of the authority that Montfaucon enjoyed. It was thus that the tomb of Childeric was once augmented with twenty or so Egyptian scarabs ! (1976, p. 6)

Why should she see her forerunners as having made a chain of such improbable errors? There are, in fact, powerful ideological reasons why 19th- and 20th-century scholars should have wanted to remove the scarabs. The Germanic Frankish kings who founded the French monarchy are very dear to the heart of the French Right, and to those believing in collaboration between France and Germany. It is no coincidence that the symbol of Vichy France was the *francisque*, the Frankish double-headed axe – a splendid example of which was found in Childeric's thomb. Thus the presence of Egyptian scarabs in such a shrine to Aryan, northern barbarian vigour was intolerable.

89. Seznec (1953, p. 55).
90. Blanco (1984, p. 2260; Wigtil (1984, pp. 2282–97).
91. Festugière (1945, vol. 1, pp. xv–xvi; vol. 2, pp. 267–75). Scott (1924–36, vol. 1, pp. 48–50); *pace* Dieckmann (1970, pp. 30–31), who seems unaware of these copies and the Hermetic aspects of pre-15th-century humanism.
92. Blunt (1940, pp. 20–1).
93. Cited in Wind (1980), p. 10.
94. Blanco (1984, pp. 2256–60).
95. Dieckmann (1970, pp. 27–30); Iversen (1961, p. 65); Seznec (1953, pp. 99–100) and Boas (1950).

96. Gardiner (1927, p. 11).

97. See Wind (1980, pp. 230–5); Dieckmann (1970, pp. 32–4), and *pace* Blunt (1940, pp. 1–22).

98. Wind (1980, p. 7).

99. Bruno, *Spaccio*, Dial. 3, in *Dialeghi italiani*, pp. 799–800, cited in Yates (1964), p. 223.

100. Yates (1964, pp. 12–14); there is an anachronism in her choice of the examples of the *Symposion* and the *Republic*. For the Renaissance as for Late Antiquity, Plato's best-known text was the *Timaios* which, unlike the other two, had explicit references to Egyptian wisdom.

101. Wind (1980, p. 245).

102. The argument that such mysteries and initiations existed in Middle if not Old Kingdom Egypt will be set out in vol. 3.

103. Yates (1964, pp. 84–116); Dieckmann (1970, pp. 38–44).

104. Yates (1964, p. 116).

105. Yates (1964, pp. 360–97).

106. Yates (1964, p. 85).

107. Yates (1964, p. 154); see also Rattansi (1975, pp. 149–66); Kuhn (1970, esp. pp. 128–30).

108. Festugière (1945–1954, vol. 2, p. 319), quoted by Yates (1964, p. 36).

109. E. Rosen (1970; 1983).

110. For a survey of this influence, see Swerdlow and Neugebauer (1984, pp. 41–8). I am very grateful to Dr Jamil Ragep for help in this section.

111. See Swerdlow and Neugebauer (1984, pp. 50–1). The influence of Hermeticism on astronomy did not end with Copernicus. A century later, the great astronomer Johann Kepler was deeply immersed in Neo-Platonism or Neo-Pythagorean-ism. See Haase (1975, pp. 427–38); Fleckenstein (1975, pp. 519–33). The Hermeticism of Bruno and 17th-century scientists will be discussed below.

112. Blanco (1984, p. 2261).

113. Eliot (1906, ch. 6, pp. 80–4).

114. See Sauneron *et al.* (1970–1, Introduction). See also Khattab (1982).

115. Hill (1976, p. 3); Rattansi (1963, pp. 24–32).

116. Seznec (1953, p. 238).

117. Seznec (1953, pp. 253–4).

118. Yates (1964, p. 6).

119. See Note 99 above.

120. Yates (1964, p. 351).

121. Yates (1964, pp. 164–5).

122. Daneau, 1578, p. 9, cited in Manuel (1983, p. 6). I have been able to trace the connection as late as Warburton (1736–9, vol. 3, p. 398). See also McGuire and Rattansi (1966, p. 130), who trace the association back to the Frisian scholar Arcerius in a note to his translation of Iamblichus' *De vita Pythagorae*, published in

1598. They also point out his linking of Moschos to Mochos (see above, Note 70). These arguments are not quite as crazy as they seem. There certainly was a tradition of Egypt's having borrowed knowledge from 'Syria', which we can now reasonably equate with Phoenicia, Syria and Mesopotamia. Furthermore, there is no substantial objection to linking Moschos with the Hebrew or Aramaic Môšeh, as šîn was sometimes transcribed into Greek as *sch* and the *-os* is clearly a Greek nominal ending. This is not to say that the Israelites had comparable – let alone superior – 'scientific' knowledge to the Egyptians. Furthermore, transcriptions *šsch* are late; this would provide phonetic backing to the hypothesis that these traditions are from Hellenistic times, when there was a belief that the Jews were great astronomers (see Theophrastos, *Peri Euseb*, 1.8, cited in M. Stern (1974, vol. 1, p. 10). See also Momigliano (1975, pp. 85–6).

Chapter III
THE TRIUMPH OF EGYPT
IN THE 17TH AND 18TH CENTURIES

1. Yates (1964, p. 401); see also Dieckmann (1970, pp. 104–5).
2. Scott (1924–36, vol. 1, pp. 41–3); Blanco (1984, pp. 2263–4).
3. Cudworth (1743, p. 320); cited in Yates (1964, p. 429); Dieckmann (1970, pp. 105–7). For more on the Cambridge Platonists and Hermeticism, see Rattansi (1975, pp. 160–5); Patrides (1969, pp. 4–6). Scholars writing before Frances Yates do not seem to have seen their Hermetic interests as significant. See Cassirer (1970 – written many years earlier) and Colie (1957).
4. See above, ch. II, Note 48.
5. Yates (1964, pp. 398–9). See also Blanco (1984, p. 2264); Scott (1924–36, vol. 1, p. 43).
6. Yates (1964, pp. 432–55); Blanco (1984, p. 2264); for Fludd and hieroglyphics, see Dieckmann (1970, pp. 76–7).
7. See Godwin (1979); Iversen (1961, pp. 89–90); Dieckmann (1970, pp. 97–9).
8. Kircher (1652, vol. 3, p. 568; trans. Yates, 1964, pp. 417–18).
9. Tompkins (1973, p. 30). It is a tragedy that Tompkins's brilliant and scholarly book has been stripped of its scholarly apparatus. See also Iversen (1961, pp. 94–6).
10. Gardiner (1957, pp. 11–12); Iversen (1961, pp. 90–8).
11. For the possibility of the connection, see Yates (1964, pp. 407–15); Dieckmann (1970, pp. 71–5).
12. Yates (1972, pp. 180–92); see also Dieckmann (1970, pp. 103–4).
13. Hill (1976, p. 8).
14. Hill (1968, p. 290); Rattansi (1963, pp. 24–6).
15. For the impact of millenarianism, which was also very important in these circles, see Popkin (1985, pp. xi–xix). I have not covered the literature on the subject, but

I feel sure someone must have made the connection between this kind of millenarianism and the Kabbalist attempt to recover – through study – the light fragmented at the Creation.

16. Yates (1964, pp. 423–31); Popkin (1985, p. xii).

17. Bullough (1931, p. 12), quoted in Patrides (1969, p. 6). For Cudworth and hieroglyphics, see Dieckmann (1970, pp. 105–7).

18. For arguments in favour, see Rattansi (1973, pp. 160–5). Against this, see McGuire (1977, pp. 95–142).

19. Manuel (1974, pp. 44–5).

20. Tompkins (1978, pp. 30–3).

21. See McGuire and Rattansi (1966, p. 110).

22. For the bibliographic complications, see Westfall (1980, p. 434). See also Pappademos (1984, p. 94).

23. Shishak is now put in the 9th century BC. For a full discussion of the details, see Manuel (1963, esp. pp. 101–2). See also Westfall (1980, pp. 812–21); Iversen (1961, p. 103).

24. Friedrich (1951, p. 4) saw the relationship between Phoenician and Hebrew as similar to that between Dutch and High German. Albright (1970, p. 10) described Hebrew 'as a dialectical variant of Canaanite'. Menaham Stern writes (1974, p. 12): 'Since there is practically no difference between the Hebrew and Phoenician languages . . .'

25. This topic will be discussed in detail in vol. 2.

26. Bodin (1945, p. 341).

27. Bochart (1646).

28. Fénelon (1833, Bk 2, pp. 22–40).

29. Cited in Charles-Roux (1929, p. 4).

30. Vico had formed the basis for this scheme by 1721, when it appeared in his *De Constantia Jurisprudentia* (conclusion). The parallel with writing systems came in the first edition of his *Scienza Nuova* (see Bk 4, ch. 3) in 1725. For the discussion of Kadmos, see *De Constantia*, ch. 17. See also Dieckmann (1970, pp. 119–24). I am indebted to Gregory Blue for these references.

31. Montesquieu (1748, 15.5).

32. Gibbon (1794, vol. 1, pp. 41–2). For more on the 18th-century enthusiasm for Egypt, see Iversen (1961, pp. 106–23).

33. Barthélemy (1763, p. 222).

34. Barthélemy (1763, p. 226). For a hostile assessment of this paper, see Badolle (1926, pp. 76–8).

35. Banier (1739).

36. Bryant (1774, esp. vol. 1, p. xv).

37. Frye (1962, pp. 173–5); F. M. Turner (1981, pp. 78–9).

38. Braun (1973, pp. 119–27); Pocock (1985, pp. 19–23).

39. As early as 1712 de la Croze had tried to link the two scripts. See his letter quoted

in Barthélemy (1763, p. 216). The most famous attempts were those made by de Guignes (1758) and J. T. Needham (1761).

40. Not surprisingly, this extremely fertile field has received very little attention from 19th- and 20th-century historians. But see Pinot (1932); Maverick (1946); Appleton (1951); and Honour (1961). Raymond Schwab (1950) is profoundly misleading in this respect; see below, ch. V, Notes 7–10.

41. R. F. Gould (1904, pp. 240–5).

42. Knoop and Jones (1948, pp. 64–6).

43. For an extended discussion of these manuscripts, see Gould (1904, pp. 262–85).

44. See Lumpkin (1984, p. 111).

45. This is indicated by the fact that the craftsman was called Hiram Abif in Coverdale's translation of the Bible in the 1540s. The name does not appear in the King James Version of the early 17th century.

46. Gould (1904, p. 243).

47. Yates (1972, p. 210). These two beliefs were also central to the Knights Templars, who made a cult of the Dome of the Rock as the successor to the Temple. They also saw themselves as an elite, transcending the religious differences – in this case those between Christianity and Islam – of the vulgar. They were active from 1118 until they were broken up as heretical by the king of France in 1314 after the fall of Acre, their last stronghold in Palestine. The Freemasons consider themselves to be descended from the Templars (Steel-Maret, 1893, p. 2).

48. Popkin (1985, pp. xii–xiii).

49. For Spinoza and his influence on the Cambridge Neo-Platonists, see Colie (1957, pp. 66–116).

50. Jacob (1976, pp. 201–50; 1981, esp. pp. 151–7); Manuel (1983, pp. 36–7); Force (1985, pp. 100, 113).

51. Manuel (1983, p. 36). Later Masonic discomfort about the important role of Toland in the reformation of the craft can be seen from his omission from their standard histories.

52. Force (1985, p. 100).

53. Knight (1984, pp. 236–40).

54. Diogenes Laertius, VIII. 90.

55. Tompkins (1973, p. 214).

56. For a discussion of this see Yates (1964, pp. 55–7).

57. Yates (1964, pp. 370–2).

58. See Yates (1964, pp. 367–73).

59. For the intricacies of the *querelle*, see Farnham (1976, pp. 171–80); Furhmann (1979, pp. 107–28); Simonsuuri (1979, pp. 1–45).

60. For earlier attempts to merge the two cults, see Farnham (1976, p. 39). For other attempts to set up national religious festivals, see Bloch (1924, pp. 360–70).

61. Some thinkers were aware of the greater splendour of the court of the Manchu Emperor Kang Xi (Honour, 1961, pp. 21–5, 93).

62. Marin (1981, pp. 246–7).

63. Voltaire (1886, ch. 32, pp. 408–9).

64. Fuhrmann (1979, p. 114). Dr Farnham (1976, p. 177) exaggerates his commitment to Homer and the Ancients.

65. Beuchot (1854, pp. 169–71).

66. Terrasson (1715).

67. Manetho was quoted by Josephus in *Contra Apionem*, I.98.

68. Terrasson (1731). For a thoroughly hostile assessment of *Sèthos*, see Badolle (1926, pp. 275–6). See also Iversen (1961, pp. 121–2). For a discussion of this in the context of the theme of the *Bildungsroman* in the 18th century, see Honolka (1984, pp. 144–54).

69. Terrasson (1731, esp. Bk 2).

70. Terrasson (1731, Bk 7, p. 4).

71. Chailley (1971); Nettl (1957). The other major source for *The Magic Flute* was Ignaz von Born's 'Über die Mysterien der Ägyptier', in *Journal für Freymaurer*, vol. 1 (1784). See Iversen (1961, p. 122); Honolka (1984, p. 144). In 1773, when he was seventeen and before he became a Mason, Mozart wrote the score for an opera by Gebler called *Thamos, King of Egypt*, which was also based on *Sèthos*. See K. Thomson (1977, pp. 24–31); Honolka (1984, pp. 142–4). Apart from its intrinsic merit, the survival of *The Magic Flute* – despite the fact that its libretto was unsuitable for the Romantic period – would seem to be linked to the fact that it was the first major opera in German. In the years immediately following its production there was no objection to its theme. Goethe wrote a sequel to it in 1795. See Iversen (1961, p. 122).

72. Rheghellini de Schio (1833, pp. 7–8).

73. Manuel (1959, pp. 85–125).

74. Manuel (1959, pp. 44–5).

75. Manuel (1959, pp. 245–58).

76. De Santillana (1963, p. 819).

77. Manuel (1959, pp. 259–70).

78. De Santillana (1963, p. 819).

79. Dupuis (1795, vol. 1, p. 14). He cited Tatian, an Assyrian Christian of the 2nd century who wrote a *Letter to the Greeks* in which he mentioned Persian magic, Phoenician letters and Egyptian geometry and historical writing (ch. 1).

80. Auguis (1822, p. 10).

81. Charles-Roux (1929, p. 13; 1937, p. 2). Another – though 'lesser' – factor was the tradition of St Louis's ill-fated expedition to Egypt during the Crusades.

82. R. F. Gould (1904, pp. 451–5); Beddaride (1845, pp. 96–140).

83. See Iversen (1961, p. 132).

84. Madelin (1937, pp. 235–7). *La Décade Égyptienne* (1798, vol. I, pp. 1–4); Tompkins (1978, pp. 49–50).

85. Said (1978, pp. 113–226).

86. Tompkins (1978, pp. 45–51, 201–6).

87. For the deficiencies of Xenophon as a writer and *Anabasis* as a text as introductions to Greek, see Pharr (1959, pp. xvii–xxxii). The Latin equivalent to Xenophon was Caesar's *Gallic Wars*.

88. Madelin (1937, vol. 2, p. 248).

89. Gibbon (1794, pp. 41, 137). For his consistent anti-Semitism, see Pocock (1985), p. 12.

90. For a comparison with *Sèthos*, see Badolle (1926, p. 275).

91. Badolle (1926, pp. 397–8).

92. Barthélemy (1789, pp. 2–5). For Fréret's views, see ch. I, Note 92.

93. Barthélemy (1789, p. 62).

94. Mitford (1784, vol. 1, p. 6). For the influence of Mitford's history, see F. M. Turner (1981, pp. 203–7).

95. Mitford (1784, vol. 1, p. 19). We now know that Cretan palatial civilization was set up long before Mitford's 'Egyptian upheavals', which must refer to the Hyksos period.

96. Musgrave (1782, pp. 4–5).

Chapter IV
HOSTILITIES TO EGYPT IN THE 18TH CENTURY

1. See ch. III, Note 7; Iversen (1961, pp. 5, 89–99); Blanco (1984, pp. 2263–4); Godwin (1979, esp. pp. 15–24).

2. Colie (1957, pp. 2–4); Pocock (1985, p. 12).

3. Pocock (1985, p. 13). This is not to say that the Cambridge Platonists were unconcerned by Spinoza and by what they saw as his pantheist or 'hylozoick' atheism (Colie, 1957, pp. 96–7).

4. Westfall (1980, p. 815).

5. *Ibid.*; Manuel (1959, pp. 90–5).

6. Pocock (1985, p. 23); Colie (1957, p. 96).

7. See Josephus, *Against Apion*; Clement, *Stromata*. For Tatian, see also ch. II, Note 76.

8. See above, ch. II, Note 121.

9. Hare (1647, pp. 12–13), quoted in MacDougall (1982, p. 60).

10. For a survey of the historiography of this link between Protestantism and Greek studies, see Lloyd-Jones (1982b, p. 19).

11. Pfeiffer (1976, pp. 143–58; Wilamowitz-Moellendorf (1982, pp. 79–81). It is generally considered that the *digamma* is an ancient letter because it does not exist in the Ionian alphabet, which became standard in Greece at the end of the

Peloponnesian War in 403 BC. I argue in Bernal (1987a; forthcoming, 1988) that the Ionian alphabet is much older than the Dorian alphabets which contained the *F*, and that the letter was therefore introduced into the Greek alphabet around 1000 BC – much later than *c.* 1600, when I date the transmission of the alphabet as a whole. That is not to deny Bentley's discovery of the phoneme w, although I believe that some of the failures to elide may be the result of Greek borrowing, or at least reflexes or awareness, of a Semitic or Egyptian *'ayin.* See vol. 2.

12. Bentley (1693).

13. Jacob (1981, p. 89).

14. Bentley (1693). For more on Bentley and the Boyle Lectures, see Pfeiffer (1976, pp. 146–7).

15. For the deist implications of Bentley's Boyle lectures themselves, see Force (1985, pp. 65–6). For further doubts about his orthodoxy, see Westfall (1980, pp. 650–1). There were, of course, Christians who objected to both Newton and Bentley; see Force (1985, p. 64).

16. Potter (1697); B. H. Stern (1940, p. 38, n. 49); Smith (1848). For some later ramifications of the alliance between Ancient Greece and Christianity, see Bernal (1986, pp. 11–12).

17. *De Rerum Nat,* VI.I. As mentioned above, Lucretius was an Epicurean. For the Greek nationalism or chauvinism of this school, see ch. I, Note 170.

18. Potter (1697, Bk 1, pp. 1–3; Bk 2, pp. 1–2).

19. Warburton (1739, vol. 4, p. 403). For more on Warburton and Egypt, see Dieckmann (1970, pp. 125–8); Iversen (1961, pp. 103–5).

20. Pocock (1985, p. 11).

21. Manuel (1959, pp. 69, 191–3).

22. Warburton (1739, vol. 4, pp. 5–26); Manuel (1959, pp. 107–12).

23. Warburton (1739, vol. 4, pp. 229–41).

24. For a bibliography on Brucker, see L. Braun (1973, p. 120).

25. Pocock (1985, p. 22).

26. *Ibid.*

27. Montesquieu (1721, Letters 97, 104, 135; cited by Rashed, 1980, p. 9).

28. *Epinomis,* 987D.

29. See, for instance, the *Kokusai* (national essence) movement which arose in reaction to the rapid Westernization of Japan in the 1870s and 80s (Pyle, 1969, pp. 60–9); Teters (1962, pp. 359–71).

30. Goldsmith (1774, vol. 2, pp. 230–1).

31. Turgot (1808–15, vol. 2, pp. 52–92, 255–328).

32. Turgot (1808–15, vol. 2, pp. 55, 315).

33. Manuel (1959, p. 69).

34. Montesquieu (1748, Bk 18, ch. VI). This is, of course, in direct contradiction to the later 'hydraulic theory' – hinted at by Marx and developed by Wittfogel – that water control leads to 'Oriental Despotism'. Unlike the 19th- and 20th-

century thinkers, Montesquieu had the example of Holland on his side. For a bibliography on the Asiatic Mode of Production, see Bernal (1987b).

35. Turgot (1808–15, vol. 2, pp. 65, 253, 314–16). Elsewhere (p. 71) he wrote: 'Plato sowed flowers; the charm of his eloquence even embellished his errors.' For the persistence into the 19th century of the view of Plato as a seductive poet rather than a philosopher, see Wismann (1983, p. 496).

36. Turgot (1808–15, vol. 2, pp. 276–9).

37. Turgot (1808–15, vol. 2, p. 70).

38. Turgot (1808–15, vol. 2, pp. 66–7).

39. See ch. III, Notes 33, 34.

40. Turgot (1808–15, vol. 2, pp. 330–2).

41. Child (1882–98, vol. 3, pp. 233–54). This lack of concern with the Jews' colour is in stark contrast to Walter Scott's reconstruction of the period in *Ivanhoe*, in which their darkness is repeatedly emphasized. This, of course, was written in the early 19th century, when there was obsessive interest in 'ethnic' or 'racial' differences.

42. For a general survey of medieval attitudes to Blacks, see Devisse (1979, pt 1). See also Child (1882–98, vol. 1, pp. 119–21).

43. Child (1882–98, vol. 3, pp. 51–74).

44. *Politics*. VII.7 (trans. Sinclair, 1962, p. 269).

45. Bracken (1973, pp. 81–96; 1978, pp. 241–60). See also Poliakov (1974, pp. 145–6).

46. See, for example, Locke (1689, Bk 5, p. 41).

47. Locke (1689, Bk 4).

48. Locke (1689, Bk 5, pp. 25–45). For a discussion of this, see Bracken (1973, p. 86).

49. Jordan (1969, p. 229).

50. Locke (1688, Bk 3, p. 6, quoted and discussed in Jordan, 1969, pp. 235–6). For other examples of Locke's racism, see Bracken (1978, p. 246).

51. See Bracken (1978, p. 253).

52. Footnote to 'Of National Characters', cited in Jordan (1969, p. 253); Bracken (1973, p. 82); Popkin (1974, p. 143); and S. J. Gould (1981, pp. 40–1).

53. For the reference to Pseudo-Plato, see *Epinomis*, 987D. For Bodin, see ch. III, Note 26.

54. See, for instance, Montesquieu (1748, Bk 8, p. 21).

55. For a more extended attack on trees, see Bernal (forthcoming, 1988).

56. To some extent, the 18th-century French cultural conquest of Europe was shared by the Italians, who were generally acknowledged to be the finest musicians and painters, and still had a formidable scientific tradition.

57. See Blackall (1958, pp. 1–35).

58. Berlin (1976, pp. 145–216); Iggers (1968, pp. 34–7).

59. Trevor-Roper (1983).

60. Berlin (1957, pp. 145–216).

61. For a description of Homer's role in Classical Greek culture, see Finley (1978, pp. 19–25). Homer's title of 'the poet' can be linked to the plausible derivation of his name from the Egyptian *ḥm(w)t-r*, Coptic *ḥmēr* (spell, act(or) of speech).

62. Le Fèvre (1664, p. 6); cited in Farnham (1976, p. 146).

63. Dacier (1714, pp. 10–12); quoted in Simonsuuri (1979, pp. 53–5). See also Farnham (1976, pp. 171–9).

64. Voltaire (letter to M. Damilaville, 4 Nov. 1765); cited in Santangelo (n.d., p. 6).

65. Vico (1730). For discussions of this, see Manuel (1959, pp. 154–5); Simonsuuri (1979, pp. 90–8).

66. See Blackwell (1735); Simonsuuri (1979, pp. 53–5).

67. *Timaios*, 22B (trans. Bury, 1925, p. 33). Despite the problems with the early dating of the word *ìd* (child) and the late dating of *pꜣ* (the), the most plausible etymology for the Greek word *pais, paidos* is *pꜣ' id* (the child). The Indo-European root **pu* or **pur* seems much less likely. The Egyptian *ìd* is almost certainly the origin of the Greek suffix *-ad* (children) and the patronymic *-ides*.

68. For the first use of the term 'Romantic Hellenism' see H. Levin (1931). See also B. H. Stern (1940, p. vii).

69. Simonsuuri (1979, pp. 104–6). Shaftesbury was also hostile to Egypt and hieroglyphics.

70. St Clair (1983, p. 176). See also Jenkyns (1980, pp. 8–9); B. H. Stern (1940); Simonsuuri (1979, pp. 133–42).

71. For a vivid description of this process, and the results it can produce, see Edmund Wilson's description of the historian Michelet (1960, pp. 12–31).

72. Jenkyns (1980, pp. 8–9); Turner (1981, pp. 138–40); Simonsuuri (1979, pp. 133–42); Wilamowitz-Moellendorf (1982, p. 82).

73. Harris (1751, p. 417).

74. Duff (1767, pp. 27–9).

75. Wilamowitz-Moellendorf (1982, p. 83).

76. Musgrave (1782, esp. pp. 4–5). He coupled this dissertation with another criticizing Newton's Chronology.

77. Winckelmann (1764, p. 128).

78. Winckelmann (1764, p. 97).

79. Turgot (1808–15, vol. 2, pp. 256–61). See also L. Braun (1973, pp. 256–61); Comte (1830–42).

80. For a devastating debunking of this ridiculous view, see Jean Capart (1942, pp. 80–119). For a discussion on the confusion of Winckelmann's ideas on hieroglyphics, see Dieckmann (1970, pp. 137–41).

81. These views were not restricted to Aristotle. See, for instance, the very unflattering portraits of Egyptians on the Caeretan *hydria* illustrating the legend of Bousiris (Boardman, 1964, plate 11 and p. 149). While both point out that Bousiris has black attendants and that Bousiris himself is portrayed as one on

another vase, neither Boardman nor Snowden (1970, p. 159) mentions the fact that the 'Greek hero Herakles' is depicted as a curly-haired African Black! This is something that the Aryan Model is completely unable to handle. For reasons Herakles should have been seen in this way, see vol. 3.

82. Winckelmann (1764, Bks 1 and 2). See also Iversen (1961, pp. 114–15). For British predecessors holding these general beliefs, see B. H. Stern (1940, pp. 79–81).

83. See ch. V, Notes 155–6 for the 'Egyptian way of death' in the 19th century.

84. See Butler (1935, pp. 11–48); *pace* Pfeiffer (1976, p. 169).

85. See Jenkyns (1980, pp. 148–54); F. M. Turner (1981, pp. 39–41).

86. See Butler (1935, pp. 294–300); Kistler (1960, pp. 83–92).

87. Pfeiffer (1976, p. 170).

88. Quoted by Pfeiffer (1976, p. 169).

89. Butler (1935, pp. 11–48).

90. See Clark (1954).

91. Trevelyan (1981, p. 50); Lloyd-Jones (1981, pp. xii–xiii).

92. Trevelyan (1981, pp. 50–4); Butler (1935, pp. 70–80); Pfeiffer (1976, p. 169).

93. L. Braun (1973, p. 165).

94. For the Romanticism in late-18th-century Germany, see above; for the racism, see Gilman (1982, pp. 19–82).

95. Three of the earliest four references to *philosophia* are associated with Egypt. As mentioned above, (ch. I, Note 136), Isokrates specifically derived it from that country. The difficulty modern scholars have in recognizing this can be seen in Malingrey (1961), who consistently translates *philosophia* as the 'civilization' of Egypt. See Froidefond (1971, pp. 252–3).

96. Quoted in L. Braun (1973, p. 111) from Heumann (1715, p. 95), which I have been unable to see.

97. *Stromateis*, I.4. For Epicurean chauvinism and the possibility that it was linked to rivalry with the 'Phoenician' Stoics, see above, Note 17.

98. See Note 28 above.

99. For the low status of German at the beginning of the 18th century, see above, Note 57.

100. 1715, vol. 1, p. 637 (quoted in L. Braun, 1973, p. 113).

101. See Notes 24–6 above.

102. See Tiedemann (1780); L. Braun (1973, pp. 165–7).

103. See Hunger (1933); Butterfield (1955, esp. p. 33); Marino (1975, pp. 103–12).

104. Marino (1975, pp. 103–12); L. Braun (1973, pp. 165–7).

105. For the degrees to which 18th-century Germans were aware of Vico's work and to which they denied his influence, see Croce (1947, vol. 1, pp. 504–15). See also Momigliano (1966c, pp. 253–76).

106. Meiners (1781–2, vol. 1, p. xxx), quoted in L. Braun (1973, pp. 175–6).

107. De Santillana (1963, p. 823).

108. See below, ch. VII, Note 25.

109. Meiners (1781–2 vol. I, pp. 123–4, 1811–15). See also Poliakov (1974, pp. 178–9).

110. Baker (1974, pp. 24–7); Jordan (1969, p. 222); Bracken (1973, p. 86); Gerbi (1973, pp. 3–34).

111. For Vico and the post-diluvian population of the world, see Manuel (1955, pp. 154–5).

112. Herder (1784–91, Bk 6, p. 2 and Bk 10, pp. 4–7), cited by Harris-Schenz (1984, p. 28). The explorer Georg Forster, who was very much part of the Göttingen circle, assumed that 'Whites' came from the Caucasus (Forster, 1786).

113. Arya is, of course, an ancient term in the Indo-Aryan languages and Greek. Its earliest modern use seems to have been in Sir William Jones (1794, sect. 45).

114. Gobineau (1983, p. 656); Graves (1955, vol. 2, p. 407).

115. Moscati et al. (1969, p. 3). The idea that there was a relationship between Hebrew, Aramaic and Arabic was, of course, known since Antiquity and was used by scholars long before Schlözer. See, for example, the references to Barthélemy in the last chapter.

116. Poliakov (1974, p. 188).

117. See R. S. Turner (1985).

118. For a short bibliography on Heyne, see Pfeiffer (1976, p. 171, n. 5).

119. See, for example, the attack led by Heyne on the authenticity of *Iliad*, IX.383–4, which praises the riches of the Egyptian Thebes. See P. Von der Mühl (1952, p. 173).

120. S. Gould (1981, p. 238).

121. Wilamowitz-Moellendorf (1982, p. 96).

122. Pfeiffer (1976, p. 171).

123. R. S. Turner (1983a, p. 460).

124. Manuel (1959, p. 302).

125. For Forster and Heyne, see Leuschner (1958–82, esp. vol. 14). For Forster's anthropology, see vol. 8, pp. 133, 149–53; Harris-Schenz (1984, pp. 30–1).

126. For Heyne's vehemence and the personal explanation, see Momigliano (1982, p. 10). For the claim that Göttingen took a 'middle way' between the extremes of revolution and reaction, see Marino (1975, pp. 358–71). For the hostility of the Göttingen school to the Revolution, see ch. VI, Notes 9–16 below. Another reason for Forster's going to Paris was to study Indian languages and prepare for a voyage there. For this and the Romantic entanglement, see Schwab (1984, p. 59). After Forster's death, Caroline worked with and married August Wilhelm Schlegel, the translator of Shakespeare and Sanskritist. On their divorce she married the philosopher Friedrich Wilhelm Schelling. Her fame today comes from her letters, which provide a brilliant portrait of the early German Romantics (Nissen, 1962, pp. 108–9).

Chapter V
Romantic Linguistics: the rise of India and the fall of Egypt, 1740–1880

1. Herder did in fact write at length on Egypt and hieroglyphs. However, as Liselotte Dieckmann puts it: 'The whole long discussion of Egypt serves only the purpose of showing how the Song of Creation was nationalized in Egypt' (1970, p. 153; see also pp. 146–54). For the 18th-century attitude to Greek as a purely poetic language, see ch. IV, Note 38.

2. For an attack on the traditional approach, see Masica (1978, pp. 1–11). See also Scollon and Scollon (1980, pp. 73–176).

3. For Rask and Bopp, see Pedersen (1959, pp. 241–58).

4. For Indo-German, see Meyer (1892, pp. 125–30), cited in Poliakov (1974, p. 191).

5. For Indo-European, see Siegert (1941–42, pp. 73–99), cited in Poliakov (1974, p. 191). For Bopp's use of Indo-European, see Intro. to Bopp (1833), cited in Poliakov (1974, p. 191) and Pedersen (1959, p. 262, n. 2).

6. Schlegel (1808, p. x, trans. Millington, 1849, p. 10).

7. Schwab (1984, p. 11); Rashed (1980, p. 10).

8. As illustrations, see the following, written by Sir William Jones in 1784: 'Since *Egypt* appears to have been the grand source of knowledge for the *western* and *India* for the more *eastern* parts of the globe . . .' (1807, p. 387). In the library catalogue of Göttingen as established by Heyne in the 1760s and 70s, Egyptian mythology was placed under 'Western'. At some point in the 19th century it was transferred to the 'Oriental' section.

9. Boon (1978, pp. 334–8); Schwab (1984, pp. 27–33). He portrays this merely as a 'prehistory' to 'true' scholarship.

10. Jones (1807, p. 34). See also Schwab (1984, pp. 33–42).

11. See Thapar (1975; 1977, pp. 1–19). See also Leach (1986).

12. Schwab (1984, pp. 51–80).

13. Schwab (1984, pp. 195–7).

14. Schwab (1984, p. 59) and see above, ch. III, Note 88.

15. Schwab (1984, pp. 78–80).

16. See below, chs VI and IX.

17. Schwab (1984, p. 59).

18. Letter to Ludvig Tieck, 15 Dec. 1803 (Tieck, 1930, p. 140; cited in Poliakov, 1974, p. 191).

19. Schlegel (1808, p. 85); see Schwab (1984, p. 175); Timpanaro (1977, pp. xxii–xxiii). For my conviction that Jones was right and Schlegel – and later Bopp – wrong on this, see the Introduction, p. 11 and vol. 2.

20. Schlegel (1808, trans. Millington, 1849, pp. 506–7); cited in Poliakov (1974, p. 191).

21. Schlegel (1808, pp. 60–70). See also Timpanaro (1977, pp. xxii–iii).

22. Schlegel (1808, pp. 68–9; trans. Millington, 1849, pp. 456–7). See also Rashed (1980, p. 11).

23. Poliakov (1974, p. 191).

24. Schlegel (1808, p. 55; trans. Millington, 1849, p. 451).

25. Timpanaro (1977, p. xix).

26. Poliakov (1974, p. 191).

27. Timpanaro (1977, p. xx–xxi).

28. See below, chs VII and VIII.

29. Schlegel (1808, pp. 41–59; trans. Millington, 1849, pp. 439–53); Timpanaro (1977, p. xix).

30. Timpanaro (1977, p. xix).

31. For the Afroasiatic language family, see the Introduction and vol. 2. For Barthélemy, see ch. III, Note 34 above.

32. Schlegel (1808, pp. 55–9, trans. Millington, 1849, pp. 451–3).

33. Humboldt (1903–36, vol. 4, pp. 284–313). See Sweet (1978–80, vol. 2, pp. 403–4). In his review of Sweet, Professor Lloyd-Jones points out that Humboldt was not always consistent on this (1982a, p. 73).

34. Humboldt (1903–36, vol. 5, pp. 282–92).

35. Humboldt (1903–36, vol. 5, p. 293). Schlegel had made a similar comparison between the two languages (1808, pp. 45–50.

36. See Humboldt's letters, reprinted in Schlesier (1838–1840, vol. 5, p. 300) and in von Sydow (1906–16, vol. 7, p. 283). See also Sweet (1978–80, vol. 2, pp. 418–25).

37. Schwab (1984, pp. 482–6).

38. For Grotefend and his successors, see Pedersen (1959, pp. 153–8); Friedrich (1957, pp. 50–68).

39. Said (1974, pp. 123–30). There is a misprint on his p. 124: '1769' should read '1799'.

40. Said (1974, pp. 59–92).

41. See Cordier (1904–24).

42. Cordier (1898, p. 46).

43. Schwab (1984, pp. 24–5). Schwab shared many of the prejudices of the men he wrote about. His own distaste for Egypt is apparent throughout the book.

44. Schwab (1984, p. 488), citing the Russian writer V. V. Bartold.

45. Said (1974, pp. 122–48); Rashed (1980, pp. 10–11).

46. See Rahman (1982, pp. 1–9).

47. In the cases of Islamic, Indian and Chinese civilizations, the borrowing from their later forms is quite clear. Even the undoubted Western achievements in reading and understanding the languages written in cuneiform would have been impossible without the continuity of Persian, Jewish and Arabic cultures. For Champollion's use of the Hermetic tradition and Coptic in his decipherment of hieroglyphics, see below.

48. It is absurd to deny the title of 'historian' to Sima Qian and the succeeding writers and compilers of the Chinese dynastic histories, or to the great Ibn Khaldun and later Moslem 'historians'. For a discussion of this in the Islamic context, see Abdel-Malek (1969, pp. 199–230). A survival of the view that only Aryans can write history comes in the claim that the Indo-European-speaking Hittites invented it in the Ancient Near East. See, for instance, Butterfield (1981, pp. 60–71).

49. The impact of Africa and Asia on ancient Europe is the theme of this work. I hope in the future to work on later extra-European influences. For Europe as the only 'scientific' continent, see Rashed (1980).

50. Gobineau (1983, vol. 1, p. 221).

51. Said (1974, esp. pp. 73–110).

52. Chaudhuri (1974).

53. De Tocqueville (1877, p. 241; trans. Gilbert, 1955, p. 163). For an excellent survey of this transformation, see Blue (1984, p. 3).

54. Humboldt (1826; 1903–36, vol. 5, p. 294).

55. Schleicher (1865), cited in Jespersen (1922, pp. 73–4).

56. C. Bunsen (1848–60, vol. 4, p. 485). The notion that true history did not exist in the East goes back at least as far as Hegel.

57. For the uphill struggle of orthodox Christians on this, see Curtin (1964, pp. 228–43). For 19th-century supporters of polygenesis, see Gould (1981, pp. 30–72). See also Curtin (1971, pp. 1–33).

58. See ch. VI below for its use by Niebuhr and other historians.

59. Cordier (1899, p. 382).

60. See, for instance, Bernier (1684), cited in Poliakov (1974, p. 143).

61. *Punch*, 10 Apr. 1858, cited in Dawson (1967, p. 133) and Blue (1984, p. 3).

62. Cuvier (1831, vol. 1, p. 53); quoted in Curtin (1971, p. 8).

63. Gobineau (1983, vol. 1, pp. 340–1).

64. Cuvier (1831, vol. 1, p. 53); quoted in Curtin (1971, p. 8).

65. Gobineau (1983, vol. 1, pp. 339–40).

66. Gobineau wrote: 'I need not add that the word honour, like the concept of civilization which contains it, are equally unknown to the Yellows and the Blacks' (1983, vol. 1, p. 342).

67. See Introduction.

68. Bk II.104.

69. See ch. IV, Note 81 above.

70. See Devisse (1979) 1, p. 43 for the early Christian picture; 2, pp. 82–4.

71. Devisse 2, pp. 136–94.

72. See Yates (1964, Frontispiece and pls 3–5).

73. For parallels between images of Blacks and Gypsies see Child (1882–98, vol. 3, pp. 51–74). The fact that there was clearly considerable confusion in this area is shown by the traditional English depiction of a Turk's head as that of an African Black. See above, ch. IV, Notes 42–50.

74. This tradition, and its use in the 17th century, are discussed by Jordan (1969, p. 18).
75. Bernier (1684); cited in Poliakov (1974, p. 143).
76. Gilman (1982, pp. 61–9).
77. Johnson (1768). See also Moorehead (1962, p. 38). Fifty years later, Coleridge still toyed with the view of Abyssinia as the centre of an idealized Orient. See Shaffer (1975, pp. 119–21).
78. Cuvier (1831, vol. 1, p. 53); quoted in Curtin (1971, pp. 8–9).
79. See Hartleben (1909, vol. 2, p. 185); Bruce (1795, vol. 1, pp. 377–400); Volney (1787, pp. 74–7); Dupuis (1822, vol. 1, p. 73).
80. Winckelmann (1964, p. 43); trans. in Gilman (1982, p. 26).
81. De Brosses (1760). See Manuel (1959, pp. 184–209). I can find no 18th- or, for that matter, 20th-century references suggesting the obvious thought that the 'Negro fetishes' themselves could have symbolic or allegorical functions. See Horton (1967, 1973). Such is the power of racism!
82. Herder (1784, vol. 1, p. 43).
83. See Rawson (1969, pp. 350–1); Jordan (1969, p. 237).
84. See Blumenbach (1865, pp. 264–5).
85. Curtin (1971, p. 9).
86. Gobineau (1983, vol. 1, p. 347). For Schlegel's theory, see below.
87. Jordan (1969, pp. 580–1).
88. Wells (1818, pp. 438–1); cited in Curtin (1964, p. 238).
89. Jeremiah 13:23.
90. See its reproduction as the Frontispiece to Diop (1974) and in Tompkins (1973, p. 76).
91. Gran (1979, pp. 11–27).
92. Abdel-Malek (1969, pp. 23–64); Gran (1979, pp. 111–31).
93. Abdel-Malek (1969, p. 31).
94. Sabry (1930, pp. 80–2); St Clair (1972, pp. 232–8).
95. Sabry (1930, pp. 95–7); St Clair (1972, pp. 240–3).
96. Quoted in Sabry (1930, p. 135).
97. Sabry (1930, p. 396).
98. Sabry (1930, pp. 395–401).
99. Sabry (1930, pp. 405–541); R. and G. Cattaui (1950, pp. 138–216).
100. Abdel-Malek (1969, pp. 32–46).
101. Abdel-Malek (1969, pp. 47–64).
102. De Tocqueville reconciled his racialism with the undeniable economic and social successes of the Cherokees by attributing their progress to a large number of half-breeds (1837, vol. 3, p. 142). See Gobineau (1983, vol. 1, p. 207, footnote).

The big exception to this pattern is Japan, the scale and power of which would have made it extraordinarily difficult to fit into the colonial system and which must be seen in conjunction with what, to the Westerners, was the much bigger fish of China. Even so, evident Japanese successes were explained away as some form of 'cheating'. And until the Second World War it was insisted, on the grounds of racial stereotypes, that the Japanese were physically incapable of fighting Western Europeans.

103. See below, ch. VII, Note 27.

104. See, for instance, the triumphant Black standing behind the open-breasted, white Greece in Delacroix's famous picture *Greece Expiring on the Ruins of Missolonghi*.

105. For reading Dupuis, 'Letter to Thelwall', 19 Nov. 1796; for liking Berkeley, 'Letter to Poole', 1 Nov. 1796 and 'To Thelwall', 17 Dec. 1796. This and the following section are closely based on Bernal (1986, pp. 21–3).

106. 4 November 1816, cited in Manuel (1959, p. 278).

107. Hartleben (1906, vol. 1, p. 140). Iversen (1961, p. 143) notes the king's reconciliation with Champollion, but does not explain it.

108. Gardiner (1957, p. 14).

109. For Jomard's interpretation of the zodiac, see Tompkins (1973, p. 49). For the possibility that it did in fact represent a much older tradition, see pp. 168–75.

110. Letter of Montmorency-Laval, 22 Jun. 1825, in Hartleben (1909, vol. 1, p. 228).

111. See, for instance, Champollion's letters to the Abbé Gazzera, 29 Mar. and 19 Aug. 1826; and his journal for 18 Jun. 1829 (Hartleben, 1909, vol. 1, pp. 304, 348; vol. 2, p. 335). See also Marichal (1982, pp. 14–15).

112. Marichal (1982, p. 28); Leclant (1982, p. 42).

113. *Middlemarch*. Eliot gave a splendid double message in her choice of the unusual name Casaubon. She was clearly aware that the original was both a scholar from bygone days and a pioneer of the new sceptical scholarship.

114. Humboldt, Gegen Aenderung des Museumsstatuts, 14 Juni 1833 (1903–1936, vol. 12, pp. 573–81); cited in Sweet (1978–80, vol. 2, pp. 453–4).

115. F. Bunsen (1868, vol. 1, p. 244). This was at least partly because it would involve learning Coptic.

116. F. Bunsen (1868, vol. 1, p. 254).

117. Letter to his sister Christina, 28 Dec. 1817, in F. Bunsen (1868, vol. 1, p. 137).

118. F. Bunsen (1868, vol. 1, p. 244); C. Bunsen (1848–80, vol. i, pp. i, ix).

119. C. Bunsen (1868–70, vol. 1, p. 210).

120. See, for instance, the embattled tone of R. Brown (1898). For the later developments see below, ch. IX, Note 4.

121. For the plausibility of these views in the light of the mass of more recent information, see the bibliography on the subject in vol. 2.

122. C. Bunsen (1848–60, vol. 4, p. 485).

123. Hegel (1975, pp. 196–202).

124. Hegel (1892, vol. 1, pp. 117–47, 198).

125. C. Bunsen (1848–60, vol. 4, pp. 440–3).

126. Beth (1916, p. 182).

127. De Rougé (1869, p. 330); cited in Hornung (1983, p. 18). According to Budge (1904, vol. 1, p. 142), Champollion Figeac, the devoted elder brother of Jean-François, believed in Egyptian monotheism. Hornung (1983, p. 18) uses the significant phrase 'had already proposed'. This supposes that the modern discipline of Egyptology should be cut off completely from its 'prehistory', and that everything in it was a new discovery.

128. Brugsch (1891, p. 90); cited in Hornung (1983, p. 22) and Renouf (1880, p. 89). Hornung (1983, p. 23).

129. Preface to 2nd edn, cited in Hornung (1983, p. 19).

130. Hornung (1983, p. 24).

131. Lieblein (1884), quoted in Budge (1904, vol. 1, pp. 69–70).

132. Maspero (1893, p. 277).

133. It is interesting to note that an enlightened interest in non-European civilizations was maintained when Maspero's son Jean became a distinguished Sinologist. He was killed fighting with the Resistance in the Second World War.

134. Maspero (1893, p. 277, trans. Budge, 1904, vol. 1, p. 142).

135. *Ibid.*

136. Budge (1904, vol. 1, p. 143).

137. Budge (1904, vol. 1, p. 68). For a derivation of the Greek ἄνθος (flower) but originally (growth) from *nṯr*, see vol. 2.

138. See Hornung (1983, pp. 24–32).

139. Bezzenberger (1883, p. 96).

140. Erman (1883, p. 336); the challenge came from Weise (1883, p. 170).

141. Erman (1883, pp. 336–8). Naturally, I maintain that the reason it is so remarkably easy to find correspondences between Egyptian and Greek words is that between 20 and 25 per cent of the Greek vocabulary does in fact derive from Egyptian!

142. Gardiner (1986, p. 23).

143. See ch. II, Note 57.

144. See ch. II, Note 57.

145. Kern (1926, p. 136, n. 1).

146. Gardiner (1927, pp. 4, 24). It must be emphasized that Gardiner's Egyptians were categorically different from Winckelmann's Greeks in their lack of poetry and spirituality. Late-19th- and early-20th-century Egyptology was very reluctant to recognize the sophistication of Egyptian literature. See the recent discussion of the 'prosaic' *Tale of Sinuhe* (Baines, 1982). Similarly, there was a tendency to describe Egyptian 'Wisdom Literature' as utilitarian and not religious. This has been abandoned in the last twenty years. See R. J. Williams (1981, p. 11).

147. Gardiner (1942, p. 53).

148. Gardiner (1942, p. 65).

149. Hornung (1983, p. 24).

150. Murray (1931; 1949). See Černy (1952, p. 1).

151. Drioton (1948).

152. Brunner (1957, pp. 269–70). See also the bibliography in Hornung (1983, pp. 28–9).

153. Curl makes this point (1982, p. 107).

154. See Iversen (1961, pp. 131–3); Curl (1982, pp. 107–52); Tompkins (1978, pp. 37–55).

155. Curl (1982, pp. 153–72).

156. Farrell (1980, pp. 162–70). He does not discuss the possible influence of Masonry in the 'Egyptianizing' of American funeral customs. It would be interesting, for instance, to consider the impact of Washington's splendid Masonic funeral. It may be inevitable that scholars, like everyone else, should kick their predecessors in the teeth, but it is still sad that Professor Farrell should be so contemptuous towards Jessica Mitford (p. 213), who opened up this important field, and from whom he stole his title.

157. Mayes (1959, p. 295); Wortham (1971, p. 92).

158. Brodie (1945, pp. 50–3); Franklin (1963, pp. 70–9); Irwin (1980). This is not to deny the significance of hieroglyphs in 19th-century European literature (see Dieckmann, 1970, pp. 128–37); I merely claim that they were more central in the USA.

159. Iversen (1961, p. 121).

160. Manuel (1956, pp. 155–6); for the centrality of Egypt to Swedenborg's thought, see Dieckmann (1970, pp. 155–60); for Theosophy, see Blavatsky (1930; 1931).

161. Abdel-Malek (1969, p. 190). In n. 4 on that page, he cites a letter from Jean Dautry in which the latter wrote: 'In neither his published nor his unpublished works did St Simon ever mention the Suez canal, but he must almost certainly have referred to it in his conversations about transoceanic communications.'

162. Abdel-Malek (1969, pp. 189–98). For a visual image of the awakening, see the bronze medallion struck commemorating the publication of *La Description de l'Égypte*, dated 1826. The obverse portrays the rediscovery of Egypt: an Egyptian queen is unveiled by a standing figure of Gallia, represented as a victorious Roman general. The reverse shows a series of Egyptian gods and goddesses. This is on the dust jacket of Curl (1982).

163. See Abdel-Malek (1969, p. 302); Curl (1982, p. 187). Verdi also composed an Egyptian national anthem.

164. Curl (1982, pp. 173–94).

165. Black (1974, pp. 4–6).

166. Elliot Smith (1911, pp. 63–130).

167. It does not, however, rule out the possibility that monuments from the 3rd millennium – like Silbury Hill – or from the 2nd – like the later stages of Stonehenge – were influenced by developments in Egypt and the East Mediterranean.

168. This is in no way to deny the fundamentally local nature of American agriculture and the civilizations based upon it, or the possibility that the mummification found in the Atacama desert could be from the 4th millennium BC, and therefore indigenous. On the other hand, it is also very likely that American cultures – at least since the Olmec civilization, found in Eastern Mexico and dating to the early 1st millennium BC – have received considerable African influence; see Van Sertima (1976; 1984). For equally compelling evidence for East Asian influence on America, see Needham and Lu (1985). For an attack on extracontinental influences on Pre-Columbian America, see Davies (1979). He is especially hostile to the notion of African initiative and influence (pp. 87–93). While 'diffusionism' has been greatly influenced by imperialism, in this case isolationism would seem to be related to the belief that only Europe, the 'universal continent', can connect the others.

169. Langham (1981, pp. 134–99).

170. Elkin (1974, pp. 13–14); Langham (1981, pp. 194–9).

171. Jomard (1829a; 1829b); see also Tompkins (1978, pp. 44–51).

172. See above, Note 109.

173. See Tompkins (1978, pp. 93–4).

174. Tompkins (1978, p. 169).

175. Tompkins (1978, pp. 77–146).

176. Tompkins (1978, pp. 96–107).

177. Petrie (1931); Tompkins (1978, p. 107).

178. Schwaller de Lubicz (1958; 1961; 1968). See also Tompkins (1978, pp. 168–75).

179. Stecchini (1957; 1961; 1978).

180. See de Santillana (1963); de Santillana and von Derchend (1969). For the precession of the equinoxes, see ch. II, Note 9.

181. See Neugebauer (1945). For Copernicus, see ch. II, Notes 110–11.

182. Neugebauer and Parker (1960–9). For the contempt, see for instance Neugebauer (1957, pp. 71–4).

183. Neugebauer (1957, p. 78).

184. Neugebauer (1957, p. 96).

185. *Ibid.*

186. Lauer (1960, p. 11).

187. Lauer (1960, p. 10).

188. Lauer (1960, pp. 4–5; 13–14; 21–4). For the question of the cubit, see Tompkins (1978, p. 208).

189. Lauer (1960, pp. 1–3).

190. Brunner (1957, pp. 269–70). He does not specify the Pyramids in his claim here.

191. Lauer (1960, p. 10).

192. Drioton and Vandier (1946, p. 129); cited in Lauer (1960, p. 4).

193. Drioton, preface to Lauer (1948); cited in Tompkins (1978, p. 208).

194. See Brunner (1957); Brunner-Traut (1971).

Chapter VI
HELLENOMANIA, 1

1. For this, see ch. IV, Notes 123, 124 above.

2. See above, ch. IV, Notes 63–7. For Wolf and Bentley, see Wilamowitz-Moellendorf (1982, pp. 81–2).

3. There is no doubt that Homer was thought to be a oral performer in Antiquity; this tradition is strengthened by the most plausible Egyptian etymology for his name, or a general word for poet, from 'art of utterance'. See above, ch. III, Note 61. Wolf did not go into the problems of the origin of the Greek alphabet. His supposition on this was shared by the promoters of the Extreme Aryan Model in the 20th century. I believe that, despite the undoubted associations with orality, the epics are sophisticated written documents coming from a long literate tradition. For more on Homer, see ch. I, Note 59 above. For a discussion of the 20th-century scholars and my arguments in favour of placing the introduction of the Greek alphabet in the middle of the 2nd millennium BC, well before Homer, see Bernal (1987a; forthcoming, 1988).

4. Wolf (1804); see also Pfeiffer (1976, pp. 173–7); F. M. Turner (1981, pp. 138–9).

5. For the Scots and Wood, see ch. IV, Notes 71–2 above. For the professionalization, see R. S. Turner (1983a; 1985).

6. Monro (1911, p. 771).

7. See Pfeiffer (1976, p. 173).

8. See above, ch. IV, Notes 122–3.

9. Humboldt (1793).

10. Humboldt (1793); see also Sweet (1978–80, vol. 1, p. 126).

11. For the initial idea of *Bildung* for the masses, see Hohendahl (1981, pp. 250–72). For the actual result, see R. S. Turner (1983b, p. 486).

12. Letter, 6 Feb. 1793, in Humboldt (1841–52, vol. 5, p. 34); quoted in Sweet (1978–80, vol. 1, p. 131). For more on the subject, see Seidel (1962, pp. xix–xxix).

13. See above, ch. III, Note 91. *Pace* Wilamowitz-Moellendorf, who attributes much of its success to its oblique references to contemporary Frenchmen. However, he also admitted (1982, p. 103) that it gave a good picture of Classical Athens.

14. Schiller (1967, pp. 24–43). For Göttingen's allegedly middle way between revolutionary and reactionary extremes, see Marino (1975, pp. 358–71).

15. Sweet (1978–80, vol. 2, p. 46).

16. Wolf (1804, 2nd edn, p. xxvi); quoted with complete approval by Pfeiffer (1976, p. 174).

17. Humboldt (1903–36, vol. 4, p. 37, trans. Iggers, 1967, p. 59). For further discussion of this piece, see Iggers (1968, pp. 56–62); Sweet (1978–80, vol. 2, pp. 431–40).

18. Humboldt (1903–36, vol. 3, p. 188, trans. in Cowan, 1963, p. 79).

19. See above, ch. IV, Note 102.

20. See above, ch. IV, Notes 57–8; ch. V, Notes 1–3.

21. R. L. Brown (1967, pp. 12–13); Humboldt (1903–36, vol. IV, p. 294).

22. See above, ch. IV, Note 9.

23. Poliakov (1974, p. 77). For the poet Klopstock on this, see p. 96. There is a translation of one of Fichte's speeches on this in R. L. Brown (1967, pp. 75–6).

24. Humboldt (1903–36, vol. I, p. 266).

25. Iggers (1967, p. 59). Ideas of this type occur in Hegel and many other contemporary thinkers.

26. The only possible objection to this is the utopian aspect of Humboldt's original concept of *Bildung* (see above, Note 11). Professor Canfora (1980, pp. 39–56) argues that there was a right-wing *usurpazione* of Classics at the turn of the 19th century. However, he takes the Jacobin use of Antiquity as his base. Following conventional wisdom in Northern Europe, I do not include this in the tradition of *Altertumswissenschaft/*Classics.

27. Another conservative avenue was, of course, 'the Orient' and India. See above, ch. V, Notes 6–36. This section is closely based on Bernal (1986, pp. 24–7).

28. Highet (1949, pp. 377–436); St Clair (1972, pp. 251–62).

29. For the public schools, see below, ch. VII, Notes 4–10; for Aryan Christianity, see ch. VIII, Notes 38–42.

30. For the degree of this alienation and concern with the Mediterranean in these circles *before* the Greek War of Independence, see M. Butler (1981, pp. 113–37).

31. St Clair (1972, pp. 119–27).

32. St Clair (1972, pp. 334–47). The great exception to this is ΦBK, which was founded before the others and has always retained a very different character. For 'Father' Jahn, his exercises and his book burnings see Mosse (1964, pp. 13–30); F. R. Stern (1961, pp. 1–25).

33. For the impact of the Marbles on British appreciation of Greek art and Greece itself in this period, see St Clair (1983, pp. 166–202).

34. Haydon (1926, p. 68).

35. Knowles (1831, p. 241).

36. Shelley (1821, Preface).

37. In Flaubert's *Madame Bovary*, set in the 1820s, the heroine had read Scott and had a cult of Mary Queen of Scots (ch. 6). For the invention of the tradition, see Trevor-Roper (1983, pp. 29–30).

38. St Clair (1972, pp. 164–84).

39. *Courrier Français*, 7 Jun. 1821, p. 2b, quoted in Dimakis (1968, p. 123).

40. For the first view, see Borrow (1843); Irving (1829) and Prescott's many works on Spanish history. For the later 'racial' interpretation, see Hannay (1911).

41. See Fallmerayer (1835); and St Clair (1972, esp. pp. 82–4).

42. Rawson (1969, p. 319).

43. See Kistler (1960); E. M. Butler (1935, pp. 294–300).

44. See Rawson (1969, pp. 338–43). See the constant references to the Dorians as models in Speer (1970, esp. pp. 63, 159).

45. Rawson (1969, pp. 330–43).

46. Bury (1900, p. 62).

47. Cartledge (1979, p. 119) cites a marginal note by Professor Wade-Geary referring to Mothone, a city in Messenia conquered by the Spartans, as 'the Ulster in the Messenian Ireland'. Cartledge himself uses the analogy elsewhere (p. 116), but in an anti-English/Spartan sense.

48. Ridgeway also wrote books on Scottish history and ballads (Conway, 1937). See also Stewart (1959, pp. 17–18).

49. Michelet was a student of his. Hegel (1892, vol. 1, trans.' note).

50. Hegel (1975, pp. 154–209).

51. Hegel (1975, ch. 6, n. 127).

52. Hegel (1892, vol. 1, pp. 117–47).

53. Hegel (1892, vol. 1, pp. 197–8).

54. Hegel (1892, vol. 1, pp. 149–50).

55. See above, ch. IV, Note 28.

56. For more on this, see Bernal (1987b).

57. Marx (1939, pp. 375–413, trans. 1973, pp. 471–513). For more on this, see Bernal (1987b).

58. Marx (trans. 1973, p. 110).

59. While I am convinced that the vast majority of Greek mythological themes came from Egypt or Phoenicia, it is equally clear that their selection and treatment was characteristically Greek, and to that extent they did reflect Greek society.

60. See esp. Heeren (1832–4, vol. 1, pp. 470–1; vol. 2, pp. 122–3).

61. Humboldt to his wife Caroline, 18 Nov. 1823, in von Sydow (1906–16, vol. 7, pp. 173–4). See also Heine (1830–31, vol. 2, p. 193).

62. See, for instance, Hansberry (1977, pp. 27, 104, 109).

63. C. Bunsen (1859, pp. 30–5); Witte (1979, pp. 17–19).

64. Yavetz (1976, pp. 276–96).

65. Rytkönen (1968, pp. 21, 222). See also Witte (1979, p. 191).

66. Momigliano (1980, p. 567).

67. Momigliano (1982, p. 8).

68. C. Bunsen (1859, pp. 336–7, 340); F. Bunsen (1868, vol. 1, p. 195).

69. Witte (1979, p. 136). Letter to Mme Hensler, 17 Mar. 1821.

70. Rytkönen (1968, pp. 280–2); C. Bunsen (1859, pp. 485–9).

71. Rytkönen (1968, p. 220); Momigliano (1982, pp. 8–9).

72. Witte (1979, p. 21); C. Bunsen (1859, pp. 38–42).

73. Witte (1979, p. 18).

74. Momigliano (1982, p. 7).

75. He made it clear that the latter was the lesser evil; see C. Bunsen (1859, p. 125).

76. E. Fueter (1936, pp. 467–70); C. P. Gooch (1913, pp. 16–17); H. Trevor-Roper (1969).
77. p. xiii, cited in Rytkönen (1968, p. 306).
78. F. Bunsen (1868, vol. 1, p. 337). For the others, see Witte (1979, p. 185) and Bridenthal (1970, p. 98).
79. Letter to Moltke, 9 Dec. 1796, cited in Bridenthal (1970, p. 98).
80. Witte (1979, p. 167).
81. Rytkönen (1968, pp. 67, 219).
82. See ch. V, Note 115.
83. See his letters to Altenstein, 4 Jan. 1808 and Schuckman, 2 May 1811; see Witte (1978, p. 20) and Rytkönen (1968, pp. 175–6).
84. Witte (1979, p. 185).
85. Anon. article on Niebuhr in the *Encyclopaedia Britannica*, 11th edn, 1911.
86. Momigliano (1966d, pp. 6–9). M. Pallotino (1984, p. 15) rightly points out that Mitford and Giuseppe Micali, the historian of ancient Italy, anticipated Niebuhr's 'modern' historical methods.
87. Cited without reference by Gooch (1913, p. 19).
88. Bridenthal (1970, p. 2); Fueter (1936, p. 467); Witte (1978, p. 82); Trevor-Roper (1969). Professor Momigliano's case that Niebuhr could have been right (1957, pp. 104–14; 1977, pp. 231–51) in no way diminishes the importance of the Romantic influence. Macaulay's *Lays of Ancient Rome*, first published in 1842, was based on Niebuhr's hypothesis.
89. Momigliano (1982, pp. 3–15).
90. Quoted in Momigliano (1982, p. 9).
91. Michelet (1831, vol. 1, p. xi).
92. See ch. VII, Notes 7–10.
93. Niebuhr (1847–51, vol. 1, pp. xxix–xxxi).
94. Wilcken (1931), cited in Witte (1979, p. 183). For Wilcken under the Nazis, see Canfora (1980, p. 136).
95. Letter from Kiel, in C. Bunsen (1868, pp. 35–40).
96. See above, ch. V, Notes 56–8. See also below, ch. VIII, Notes 24–8.
97. See Iggers (1968, p. 30); Shaffer (1975, p. 85).
98. See the quotation from the wise Sidonia in Disraeli's *Tancred*, vol. 3, ch. 1:
 'All is race, there is no other truth.'
 'Because it includes all others,' said Lord Henry.
 'You have said it.'
99. See Witte (1979, p. 20).
100. See Rytkönen (1968, p. 182); Niebuhr (1852, Lecture, VII, Pt 1, vol. 1, pp. 98–9). Some years earlier Niebuhr had expressed the wish to settle Asia with Europeans: 'I imagine German colonies in Bithynia etc.' See his letter to Mme Hensler, 16 Aug. 1821, in C. Bunsen (1859, p. 410).
101. Niebuhr (1852, Lecture, XX vol. 1, pp. 222–3).

102. See above, ch. V, Notes 111–12.

103. Niebuhr (1852, Lecture, V, vol. 1, p. 77). See also Lecture, VII, pp. 97–9.

104. Niebuhr (1852, Lecture, VI, vol. 1, pp. 83–4).

105. See, for instance, his letter to Mme Hensler, 17 Mar. 1821, in C. Bunsen (1859, p. 405).

106. Niebuhr (1852, Lecture, XX, vol. 1, p. 223).

107. Niebuhr (1852, Lecture, IX, vol. 1, p. 117).

108. Hoefer (1852–77, vol. 8, cols 721–5).

109. These 'Cyclopean' buildings may well have a common ancestry in Anatolia. The walls and gates of Mycenae and other Mycenaean cities and fortifications would seem to be the result of the wave of Anatolian influence associated in legend with the conquest of Pelops in the 14th century BC. The buildings of this type in Italy can be associated with the Etruscans, whom ancient tradition maintained had come from North-West Anatolia. Thus I believe that this style was introduced after the major Egyptian influence on Greece at the beginning of the Late Bronze Age, but before the chief Phoenician one in the 10th and 9th centuries.

110. For a discussion of Inachos, see ch. I, Notes 93–7.

111. See Petit-Radel (1815).

112. Pfeiffer (1976, p. 186); Gooch (1913, pp. 16–17); Wilamowitz-Moellendorf (1959, pp. 67; 1982, p. 127) describes him in similar terms.

113. See Miller's title *Prolegomena zu einer wissenschaftlichen Mythologie*, translated by Leitch (1844) as *Introduction to a Scientific System of Mythology*. For a discussion of this, and Kant's use of the terms, see Neschke-Hentschke (1984, p. 484).

114. See R. S. Turner (1983a).

115. Gooch (1913, p. 35).

116. Donaldson (1858, p. vii).

117. Donaldson (1858, pp. vii–xxxix). It is striking that Müller was not dismissed along with his friends and colleagues – including the Grimm brothers – 'the Göttingen Seven', who in 1837 had protested the illiberal actions of the King of Hanover.

118. His work on the Etruscans won the prize offered by the Prussian Academy: 'To explain and exhibit critically the nature and constitution of the training of the Etruscan nation'. See Donaldson (1858, p. xxii). Beyond reflecting the Etrusco-mania of the turn of the 18th century, which was especially promoted by the Bonapartes, who may have seen themselves as Etruscans, some Germans identified themselves with this ancient people (see Poliakov, 1974, pp. 65–6; Borsi, 1985). Niebuhr claimed, in his first edition, that the Etruscans had come from north of the Alps, which would explain the interest of the Prussian Academy. Note also the concern with the *Bildung* of the Etruscans, about which virtually nothing was known.

119. Pausanias, XI.36.3 (trans. P. Levi, 1971. vol. 1, p. 387).

120. Plutarch had used the word *philobarbaros*, to attack Herodotos. See above, ch. I, Note 183. Another modern term for this is the *interpretatio Graeca*, for a

remarkably balanced view of which see Griffiths (1980). I maintain that the name Minyans – found in the rich plains of Boiotia ('cattle country') and Messenia in the Peloponnese – came from the Egyptian *mniw* meaning 'herdsmen' (see vol. 2).

121. For Indophilia, see above, ch. V, Notes 6–17. See also Creuzer (1810–12); Momigliano (1946, pp. 152–163, repr. 1966, pp. 75–90). For a short bibliography on F. Schlegel, Creuzer and Görres, see Feldman and Richardson (1972, pp. 383, 389).

122. For an attack on Creuzer, see Müller (1825, pp. 331–6); for one on Dupuis, see Müller (1834, pp. 1–30).

123. For the 'argument from silence', see the Introduction, p. 9.

124. Müller (1825, pp. 128–9; trans. 1844, pp. 68–9).

125. Müller (1825, pp. 218–19; trans. 1844, pp. 158–9). This certainly existed in Antiquity, but I see no reason to doubt that there were more or less equivalent forces for differentiation.

126. Müller (1825, p. 221; trans. 1844, p. 161).

127. Müller (1825, pp. 232–4; trans. 1844, p. 173–4).

128. Müller (1825, pp. 239–40; trans. 1844, p. 179).

129. For the possibility that Kekrops' colonizations represent Egyptian influence from expeditions during the 12th Dynasty, see vol. 2. See also the Introduction, p. 19.

130. Müller (1820–4, vol. 1, pp. 106–8).

131. For Herodotos on the other settlements, see above, ch. I, Notes 117–24; for Kekrops, see VIII.44.

132. *Menexenos*, 245.C–D; Müller (1820–4, vol. 1, p. 107). For the distinction between Athenian 'purity' and the Eastern conquests of other parts of Greece, see above, ch. IV, Note 18.

133. For my opinions about the name Danaos, see ch. I, Notes 107–10.

134. Müller (1820–4, vol. 1, p. 109).

135. For this see above, ch. I, Note 57.

136. Müller (1820–4, vol. 1, p. 112).

137. Müller (1820–4, vol. 1, pp. 108, 113).

138. Herodotos, II.51. Mr Casaubon knew about this connection with the Kabeiroi (see *Middlemarch*, ch. 20). See also Astour (1967a, p. 155); Dupuis (1795, vol. 1, p. 95).

139. Müller did not mention Herodotos (III.37) having implied a link between the Kabeiroi and the cult of Ptah, the Egyptian god of metalwork.

140. Usener (1907, p. 11). For a fascinating study of Usener, see Momigliano (1982, pp. 33–48).

141. For Movers, see below, ch. VIII, Note 86.

142. Müller (1820–4, vol. 1, p. 122).

143. Müller (1825, pp. 282–3; trans. 1844, pp. 221–2).

144. Despite the obscurity of her publications on the issue of Near Eastern influence

on Greek mythology, Jane Harrison (1925, p. 84) saw beyond this when she compared the brilliant Semitist Robertson-Smith – whose religious background had allowed him to stay within the Broad Aryan Model and maintain that there had been Near Eastern influence on Greece – to the Classicist Frazer, who argued much less threateningly for anthropological parallels:

> Robertson-Smith, exiled for heresy, had seen the star in the East; in vain, we classical deaf adders stopped our ears and closed our eyes. But at the mere sound of the magical words 'Golden Bough', the scales fell – we heard and understood.

145. Müller (1825, p. 285; trans. 1844, p. 224).
146. Foucart (1914, pp. 2–3). For more on Foucart, see above, ch. V, Note 145; and vol. 3.
147. Müller (1825, pp. 285–6; trans. 1844, pp. 224–5).
148. Müller (1825, p. 290; trans. 1844, p. 229).
149. Feldman and Richardson (1972, p. 417).
150. Müller (1825, p. 290; trans. 1844, p. 229).
151. See the Introduction and vols 2 and 3.
152. See Astour (1967a, pp. 128–58); R. Edwards (1979, pp. 64–114).
153. See Nissen (1962, pp. 12, 117).
154. Wilamowitz-Moellendorf (1982, p. 105).
155. F. M. Turner (1981, p. 79).
156. Feldman and Richardson (1972, pp. 416–18). See also the bibliography in F. M. Turner (1981, p. 79). Turner also takes Müller very seriously.
157. Pfeiffer (1976, p. 187).
158. For an attempt to justify this, see Momigliano (1982, p. 33).

Chapter VII
HELLENOMANIA, 2

1. For Isokrates' claim, see ch. I, Note 131. The quotation comes from C. Bunsen; see F. Bunsen (1868, vol. 1, p. 111).
2. Shaffer (1975, p. 25).
3. Cousin (1841, pp. 35–45). Cousin appears to have developed his central idea on 'eclecticism' and the central role of Plato from Combes-Dounous, who wrote at the beginning of the century; see Wismann (1983, pp. 503–7). Though he seems to have been reluctant to do so, Combes-Dounous could not deny Plato's borrowing of the idea of the immortality of the soul from Egypt and the East. See Combes-Dounous (1809, esp. vol. 1, p. 141). By the 1830s, it was safe for Cousin to attribute it to Greek genius.
4. Bunsen, letter to Arnold, 4 Mar. 1836 (F. Bunsen, 1868, vol. 1, pp. 420–2). For the Prussian professorial autocracy, see R. S. Turner (1983a; 1985).

5. See Lloyd-Jones (1982a, pp. 16–17).

6. See the letter from H. G. Liddell (Alice's father, and writer of the first great Greek–English dictionary) to H. H. Vaughan, 18 Dec. 1853, cited in Bill (1973, p. 136).

7. This was set out by Bolgar (1979, pp. 327–38).

8. He found Germans less attractive. See his letter to Bunsen, Easter Monday 1828, in F. Bunsen (1868, pp. 316–19).

9. See T. Arnold (1845, pp. 44–50). Race was also the only detectable historical principle of Arnold's star pupil Vaughan when he became professor at Oxford; see Bill (1973, pp. 182–5).

10. See Bill (1973, pp. 8–10).

11. See anon. on Thirlwall in the *Encyclopaedia Britannica* (1911) and J. C. Thirlwall (1936, pp. 1–24).

12. For more on Schleiermacher, see Shaffer (1975, pp. 85–7 and elsewhere). For his belief in an Aryan Christianity, see ch. VIII, Notes 29–30.

13. J. C. Thirlwall (1936, pp. 56–7).

14. Merrivale (1899, p. 80), which I have been unable to find; cited in J. C. Thirlwall (1936, p. 57); Brookfield (1907, p. 8).

15. See Annan (1955, pp. 243–87); P. Allen (1978, p. 257).

16. Thirlwall (1936, p. 200); F. Bunsen (1868, vol. 1, p. 601).

17. Thirlwall (1936, p. 165). This is not a bad description of the situation in 1987!

18. Cited in Thirlwall (1936, p. 164).

19. Macaulay (1866–71, vol. 7, pp. 684–5); cited in Jenkyns (1980, p. 14). See the interesting discussion in F. M. Turner (1981, pp. 204–6).

20. Grote (1826, p. 280). See F. M. Turner (1981, pp. 207–8).

21. Cited in Thirlwall (1936, p. 97); F. M. Turner (1981, pp. 203–16); Momigliano (1966b, pp. 57–61).

22. For these arguments, see above, ch. III, Notes 94–5.

23. C. Thirlwall (1835, vol. 1, p. 63).

24. C. Thirlwall (1835, vol. 1, p. 64).

25. C. Thirlwall (1835, vol. 1, p. 67).

26. C. Thirlwall (1835, vol. 1, p. 71).

27. C. Thirlwall (1835, vol. 1, p. 74).

28. For Egyptian activities in the Aegean at the time, see above, ch. V, Notes 91–9.

29. C. Thirlwall (1835, vol. 1, p. 74).

30. J. C. Thirlwall (1936, pp. 98–101).

31. Momigliano (1966b, p. 61).

32. *Ibid.*

33. Momigliano (1966b, p. 60); Pappe (1979, pp. 297–302).

34. Momigliano (1966b, p. 61).

35. Momigliano (1966b, p. 62).

36. Momigliano (1966b, p. 63).

37. K. O. Müller (1825, p. 59; trans. 1844, p. 1).
38. Müller (1825, pp. 249–51; trans. 1844, pp. 189–90); Grote (1846–56, vol. 2, pp. 157–9, 182–204).
39. Müller (1825, p. 108; trans. 1844, pp. 189–90); Grote (1846–56, vol. 2, p. 477).
40. F. M. Turner (1981, pp. 90–1); Momigliano (1966b, pp. 56–74).
41. Momigliano (1966b, p. 63). For a discussion of Grote's approach to mythology and the influence of Müller upon it, see F. M. Turner (1981, pp. 87–8).
42. Grote (1846–56, vol. 1, p. 440).
43. Momigliano (1966b, pp. 63–4).
44. For a bibliography concerning Canaanite and Phoenician finds at Thebes, see R. Edwards (1979, p. 132, n. 145); Porada (1981). For the 12th-dynasty expeditions, see Farag (1980, pp. 75–81). For my ideas on this, see the Introduction (p. 19) and vol. 2.
45. This refers to the treatment of Paul Foucart, Victor Bérard, Cyrus Gordon, Michael Astour, Saul Levin, Ruth Edwards and others.
46. Momigliano (1966b, pp. 64–7).
47. Smith (1854, pp. 14–15).
48. See Introduction, pp. 14–21. The Revised Ancient Model will be discussed at more length in vol. 2.
49. Thucydides, I.3.
50. See above, ch. I, Notes 39–41.
51. Curtius (1857–67, vol. 1, p. 26; trans. 1886, vol. 1, p. 39).
52. Quoted without specific reference by Pallotino (1978, p. 37). For a fascinating description of Mommsen's sceptical position and others' opposition to it, see Gossman (1983, esp. pp. 21–41).
53. See Sandys (1908, vol. 3, p. 207).
54. Stuart-Jones (1968, p. x).
55. For more discussion of this, see vol. 2.
56. See Sandys (1908, vol. 3, pp. 228–9).
57. Wilamowitz-Moellendorf (1982, p. 153).
58. Curtius (1857–67, vol. 1, p. 27; trans. 1886, vol. 1, p. 41).
59. Curtius (1857–67, vol. 1, p. 30; trans. 1886, vol. 1, p. 45).
60. See above, ch. VI, Notes 46–7.
61. Curtius (1857–67, vol. 1, pp. 30–1; trans. 1886, vol. 1, pp. 45–6). I can find no explicit mention of it, but it would seem overwhelmingly likely that Curtius and other German scholars saw analogies between the land-based and morally superior Germans and Dorians and their sea-based talented – but unreliable – 'cousins', the English/Ionians.
62. Curtius (1857–67, vol. 1, p. 31; trans. 1886, vol. 1, pp. 45–6).
63. *Ibid.*
64. Curtius (1857–67, vol. 1, p. 20; trans. 1886, vol. 1, p. 32).
65. Curtius (1857–67, vol. 1, p. 19; trans. 1886, vol. 1, p. 34).

66. Curtius (1857–67, vol. 1, p. 41; trans. 1886, vol. 1, p. 58).
67. Curtius (1857–67, vol. 1, pp. 41–3; trans. 1886, vol. 1, pp. 58–61). For Bunsen's scheme, see ch. V, Note 125. Homer's single mention of 'barbarian' – i.e. non-Greek – was in reference to Carians (*Iliad*, II.867).
68. Curtius (1857–67, vol. 1, pp. 58–61; trans. 1886, vol. 1, pp. 81–3).
69. For a vivid portrait of him, see Stewart (1959, pp. 16–18).
70. Ridgeway (1901, vol. 1, p. 88).

Chapter VIII
THE RISE AND FALL OF THE PHOENICIANS, 1830–85

1. Humboldt to Caroline, 29 Feb. 1816 (Sydow, 1906–16, vol. 5, pp. 194–5; cited in Sweet, 1978–80, vol. 2, p. 208).
2. Poliakov (1974, pp. 37–46, 210–13).
3. See ch. IV, Notes 113–14.
4. Disraeli (1847, Bk 3, ch. 7; Bk 5, ch. 6); Eliot (1876, Bk 5, ch. 40).
5. Poliakov (1974, p. 197).
6. Knox (1862, p. 1); quoted in Poliakov (1974, p. 232).
7. Quoted in Curtin (1971, p. 16); see also Curtin (1964, pp. 375–80).
8. Knox (1862, p. 194); quoted in Poliakov (1974, p. 362).
9. Poliakov (1974, p. 233).
10. Letter to Gobineau, 26 Jun. 1856, cited in Boissel (1983, pp. 1249–50).
11. Michelet (1831, Bk 2, ch. 3).
12. Burnouf (1872, pp. 318–19; trans. 1888, pp. 190–1).
13. Poliakov (1974, p. 234). For Gobineau's images of the Yellows and Blacks, see above, ch. V, Notes 63–5.
14. See Gaulmier (1983, pp. lxxii–xi).
15. Cited in Poliakov (1974, p. 235). For the relationship seen in the 19th century among all deviants from the white, adult, male norm – non-Whites, children, the mad and women – see Gilman (1982, pp. 1–18).
16. For a general survey of Gobineau's scheme, see Poliakov (1974, p. 234).
17. Gobineau (1983, pp. 349–63).
18. Gobineau (1983, pp. 364–478).
19. *Ibid.*, especially pp. 415–17.
20. Letter of 30 Jul. 1856, quoted in Poliakov (1974, p. 238).
21. For Barthélemy, see ch. III, Note 24; for Bochart, see ch. III, Note 27.
22. R. L. Brown (1967, p. 57).
23. See ch. V, Note 25.
24. Renan (1855); cited in Gaulmier (1977, p. 48). Most of this is cited in Rashed (1980, p. 12). See also Said (1978, p. 139). It is interesting that Renan chose a Greek and a German as examples of true European philosophers. He would have

found himself in difficulties if he had cited Locke and Hume, who wrote largely in English, an isolating language.

25. Renan (1855); cited in Gaulmier (1977, p. 47).

26. For Renan's notion that by studying Semitic culture he was in some sense creating it, see Said (1978, p. 140).

27. Renan (1855); cited in Gaulmier (1977, p. 47); see also Faverty (1951, p. 169).

28. See Faverty (1951, pp. 167–74); Said (1978, pp. 137–48).

29. See above, ch. V, Notes 117–20. This is, of course, the theme of Said (1978).

30. Renan (1858, p. 359). As far as I am aware, Renan never faced up to the problems these parallels posed for this theory of climatic determinism. The English could hardly have developed these characteristics from the blazing sun!

31. Cited in Faverty (1951, p. 76).

32. See Faverty (1951, esp. pp. 111–61).

33. See M. Arnold (1906). The great 19th-century romanticizer of the Gypsies, George Borrow, was extremely interested in their language and those of other Eastern Indo-European speakers like the Armenians (1851, chs 27, 47). Borrow's descriptions of the Gypsy natural philosopher Jasper Petulengro (1857, ch. 9) were extremely popular in Victorian and Edwardian England; see Borrow (1851; 1857). The British cult of the Gypsy/Bohemian was not accepted in Germany. When it came to the Holocaust, their Indo-European language was no more protection to them than the Jews' Germanic one, Yiddish.

34. See Faverty (1951, p. 167).

35. Faverty (1951, pp. 162–85).

36. For Matthew Arnold's 'Hellenism' as a major factor in Britain's decline in the late 19th and early 20th centuries, see Wiener (1981, pp. 30–7).

37. M. Arnold (1869, p. 69). Note the use of the Saxon word 'growth' and the dynamism implied in 'movement'. For links between Hellenism and Aryanism, see Hersey (1976).

38. See above, ch. V, Note 119.

39. Russell (1895, vol. 1, p. 383).

40. For more on Schleiermacher in England, see Shaffer (1975, esp. pp. 85–7). For Cousin, see Gaulmier (1978, p. 21).

41. Poliakov (1974, p. 310). There is an interesting 20th-century parallel to this in the progression from Kenneth Clark's 'soft-core' racism to the 'hard-core' version of his son.

42. See Poliakov (1974, pp. 307–9); Mosse (1964, pp. 15–30); F. R. Stern (1961, pp. 35–52). Many of Lagarde's ideas were extensions of those of Renan.

43. Hardy (1891, ch. 25).

44. Gladstone (1869).

45. See F. M. Turner (1981, pp. 159–70); Lloyd-Jones (1982a, pp. 110–25).

46. Rawlinson (1889, p. 23).

47. M. Arnold (1906, p. 25). These were very much the words of Arnold's contem-

porary Ernst Curtius when writing about the 'retreat' of the Semites. See above, ch. VII, Note 6. See also T. S. Eliot (1971, pp. 46–7).

48. Quoted by Evans (1909, p. 94). Evans, who was by this time projecting non-Semitic Minoans everywhere, including Phoenicia, agreed with the Grand Old Man.

49. Michelet (1962, p. 68).

50. Michelet (1831, pp. 177–8).

51. See ch. III, Note 27.

52. Gesenius (1815, p. 6). The classification of Semitic languages is in fact a very disputed subject which has been made much more complicated today by the discovery of several more ancient and modern ones. For more discussion of my views on this, see Bernal (1980). There has never been any doubt about Gesenius' identification of Phoenician with Hebrew rather than with the Berber languages.

53. Gesenius (1815, p. 4); Gobineau (1983, pp. 380–1).

54. Gobineau (1983, p. 388).

55. Gobineau (1983, p. 149).

56. Gobineau (1983, p. 1135).

57. Gobineau (1983, p. 1141).

58. Gobineau (1983, p. 396).

59. Gobineau (1983, pp. 369–72).

60. Gobineau (1983, pp. 399–401).

61. Gobineau (1983, pp. 401–5).

62. Gobineau (1983, pp. 195, 413–17).

63. Gobineau (1983, pp. 378–9, 379, n. 2).

64. Michelet (1831, pp. 203–11). According to Polybios, Spendios was a Campanian from Southern Italy.

65. See Benedetto (1920, pp. 21–39); A. Green (1982, pp. 28–31). For a critical treatment of this fascination, see Said (1978, esp. pp. 180–97). As Jean Bruneau points out (Flaubert, 1973, vol. 2, p. 1354): 'Of all Flaubert's works, *Salammbô* is without doubt the least studied. There is no good edition and its genesis is badly known.' See also Bruneau's bibliography on the subject.

66. Benedetto (1920, p. 39); A. Green (1982, p. 28); Starkie (1971, p. 14). My claim that the Mutiny triggered Flaubert's interest in this topic and remained an important modern parallel in his mind does not in any way try to discredit the important parallels Dr Green has shown between *Salammbô* and the French Revolution of 1848; see A. Green (1982, pp. 73–93).

67. Letter, early May 1861; quoted in English by Starkie (1971, p. 22).

68. See Starkie (1971, pp. 20–2).

69. See Starkie (1971, pp. 58–9).

70. See Benedetto (1920). For the anti-Semitism of this School, which was dominated by Julius Beloch, see below.

71. I agree here with Professor Lloyd-Jones. See Wilamowitz-Moellendorf (1982, p. 103, n. 405).
72. Michelet, who revelled in describing the horrors of the Mercenary War, describes the Third Servile one in a very matter-of-fact way. He completely omits the lining of the road from Capua to Rome with 6,000 crucified slaves after the Roman victory (1831, vol.2, pp. 198–203).
73. Although Zola published *Nana* only in 1880, he began his realistic novels of Parisian life and corruption in the 1860s.
74. See Starkie (1971, pp. 23–6).
75. See Said (1978, pp. 182–5).
76. This was established by Eissfeldt (1935). See also Spiegel (1967, p. 63); A. R. W. Green (1975, pp. 179–83).
77. Flaubert (1862, ch. 13). The many and crucially important ramifications of this subject have, for obvious reasons, been very little studied. They deserve serious and detailed treatment, which I am unable to give them here.
78. See Benedetto (1920, pp. 196–215); Spiegel (1967, pp. 62–3); A. R. W. Green (1975, pp. 182–3).
79. See Harden (1971, p. 95); Herm (1975, pp. 118–19); Warmington (1960, p. 164) is very hostile to Flaubert.
80. Cited by Herm (1975, p. 118). While I have no reason to doubt it, I have not been able to find the original. See Kunzl (1976, pp. 15–20).
81. See Lohnes and Strothmann (1980, p. 563). The authors make it a point of principle to quote wherever possible from German sources.
82. After the fall of the German Empire in 1918 and the rise of Mussolini in 1922, the latter's identification with Rome led to an Italian revival of the identification of the enemy, England, with Carthage. See Cagnetta (1979, pp. 92–5).
83. See, for instance, 1820–4, vol. 1, p. 8.
84. Movers (1840–50, vol. 2, pt 1, pp. 265–302).
85. Movers (1840–50, vol. 2, pt 1, pp. 300–3, 420).
86. See Astour (1967a, p. 93).
87. Gobineau (1983, vol. 1, pp. 664–5).
88. Gobineau (1983, vol. 1, p. 663).
89. Gobineau (1983, vol. 1, p. 663).
90. Gobineau (1983, vol. 1, p. 367).
91. Gobineau (1983, vol. 1, p. 662).
92. Gobineau (1983, vol. 1, pp. 420–63). For Schlegel on this, see ch. V, Note 20.
93. Gobineau (1983, vol. 1, pp. 660–85).
94. He had more trouble explaining Odysseus, the epitome of Semitic Greece from northern Ithake (vol. 1, p. 661).
95. See the articles he wrote on this theme, mentioned in Gaulmier (1983, p. lxx).
96. Gobineau (1983, vol. 1, pp. 716–932).

97. For Bunsen, see above, ch. V, Note 125; for Curtius, ch. VII, Notes 67–8; for Smith, ch. VII, Note 47; and Rawlinson (1869, pp. 119–20).
98. Gladstone (1869, p. 129).
99. Gardner (1880, p. 97); Vermeule (1975, p. 4).
100. Dunker (trans. 1883, vol. 1, p. 59).
101. Holm (trans. 1894, pp. 47, 101–2).
102. For Thirlwall, see ch. VII, Note 29; for Stubbings, see ch. X, Note 24 below.
103. Marsh (1885, p. 191).
104. See Friedrich (1957, pp. 59–69).
105. Winckler (1907, p. 17). See also T. Jones (1969, pp. 1–47). For my views on this, see the Introduction, pp. 11 and 12.
106. See, for instance, Reinach (1893, pp. 699–701). This will also be noted below.
107. Walcot (1966, pp. 1–54).

Chapter IX
THE FINAL SOLUTION OF THE PHOENICIAN PROBLEM, 1885–1945

1. Tsountas and Manatt (1897, p. 326).
2. Frothingham (1891, p. 528).
3. Van Ness Myers (1895, p. 16).
4. R. Brown (1898, p. ix).
5. Reinach (1892b, p. 93); cited in Reinach (1893, p. 724).
6. Necrologue, *Revue Archéologique* 36 (1932) and the anon. article on Reinach in *Encyclopaedia Judaica*.
7. Reinach (1893, p. 543).
8. Reinach (1893, p. 541).
9. Reinach (1892b; 1893, pp. 541–2). For the elevation of Lithuanian, Saussure's historical linguistics and the Neo-Grammarians, see Pedersen (1959, pp. 64–7, 277–300).
10. Reinach (1893, pp. 561–77).
11. Reinach (1893, p. 572).
12. Reinach (1893, p. 704).
13. Reinach (1893, p. 726).
14. Beloch (1894).
15. Momigliano (1966a, p. 247).
16. Momigliano (1966a, pp. 259–60).
17. Beloch (1893, vol. 1, p. 34, n. 1).
18. Lloyd-Jones (1982c, p. xx).
19. Momigliano (1966a, p. 258).
20. See above, ch. VI, Note 94.
21. See the striking conjunction of the two in Beloch (1894, p. 114).
22. Beloch (1894, p. 126).

23. Beloch (1894, p. 125).
24. Beloch (1894, p. 128).
25. Beloch (1894, p. 112).
26. For Canaanite terms see, for instance, *byblinos* (cordage), related to the city name Byblos; *'ēlāh, elatē* (oar) from *'ēlāh/'ēlat* (mighty tree, post); *gaulos* (vessel) from *gullāh* (vessel). To my mind, Chantraine (1928, p. 18) dismisses the Indo-European **ku(m)bara* (shaft) as an etymon for *kubern-* (steering oar) too readily. However, there would also seem to be influence from the Semitic root √kbr (great). Chantraine admitted the possibility of the Egyptian etymology for *baris*, but – writing in the 1920s – he denied the Semitic loans, attributing the vast majority of maritime words that cannot be explained in terms of Indo-European to the 'Pre-Hellenes' or 'Mediterranean stock'. For the Egyptian etymologies, see vol. 2.

    For pictures of Egyptian boats, see the murals uncovered at Thera reproduced in *Thera and the Aegean World: Papers Presented at the Second International Scientific Congress, Santorini, Greece, August 1978* (ed. C. Doumas, London, 1979).
27. See Bass (1967); Helm (1980, pp. 95, 223–6).
28. Beloch (1894, pp. 124–5).
29. See above, ch. I, Notes 58–68; Beloch (1894, p. 112).
30. Bunnens (1979, pp. 6–7).
31. See Armand Bérard (1971, pp. vii–xviii).
32. V. Bérard (1894, pp. 3–5).
33. V. Bérard (1894, pp. 7–10).
34. Kropotkin (1899, pp. 385–400).
35. V. Bérard (1902–03; 1927–9).
36. Herodotos, I.105.
37. Bérard (1902–03, vol. 2, pp. 207–10); Astour (1967a, p. 143). Neither of these believed in significant Egyptian influence, so they failed to note that Skandeia – which has no Indo-European etymology – probably derives from the Egyptian *shmty* (the double crown of Egypt), which, with the article *pꜣ-*, was transcribed into Greek as *psent*. I believe that many, if not most, of Bérard's doublets are in fact between Egyptian and Semitic rather than between Greek and Semitic.
38. Petrie (1894–1905, vol. 2, pp. 181–3).
39. Weigall (1923, p. 69).
40. Gardiner (1961, pp. 213–14).
41. King and Hall (1907, pp. 385–6).
42. Weigall (1923, p. 127).
43. Freud (1939).
44. Vercoutter (1953, pp. 98–122); Helck (1979, pp. 26–30).
45. See Evans (1909, p. 109). He gave reasons for accepting Septimius' report; see also Gordon (1966b, p. 16).
46. Ch. VII, Note 68.

47. See above, ch. 8, Note 48. For Evans' invention of the term 'Minoan', see 1909 (p. 94).

48. Stobart (1911, p. 32), quoted in Steinberg (1981, p. 34).

49. King and Hall (1907, p. 363).

50. See Dörpfeldt (1966, pp. 366–94); E. Meyer (1928–36, vol. 2, pt 2, pp. 113–22). See also Giles (1924, p. 27).

51. Bury (1900, p. 77). This passage remains in the 3rd edn, revised by R. Meiggs in 1951 (p. 77).

52. See, for example, Baron (1976, pp. 168–71).

53. Oren (1985, pp. 38–63).

54. *Cornell Alumni News* 84, 9 July 1981, p. 7. I am indebted to Dr Paul Hoch for this reference.

55. Childe (1926, p. 4).

56. Myres (1924, p. 3).

57. Myres (1924, pp. 21–3).

58. Myres (1924, pp. 26–7).

59. S. A. Cook (1924, p. 195).

60. S. A. Cook (1924, p. 196).

61. Frankfort (1946, pp. 3–27); for a splendid discussion of this issue in European thought of the late 19th and early 20th centuries, see Horton (1973, pp. 249–305).

62. S. A. Cook (1924, p. 203).

63. This point is made in Barnard (1981, p. 29).

64. Nilsson (1950, p. 391).

65. Blegen and Haley (1927, pp. 141–154).

66. Blegen and Haley (1927, p. 151).

67. Laroche (1977?, p. 213).

68. Kretschmer (1924, pp. 84–106). See also Georgiev (1973, p. 244).

69. For a detailed discussion of these 'elements', see vol. 2.

70. See ch. V, Note 125; ch. VII, Note 68. For the confusion between Phoenicians and Minoans, see Burns (1949, p. 687).

71. For a bibliography of German attempts to prove this, see Jensen (1969, p. 574). See also Waddell (1927); Graves (1948, pp. 1–124); Georgiev (1952, pp. 487–95).

72. Josephus, *Contra Apionem*, I.11.

73. See Note 11 above.

74. Beloch (1894, pp. 113–14).

75. *Iliad*, VI.168–9.

76. Carpenter (1933, pp. 8–28).

77. For my conviction that the Greek alphabet was initially formed from a Semitic one which used vowels, at least for the transcription of foreign sounds, see Bernal (1987a; forthcoming, 1988).

78. Carpenter (1933, p. 20).
79. Woolley (1938, p. 29).
80. See Jeffery (1961, p. 10, n. 3).
81. Jeffery (1961, p. 7).
82. See above, Note 33.
83. Bury (1900, p. 77). See above, Note 51.
84. See ch. VIII, Notes 83–5.
85. For my arguments that there was heavy Phoenician influence on the Aegean, at least from the 10th century, and that the Greek *polis* and Slave Society as a whole derived from Phoenicia, see Bernal (1987b).
86. Carpenter (1938, p. 69).
87. Jensen (1969, p. 456).
88. Ullman (1934, p. 366).
89. Carpenter (1938, pp. 58–69).
90. See Parry (1971).
91. See Z. S. Harris (1939, p. 61). For Albright's shifts on the dating of the critical inscription on the sarcophagus of Ahiram to bring it down to one that could fit with the predominant dating, see Garbini (1977, pp. 81–3). See also Bernal (1987a; forthcoming, 1988); Tur-Sinai (1950, pp. 83–4).

Chapter X
THE POST-WAR SITUATION

1. Oren (1985, pp. 173–286).
2. See, for instance, Holm (1894, vol. 1, p. 13).
3. See Grumach (1968/9); Hood (1967).
4. For a description of the decipherment, see Chadwick (1973a, pp. 17–27).
5. See Friedrich (1957, pp. 124–31).
6. See Chadwick (1973a, pp. 24–7).
7. See Georgiev (1966; 1973, pp. 243–54); Renfrew (1973, pp. 265–79). For a survey of my own views on this, see the Introduction, pp. 13–17.
8. This is not to say that all supporters of the isolationist paradigm have been anti-colonialist, nor all the diffusionists hostile to colonialism.
9. Crossland and Birchall (1973, pp. 276–8).
10. See Carpenter (1958; 1966). See also Snodgrass (1971, pp. 18–23).
11. Vian (1963).
12. Bury (1951, p. 66).
13. Kantor (1947, p. 103).
14. Baramki (1961, p. 10).
15. Albright (1950; 1975).
16. Culican (1966).
17. Thomson (1949, pp. 124, 376–7); Willetts (1962, pp. 156–8).

18. Baramki (1961, pp. 11, 59); Jidejian (1969, pp. 34–7, 62).
19. Huxley (1961, esp. pp. 36–7); see also below, Notes 64–5.
20. Stubbings (1973, vol. 2, pt 1, pp. 627–58). This fascicule was first published in 1962.
21. Stubbings (1973, pp. 631–5).
22. Vermeule (1960, p. 74); cited in Astour (1967a, p. 358).
23. See Chadwick (1976); Dickinson (1977); Hammond (1967); Hooker (1976); Renfrew (1972) and Taylour (1964). The best expression of this view comes in Muhly (1970b, pp. 19–64). However, his shifting positions will be discussed below. Vermeule (1964) also held these views, but she too has broadened her position greatly since then.
24. Stubbings (1973, p. 637). The changes that took place in Egypt include the development of what is generally agreed to be a new language: Late Egyptian; the first widespread use of bronze and the introduction of such things as the horse, the chariot, the sword, the composite bow and the shadouf.
25. Bass (1967); for his preliminary report, see 1961 (pp. 267–86).
26. See Symeonoglou (1985, pp. 226–7).
27. For a survey of these, see R. Edwards (1979, pp. 132–3).
28. For a bibliography on this, see R. Edwards (1979, p. 118, notes 122–3).
29. See the reviews of the work of Stevenson Smith by Mellink (1967, pp. 92–4) and Muhly (1970a, p. 305).
30. See, for instance, Akurgal (1968, p. 162); Stubbings (1975, pp. 181–2).
31. See Astour (1967a, pp. 350–5).
32. See, for instance, the work of Professor G. S. Kirk.
33. See Walcot (1966); West (1971).
34. See Fontenrose (1959).
35. Webster (1958, p. 37).
36. See Szemerenyi (1964; 1966; 1974); Mayer (1964; 1967). For further discussion of their work, see vol. 2.
37. See Levin (1968; 1971a; 1971b; 1973; 1977; 1978; 1979; 1984). For his work on the two language families, see 1971a. As mentioned in the Introduction (p. 54), there has been a substantial revival in the last few years of the idea of a genetic relationship between Afroasiatic and Indo-European.
38. See Brown (1965; 1968a; 1968b; 1969; 1971).
39. See Masson (1967); for the praise see, for example, Rosenthal (1970, p. 338).
40. There were, of course, important exceptions; notably the works of Umberto Cassuto (1971) and Spiegel (1967).
41. See the autobiographical section in Gordon, 1971 (pp. 144–59).
42. See Cross (1968, pp. 437–460); Friedrich (1968, pp. 421–4), Bunnens (1979, pp. 43–4); Davies (1979, pp. 157–8). For my own views on this, see ch. V, Note 168.

43. Gordon (1971, p. 157).

44. Gordon (1971, p. 158). For the concession, see Chadwick (1973a, pp. 387–8).

45. See Gordon (1962a; 1963a; 1966b; 1968a; 1968b; 1969; 1970a; 1970b; 1973; 1975; 1980; 1981). See also Astour (1967b, pp. 290–5). For Eteocretan, see above, ch. I, Note 16.

46. See Dahood (1981a; 1981b); Garbini (1981); Gelb (1977; 1981); Keinast (in Cagni, 1981).

47. See Gordon (1971, p. 161).

48. This has not prevented Afrikaner leaders from rediscovering their very real affinities with the ancient Israelites now that they have found it politic to establish an alliance with modern Israel.

49. See Chanaiwa (1973).

50. See Chadwick (1973b, vol. 2, pt 1, pp. 609–26; 1973a, pp. 595–605).

51. See, for instance, Duhoux (1982, pp. 223–33).

52. See Stieglitz (1981, pp. 606–16).

53. See Neiman (1965, pp. 113–15); Sasson (1966, pp. 126–38).

54. Astour (1967a, pp. xii–xvii).

55. See above, Note 33. A little later, Kirk (1970) took up very much the same themes.

56. For Edwards' objections, see 1979 (pp. 139–61). She makes some valid points without destroying his overall case.

57. Astour (1967a, pp. 357–8).

58. Muhly (1965, p. 585).

59. Muhly (1965, p. 586).

60. For the modern admiration, see ch. IX, Note 18.

61. Muhly (1970b, pp. 19–64).

62. Billigmeier, (1976, esp. pp. 46–73).

63. The publisher was J. C. Gieben of Amsterdam, and the book was to have had the title *Kadmos and Danaos: A Study of Near Eastern Influence on the Late Bronze Age Aegean.*

64. Levin (1971a, p. ix).

65. R. Edwards (1979, p. x).

66. R. Edwards (1979, pp. 139–61).

67. R. Edwards (1979, pp. 17–113). For her specific arguments, see ch. I, Notes 52–7.

68. R. Edwards (1979, pp. 201–3).

69. R. Edwards (1979, pp. 172–3).

70. R. Edwards (1979, p. 171, n. 182).

71. Van Berchem (1967, pp. 73–109, 307–38).

72. Bunnens (1979, esp. pp. 5–26).

73. Helm (1980, pp. 97, 126).

74. Muhly (1984, pp. 39–56).

75. Muhly (1985, pp. 177–91).
76. Tur-Sinai (1950, pp. 83–110, 159–180, 277–302); Naveh (1973, pp. 1–8). For the original but uninfluential work of Bundgard in the 1960s, see Bernal (forthcoming, 1988).
77. Naveh (1973, pp. 1–8).
78. For the dating of the inscription to the 13th century BC, see Garbini (1977); Bernal (1985b; 1987a; forthcoming (1988)).
79. Jeffery (1982, p. 823, n. 8).
80. Jeffery (1982, p. 832).
81. McCarter (1975, p. 126).
82. See, for instance, Millard (1976, p. 144).
83. Cross (1979, pp. 108–11). While I support nearly everything in this splendid statement, I do not agree with his belief in the special antiquity of the alphabets of Crete, etc., see Bernal (1987b; forthcoming (1988)).
84. Cross (1980, p. 17).
85. See Millard and Bordreuil (1982, p. 140); Kaufman (1982), for whose glee see pp. 142, 144, n. 18.
86. See, for instance, Burzachechi (1976, pp. 82–102).
87. Stieglitz (1981, pp. 606–16).
88. Bernal (1983a; 1983b).
89. Röllig and Mansfeld (1970, pp. 265–70).
90. Evans (1909, pp. 91–100); Dussaud (1907, pp. 57–62).
91. See Bernal (1983a; 1983b; 1985b; 1987b; forthcoming (1988)).
92. See Murray (1980, pp. 300–1, 80–99). For the Greek borrowing of these institutions, see Bernal (1987b). The forthcoming Vol. III, 2 of *The Cambridge Ancient History* will contain articles on the Phoenicians. This volume, however, is supposed to cover the 8th to the 6th centuries. The significance of the omission from Vol. III, 1 is that it denies the importance of Phoenician influence on Greece before 750 BC.
93. Morenz (1969, p. 44; for language, see pp. 20, 175).
94. Morenz (1969, pp. 38, 39).
95. Morenz (1969, p. 49).
96. Morenz (1969, pp. 56–7).
97. Morenz (1969, pp. 44–8).
98. Snowden (1970).
99. James (1954).
100. James (1954, p. 158).
101. I was led to it by Dr James Turner only after many years of research in this area.
102. Diop (1974; 1978; 1985a; 1985b). See esp. 1974, pp. xii–xvii, p. 1. For my own views on this subject, see ch. V, Notes 65–90.
103. Carruthers (1984, p. 34).

104. Carruthers (1984, p. 35). See Dubois (1975, pp. 40–2; 1976, pp. 120–47); J. H. Franklin (1974); Noguera (1976).
105. Carruthers (1984, p. 35). See Diop (1974; 1978; 1985a; 1985b); Ben Jochannan (1971); and C. Williams (1971).
106. Apart from Morenz, there are one or two exceptions to this. Billigmeier's acceptance of the myths concerning the Egyptian Danaos has been mentioned above (see Note 62). Even more significant are the indications that Professor Emily Vermeule is considering the possibility of major Egyptian influence on Greece. See her reference (1979, pp. 69–80) to the fundamental similarities between the Egyptian and the Greek beliefs about death.

APPENDIX

1. See ch. I, Notes 17 and 18. See also Macalister (1914, p. 2); Mazars (1971, p. 166), both cited in Joffe (1980, p. 2).
2. Sandars (1978, p. 145). I shall not here go into the question of the head-dresses portrayed so vividly on Egyptian reliefs, because they do not give clear indications of whether their wearers come from the Aegean or Anatolia.
3. Barnett (1975, p. 373).
4. Albright (1975, p. 513).
5. Barnett (1975, pp. 363–6). For a more sceptical approach, see Astour (1967a, pp. 53–67; 1972, pp. 454–5).
6. Quoted in Strabo, XIV.4.3. (trans. Jones, p. 325). Astour (1972, pp. 454–5) rightly points out the extraordinary confusion surrounding reports of the migrations of various Greek and Lydian Mopsoi.
7. Quoted in Astour (1967a, p. 11); Sandars (1978, p. 119).
8. See Gardiner (1947, vol. I, pp. 124–5). For the Danaans, see ch. I, Notes 106–11.
9. Astour (1972, p. 457).
10. See Rendsberg (1981).
11. Astour (1972, p. 458).
12. Strange (1973).
13. Lipinsky (1978, pp. 91–7); Pope (1980, pp. 170–5). See also *Black Athena*, vol. 3.
14. See Astour (1967a, pp. 1–4). For a discussion of the phonetic relationship between Muksas and Mps, see vol. 2 and Bernal (forthcoming, 1988).
15. Amos 9:7; Jer. 47:4; Gen. 10:14; with textual emendation, Ezek. 25:15–17; Zeph. 2:4–7.
16. See 2 Sam. 15:18–22; 1 Sam. 27. On David's relations to the Philistines, *pace* J. Strange (1973).
17. See M. Dothan (1973); Muhly (1973); Popham (1965). T. Dothan (1982, pp. 291–6); Snodgrass (1971, pp. 107–9), and Helck (1979, pp. 135–46).

18. T. Dothan (1982, pp. 20–2, 291–6). She has in her favour the fact that 'feathered crowns' or stiffened hair of the type worn by the Prst has not been attested in Greece. Neither, however, have they been attested in the Balkans or Western Anatolia. Furthermore the T(t̲)kr and the Dnn, who must surely have come from Greece, shared the same style. See Sandars (1978, p. 134).

19. For a recent survey of this, see Helm (1980, p. 209).

20. Nehemiah 13:23–4.

21. For Yhd, J. Naveh (personal communication, Jerusalem, Jun. 1983); for Yhw, see Seltman (1933, p. 154).

22. Gardiner (1947, vol. 1, p. 202).

23. Tcherikover (1976, pp. 87–114).

24. Gardiner (1947, vol. 1, p. 202). I believe that Marna derives from the Egyptian M3nw, the mysterious 'Mountain of Sunset in the West', a name which could be applied to Crete. The New Kingdom place name Mnnws, which has been plausibly, though not conclusively, identified with Minos and Crete, could well derive from this. See Vercoutter (1956, pp. 159–82); for more on this see vol. 2.

GLOSSARY

affixing or agglutination	Addition of prefixes, suffixes or infixes to words without affecting their roots. It is a term used to describe languages not included among the **inflected** or **isolating** ones. The best-known affixing languages are the Altaic ones, of which the central examples are Turkish and Mongol, but this family may include other languages as far apart as Japanese and Hungarian.
Afroasiatic	Otherwise known as Hamito-Semitic, a linguistic 'superfamily' consisting of a number of language families including **Berber**, Chadic, **Egyptian**, **Semitic** and East, South and Central Cushitic.
Akkadian	The **Semitic** language of ancient Mesopotamia, heavily influenced by and influencing **Sumerian**. It was replaced by Aramaic around the middle of the 1st millennium BC.
Allogenes	Foreigners in Greek cities with rights greater than those of slaves but less than those of citizens.
Anatolia	Ancient region, more or less contiguous with modern Turkey.
Anatolian	The **Indo-Hittite** but non-**Indo-European** languages of Anatolia. They include **Hittite**, Palaic,

	Luvian, **Lycian**, **Lydian** and probably **Carian** and **Etruscan**.
Aramaic	A West Semitic language, originally spoken in parts of what is now Syria, that became the lingua franca of the **Assyrian**, **Neo-Babylonian** and much of the **Persian** empires. It replaced the **Canaanite** dialects of **Phoenician** and **Hebrew** in the East Mediterranean during the middle of the 1st millennium BC. It was in its turn replaced by Greek and Arabic, though it still survives in some remote villages.
Archaic Greece	Greece from the 8th to the 6th century BC; the period in which the Greek cities or *poleis*, and what Marxists call Slave Society, were established.
Armenian	Indo-European language of an ancient people of Eastern Anatolia. It is sometimes supposed to be especially close to Greek. However, as the earliest surviving texts go back to only the 4th century AD, the similarities may be the result of Greek influence or common contacts with Semitic.
Aryan	Term used to describe the speakers of the Indo-Iranian branch of the **Indo-European** language family. They appear to have invaded Iran and India in the 1st half of the 2nd millennium BC. In the late 19th century AD the term came to be used for the Indo-European 'race' as a whole.
Assyria	An ancient kingdom in Northern Mesopotamia dating back to the middle of the 3rd millennium. Its greatest periods were at the end of the 2nd millennium and between 900 and 600 BC. Its language was originally a dialect of **Akkadian**.
Atlantis	Land sunk beneath the Atlantic Ocean described by Plato; plausibly identified with **Thera** by modern writers.
atomism	The belief that matter is made up of minute indivisible particles, held by Demokritos – who had studied with Pythagoreans and in Egypt – in the 5th century BC. It later became current among the Epicureans. In the 19th century it was revived by John Dalton.
autochthonous	Native or aboriginal.

Babylon   Ancient city in South Central Mesopotamia. Seat of several important kingdoms and finally of the Neo-Babylonian Empire between 600 and 538 BC.

Berber   The languages spoken by the original inhabitants of North-West Africa. They are still spoken in mountainous or remote areas from the Western Desert in Egypt to Morocco.

Bohairic   **Coptic** dialect originally spoken in the Western Delta, later standard throughout Christian Egypt.

Boiotia   Region of central Greece known for its wealth and power in the Bronze Age. Its major geographical feature was the shallow lake Kopais, much of which was drained at some time around the end of the Early Bronze Age. Boiotia's chief city was Thebes.

Byblos   Ancient port city in what is now Southern Lebanon. In close touch with Egypt since the 4th millennium, it was the most important Levantine city until it was eclipsed by the rise of **Sidon** at the end of the 2nd millennium.

byname   A subsidiary name.

calque   The literal borrowing of an expression or idiom from another language.

Canaanite   A Semitic language, heavily influenced by Egyptian, spoken in Southern Syro-Palestine between 1500 and 500 BC, when it was displaced by **Aramaic**. **Phoenician** and **Hebrew** are the best-known later Canaanite dialects. 'Canaanite' is also used to describe the material culture of Southern Syro-Palestine in the Late Bronze Age, *c*.1500–1100 BC.

Caria   Region in South-West Anatolia. Its language was probably **Anatolian** but may have been non-**Indo-Hittite**. Alphabetic inscriptions in Carian date from the 6th century BC.

Catharism   The name comes from the Greek *Kathar*- 'pure.' A group of **Manichaean** heresies in medieval Europe, first reported in Bulgaria in the 9th century. The most famous centre was the one in Languedoc in the 12th century, also known as Albigensianism.

ceramic period   A period of time reconstructed by archaeologists on the basis of pottery styles.

Classical Greece   Greece in the 5th and 4th centuries BC, the period

which is generally held to have seen the greatest and
'purest' products of Greek genius.

Common Era — Term used by non-Christians in general and Jews
in particular, to avoid the sectarianism of the term
AD, Anno Domini.

Coptic — The language and culture of Christian Egypt.
Spoken until the 15th or 16th century AD, it remains
the liturgical language of Egyptian Christians.
Written in the Greek alphabet, with some additional
letters derived from **Demotic**, it is the latest form of
the Egyptian language.

cuneiform — A script system developed in Mesopotamia in
which nail-shaped wedges were pressed into wet clay.

Dark Ages (Greek) — Name given to the period of Greek history after the
fall of the Mycenaean palaces in the 12th century BC
and before the rise of Archaic Greece in the 8th.

Dark Ages (Christian) — Name conventionally given to the period after the
fall of the Western Roman Empire in the 5th
century AD and before the Middle Ages, which are
usually seen as beginning in the 9th or 10th.

Dead Sea Scrolls — These scrolls were found in caves above the Dead
Sea in the 1940s. Most of them are concerned with
the religious and institutional lives of Jewish sects
living nearby from the 3rd century BC to the 2nd
century AD. They cast a very interesting light on the
Essenes and the origins of Christianity.

deists — A group of 17th- and 18th-century thinkers who
rejected formal religion but argued that the
existence of God can be demonstrated from nature.
Their doubts on the divinity of Christ also led them
to Arianism or Unitarianism.

Demotic — Strictly speaking, Demotic is the script derived from
Hieroglyphic and **Hieratic**, used in Egypt after the
7th century BC. The word is also used to describe
the language of this period.

dendrochronology — The method of determining the age of wood and
archaeological contexts by counting tree rings.

dentals — Consonants formed with the tongue against the
teeth, as for example d and t.

determinative — Element in the hieroglyphic representation of a
word signifying its meaning as opposed to its sound.

Diodoros Sikeliotes	Greek historian from Sicily, *c*.80–*c*.20 BC, known for his *Library of History*.
Dorians	A Greek tribe originating from North-Western Greece who overran much of Southern Greece in the 12th century BC. The most famous Dorian state was Sparta.
Early Helladic	**Ceramic period** applied to Mainland Greece in the Early Bronze Age, *c*.2900 BC–2000 BC.
Early Minoan	**Ceramic period** in Crete in the early Bronze Age, *c*.3000–2000 BC.
Ebla	An ancient Syrian city first excavated in the 1970s. It had a massive trading network and empire throughout Syro-Palestine in around 2500 BC.
Eblaite	The language of Ebla, an independent Semitic language that can usefully be seen as a predecessor of **Canaanite**.
Egyptian	This is used here to refer not to the Arabic dialect spoken in Egypt today but to the language of Ancient Egypt, which was an independent **Afroasiatic** language. It is subdivided into Old Egyptian, spoken during the Old Kingdom from *c*.3250 to 2200 BC; and Middle Egyptian, spoken during the Middle Kingdom from 2200 to 1750 BC, which remained the official language for the next 1,500 years. When 'Egyptian' is used without epithet it usually refers to this. Late Egyptian was spoken by the 16th century, but it was not commonly used in writing until the end of the millennium. It was, I argue, Late Egyptian that had the greatest influence on Greek. For the later stages, **Demotic** and **Coptic**, see above.
Egypto-Paganism	My own term for the pagan religion of the Hellenistic and Roman periods, with its insistence on the centrality and originality of Egypt in polytheist religion.
epiclesis	Surname or additional name.
Epicurean	School of thought founded by Epicurus, according to which the purpose of philosophy was to make life happy through intellectual pleasure or serenity. It was later known for the oversimplified formula 'eat, drink and be merry, for tomorrow we die', and was

considered by monotheists as the epitome of atheist materialism.

Epicurus   Greek founder of Epicureanism, 341–270 BC.

Eratosthenes   c.275–195. Greek scholar and librarian of the great library at Alexandria. The first Greek to measure the circumference and tilt of the world.

Essenes   An ascetic Jewish sect who lived in communities in the Judaean and other deserts around the time of Christ. The **Dead Sea Scrolls** have been plausibly attributed to the Essenes, and tend to confirm the theory that the Essene religious organization and beliefs played an important role in the emergence of Christianity.

Etruscan   Civilization of ancient Italy. The predominant view in Antiquity was that the Etruscans came from **Lydia** in North-West Anatolia. The language – which is not well understood – could well be **Anatolian**. A very closely related language has been found on inscriptions from the nearby island of **Lemnos**. **Etruscan** seems to have been heavily influenced by Phoenician civilization from the 9th to the 6th century BC. It was itself a central influence in the formation of Latin culture.

Eudoxos   Great Greek astronomer and mathematician from Knidos on the Anatolian coast. Studied in Egypt. Born c.400, died c.350 BC.

Euhemeros   Philosopher – probably of Phoenician origin – who flourished around 300 BC.

euhemerism   Doctrine of Euhemeros according to which what were commonly worshipped as gods were actually deified heroes. By extension the word is used to mean the explanation or reduction of religious beliefs in rational terms.

genetic   A 'genetic' relationship between languages is one in which they are supposed to come from a single parent or ancestral language. For example, French and Romanian have a 'genetic' relationship because, for all their differences, both derive from Vulgar Latin.

Gnostic   Name of Christian and Jewish sects which maintained that behind the religion of the ordinary believers lay another, higher one, accessible only to those who 'know', the Greek *gnō-*.

Gymnosophist   Naked philosophers, name given by Greeks to Indian or Ethiopian holy men.

Harappa   The names of this site or another, Mohenjo Daro, are used for the ancient civilization that flourished in North-West India from *c.*2500 BC to 1700, when it was destroyed, probably by the invading **Aryans** from the north. The writing of this civilization has not been deciphered, but it is likely that its language belonged to the Dravidian language family, dominant today in South India and still spoken in pockets in Western Pakistan.

Hasidîm   Name from the Hebrew *hâsîd* (pious) used to denote two Jewish religious movements: the first between 300 and 175 BC in resistance to the **Seleucid** attempts to Hellenize the Jews, and the second in the 18th century of the Common Era as a Messianic reaction against the rationalism of Talmudic Judaism.

Hebrew   Canaanite dialect spoken in the kingdoms of Israel, Judah and Moab between 1500 and 500 BC. For religious reasons it is often treated as the distinct language which, with the disappearance of the other Canaanite dialects, it has since become.

Helladic   Name given to three **ceramic periods** on Mainland Greece, roughly approximating to the **Minoan ceramic periods** in Crete.

Hellenic   Greek or Greek-speaking, but particularly associated with Thessaly in northern Greece. Since the late 18th century, the word has gained many connotations of nobility and of northern and Aryan 'blood'.

Hellenistic   The name given to Greek culture throughout the East Mediterranean from the conquests of Alexander the Great in the late 4th century BC to the incorporation of the region into the Roman Empire in the 1st century BC.

Hellespont   Strait linking the Mediterranean and Black Seas and dividing Asia from Europe.

Hermetic Texts   A collection of mystical, magical and philosophical documents, probably first written in Demotic in the second half of the 1st millennium BC and/or in Coptic between 200 and 400 AD, attributed to the god Thoth/Hermes. They later became central to **Hermeticism**.

Hermeticism	Belief in the magical, mystical and philosophical power of the **Hermetic Texts**. The Hermeticist movement existed in Late Antiquity and again in the Renaissance.
Herodotos	Earliest Greek historian from Halikarnassos in Asia Minor, born *c.*485 BC, died *c.*425 BC.
Hieratic	Egyptian script gradually developed from **Hieroglyphic** about 2000 BC. It changed the formal pictorial Hieroglyphic into a cursive script that was still based on the same principles.
Hieroglyphic	Egyptian script first attested in the late 4th millennium. It is made up of phonetic signs for letters, double letters, triple letters and 'determinatives' which indicate the category of the word's meaning.
Hittite	Empire in central Anatolia during the 2nd millennium BC. Its language was an **Anatolian** one and was written in a form of cuneiform.
Hurrian	Name of a people who lived in Eastern Anatolia and Syria in the 2nd millennium BC. Their extinct language was neither Indo-Hittite nor Afroasiatic.
Indo-European	Language family including all European languages – except for Basque, Finnish and Hungarian – the Iranian and North Indian languages, and **Tokharian**. Although **Phrygian** and **Armenian** were situated in Anatolia they are Indo-European languages, not Anatolian.
Indo-Hittite	A language superfamily including both the **Anatolian** and **Indo-European** families.
inflected languages	Languages like Greek, Latin and German that rely to a great extent on inflection or changing word shapes or morphology to convey meaning; opposed to **isolating** and **affixing** languages.
interdentals	Consonants formed by putting the tongue between the teeth, as in th.
Ionians	Central and Southern Greek people who survived the **Dorian** conquest, some of whom migrated to

	the western coast of **Anatolia**. Their most famous state was Athens.
Isokrates	Greek orator, teacher and pupil of Sokrates, 436–338 BC.
isolating languages	Languages like Chinese and English that have relatively little inflection but rely heavily on syntax or the positioning of words in a sentence to convey meaning; opposed to **inflected** and **affixing** languages.
Kekrops	Legendary founder and king of Athens. He was generally portrayed as **autochthonous**, although a minority tradition saw him as coming from Egypt. Some evidence supporting the latter is given in the Introduction.
labials	Consonants formed with the lips: b, p, m and so on.
labiovelars	Velars completed with a rounding of the lips, as for instance in our qu, kʷ, and gʷ.
laryngeals	Sounds made in the larynx or the throat as a whole; more precisely they can be divided into velar fricatives – ḫ and ǵ – pharyngeals – ḥ and ʿ – and the laryngeals – ʾ and h. All these, except for ǵ, exist throughout Semitic and Egyptian, but all except h have disappeared from Indo-European.
Late Helladic or Mycenaean	**Ceramic period** in Mainland Greece from *c.*1650–1100 BC.
Late Minoan	**Ceramic period** in Crete from *c.*1650–1450 BC, when the island became dominated by Greeks.
Lemnos	Island in the North-West Aegean where a non-Indo-European language related to **Etruscan** was spoken in Classical times.
Linear A	**Syllabary** used in Crete and elsewhere before the establishment of Greek on the island.
Linear B	**Syllabary** derived from **Linear A**, attested in Mycenaean Greece and Crete from about 1400 BC but probably written well before that date.
liquids	Consonants like l and r which 'flow'.
Lycia	Region in Southern Anatolia. The Lycian language was Anatolian and was an indirect descendant of Hittite. Alphabetic inscriptions in it date from the 5th century BC.
Lydia	Region of North-West Anatolia. The Lydian language belonged to the **Anatolian** family.

Tradition maintained that the **Etruscans** came
from Lydia. Alphabetic inscriptions in it date from
the 5th century BC.

Manichaeism | Religion founded by the Persian religious reformer
Mani in the 3rd century AD. It took the **Zoroastrian**
dualism still further and denied all matter or flesh as
evil. Believers were divided into an elite, who
practised strict celibacy and austerity, and the
ordinary members, who were allowed to marry and
live – austerely – in the world. Manichaeism was
crushed by Christianity in the 6th century.
However, Manichaean 'heresies' were relatively
common in the Middle Ages. The best known of
these was **Catharism** or Albigensianism.

materialism | Belief that the world is made of matter, first
promoted in Greece by Demokritos in the 5th and
4th centuries BC.

metathesis | Alternation or switching of consonantal or vocalic
position in language.

Middle Helladic | **Ceramic period** for Mainland Greece for the
period *c.*2000–1650 BC.

Middle Minoan | **Ceramic period** applied to Cretan Culture –
roughly contemporary with the Egyptian Middle
Kingdom – *c.*2000–1650 BC.

Minoan | Name – derived by Arthur Evans from Minos, the
legendary king of Crete – applied to the cultures of
Crete before the arrival there of Greek speakers,
and to three **ceramic periods**, also established by
Evans.

monism | In this book monism is used to indicate the idea that
all things must have single causes.

monogenesis | The belief in single origins, largely restricted in this
book to humanity and language. The opposite of
polygenesis.

Mycenae | City near Argos in the North-Eastern Peloponnese,
famous as the leading city in the Bronze Age.

Mycenaean | Name of the Bronze Age material culture first
discovered at Mycenae and, by extension, Greek
culture in the Late Bronze Age.

nasals | Consonants like m and n formed with the nasal
passage. Nasalization is the common feature of the

introduction of nasals before stops: m before b or p; n before d or t; and ng before g or k.

Neo-Platonism Philosophy established in Egypt in the 2nd century AD which promoted Platonic idealist and mystical philosophy and Egypto-Greek religion. It was crushed by Christian authority early in the 6th century but survived in Christian form in the Middle Ages. It was revived – under more or less Christian guise – in the Renaissance.

nominalism The view that ideal forms or universals are merely names. The opposite of realism or essentialism.

Olympian Festival and Games Religious festival and games held at Olympia in the North-West Peloponnese every four years from 776 BC until they were discontinued by the Christian emperor Theodosius at the end of the 4th century AD. Revived according to the Aryan Model at the end of the 19th century.

Orphics Followers of the divine Orpheus. Very much like the Pythagoreans, the Orphics promoted Egyptian religious beliefs and were especially concerned with personal immortality.

pantheism Belief that God is in all things and all things are God. This world-view, which closely resembled that of Egyptian and Greek religion, became significant in the 17th century, especially after the publication of the works of Spinoza.

Pausanias Writer of an extensive *Guide to Greece*, who lived in the 2nd century AD.

Pelasgians According to Classical tradition, the earliest inhabitants of Greece.

Persian Empire Founded by Cyrus the Great in the mid-6th century BC, it dominated the Middle East, Asia Minor and the Aegean until pushed back by the Greeks. It was finally destroyed by Alexander the Great in the 2nd half of the 4th century BC.

Philistines Invaders of Egypt and the Levant from Anatolia and the Aegean in the late 13th and 12th centuries BC.

Phoenicia Cities along a strip of coast stretching from the present-day Lebanon to Northern Israel, the most famous of which were **Byblos**, **Tyre** and **Sidon**. The name Phoenicia refers to this region throughout Antiquity. However, it generally indicates the greatest period in the cities' history, between 1100 and 750 BC. The Phoenician 'language' was like **Hebrew**, a dialect of **Canaanite**. The alphabet is often referred to as a Phoenician invention. It may well have originated in the region, but it was developed long before the Phoenician period.

phoneme
: The minimal significant unit of sound within a language.

phonetic correspondences
: Sounds that are actually or etymologically similar.

Phrygia
: Region in Northern Anatolia. It was a powerful state in the first half of the 1st millennium BC. Its language, which was written alphabetically, was not Anatolian but Indo-European, and closely related to Greek.

Physiocrats
: A group of French philosophers and officials, overlapping with the Encyclopaedists, who played an important role in the rationalization of administration and strengthening of the state in the middle of the 18th century. Their most prominent figure, François Quesnay, established a complete system of economics according to which – following Chinese economic theory – all wealth came from land.

pictogram
: Writing in which the object signified is pictured or directly represented.

polygenesis
: The belief in multiple origins, in particular of humanity and language. The opposite of **monogenesis**.

prothetic or prosthetic
: Vowels placed at the beginning of words to avoid initial consonants. The placing of prothetic vowels is particularly common before double consonants.

Proto-Greek
: The unattested language or people reconstructed as having been the origin of Greek or the Greeks.

Ptolemaic
: Name given to Egyptian culture under the rule of the Ptolemies.

Ptolemy
: Name of a succession of descendants of Ptolemy I, a general of Alexander the Great who seized power in Egypt after Alexander's death. The last ruler of this dynasty was Kleopatra VII, loved by both Caesar and Antony, who died dramatically in 30 BC.

puttini Small boys in artistic representation.

Pythagoreans Followers of Pythagoras organized into a 'brotherhood' along what were generally seen to be Egyptian lines. The Pythagoreans played an important political, religious and scientific role in the Greek society of Sicily and Southern Italy in the 5th and 4th centuries BC.

Pythagoras Greek philosopher and mathematician, *c.*582–500 BC. He studied in Egypt and brought back Egyptian mathematical and religious principles, and founded the Pythagorean brotherhood.

root Essential part of a word which remains after all other elements have been removed.

Seleucid The name of a dynasty established in Syria and Mesopotamia by Alexander's general, Seleukos.

semantic Relating to signification or meaning.

sibilants Consonants with a hissing sound like s, š, ṣ and z.

Sidon Ancient Phoenician city dedicated to the sea god Sid. Its apogee was in the very early Iron Age, therefore 'Sidonian' is used for Phoenician in general in the early historical books of the Bible and in Homer. Its dominance was replaced by that of its rival **Tyre** in about the 9th century BC.

stele Upright slab with sculptured designs or inscriptions.

stem Verbal form derived from a root by special **vocalization** or the addition of various prefixes or suffixes.

stop A complete consonantal explosion of breath, as in the sounds represented by our letters b, p, d, t, g and k.

Stoicism Philosophy founded by **Zeno of Kition** which flourished in **Hellenistic** and Roman times. Stoics maintained that the world is material and that a universal working force – God – pervades everything. They stressed putting aside passion in order to follow duty and gain true freedom.

Strabo Greek geographer of the 1st century BC and 1st century AD.

theogony Ancestry and birth of the gods; it was the name and subject of a number of poems, the most famous being that of Hesiod.

Thera | Volcanic island 70 miles north of Crete. It suffered a major eruption during the 2nd millennium BC, the conventional dates for which are *c.*1500–1450. I argue, however, that it took place 150 years earlier, in 1626 BC.

Thucydides | Greek historian of the Peloponnesian War, born *c.*460 BC, died 400 BC.

Tokharian | Indo-European language spoken in the 1st millennium AD in the now Turkic-speaking, Western Chinese 'autonomous region' of Sinkiang. Tokharian shares several features with Western Indo-European languages which are not present in the Indo-Aryan languages. It therefore provides critical information on the nature of early Indo-European.

toponym | Place name.

trireme | Greek galley with three banks of oars.

Tyre | Ancient Phoenician city. Its period of greatest glory was from the 10th to the 9th century BC, but it remained an important political and cultural centre until its destruction by Alexander the Great in 333 BC.

velars | **Stops** formed with the tongue at the back of the mouth, as for example k and g.

vocalization | Infusing a consonantal structure with vowels.

Zeno of Kition | A Phoenician who moved to Athens. The founder of **Stoicism**, *c.*336–264 BC.

Zoroastrianism | The state religion of the Persian Empire, founded by the religious reformer generally thought to have lived in the 7th century BC but probably much earlier, in the 2nd millennium. It maintained that the universe was the scene of a perpetual and finely balanced struggle between good and evil. Zoroastrianism was weakened by Alexander's conquest, and virtually destroyed by Islam. It may still survive in tiny pockets in Khomeini's Iran, and it is still flourishing throughout the world as the religion of the Parsees.

BIBLIOGRAPHY

Abdel-Malek, A. (1969) *Idéologie et renaissance nationale: l'Égypte moderne*. Paris: Éditions Anthropos, 2nd edn.

Abel, L. S. (1966) *Fifth Century BC Concepts of the Pelasgians*. Stanford University, MA thesis.

Abou-Assaf, A., Bordreuil, P. and Milliard, A. R. D. (1982) *La Statue de Tell Fekheriyé: et son inscription bilingue assyro-araméenne*. Études Assyriologiques Éditions recherche sur les civilisations no. 7, Paris.

Ahl, F. (1985) *Metaformations: Soundplay and Wordplay in Ovid and Other Classical Poets*. Ithaca, NY: Cornell University Press.

Akurgal, E. (1968) *The Art of Greece: Its Origins in the Mediterranean and the Near East*. New York: Crown Publishers.

Albright, W. F. (1950) 'Some Oriental glosses on the Homeric problem', *American Journal of Archaeology* 54:162–76.

— (1968) *Yahweh and the Gods of Canaan: A Historical Analysis of Two Contrasting Faiths*, London: Athlone.

— (1970) 'The biblical period', in L. Finkelstein, *The Jews Their History*. New York: Schocken, pp. 1–71.

— (1975) 'Syria, the Philistines and Phoenicia', *Cambridge Ancient History*, 3rd edn, vol. II, pt 2, *History of the Middle East and the Aegean Region 1380–1000 BC*, pp. 507–16.

Allen, P. (1978) *The Cambridge Apostles: The Early Years*. Cambridge University Press.

Allen, T. G. (1974) (trans.) *The Book of the Dead or Going Forth by Day*. Chicago: Oriental Institute.

Annan, N. (1955) 'The intellectual aristocracy', in J. H. Plumb, ed., *Studies in Social History: A Tribute to G. M. Trevelyan.* London: Longman, pp. 243–87.

Apollodoros (1921) *The Library,* J. G. Frazer, trans., 2 vols. Cambridge, Mass.: Loeb.

Appleton, W. W. (1951) *A Cycle in Cathay, The Chinese Vogue in England in the 17th and 18th Centuries.* New York: Columbia University Press.

Arbeitman, Y. and Bomhard A. R., eds (1981) *Bono Homini Donum: Essays in Historical Linguistics, in Memory of J. Alexander Kerns,* 2 vols. Amsterdam: John Benjamin.

Arbeitman, Y. and Rendsburg, G. (1981) 'Adana revisited: 30 years later', *Archiv Orientální* 49: 145–57.

Aristotle, *De Caelo.*

—— *Metaphysica.*

—— *Meteriologica.*

—— (1962) *Politics,* T. A. Sinclair, trans. London: Penguin.

Arnold, M. (1869) *Culture and Anarchy.* London: Smith Elder.

—— (1883) *Literature and Dogma.* London: Smith Elder.

—— (1906) *The Scholar Gypsy and Thyrsis.* London: Macmillan. See F. W. E. Russell.

Arnold, T. (1845) *Introductory Lectures on Modern History.* New York.

—— (1864) *A French Eton.* London.

Arrian (1929) *Anabasis of Alexander,* E. Iliff, trans. Robson. New York: Putnam.

Astour, M. C. (1967a) *Hellenosemitica: An Ethnic and Cultural Study in West Semitic Impact on Mycenaean Greece.* Leiden: Brill.

—— (1967b) 'The problem of Semitic in Ancient Crete', *Journal of the American Oriental Society* 87: 290–5.

—— (1972) 'Some recent works on Ancient Syria and the Sea People', *Journal of the American Oriental Society* 92.3: 447–59.

Auguis, P. R. (1822) Introduction, in vol. 7 (pp. 1–26) of Dupuis, *Origine de tous les cultes, ou la religion universelle,* 12 vols. Paris.

Badolle, M. (1926) *L'Abbé Jean-Jacques Barthélemy (1716–1795) et l'Hellénisme en France dans la seconde moitié du XVIIIe siècle.* Paris: Presses Universitaires de France.

Baines, J. (1982) 'Interpreting *Sinuhe*', *Journal of Egyptian Archaeology* 68: 31–44.

Baker, J. R. (1974) *Race.* London: Oxford University Press.

Baldwin Smith, E. (1918) *Early Christian Iconography and the School of Provence.* Princeton: University Press.

Banier, A. (1739) *The Mythology of the Ancients Explained,* anon. trans. London: A. Millar.

Baramki, D. (1961) *Phoenicia and the Phoenicians.* Beirut: Khayats.

Barnard, K. (1981) *The Paradigm of Race and Early Greek History,* paper for an undergraduate course, Government 352. Cornell.

Barnett, R. D. (1956) 'Ancient Oriental influence on Archaic Greece', *The Aegean and the Near-East, Studies Presented to Hetty Goldman,* ed. S. Weinberg. Locust Valley, NY: Augustin, pp. 212–38.

—— (1960) 'Some contacts between Greek and Oriental religions', *Éléments orientaux dans la religion grecque ancienne*, ed. O. Eissfeldt. Paris: Presses Universitaires de France, pp. 143–53.

—— (1975) 'The Sea Peoples', *Cambridge Ancient History*, 3rd edn, vol. II, pt 2, pp. 359–78.

Baron, S. W. (1952) *A Social and Religious History of the Jews*. New York: Columbia University Press, vols 1–2.

—— (1976) *The Russian Jew under Tsars and Soviets*. New York: 2nd enl. edn.

Barthélemy, J-J. (1750) 'Réflexions sur quelques monuments et sur les alphabets qui en résultent', *Recueils des Mémoires de l'Académie des Inscriptions* 30: 302–456.

—— (1763) 'Réflexions générales sur les rapports des langues égyptienne phénicienne et grecque', *Recueils des Mémoires de l'Académie des Inscriptions* 32: 212–33.

—— (1789) (1788) *Voyage du jeune Anacharsis en Grèce vers le milieu du IVe siècle avant l'ère vulgaire*. Paris.

Bass, G. (1961) 'Cape Gelidonya Wreck: preliminary report', *American Journal of Archaeology* 65: 267–86.

—— (1967) 'Cape Gelidonya: a Bronze Age shipwreck', *Transactions of the American Philosophical Society* 57: pt 8.

Baumgarten A. J. (1981) *The Phoenician History of Philo of Byblos: A Commentary*. Leiden: Brill.

Beck, R. (1984) 'Mithraism since Franz Cumont', in H. Temporini and W. Haase, eds (1972–) *Aufstieg und Niedergang der römischen Welt: Geschichte und Kultur Roms im Spiegel der neueren Forschung*, 21 vols. Berlin/New York. vol. 17.4. *Religion: (Heidentum: römische Götterkulte, orientalische Kulte in der römischen Welt [Forts.])* ed. W. Haase, pp. 2003–112.

Beckarath, J. von (1980) *Kalender*, in Helck and Otto, cols 297–9.

Beddaride, M. (1845) *De l'Ordre Maçonique de Misraim*. Paris.

Beer, A. and Beer, P. (1975) *Kepler Four Hundred Years: Proceedings of Conferences Held in Honour of Johannes Kepler*. Oxford: Pergamon.

Beloch, J. (1893) *Griechische Geschichte*, Strasbourg.

—— (1894) 'Die Phoeniker am aegäischen Meer', *Rheinisches Museum* 49: 111–32.

Benedetto, L. F. (1920) *Le Origini di 'Salammbô'*. Florence: Istituto di Studi Superiori Pratici in Firenzi Sezione di filologia e filosofia.

Ben Jochannan, Y. (1971) *Black Man of the Nile, Africa, Africa the Mother of Civilization*. New York: Alkebu Lan Books.

Bentley, R. (1693) *A Confutation of Atheism from the Structure and Origin of Humane Bodies*. London.

Benz, F. L. (1972) *Personal Names in the Phoenician and Punic Inscriptions*. Rome: Biblical Institute.

Bérard, A. (1971) Préface, in V. Bérard, *Les Navigations d'Ulysse*, 3 vols. Paris: Librairie Armand Colin.

Bérard, J. (1951) 'Philistines et préhellènes', *Revue Archéologique*, série 6: 129–42.

—— (1952) 'Les hyksos et la légende d' io: Recherches sur la période pré-mycenienne, *Syria* 29: 1–43.

Bérard, V. (1894) *De l'origine des cultes arcadiens: Essai de méthode en mythologie grecque.* Paris: Bibliothèque des Écoles Françaises d'Athènes et de Rome.

—— (1902–3) *Les Phéniciens et l'Odysée*, 2 vols. Paris: Librairie Armand Colin.

—— (1927–9) *Les Navigations d'Ulysse.* Paris: Librairie Armand Colin.

Berlin, I. (1976) *Vico and Herder: Two Studies in the History of Ideas.* London: Hogarth.

Bernal, M. (1980) 'Speculations on the disintegration of Afroasiatic', paper presented at the 8th conference of the North American Conference of Afroasiatic Linguistics, San Francisco, April and to the 1st International Conference of Somali Studies, Mogadishu, July.

—— (1983a) 'On the westward transmission of the Canaanite alphabet before 1500 BC', paper presented to the American Oriental Society, Baltimore (April).

—— (1983b) 'On the westward transmission of the Semitic alphabet before 1500 BC', paper read at the Hebrew University, Jerusalem (June).

—— (1985a) 'Black Athena: the African and Levantine roots of Greece', *African Presence in Early Europe, Journal of African Civilizations* 7.5: 66–82.

—— (1985b) Review of *Sign, Symbol, Script: An Exhibition on the Origins of the Alphabet*, in *Journal of the American Oriental Society* 105.4: 736–7.

—— (1986) 'Black Athena denied: the tyranny of Germany over Greece', *Comparative Criticism* 8: 3–69.

—— (1987a) 'On the transmission of the alphabet to the Aegean before 1400 BC', *Bulletin of the American Schools of Oriental Research.*

—— (1987b) 'First land then sea: thoughts about the social formation of the Mediterranean and Greece', in E. Genovese and L. Hochberg, eds *Geography in Historical Perspective.* Oxford: Blackwell.

—— (1988) *Cadmean Letters: The Westward Diffusion of The Semitic Alphabet Before 1400 BC.* Winona Lake: Eisenbrauns.

Bernier, F. (1684) *Nouvelle Division de la terre par les différentes espèces ou races qui l'habitent.* Paris.

Beth, K. (1916) 'El und Neter', *Zeitschrift für die alttestamentliche Wissenschaft* 36: 129–86.

Beuchot, A. 'Jean Terrasson, 1852–77', *Biographie Universelle: Ancienne et Moderne.* Paris, vol. 41, pp. 169–71.

Bezzenberger, A. (1883) 'Aus einem briefe des herrn dr. Adolf Erman', *Beiträge zur Kunde der indogermanischen Sprachen* 7: 96.

Bietak, M. (1979) *Avaris and Piramesse: Archaeological Exploration in the Eastern Nile Delta. Proceedings of the British Academy* 65. London.

Bill, E. G. W. (1973) *University Reform in Nineteenth Century Oxford: A Study of Henry Halford Vaughan.* Oxford: Clarendon.

Billigmeier, J. C. (1976) *Kadmos and the Possibility of a Semitic Presence in Helladic Greece.* University of California, Santa Barbara, thesis.

Black, H. D. (1974) 'Welcome to the centenary commemoration', in Elkin and Macintosh, eds *Grafton Elliot Smith*. Sydney University Press, pp. 3–7.

Blackall, E. (1958) *The Emergence of German as a Literary Language, 1700–1775*. Cambridge University Press.

Blackwell, T. (1735) *Enquiry into the Life and Writings of Homer*. London.

Blanco, A. G. (1984) 'Hermeticism: bibliographical approach', in H. Temporini and W. Haase, eds (1972–) *Aufstieg und Niedergang der römischen Welt: Geschichte und Kultur Roms im Spiegel der neueren Forschung*, 21 vols. Berlin/New York. Vol. 17.4. *Religion: (Heidentum: römische Götterkulte, orientalische Kulte in der römischen Welt [Forts.])* ed. W. Haase, pp. 2240–81.

Blavatsky, H. P. (1930) *The Secret Doctrine . . .* Los Angeles: The Theosophy Co.

—— (1931) *Isis Unveiled . . .* Los Angeles: The Theosophy Co.

Blegen, C. W. and Haley, J. (1927) 'The coming of the Greeks: the geographical distribution of prehistoric remains in Greece', *American Journal of Archaeology* 32: 141–52.

Bloch, M. (1924) *Les Rois Thaumaturges: Étude sur le caractère surnaturel attribué à la puissance royale particulièrement en France et en Angleterre*. Strasbourg and Paris: Publications de la Faculté des Lettres de l'Université de Strasbourg.

Bloomfield, M. W. (1952) *The Seven Deadly Sins*. East Lansing: Michigan State University Press.

Blue, G. (1984) *Western Perceptions of China in Historical Perspective*. Talk at the China Summer School, Selwyn College, Cambridge.

Blumenbach, J. F. (1795) *De Generis Humani Varietate Nativa*. Göttingen, 3rd. edn.

—— (1865) *Anthropological Treatises of Johann Friedrich Blumenbach*, ed. and trans. T. Bendyshe. London.

Blunt, A. (1940) *Artistic Theory in Italy: 1450–1600*. Oxford: Clarendon.

Boardman, J. (1964) *The Greeks Overseas: The Archaeology of Their Early Colonies and Trade*. London: Penguin.

Boas, G. (1950) trans. *The Hieroglyphics of Horapollo*. New York: Pantheon.

Bochart, S. (1646) *Geographia Sacræ Pars Prior: Phaleg seu de Dispersione Gentium et Terrarum Divisione Facta in Ædificatione Turris Babel etc. Pars Altera: Chanaan, seu de Coloniis et Sermone Phœnicum*. Munich.

Bodin, J. (1945) *Method for the Easy Comprehension of History*, B. Reynolds, trans. New York: Columbia University Press.

Boissel, J. (1983) 'Notices, notes et variantes', in Gobineau, *Oeuvres*, vol. 1, pp. 1177–471.

Bolgar, R. R. (1979) 'Classical influences in the social, political and educational thought of Thomas and Matthew Arnold', in Bolgar, ed., *Classical Influences on Western Thought AD 1650–1870: Proceedings of an International Conference held at King's College, Cambridge, March 1977*. Cambridge University Press, pp. 327–38.

—— (1981) 'The Greek legacy', in Finley, pp. 429–72.

Bollack, M. and Wismann, H. (1983) *Philologie und Hermeneutik im 19. Jahrhundert*

II: Philologie et herméneutique au 19ème siècle. Göttingen: Vandenhoek und Ruprecht.

Bomhard, A. (1976) 'The placing of the Anatolian languages', *Orbis* 25.2: 199–239.

—— (1984) *Toward Proto-Nostratic: A New Approach to the Comparison of Indo-European and Afroasiatic.* Amsterdam: John Benjamin.

Boon, J. (1978) 'An endogamy of poets and vice versa; exotic ideas in Romanticism and Structuralism', *Studies in Romanticism* 18: 333–61.

Bopp, F. (1833) *Vergleichende Grammatik des Sanskrit, Zend, Griechischen, Lateinischen, Litthauschen, Gothischen und Deutschen.* Berlin, trans. E. B. Eastwick, as *A Comparative Grammar of the Sanskrit, Zend, Greek, Latin, Lithuanian, Gothic, German and Slavonic Languages*, 3 vols. London, 1845–50.

Bordreuil, P. (1982) see Abou-Assaf.

Borrow, G. (1843) *The Bible in Spain.* London: John Murray.

—— (1851) *Lavengro.* London: John Murray.

—— (1857) *Romany Rye.* London: John Murray.

Borsi, F. *et al.* (1985) *Fortuna degli etruschi.* Milan: Electa.

Boylan, P. (1922) *Thoth the Hermes of Egypt: A Study of Some Aspects of Theological Thought in Ancient Egypt.* London: Oxford University Press.

Bracken, H. (1973) 'Essence, accident and race', *Hermathena* 116: 91–6.

—— (1978) 'Philosophy and racism', *Philosophia* 8: 241–60.

Brady, T. H. (1935) 'The reception of Egyptian cults by the Greeks (330–300 BC)', *The University of Missouri Studies* 10: 1.

Braun, L. (1973) *Histoire de l'histoire de la philosophie.* Paris: Ophrys.

Braun, T. F. R. G. (1982) 'The Greeks in the Near East', *Cambridge Ancient History*, 2nd edn, vol. 3, pt 3, *The Expansion of the Greek World, Eighth to Sixth Centuries BC*, pp. 1–31.

Breasted, J. H. (1901) 'The philosophy of a Memphite priest', *Zeitschrift für ägyptische Sprache und Altertumskunde* 39: 39–54.

—— (1912) *The Development of Religion and Thought in Ancient Egypt.* Chicago: Scribner.

Bridenthal, R. (1970) *Barthold George Niebuhr, historian of Rome: a Study in Methodology.* Columbia University, thesis.

Brodie, F. M. (1945) *No Man Knows My History: The Life of Joseph Smith the Mormon Prophet.* New York: Knopf.

Brookfield, F. (1907) *The Cambridge Apostles.* New York: Scribner.

Brosses, C. de (1760) *Du Culte des dieux fétiches ou parallèle de l'ancienne religion de l'Égypte avec la religion actuelle de Nigritie.* Paris.

Brown, J. P. (1965) 'Kothar, Kinyras and Kytheria', *Journal of Semitic Studies* 10: 197–219.

—— (1968a) 'Literary contexts of the common Hebrew Greek vocabulary', *Journal of Semitic Studies* 13: 163–91.

—— (1968b) 'Cosmological myth and the Tuna of Gibraltar', *Transactions of the American Philological Association* 99: 37–62.

— (1969) 'The Mediterranean vocabulary of the vine', *Vetus Testamentum* 19: 146–70.

— (1971) 'Peace symbolism in ancient military vocabulary', *Vetus Testamentum* 21: 1–23.

— (1979–80) 'The sacrificial cult and its critique in Greek and Hebrew', pt 1, *Journal of Semitic Studies* 24: 159–74; pt 2, *Journal of Semitic Studies* 25: 1–21.

Brown, R. (1898) *Semitic Influences in Hellenic Mythology*. London: Williams and Norgate.

Brown, R. L. (1967) *Wilhelm von Humboldt's Conception of Linguistic Relativity*. The Hague and Paris: Mouton.

Bruce, J. (1795) *Travels to Discover the Sources of the Nile, In the Years 1768, 1769, 1770, 1771, 1772 and 1773*, 5 vols. London: G. G. and J. Robinson.

Brugsch, H. (1879–80) *Dictionnaire géographique*. Leipzig.

— (1891) *Religion und Mythologie der alten Ägypter*. Leipzig.

Brunner, H. (1957) 'New aspects of Ancient Egypt', *Universitas* 1.3: 267–79.

Brunner-Traut, E. (1971) 'The origin of the concept of the immortality of the soul in Ancient Egypt', *Universitas* 14.1: 47–56.

Bryant, J. (1774) *A New System or an Analysis of Ancient Mythology*, 3 vols. London.

Buck, R. J. (1979) *A History of Boiotia*. Edmonton: University of Alberta Press.

Budge, W. (1904) *The Gods of the Egyptians: or Studies in Ancient Egyptian Mythology*, 2 vols. London: Methuen.

Bullough, G. (1931) *Philosophical Poems of Henry More, Comprising Psychozoia and Minor Poems*. Manchester University Press.

Bunnens, G. (1979) *L'expansion phénicienne en méditerranée: essai d'interprétation fondé sur une analyse des traditions littéraires*. Brussels and Rome: Institut historique belge de Rome.

Bunsen, C. (1848–60) *Egypt's Place in Universal History*, C. H. Cotrell, trans. 5 vols. London: Longman.

— (1852) *The Life and Letters of Barthold George Niebuhr, with Essays on his Character and Influence*, 2 vols. London.

— (1859) *The Life and Letters of Barthold George Niebuhr*. New York.

— (1868) Statement of a Plan of Intellectual Labour Laid Before Niebuhr, at Berlin, January 1816. Trans. F. Bunsen, vol. 1, pp. 85–90.

— (1868–70) *God in History, or the Progress of Man's Faith in the Moral Order of the World*, S. Winckworth, trans., 3 vols. London: Longman.

Bunsen, F. (1868) *A Memoir of Baron Bunsen . . . Drawn chiefly from family papers by his widow Frances Baroness Bunsen*, 2 vols. London: Longman.

Burnouf, E. (1872) 'La science des religions', Paris; trans. J. Liebe (1888) as *The Science of Religion*, London.

Burn, A. R. (1949) 'Phoenicians', *Oxford Classical Dictionary*, pp. 686–88.

Burton, A. (1972) *Diodorus Siculus, Book 1: a Commentary*. Leiden: Brill.

Bury, J. B. (1900) *A History of Greece to the Death of Alexander the Great*. London: Macmillan.

— (1951) *A History of Greece to the Death of Alexander the Great.* London: Macmillan, 3rd edn., rev. R. Meiggs.

Burzachechi, C. (1976) 'L'adozione dell'alfabeto nel mondo greco', *Parola del Passato* 31: 82–102.

Butler, E. M. (1935) *The Tyranny of Greece over Germany. A Study on the Influence Exercised by Greek Art and Poetry over the Great German Writers of the Eighteenth, Nineteenth and Twentieth Centuries.* Cambridge University Press.

Butler, M. (1981) *Romantics Rebels and Reactionaries: English Literature and its Background, 1760–1830.* Oxford University Press.

Butterfield, H. (1955) *Man and His Past: the Study of Historical Scholarship.* Cambridge University Press.

— (1981) *The Origins of History.* ed. A. Watson. New York: Basic Books.

Cagnetta, A. (1979) *Antichisti e impero fascista.* Bari: Dedalo.

Cagni, L., ed. (1981) *La Lingua di Ebla: Atti del convegno internationale (Napoli, 21–23 aprile 1980).* Naples: Istituto Universitario Orientale, Seminario di Studi Asiatici, 14.

Canfora, L. (1980) *Ideologie del Classicismo.* Turin: Einaudi.

Capart, J. (1942) 'Egyptian art', in Glanville, *Legacy of Egypt.* Oxford: Clarendon, pp. 80–119.

Carpenter, R. (1933) 'The antiquity of the Greek alphabet', *American Journal of Archaeology* 37: 8–29.

— (1938) 'The Greek alphabet again', *American Journal of Archaeology* 42: 58–69.

— (1958) 'Phoenicians in the west', *American Journal of Archaeology* 62: 35–53.

— (1966) *Discontinuity in Greek Civilization.* Cambridge.

Carruthers, J. (1984) *Essays in Ancient Egyptian Studies.* Los Angeles.

Cartledge, P. (1979) *Sparta and Lakonia: A Regional History 1300–362 BC.* London: Routledge & Kegan Paul.

Cassirer, E. (1970) *The Platonic Renaissance in England,* J. P. Pettegrove, trans. New York: Gordian Press.

Cassuto, U. (1971) *The Goddess Anath: Canaanite Epics of the Patriarchal Age,* I. Abraham, trans. Jerusalem: Magness.

Cattaui, R. and G. (1950) *Mohamed-Aly en Europe.* Paris: Geuthner.

Černy, J. (1952) *Egyptian Religion.* London: Hutchinson.

Chadwick, J. (1973a) *Documents in Mycenaean Greek.* 2nd edn. Cambridge University Press.

— (1973b) 'The Linear B tablets as historical documents', *Cambridge Ancient History,* 3rd edn, vol. 2, pt 1, *The Middle East and the Aegean Region, c.1800–1380 BC,* pp. 609–26.

— (1976) *The Mycenaean World.* London: Cambridge University Press.

Chailley, J. (1971) *The Magic Flute, Masonic Opera,* H. Weinstock, trans. New York: Knopf.

Champollion, J. F. (1814) *L'Égypte sous les Pharaons: ou recherches sur la géographie, la religion, la langue, les écritures et l'histoire de l'Égypte avant l'invasion de Cambyse.* Grenoble.

—— (1909) see Hartleben, H.

Chanaiwa, D. (1973) *The Zimbabwe Controversy: A Case of Colonial Historiography.* Syracuse, NY: Program of Eastern African Studies.

Chandler, R. (1769) *Ionian Antiquities, Published with Permission with the Society of Dilletanti.* London.

Chang, K. C. (1980) *Shang Civilization.* New Haven: Yale University Press.

Chantraine, P. (1928) 'Sur le vocabulaire maritime des grecs', in *Étrennes de linguistique: offertes par quelques amis à Émile Benveniste.* Paris: Geuthner, pp. 1–25.

—— (1968–75) *Dictionnaire étymologique de la langue grecque,* 4 vols. Paris: Klincksieck.

Charles-Roux, F. (1929) 'Le projet français de conquête de l'Égypte sous le règne de Louis XVI', *Mémoires de l'Institut d'Égypte* 14: 1–85.

—— (1937) *Bonaparte Governor of Egypt,* E. W. Dickes, trans. London: Methuen.

Chaudhuri, N. C. (1974) *Scholar Extraordinary: The Life of Professor the Right Honourable Max Müller PC.* London: Chatto & Windus.

Child, F. J. (1882–98) *The English and Scottish Popular Ballads,* 5 vols. Boston.

Childe, G. F. (1926) *The Aryans.* London: Kegan Paul.

Cicero, *The Nature of the Gods.*

—— *Tusculanae Disputationes.*

Clark, W. M. (1954) *Christoph-Martin Wieland and the Legacy of Greece: Aspects of his Relationship to Greek Culture.* Columbia University, PhD thesis.

Clement of Alexandria, *Stromata.*

—— *Protrepticus.*

Coleridge, S. T., see Griggs, E. L.

Colie, R. L. (1957) *Light and Enlightenment: A Study of the Cambridge Platonists and the Dutch Arminians.* Cambridge University Press.

Combes-Dounous (1809) *Essai Historique sur Platon, et coup d'œil rapide sur l'histoire du Platonisme depuis Platon jusqu'à nous.* Paris.

Comte, A. (1830–42) *Cours de philosophie positive,* 6 vols. Paris: Bachelier.

Conan-Doyle, A. (1968) *The Adventure of the Devil's Foot,* in *The Annotated Sherlock Holmes,* 2 vols. London: Murray, pp. 508–26.

Conway, R. S. (1937) 'William Ridgeway', *Dictionary of National Biography: Twentieth Century 1922–1930.* Oxford University Press, pp. 720–2.

Cook, A. B. (1914–40) *Zeus: A Study in Ancient Religion,* 3 vols, 5 pts. Cambridge University Press.

Cook, R. M. (1937) 'Amasis and the Greeks in Egypt', *Journal of Hellenic Studies* 57: 227–37.

Cook, S. A. (1924) 'The Semites', *Cambridge Ancient History,* 1st edn, vol. 1, pp. 181–237.

Cordier, H. (1898) 'Les études chinoises: 1895–1898', Suppl. to *T'oung-Pao* 9: 44–51.

—— (1899) 'Deux voyageurs dans l'Extrême Orient au XVe et au XVIe siècles: essai bibliographique, Nicolò de Conti-Lodovico de Varthema', *T'oung-Pao*, 10: 380–404.

— (1904–24) *Bibliotheca Sinica: dictionnaire bibliographique des ouvrages relatifs à l'Empire Chinois*, 2nd edn, 5 vols. Paris: Librairie Orientale et Américaine.

Corpus Hermeticum (1945–54) text established by A. D. Nock, trans. (into French) by A.-J. Festugière, 4 vols. Paris.

Cory, I. P. (1832) *Sanchunation, Ancient Fragments of the Phoenician, Chaldaean, Egyptian, Tyrian, Carthaginian, Indian, Persian and Other writers, With an Introductory Dissertation and an Inquiry into the Philosophy and Trinity of the Ancients*. London.

Cousin, V. (1841) *Cours de l'histoire de la philosophie: Introduction à l'histoire de la philosophie*. Paris.

Cowan, M. (1963) *An Anthology of the Writings of Wilhelm von Humboldt: Humanist Without Portfolio*. Detroit: Wayne State University Press.

Cramer, M. (1955) *Das altägyptische Lebenszeichen (Ankh) im christlichen (koptischen) Ägypten*. Wiesbaden: Harrasowitz.

Creutzer, F. (1810–12) *Symbolik und Mythologie der alten Völker besonders der Griechen*, 4 vols. Leipzig/Darmstadt.

Croce, B. (1947) *Bibliographica Vichiana*, 2 vols. Naples: Atti dell'Accademia Pontaniana.

Crombie, A. C. (1963) ed. *Scientific Change: Historical Studies in the Intellectual, Social and Technical Conditions for Scientific Discovery and Technical Invention, from Antiquity to the Present: Symposium on the History of Science Held at the University of Oxford, 9–15 July 1961*. London: Heinemann.

Cromey, R. D. (1978) 'Attic Παιανια and Παιονιδαι', *Glotta* 56: 62–9.

Cross, F. M. (1968) 'The Phoenician inscription from Brazil. A nineteenth century forgery', *Orientalia* 37: 437–60.

— (1974) 'Leaves from an epigraphist's notebook', *The Catholic Biblical Quarterly* 36: 490–3.

— (1979) 'The early alphabetic scripts', in Cross, ed. *Symposia, Celebrating the Seventy-Fifth Anniversary of the American Schools of Oriental Research (1900–1975)*. Cambridge, Mass., pp. 97–123.

— (1980) 'Newly found inscriptions in Old Canaanite and Early Phoenician scripts', *Bulletin of the American Schools of Oriental Research* 238: 1–21.

Crossland, R. A. and Birchall, C. (1973) *Bronze Age Migrations in the Aegean: Archaeological and Linguistic Problems of Greek Prehistory*. London: Duckworth.

Crum, W. (1939) *A Coptic Dictionary*. Oxford: Clarendon.

Cudworth, R. (1743) (1676) *The True Intellectual System of the Universe*, 2nd edn. London.

Culican, W. (1966) *The First Merchant Venturers: The Ancient Levant in History and Commerce*. London: Thames & Hudson.

Cumont, F. (1929) *Les religions orientales dans le paganisme romain*, 3rd edn. Paris: Annales du Musée Guimet, Bibliothèque de Vulgarisation.

—— (1937) *L'Égypte des Astrologues*. Brussels: Fondation Égyptologique de La Reine Elizabeth.

Curl, J. S. (1982) *The Egyptian Revival, An Introductory Study of a Recurring Theme in the History of Taste*. London: Allen & Unwin.

Curtin, P. (1964) *The Image of Africa: British Ideals and Action, 1780–1850*. Madison: Wisconsin University Press.

—— (1971) *Imperialism: the Documentary History of Western Civilization*. New York: Harper & Row.

Curtius, E. (1857–67) *Griechische Geschichte*, 4 vols. Berlin, trans. A. W. Ward (1886) as *History of Greece*, 5 vols. New York.

Cuvier, G. (1817) *Le règne animal distribué d'après son organisation*. Paris, trans. M. Mac Murtrie (1831) as *The Animal Kingdom*, 4 vols. New York.

Dacier, A. Le F. (1714) *Des Causes de la Corruption du goût*. Paris.

Dahood, M. (1981a) 'The linguistic classification of Eblaite', in Cagni, pp. 177–89.

—— (1981b) 'Afterward: Ebla, Ugarit and the Bible', in Pettinato, *The Archives of Ebla*, pp. 271–321.

Daniélou, J. (1964) *Primitive Christian Symbols*, D. Attwater, trans. Baltimore: Helicon.

Dart, R. A. (1974) 'Sir Grafton Elliot Smith and the evolution of man', *Grafton Elliot Smith: The Man and his Work*. Sydney University Press, pp. 25–38.

Davies, N. (1979) *Voyagers to the New World*. London: Macmillan.

Davis, W. M. (1979) 'Plato on Egyptian art', *Journal of Egyptian Archaeology* 66: 121–7.

Dawson, R. (1967) *The Chinese Chameleon: An Analysis of European Conceptions of Chinese Civilization*. London: Oxford University Press.

Delatte, A. (1922) *La vie de Pythagore de Diogène Laerce*. Brussels: Académie Royale de Belgique, Classe de Lettres etc.

Delia, R. (1980) *A Study in the Reign of Senwosret III*, Columbia University, PhD thesis.

Derchain, M.-T. & P. (1975) 'Noch einmal "Hermes Trismegistos"', *Göttinger Miszellen* 15:7–10.

Derchain, P. (1962) 'L'authenticité de l'inspiration égyptienne dans le "Corpus Hermeticum"', *Revue de l'Histoire des Religions*: 175–98.

—— (1980) 'Kosmogonie'. Helck and Otto, cols 747–56.

Des Places, E. (1964) 'Les *Mystères d'Égypte* et les *Oracles Chaldaïques*', *Oikumene*: 455–60.

—— (1975) 'La religion de Jamblique', *Entretiens sur l'Antiquité classique* 21: 69–94.

—— (1984) 'Les oracles Chaldaïques', in H. Temporini and W. Haase, eds (1972–) *Aufstieg und Niedergang der römischen Welt: Geschichte und Kultur Roms im Spiegel der neueren Forschung*, 21 vols. Berlin/New York, vol. 17.4. *Religion: (Heidentum: römische Götterkulte, orientalische Kulte in der römischen Welt [Forts.])*, ed. W. Haase, pp. 2300–35.

Devisse, J. (1979) *L'image du noir: dans l'art occidental 2. Des premiers siècles chrétiens aux 'grands découverts'* pt 1: *De la menace démoniaque à l'incarnation de la sainteté*; pt 2: *Les*

Africains dans l'ordonnance chrétienne du monde (XIVᵉ–XVIᵉ siècle) Lausanne: Fondation de la menil.

Dickinson, O. T. P. K. (1977) *The Origins of Mycenaean Civilization.* Gotenborg: Studies in Mediterranean Archaeology No. 49.

Dieckmann, L. (1970) *Hieroglyphics: The History of a Literary Symbol.* St Louis: Washington University Press.

Dimakis, J. (1968) *La guerre de l'indépendance grecque vue par la presse française (période 1821–1824): contribution à l'étude de l'opinion publique et du mouvement philhellénique en France.* Thessalonika.

Diodoros Sikeliotes (1933–67) *The Library of History,* 12 vols, C. H. Oldfather, trans. Cambridge, Mass. (vols 11 and 12 trans. F. R. Walton and R. M. Geer).

Diogenes Laertius (1925) *Lives of Eminent Philosophers,* R. D. Hicks, trans. 2 vols. Cambridge, Mass.

Diop, C. A. (1974) *The African Origin of Civilization: Myth or Reality?,* M. Cook, trans. Westport, Conn.: L. Hill.

—— (1978) *The Cultural Unity of Black Africa.* Chicago.

—— (1985a) 'Africa: cradle of humanity', *Nile Valley Civilizations:* pp. 23–8.

—— (1985b) 'Africa's contribution to world civilization: the exact sciences', *Nile Valley Civilizations:* pp. 69–83.

Disraeli, B. I. (1847) *Tancred; or the New Crusade.* Liepzig: Tauschnitz.

Dods, M. and Smith, T. (trans.) (1867) *Tatian, Theophilus and the Clementine Recognition,* vol. 3, *The Ante-Nicene Christian Library.* Edinburgh, pp. 1–39, esp. 35–6.

Dolgopolskii, A. B. (1973) *Sravitelno-istoricheskaya fonetika kushchitskikh yazykov.* Moscow: Nauka.

Donaldson, J. W. (1858) Introduction in Müller, *A History of the Literature of Ancient Greece,* 3 vols. London, vol. 1, pp. i–xxxix.

Doresse, J. (1960) *The Secret Books of the Egyptian Gnostics.* London: Hollis & Carter.

Dörpfeldt, W. (1966) (1935) *Alt-Olympia: Untersuchungen und Ausgrabungen zur Geschichte des ältesten Heiligtums von Olympia und der älteren griechischen Kunst* (reprint). Osnabrück: Zeller.

Dothan, M. (1973) 'Philistine material culture and its Mycenaean affinities', in Karageorghis, ed. *The Mycenaeans in the East Mediterranean.* Nicosia.

Dothan, T. (1982) *The Philistines and their Material Culture.* Jerusalem and New Haven: Yale University Press.

Doumas, C. (1979) *Thera and the Aegean World: Papers Presented at the Second International Scientific Congress, Santorini, Greece, August 1978.* London.

Dow, S. (1937) 'The Egyptian cults in Athens', *Harvard Theological Review* 30, 4: 183–232.

Drioton, E. (1948) 'Le monothéisme de l'ancienne Égypte', *Cahiers d'histoire égyptienne* 1: 149–68.

—— (1948a) Preface, in Lauer, *Le Problème des Pyramides d'Égypte.*

Drioton, E. and Vandier, J. (1946) *L'Égypte*. Clio. Paris: Introduction aux études historiques.

Dubois, W. E. B. (1975) *The Negro*. New York: Kraus-Thompson Organization.

—— (1976) *The World and Africa*. New York: Kraus-Thompson Organization.

Duff, W. (1767) *An Essay on Original Genius: and its various Modes of Exertion in Philosophy and the Fine Arts, Particularly in Poetry*. London.

Duhoux, Y. (1982) *L'Étéocrétois: Les textes, la langue*. Amsterdam: J. C. Gieben.

Duke, T. T. (1965) review, *The Classical Journal* 61.3: 131–6 (p. 133).

Dumas, F. (1976) *Le Tombeau de Childéric*. Paris: Le Cabinet.

Dunand, F. (1973) *Le culte d'isis dans le bassin de la Méditerranée*, 3 vols. Vol. II: *Le culte d'isis en Grèce*. Leiden: Brill.

Dunker, M. (1880) *Griechische Geschichte*, S. F. Alleyne, trans. (1883), 3 vols. London.

Dupuis, C. F. (1822) (1795) *Origine de tous les cultes, ou la religion universelle*, 12 vols in 7. Paris.

—— (An XII) Discours prononcé à la rentrée du Collège de France Le 1er Frimaire.

Dussaud, R. (1907) *Les Arabes en Syrie avant l'Islam*. Paris: Leroux.

—— (1931) 'Victor Bérard (necrologue)', *Syria* 12: 392–3.

Earp, F. R. (1953) 'The date of the Supplices of Aeschylus', *Greece and Rome*: 118–23.

Edwards, G. P. (1971) *The Language of Hesiod in its Traditional Context*. Oxford: Blackwell.

Edwards, I. E. S. (1947) *The Pyramids of Egypt*. London: Penguin.

Edwards, R. (1979) *Kadmos the Phoenician: A Study in Greek Legends and the Mycenaean Age*. Amsterdam: Hakkert.

Eissfeldt, O. (1935) 'Molk als Opferbegriff im Punischen und Hebräischen und das Ende des Gottes Moloch', *Beiträge zur Religiongeschichte des Altertums*, vol. 3.

—— (1960) 'Phönikische und griechische Kosmogonie', in *Éléments orientaux dans la religion grecque ancienne*. Paris, pp. 1–15.

Eliot, G. (1906) (1864) *Romola*, 2 vols. Chicago: Mc Clarg.

—— (1871–2) *Middlemarch*, 2 vols. London and Edinburgh.

—— (1876) *Daniel Deronda*, 2 vols. Edinburgh and London.

Eliot, T. S. (1971) *The Complete Poems and Plays: 1909–1950*. New York: Harcourt Brace.

Elkin, A. P. (1974) 'Sir Grafton Elliot Smith: the man and his work; a personal testimony', in *Grafton Elliot Smith: the Man and His Work*. Sydney University Press, pp. 8–15.

—— (1974a) 'Elliot Smith and the diffusion of culture', in *Grafton Elliot Smith: the Man and His Work*. Sydney University Press, pp. 139–59.

Elliot Smith, G. (1911) *The Ancient Egyptians and their Influence Upon the Civilization of Europe*. London: Harper.

—— (1923) *The Ancient Egyptians and the Origin of Civilization*. London: Harper.

Erman, A. (1883) 'Aegyptische Lehnwörte im Griechischen', *Beiträge zur Kunde der indogermanischen Sprachen* 7: 336–8.

Erman, A. and Grapow, H. (1982) *Wörterbuch der ägyptischen Sprache*, 7 vols. Berlin: Akademie Verlag.

Eusebius (1866) *Chronicorum*, trans. from the Armenian by H. Petermann, ed. A. Schoene. Berlin: Weidmann.

Evans, A. (1909) *Scripta Minoa*. Oxford: Clarendon.

—— (1921–35) *The Palace of Minos*, 4 vols in 6. London: Macmillan.

Fallmerayer, J. P. (1835) *Welchern Einfluss hatte die Besetzung Griechenlands durch die Slawen auf das Schicksal der Städte Athen und der Landschaft Attika*. Stuttgart and Tübingen.

Fan Xiangyong (1962) *Guben Zhushu Jinian Jixiao Dipu*. Shanghai.

Farag, S. (1980) 'Une inscription memphite de la XIIᵉ dynastie', *Revue d'Égyptologie* 32: 75–81.

Farnell, L. R. (1895–1909) *The Cults of the Greek States*, 5 vols. Oxford: Clarendon.

Farnham, F. (1976) *Madame Dacier: Scholar and Humanist*. Monterey: Angel Press.

Farrell, J. J. (1980) *Inventing the American Way of Death*. Philadelphia: Temple University Press.

Faverty, F. (1951) *Matthew Arnold: The Ethnologist*. Evanston, Ill.: Northwestern University Press.

Fay, B. (1961) *La francmaçonnerie et la révolution intellectuelle du XVIIIᵉ siècle*. Paris: Libraire Français.

Feldman, B. and Richardson R. D. (1972) *The Rise of Modern Mythology 1680–1860*. Bloomington and London: Indiana University Press.

Fénelon, F. de S. de la M. (1833) (1699) *Télémaque, fils d'Ulysse*. Philadelphia.

Festugière, R. P. (1944–9) *La révélation d'Hermès Trismégiste*, 3 vols. Paris: Lecoffre, vol. 1, *L'astrologie et les sciences occultes*.

—— (1945) trans. *Corpus Hermeticum*, 4 vols. Paris: Société d'édition 'Les Belles Lettres'.

—— (1961–5) *Les Moines d'Orient*, 4 vols in 3. Paris: Éditions du Cerf.

—— (1966–8) *Prolius, Commentaire sur le Timée*, 5 vols. Paris.

Finkelstein, L. (1970) *Akiba: Scholar, Saint and Martyr*. New York: Atheneum.

Finley, M. I. (1978) *The World of Odysseus*. New York, rev. reset edn.

—— (1980) *Ancient Slavery and Modern Ideology*. New York.

—— (1981) *The Legacy of Greece: A New Appraisal*. Oxford: Clarendon.

Flaubert, G. (1857) *Madame Bovary*. Paris.

—— (1862) *Salammbô*. Paris.

—— (1973) *Oeuvres*, 3 vols., ed. and ann. J. Bruneau. Paris: Pléiades.

Fleckenstein (1975) 'Kepler and Neoplatonism', in Beer, pp. 519–33.

Fontenrose, J. (1959) *Python: a Study in Delphic Myth and its Origins*, Berkeley: University of California Press.

Force, J. E. (1985) *William Whiston: Honest Newtonian*. Cambridge University Press.

Forrest, W. G. G. (1982) 'Central Greece and Thessaly', *Cambridge Ancient History*, 2nd edn, vol. 3, pt 3, *The Expansion of the Greek World, Eighth to Sixth Centuries BC*. eds. J. Boardman and N. G. L. Hammond, pp. 286–99.

Forster, G. (1786) 'Noch etwas über die Menschenraßen', *Der Teutsche Merkur*. Aug.

—— (1958–) Georg Forsters Werke. Berlin: Akademie der Wissenschaften der D.D.R. Zentralinstitut für Literaturgeschichte.

Foucart, G. (1914) *Les Mystères d'Eleusis*. Paris: A. Picard.

Frankfort, H. and H. A. (1946) 'Myth and reality', in *The Intellectual Adventure of Ancient Man*. University of Chicago Press.

Franklin, J. H. (1947) *From Slavery to Freedom: A History of American Negroes*. New York: Knopf.

Franklin, H. B. (1963) *The Wake of the Gods: Melville's Mythology*. Stanford: Stanford University Press.

Frazer, J. (1890–1915) *The Golden Bough: A Study in Magic and Religion*, 9 vols. London: Macmillan.

—— (1898) *Pausanias's Description of Greece*, 6 vols. London.

—— (1911) *The Dying God, The Golden Bough*, vol. 3. London: Macmillan.

—— (1921) *Apollodoros; The Library*, 2 vols. Cambridge, Mass. See Apollodoros.

Freeman-Greville, G. S. P. (1962) *The East African Coast: Select Documents from the First to the Earlier Nineteenth Centuries*. Oxford: Clarendon.

Fréret, N. (1784) 'Observations générales sur l'origine et sur l'ancienne histoire des premiers habitants de la Grèce', *Académie des Inscriptions, 1784–1793* 47 (published 1809). *Mémoire de Littérature*: 1–149.

Freud, S. (1939) *Moses and Monotheism*, Katherine Jones, trans. London: Hogarth.

Friedrich, J. (1951) *Phönizisch-punische Grammatik*. Rome: Analecta Orientalia.

—— (1957) *Extinct Languages*, F. Gaynor, trans. New York: Philosophical Library.

—— (1968) 'Die Unechtheit der phönizischen Inschrift aus Parahyba', *Orientalia* 37: 421–4.

Froidefond, C. (1971) *Le mirage égyptien dans la littérature grecque d'Homère à Aristote*. Paris: Ophrys.

Frothingham, A. (1891) 'Archaeological news', *American Journal of Archaeology* 6: 476–566.

Frye, N. (1962) *Fearful Symmetry*. Boston: Beacon.

Fueter, E. (1936) *Geschichte der neueren Historiographie*. Berlin and Munich: R. Oldenberg.

Fuhrmann, M. (1979) 'Querelle des Anciens et des Modernes, der Nationalismus und die deutsche Klassik', in Bolgar, *Classical Influences*, pp. 107–28.

Fung Yu-lan (1952) *A History of Chinese Philosophy*, D. Bodde, trans., 2 vols. Princeton University Press.

Gamer-Wallert, I. (1977) 'Fische, religiös', in Helck and Otto, cols 228–34.

Garbini, G. (1977) 'Sulla datazione dell'iscrizione di Ahiram', *Annali dell'Istituto Orientale di Napoli* 627: 81–9.

538 BLACK ATHENA

—— (1978) 'La Lingua di Ebla', *La Parola del Passato* 181: 241–51.

—— (1981) 'Considerations on the language of Ebla', in Cagni, pp. 75–82.

Gardiner, A. H. (1927) *Egyptian Grammar*. Oxford: Clarendon.

—— (1942) 'Writing and literature', in S. R. A. Glanville, ed., *The Legacy of Egypt*. Oxford: Clarendon, pp. 53–79.

—— (1947) *Ancient Egyptian Onomastica*, 3 vols. Oxford University Press.

—— (1957) *Egyptian Grammar*, 3rd edn. Oxford: Clarendon.

—— (1961) *Egypt of the Pharaohs*. Oxford: Clarendon.

—— (1986) (1945–55) *My Early Years*, ed. J. Gardiner. Isle of Man: Andreas.

Gardner, P. (1880) 'Stephani on the tombs at Mycenae', *Journal of Hellenic Studies* 1: 94–106.

Garvie, A. F. (1969) *Aeschylus' Supplices: Play and Trilogy*. Cambridge University Press.

Gaster, T. H. (1964) *The Dead Sea Scriptures: In English Translation*. Garden City New York: Anchor Books.

Gaulmier, J. (1978) *Ernest Renan: Judaisme et Christianisme: textes présentés par Jean Gaulmier*. Paris.

—— (1983) Introduction to Gobineau, *Oeuvres*, vol. 1, pp. i–lxxxvii.

Gauthier, H. (1925–31) *Dictionnaire des noms géographiques contenus dans les textes hiéroglyphiques*, 5 vols. Cairo: L'Institut Français d'archéologie orientale.

Gelb, I. J. (1977) 'Thoughts about Ibla: A Preliminary Evaluation, March 1977', *Syro-Mesopotamian Studies* 1.1: 1–26.

—— (1981) 'Ebla and the Kish civilization', in Cagni, pp. 9–73.

Georgiev, V. I. (1952) 'L'origine minoenne de l'alphabet phénicienne', *Archív Orientální* 20: 487–95.

—— (1966) *Introduzione alla storia delle lingue indoeuropee*. Rome: Edizione de l'Ateneo.

—— (1973) 'The arrival of the Greeks in Greece: the linguistic evidence', in Crossland and Birchall, pp. 243–54.

Gerbi, A. (1973) *Dispute of the New World: The History of a Polemic, 1750–1900*, rev. and enl. edn. Pittsburgh: University of Pittsburgh Press.

Gesenius, F. H. W. (1815) *Geschichte der hebräischen Sprache und Schrift*. Leipzig.

Gibbon, E. (1776–88) *The Decline and Fall of the Roman Empire*, 6 vols. London.

—— (1794) 'Memoirs of my life and writings', *Miscellaneous Works of Edward Gibbon Esquire with Memoirs of His Life and Writings, Composed by Himself: Illustrated from His Letters with Occasional Notes and Narrative by John Lord Sheffield*, 2 vols. London, vol. 1, pp. 1–185.

Giles, P. (1924) 'The peoples of Europe', *Cambridge Ancient History*, vol. 2, *The Egyptian and Hittite Empires to c. 1000 BC*. Cambridge University Press, pp. 20–40.

Gillings, R. J. (1973) *Mathematics in the times of the Pharaohs*. Cambridge, Mass.

Gilman, S. (1982) *On Blackness without Blacks: Essays on the Image of the Black in Germany*. Boston.

Gimbutas, M. (1970) 'Proto-Indo-European culture: the Kurgan culture during the fifth, fourth and third millennia', *Indo-European and Indo-Europeans: Papers Presented at the Third Indo-European Conference at the University of Pennsylvania*, eds. G. Cardona, H. M. Hoenigswald and A. Senn. Philadelphia: University of Pennsylvania Press, pp. 155–97.

Gladstone, W. (1869) *Juventus Mundi: The gods and men of the heroic age*. London: Macmillan.

Glanville, S. (1942) *The Legacy of Egypt*. Oxford: Clarendon.

Gobineau, J. A. de (1983) *Oeuvres*, 2 vols. Paris: Pléiades.

Godwin, J. (1979) *Athanasius Kircher: A Renaissance Man and the Quest for Lost Knowledge*. London: Thames & Hudson.

Goldin, J. (1967) Introduction, in Spiegel, *The Last Trial*, pp. i–xxvi.

Goldsmith, O. (1774) *History of the Earth*, 8 vols. London.

Gomme, A. W. (1913) 'The legend of Cadmus and the Logographi', *Journal of Hellenic Studies*, pp. 53–72, 223–45.

Gooch, C. P. (1913) *History and Historians in the Nineteenth Century*. London: Longman.

Goodenough, W. H. (1970) 'The evolution and pastoralism and Indo-European origins', in *Indo-European and Indo-Europeans: Papers Presented at the Third Indo-European Conference at the University of Pennsylvania*, eds. G. Cardona, H. M. Hoenigswald and A. Senn, pp. 253–65.

Gordon, C. (1962a) 'Eteocretan', *Journal of Near Eastern Studies* 21: 211–14.

—— (1962b) *Before the Bible: The Common Background of Greek and Hebrew Civilizations*. New York: Harper & Row.

—— (1963a) 'The Dreros bilingual', *Journal of Semitic Studies* 8: 76–9.

—— (1963b) 'The Mediterranean factor in the Old Testament', *Supplements to Vetus Testamentum* 9: 19–31.

—— (1965) *Ugaritic Textbook, Analecta Orientalia* 18. Rome: Pontificum Institutum Biblicum.

—— (1966) *Evidence for the Minoan Language*. Ventnor.

—— (1968a) 'The present status of Minoan studies', *Atti*: 383–8.

—— (1968b) 'Northwest Semitic texts in Latin and Greek letters', *Journal of the American Oriental Society* 88: 285–9.

—— (1968c) 'The Canaanite text from Brazil', *Orientalia* 37: 425–36.

—— (1968d) 'Reply to Professor Cross', *Orientalia* 37: 461–3.

—— (1969) 'Minoan', *Athenaeum* 47: 125–35.

—— (1970a) 'Greek and Eteocretan unilinguals from Praisos and Dreros', *Berytus* 19: 95–8.

—— (1970b) 'In the wake of Minoan and Eteocretan', Πρακτικά του Α' Διέθνουσ 'Ανθρωπιστικού Συμποσίου ἐν Δελφοῖς 1: 163–71.

—— (1971) *Forgotten Scripts: The Story of their Decipherment*. London: Penguin.

—— (1975) 'The decipherment of Minoan and Eteocretan', *Journal of the Royal Asiatic Society*: 148–58.

—— (1980) 'A new light on the Minoan language', Πεπραγμένα: 205–9.

—— (1981) 'The Semitic language of Minoan Crete', in Arbeitman and Bomhard, pp. 761–82.

—— (1983) 'The Greek unilinguals from Praisos and Dreros and their bearing on Eteocretan and Minoan', Πεπραγμένα τοῦ Γ' Διεθνους Κρητολογικοῦ Συνεδρίου: 97–103.

Gossman, L. (1983) 'Orpheus Philologus: Bachofen versus Mommsen on the study of Antiquity', *Transactions of the American Philosophical Society* 73: pt 5.

Gould, R. F. (1904) *A Concise History of Freemasonry*. London: Gale and Polden.

Gould, S. J. (1981) *The Mismeasure of Man*. New York: Norton.

Gran, P. (1979) *Islamic Roots of Capitalism: Egypt 1760–1840*. Austin: University of Texas Press.

Graves, R. (1948) *The White Goddess*. London: Faber & Faber.

—— (1955) *Greek Myths*, 2 vols. London: Penguin.

Green, A. (1982) *Flaubert and the Historical Novel*. Cambridge University Press.

Green, A. R. W. (1975) *The Role of Human Sacrifice in the Ancient Near East*. Missoula, Montana: Scholars Press for the American Schools of Oriental Research.

Griffiths, G. J. (1970) *Plutarch's De Iside et Osiride*. Cambridge University Press.

—— (1975) *Apuleius of Madauros, The Isis Book (Metamorphosis, Book XI)*. Leiden: Brill.

—— (1980) 'Interpretatio Graeca', in Helck and Otto, vol. III, cols 167–72.

—— (1982) 'Plutarch', in Helck and Otto, vol. IV, cols 1065–7.

Griggs, E. L. (1956–71) *Collected Letters of Samuel Taylor Coleridge*, 5 vols. Princeton University Press and Oxford: Clarendon.

Grimm, G. (1969) *Die Zeugnisse ägyptischer Religion und Kunstelemente in römischen Deutschland*. Leiden: Brill.

Grote, G. (1826) 'Mitford's *History of Greece*', in the *Westminster Review* 5: 280–331.

—— (1846–56) *A History of Greece*, 12 vols. London.

Grumach, E. (1968/9) 'The coming of the Greeks', *Bulletin of the John Rylands Library* 51: 73–103, 400–30.

Guignes, C. L. J. de (1758) *Mémoire dans lequel on prouve que les chinois sont une colonie égyptienne*. Paris.

Haase, R. (1975) 'Kepler's harmonies between Pansophia and Mathesis Universalis', in Beer and Beer, pp. 427–38.

Hammond, N. G. L. (1967) *A History of Greece to 322 BC*, 2nd edn. Oxford: Clarendon.

Hani, J. (1976) *La Religion égyptienne dans la pensée de Plutarque*, collection d'études mythologiques. Centre de Recherche Mythologique de l'Université de Paris. Paris: 'Les Belles Lettres'.

Hannay, D. (1911) 'Spain, history', *Encyclopaedia Britannica*, 11th edn.

Hansberry, L. W. (1977) *Africa and the Africans as seen by Classical Writers: The Leo*

William Hansberry African History Notebook, 2 vols, ed. J. E. Harris. Washington: Howard University Press.

Harden, D. (1971) *The Phoenicians.* London: Penguin.

Hardy, T. (1891) *Tess of the d'Urbervilles.*

Hare, J. (1647) *St Edward's Ghost: or, Anti-Normanisme. Being a Patheticall Complaint and Motion in the behalfe of our English Nation against her grand (yet neglected) grievance, Normanisme.* London.

Harris, J. (1751) *Hermes: Or, a Political Inquiry, Concerning Language and Universal Grammar.* London.

Harris, Z. S. (1939) *The Development of the Canaanite Dialects: An Investigation in Linguistic History.* New Haven: American Oriental Society.

Harris-Schenz, B. (1984) *Black Images in Eighteenth Century German Literature.* Stuttgart: Heinz.

Harrison, J. (1903) *Prolegomena.* Cambridge University Press.

—— (1925) *Reminiscences of a Student's Life.* London: Hogarth.

Hartleben, H. (1906) *Champollion sein Leben und sein Werk*, 2 vols. Berlin: Weidmann.

—— (1909) *Lettres de Champollion le Jeune recuellies et annotées*, 2 vols. Paris: Bibliothèque Égyptologique.

Havelock, A. E. (1982) *The Literate Revolution in Greece and its Cultural Consequences.* Princeton University Press.

Haydon, B. R. (1926) *Autobiography and Memoirs*, new edn, ed. Aldous Huxley. London: P. Davies.

Heeren, A. H. L. (1824) *Ideen über die Politik, den Vehrkehr und den Handel der vornehmsten Völker der alten Welt*, 2 vols, Göttingen, trans. B. W. Talboys (1832–4) as *Reflections on the Politics, Intercourse, and Trade of the Principal Nations of Antiquity*, 2 vols. Oxford.

Hegel, G. W. F. (1892) *Lectures on the History of Philosophy*, E. S. Haldane and F. H. Simson, trans., 3 vols. London.

—— (1967) *Philosophy of Right*, trans. with notes by T. M. Knox. London: Oxford University Press.

—— (1975) *Lectures on the Philosophy of World History: Introduction: Reason in History*, H. B. Nisbet, trans. Cambridge University Press.

Heine, H. (1830–1) *Reisebilder*, 2 vols. Hamburg.

Helck, W. (1962) 'Osiris', in *Pauly Wissowa*, suppl. 9: 469–513.

—— (1971) *Die Beziehungen Ägyptens zu Vorderasien im 3. und 2. Jahrtausend v. Chr.* 2nd improved edn, Wiesbaden.

—— (1979) *Die Beziehungen Ägyptens und Vorderasiens zur Ägäis bis ins 7. Jahrhundert v. Chr.* Darmstadt: Wissenschaftliche Buchgesellschaft.

Helck, W. and Otto, E. (1975) *Lexikon der Ägyptologie*, vol. I. Wiesbaden: Harrasowitz.

—— (1977) —— vol. II.

—— (1980) —— vol. III.

—— (1982) —— vol. IV.

Heliodoros (1935) *Aithiopika*, J. Maillon, trans., 2 vols. Paris: 'Belles Lettres'.

Helm, P. R. (1980) *'Greeks' in the Neo-Syrian Levant and 'Assyria' in Early Greek Writers*. Philadelphia, PhD thesis.

Hemmerdinger, B. (1969) 'Noms communs d'origine égyptienne', *Glotta* 44: 238–47.

Herder, J. G. (1784–91) *Ideen zur Philosophie der Geschichte der Menschheit*, 4 vols. Riga and Leipzig.

Herm, G. (1975) *The Phoenicians: The Purple Empire of the Ancient World*, C. Hillier, trans. New York.

Herodotos (1954) *Herodotus: The Histories*, A. de Selincourt, trans. London.

Hersey, G. (1976) '"Aryanism" in Victorian England', *Yale Review* 66: 104–13.

Hester, D. A. (1965) 'Pelasgian a new Indo-European language?' *Lingua* 13: 335–84.

Heumann (1715) *Acta Philosophorum*. Halle.

Highet, G. (1949) *The Classical Tradition: Greek and Roman Influences on Western Literature*. New York and London: Oxford University Press.

Hill, C. (1968) *The World Turned Upside Down*. London: Temple Smith.

—— (1976) *Science and Magic in Seventeenth Century England*, text of a lecture given at the J. D. Bernal Peace Library, 19 Oct. 1976.

Hodge, C. (1976) 'Lisramic (Afroasiatic): an overview', in M. L. Bender, ed., *The Non-Semitic Languages of Ethiopia*. East Lansing, Mich., pp. 43–65.

Hoefer (1852–77) *Nouvelle Biographie générale*, 46 vols. Paris.

Hohendahl, P. U. (1981) 'Reform als Utopie: Die preußiche Bildungspolitik 1809–1817', in W. Voßkamp, ed., *Utopieforschung: Interdisziplinäre Studien zur neuzeitlichen Utopie*, vol. 3, pp. 250–72.

Holm, A. (1886–94) *Griechische Geschichte von ihrem Ursprunge bis zum Untergange der Selbständigheit des griechischen Volkes*, 4 vols, Berlin, trans. 1894 as *History of Greece*. London: Macmillan.

Honolka, K. (1984) *Papageno: Emanuel Schikaneder: Der Große Theartermann der Mozart-Zeit*. Salzburg: Residenz Verlag.

Honour, H. (1961) *Chinoiserie: The Vision of Cathay*. London: John Murray.

Hood, S. (1967) *Home of the Heroes: The Aegean Before the Greeks*. London: Thames & Hudson.

Hooker, J. T. (1976) *Mycenaean Greece*. London: Routledge & Kegan Paul.

Hopfner, T. (1922/3) *Fontes Historiae Religonis Aegyptiacae*, 2 vols. Bonn: Marci et Weberi.

—— (1940–1) *Plutarch über Isis und Osiris*, 2 vols. Prague: Orientalisches Institut.

Hornung, E. (1971) *Der Eine und die Vielen: Ägyptische Gottesvorstellungen*. Darmstadt, trans. J. Baines (1983) as *Conceptions of God in Ancient Egypt: The One and the Many*. London: Routledge & Kegan Paul.

Horton, R. (1967) 'African traditional thought and Western science', *Africa* 37: 50–71, 155–87.

—— (1973) 'Lévy-Brühl, Durkheim and the scientific revolution', in R. Horton and R.

Finnegan, eds *Modes of Thought: Essays on Thinking in Western and Non-Western Societies*. London: Faber & Faber.

Humboldt, W. von. (1793) 'Über das Studium des Altertums und des Griechischen insbesondre', *Gesammelte Schriften*, vol. I, pp. 255–81.

—— (1821) 'Ueber die Aufgabe des Geschichtsschreibers', *Gesammelte Schriften*, vol. 4, pp. 35–56.

—— (1826) 'Lettre à Monsieur Abel-Remusat sur la nature des formes grammaticales en générale, et sur la génie de la langue chinoise en particulier', *Journal Asiatique* 9:115; reprinted, *Gesammelte Schriften*, vol. 5, pp. 254–308.

—— (1841–52) *Wilhelm von Humboldts gesammelte Werke*, ed. C. Brandes, 7 vols in 4. Berlin.

—— (1903–36) *Wilhelm von Humboldts gesammelte Schriften*, 17 vols. Berlin: Leitzmann and Gebhardt.

Hunger, K. (1933) *Die Bedeutung der Universität Göttingen für die Geschichtsforschung am Ausgang des achtzehnten Jahrhunderts*. Berlin: E. Ebering.

Huxley, G. (1961) *Crete and the Luvians*. Oxford: the author.

Iggers, G. I. (1967) [trans. of W. von Humboldt's] 'The task of the historian', *History and Theory* 6: 57–71.

—— (1968) *The German Conception of History: The National Tradition of Historical Thought from Herder to the Present*. Middletown, Conn.: Wesleyan University Press.

Irving, W. (1829) *The Conquest of Granada*. New York.

—— (1852) *The Alhambra*. New York.

Irwin, J. T. (1980) *American Hieroglyphics: the Symbol of Egyptian Hieroglyphics in the American Renaissance*. New Haven: Yale University Press.

Isokrates (1928–44), 3 vols, 1 & 2 trans. G. Norlin; 3, trans. L. Van Hook. Cambridge, Mass.: Loeb.

Iversen, E. (1957) 'The Egyptian origin of the Archaic Greek canon', *Mitteilungen des Deutschen Archäeologischen Instituts Abt. Kairo* 15: 134–47.

—— (1961) *The Myth of Egypt and its Hieroglyphs in European Tradition*. Copenhagen: Gad.

Jacob, M. C. (1976) *The Newtonians and the English Revolution 1689–1720*. Ithaca, NY: Cornell University Press.

—— (1981) *The Radical Enlightenment: Pantheists, Freemasons and Republicans*. London: Allen & Unwin.

Jacoby, F. (1904) *Das Marmor Parium*, ed. and ann. Weidmann. Berlin.

—— (1923–9) *Fragmente der griechischen Historiker*, ed. and ann. Weidmann. Berlin.

James, G. G. M. (1954) *Stolen Legacy, The Greeks were not the authors of Greek Philosophy, but the people of North Africa, commonly called the Egyptians*. New York: Philosophical Library.

Jeanmaire, H. (1951) *Dionysos*. Paris: Payot.

Jeffery, L. H. (1961) *The Local Scripts of Archaic Greece: A Study in the Origin of the Greek Alphabet and its Development from the Eighth to the Fifth Centuries BC*. Oxford: Clarendon.

—— (1976) *Archaic Greece: The City-States c. 700–500 BC*. London/New York: St Martin's.

—— (1982) 'Greek alphabetic writing', *Cambridge Ancient History*, vol. 3, pt 1, pp. 819–33.

Jenkyns, R. (1980) *The Victorians and Ancient Greece*. Oxford: Blackwell.

Jensen, H. (1969) *Sign, Symbol and Script: An Account of Efforts to Write*, 3rd rev. edn, trans. G. Unwin. New York: Putnam.

Jespersen, O. (1922) *Language: its Nature, Development and Origin*. London: Allen & Unwin.

Jidejian, N. (1969) *Tyre Through the Ages*. Beirut: Dar el-machreq.

Joffe, A. H. (1980) *Sea Peoples in the Levant*. Cornell, Department of Near Eastern Studies, undergraduate thesis.

Johansen, H. F. and Whittle, E. W. (1980) *Aeschylus: the Suppliants*, 3 vols. Aarhus: Gyldenda.

Johnson, S. (1768) *The History of Rasselas Prince of Abissinia: An Asiatic Tale*. Philadelphia.

Jomard, E. F. (1829a) *Description générale de Memphis et ses pyramides*. Paris.

—— (1829b) *Remarque sur les pyramides*. Paris.

Jones, T. (1969) *The Sumerian Problem*. London, New York, Toronto and Sydney: John Wiley & Sons.

Jones, W. (1784) 'On the gods of Greece, Italy and India', in *The Works of Sir William Jones, with the Life of the Author by Lord Teignmouth*, 13 vols, London, 1807, vol. 1, pp. 319–97.

—— (1786) 'Third anniversary discourse before the Asiatick Society (of Bengal)', in *The Works of Sir William Jones, with the Life of the Author by Lord Teignmouth*, 13 vols, London, 1807, vol. 1, pp. 25–39.

—— (1794) *The Laws of Manu*. Calcutta.

Jordan, W. D. (1969) *White Over Black: American Attitudes Toward the Negro: 1550–1812*. Baltimore: Penguin.

Josephus, *Contra Apionem*.

——*Antiquitates Judaicae*.

Juster, J. (1914) *Les Juifs dans l'Empire romaine*, 2 vols. Paris: Geuthner.

Kantor, H. J. (1947) 'The Aegean and the Orient in the second millennium BC', *American Journal of Archaeology* 51: 1–103.

Kaufman, S. A. (1982) 'Reflections on the Assyrian–Aramaic bilingual from Tell Fakhariyeh', *MAARAV* 3/2: 137–75.

Keightly, D. N. (1978) *Sources of Shang History: The Oracle Bone Inscriptions of Bronze Age China*. Berkeley: University of California Press.

—— (1983) ed., *The Origins of Chinese Civilization*. Berkeley: University of California Press.

Keinast, B. (1981) 'Die Sprache von Ebla und das Altsemitische', in Cagni, pp. 83–98.

Kern, O. (1926) *Die Religion der Griechen*. Berlin: Weidmann.

Khattab, A. (1982) *Das Ägyptenbild in den deutschsprachigen Reisebeschreibungen der Zeit von 1285–1500*. Frankfort a.M.: Europäische Hochschulschriften Reihe 1 Deutsche Sprache und Literatur.

King, L. W. and Hall, H. R. (1907) *Egypt and Western Asia in the Light of Recent Discoveries*. London: Grolier Society.

Kinkel, I. G. (1877) *Epicorum Graecorum Fragmenta*. Leipzig.

Kircher, A. (1652) *Oedipus Aegyptiacus*. Rome.

Kirk, G. S. (1970) *Myth: its Meanings and Functions in Ancient and Other Cultures*. Berkeley and Cambridge: University of California Press.

Kistler, M. O. (1960) 'Dionysian elements in Wieland', *Germanic Review* 25.1: 83–92.

Klausner, J. (1976) 'The First Hasmonean rulers: Jonathan and Simeon', in A. Schalit, ed. *World History of the Jewish People: VI, The Hellenistic Age*. London: W. H. Allen, pp. 183–210.

Knight, S. (1984) *The Brotherhood: The Secret World of the Freemasons*. London, New York: Granada.

Knoop, D. and Jones, G. P. (1948) *The Genesis of Freemasonry: An Account of the Rise and Development of Freemasonry in its Operative, Accepted and Early Speculative Phases*. University of Manchester Publications.

Knowles, J. (1831) *The Life and Writings of Henry Fuseli, Esq. M.A., R.A.* London.

Knox, R. (1862) *The Races of Men: A Philosophical Inquiry into the Influence of Race over the Destinies of Nations*. London, 2nd edn.

Kretschmer, P. (1924) 'Das nt-suffix', *Glotta* 13: 84–106.

Kroll, J. (1923) 'Kulturhistorisches aus astrologischen Texten', *Klio* 18: 213–25.

Kropotkin, P. (1899) *Memoirs of a Revolutionist*. New York and Boston: Houghton Mifflin.

Kuhn, T. (1970) *The Structure of Scientific Revolutions*, 2nd edn. Chicago University Press.

Kunzl, A. (1976) *Der Gegensatz Rom-Kartago im Spiegel historisch-politischer Äusserungen der Zeit um den Ersten Weltkrieg*. Erlangen, thesis.

Lafont, R., Labal, P., Duvernoy, J., Roquebert Martel, P. and Pech, R. (1982) *Les Cathares en Occitanie*. Paris: Fayard.

La Marche, V. C. and Hirschbeck, K. K. (1984) 'Frost rings in trees as records of major volcanic eruptions', *Nature* 307, 12 Jan. pp. 121–6.

Lambert, R. (1984) *Beloved and God: the Story of Hadrian and Antinous*. New York: Viking.

Lane-Fox, R. (1980) *The Search for Alexander*. Boston and Toronto.

Langham, I. (1981) *The Building of British Social Anthropology: W. H. R. Rivers and his Cambridge Disciples in the Development of Kinship Studies, 1898–1931*. Dordrecht, Boston and London: J. D. Reidel.

Laroche, E. (1977?) 'Toponymes et frontières linguistiques en Asie Mineure', in *La Toponymie Antique: Actes du Colloque de Strasbourg, 12–14 juin 1975*. Leiden: Brill, pp. 205–13.

Lattimore, R. (1939) 'Herodotus and the names of the Egyptian gods', *Classical Philology* 34: 357–65.

Lauer, J. F. (1948) *Le Problème des Pyramides d'Égypte*. Paris: Payot.

—— (1960) *Observations sur les pyramides*. Cairo: Institut Français d'Archéologie Orientale.

Leach, E. (1966) 'The legitimacy of Solomon, some structural aspects of Old Testament history', *European Journal of Sociology* 7: 58–101.

—— (1986) *Aryan Invasions over Four Millennia*, Wenner-Gren Symposium no. 100, 'Symbolism Through Time'. Fez: 12–21 Jan.

Leclant, J. (1972) *Inventaire Bibliographique des Isiaca: Répertoire analytique des travaux relatifs à la diffusion des cultes isiaques, A–D*. Leiden: Brill.

—— (1974) *E–K*.

—— (1982) 'Champollion et le Collège de France', *Bulletin de la Société Française d'Égyptologie* 95: 32–46.

Lee, H. D. P. (1955) *Plato: The Republic*. London: Penguin.

Le Fèvre, T. (1664) *Les Poètes grecs*. Saumur.

Lehmann, W. P. (1973) *Historical Linguistics: an Introduction*. New York: Holt, Reinhart & Winston.

Levi, P. (1971) *Pausanias' Guide to Greece*, 2 vols. London: Penguin.

Levin, H. (1931) *The Broken Column; a Study in Romantic Hellenism*. Cambridge, Mass.: Harvard University Press.

Levin, S. (1968) 'Indo-European penetration of the civilized Aegean world as seen in the "Horse" tablet of Knossos (Ca895)', *Attie memorie del 1° congresso internazionale di micinilogia. Roma, 27 Settembre–3 Ottobre 1967*, pp. 1179–85.

—— (1971a) *The Indo-European and Semitic Languages*. Albany: State University of New York Press.

—— (1971b) 'The etymology of νέκταρ exotic scents in early Greece', *Studi Micenei ed Egeo-Anatolici* 13: 31–50.

—— (1973) 'The accentual system of Hebrew, in comparison with the ancient Indo-European languages', *Fifth World Congress of Jewish Studies*, 4: 71–7.

—— (1977) 'Something stolen : a Semitic participle and an Indo-European neuter substantive', in P. Hopper, ed., *Studies in Descriptive and Historical Linguistics: Festschrift for Winfred P. Lehmann*. Amsterdam: John Benjamin, pp. 317–39.

—— (1978) 'The perfumed goddess', *Bucknell Review* 24: 49–59.

—— (1979) 'Jocasta and Moses' mother Jochabed, Teiresias-Teipeσιασ, suppl. 2: 49–61.

—— (1984) 'Indo-European descriptive adjectives with 'Oxytone' accent and Semitic stative verbs', *General Linguistics* 24.2: 83–110.

Lewy, H. (1895) *Die semitischen Fremdwörter im Griechischen*. Berlin.

Lieblein, J. (1884) *Egyptian Religion*. Christiania and Leipzig.

Linforth, I. M. (1911–16) 'Epaphos and the Egyptian Apis', *University of California Publications in Classical Philology* 2: 81–92.

—— (1926) 'Greek gods and foreign gods in Herodotus', *University of California Publications in Classical Philology* 9.1: 1–25.

—— (1940) 'Greek and Egyptian gods (Herodotus II, 50, 52), *Classical Philology* 35: 300–1.

Lipinsky, E. (1978) 'Ditanu', *Studies in Bible and the Ancient Near East, Separatum*: 91–110.

Lloyd, A. B. (1976) *Herodotos Book II*, vol. II: *Commentary 1–98*. Leiden: Brill.

Lloyd-Jones, H. (1981) Foreword, in Trevelyan, *Goethe and the Greeks*, pp. i–xlvii.

—— (1982a) *Blood for the Ghosts: Classical Influences in the Nineteenth and Twentieth Centuries*. London: Duckworth.

—— (1982b) *Classical Survivals: The Classics in the Modern World*. London: Duckworth.

—— (1982c) 'Introduction to Wilamowitz-Moellendorf', *History of Classical Scholarship*: i–xxxii.

Lochner-Hüttenbach, F. (1960) *Die Pelasger*. Vienna.

Locke, J. (1688) *Essay Concerning Human Understanding*. London.

—— (1689) *The True End of Civil Government*. London.

Lockyer, J. N. (1893) *The Early Temple and Pyramid Builders*. Washington.

—— (1894) *The Dawn of Astronomy*. London.

Lohnes, W. F. W. and Strothmann, F. W. (1980) *German: a Structural Approach*, 3rd edn. New York: Norton.

Lorimer, H. L. (1950) *Homer and the Monuments*. London: Macmillan.

Lucretius, *De Rerum Natura*.

Lumpkin, B. (1984) 'Mathematics and engineering in the Nile Valley', *Journal of African Civilizations* 6.2: 102–19.

Macaulay, T. B. (1842) *Lays of Ancient Rome*. London.

—— (1866–71) *The Works of Lord Macaulay Edited by His Sister, Lady Trevelyan*, 8 vols. London.

McCarter, K. (1975) *The Antiquity of the Greek Alphabet and the Early Phoenician Scripts*. Missoula, Montana: Scholars Press for Harvard Semitic Museum.

MacDougall, H. A. (1982) *Racial Myth in English History*. Montreal, Hanover Vt. and London: Harvest House, University Press of New England .

Macqueen, J. G. (1975) *The Hittites and Their Contemporaries in Asia Minor*. London: Thames & Hudson.

McGready, A. G. (1969) 'Egyptian words in the Greek vocabulary', *Glotta* 44: 247–54.

McGuire, J. E. (1977) 'Neoplatonism and Active Principles: Newton and the Corpus Hermeticum', in Westman and McGuire, pp. 95–142.

McGuire, J. E. and Rattansi, P. M. (1966) 'Newton and the pipes of Pan', *Notes and Records of the Royal Society* 21: 108–43.

Madelin, L. (1937) *Histoire du consulat et de l'empire*, 8 vols. Paris: Hachette, vol. 2, *L'ascension de Bonaparte*.

Malingrey, A. M. (1961) *Philosophy: Étude d'un groupe de mots dans la littérature grecque des Présocratiques au IVᵉ s. ap. J.-C.* Paris: Klincksieck.

Mallet, D. (1888) *Le Culte de Neïth à Saïs*. Paris.

Manuel, F. E. (1956) *The New World of Henri Saint Simon*. Cambridge, Mass.: Harvard University Press.

—— (1959) *The Eighteenth Century Confronts the Gods*. Cambridge, Mass.: Harvard University Press.

—— (1963) *Isaac Newton, Historian*. Cambridge, Mass.: Harvard University Press.

—— (1974) *The Religion of Isaac Newton*. Oxford: Clarendon.

—— (1983) *The Changing of the Gods*. Hanover Vt. and London.

Marichal, R. (1982) 'Champollion et l'Académie', *Bulletin de la Société Française d'Égyptologie* 95: 12–31.

Marin, L. (1981) *Le Portrait du Roi*. Paris: Minuit.

Marino, L. (1975) *I maestri della Germania, Göttingen 1770–1820*. Turin: Einaudi.

Marsh, (1885) 'Review of *A History of Art in Phoenicia and its Dependencies*, by G. Perrot and C. Chipiez', *American Journal of Archaeology* 1: 190–5.

Marx, K. (1939) *Grundrisse der Kritik der politischen Ökonomie, Verlag für fremdsprachige Literatur*. Moscow and Berlin. trans. Martin Nicolaus (1973) as *Karl Marx, Grundrisse*. New York: Vintage Books.

—— (1983) *Das Kapital: Kritik der politischen Ökonomie, erster Band, Hamburg 1867 Text*. Ser. 2, vol. 5, in *Karl Marx – Friedrich Engels, Gesamtausgabe (MEGA)* 1975–1983. Berlin: Dietz Verlag.

Masica, C. P. (1978) *Defining a Linguistic Area: South Asia*. Chicago University Press.

Maspero, G. (1893) *Études de mythologie et d'archéologie égyptiennes*. Paris.

Masson, E. (1967) *Recherches sur les plus anciens emprunts sémitiques en grec*. Paris: Klincksieck.

Matz, F. (1973) 'The zenith of Minoan civilization', *The Cambridge Ancient History*, 3rd edn, vol. 2, pt 1, *The Middle East and the Aegean c. 1800–1380 BC*, pp. 557–81.

Maverick, L. (1946) *China a Model for Europe*. San Antonio: Paul Anderson.

Maximus of Tyre (1910) ed. H. Hobein. Leipzig: Teubner.

Mayer, M. L. (1964) 'Note etimologiche III', *Acme* 17: 223–9.

—— (1967) 'Note etimologiche IV', *Acme* 20: 287–91.

Mayes, S. (1959) *The Great Belzoni*. London: Putnam.

Mazar, B. (1971) *World History of the Jewish People*, vol. 3. London: W. H. Allen.

Meiners, C. (1781–2) *Geschichte des Ursprungs, Fortgangs und Verfalls der Wissenschaft in Griechenland und Rom*. Lemgo.

—— (1811–15) *Untersuchungen über die Verscheidenheiten der Menschenrassen*, 3 vols. Tübingen.

Mellink, M. J. (1967) Review of *Interconnections in the Bronze Age* by W. S. Smith. *American Journal of Archaeology* 71: 92–4.

Merkelbach, R. and West, M. L. (1967) *Fragmenta Hesiodea*. Oxford: Clarendon.

Meyer, E. (1892) *Forschungen zur alten Geschichte*, 2 vols. Halle.

—— (1921) *Ursprung und Anfange des Christentums, II. Die Entwicklung des Judentums und Jesus von Nazaret*. Stuttgart and Berlin: Cotta.

—— (1928–36) *Geschichte des Altertums*, 4 vols. Stuttgart and Berlin: Cotta.

Meyer, G. (1892) 'Von wem stammt die Bezeichnung Indogermanen?', *Indogermanische Forschungen* 2: 125–30.

Michael, H. N. and Weinstein, G. A. (1977) 'New radio carbon dates from Akrotiri', *Thera. Temple University Aegean Symposium* 2: 27–30.

Michelet, J. (1831) *Histoire Romaine*, 2 vols. Paris.

—— (1962) (1831) *Introduction à l'histoire universelle*. Paris: A. Colin.

Millard, A. R. (1976) 'The Canaanite linear alphabet and its passage to the Greeks', *Kadmos* 15: 130–44.

Millard, A. R. and Bordreuil, P. (1982) 'A statue from Syria with Assyrian and Aramaic inscriptions', *Biblical Archaeologist* 45.3: 135–41. See also under Abou-Assaf.

Mitford, W. (1784–1804) *The History of Greece*, 8 vols. London.

Momigliano, A. (1946) 'Friedrich Creuzer and Greek historiography', *Journal of the Warburg and Courtauld Institute* 9: 152–63.

—— (1957) 'Perizonus, Niebuhr and the character of the early Roman tradition', *Journal of Roman Studies* 47: 104–14, repr. in his *Essays on Ancient and Modern Historiography* (1977). Oxford, pp. 231–51.

—— (1966a) 'Giulio Beloch', in *Dizionario Biografico degli Italiani*, vol. 8, pp. 32–45, repr. in *Terzo Contributo alla storia degli studi classici e del mondo antico*, 1966. Rome, pp. 239–65.

—— (1966b) 'George Grote and the study of Greek history', *Studies in Historiography* (1966) London, pp. 56–74.

—— (1966c) 'Vico's scienza nuova: Roman "Bestioni" and Roman "Eroi"', *History and Theory* 5: 3–23, repr. in *Essays on Ancient and Modern Historiography* (1977), pp. 253–76.

—— (1966d) 'Ancient history and the antiquarian', *Studies in Historiography*, pp. 6–9.

—— (1968) *Prime linee di storia della tradizione Maccabaica*. Amsterdam: Hakkert.

—— (1975) *Alien Wisdom: The Limits of Hellenization*. Cambridge University Press.

—— (1980) 'Alle origini dell'interesse su Roma arcaica, Niebuhr e l'India', *Rivista Storica Italiana* 92: 561–71.

—— (1982) "New paths of Classicism in the nineteenth century', *History and Theory Beiheft* 21.

Monro, D. B. (1911) 'Wolf, Friedrich August', *Encyclopaedia Britannica*, 11th edn, vol. 28, pp. 770–1.

Montesquieu, C. de (1721) *Lettres Persanes*. Paris.

—— (1748) *L'esprit des lois*. Paris.

Moorehead, A. (1962) *The Blue Nile*. New York: Harper & Row.

More, H. (1931) *Philosophical Poems of Henry More*. G. Bullough, ed. Manchester University Press.

Morenz, S. (1969) *Die Begegnung Europas mit Ägypten*. Zürich and Stuttgart: Artemis.

—— (1973) *Egyptian Religion*, A. E. Keep, trans. London: Methuen.

Moscati, S. (1968) *Fenici e cartaginesi in Sardegna*. Milan: A. Mondadori.

Moscati, S., Spitaler, A., Ullendorf, E., and von Soden, W. (1969) *An Introduction to the Comparative Grammar of the Semitic Languages: Phonology and Morphology*. Wiesbaden: Harrasowitz.

Mosse, G. (1964) *The Crisis of German Ideology: Intellectual Origins of the Third Reich*. New York: Grosse & Dunlap.

Mosshammer, A. A. (1979) *The Chronicle of Eusebius and the Greek Chronographic Tradition*. Lewisburg: Bucknell University Press.

Movers, F. C. (1841–50) *Die Phönizier*, 2 vols, 4 books. Bonn and Berlin.

Muhly, J. D. (1965) Review of *Hellenosemitica*, by M. C. Astour. *Journal of the American Oriental Society* 85: 585–8.

—— (1970a) Review of *Interconnections in the Ancient Near East*, by W. S. Smith. *Journal of the American Oriental Society* 90: 305–9.

—— (1970b) 'Homer and the Phoenicians: The relations between Greece and the Near East in the Late Bronze Age and Early Iron Ages', *Berytus* 19: 19–64.

—— (1973) 'The Philistines and their pottery', paper presented to the *Third International Colloquium on Aegean Prehistory*. Sheffield.

—— (1979) 'On the Shaft Graves at Mycenae', *Studies in Honor of Tom B. Jones*, M. A. Powell and R. M. Sack, eds. Neukirchen-vlugn: Butzon & Bercker kevelaer, pp. 311–23.

—— (1984) 'The role of the Sea Peoples in Cyprus during the L.C. III period,' in *Cyprus at the Close of the Late Bronze Age*, V. Karageorgis, ed. Nicosia: G. Leventis Foundation, pp. 39–56.

—— (1985) 'Phoenicia and the Phoenicians', *Biblical Archaeology Today: Proceedings of the International Congress on Biblical Archaeology, Jerusalem, April 1984*, A. Biran *et al.*, eds Jerusalem: Israel Exploration Society, Israel Academy of Sciences and Humanities American Schools of Oriental Research, pp. 177–91.

Müller, C. (1841–70) *Fragmenta Historicorum Graecorum*. Paris.

Müller, K. O. (1820–4) *Geschichte hellenischer Stämme und Städte*, 3 vols. Breslau. Vol. 1, *Orchomenos und die Minyer*, vols II and III, *Die Dorier*; vols 2 and 3 trans. H. Tufnell and G. C. Lewis as *The History and Antiquities of the Doric Race* (1830) 2 vols. London.

—— (1825) *Prolegomena zu einer wissenschaftlichen Mythologie*. Göttingen. trans. J. Leitch as *Introduction to a Scientific System of Mythology* (1844) London.

—— (1834) 'Orion', *Rheinisches Museum* 2: 1–30.

—— (1858) *A History of the Literature of Ancient Greece, Continued by J. W. Donaldson*, 3 vols. London.

Murray, G. (1951) *Five Stages of Greek Religion*. Oxford: Clarendon.

Murray, M. (1931) *Egyptian Temples*. Marston, London: Sampson Low.

—— (1949) *The Splendour that was Egypt*. London: Sidgwick & Jackson.

Murray, O. (1980) *Early Greece*. Brighton: Harvester/Atlantic Highlands, NJ: Humanities.

Musgrave, S. (1782) *Two Dissertations: 1) On the Grecian Mythology: 2) An Examination of Sir Isaac Newton's Objections to the Chronology of the Olympiads*. London.

Myres, J. L. (1924) 'Primitive man in geological time', *Cambridge Ancient History*, 1st edn, vol. 1, pp. 1–97.

Naveh, J. (1973) 'Some Semitic epigraphical considerations on the antiquity of the Greek alphabet', *American Journal of Archaeology*: 1–8.

—— (1982) *Early History of the Alphabet: An Introduction to West Semitic Epigraphy and Paleography*. Jerusalem: Magnes/Leiden: Brill.

Needham, J. and Lu, G. D. (1985) *Transpacific Echoes and Resonances: Listening Once Again*. Singapore: World Scientific.

Needham, J. T. (1761) *De Inscriptione quadam Ægyptiaca Taurini inventa et Characteribus Ægyptiis olim et Sinis communibus exarata idolo cuidam antiquo in regia universitate servato ad utrasque Academias Londonensem et Parisiensem Rerum antiquarum, investigationi et studio præpositas data Epistola*. Rome.

Neiman, D. (1965) 'Phoenician place names', *Journal of Near Eastern Studies* 24: 113–15.

Neschke-Hetschke, A. B. (1984) 'Discussion', in Bollack and Wismann, pp. 483–4.

Nettl, P. (1957) *Mozart and Masonry*. New York: Philosophical Library.

Neugebauer, O. (1945) *Mathematical Cuneiform Texts*. New Haven: American Oriental Society and the American Schools of Oriental Research.

—— (1950) 'The alleged Babylonian discovery of the precession of the equinoxes', *Journal of the American Oriental Society* 70: 1–8.

—— (1957) *The Exact Sciences in Antiquity*. Providence.

Neugebauer, O. and Parker, R. A. (1960–9) *Egyptian Astronomical Texts*, 4 vols. Providence and London: Brown University Press. See also Swerdlow.

Neusner, J. (1965–70) *A History of the Jews in Babylonia*, 5 vols. Leiden: Brill.

Newton, I. *A Dissertation upon the Sacred Cubit of the Jews and the Cubits of several Nations: in which from the dimensions of the Greatest Pyramid as taken by Mr. John Greaves, the ancient Cubit of Memphis is determined.*

—— *Principia Mathematica.*

—— *The Origins of Gentile Theology.*

Niebuhr, B. (1828–31, enl. edn) *Romische Geschichte*, 2 vols. Berlin.

—— (1847) *Vorträge über alte Geschichte an der Universität zu Bonn gehalten*, 3 vols. Berlin. trans. L. Schmitz as *Lectures on Ancient History from the Earliest Times to the Taking of Alexandria by Octavius* (1852) 3 vols. Philadelphia.

—— (1847–51) *The History of Rome*, J. C. Hare and C. Thirwall, trans. 4th edn, 3 vols. London.

Nilsson, M. P. (1932) *The Mycenaean Origin of Greek Mythology*. Berkeley: University of California Press.

—— (1950) *The Minoan Mycenaean Religion*. 2nd rev. edn. Lund. C. W. K. Gleerup.

Nissen, W. (1962) *Göttinger Gedenktafeln: Ein biographischer Wegweiser*. Göttingen: Vandenhoek & Ruprecht.

—— (1975) 'Ergänzungen', *Göttinger Gedenktafeln: Ein biographischer Wegweiser*. Göttingen.

Noguera, A. (1976) *How African was Egypt: A Comparative Study of Egyptian and Black African Cultures*. New York: Vantage Press.

Nonnos, (1940) *Dionysiaca*, 3 vols, trans. W. H. D. Rouse, notes by H. J. Rose and L. R. Lind (Loeb). Cambridge, Mass.

Oren, D. A. (1985) *Joining the Club: A History of Jews at Yale*. New Haven: Yale University Press.

Otto, E. (1975) 'Ägypten im Selbstbewußtsein des Ägypters', in Helck and Otto, cols 76–8.

Paaw, C. de (1773) *Recherches philosophiques sur les Égyptiens et les Chinois*. Berlin.

Pagels, E. (1979) *The Gnostic Gospels*. New York: Random House.

Pallotino, M. (1978) *The Etruscans*, rev. and enl. edn, trans. J. Cremona, ed. D. Ridgeway. London: Penguin.

—— (1984) *Storia della Prima Italia*. Milan: Rusconi.

Pang, K. D. and Chou, H. H. 'Three very large volcanic eruptions in Antiquity and their effects on the climate of the Ancient World', paper abstract in *Eos* 66.46. 12 Nov. 1985: 816.

Pappademos, J. (1984) 'The Newtonian synthesis in physical science and its roots in the Nile Valley', *Journal of African Civilizations* 6.2: 84–101.

Pappe, H. O. (1979) 'The English Utilitarians and Athenian democracy', in Bolgar, *Classical Influences . . .* , pp. 297–302.

Parke, H. W. (1967) *The Oracles of Zeus: Dōdōna, Olympia and Ammon*. Oxford: Blackwell.

Parker, R. A. and Neugebauer, O. (1960–4) *Egyptian Astronomical Texts*, 4 vols. London: Lund Humphries for Brown University Press.

Parmentier, L. (1913) *Recherches sur le traité d'Isis et d'Osiris de Plutarque*. Brussels: Académie Royale de Belgique.

Parry, M. (1971) *The Making of Homeric Verse: The Collected Papers of Milman Parry*. Oxford: Clarendon.

Patrides, C. A. (1969) *The Cambridge Platonists*. Cambridge University Press.

Paulys Real-Encyclopädie der classischen Altertumswissenschaft, ed. G. Wissama *et al.* (1894–). Stuttgart, München.

Pausanias, *Guide to Greece*, see Frazer and Levi.

Pedersen, H. (1959) *The Discovery of Language: Linguistic Science in the Nineteenth Century*, J. W. Spargo, trans. Bloomington: Indiana University Press.

Pendlebury, J. D. S. (1930a) *Aegyptiaca*. Cambridge University Press.

—— (1930b) 'Egypt and the Aegean in the Late Bronze Age', *Journal of Egyptian Archaeology* 16: 75–92.

Petit-Radel, F. (1815) 'Sur l'origine grecque du fondateur d'Argos', *Mémoires de l'Institut Royal de France, Classe d'Histoire et de Littérature Ancienne* 2: 1–43.

Petrie, W. M. F. (1883) *The Pyramids and Temples of Gizeh*. London.

—— (1893) *The Great Pyramid*. London.

—— (1894–1905) *A History of Egypt*, 3 vols. London.

—— (1908) 'Historical references in Hermetic writings', in *Transactions of the Third International Congress of the History of Religions*, Oxford 1: 196–225.

—— (1909) *Personal Religion in Egypt before Christianity*. New York: Harpers Library of Living Thought.

—— (1931) *70 Years of Archaeology*. London: Sampson Low.

Pettinato, G. (1978) 'L'Atlante Geografico nel Vicino Oriente antico Attestate ad Ebla ed ad Abu Salabikh', *Orientalia* 46: 50–73.

—— (1979) *Ebla: un impero inciso nell'argilla*. Milan: Mondadori, trans. (1981) as *The Archives of Ebla: An Empire Inscribed in Clay, with an Afterword by Mitchell Dahood S. J.* Garden City: Doubleday.

Pfeiffer, R. (1976) *History of Classical Scholarship: From 1300–1850*. Oxford: Clarendon.

Pharr, C. (1959) *Homeric Greek: A Handbook for Beginners*, 2nd edn. Norman, Okla.: University of Oklahoma Press.

Picard, C. (1937) 'Homère et les religions de l'Égypte', *Revue archéologique* 6ᵐᵉ Série, 10: 110–13.

—— (1948) *Les Religions Préhelleniques*. Paris: Presses Universitaires de France.

Pierce, R. H. (1971) 'Egyptian loan words in Ancient Greek?', *Symbolae Osloenses* 46: 96–107.

Pinot, V. (1932) *La Chine et l'esprit philosophique en Europe 1640–1740*. Paris: Geuthner.

Plato, (1914–192?) 12 vols, H. N. Fowler, trans. *Kratylos*.

—— *Kritias*.

—— *Menexenos*.

—— *Republic*.

—— *Timaios*, see Lee, 1955.

Platon, N. and Stassinopouloutouloupa, E. (1964) 'Oriental seals from the Palace of Cadmus: unique discoveries in Boeotian Thebes', *Illustrated London News*, 28 November: 859–61.

Plutarch, *De Iside et Osiride*, trans. F. C. Babbit (1934–5) in *Plutarch's Moralia*, 16 vols (Loeb). Cambridge, Mass.: Harvard University Press/London: Heinemann, vol. 5, pp. 7–191.

—— *De Herodoti Malignitate*, trans. L. Pearson and F. H. Sandbach in *Plutarch's Moralia*, vol. 11, pp. 9–133.

Pocock, J. G. A. (1985) 'Gibbon as an Anglican manqué: clerical culture and the *Decline and Fall*', Miriam Leranbaum Memorial Lecture, SUNY, Binghamton, 17 April.

Poliakov, L. (1974) *The Aryan Myth: A History of Racist and Nationalist Ideas in Europe*, E. Howard, trans. London: Chatto & Windus and Heinemann for Sussex University Press.

Polomé, E. C. (1981) 'Can graphemic change cause phonemic change?', in Arbeitman and Bomhard, pp. 881–8.

Pope, M. (1973) *Job: A New Translation with Introduction and Commentary*, 3rd edn. Garden City, NY: Anchor.

—— (1980) 'The cult of the dead at Ugarit', in G. Young, ed. *Ugarit in Retrospect: 50 Years of Ugarit and Ugaritic*. Winona Lake: Eisenbraun, pp. 170–5.

Popham, M. (1965) 'Some Late Minoan pottery from Crete', *Annual of the British School at Athens* 60: 316–42.

Popkin, R. H. (1974) 'The philosophical basis of modern racism', in C. Walton and J. P. Anton, eds *Philosophy and the Civilizing Arts*, pp. 126–65.

—— (1985) Introduction to Force, pp. xi–xix.

Popper, K. R. (1950) *The Open Society and its Enemies*, 2 vols. Princeton University Press.

Porada, E. (1965) 'Cylinder seals from Thebes: a preliminary report', *American Journal of Archaeology* 69: 173.

—— (1966) 'Further notes on the cylinders from Thebes', *American Journal of Archaeology* 70: 194.

—— (1981) 'The cylinder seals found at Thebes in Boiotia, with contributions on the inscriptions from Hans G. Güterbock and John A. Brinkman', *Archiv für Orientforschung* 28: 1–78.

Porphery, *Vita Plotini*.

Potter, J. (1697) *Archæologia Græca, or the Antiquities of Greece*, 4 vols. London.

Praetorius, G. F. (1902) 'Zur Geschichte des griechischen Alphabets', *Zeitschrift der Deutschen Morgenländischen Gesellschaft* 56: 676–80.

Pulleybank, E. G. (1955) *The Background of the Rebellion of An Lu-shan*. Cambridge University Press.

Pyle, K. B. (1969) *The New Generation in Meiji Japan: Problems of Cultural Identity 1885–1895*. Stanford University Press.

Rahman, A. (1982) *Science and Technology in Medieval India*. New Delhi: Vikas.

—— (1983) *Intellectual Colonization: Science and Technology in West–East Relations*. New Delhi: Vikas.

Rashed, R. (1980) 'Science as a Western phenomenon', *Fundamenta Scientiae* 1: 7–21.

Rattansi, P. M. (1963) 'Paracelsus and the Puritan revolution', *Ambix* 11: 24–32.

—— (1973) 'Some evaluations of reason in sixteenth- and seventeenth-century natural philosophy', in Teich and Young, pp. 148–66.

Rawlinson, G. (1869) *A Manual of Ancient History*. Oxford.

—— (1889) *History of Phoenicia*. London.

Rawson, E. (1969) *The Spartan Tradition in European Thought*. Oxford: Clarendon.

Ray, J. D. (1976) *The Archive of Hor*. London: Egypt Exploration Society.

Reghellini de Schio (1833) *La Maçonnerie considérée comme le résultat des religions égyptienne, juive et chrétienne*. Paris.

Reinach, S. (1892a) *L'Origine des Aryens: Histoire d'une Controverse*. Paris.

—— (1892b) 'Résumé of Tsountas', in *Revue Archéologique* 1: p. 93.

—— (1893) 'Le mirage oriental', *Anthropologie* 4: 539–78, 699–732.

Renan, E. (1855) *Histoire générale et système composée des langues sémitiques*. Paris.

—— (1858) *Études d'histoire religieuse*, 3rd edn. Paris.

—— (1868) 'Mémoire sur l'origine et caractère véritable de l'histoire phénicienne qui porte le nom de Sanchunation', *Mémoires de l'Académie des inscriptions et Belles-Lettres* 23: 241–334.

Rendsberg, G. (1982) 'A new look at Pentateuchal HW'', *Biblica* 63: 351–69.

Renfrew, C. (1972) *The Emergence of Civilization: The Cyclades and the Aegean in the Third Millennium BC.* London: Methuen.

—— (1973) 'Problems in the general correlation of archaeological and linguistic strata in prehistoric Greece: the model of autochthonous origin', in Crossland and Birchall, pp. 265–79.

Renouf, P. I. P. (1880) *Lectures on the Origin and Growth of Religion.* London.

Ridgeway, W. (1901) *The Early Age of Greece,* 2 vols. Cambridge University Press.

Robertson Smith, W. (1894) *The Religion of the Semites: The Fundamental Institutions.* Cambridge.

Röllig, V. W. and Mansfeld, G. (1970) 'Zwei Ostraka vom Tell Kāmid el Loz und ein neuer Aspekt für die Entstehung des kanaanäischen Alphabets', *Die Welt des Orients* 5. 2: 265–70.

Rosen, E. (1970) 'Was Copernicus a Hermeticist?', *Minnesota Studies in the Philosophy of Science* 5: 164–9.

—— (1983) 'Was Copernicus a Neoplatonist?', *Journal of the History of Ideas* 44.3: 667–9.

Rosen, G. (1929) *Juden und Phönizier.* Tübingen: Mohr.

Rosenthal, F. (1970) Review of *Recherches sur les plus anciens emprunts sémitiques en grec,* by E. Masson, in *Journal of the American Oriental Society* 90: 338–9.

Rothblatt, S. *The Revolution of the Dons: Cambridge and Society in Victorian England.* Cambridge University Press.

Rougé, E. de (1869) 'Conférence sur la religion des anciens Égyptiens', *Annales de philosophie chrétienne,* 5th ser. 328–30.

Russell, B. (1961) *History of Western Philosophy: and its Connections with Political and Social Circumstances from the Earliest Times to the Present Day,* new edn. London: Allen & Unwin.

Russell, F. W. E. (1895) *The Letters of Matthew Arnold,* 2 vols. New York.

Rytkönen, S. (1968) *B. G. Niebuhr als Politiker und Historiker.* Helsinki: Annales Academiae Scientiarum Fennicae, ser. B. vol. 156.

Sabry, M. (1930) *L'Empire Égyptien sous Mohamed-Ali et La Question d'Orient (1811–1849).* Paris: Geuthner.

Saggs, H. W. F. (1962) *The Greatness that was Babylon.* New York: Hawthorn Books.

Said, E. (1978) *Orientalism.* New York and London: Vintage.

St Clair, W. (1972) *That Greece Might Still be Free: The Philhellenes in the Greek War of Independence.* London: Oxford University Press.

—— (1983) *Lord Elgin and the Marbles.* 2nd rev. edn. Oxford University Press.

Saldit-Trappmann, R. (1970) *Tempel der ägyptischen Götter in Griechenland und an der Westküste Kleinasiens.* Leiden: Brill.

Sandars, N. K. (1978) *The Sea Peoples: Warriors of the Ancient Mediterranean 1250–1150 BC.* London: Thames & Hudson.

Sandmel, S. (1979) *Philo of Alexandria: An Introduction.* New York/Oxford: Oxford University Press.

Sandys, J. E. (1908) *A History of Classical Scholarship,* 3 vols. Cambridge University Press.

Santangelo, G. S. (1984) *Madame Dacier, una filologa nella 'Crisi' (1672–1720).* Rome: Bulzoni.

Santillana, G. de (1963) 'On forgotten sources in the history of science', in A. C. Crombie, ed. *Scientific Change: Historical Studies in the Intellectual, Social and Technical Conditions for Scientific Discovery and Technical Invention, from Antiquity to the Present.* London, pp. 813–28.

Santillana, G. de and von Dechend, H. (1969) *Hamlet's Mill: an Essay in Myth and the Frame of Time.* Boston: Gambit.

Sasson, J. M. (1966) 'Canaanite maritime involvement in the second millennium BC', *Journal of the American Oriental Society* 86: 126–38.

Sauneron, S. *et al.* (1970–) *Collection des voyageurs occidentaux en Égypte.* Cairo: Institut Français d'archéologie orientale.

Schiller, F. von (1967) *Über die ästhetische Erziehung des Menschen: in einer Reihe von Briefen (On the Aesthetic Education of Man: In a Series of Letters),* E. M. Wilkinson and L. A. Willoughby, trans. Oxford.

Schlegel, F. von (1808) *Über die Sprache und Weisheit der Indier.* Heidelberg. trans. as 'On the language and philosophy of the Indians' by E. J. Millington (1949) in *Aesthetic and Miscellaneous Works of Friedrich von Schlegel.* London.

—— (1939) *Cours d'histoire universelle (1805–1806).* J. J. Anstett, ed. Paris: Patissier.

Schleicher, A. (1865) *Über die Bedeutung der Sprache für die Naturgeschichte des Menschen.* Weimar: H. Böhlen.

Schlesier, G. (1838–40) *Schriften von Friedrich von Gentz,* 5 vols. Mannheim.

Scholem, G. G. (1960) *Jewish Gnosticism, Merkehbah Mysticism and the Talmudic Tradition.* New York: Jewish Theological Seminary of America.

—— (1965) *On the Kabbalah and its Symbolism,* R. Mannheim, trans. New York: Schocken.

—— (1970) *Kabbalah.* New York: Quadrangle.

—— (1974) *Major Trends in Jewish Mysticism.* New York: Schocken.

Schwab, R. (1950) *La Renaissance Orientale.* Paris: Bibliothèque Historique.

—— (1984) G. Patterson-Black and V. Reinking, trans. New York: Columbia University Press.

Schwaller de Lubicz, R. A. (1958) *Le Temple de l'homme: Apet du sud à Louqsor.* Paris: Caractères.

—— (1961) *Le Roi de la théocratie pharaonique.* Paris: 'Homo Sapiens'.

—— (1968) *Le Miracle égyptien.* Paris: Flammarion.

Scollon, R. and S. B. K. (1980) *Linguistic Convergence: An Ethnography of Speaking: At Fort Chipewyan, Alberta.* New York, San Francisco and London: New York Academic Press.

Scott, W. (1924–36) *Hermetica*, 4 vols. Oxford: Clarendon.

Seidel, S. (1962) *Der Briefwechsel zwischen Friedrich Schiller und Wilhelm von Humboldt*, 2 vols. Berlin: Aufban Verlag.

Selem, P. (1980) *Les Religions orientales dans la Pannonie Romaine: Partie en Yougoslavie*. Leiden: Brill.

Seltman, C. (1933) *Greek Coins: A History of Metallic Currency and Coinage Down to the Fall of the Hellenistic Kingdoms*. London: Methuen.

Seznec, J. (1953) *The Survival of the Pagan Gods: The Mythological Tradition and its Place in Renaissance Humanism and Art*, B. E. Sessions, trans. New York: Pantheon.

Shaffer, E. S. (1975) *Kublai Khan and the Fall of Jerusalem: The Mythological School of Biblical Criticism and Secular Literature 1770–1880*. Cambridge University Press.

Shelley, P. B. (1821) *Hellas*. London.

Sheppard, J. T. (1911) 'The first scene of the Suppliants of Aeschylus', *Classical Quarterly* 5: 220–9.

Siegert, H. (1941–2) 'Zur Geschichte der Begriffe "Arische" und "arich"', *Wörter und Sachen* 4: 73–99.

Simonsuuri, K. (1979) *Homer's Original Genius: Eighteenth Century Notions of the Early Greek Epic (1688–1798)*. Cambridge University Press.

Smelik, K. A. D. and Hemelrijk, E. A. (1984) '"Who knows not what monsters demented Egypt worships?" Opinions on Egyptian animal worship in Antiquity as part of the ancient conception of Egypt', in H. Temporini and W. Haase, eds *Aufstieg und Niedergang der römischen Welt: Geschichte und Kultur Roms im Spiegel der neueren Forschung*. 17.4, *Religion: (Heidentum: römische Götterkulte, orientalische Kulte in der römischen Welt [Forts.])*, ed. W. Haase, pp. 1852–2000.

Smith, W. (1848) *A Classical Dictionary of Greek and Roman Biography, Mythology and Geography*. London.

—— (1854) *A History of Greece: From the Earliest Times to the Roman Conquest*. New York.

Smyth, C. P. (1864) *Our Inheritance in the Great Pyramid*. London.

—— (1867) *Life and Work at the Great Pyramid*. Edinburgh.

—— (1874) *The Great Pyramid & the Royal Society*. London.

Snodgrass, A. (1971) *The Dark Age of Greece: An Archaeological Survey of the Eleventh to the Eighth centuries BC*. Edinburgh University Press.

Snowden, F. M. S. (1970) *Blacks in Antiquity: Ethiopians in the Greco-Roman Experience*. Cambridge, Mass.: Harvard University Press.

Sourvinou-Inwood, C. (1973) 'The problem of the Dorians in tradition and archaeology', paper presented to *the Third International Colloquium on Aegean Prehistory*, Sheffield.

Speer, A. (1970) *Inside the Third Reich*, R. and C. Winston, trans. London: Weidenfeld & Nicolson.

Spiegel, S. (1967) *The Last Trial: On the Legends and Lore of the Command to Abraham to Offer Isaac as a Sacrifice: The Akedah*, J. Goldin, trans. New York: Pantheon.

Spyropoulos, T. (1972) 'Αἰγυπτιακὸς 'Εποικισμὸς ἐν Βοιωτίαι', *'Αρχαιολογικὰ 'Ανάλεκτα ἐξ 'Αθηνῶν* 5: 16–27.

—— (1973) 'Εἰσαγωγὴ εἰς τὴν Μελέτην τοῦ Κωπαϊκοῦ Χώρου', *Αρχαιολογικὰ 'Ανάλεκτα ἐξ 'Αθηνῶν* 6: 201–14.

Starkie, E. (1971) *Flaubert the Master: A Critical and Biographical Study (1856–1880)*. New York: Atheneum.

Stecchini, (1957) 'The Delphian column of the dancers', *American Journal of Archaeology* 61: 187, note.

—— (1961) 'A history of measures', *American Behavioral Scientist* 4.7: 18–21.

—— (1978) 'Notes on the relation of ancient measures to the Great Pyramid', in Tompkins, *The Secrets of the Great Pyramid*, pp. 287–382.

Steel-Maret (1893) 'La Franc-Maçonnerie: ses origines, ses mystères et son but', in *Archives Secrètes de la Franc-Maçonnerie*. Lyon.

Steinberg, R. (1981) *Modern Shadows on Ancient Greece: Aegean-Levantine Connections in the Late Bronze Age*. Cornell University, MA thesis.

Stella, L. A. (1951–2) 'Chi furono i Populi del Mare', *Rivista di antropologia* 39: 3–17.

Stern, B. H. (1940) *The Rise of Romantic Hellenism in English Literature, 1732–1786*. Menasha, Wisconsin: G. Banta.

Stern, F. R. (1961) *The Politics of Cultural Despair; a Study in the rise of the Germanic ideology*. Berkeley: University of California Press.

Stern, M. (1974) *Greek and Latin Authors on Jews and Judaism*, vol. I, *From Herodotus to Plutarch*. Jerusalem: Israel Academy of Humanities and Sciences.

Stewart, J. G. (1959) *Jane Ellen Harrison: A Portrait from Letters*. London: Merlin.

Stieglitz, R. R. (1981) 'The letters of Kadmos: mythology, archaeology and eteocretan', ανντψπο απο τον α' (2) τομο των πεπραγμενων τον δ' διέθνονσ κρητολογικὸν σννεδριὸν ('Ηράκλειο, 29, Αὐγούστου-3 Σεπτεμβρίου 1976). Athens.

Stobart, J. C. (1911) *The Glory that was Greece*. Philadelphia: Lippincott.

Strabo (1929) *The Geography*, H. L. Jones, trans. 8 vols. Cambridge, Mass.: Loeb.

Strange, J. (1973) 'Biblical material on the origin of the Philistines', paper presented to the *Third International Colloquium on Aegean Prehistory*, Sheffield.

Strauss, B. S. (forthcoming) *Politics and Society in Athens After the Peloponnesian War, 403–386 BC*. Ithaca: Cornell University Press.

Stricker, B. H. (1949) 'The Corpus Hermeticum', *Mnemosyne*, Series 4, vol. 2: 79–80.

Stuart-Jones, H. (1968) Preface, *Greek–English Lexicon: Liddell and Scott*. Oxford, pp. i–xii.

Stubbings, F. H. (1973) 'The rise of Mycenaean civilization', *The Cambridge Ancient History*, 3rd edn, vol. 2, pt 1, *The Middle East and the Aegean 1800–1380 BC*, pp. 627–58.

—— (1975) 'The expansion of Mycenaean civilization', *The Cambridge Ancient History*,

3rd edn, vol. 2, pt 11, *The Middle East and the Aegean Region c.1380–1000 BC*, pp. 165–87.

Sturtevant, E. H. (1942) *Indo-Hittite Laryngeals*. Baltimore: Linguistic Society of America.

Sweet, P. R. (1978–80) *Wilhelm von Humboldt: A Biography*, 2 vols. Columbus: Ohio State University Press.

Swerdlow, N. M. and Neugebauer, O. (1984) *Mathematical Astronomy in Copernicus's De Revolutionibus*, 2 pts. New York/Berlin: Springer.

Sydow, A. von (1906–16) *Wilhelm und Caroline in ihren Briefe*, 7 vols. Berlin: Mittler und Sohn.

Symeonoglou, S. (1985) *The Topography of Thebes: From the Bronze Age to Modern Times*. Princeton University Press.

Szemerenyi, O. (1964) 'Structuralism and substratum: Indo-Europeans and Aryans in the Ancient Near East', *Lingua* 13: 1–29.

—— (1966) 'Iranica II', *Die Sprache* 12: 190–205.

—— (1974) 'The origins of the Greek lexicon: *Ex Oriente Lux*', *Journal of Hellenic Studies* 94: 144–57.

Sznycer, M. (1979) 'L'inscription phénicienne de Tekké près de Cnossos', *Kadmos* 18: 89–93.

Tatian, see Dods and Smith.

Taylor, A. E. (1929) *Plato: The Man and His Work*, 3rd edn. London: Methuen.

Taylor, T. (1821) *Iamblichus on the Mysteries of the Egyptians, Chaldaeans and Assyrians*. Walworth.

Taylour, W. (1964) *The Mycaeneans*. London: Thames & Hudson.

Tcherikover, V. (1959) *Hellenistic Civilization and the Jews*, S. Applebaum, trans. Philadelphia.

—— (1976) *Hellenistic Palestine in the Hellenistic Age: Political History of Jewish Palestine from 332 BCE to 67 BCE*, ed. A. Schalit, vol. 6 in *The World History of the Jewish People*. London: W. H. Allen.

Teich, M. and Young, R. (1973) *Changing Perspectives in the History of Science: Essays in Honour of Joseph Needham*. London: Heinemann.

Terrasson, J. (1715) *Dissertation critique sur l'Iliad d'Homère, où à l'occasion de ce poème, on cherche les règles d'une poétique fondée sur la raison et sur les exemples des anciens et des modernes*, 2 vols. Paris.

—— (1731) *Sèthos, histoire ou vie tirée des monuments de l'ancienne Égypte*. Paris.

Teters, B. (1962) 'The Genro In and the National Essence Movement', *Pacific Historical Review* 31: 359–71.

Thapar, R. (1975) *The Past and Prejudice*. New Delhi: National Book Trust.

—— (1977) 'Ideology and the interpretation of early Indian history', in *Society and Change: Essays in Honour of Sachin Chaudhuri*. New Delhi, pp. 1–19.

Thirlwall, C. (1835–44) *A History of Greece*, 8 vols. London.

Thirlwall, J. C. Jr (1936) *Connop Thirlwall, Historian and Theologian*. London: Society for the Promotion of Christian Knowledge.

Thissen, H.-J. (1980) 'Manetho', in Helck and Otto, *Lexikon*, vol. III, cols 1179–81.

Thomson, G. (1941) *Aeschylus and Athens – A Study in the Social Origin of Drama*. London: Lawrence & Wishart.

—— (1949) *Studies in Ancient Greek Society 1: The Prehistoric Aegean*. London: Lawrence & Wishart.

Thomson, K. (1977) *The Masonic Thread in Mozart*. London: Lawrence & Wishart.

Thucydides, (1954) *The Peloponnesian War*, R. Warner, trans. London: Penguin.

—— (1980) *Histories*, C. F. Smith, trans. (Loeb). London: Heinemann/Cambridge, Mass.: Harvard University Press.

Tieck, L. (1930) *Ludwig Tieck und die Brüder Schlegel, Briefe mit Einleitung und Anmerkungen*, H. Lüdete, ed., Frankfurt a. M.: Baer.

Tiedemann, P. (1780) *Griechenlands erste Philosophen oder Leben und System des Orpheus, Pherekydes, Thales und Pythagoras*. Leipzig.

—— (1793) *Geist der spekulativen Philosophie*. Marburg.

Timpanaro, S. (1977) Introduction to Schlegel, *Über die Sprache und Weisheit der Indier*. Amsterdam.

Tocqueville, A. de (1837) *De la Démocratie en Amérique*, 3 vols. Brussels.

—— (1877) *L'ancien régime et la révolution*, 8th edn. Paris; trans. S. Gilbert (1955) as *The Old Regime and the French Revolution*. New York.

Tompkins, P. (1978) *The Secrets of the Great Pyramid*. London: Penguin.

Trevelyan, H. (1981) *Goethe and the Greeks*, 2nd edn. Cambridge University Press.

Trevor-Roper, H. (1969) *The Romantic Movement and the Study of History* (John Coffin Memorial Lecture). London: Athlone.

—— (1983) 'The Highland tradition of Scotland', in Hobsbawm and Ranger, *The Invention of Tradition*. Cambridge University Press, pp. 15–41.

Tsountas, C. and Manatt, J. (1897) *The Mycenaean Age*. Boston.

Turgot, A. (1808–15) *Oeuvres de M. Turgot Ministre d'État, Précédées et accompagnées de Mémoires et de Notes sur sa Vie, son Administration et ses Ouvrages*, 9 vols. Paris.

Turner, F. M. (1981) *The Greek Heritage in Victorian Britain*. New Haven: Yale University Press.

Turner, R. S. (1983a) 'Historicism, *Kritik*, and the Prussian professoriate', in Bollack and Wismann, pp. 450–78.

—— (1983b) 'Discussion', in Bollack and Wismann, p. 486.

—— (1985) 'Classical philology in Germany: toward a history of the discipline', Paper presented to *The Fabrication of Ancient Greece 1780–1880*, Conference held at Cornell 22–23 April 1985.

Tur-Sinai, S. (1950) 'The origin of the alphabet', *The Jewish Quarterly Review* 61: 83–110, 159–80, 277–302.

Ullman, B. L. (1934) 'How old is the Greek alphabet?', *American Journal of Archeology* 38: 359–81.

Usener, H. (1907) 'Philologie und Geschichtswissenschaft', in *Vorträge und Aufsätze*, 2 vols. Leipzig, vol. 2, p. 11.

Van Berchem, D. (1967) 'Sanctuaires d'Hercule-Melqart: contribution à l'étude de l'expansion Phénicienne en Méditerranée', *Syria*: 73–109, 307–38.

Van Ness Myers, P. (1895) *A History of Greece for Colleges and High Schools*. Boston.

Van Sertima, I. (1976) *They Came Before Columbus*. New York: Random House.

—— (1984) 'Nile Valley presence in America BC', *Journal of African Civilizations* 6.2: 221–46.

Vaux de Foletier, F. de (1970) *Mille ans d'histoire des Tsiganes*. Paris: Fayard.

Vercoutter, J. (1956) *L'Égypte et le monde égéen préhellénique*. Paris: Maisonneuve.

—— (1975) 'Apis', in Helck and Otto, vol. 1, cols 338–50.

Vermeule, E. (1960) 'The fall of the Mycenaean Empire', *Archaeology* 13.1: 66–75.

—— (1964) *Greece in the Bronze Age*. Chicago University Press.

—— (1975) *The Art of the Shaft Graves of Mycenae*. Cincinnati: University of Cincinnati.

—— (1979) *Aspects of Death in Early Greek Art and Poetry*. Berkeley and Los Angeles: University of California Press.

Vesey-Fitz-Gerald, B. (1973) *Gypsies of Britain: an Introduction to their History*, 2nd edn. Newton Abbot: David and Charles.

Vian, F. (1963) *Les origines de Thèbes: Cadmos et les Spartes*. Paris: Études et Commentaires No. 48.

Vico, G. B. (1721) *De Constantia Jurisprudenta*. Naples.

—— (1725) *La Scienza Nuova*. Naples.

—— (1730) *La Scienza Nuova Seconda*. Naples.

Virgil (1935) *Works*, H. R. Fairclough, trans., 2 vols (Loeb). London: Heinemann/ Cambridge, Mass.: Harvard University Press.

Volney, C. F. C. (1787) *Voyages en Syrie et en Égypte*. Paris.

Voltaire, F. M. (1886) (1768) *Siècle de Louis XIV*. Paris.

Von der Mühll, P. (1952) *Kritisches Hypomnema zur Ilias*. Basel: Rheinhardt.

Voss, von M. H. (1980) 'Horuskinder', in Helck and Otto, vol. III, cols 52–3.

Wace, A. J. B. (1924) 'Greece and Mycenae', *Cambridge Ancient History*, 1st edn, vol. 2, *The Egyptian and Hittite Empires to c. 1000 BC*, pp. 431–72.

Waddell, L. A. (1927) *The Aryan Origin of the Alphabet*. London: Luzac.

Walcot, P. (1966) *Hesiod and the Near East*. Cardiff: University of Wales Press.

Wallace, W. P. (1966) 'The early coinages of Athens and Euboia', *Numismatic Chronicle*, 7th series. 6: 23–44.

Walton, C. and Anton, J. P. (1974) *Philosophy and the Civilizing Arts*.

Warburton, W. (1738–41) *The Divine Legation of Moses, demonstrated, on the principles of a religious deist from the omission of the doctrine of a future state of reward and punishment in the Jewish dispensation*. London.

Wardle, K. A. (1973) 'North West Greece in the Late Bronze Age: the archaeological background', paper presented to the *Third International Colloquium on Aegean Prehistory*, Sheffield.

Warmington, B. H. (1960) *Carthage*. London: Robert Hale.

Warren, P. M. (1965) 'The first Minoan stone vases and early Minoan chronology', *Kretika Chronika* 19: 7–43.

—— (1967) 'Minoan stone vases as evidence for Minoan foreign connections in the Aegean Late Bronze Age', *Proceedings of the Prehistoric Society* 33: 37–48.

Webster, T. B. L. (1958) *From Mycenae to Homer*. London: Methuen.

Weigall, A. (1923) *The Life and Times of Akhnaton*. New York: Putnam.

Weir Smyth, H. (1922) *Aeschylus*, 2 vols (Loeb). London: Heinemann/Cambridge, Mass.: Harvard University Press.

Weise, O. (1883) 'Miscellen', *Beiträge zur Kunde der Indogermanischen Sprachen* 7: 167–71.

Wells, W. C. (1818) *An Account of the Female of the White Race of Mankind, Part of Whose Skin Resembles that of a Negro; with some Observations on the Causes of the Differences in Colour and Form Between the White and the Negro Races of Men Appended to Two Essays: One upon Single Vision with Two Eyes and the other . . .* London.

Wessetzky, V. (1961) *Die ägyptische Kulte zur Römerzeit in Ungarn*. Leiden: Brill.

West, M. L. (1971) *Early Greek Philosophy and the Orient*. Oxford: Clarendon.

Westfall, R. S. (1980) *Never a Rest: A Biography of Isaac Newton*. Cambridge University Press.

Westman, R. S. and McGuire, J. E. (1977) *Hermeticism and the Scientific Revolution: Papers read at a Clark Library Seminar Los Angeles: William Andrews Clark Memorial Library*. Los Angeles: Unversity of California Press.

Whiston, W. (1957) (1720?) *Concerning God's Command to Abraham to Offer up Isaac, his Son, for a Sacrifice*. Dissertation II added to *The Life and Works of Flavius Josephus*. Philadelphia, pp. 914–21.

White, H. G. E. (1914) *Hesiod: The Homeric Hymns and Homerica*. Cambridge, Mass.: Loeb edn.

Wiener, M. J. (1981) *English Culture and the Decline of the Industrial Spirit, 1850–1980*. Cambridge University Press.

Wigtil, D. N. (1984) 'Incorrect apocalyptic: The Hermetic "Asclepius" as an improvement on the Greek original', in H. Temporini and W. Haase, eds *Aufstieg und Niedergang der römischen Welt: Geschichte und Kultur Roms im Spiegel der neueren Forschung. 17.4. Religion: (Heidentum: römische Götterkulte, orientalische Kulte in der römischen Welt [Forts.])*, ed. W. Haase, pp. 2282–97.

Wilamowitz-Moellendorf, U. von (1919) *Platon*. Berlin: Weidmann.

—— (1931) *Der Glaube der Hellenen*, 2 vols. Berlin: Weidmann.

—— (1959) *Geschichte der Philologie*, 3rd. edn (1927) repr. Leipzig: Teubner.

—— (1982) *History of Classical Scholarship*, A. Harris, trans. London and Baltimore: Johns Hopkins University Press.

Wilcken, U. (1928) 'Alexander Zug in die Oase Siwa', *Sitzungberichte der preußischen Akademie der Wissenschaften* VIII: 576–603.

—— (1930) 'Alexander Zug von Ammon: Epiteg', *Sitzungberichte der Preußischen Akademie der Wissenschaften* X: 159–76.

—— (1931) 'Eine Gedächtnisrede auf Barthold Georg Niebuhr', *Bonner akademische Reder* 10. Bonn.

Willetts, R. (1962) *Cretan Cults and Festivals*. London: Routledge & Kegan Paul.

Williams, C. (1971) *The Destruction of Black Civilization: great issues of a race from 4500 BC to 2000 BC*. Dubugne, Iowa: Kendall/Hunt.

Williams, R. J. (1981) 'The sages of Ancient Egypt in the light of recent scholarship', *Journal of the American Oriental Society* 101/1: 1–19.

Wilson, E. (1960) *To the Finland Station*. New York: p.b. edn.

Winckelmann, J. (1964) (1764) *Geschichte der Kunst des Altertums*, ed. W. Senff. Weimar.

Winckler, H. (1907) *The History of Babylonia and Assyria*, J. A. Craig, trans. New York: Scribner.

Wind, E. (1968) *Pagan Mysteries in the Renaissance*, rev. edn. (1980) p.b. Oxford: Oxford University Press.

Wismann, H. (1983) 'Modus operandi, analyse comparé des études platoniciennes en France et en Allemagne au 19ème siècle', in Bollack and Wismann, pp. 490–513.

Witte, B. C. (1979) *Der preußische Tacitus: Aufstieg, Ruhm und Ende des Historikers Barthold Georg Niebuhr 1776–1831*. Düsseldorf: Droste.

Wolf, F. A. (1804) *Prolegomena ad Homerum*. 2nd edn. Halle.

Wood, R. (1767) *A Comparative View of the Antient and Present State of the Troade. To which is Prefixed an Essay on the Original Genius and Writings of Homer*. London.

—— (1775) *An Essay on the Original Genius of Homer, with a Comparative View of the Antient and Present State of the Troade*, ed. J. Bryant. London.

Woolley, L. (1938) 'Excavations at Al Mina, Sueidia, 1 & 2', *Journal of Hellenic Studies* 58: 1–30, 133–70.

Wortham, J. D. (1971) *British Egyptology 1549–1906*. Newton Abbot: David & Charles.

Yadin, Y. (1965) '"And Dan, why did he remain in the ships?"', *Australian Journal of Biblical Archaeology*, 1.1: 19–23.

—— (1973) 'And Dan, why did he remain in the ships?', in J. Best, ed. *The Arrival of the Greeks*. Amsterdam: Hakkert, pp. 55–74.

Yates, F. (1964) *Giordano Bruno and the Hermetic Tradition*. London: Routledge & Kegan Paul.

—— (1967) 'The Hermetic tradition in Renaissance science', in C. S. Singleton, ed., *Art, Science and History in the Renaissance*. Baltimore, pp. 255–74.

—— (1972) *The Rosicrucian Enlightenment*. London: Routledge & Kegan Paul.

Yavetz, Z. (1976) 'Why Rome? Zeitgeist and Ancient historians in early 19th century Germany', *American Journal of Philology* 97: 276–96.

Yoyotte, J. (1982) 'Le Panthéon égyptien de J.-F. Champollion', *Bulletin de la Société Française d'Égyptologie: séance solennelle consacrée à la commémoration du cent-cinquantenaire de la mort de J.-F. Champollion* 95: 76–108.

Zafiropulo, J. and Monod, C. (1976) *Sensorium Dei dans l'hermétisme et la science*. Paris: 'Les Belles Lettres'.

Zervos, C. (1920) *Un Philosophe néoplatonicien du XIe s.: Michel Psellos, sa vie, son œuvre, ses luttes philosophiques, son influence*. Paris: Leroux.

Zucker, F. (1950) 'Athen und Aegypten bis auf den Beginn der hellenstischer Zeit', *Antike und Orient*: 140–65. Leipzig.

INDEX